RESTATEMENT OF THE LAW THIRD

THE AMERICAN LAW INSTITUTE

RESTATEMENT OF THE LAW

UNFAIR COMPETITION

As Adopted and Promulgated

BY

THE AMERICAN LAW INSTITUTE

AT WASHINGTON, D.C.

May 11, 1993

§§ 1–End

TABLES and INDEX

ST. PAUL, MINN.
AMERICAN LAW INSTITUTE PUBLISHERS
1995

Printed in the United States of America

ISBN 0–314–04251–2

TEXT IS PRINTED ON 10% POST CONSUMER RECYCLED PAPER

PRINTED WITH SOY INK

1st Reprint—1995

The American Law Institute

COUNCIL

The Executive Office
THE AMERICAN LAW INSTITUTE
4025 Chestnut Street
Philadelphia, Pennsylvania 19104

* *Counselor Emeritus*
** *Director Emeritus*
*** *Executive Vice President Emeritus*
**** *Chairman Emeritus*

REPORTERS

ROBERT C. DENICOLA, University of Nebraska College of Law, Lincoln, Nebraska

HARVEY S. PERLMAN, University of Nebraska College of Law, Lincoln, Nebraska [from 1989]

ADVISERS *

MILES J. ALEXANDER, Atlanta, Georgia

WILLIAM M. BORCHARD, New York, New York

RALPH S. BROWN, Yale Law School, New Haven, Connecticut

MARIE V. DRISCOLL, New York, New York [from 1988]

KENNETH B. GERMAIN, Cincinnati, Ohio

JEROME GILSON, Chicago, Illinois

MILTON HANDLER, New York, New York [from 1988]

ANNE S. JORDAN, Menlo Park, California [from 1988]

BENJAMIN KAPLAN, Harvard University Law School, Cambridge, Massachusetts

BRUCE P. KELLER, New York, New York [from 1989]

EDMUND W. KITCH, University of Virginia School of Law, Charlottesville, Virginia

WILLIAM M. LANDES, University of Chicago Law School, Chicago, Illinois [from 1988]

DAVID L. LANGE, Duke University School of Law, Durham, North Carolina

J. THOMAS McCARTHY, University of San Francisco Law School, San Francisco, California

JON O. NEWMAN, Judge, United States Court of Appeals for the Second Circuit, Hartford, Connecticut

HELEN WILSON NIES, Chief Judge, United States Court of Appeals for the Federal Circuit, Washington, District of Columbia

JAMES L. OAKES, Chief Judge, United States Court of Appeals for the Second Circuit, Brattleboro, Vermont

HARVEY S. PERLMAN [to 1989]

LOUIS H. POLLAK, Judge, United States District Court for the Eastern District of Pennsylvania, Philadelphia, Pennsylvania [from 1989]

ARTHUR H. SEIDEL, Philadelphia, Pennsylvania

MICHAEL TRAYNOR, San Francisco, California

---

* Status as of May 11, 1993

ADVISERS

DONALD F. TURNER, Georgetown University Law Center, Washington, District of Columbia [from 1988 to 1992]

SYLVIA H. WALBOLT, St. Petersburg, Florida [from 1988]

CHARLES ALAN WRIGHT, University of Texas School of Law, Austin, Texas

EX OFFICIO *

ROSWELL B. PERKINS, New York, New York
President, The American Law Institute

GEOFFREY C. HAZARD, JR., New Haven, Connecticut
Director, The American Law Institute

---

* Status as of May 11, 1993

MEMBERS CONSULTATIVE GROUP

(as of April 1, 1993)

BURTON C. AGATA, Hempstead, New York

WALTER H. ALFORD, Atlanta, Georgia

IRWIN M. ALTERMAN, Farmington Hills, Michigan

RICHARD ALAN ARNOLD, Miami, Florida

GRADY AVANT, JR., Detroit, Michigan

TYLER A. BAKER III, Dallas, Texas

ROBERT L. BANSE, Princeton, New Jersey

JOHN J. BARRY, Newark, New Jersey

PETER V. BAUGHER, Chicago, Illinois

JANIS M. BERRY, Boston, Massachusetts

DAVID E. BIRENBAUM, Washington, D.C.

ALLEN D. BLACK, Philadelphia, Pennsylvania

RICHARD A. BOOTH, Rockville, Maryland

ROBERT S. BRAMSON, Bala Cynwyd, Pennsylvania

CHARLES F. BREGA, Denver, Colorado

KATHLEEN F. BRICKEY, St. Louis, Missouri

WARREN BRODY, Roselle, New Jersey

ALEXANDRA A. BROOKSHIRE, Seattle, Washington

JACK E. BROWN, Phoenix, Arizona

RAYMOND F. BURKE, White Plains, New York

W. AMON BURTON, JR., Austin, Texas

STEPHEN CALKINS, Detroit, Michigan

TERRY CALVANI, Washington, D.C.

RICHARD F. CAMPBELL III, Oklahoma City, Oklahoma

RONALD G. CARR, Washington, D.C.

WILLIAM R. CASTO, Lubbock, Texas

BENJAMIN R. CIVILETTI, Baltimore, Maryland

RUTLEDGE C. CLEMENT, JR., New Orleans, Louisiana

MILO G. COERPER, Washington, D. C.

CALVIN J. COLLIER, Northfield, Illinois

WAYNE DALE COLLINS, New York, New York

FREDERICK U. CONARD, JR., Hartford, Connecticut

WILLIAM L. CROWE, SR., New Orleans, Louisiana

RICHARD D. CUDAHY, United States Court of Appeals for the Seventh Circuit, Chicago, Illinois

JOHN B. DAVIDSON, Chicago, Illinois

RICHARD E. DAY, Columbia, South Carolina

JOSEPH W. DELLAPENNA, Villanova, Pennsylvania

RICHARD F. DOLE, JR., Houston, Texas

ROLAND W. DONNEM, Cleveland, Ohio

MEMBERS CONSULTATIVE GROUP

DAVID S. DOTY, U.S. District Court for the District of Minnesota, Minneapolis, Minnesota

ROCHELLE C. DREYFUSS, New York, New York

DIANE DURGIN, Atlanta, Georgia

PETER D. EHRENHAFT, Washington, D.C.

A. MICHAEL FERRILL, San Antonio, Texas

RALPH ADAM FINE, Wisconsin Court of Appeals, Milwaukee, Wisconsin

GERARD M. FINKEL, Columbia, South Carolina

PETER FLYNN, Chicago, Illinois

ELEANOR M. FOX, New York, New York

RICHARD T. FRANCH, Chicago, Illinois

LEWIS R. FRIEDMAN, New York State Supreme Court, New York, New York

JAKE E. GALLEGOS, Sante Fe, New Mexico

PETER M. GERHART, Cleveland, Ohio

JOHN J. GIBBONS, Newark, New Jersey

DANIEL J. GIFFORD, Minneapolis, Minnesota

R. NICHOLAS GIMBEL, Philadelphia, Pennsylvania

JANE GINSBURG, New York, New York

JOSEPH GOLDBERG, Albuquerque, New Mexico

WENDY J. GORDON, Newark, New Jersey

ROBERT A. GORMAN, Philadelphia, Pennsylvania

OSCAR S. GRAY, Baltimore, Maryland

J. FOY GUIN, JR., United States District Court for the Northern District of Alabama, Birmingham, Alabama

SHELDON W. HALPERN, Columbus, Ohio

JAMES J. HANKS, JR., Baltimore, Maryland

RICHARD E. V. HARRIS, San Francisco, California

THOMAS P. HESTER, Chicago, Illinois

CASWELL O. HOBBS, Washington, D.C.

STEPHEN J. HOLTMAN, Cedar Rapids, Iowa

DOUGLAS G. HOUSER, Portland, Oregon

MICHAEL J. HUTTER, JR., Albany, New York

LESLIE W. JACOBS, Cleveland, Ohio

ARTHUR H. KAHN, Philadelphia, Pennsylvania

MICHAEL ALEXANDER KAHN, San Francisco, California

ARTHUR M. KAPLAN, Philadelphia, Pennsylvania

JOSEPH A. KATARINCIC, Pittsburgh, Pennsylvania

JUDITH S. KAYE, New York Court of Appeals, New York, New York

RICHARD A. KILLWORTH, Dayton, Ohio

JAMES B. KOBAK, JR., New York, New York

HARVEY C. KOCH, New Orleans, Louisiana

MEMBERS CONSULTATIVE GROUP

PETER G. KUMPE, Little Rock, Arkansas

SYBIL H. LANDAU, New York, New York

MATTHEW L. LARRABEE, San Francisco, California

JOHN HENRY LEWIN, JR., Baltimore, Maryland

HENRY R. LORD, Baltimore, Maryland

HOUSTON PUTNAM LOWRY, Farmington, Connecticut

JOHN SHAFROTH LUTZ, Denver, Colorado

MYLES V. LYNK, Washington, D.C.

PETER B. MAGGS, Urbana, Illinois

DAVID H. MARKS, New York, New York

KIRK MARTIN McALPIN, Savannah, Georgia

JOHN P. McKENNA, Washington, D.C.

CHARLES R. McMANIS, St. Louis, Missouri

JAMES A. MEDFORD, Greensboro, North Carolina

A. DOUGLAS MELAMED, Washington, D.C.

JUDITH A. MILLER, Washington, D.C.

W. ROBERT MORGAN, San Jose, California

DANIEL T. MURPHY, Richmond, Virginia

FRED F. MURRAY, Washington, D.C.

PAUL V. NIEMEYER, Baltimore, Maryland

LEWIS A. NOONBERG, Baltimore, Maryland

VANCE K. OPPERMAN, Minneapolis, Minnesota

JACK OWENS, Modesto, California

HENRY L. PARR, JR., Greenville, South Carolina

JERRY J. PHILLIPS, Knoxville, Tennessee

ALAN E. POPKIN, St. Louis, Missouri

FRANKLIN POUL, Philadelphia, Pennsylvania

PHILLIP A. PROGER, Washington, D.C.

FREDERICK A. PROVORNY, Washington, D.C.

LEO J. RASKIND, Minneapolis, Minnesota

BRYCE REA, JR., Washington, D.C.

BERNARD D. REAMS, JR., St. Louis, Missouri

BARBARA A. REEVES, Los Angeles, California

THOMAS W. RHODES, Atlanta, Georgia

DAVID A. RICE, Chestnut Hill, Massachusetts

C. KENNETH ROBERTS, Irving, Texas

A. JAMES ROBERTSON II, San Francisco, California

RUSSELL M. ROBINSON II, Charlotte, North Carolina

H. C. ROEMER, Winston-Salem, North Carolina

KEITH E. ROUNSAVILLE, Tampa, Florida

BENJAMEN T. ROWE, Mobile, Alabama

STEPHEN RUBIN, Washington, D.C.

MEMBERS CONSULTATIVE GROUP

JOHN L. SALTONSTALL, JR., Sacramento, California

VALERIUS SANFORD, Nashville, Tennessee

JOHN H. SCHAFER, Washington, D.C.

GORDON W. SCHMIDT, Pittsburgh, Pennsylvania

HERBERT F. SCHWARTZ, New York, New York

HAROLD F. SEE, Tuscaloosa, Alabama

DAVID J. SEIPP, Boston, Massachusetts

MARC M. SELTZER, Los Angeles, California

MICHAEL L. SHAKMAN, Chicago, Illinois

STEPHEN M. SHAPIRO, Chicago, Illinois

DAVID E. SHIPLEY, University, Mississippi

JOSEPH SIMS, Washington, D.C.

DOLORES K. SLOVITER, United States Court of Appeals for the Third Circuit, Philadelphia, Pennsylvania

ALISON L. SMITH, Houston, Texas

THEODORE M. SPACE, Hartford, Connecticut

SUSAN R. STEINGASS, Madison, Wisconsin

PATRICK J. SULLIVAN, Encivitas, California

ROBERT P. TAYLOR, San Francisco, California

GERALD J. THAIN, Madison, Wisconsin

DEBRA A. VALENTINE, Washington, D.C.

LEWIS H. VAN DUSEN, JR., Philadelphia, Pennsylvania

ROBERT M. WALMSLEY, JR., New Orleans, Louisiana

PRISCILLA PETERSON WEAVER, Chicago, Illinois

WILLIAM H. WEBB, Pittsburgh, Pennsylvania

NANCY F. WECHSLER, New York, New York

EDWARD L. WEIDENFELD, Washington, D.C.

DAVID H. WEINSTEIN, Philadelphia, Pennsylvania

JUDY LYNN WHALLEY, Washington, D.C.

PAUL MARTIN WOLFF, Washington, D.C.

PAUL A. WOLKIN, Philadelphia, Pennsylvania

DOUGLAS P. WOODLOCK, United States District Court for the District of Massachusetts, Boston, Massachusetts

SHARON M. WOODS, Detroit, Michigan

HENRIETTA WRIGHT, Washington, D.C.

ROBERT C. WRIGHT, San Diego, California

JOHN HARDIN YOUNG, Alexandria, Virginia

DIANE L. ZIMMERMAN, New York, New York

FOREWORD

The Institute is pleased to publish herewith Restatement of the Law Third, Unfair Competition.

This Restatement treats the common law principles and analogous statutory rules that collectively comprise the law of unfair competition. Although the common law action for unfair competition evolved originally to afford relief against a competitor's misrepresentation of the source of goods or services, the term "unfair competition" now describes an array of legal actions addressing methods of competition that improperly interfere with the legitimate commercial interests of other sellers in the marketplace. Included within this Restatement are causes of action for passing off, deceptive advertising, and the infringement of trademarks, trade secrets, and publicity rights.

Federal and state statutes play a significant, sometimes dominant role in many of the substantive areas encompassed within this Restatement. For the most part the federal legislation does not preempt state law, and both federal and state unfair competition statutes generally rely without significant elaboration on concepts derived from the common law. The interstate character of modern business accentuates the interest in uniformity—an interest advanced by a consistent interpretation of both the common law rules and derivative statutory provisions that define the boundaries of fair competition. Except as otherwise noted, the principles discussed in this Restatement are applicable to actions at common law and to the interpretation of analogous federal and state statutory codifications.

This Restatement is the Institute's first independent work on the subject. The subject of unfair competition was to have been addressed in the Restatement, Second, of Torts, as it had been in the original Restatement of Torts. However, it was eventually decided that the law of unfair competition had evolved to the point that it was no longer appropriate to treat it as a subcategory of the law of Torts. See 4 Restatement, Second, Torts, Introduction and Introductory Note to Division Nine. Subsequently—over the last 30 years or so—there has been enormous development of the law, as well as of the technology and techniques of business competition. There has been a parallel increase in the commercial and financial significance of intellectual property generally, including that defined through the law of unfair competition. Over approximately the same period theoretical explorations, often under the rubric of law and economics, have yielded a much more sophisticated understanding of the law and of the relationship between the values inherent in business competition and other social and political values, including the protection of free speech in a commercial context. It is thus timely that this work now be presented.

The Reporters, aided by the Advisers, the Members Consultative Group, and suggestions from outside commentators, have been fully alive to the foregoing developments. Those having occasion to consult this work, whether specialists in the field or otherwise interested, will find it an admirable example of professional scholarship. The writing is crisp, the underlying analysis is clear, and the Illustrations are pointed. Ample and careful supporting references have been provided in the Reporter's Notes.

The Reporters have carried the enterprise forward in estimable fashion, presenting their views thoughtfully and forcefully but being always respectful of suggestions and receptive to those that improved the work. We congratulate them on setting a high standard and thank our colleagues on the Advisory Committee and the Members Consultative Group for upholding that standard through their contributions.

GEOFFREY C. HAZARD, JR.
Director
The American Law Institute

April 29, 1994

SUMMARY OF CONTENTS

*

TABLE OF CONTENTS

Topic 2. Acquisition and Priority of Rights

Topic 3. Infringement of Rights

Topic 4. Defenses and Limitations on Relief

Topic 5. Licensing and Assignment of Rights

Topic 6. Remedies

CHAPTER FOUR

APPROPRIATION OF TRADE VALUES

TABLE OF CONTENTS

Topic 1. Misappropriation

Topic 2. Trade Secrets

Topic 3. Right of Publicity

Cite thus:

Restatement Third,
Unfair Competition § _____

Restatement of the Law Third

The American Law Institute

Restatement of the Law
Unfair Competition

*

CHAPTER ONE

THE FREEDOM TO COMPETE

---

§ 1. General Principles

One who causes harm to the commercial relations of another by engaging in a business or trade is not subject to liability to the other for such harm unless:

(a) the harm results from acts or practices of the actor actionable by the other under the rules of this Restatement relating to:

(1) deceptive marketing, as specified in Chapter Two;

(2) infringement of trademarks and other indicia of identification, as specified in Chapter Three;

(3) appropriation of intangible trade values including trade secrets and the right of publicity, as specified in Chapter Four;

or from other acts or practices of the actor determined to be actionable as an unfair method of competition, taking into account the nature of the conduct and its likely effect on both the person seeking relief and the public; or

(b) the acts or practices of the actor are actionable by the other under federal or state statutes, international agreements, or general principles of common law apart from those considered in this Restatement.

Comment:

a. The freedom to compete. The freedom to engage in business and to compete for the patronage of prospective customers is a fundamental premise of the free enterprise system. Competition in the marketing of goods and services creates incentives to offer quality products at reasonable prices and fosters the general welfare by promoting the efficient allocation of economic resources. The freedom to compete necessarily contemplates the probability of harm to the commercial relations of other participants in the market. The fundamental rule stated in the introductory clause of this Section promotes competition by insuring that neither new entrants nor existing competitors will be subject to liability for harm resulting solely from the fact of their participation in the market.

The freedom to compete implies a right to induce prospective customers to do business with the actor rather than with the actor's competitors. This Section permits a seller to seek to divert business not only from competitors generally, but also from a particular competitor. This Section is applicable to harm incurred by persons with whom the actor directly competes and to harm incurred by other persons affected by the actor's decision to enter or continue in business. Thus, the actor is not subject to liability to indirect competitors or to employees or suppliers of others who may be harmed by the actor's presence in the market. Liability is imposed under this Section, and under this Restatement generally, only in connection with harm resulting from particular methods of competition determined to be unfair.

The principle embodied in this Section is often loosely described as a "privilege" to compete. That characterization, however, is sometimes taken to imply that any intentional interference in the commercial relations of another is prima facie tortious, with the burden on the actor to establish an applicable privilege as an affirmative defense. There is as yet no consensus with respect to the allocation of the burdens of pleading and proof under the general tort of intentional interference with prospective economic relations. See Restatement, Second, Torts § 767, Comment *k*. However, in the case of harm resulting from competition in the marketplace, the privilege rationale appears inconsistent with the basic premise of our free enterprise system. Rather than adopting the view that such harm is prima facie tortious subject to a competitive privilege, this Restatement rejects the privilege rationale in favor of a general principle of non-liability. A person alleging injury through competition must therefore establish facts sufficient to subject the actor to liability under one or more of the rules enumerated in this Section.

This Section does not preclude the imposition of liability when the actor's participation in the market is itself unlawful. One who engages in a particular business or trade in violation of a statute prohibiting such activity, either absolutely or without prescribed permission, may be subject to liability to others engaged in the business or trade if one of the purposes of the enactment is to protect the others against unauthorized competition and the recognition of a private right of action is not inconsistent with the legislative intent. This result is an application of the general principles relating to the imposition of tort liability for violations of legislative enactments that do not explicitly authorize a private cause of action. See Restatement, Second, Torts § 874A.

Intentional interference with another's commercial relations by means other than the actor's participation in the market is not within the scope of this Section. Such conduct may subject the actor to liability under the general rules on interference with prospective economic relations stated in Restatement, Second, Torts § 766B.

Illustrations:

1. *A*, the owner of a bakery, employs *B*, a baker, and sells products made with ingredients purchased from *C*, a supplier. *D* opens a competing bakery and *A* is compelled to go out of business. *D* is not subject to liability to *A*, *B*, or *C*.

2. *A* and *B* are competing distributors of shoes. *A* induces *C* not to purchase *B* 's house. *A* 's interference is not within the scope of this Restatement. *A* may be subject to liability to *B* for intentionally interfering with *B* 's prospective economic relations under the rule stated in Restatement, Second, Torts § 766B.

3. A federal statute prohibits *A*, a governmental corporation, from selling electricity outside a designated geographic area. *B*, a private utility company, commences an action seeking to enjoin sales by *A* in localities served by *B* that are outside the designated area. If the court concludes that a purpose of the statute is to protect private utilities from competition by *A* and that the recognition of a private remedy is not inconsistent with the legislative intent, *A* may be subject to liability to *B*.

b. "Subject to liability"; "harm". This Restatement uses the words "subject to liability" to denote the fact that the actor's conduct is such as to make it liable to another if the conduct is the legal cause of the other's injury and the actor has no defense applicable to the particular claim. See Restatement, Second, Torts § 5. The phrase carries no implications with respect to the remedies available to the injured party. In particular, it does not imply that the injured party is entitled to monetary relief. The word "harm" as used in this Restatement denotes the existence of loss or detriment in fact, whether or not the loss or detriment results from an invasion of a legally protected interest. See *id.*, § 7.

c. Motives of the actor. Several cases recite, mostly in dicta, that one who engages in competition solely or primarily for the purpose of causing harm to another is subject to liability to the other, apparently without regard to the nature of the actor's business methods. The prior Restatement of this topic incorporated a narrow version of this principle, requiring both a malicious motive and an intention on the part of the actor to terminate the business after the infliction of harm. Restatement of Torts § 709. However, both the case law and the prior Restatement declined to invoke the rule when the actor's conduct was directed at least in part to the advancement of its own competitive interests. This proposition necessitated a distinction between "good faith" competition, which would not subject the actor to liability even if motivated in part by ill will toward the other, and "simulated competition" that was undertaken merely as a means of inflicting harm.

The rule purporting to impose liability upon one who engages in business solely for the purpose of harming another has had little practical effect. When harm results from the actor's participation in a bona fide business or trade, courts are quick to find a concurrent commercial motive sufficient to preclude the imposition of liability even in the face of evidence of genuine ill will. When the rule has been invoked to support the imposition of liability, the actor's conduct has typically involved unfair methods of competition sufficient in themselves to subject the actor to liability. In the absence of such misconduct, the rule invites misuse by affording a colorable claim through which an established business can restrict legitimate competition and harass new entrants in the market. The public benefits derived from competition are independent of the actor's motivation, and even an intention to withdraw from the market will not ordinarily threaten the public interest in light of the opportunity for entry by others. Under the rule stated in this Section, an actor who causes harm to another merely by engaging in a business or trade is not subject to liability regardless of motive. Liability is thus determined by an analysis of the business methods employed by the actor and not by the actor's motivation.

Although a malicious motive is not sufficient in itself to subject an actor to liability, a competitor motivated by ill will may be tempted to pursue impermissible means of competition in order to insure or enhance the harm to another. Evidence of such ill will may therefore justify close scrutiny of the actor's methods under the various rules enumerated in this Section. The actor's motives may also be relevant to the application of rules of liability outside the scope of this Restatement, including state and federal antitrust laws.

Illustration:

4. *A*, a manufacturer of medicines, quarrels with *B*, a newspaper publisher, because of *B* 's articles ridiculing *A* 's medicines. *A*, after threatening to drive *B* out of business, establishes a competing newspaper. *A* 's newspaper is successful and *B* is eventually forced to cease publication. *A* is not subject to liability to *B*.

d. Deceptive marketing. Competitive markets cannot operate efficiently unless consumers have access to information about the goods and services offered by competing sellers. Much of the information available to prospective purchasers is provided by sellers in the form of advertising. If the message that it communicates is accurate, advertising can function as a convenient, low-cost source of information that assists consumers to choose intelligently among competing products. False or deceptive advertising, however, can result in improvident expenditures or force consumers to spend additional resources in an effort to acquire more reliable information. Deceptive advertising also threatens harm to other sellers who are thereby deprived of the opportunity to compete on the merits of their goods and services. Recognition of a right of action for deceptive marketing in favor of other sellers, however, raises complex issues. It is often difficult to establish a clear nexus between the misrepresentations of one seller and injury to the business relations of another seller. Further, unless the cause of action for deceptive advertising is carefully circumscribed, it may inhibit the dissemination of useful information and function as a barrier to vigorous competition. The scope of liability for deceptive advertising must also reflect the constitutional protection afforded to commercial speech.

The rules stated in Chapter Two describe the circumstances in which a seller may be subject to liability for injuries to the commercial relations of other sellers resulting from the use of deceptive representations in the marketing of goods or services.

e. Trademark infringement. A trademark is a word, name, symbol, device, or other designation used by a manufacturer or seller to identify its goods or services and distinguish them from goods or services manufactured or sold by others. The protection of trademarks and other indicia of origin or sponsorship is a fundamental feature of the law of unfair competition.

By indicating the source or sponsorship of the goods or services with which they are used, trademarks communicate to prospective purchasers information relating to the quality and other characteristics of the product. The deceptive use of another's trademark can be seen as a form of deceptive marketing, and the protection of trademarks thus implicates many of the interests identified in Comment *d*. The recognition of rights in trademarks also serves to protect and encourage investments in good will by insuring the trademark owner an opportunity to capture the benefits of a favorable reputation created through expenditures on quality, service, or promotion.

The rules governing the protection of trademarks must also be responsive to the public interest in fostering vigorous competition. In defining protectable subject matter and in delineating the scope of exclusive rights, the law cannot neglect the legitimate interests of other competitors. In some cases the recognition of exclusive rights in favor of a particular seller may undermine the ability of other sellers to communicate useful information to consumers or deprive competitors of access to product features necessary for effective competition. The scope of exclusive rights in trademarks must also accommodate the interest in free expression.

The rules governing the acquisition and protection of rights in trademarks and related subject matter are stated in Chapter Three.

f. Appropriation of trade values. An important function of the law of unfair competition is to delimit the circumstances in which a person may prohibit the appropriation by another of intangible business assets created through an investment of time, money, or effort. The law of trademarks and the general proscription against passing off, for example, prohibit the appropriation of another's good will through misrepresentations relating to source. Other appropriations can be more direct, as when a competitor utilizes the work-product of another in competition with the creator. The federal patent and copyright statutes offer a complex regime of protection for some intangible assets, but the common law also imposes limitations on the appropriation of intangible assets.

The recognition of rights in intangible business assets generally proceeds from the premise that protection is necessary in order to insure adequate incentive for the investment of resources necessary to produce such assets. This incentive rationale is frequently augmented by references to the perceived unjust enrichment resulting from an appropriation of the fruits of another's investment. The recognition of exclusive rights in intangible business assets, however, must also take account of the anticompetitive consequences inherent in restrictions on the free flow of ideas and information. Thus, in many instances the incentive and unjust enrichment rationales may be outweighed by the advantages of unrestricted imitation and dissemination as embodied in the concept of a public domain. The common law has generally accorded rights against the appropriation of intangible business assets only when the recognition of rights is supported by additional interests justifying protection, and then only when the scope of the resulting rights can be clearly defined. In the case of trade secrets, for example, the owner's rights reflect the protection traditionally accorded confidential relationships as well as the interest in security against wrongful physical intrusions. Appropriation of the commercial value of another's name or likeness implicates interests in privacy and personal autonomy. The recognition of rights in intangible assets must also reflect the appropriate relationship between common law and legislation and the permissible sphere of state authority in light of the extensive regime of federal intellectual property law. Rules relating to the appropriation of intangible business assets, including the protection of trade secrets and the recognition of a right of publicity, are stated in Chapter Four.

g. Unfair methods of competition. A primary purpose of the law of unfair competition is the identification and redress of business practices that hinder rather than promote the efficient operation of the market. Certain recurring patterns of objectionable practices form the basis of the traditional categories of liability specifically enumerated in Subsection (a)(1)-(3). However, these specific forms of unfair competition do not fully exhaust the scope of statutory or common law liability for unfair methods of competition, and Subsection (a) therefore includes a residual category encompassing other business practices determined to be unfair.

It is impossible to state a definitive test for determining which methods of competition will be deemed unfair in addition to those included in the categories of conduct described in the preceding Comments. Courts continue to evaluate competitive practices against generalized standards of fairness and social utility. Judicial formulations have broadly appealed to principles of honesty and fair dealing, rules of fair play and good conscience, and the morality of the marketplace. The case law, however, is far more circumscribed than such rhetoric might indicate, and courts have generally been reluctant to interfere in the competitive process. An act or practice is likely to be judged unfair only if it substantially interferes with the ability of others to compete on the merits of their products or otherwise conflicts with accepted principles of public policy recognized by statute or common law.

As a general matter, if the means of competition are otherwise tortious with respect to the injured party, they will also ordinarily constitute an unfair method of competition. A competitor who interferes with the business of another by acts or threats of violence directed at the other, for example, is subject to liability for unfair competition. So also is one who interferes by instituting or threatening to institute groundless litigation against a competitor. Similarly, if a competitor interferes with the commercial relations of another by engaging in defamation or by establishing or maintaining an unlawful restraint of trade, the conduct also constitutes unfair competition. Liability for unfair competition under the residual rule stated in Subsection (a), however, is not limited to conduct that is otherwise tortious with respect to the party seeking relief. Thus, interference in the commercial relations of a competitor resulting from unlawful threats directed at customers of the competitor will also constitute unfair competition.

In assessing the propriety of the actor's conduct, a primary consideration is the social utility of the conduct as a means of competition. If the conduct is likely to interfere in a substantial manner with the ability of prospective purchasers to choose on the merits of the competing products, it will ordinarily be considered unfair. In some circumstances, for example, a court may conclude that a failure to disclose to prospective consumers particular information that is crucial to an intelligent purchasing decision constitutes unfair competition.

Some applications of the residual rule of liability specified in Subsection (a) can be seen as extensions of the established categories of unfair competition. A competitor who diverts business from another by means of fraudulent misrepresentations or through the wrongful use of confidential information, for example, may in some circumstances be subject to liability for unfair competition even if the conduct is not specifically actionable under the rules relating to deceptive marketing or the appropriation of trade secrets. However, in determining whether it is appropriate to conclude that an act or practice is unfair despite the fact that a restrictive element of traditional doctrine precludes the imposition of liability under an established category of unfair competition, careful consideration must be given to the nature of the restriction. If the restriction expresses an important policy of the law against the imposition of liability in such circumstances, the conduct should not be actionable as unfair competition.

A person seeking relief under the residual rule stated in Subsection (a) bears the burden of establishing that the method of competition employed by the actor is unfair. The use of equitable remedies has contributed to the development of the law by facilitating the condemnation of practices not previously determined to be unlawful. A person likely to be damaged by the unfair competition of another may obtain an injunction against a continuation of the conduct. The court may also award appropriate monetary relief.

Liability at common law for acts of unfair competition has been supplemented by the widespread enactment of the Unfair Trade Practices and Consumer Protection Act, which commonly prohibits "unfair methods of competition and unfair or deceptive acts or practices." See the Statutory Note following this Section. The private right of action available under many of these statutes has been pursued primarily as an alternative to traditional contract and tort actions by disappointed purchasers attracted by the generous remedial provisions of the Act. In a number of jurisdictions, however, competitors also have standing to seek redress under the Act for harm to their commercial relations. Application of the Act in this latter context has thus far been generally limited to conduct falling within the traditional categories of unfair competition law. However, the broad substantive standards embodied in many of these statutes provide a flexible statutory counterpart to the general common law proscription against unfair competition.

Illustrations:

5. *A* manufactures a computer designed for use by school children. *B*, a manufacturer of a competing product, sends letters to wholesalers and distributors stating that *A* 's computer infringes a patent owned by *B*. The letters contain a threat to institute an infringement action against anyone who markets *A* 's product. *B* knows that *A* 's product does not infringe the patent and has no intention of commencing the threatened litigation. *B* is subject to liability to *A*.

6. *A* is the local distributor for a brand of wall paneling. *B*, a builder, makes a contract to install wall paneling in a school being constructed by *C*, a school district. *C* requests *B* to solicit bids for the wall paneling from suppliers. *B* then arranges to become the local distributor for a brand of paneling similar to that sold by *A*. Without informing *A* of this fact, *B* obtains a bid from *A* but alters *A* 's figures to increase the price before submitting *A* 's bid, together with its own lower bid, to *C*. *C* awards the supply contract to *B*. *B* is subject to liability to *A*.

7. *A* is involved in a dispute with *B*, a former licensee, concerning the use by *B* of a trade name similar to *A* 's. *A* files a change of address form under *B* 's name at the local post office, listing its own address as the new address of *B* 's business. As a result of the diversion of mail, *B* loses the opportunity to bid on several contracts. *A* is subject to liability to *B*.

h. Liability under other rules. The succeeding Chapters of this Restatement treat the common law and statutory rules governing liability for the specific forms of unfair competition enumerated in Subsection (a)(1)-(3). Other conduct undertaken to advance the competitive interests of the actor may result in liability under the various federal and state statutes regulating aspects of the competitive process beyond those considered in this Restatement. The federal copyright and patent statutes, for example, prohibit the unauthorized appropriation of another's writings and discoveries. Federal and state statutes afford private remedies against price discrimination, and state "sales below cost" statutes subject a seller to liability to competitors for other specified pricing practices. Similarly, if the actor's conduct threatens to reduce or eliminate competition, liability may arise under federal and state antitrust law.

A competitor may also be subject to liability to other participants in the market if its methods of competition violate generally applicable principles of tort and contract law. A seller who seeks to improve its position in the market through physical violence to the person or property of a competitor, for example, may be subject to liability under traditional rules of tort law. If the actor has made an enforceable promise not to compete with another, competition may subject it to liability under general principles of contract law. Unreasonable interference with the use of real property owned by a competitor may be actionable under rules relating to nuisance. Statements derogatory to the personal reputation of a competitor or to the quality of its goods or services may be actionable as defamation or disparagement.

As the other party's economic relations approach the status of formal contract rights, the freedom of a competitor to interfere with those expectancies is also circumscribed by the protection afforded in tort against intentional interference with contracts. See Restatement, Second, Torts §§ 766–774A. The freedom to compete embodied in this Section extends only to interference with prospective economic relations and does not insulate the actor from liability for intentional interference with a competitor's contract rights. The characterization of economic relations as prospective or contractual, however, is itself influenced by the policies underlying recognition of the freedom to compete. Many cases, for example, recognize a right to induce a third person to terminate a contract with a competitor if the agreement is terminable at will.

The rules in this Restatement relating to liability for unfair methods of competition supplement rather than displace these general principles of common law.

Illustration:

8. *A* and *B* are engaged in the sale of gasoline and convenience foods on adjoining properties. In order to block the view

of *B*'s premises from a nearby highway, *A* constructs a wall 14 feet in height at the boundary of the properties and places a sign marked "Exit Only" near the entrance to *B*'s property. *A* may be subject to liability to *B* under general principles of tort law relating to nuisance.

STATUTORY NOTE

The Unfair Trade Practices and Consumer Protection Act was developed by the Federal Trade Commission and published by the Council of State Governments in 1967. The current version appears at 29 Suggested State Legislation 141 (1970). The Act has served as the basis for widespread state legislation.

Every state has now adopted legislation of general applicability proscribing unfair or deceptive acts or practices in trade. In some states the proscription extends to a specific list of prohibited activities; in others the statutes refer to "false, misleading, or deceptive" acts. In a number of jurisdictions the statutes incorporate the language in § 5(a)(1) of the Federal Trade Commission Act, 15 U.S.C.A. § 45(a)(1), prohibiting "unfair methods of competition and unfair or deceptive acts or practices in the conduct of any trade or commerce."

Although in several jurisdictions the Unfair Trade Practices and Consumer Protection Act relies exclusively on enforcement by public officials, in the vast majority of states private actions may also be maintained. In many of these states the private action is limited to consumers or other purchasers injured as a result of a seller's unfair or deceptive acts or practices. In a significant number of jurisdictions, however, the statutory language is sufficiently broad to accommodate actions by competitors seeking redress for harm to their commercial relations resulting from the unfair or deceptive acts of competing sellers. Judicial decisions in a number of states recognize a private right of action on behalf of injured competitors.

The Unfair Trade Practices and Consumer Protection Act or an analogous statute is in effect as follows:

Alabama . . . . ALA. C. § 8–19–1 et seq.
Alaska . . . . ALASKA S. § 45.50.471 et seq.
Arizona . . . . ARIZ. R.S.A. § 44–1521 et seq.
Arkansas . . . . ARK. C.A. § 4–88–101 et seq.
California . . . . CAL. Bus. & Prof.C. § 17000 et seq.
Colorado . . . . COLO. R.S.A. § 6–1–101 et seq.
Connecticut . . . . CONN. G.S.A. § 42–110a et seq.
Delaware . . . . DEL. C., tit. 6, § 2511 et seq.
Dist. of Columbia . . . . . . D.C. C.A. § 28–3901 et seq.

Florida	FLA. S.A. § 501.201 et seq.
Georgia	GA. C.A. § 10–1–390 et seq.
Hawaii	HAW. R.S. § 480–1 et seq.
Idaho	IDAHO C.A. § 48–601 et seq.
Illinois	ILL. C.S., ch. 815, § 505/1 et seq.
Indiana	IND. A.S. § 24–5–0.5–1 et seq.
Iowa	IOWA C.A. § 714.16
Kansas	KAN. S.A. § 50–623 et seq.
Kentucky	KY. R.S. § 367.110 et seq.
Louisiana	LA. S.A. § 51:1401 et seq.
Maine	ME. R.S.A., tit. 5, § 206 et seq.
Maryland	MD. Com.L. C.A. § 13–301 et seq.
Massachusetts	MASS. G.L.A., ch. 93A, § 1 et seq.
Michigan	MICH. C.L.A. § 445.901 et seq.
Minnesota	MINN. S.A. § 325F.68 et seq.
Mississippi	MISS. C.A. § 75–24–1 et seq.
Missouri	MO. R.S. § 407.010 et seq.
Montana	MONT. C.A. § 30–14–101 et seq.
Nebraska	NEB. R.S. § 59–1601 et seq.
Nevada	NEV. R.S.A. § 598.0903 et seq.
New Hampshire	N.H. R.S.A. § 358–A:1 et seq.
New Jersey	N.J. S.A. § 56:8–1 et seq.
New Mexico	N.M. S.A. § 57–12–1 et seq.
New York	N.Y. Gen.Bus.L. § 349 et seq.
North Carolina	N.C. G.S. § 75–1.1 et seq.
North Dakota	N.D. Cent.C. § 51–15–01 et seq.
Ohio	OHIO R.C. § 1345.01 et seq.
Oklahoma	OKLA. S.A., tit. 15, § 751 et seq.
Oregon	OR. R.S. § 646.605 et seq.
Pennsylvania	PA. S.A., tit. 73, § 201–1 et seq.
Puerto Rico	P.R. L.A., tit. 10, § 257 et seq.
Rhode Island	R.I. G.L.A. § 6–13.1–1 et seq.
South Carolina	S.C. C.A. § 39–5–10 et seq.
South Dakota	S.D. Comp. L.A. § 37–24–1 et seq.
Tennessee	TENN. C.A. § 47–18–101 et seq.
Texas	TEX. Bus. & Com.C. § 17.41 et seq.
Utah	UTAH C.A. § 13–11–1 et seq.
Vermont	VT. S.A., tit. 9, § 2451 et seq.
Virginia	VA. C.A. § 59.1–196 et seq.
Washington	WASH. R.C.A. § 19.86.010 et seq.
West Virginia	W.VA. C.A. § 46A–6–101 et seq.
Wisconsin	WIS. C.A. § 100.20
Wyoming	WYO. S.A. § 40–12–101 et seq.

REPORTERS' NOTE

This Section describes the circumstances in which a person may be subject to liability for harm to the commercial interests of others resulting from the operation of a trade or business. It reaffirms the general freedom to compete embodied in the former statement of the rule, Restatement of Torts § 708 (1938), but abandons the exception relating to competition motivated by ill will contained in § 709. The rule of former § 710 relating to competition in violation of legislative restrictions is discussed in Comment *a*.

Comment a. The freedom to compete for the business of prospective customers recognized in this Section is in accord with the general rules limiting liability for intentional interference with the prospective economic relations of others stated in Restatement, Second, Torts §§ 766B, 768.

The view that all intentional interference with the economic relations of others is prima facie tortious has long been subject to criticism. "It is silly to say all the leading cigarette companies are committing prima facie torts every day by trying to take business away from each other; that they could start suits for damages or injunctions and force the defendant to establish justification. * * * Of course, in nine hundred and ninety-nine cases out of a thousand, the tort is justified; but is it worth while to take all this trouble to march up the hill and then march down again?" Chafee, Unfair Competition, 53 Harv. L.Rev. 1289, 1304 (1940).

The Restatement, Second, of Torts, in discussing the general principles of liability for intentional interference with economic relations, recognizes that the requirements for establishing a prima facie case and for setting up an affirmative defense based on privilege remain unsettled. "The result is that there is little consensus on who has the burden of raising the issue of whether the interference was improper or not and subsequently of proving that issue * * *." Restatement, Second, Torts § 767, Comment *k*. With respect to interference resulting from business competition, however, it suggests that "the question of whether the actor was competing with the other for the prospective business of a third party might be treated as a matter of culpability (cf. § 768), for which the burden of pleading and proving would be on the plaintiff." *Id.*; cf. § 768, Comment *a*. See, e.g., Allied Financial Services, Inc. v. Foremost Insurance Co., 418 F.Supp. 157 (D.Neb.1976) (general allegation that by competing with plaintiff and employing others to do so defendant caused the plaintiff to lose commissions does not state a cause of action); Katz v. Kapper, 7 Cal.App.2d 1, 5, 44 P.2d 1060, 1062 (1935) (sustaining a demurrer to a complaint that failed to charge defendants "with making any effort to deprive plaintiff of his trade except by transferring the same to themselves"); cf. A.F. Arnold & Co. v. Pacific Professional Insurance, Inc., 27 Cal.App.3d 710, 716, 104 Cal.Rptr. 96, 100 (1972) ("On the other hand, it is necessary to avoid a situation where every *bona fide* competitor might find himself put to justifying the conduct of his business at the whim of a rival. * * * Where only a *bona fide* competitive situation is alleged, and no more, no cause of action would seem to exist.") (dictum).

The problem of allocating burdens of pleading and proof with respect to liability for intentional interference with economic relations was considered at length in Top Service Body Shop, Inc. v. Allstate Insurance Co., 283 Or. 201, 582 P.2d 1365 (1978). Rejecting the prima facie tort approach, the court concluded that "such a claim is made out when interference resulting in injury to another is wrongful by some measure beyond the fact of the interference itself." *Id.* at 1371. This view was subsequently adopted in Leigh Furniture and Carpet Co. v. Isom, 657 P.2d 293 (Utah 1982), requiring plaintiff to prove that the interference was done for an improper purpose or by improper means. See also, e.g., Gregg v. U.S. Industries, Inc., 887 F.2d 1462 (11th Cir.1989) (plaintiff must show that the interference was unjustified) (Florida law); Flintridge Station Associates v. American Fletcher Mortgage Co., 761 F.2d 434 (7th Cir.1985) (same) (Indiana law); Machine Maintenance & Equipment Co. v. Cooper Industries, Inc., 661 F.Supp. 1112 (E.D.Mo.1987) (plaintiff must show absence of justification; competition is a justification) (Missouri law); Nesler v. Fisher & Co., 452 N.W.2d 191 (Iowa 1990) (plaintiff must show that the interference was improper); Wagenseller v. Scottsdale Memorial Hosp., 147 Ariz. 370, 710 P.2d 1025 (1985) (en banc); Blake v. Levy, 191 Conn. 257, 464 A.2d 52 (1983); M & M Rental Tools, Inc. v. Milchem, Inc., 94 N.M. 449, 612 P.2d 241 (App.1980). But see Ocean State Physicians Health Plan, Inc. v. Blue Cross & Blue Shield, 883 F.2d 1101 (1st Cir. 1989), cert. denied 494 U.S. 1027, 110 S.Ct. 1473, 108 L.Ed.2d 610 (1990) (justification is a defense) (Rhode Island law); Thompson v. Allstate Insurance Co., 476 F.2d 746 (5th Cir. 1973) (same) (Alabama law); Alyeska Pipeline Service Co. v. Aurora Air Service, Inc., 604 P.2d 1090 (Alaska 1979) (prima facie case established by showing intentional interference with contract terminable at will). The latter case is criticized in Dobbs, Tortious Interference with Contractual Relationships, 34 Ark.L.Rev. 335 (1980).

Illustration 1 is based on Illustration 1 to former § 708. The rule precluding the imposition of liability for harm resulting from the mere fact of competition is sometimes traced to the Schoolmasters' Case, Y.B. Hilary 11, H.IV, f. 47, pl. 21 (1410), in which two masters of a long-established grammar school were held to have no cause of action against an interloper who opened a rival school. "If I have a mill and my neighbor constructs another mill, as a result of which the profit of my mill is diminished, I state no action against him * * *." *Id.* For a more recent application of this principle, see RCM Supply Co. v. Hunter Douglas, Inc., 686 F.2d 1074 (4th Cir.1982) (damage award reversed because of the failure to instruct the jury on the "competitive privilege").

Illustration 2 is taken from Illustration 2 to Restatement, Second, Torts § 768.

Illustration 3 is based on Hardin v. Kentucky Utilities Co., 390 U.S. 1, 88 S.Ct. 651, 19 L.Ed.2d 787 (1968). See Smalley Transportation Co. v. Moed's Transfer Co., 373 So.2d 55 (Fla.App. 1979), permitting recovery of damages in an action by a competitor against a carrier operating without the required state approval. See also National Bank of Detroit v. Wayne Oakland Bank, 252 F.2d 537 (6th Cir. 1958); Commercial State Bank v. Gidney, 174 F.Supp. 770 (D.D.C. 1959), affirmed 278 F.2d 871 (D.C.Cir.1960). On the principles governing the recognition of a private right of action for the violation of a statutory duty, see Cort v. Ash, 422 U.S. 66, 95 S.Ct. 2080, 45 L.Ed.2d 26 (1975); Touche Ross & Co. v. Redington, 442 U.S. 560, 99 S.Ct. 2479, 61 L.Ed.2d 82 (1979).

Cases involving private actions brought by competitors to enforce professional licensing statutes have yielded inconsistent results. Compare Massachusetts Society of Optometrists v. Waddick, 340 Mass. 581, 165 N.E.2d 394 (1960), and Delaware Optometric Corp. v. Sherwood, 36 Del.Ch. 223, 128 A.2d 812 (1957), with Burden v. Hoover, 9 Ill.2d 114, 137 N.E.2d 59 (1956). See Callmann, Unfair Competition, Trademarks, and Monopolies § 16.04 (4th ed.).

Comment c. The Reporter's Explanatory Notes to Restatement of Torts § 709, which imposed liability on "[o]ne who engages in a business primarily for the purpose of causing loss of business to another and with the intention of terminating the business when that purpose is accomplished," conceded that "[t]he cases in which liability was actually imposed are very few." Restatement of Torts (Tent. Draft No.17 1938). The Section was based primarily on the decisions in Tuttle v. Buck, 107 Minn. 145, 119 N.W. 946 (1909), and Dunshee v. Standard Oil Co., 152 Iowa 618, 132 N.W. 371 (1911).

In *Tuttle*, the court sustained an order overruling a demurrer to a complaint alleging that the defendant banker "wrongfully, unlawfully, and maliciously" attempted to destroy the business of plaintiff, a barber, by establishing, "for the sole and only purpose of injuring the trade of the plaintiff," a competing shop staffed with a salaried barber under an agreement whereby all income was to be paid to the defendant. In an Illustration to § 709 based on the case, the agreement was described as one in which the employee retained all receipts, thereby minimizing the defendant's competitive interest. See § 709, Illustration 1. In *Dunshee*, the court held that a wholesale oil dealer who had entered the retail market in order to drive out a retailer who had ceased doing business with the wholesaler was subject to liability if "there was no real purpose or desire to establish a competing business, but, under the guise or pretense of competition, to accomplish a malicious purpose to ruin the [plaintiff] or drive it out of business, intending themselves to retire therefrom when their end had been secured." 152 Iowa at 626, 132 N.W. at 374. See also Memphis Steam Laundry–Cleaners, Inc. v. Lindsey, 192 Miss. 224, 5 So.2d 227 (1941); Boggs v. Duncan–Schell Furniture Co., 163 Iowa 106, 143 N.W. 482 (1913) (condemning "simulated competition"). Liability in each of the foregoing cases, however, might instead be justified by the nature of the defendant's conduct. In *Dunshee* there was evidence of passing off and other improper interference with orders to the plaintiff from its customers; in *Boggs* the injury to plaintiff resulted primarily from the defendant's false advertising; in *Memphis Steam Laundry–Cleaners* the defendant's actions might well have been unlawful under antitrust law. Even the complaint in Tuttle v. Buck alleged the making of "false and malicious reports and accusations" by the defendant.

Discussions questioning the utility of inquiries into the actor's motives include Dobbs, Tortious Interference with Contractual Relationships, 34 Ark.L.Rev. 335, 347–50 (1980); Perlman, Interference with Contract and Other Economic Expectancies: A Clash of Tort and Contract Doctrine, 49 U.Chi.L.Rev. 61, 94–97 (1982); Myers, The Differing Treatment of

Efficiency and Competition in Antitrust and Tortious Interference Law, 77 Minn.L.Rev. 1097 (1993). "The defendant's state of mind in engaging in competition does not alone provide a basis for liability." Augat, Inc. v. Aegis, Inc., 409 Mass. 165, 177, 565 N.E.2d 415, 422 (1991) (citing Restatement Third, Unfair Competition § 1, Comment *c* (Tent. Draft No.1 (1988))). "Problems inherent in proving motivation or purpose make it prudent for commercial conduct to be regulated for the most part by the improper means alternative, which typically requires only a showing of particular conduct." Leigh Furniture and Carpet Co. v. Isom, 657 P.2d 293, 307 (Utah 1982) (dictum). But see Deauville Corp. v. Federated Dept. Stores, Inc., 756 F.2d 1183 (5th Cir. 1985) (evidence of intent to harm should be submitted to the jury); Delaware Valley Transplant Program v. Coye, 722 F.Supp. 1188 (D.N.J.1989) (malicious intent is relevant) (dictum); Alyeska Pipeline Service Co. v. Aurora Air Service, Inc., 604 P.2d 1090 (Alaska 1979) (applying the ill will standard to interference with a contract terminable at will).

In its statement of the rule protecting competitors from liability for intentional interference with the prospective contractual relations of another, Restatement, Second, Torts § 768 requires that the actor's "purpose is at least in part to advance his interest in competing with the other." This language, and much of the accompanying commentary, is taken from the statement of the rule in Restatement of Torts § 768. Comments to both sections presume, however, that "[i]f the business diverted by the actor relates to his competition with his competitor, his conduct will ordinarily be directed, at least in part, to the improvement of his position in the competition." The rule stated in this Section can be said to go beyond that of Restatement, Second, Torts § 768 by eliminating in such circumstances the necessity of an inquiry into the actor's motives.

Illustration 4 is based on Illustration 2 to Restatement of Torts § 709, which was derived from Beardsley v. Kilmer, 236 N.Y. 80, 140 N.E. 203 (1923). See Miller Chemical Co. v. Tams, 211 Neb. 837, 843, 320 N.W.2d 759, 763 (1982). "The fact that hatred or desire for revenge was part of the reason is insufficient to make interference improper if the conduct is directed at least in part to advancement of his own competitive interest and social benefits arising therefrom." See also Katz v. Kapper, 7 Cal.App.2d 1, 44 P.2d 1060 (1935); Candalaus Chicago, Inc. v. Evans Mill Supply Co., 51 Ill.App.3d 38, 9 Ill. Dec. 62, 366 N.E.2d 319 (1977); United Wild Rice, Inc. v. Nelson, 313 N.W.2d 628 (Minn.1982).

Comment g. Judicial definitions of "unfair competition" are collected in McCarthy, Trademarks and Unfair Competition § 1.04. An act or practice that is determined to be unfair under this Section also constitutes a "wrongful means" of interference with the prospective contractual relations of a competitor under the rule in Restatement, Second, Torts § 768. See also *id.* § 767, Comment *c*.

Cases adjudicating claims of unfair competition brought by competitors under the Unfair Trade Practices and Consumer Protection Act include McLaughlin Ford, Inc. v. Ford Motor Co., 192 Conn. 558, 473 A.2d 1185 (1984); McDonald's Corp. v. Gunvill, 441 F.Supp. 71 (N.D.Ill.1977), affirmed 622 F.2d 592 (7th Cir.1980) (Illinois law); M & W Gear Co. v. AW Dynamometer, Inc., 97 Ill.App.3d 904, 53 Ill.Dec. 721, 424 N.E.2d 356 (1981); Roustabouts, Inc. v. Hamer, 447 So.2d 543 (La.App.1984); Datacomm Interface, Inc. v. Computerworld, Inc., 396 Mass. 760, 489 N.E.2d 185 (1986); Doliner v. Brown, 21 Mass.App.Ct. 692, 489 N.E.2d 1036 (1986); Princeton Graphics Operating, L.P. v. NEC Home Electronics, Inc., 732 F.Supp. 1258 (S.D.N.Y.1990) (New York law); Nordstrom, Inc. v. Tampourlos, 107 Wash.2d 735, 733 P.2d 208 (1987). Cases decided under the Act sometimes appeal to the Federal Trade Commission's unfairness criteria first announced in its Statement of Basis and Purpose of Trade Regulation Rule 408, Unfair or Deceptive Advertising and Labeling of Cigarettes in Relation to the Health Hazards of Smoking, 29 Fed. Reg. 8324, 8355 (1964), quoted in Federal Trade Commission v. Sperry & Hutchinson Co., 405 U.S. 233, 244 n.5, 92 S.Ct. 898, 905 n.5, 31 L.Ed.2d 170 (1972). The criteria were reformulated in an FTC Statement of Policy, Dec. 17, 1980. See Trade Reg. Rep. (CCH) ¶ 13,203.

Cases on physical interference include Evenson v. Spaulding, 150 Fed. 517 (9th Cir.1907); Standard Oil Co. v. Doyle, 118 Ky. 662, 82 S.W. 271 (1904). On the institution of legal proceedings against a competitor in bad faith as a form of unfair competition, see T.N. Dickinson Co. v. LL Corp., 227 U.S.P.Q. 145 (D.Conn. 1985). On defamation and disparagement as unfair competition, see Hayes v. Irwin, 541 F.Supp. 397 (N.D.Ga.1982), affirmed 729 F.2d 1466 (11th Cir.), cert. denied 469 U.S. 857, 105 S.Ct. 185, 83 L.Ed.2d 119 (1984). On unlawful restraints of trade as unfair competition, see Natural Design, Inc. v. Rouse Co., 302 Md. 47, 485 A.2d 663 (1984); Ron Tonkin Gran Turismo, Inc. v. Wakehouse Motors, Inc., 46 Or.App. 199, 611 P.2d 658 (1980). See also C.E. Services, Inc. v. Control Data Corp., 759 F.2d 1241 (5th Cir.), cert. denied 474 U.S. 1037, 106 S.Ct. 604, 88 L.Ed.2d 583 (1985) (allegations of predatory pricing); SuperTurf, Inc. v. Monsanto Co., 660 F.2d 1275 (8th Cir.1981) (allegation of collusion between architect and bidder).

Illustration 5 is based on Emack v. Kane, 34 Fed. 46 (C.C.Ill.1888). See, e.g., Gardiner v. Gendel, 727 F.Supp. 799 (E.D.N.Y.1989), affirmed 976 F.2d 746 (Fed.Cir.1992); Sparks v. McCrary, 156 Ala. 382, 47 So. 332 (1908). Cf. Brandt Consolidated, Inc. v. Agrimar Corp., 801 F.Supp. 164 (C.D.Ill.1992) (cause of action stated under § 43(a) of the Lanham Act).

Illustration 6 is based on Kinco, Inc. v. Schueck Steel, Inc., 283 Ark. 72, 671 S.W.2d 178 (1984). On the use of confidential information as an unfair means of competition, see, e.g., Michigan Avenue National Bank v. State Farm Insurance Cos., 83 Ill. App.3d 507, 39 Ill.Dec. 42, 404 N.E.2d 426 (1980); Adler, Barish, Daniels, Levin and Creskoff v. Epstein, 482 Pa. 416, 393 A.2d 1175 (1978), cert. denied 442 U.S. 907, 99 S.Ct. 2817, 61 L.Ed.2d 272 (1979); Island Air, Inc. v. LaBar, 18 Wash.App. 129, 566 P.2d 972 (1977).

Illustration 7 is based on Kelite Products, Inc. v. Binzel, 224 F.2d 131 (5th Cir.1955). See Newark Hardware & Plumbing Supply Co. v. Stove Manufacturers Corp., 136 N.J.L. 401, 56 A.2d 605 (Sup.Ct.), affirmed 137 N.J.L. 612, 61 A.2d 240 (Ct.Errors & App.1948), imposing liability on a retailer who knowingly accepted and sold scarce merchandise consigned to a competing retailer but inadvertently delivered to the defendant. Compare M & M Rental Tools, Inc. v. Milchem, Inc., 94 N.M. 449, 612 P.2d 241 (App.1980), declining to impose liability on a seller who took an incoming call at a competitor's office and, after identifying himself to the caller, made the sale for his own account. Cf. Nifty Foods Corp. v. Great Atlantic & Pacific Tea Co., 614 F.2d 832 (2d Cir.1980) (interference with advantageous relationships by a competitor is actionable only if the conduct is criminal or fraudulent) (New York law); Azar v. Lehigh Corp., 364 So.2d 860 (Fla.App.1978) (upholding a temporary restraining order enjoining a real estate broker from soliciting customers on the premises of a motel operated by a competing real estate developer who had invited prospective purchasers to the area at its own expense).

Comment h. State unfair competition statutes of general applicability are collected in International Trademark Association, State Trademark and Unfair Competition Law.

Limitations on the enforceability of promises not to compete are discussed in Restatement, Second, Contracts §§ 186–188.

Illustration 8 is based on Hutcherson v. Alexander, 264 Cal.App.2d 126, 70 Cal.Rptr. 366 (1968). See generally Restatement, Second, Torts §§ 822–831.

CHAPTER TWO

DECEPTIVE MARKETING

Introductory Note: This Chapter addresses the rules governing liability for injury to the commercial interests of competitors and others arising from the use of deceptive representations in the marketing of goods and services. It encompasses representations falsely describing the qualities or characteristics of a seller's goods or services, often referred to as "false advertising," and misrepresentations relating to the source of a seller's goods or services, sometimes referred to as "passing off." Actions for deceptive marketing are generally brought under § 43(a) of the Lanham Act, 15 U.S.C.A. § 1125(a), or under the various state statutes prohibiting deceptive trade practices. The rules stated in this Chapter elaborate the concepts relevant to the resolution of such actions. Sections 2 and 3 state the basic principles governing liability; the remaining Sections address specific applications of these general principles.

Misrepresentations of source or sponsorship arising from the unauthorized use of trademarks or other indicia of origin are treated in Chapter Three.

---

§ 2. Deceptive Marketing: General Principle

One who, in connection with the marketing of goods or services, makes a representation relating to the actor's own goods, services, or commercial activities that is likely to deceive or mislead prospective purchasers to the likely commercial detriment of another under the rule stated in § 3 is subject to liability to the other for the relief appropriate under the rules stated in §§ 35–37.

Comment:

a. Rationale. Unless prospective purchasers can accurately compare the products offered by competing sellers, the free enterprise system cannot operate efficiently. The use of deceptive representations in the marketing of goods and services impairs the ability of purchasers to choose intelligently among competing products. As confidence in the truth of advertising diminishes, prospective purchasers may be forced to expend additional resources in examining and sampling competing products. A seller's misrepresentations may be actionable by deceived purchasers under traditional rules of tort and contract law and also under the various state and federal consumer protection statutes. In many instances, however, the cost of obtaining relief may exceed the purchaser's potential remedy. The use of deceptive representations in the marketing of goods and services may also cause injury to the legitimate commercial interests of other sellers by unfairly depriving them of the opportunity to compete on the merits of their products in the marketplace or by threatening harm to their reputation and good will. The rules of this Chapter are concerned with the protection of these commercial interests. Although the rules are not applicable to actions by deceived purchasers, they function as an indirect form of consumer protection. The rules in this Chapter, however, also reflect the public interest in avoiding unnecessary restrictions on the dissemination of commercial information.

This Section is applicable only to representations made in connection with the marketing of goods or services. The United States Supreme Court has held that the first amendment protects communications promoting the sale of goods or services from unjustified governmental interference, but it has repeatedly affirmed that there is no constitutional prohibition on the imposition of liability in connection with false, deceptive, or misleading commercial speech. The rule of this Section is applicable only to commercial speech.

Illustrations:

1. *A*, a utility company, includes with its monthly bill an insert stating the company's views on nuclear power. The insert states that nuclear power plants are safe, clean, and economical and that use of nuclear energy reduces the nation's dependence on foreign energy sources. The representations, whether true or false, are not within the scope of this Section.

2. *A* and *B* are pharmaceutical companies engaged in the marketing of over-the-counter analgesics. In a television commercial, *A* makes a false representation that its product is more

effective than *B*'s for the relief of pain. The representation is within the scope of this Section.

b. Historical development. Liability to other sellers for commercial injuries resulting from an actor's deceptive marketing was initially confined to misrepresentations of source. Thus, use of another's trademark to falsely represent that the actor was the other, or that the actor's goods were manufactured by the other, subjected the actor to liability in an action for trademark infringement. See Chapter Three. Other misrepresentations relating to source were cognizable in an action for unfair competition. See § 4, Comment *b*. Recognition of liability in the absence of a misrepresentation relating to source was retarded by several factors: the seeming complexity of identifying appropriate plaintiffs; the fear that such liability might unduly hamper free enterprise; the development of alternative means of dealing with the problem of deceptive advertising; and the acceptance of precedents as exhaustive rather than illustrative.

During the first half of the 20th century, liability at common law was cautiously expanded beyond misrepresentations of source to misrepresentations concerning other characteristics or qualities of the seller's goods. Relying upon the "passing off" cases, however, courts generally required proof that the misrepresentation had directly diverted trade from the plaintiff to the actor. This requirement effectively precluded relief unless the plaintiff was the sole alternative source of the misrepresented goods. (An exception to this "single source" requirement was a series of cases involving misrepresentations of geographic origin, which were held actionable by a competitor doing business in the locality falsely designated as the origin of the defendant's goods.) The "single source" requirement severely limited the capacity of the common law to respond to the problem of deceptive advertising and it was forcefully criticized by contemporary commentators. The Restatement of Torts proffered a cautious expansion of liability, see § 761, but retained the requirement of proof that the misrepresentation had diverted sales from the plaintiff to the actor.

This limitation on the private right of action may have encouraged the public regulation of advertising. In the early decades of the twentieth century, many state legislatures enacted criminal prohibitions against false advertising (the so-called Printers Ink Statutes), but their impact was blunted by strict construction and sporadic enforcement. Federal legislation undertook to regulate the labeling of a wide variety of specific products. The Federal Trade Commission Act, proscribing "unfair methods of competition" and "unfair or deceptive acts or practices," established a comprehensive regulatory regime encompassing deceptive representations in advertising, but with no provision for private enforcement. More recently, state legislatures, inspired by the Federal Trade Commission's draft of the Unfair Trade Practices and Consumer Protection Act, have enacted "Little FTC Acts" augmenting public regulation at the state level. See the Statutory Note following § 1.

The expansion of the private right of action by competitors for deceptive marketing can be traced to the enactment of the Trademark Act of 1946, 15 U.S.C.A. §§ 1051–1127, commonly known as the Lanham Act. As originally enacted, § 43(a) of the Act, 15 U.S.C.A. § 1125(a), recognized a right of action against "a false designation of origin, or any false description or representation" used in connection with any goods or services in favor of "any person who believes that he is or is likely to be damaged." Some early interpretations confined § 43(a) to misrepresentations relating to source; other interpretations viewed it as a codification of existing common law liability under the "single source" doctrine. Subsequent decisions, however, established the section's general applicability to deceptive advertising and rejected the attempt to engraft the common law limitations onto the statutory tort. The 1988 revision of § 43(a) confirmed its application to both misrepresentations of source and other deceptive representations made in connection with the marketing of goods and services.

State legislation now also recognizes private rights of action in favor of businesses likely to be injured by deceptive marketing on the part of other sellers in the marketplace. A number of states have enacted the Uniform Deceptive Trade Practices Act. See the Statutory Note following this Section. Among the practices proscribed by the Act are deceptive designations of geographic origin; representations that the goods or services have characteristics, ingredients, uses, benefits, or quantities that they do not in fact possess; and false representations that goods are original or new, or are of a particular standard, quality, or grade. Injunctions may be granted under the Uniform Deceptive Trade Practices Act to persons likely to be damaged by the deceptive practice. In addition, in several states, either by express statutory authorization or judicial interpretation, competitors damaged by deceptive practices may also bring private actions under the Unfair Trade Practices and Consumer Protection Act. See § 1, Comment *g*.

Limitations on the common law cause of action for deceptive marketing have sometimes been ascribed to the potential chilling effect of broader liability and to the prospect of increased litigation. Although the development of private rights of action in favor of businesses injured by deceptive marketing has been achieved largely through legislation, the public policy implications of these statutes, the dearth of modern common law precedents articulating the "single source" limitation, and the persistent expansion of common law rights against other forms of unfair competition support the statement of a general principle of liability. In view of existing statutory rights, the marginal effect of an expansion of liability at common law is minimal. This Section thus recognizes a general principle of liability for deceptive marketing independent of specific statutory authority. The rules embodied in this Section and in the succeeding Sections of this Chapter are therefore applicable to both common law and statutory causes of action.

c. Relation to product disparagement. To be actionable under this Section, the representation must relate to the goods, services, or commercial activities of the actor; representations relating solely to the goods or services marketed by others are not within the scope of the rule as stated here. Liability at common law for misrepresentations that disparage the goods or services of others has long been subject to distinct rules shaped in part by questionable analogies to the law of defamation. The general rules governing product disparagement, or "trade libel" as it is sometimes called, are set forth in Restatement, Second, Torts §§ 623A–652 and are not repeated here. However, under the 1988 revision of § 43(a) of the Lanham Act and under § 2(a)(8) of the Uniform Deceptive Trade Practices Act, an actor who falsely disparages the goods or services of another seller is subject to liability without proof of special damages or of an intent to deceive, thus diminishing the distinctions drawn at common law between disparagement and false advertising. It is also uncertain whether the analogy to defamation will ultimately subject the statutory and common law actions for product disparagement to some or all of the constitutional restrictions that have been imposed on the action for defamation. Since disparaging statements that are made in connection with the marketing of goods or services typically fall within the classification of commercial speech, the full range of constitutional restrictions may not be applicable, but the issue remains unsettled. Although the rule of this Section is expressly limited to misrepresentations relating to the goods, services, or commercial activities of the actor, that limitation is not intended to preclude or discourage the development of a similar rule of liability at common law applicable to misrepresentations relating to the products or commercial activities of another.

The distinctions between representations relating to the goods or services of the actor and representations relating to the goods or services of another is particularly difficult to maintain when the representation is expressly or implicitly comparative. For example, a representation concerning the products of a competitor may imply that the actor's own product is different or superior to the competitor's with respect to the matter represented. Thus, if a representation directed at another's product causes prospective purchasers to infer facts about the actor's own goods or services, the representation is within the scope of this Section.

d. Likelihood of deception. In order to subject an actor to liability under this Section, the actor's representation must be likely to deceive or mislead "prospective purchasers." Prospective purchasers include any persons or legal entities to whom the actor's goods or services are marketed, whether by sale, lease, license, or other manner of commercial transaction, or to whom an offer of such a transaction is made. They may be the immediate customers of the actor or the customers of others who market the actor's products. The term "prospective purchasers" also includes persons such as purchasing agents, product consultants, end users, and others who may control or influence the purchasing decisions of others and whose deception is therefore likely to result in commercial detriment to competing sellers under the principles stated in § 3.

The likelihood that a particular representation will deceive or mislead is determined by the meaning likely to be attributed to the representation by its audience and the relationship between that meaning and the true facts. A representation may be likely to deceive or mislead because it is literally false, such as a claim that furniture is solid mahogany when it has only a mahogany veneer or that what is in fact a cotton textile is 40 percent wool. Representations that are not literally false may nevertheless be likely to deceive or mislead if the audience is likely to infer additional facts that are false. Thus, a statement may be true with respect to the facts stated but fail to include qualifying matter necessary to prevent the implication of further assertions that are false. Such half-truths may be as likely to deceive or mislead as a representation that is wholly false. So also may an ambiguous statement subject to two interpretations, one of which is false.

The meaning of any statement depends on the context in which it is made. The determination of meaning, and hence of the tendency of a representation to deceive or mislead, must accordingly be made in light of all the circumstances surrounding the representation, including the character and sophistication of the audience and the subject matter of the communication. If the representation is expressed through words alone, the words themselves are the most important evidence of meaning. When the representation is literally false, a court may conclude in the absence of credible evidence to the contrary that the representation is likely to deceive or mislead. When the tendency to deceive or mislead turns instead upon the inferences to be drawn from the representation or upon a choice among several possible interpretations, direct evidence of the meaning attached to the representation by the relevant audience may be necessary to establish a likelihood of deception. Surveys, when properly structured and conducted, can be helpful in ascertaining the meaning likely to be attributed to a representation and hence the likelihood that it will deceive or mislead. Evidence of actual deception, misunderstanding, or confusion, although not required under the rule in this Section, is relevant in determining whether the audience is likely to be deceived or misled.

The intentions of the speaker are also relevant in assessing the likelihood of deception. Although an intention to deceive is not required in order to subject a seller to liability, evidence that the representation is in fact intended to communicate a false or misleading message may justify the inference that deception is likely, since it is ordinarily appropriate to assume that a speaker who intends to deceive will be successful in doing so.

A person seeking to establish liability under this Section bears the burden of proving that the representation, as it is likely to be understood by the audience, is false or misleading. Thus, the fact that the representation lacks adequate substantiation is not in itself sufficient for the imposition of liability. However, liability may be established by proof that the representation either expressly or by implication includes a claim concerning the nature or degree of substantiation and that such substantiation does not in fact exist.

In many instances a representation may be likely to deceive or mislead only some of the prospective purchasers to whom it is directed. A person is subject to liability under this Section only if the representation is likely to deceive or mislead a significant portion of the audience. As a general matter, if the representation would deceive a reasonably prudent purchaser of the goods or services, it is likely to deceive or mislead under the rule in this Section. If a reasonably prudent purchaser would not be deceived or misled by the representation, the actor is not subject to liability in the absence of other evidence indicating that the representation is nevertheless likely to deceive or mislead a significant portion of its audience.

Imposition of liability in connection with a representation likely to deceive only a portion of the audience necessarily interferes with the communication of non-deceptive speech between the actor and that portion of the audience not likely to be misled. In determining whether the portion of the audience likely to be deceived is "significant," the potential harm to such persons and to the interests of competitors must be weighed against the harm that the imposition of liability and contemplated relief would cause to the actor and the remainder of the audience. It is thus not possible to analyze the issue solely in terms of absolute numbers or percentages. Among the relevant factors are the seriousness of the threatened injury to deceived purchasers and the extent to which the representation could be easily recast to convey the information in a form less likely to deceive or mislead.

Determining the likelihood that a representation will deceive or mislead is closely analogous to determining the likelihood of confusion under the rule governing the infringement of trademarks stated in § 20, and much of the commentary to § 20 is therefore also applicable to the rule stated here.

The fact that a seller has made a representation that is likely to deceive or mislead is not in itself sufficient to subject the seller to liability. Liability may be imposed under this Section only if the deception is also to the likely commercial detriment of the person seeking relief under the rule stated in § 3, which requires proof of both materiality and likelihood of harm.

Illustrations:

3. *A* and *B* manufacture competing non-prescription pain relievers. In a television commercial advertising *A* 's product, an actor wearing a white jacket and holding a stethoscope states that *A* 's product has been "proven faster-acting than any other non-prescription pain reliever." Existing clinical tests comparing *A* 's product to *B* 's are insufficient to establish which of the two products provides faster relief. *A* 's representation is likely to deceive or mislead.

4. *A*, a record distributor, represents that a particular record contains songs played by a well-known musician. In fact, the musician was a mere background player on the recording. If a significant number of prospective purchasers are likely to infer from *A* 's representation that the musician was a principal performer on the record, the representation is likely to deceive or mislead.

e. Non-disclosure. This Section subjects an actor to liability for false or misleading representations; a failure to disclose even material facts is not in itself actionable under the rule stated here. Similarly, the fact that a representation made by the actor would be more useful to prospective purchasers if accompanied by further disclosures is not sufficient to subject the actor to liability. However, in some circumstances the disclosure of additional facts may be necessary to avoid liability for a representation that would be misleading in the absence of further disclosure. In determining whether a representation is misleading because of a failure to make additional disclosures, it may be appropriate to consider the extent to which the information communicated by the representation is valuable to prospective purchasers despite the absence of the additional disclosures. In the absence of a misleading representation, the failure to disclose additional information will not subject the actor to liability under this Section.

On the possibility of liability for non-disclosure of material facts, see § 1, Comment *g*.

Illustration:

5. *A*, a manufacturer of video-recording equipment, fails to disclose to potential purchasers that certain uses of the equipment may subject the user to liability for copyright infringement. The non-disclosure does not subject *A* to liability under the rule stated in this Section.

f. Intent. Liability under this Section turns upon an objective evaluation of the probable consequences of the actor's conduct and not upon a determination of the actor's subjective intent. Although the intent of the actor may be relevant to a number of issues arising under this Section, including the meaning to be attributed to the words or conduct of the actor (see Comment *d*), the materiality of the representation (see § 3, Comment *b*), and the availability of monetary relief (see § 36, Comment *j* ; § 37, Comment *e*), an intent to deceive is not a necessary element of liability.

The history of the law of unfair competition reveals a persistent retreat from its initial emphasis on the actor's subjective state of mind. Because the action for trademark infringement arose as an offshoot of the common law action for deceit, an intent to deceive was originally thought to be an essential element of the cause of action. In the case of fanciful or arbitrary trademarks, the natural inference that the defendant's imitation had been adopted with an intent to deceive prospective purchasers eventually crystallized into a conclusive presumption, in effect a rule of law that proof of fraudulent intent is unnecessary. See § 9, Comment *d*. For a time, a distinction was maintained between actions for the infringement of technical "trademarks" and actions for "unfair competition" in which protection was sought for other designations that had acquired source significance. In the latter action, proof of fraudulent intent remained a requirement. The distinction between these actions, however, has been abandoned, and fraud is no longer a necessary element in an action for infringement. See § 20, Comment *c*.

Statutory actions for unfair competition have similarly abandoned the requirement of fraudulent intent. Liability for deceptive marketing under § 43(a) of the Lanham Act is not dependent on the defendant's intent. Under the Uniform Deceptive Trade Practices Act, a person causing confusion as to source, sponsorship, or affiliation, or falsely describing the characteristics, ingredients, or benefits of the goods or services is similarly subject to liability without regard to intent. In keeping with the trend of common law developments and the prevailing statutory formulations, this Section does not require proof of fraudulent intent.

g. Form of misrepresentation. There are no technical requirements as to the form or manner in which the misrepresentation is made. It may be conveyed at the point of sale through labels, packaging, or displays, or it may be contained in brochures, catalogs, or price lists, or in print, radio, or television advertising. The misrepresentation may be written or oral, or it may be conveyed through visual images or inferred from other conduct of the actor. If the misrepresentation is repeated by several actors in the marketing chain, each may be subject to liability under this Section.

Illustrations:

6. *A* sells a snack food product made from dehydrated potato granules. The packaging describes the product as "potato chips." If prospective purchasers, in the absence of additional disclosures, are likely to interpret that term to refer only to products made from whole, sliced potatoes, *A* has made a representation likely to deceive or mislead.

7. *A*, a manufacturer of synthetic mink garments, sells its products under the trademark NORMINK. If the use of that trademark is likely to cause prospective purchasers to believe that the garments are made of genuine mink, *A* has made a representation likely to deceive or mislead.

8. *A* is a manufacturer of dresses. In a magazine advertisement promoting mail order sales, *A* includes a photograph purporting to show one of the dresses. The photograph in fact depicts a dress manufactured by *A* 's competitor *B*, and the dress offered for sale by *A* is not identical to *B* 's dress. *A* has made a representation likely to deceive or mislead.

9. *A*, a manufacturer of orange juice, broadcasts a television commercial in which an actor is shown squeezing oranges and

pouring the freshly-squeezed juice directly into a carton bearing *A*'s name. *A*'s juice is in fact frozen after it is squeezed and later heated to prevent spoilage before being packaged in cartons. If prospective purchasers are likely to interpret the commercial as a statement that *A*'s product contains only freshly-squeezed, unprocessed juice, *A* has made a representation likely to deceive or mislead.

10. *A* produces wine that it bottles under labels falsely indicating its geographic origin. *A* sells the wine to *B*, a distributor, who sells it to retailers including *C*. *C* offers the wine for sale to the public. *A*, *B*, and *C* have made a representation likely to deceive or mislead.

h. Remedies. This Section subjects the maker of a representation to liability upon a showing that the representation is *likely* to deceive or mislead prospective purchasers to the *likely* commercial detriment of another; proof of actual deception or actual harm is not required. See § 3, Comment *e*. Thus, injunctive relief may be awarded even though the fact or extent of harm to the party seeking relief is uncertain. Such a remedy does not afford a windfall to the plaintiff and furthers the public interest in preserving the integrity of the marketplace. A person seeking monetary relief, however, bears the additional burden of establishing entitlement to such relief under the rules stated in §§ 36 and 37. Those rules generally require proof of actual deception resulting in demonstrable pecuniary loss to the plaintiff or demonstrable pecuniary gain to the defendant.

STATUTORY NOTE

The Uniform Deceptive Trade Practices Act was promulgated by the National Conference of Commissioners on Uniform State Laws in 1964 and revised in 1966.

The Prefatory Note to the 1964 Act states the purpose of the Act as follows:

> The Uniform Act is designed to bring state law up to date by removing undue restrictions on the common law action for deceptive trade practices. Certain objectionable practices are singled out, but the courts are left free to fix the proper ambit of the Act in case-by-case adjudications.
>
> The deceptive trade practices singled out by the Uniform Act can be roughly subdivided into conduct involving either misleading trade identification or false or deceptive advertising.

The Uniform Deceptive Trade Practices Act is in effect in the following jurisdictions:

1964 Act

Delaware . . . . DEL. C., tit. 6, § 2531 et seq.
Illinois . . . . ILL. C.S., ch. 815, § 510/1 et seq.
Maine . . . . ME. R.S.A., tit. 10, § 1211 et seq.
Oklahoma . . . . OKLA. S.A., tit. 78, § 51 et seq.

1966 Revision

Colorado . . . . COLO. R.S.A. § 6–1–101 et seq.
Georgia . . . . G.A. C.A. § 10–1–370 et seq.
Hawaii . . . . HAW. R.S. § 481A–1 et seq.
Minnesota . . . . MINN. S.A. § 325D.43 et seq.
Nebraska . . . . NEB. R.S. § 87–301 et seq.
New Mexico . . . . N.M. S.A. § 57–12–1 et seq.
Ohio . . . . OHIO R.C. § 4165.01 et seq.
Oregon . . . . OR. R.S § 646.605 et seq.

REPORTERS' NOTE

This Section is an expansion of the former rule on liability for false advertising in Restatement of Torts § 761. See generally McCarthy, Trademarks and Unfair Competition §§ 27.01–09; Callmann, Unfair Competition, Trademarks and Monopolies §§ 5.01–5.50.

Comment a. On the constitutional protection afforded to commercial speech, see, e.g., Virginia State Bd. of Pharmacy v. Virginia Citizens Consumer Council, Inc., 425 U.S. 748, 96 S.Ct. 1817, 48 L.Ed.2d 346 (1976); Central Hudson Gas & Electric Corp. v. Public Service Commission, 447 U.S. 557, 100 S.Ct. 2343, 65 L.Ed.2d 341 (1980). On the distinction between commercial and noncommercial speech, see, e.g., Cincinnati v. Discovery Network, Inc., ___ U.S. ___, 113 S.Ct. 1505, 123 L.Ed.2d 99 (1993); Bolger v. Youngs Drug Products Corp., 463 U.S. 60, 103 S.Ct. 2875, 77 L.Ed.2d 469 (1983). Imposition of liability for false or deceptive advertising under § 43(a) of the Lanham Act, 15 U.S.C.A. § 1125(a), does not infringe the first amendment rights of advertisers. E.g., Castrol, Inc. v. Pennzoil Co., 987 F.2d 939 (3d Cir. 1993); U.S. Healthcare, Inc. v. Blue Cross, 898 F.2d 914 (3d Cir.), cert. denied 498 U.S. 816, 111 S.Ct. 58, 112 L.Ed.2d 33 (1990). See, e.g., National Artists Management Co. v. Weaving, 769 F.Supp. 1224 (S.D.N.Y.1991) (the limitation of § 43(a) to misrepresentations in "commercial advertising or promotion" is intended to eliminate potential constitutional issues).

In some circumstances, federal laws may preempt state regulation of advertising. See Morales v. Trans World Airlines, Inc., ___ U.S. ___, 112 S.Ct. 2031, 119 L.Ed.2d 157 (1992) (Airline Deregulation Act of 1978, 49 U.S.C.A. § 1305(a)(1), preempts state enforcement of airfare advertising guidelines).

Illustration 1 is based on the facts of Consolidated Edison Co. v. Public Service Commission, 447 U.S. 530, 100 S.Ct. 2326, 65 L.Ed.2d 319 (1980).

See, e.g., Wojnarowicz v. American Family Association, 745 F.Supp. 130 (S.D.N.Y.1990) (§ 43(a) does not extend to statements made in pamphlets intended to influence government policies); New York Public Interest Research Group, Inc. v. Insurance Information Institute, 161 A.D.2d 204, 554 N.Y.S.2d 590 (1990) (state deceptive business practices statute was not applicable to expressions of opinion on matters of public interest).

Illustration 2 is based on American Home Products Corp. v. Johnson & Johnson, 577 F.2d 160 (2d Cir.1978). On the regulation of comparative advertising, see Symposium: Comparative Advertising, 67 Trademark Rep. 351 (1977). For an argument emphasizing the potential anticompetitive consequences of broad liability for false advertising, see Jordan and Rubin, An Economic Analysis of the Law of False Advertising, 8 J.Leg. Stud. 527 (1979).

Comment b. The older view that liability for unfair competition is limited to misrepresentations relating to source was forcefully stated in American Washboard Co. v. Saginaw Mfg. Co., 103 Fed. 281 (6th Cir.1900). A misrepresentation of geographic origin was enjoined in Grand Rapids Furniture Co. v. Grand Rapids Furniture Co., 127 F.2d 245 (7th Cir.1942). The "single source" exception was articulated by Judge Learned Hand in Ely–Norris Safe Co. v. Mosler Safe Co., 7 F.2d 603 (2d Cir.1925), although the decision was reversed on the facts in an opinion by Justice Holmes. Mosler Safe Co. v. Ely–Norris Safe Co., 273 U.S. 132, 47 S.Ct. 314, 71 L.Ed. 578 (1927). For more recent applications of the "single source" rule, see Electronics Corp. of America v. Honeywell, Inc., 428 F.2d 191 (1st Cir.1970), on remand 358 F.Supp. 1230 (D.Mass.), affirmed 487 F.2d 513 (1st Cir.1973), cert. denied 415 U.S. 960, 94 S.Ct. 1491, 39 L.Ed.2d 575 (1974); Construction Technology, Inc. v. Lockformer Co., 704 F.Supp. 1212 (S.D.N.Y.1989). Cf. Multi–Tech Systems, Inc. v. Hayes Microcomputer Prods., Inc., 800 F.Supp. 825 (D.Minn.1992), appeal dismissed 988 F.2d 130 (Fed.Cir.1993) (denying defendant's motion for summary judgment on common law false advertising claim). The limitations on the common law action were criticized in influential articles by Handler, False and Misleading Advertising, 39 Yale L.J. 22 (1929), and Callmann, False Advertising as a Competitive Tort, 48 Colum.L.Rev. 876 (1948). For a comparison of alternative modes of advertising regulation see Best, Controlling False Advertising: A Comparative Study of Public Regulation, Industry Self–Policing, and Private Litigation, 20 Ga.L.Rev. 1 (1985).

Early decisions yielding narrow interpretations of § 43(a) of the Lanham Act include Chamberlain v. Columbia Pictures Corp., 186 F.2d 923 (9th Cir.1951) (§ 43(a) codifies common law limitations); Samson Crane Co. v. Union Nat. Sales, Inc., 87 F.Supp. 218 (D.Mass.1949), affirmed mem., 180 F.2d 896 (1st Cir.1950) (§ 43(a) limited to activities akin to passing off). The first broad interpretation of the section came in L'Aiglon Apparel, Inc. v. Lana Lobell, Inc., 214 F.2d 649 (3d Cir.1954) (rejecting the claim that § 43(a) was merely declarative of existing law). The legislative history and early case law under § 43(a) are examined in Derenberg, Federal Unfair Competition Law at the End of the First Decade of the Lanham Act: Prologue or Epilogue?, 32 N.Y.U.L.Rev. 1029 (1957). The subsequent judicial expansion of the section is traced, and criticized, in Germain, Unfair Trade Practices Under Section 43(a) of the Lanham Act: You've Come a Long Way, Baby—Too Far, Maybe?, 49 Ind.L.J. 84 (1973). Developing trends are examined in Bauer, A Federal Law of Unfair Competition: What Should be the Reach of Section 43(a) of the Lanham Act?, 31 U.C.L.A. L.Rev. 671 (1984), and Keller, How Do You Spell Relief? Private Regulation of Advertising Under Section 43(a) of the Lanham Act, 75 Trademark Rep. 227 (1985).

Judicial interpretations of the original version of § 43(a) were largely codified in the 1988 revision:

> § 43(a)(1). Any person who, on or in connection with any goods or services, or any container for goods, uses in commerce any word, term, name, symbol, or device, or any combination thereof, or any false designation of origin, false or misleading description of fact, or false or misleading representation of fact, which—
>
> (A) is likely to cause confusion, or to cause mistake, or to deceive as to the affiliation, connection, or association of such person with another person, or as to the origin, sponsorship, or approval of his or her goods, services, or commercial activities by another person, or
>
> (B) in commercial advertising or promotion, misrepresents the nature, characteristics, qualities, or geographic origin of his or her or another person's goods, services, or commercial activities,
>
> shall be liable in a civil action by any person who believes that he or she is or is likely to be damaged by such act. (15 U.S.C.A. § 1125.)

The elements of a cause of action under § 43(a) were delineated in U.S. Healthcare, Inc. v. Blue Cross, 898 F.2d 914, 922–23 (3d Cir.), cert. denied 498 U.S. 816, 111 S.Ct. 58, 112 L.Ed.2d 33 (1990):

> 1) that the defendant has made false or misleading statements as to his own product [or another's]; 2) that there is actual deception or at least a tendency to deceive a substantial portion of the intended audience; 3) that the deception is material in that it is likely to influence purchasing decisions; 4) that the advertised goods travelled in interstate commerce; and 5) that there is a likelihood of injury to the plaintiff in terms of declining sales, loss of good will, etc. (quoting Max Daetwyler Corp. v. Input Graphics, Inc., 545 F.Supp. 165, 171 (E.D.Pa.1982)).

See also, e.g., Cook, Perkiss and Liehe, Inc. v. Northern California Collection Service Inc., 911 F.2d 242, 244 (9th Cir.1990) (quoting Skil Corp. v. Rockwell International Corp., 375 F.Supp. 777, 783 (N.D.Ill.1974)).

On the Uniform Deceptive Trade Practices Act, see Dole, The Uniform Deceptive Trade Practices Act: Another Step Toward a National Law of Unfair Trade Practices, 51 Minn. L.Rev. 1005 (1967) and Merchant and Consumer Protection: The Uniform Deceptive Trade Practices Act, 76 Yale L.J. 485 (1967).

Comment c. Commercial disparagement was brought within the scope of § 43(a) by the 1988 amendments to the Lanham Act. E.g., U.S. Healthcare, Inc. v. Blue Cross, 898 F.2d 914 (3d Cir.), cert. denied 498 U.S. 816, 111 S.Ct. 58, 112 L.Ed.2d 33

(1990); National Artists Management Co. v. Weaving, 769 F.Supp. 1224 (S.D.N.Y.1991). An argument for an analogous common law rule of liability for disparagement is made in Hayden, A Goodly Apple Rotten at the Heart: Commercial Disparagement in Comparative Advertising as Common–Law Tortious Unfair Competition, 76 Iowa L.Rev. 67 (1990). The question of constitutional limitations on liability for disparagement, although not in the context of commercial speech, was raised but not decided in Bose Corp. v. Consumers Union of the United States, Inc., 466 U.S. 485, 104 S.Ct. 1949, 80 L.Ed.2d 502 (1984). See U.S. Healthcare, *supra* ("actual malice" standard held inapplicable at common law and under § 43(a) to disparagement claims involving commercial speech).

Comment d. The problems inherent in determining deceptiveness are considered in Craswell, Interpreting Deceptive Advertising, 65 B.U.L.Rev. 657 (1985), which also provides a brief introduction to the economic and psychological literature on advertising.

American Home Products Corp. v. Johnson & Johnson, 577 F.2d 160, 165 (2d Cir.1978), reaffirms that § 43(a) encompasses more than literal falsehoods. "Were it otherwise, clever use of innuendo, indirect intimations and ambiguous suggestions could shield the advertisement from scrutiny precisely when protection against such sophisticated deception is most needed." The court held that the perceptions of the audience are controlling. See, e.g., Abbott Laboratories v. Mead Johnson & Co., 971 F.2d 6 (7th Cir.1992); Johnson & Johnson * Merck Consumer Pharmaceuticals Co. v. Smithkline Beecham Corp., 960 F.2d 294 (2d Cir.1992) (consumer survey failed to prove that the defendant's advertisement was misleading to its audience). "When a merchandising statement or representation is literally or explicitly false, the court may grant relief without reference to the advertisement's impact on the buying public. When the challenged advertisement is implicitly rather than explicitly false, its tendency to violate the Lanham Act by misleading, confusing or deceiving should be tested by public reaction." Coca–Cola Co. v. Tropicana Products, Inc., 690 F.2d 312, 317 (2d Cir.1982) (citations omitted). See, e.g., Castrol Inc. v. Pennzoil Co., 987 F.2d 939 (3d Cir.1993); Castrol, Inc. v. Quaker State Corp., 977 F.2d 57 (2d Cir. 1992).

A frequently quoted statement of the elements of a cause of action for deceptive advertising under § 43(a) requires that the representations "actually deceived or have the tendency to deceive a substantial segment of their audience." Skil Corp. v. Rockwell International Corp., 375 F.Supp. 777, 783 (N.D.Ill.1974). See also, e.g., Johnson & Johnson, *supra*, 960 F.2d at 298 ("statistically significant part of the commercial audience"); U.S. Healthcare, Inc. v. Blue Cross, 898 F.2d 914, 922 (3d Cir.), cert. denied 498 U.S. 816, 111 S.Ct. 58, 112 L.Ed.2d 33 (1990) ("tendency to deceive a substantial portion of the intended audience"); Stiffel Co. v. Westwood Lighting Group, 658 F.Supp. 1103, 1114 (D.N.J.1987) (misleads "a not insubstantial number of consumers"). Other cases consider the effect of the representation on a "reasonably intelligent" consumer. See Vidal Sassoon, Inc. v. Bristol–Myers Co., 661 F.2d 272 (2d Cir. 1981). The various standards are discussed in Craswell, *supra*, which emphasizes the need to consider both the costs and benefits of imposing liability in connection with a representation that is likely to deceive only a portion of its audience.

In connection with Illustration 3, compare Upjohn Co. v. Riahom Corp., 641 F.Supp. 1209 (D.Del.1986) (representation of scientific basis for a product claim held deceptive) with Sandoz Pharmaceuticals Corp. v. Richardson–Vicks, Inc., 902 F.2d 222, 229 (3d Cir.1990) (plaintiff must "prove whether consumers expect an advertising claim to be substantiated and whether they expect the level of substantiation to be greater than that which the defendant has performed"; claim held adequately substantiated), and Procter & Gamble Co. v. Chesebrough–Pond's Inc., 747 F.2d 114 (2d Cir.1984) (superiority claim not proven false). That unsubstantiated claims are not actionable per se, see U–Haul International, Inc. v. Jartran, Inc., 522 F.Supp. 1238 (D.Ariz.1981), affirmed, 681 F.2d 1159 (9th Cir. 1982), and Toro Co. v. Textron, Inc., 499 F.Supp. 241 (D.Del.1980). However, since consumers may generally assume that an advertiser has at least some support for its claims, a representation of fact that is completely unsubstantiated will ordinarily be actionable. Sandoz, *supra* (dictum). See Stiffel Co., *supra*; Johnson & Johnson v. Quality Pure Manufacturing, Inc., 484 F.Supp. 975 (D.N.J. 1979).

Illustration 4 is based on the facts in Yameta Co. v. Capitol Records, Inc., 279 F.Supp. 582 (S.D.N.Y.), reversed 393 F.2d 91 (2d Cir.1968). See, e.g., Benson v. Paul Winley Record Sales Corp., 452 F.Supp. 516 (S.D.N.Y.1978).

Comment e. Illustration 5 is based on Universal City Studios, Inc. v. Sony Corp. of America, 429 F.Supp. 407 (C.D.Cal.1977). "However, a failure to inform consumers of something, even something that they should know, is not *per se* a misrepresentation actionable under section 43(a) of the Lanham Act." McNeilab, Inc. v. American Home Products Corp., 501 F.Supp. 517, 532 (S.D.N.Y. 1980) (failure to disclose that "the pain reliever doctors recommend most" is aspirin). See also Alfred Dunhill Ltd. v. Interstate Cigar Co., 499 F.2d 232 (2d Cir.1974); American Home Products Corp. v. Johnson & Johnson, 672 F.Supp. 135 (S.D.N.Y. 1987) (dismissing a claim alleging a failure to warn). However, a cause of action under § 43(a) was upheld in Bohsei Enterprises Co. v. Porteous Fastener Co., 441 F.Supp. 162 (C.D.Cal.1977), in connection with a failure to disclose the country of origin of imported goods as required by federal law. In Lamothe v. Atlantic Recording Corp., 847 F.2d 1403 (9th Cir.1988), the court found that an incomplete attribution of authorship was misleading and not merely a failure to disclose.

Comment f. There is no requirement under § 43(a) that the false representation be made with an intent to deceive. Parkway Baking Co. v. Freihofer Baking Co., 255 F.2d 641 (3d Cir.1958); Brandt Consolidated, Inc. v. Agrimar Corp., 801 F.Supp. 164 (C.D.Ill.1992). Cf. Johnson & Johnson v. Quality Pure Mfg., Inc., 484 F.Supp. 975, 979 (D.N.J. 1979) ("When a newcomer in the field adopts a trade dress confusingly similar to that of an established merchant, even innocently, or by chance, once the similarity is brought to his attention a failure or refusal to alter the trade dress to avoid the confusion is equivalent to an original and actual intention.").

Comment g. Illustration 6 is based on Potato Chip Institute v. General Mills, Inc., 333 F.Supp. 173 (D.Neb.1971), affirmed 461 F.2d 1088 (8th Cir.1972).

Illustration 7 is based on Mutation Mink Breeders Ass'n v. Lou Nierenberg Corp., 23 F.R.D. 155 (S.D.N.Y. 1959).

Illustration 8 is based on L'Aiglon Apparel, Inc. v. Lana Lobell, Inc., 214 F.2d 649 (3d Cir.1954). See, e.g., Accurate Leather & Novelty Co. v. LTD Commodities, Inc., 18 U.S.P.Q.2d 1327 (N.D.Ill.1990) (also finding a likelihood of success on a trademark infringement theory based on the distinctiveness of the plaintiff's product depicted in the photograph. See § 16.). But cf. Vibrant Sales, Inc. v. New Body Boutique, Inc., 652 F.2d 299 (2d Cir.1981), cert. denied 455 U.S. 909, 102 S.Ct. 1257, 71 L.Ed.2d 448 (1982) (no liability under § 43(a) for use of a photograph of a competitor's product if the seller is prepared to deliver an identical product and the depicted item has not acquired secondary meaning); Merchant & Evans, Inc. v. Roosevelt Building Products Co., 963 F.2d 628 (3d Cir. 1992). But see National Presto Industries, Inc. v. Hamilton Beach, Inc., 18 U.S.P.Q.2d 1993 (N.D.Ill.1990) (finding that the use of a picture of a competitor's product misrepresented the defendant's current manufacturing capability). On the use of a competitor's product as a sample of the seller's allegedly inferior goods, see Crossbow, Inc. v. Dan–Dee Imports, Inc., 266 F.Supp. 335 (S.D.N.Y.1967) (preliminary injunction issued under § 43(a)). See also Arrow United Industries, Inc. v. Hugh Richards, Inc., 678 F.2d 410 (2d Cir.1982), finding that the use of mislabeled samples by a seller not yet capable of producing the article was an implicit misrepresentation of its record as a manufacturer. If a feature of a competitor's product is protectable as a trademark under the rule stated in § 16, the defendant's use of the product as a sample or depiction of its own goods may also subject the defendant to liability for trademark infringement. See Accurate Leather & Novelty Co., *supra.* Cf. Nike, Inc. v. Rubber Mfrs. Ass'n, 509 F.Supp. 919 (S.D.N.Y.1981) (§ 43(a) invoked to enjoin the alteration of a competitor's shoes by professional athletes to resemble those of the manufacturer whose shoes the athletes had contracted to wear).

Illustration 9 is based on Coca–Cola Co. v. Tropicana Products, Inc., 690 F.2d 312 (2d Cir.1982).

Illustration 10 is based on Stabilisierungsfonds Fur Wein v. Kaiser Stuhl Wine Distributors Pty. Ltd., 647 F.2d 200 (D.C.Cir.1981). In order to subject the actor to liability it is sufficient if the representation is likely to deceive the customers of other persons who market the actor's goods, and thus *A* in Illustration 10 has made a false representation regardless of whether *B* is deceived. Similarly, since intent to deceive is not required under this Section, *B* and *C* may be subject to liability even if they themselves have been deceived by *A*'s representation, although the remedy may be limited to injunctive relief.

§ 3. Commercial Detriment of Another

A representation is to the likely commercial detriment of another if:

(a) the representation is material, in that it is likely to affect the conduct of prospective purchasers; and

(b) there is a reasonable basis for believing that the representation has caused or is likely to cause a diversion of trade from the other or harm to the other's reputation or good will.

Comment:

a. Scope. A person is subject to liability to another for a false or misleading representation under the rule stated in § 2 only if the representation is likely to cause harm to the commercial interests of the other. This Section defines the circumstances in which such harm is likely.

b. Materiality. The materiality of a representation, like its meaning, must be determined from the perspective of the audience to whom it is directed. If a significant number of prospective purchasers are likely to attach importance to the representation in determining whether to engage in a proposed transaction, the representation is material. It is not necessary that the representation be the sole or predominant factor influencing the conduct of prospective purchasers. Nor is it necessary to demonstrate that purchasers would have acted differently in the absence of the representation. It is sufficient if the representation is likely to influence prospective purchasers to some substantial degree.

The materiality of a representation does not depend upon proof of harm to persons acting in reliance upon it. It is sufficient if the representation is likely to be considered important by prospective purchasers, regardless of whether their reliance causes demonstrable pecuniary harm. It is also unnecessary to prove that the actor foresaw or should have foreseen that the representation would be likely to influence prospective purchasers. Evidence indicating an intent to deceive, however, may justify an inference that the representation is material since a seller will not ordinarily make a fraudulent representation without believing that the representation is likely to influence prospective purchasers.

If a representation is not likely to be relied upon by its audience, it is not a material representation. Unless the circumstances indicate otherwise, however, a court may infer that prospective purchasers are likely to rely on representations that relate to matters that the purchasers ordinarily consider important. In some instances, however, the falsity of the representation will be obvious to prospective purchasers, and there is thus no likelihood of reliance. In other instances, purchasers may be likely to rely on their own investigations or experience rather than on the representations of the seller, and there is again no likelihood of reliance. In these or other circumstances in which reliance is unlikely, the representation is not material.

c. Subject matter. Material representations commonly take the form of statements that pertain directly to the quality or characteristics of the actor's goods or services, such as a representation that a piece of jewelry is made of solid gold or that a particular medical preparation will prevent baldness. However, a representation that only indirectly relates to product quality or that in some other manner relates to the desirability of the proposed transaction may also be material. Representations that concern matters that are trivial or of little or no significance to prospective purchasers are not material under the rule of this Section.

Illustrations:

1. *A* produces and markets alcoholic beverages. One of its products, sold as "Blended Scotch Whisky," is in fact made from a mixture of Scotch whisky malts and domestic spirits. If prospective purchasers are likely to believe that the product contains only spirits produced in Scotland and are also likely to attach importance to the geographic origin of the constituents, the representation is material.

2. *A* and *B* are manufacturers of shampoo. In a television advertisement, *A* represents that in tests with over 900 women, *A* 's product received higher ratings than *B* 's. Although prospective purchasers interpret the representation to mean that each test participant directly compared the two products, in fact each participant used only one of the products and rated it on a numerical scale. If prospective purchasers are likely to attach importance to the test methodology in evaluating the significance of the test results, the representation is material.

3. *A*, a manufacturer of wrenches, refers in its advertising to the "patented design" of the product. The product is not in fact covered by any patent. If prospective purchasers, because of an assumed relationship between patents and product quality, are likely to attach importance to the existence of a patent, the representation is material.

4. *A* is a supplier of uranium fuel for nuclear power plants. In negotiating long-term supply contracts with utility companies, *A* represents that it controls sources of supply sufficient to insure yearly delivery of a specified quantity of fuel. In fact its sources of supply are sufficient to insure delivery of only one-quarter of that amount, and *A* intends to purchase the remaining quantity from other suppliers. If utilities are likely to attach importance to the extent of *A* 's control over sources of supply, the representation is material.

5. *A*, a manufacturer of cheese products, represents in a television commercial that each slice of its processed cheese contains 5 oz. of milk while those of some competing brands contain only 2 oz. Although most of *A* 's cheese slices do in fact contain 5 or more ounces of milk, some contain only 4.6 oz. If prospective purchasers are not likely to attach importance to the difference between 4.6 and 5 ounces, the representation is not material.

d. Puffing. An important application of the principles described in the preceding Comments concerns certain representations by sellers sometimes characterized as "puffing" or "sales talk." The propensity of sellers to exaggerate the advantages of their wares is well known, and to some extent buyers are expected to and do understand that they should discount such claims in evaluating the merits of the proposed bargain. Buyers generally assume, for example, that a seller will make favorable representations concerning the quality of the goods or services offered for sale. Statements of praise in general terms without reference to specific facts are therefore unlikely to affect the conduct of prospective purchasers and are thus not material for purposes of the rule stated in this Section.

A distinction is sometimes drawn between statements in the form of opinion and statements of fact. Although as a general matter purchasers may be less likely to rely on a representation of the seller's opinion, the form of the statement is not controlling. In many circumstances prospective purchasers may reasonably understand a statement of opinion to be more than a mere assertion as to the seller's state of mind. Some representations of opinion may imply the existence of facts that justify the opinion, or at least that there are no facts known to the speaker that are substantially incompatible with the stated opinion. Thus, although consumers may be assumed to make some allowance for the favorable opinions expressed by sellers, they may in some instances rely on an implied representation that the seller knows of no specific facts that make the expressed opinion clearly untenable. In other instances, particularly when the seller is thought to have special knowledge or skill unavailable to the consumer, it may be expected that prospective purchasers will rely directly upon the seller's statement of opinion as to value or quality. The ultimate issue in each case is whether the representation, regardless of form, is likely to affect to some substantial degree the conduct of a significant number of prospective purchasers.

It is sometimes possible, even in instances of obvious hyperbole, to identify specific consumers who have in fact relied on the representation. This Section does not subject the actor to liability, however, unless a significant number of prospective purchasers have or are likely to rely on the representation. If a reasonably prudent purchaser of the goods or services would not rely on the representation, the actor is not subject to liability in the absence of evidence establishing that the representation is nevertheless likely to be relied upon by a significant number of prospective purchasers.

Illustrations:

6. *A*, an automobile manufacturer, states in its advertising that its cars are "the best automobiles made in America." The representation is not material.

7. *A* markets a computer chess game and states in its advertising that the game "is like having a World Champion as your opponent." In the absence of other evidence establishing that the representation is likely to be relied upon by a significant number of prospective purchasers, if the court finds that a reasonably prudent purchaser would not rely upon the representation, the representation is not material.

8. *A* operates a retail jewelry store and represents to prospective customers that the diamonds offered for sale are of "first quality." If a reasonably prudent purchaser, lacking the expertise to judge the quality of diamonds, is likely to rely upon the jeweler's statement, the representation is material.

9. *A* manufactures commemorative plates. In its advertising brochures, *A* states that its plates have all been "good investments." If a reasonably prudent purchaser would interpret *A* 's statement as an assertion that the facts known to *A* are not substantially incompatible with the stated opinion and would be likely to rely upon the statement, the representation is material.

e. Likelihood of harm. In order to subject the actor to liability, the misrepresentation must be *likely* to cause harm to the commercial interests of the person seeking relief. Proof that such harm has in fact occurred is not required; nor is it necessary to establish that harm is certain to result if the actor continues in its course of conduct. The actor is subject to liability if the evidence indicates that there is a reasonable probability that the person seeking relief has or will suffer harm as a result of the misrepresentation.

Imposition of liability under this Section serves as an indirect form of consumer protection. Thus, when the potential injury to deceived consumers is relatively great, a more modest likelihood of harm to competitors may be sufficient to subject the actor to liability.

f. Interests protected. If the actor markets goods or services of the same kind as those marketed by the person seeking relief, reliance by prospective purchasers on the actor's misrepresentation is likely to cause harm to the complainant by diverting sales to the actor. If the goods are not of the same kind, the other person may establish a likelihood of harm through evidence indicating that a significant number of consumers are nevertheless likely to substitute purchase of the actor's product for that of its own. Reliance on the misrepresentation is also likely to cause harm to another who, although not in competition with the actor, nevertheless has a direct pecuniary interest in the sale of competing products, such as the owner of a royalty interest measured by the sales of goods that compete with the actor's. The asserted injury, however, must be direct; derivative injury such as harm suffered by a competitor's employees or suppliers is not within the scope of this Section. In deciding whether the complainant's interest is sufficiently direct to justify protection, an important factor is the presence or absence of harm to a less remote party whose self-interest would normally motivate the party to vindicate the public interest by exposing the actor's deceptive representation.

The commercial harm cognizable under this Section is not limited to direct diversions of trade, and an actor may thus be subject to liability to a person with whom it does not compete. (See the similar rules regarding liability for misrepresentations of source and trademark infringement: § 4, Comment *f*; § 21, Comment *b*.) Commercial detriment sufficient to subject an actor to liability may be found in a threat of harm to the business reputation or good will of another. In determining the existence of likely commercial detriment, the dispositive question is whether the party seeking relief has a reasonable interest to be protected against the deceptive marketing of the actor.

Non-profit entities such as charitable, educational, governmental, fraternal, and religious organizations may also experience threatened or actual detriment cognizable under this Section, such as the disruption of economically valuable relations with present or potential donors, members, or customers.

Illustrations:

10. *A* manufactures solid walnut furniture; *B* manufactures walnut veneer furniture. *C* manufactures walnut veneer furniture that it falsely represents to be solid walnut. The representation by *C* is to the likely commercial detriment of both *A* and *B*.

11. *A*, a manufacturer of a depilatory product, falsely represents that a new ingredient in its product has a moisturizing effect on the skin. *B* manufactures lotions sometimes used as moisturizers after the use of depilatories. If a significant number of prospective purchasers acting in reliance on *A* 's representation are likely to refrain from using *B* 's product, the representation by *A* is to the likely commercial detriment of *B*.

12. *A*, an importer, sells sweaters manufactured in Ireland by *B*. *C* sells sweaters made in the United States, falsely representing that they are manufactured in Ireland. The representation by *C* is to the likely commercial detriment of both *A* and *B*.

13. *A* is the exclusive United States distributor of watches made in Switzerland by *B*. *C* sells watches in the United States, falsely representing that they are manufactured by *B*. The representation by *C* is to the likely commercial detriment of both *A* and *B*.

14. *A* and *B* manufacture microwave ovens; *C* publishes a magazine containing information and advice relating to consumer products. *C* publishes an article on microwave ovens that contains a favorable report on *B* 's products. Two years later, *C* publishes another article on the same topic that is highly critical of *B* 's products. *B*, in its advertising, subsequently quotes and attributes the favorable commentary from the first article with no mention of the second article. The representation by *B* is to the likely commercial detriment of both *A* and *C*.

15. *A*, the owner of master recordings featuring *B*, a well-known musician, grants to *C*, a record company, a license to produce tapes and discs embodying the recordings in exchange for royalties based on *C* 's sales. *D*, a competing record company, offers for sale a recording made 10 years earlier by *B*. *D* places a recent photograph of *B* on the cover of its recording in order to suggest that the songs reflect *B* 's current performing style. The representation by *D* is to the likely commercial detriment of *A*, *B*, and *C*.

REPORTERS' NOTE

This Section elaborates the scope of liability under the rule stated in § 2.

Comment b. The requirement of materiality is frequently stated as an element of a cause of action under § 43(a) of the Lanham Act. See, e.g., Cook, Perkiss and Liehe, Inc. v. Northern California Collection Service Inc., 911 F.2d 242, 244 (9th Cir. 1990) ("such deception is material, in that it is likely to influence the purchasing decision," quoting Skil Corp. v. Rockwell International Corp., 375 F.Supp. 777, 783 (N.D.Ill.1974)); U.S. Healthcare, Inc. v. Blue Cross, 898 F.2d 914, 922 (3d Cir.), cert. denied 498 U.S. 816, 111 S.Ct. 58, 112 L.Ed.2d 33 (1990) ("that the deception is material in that it is likely to influence purchasing decisions," quoting Max Daetwyler Corp. v. Input Graphics, Inc., 545 F.Supp. 165 (E.D.Pa.1982)); Allen Organ Co. v. Galanti Organ Builders, Inc., 798 F.Supp. 1162 (E.D.Pa.1992) (misrepresentations regarding technical specifications of electronic organs were not material to purchasing decisions). Any additional requirement of demonstrable harm to purchasers who rely on the misrepresentation would require an objective measure of consumer welfare and would also ignore the independent interests in competitors. Proof of such harm is not required under the rule in this Section. "In such matters, the public is entitled to get what it chooses, even though the choice may be dictated by caprice or by fashion or perhaps by ignorance." Federal Trade Commission v. Algoma Lumber Co., 291 U.S. 67, 78, 54 S.Ct. 315, 320, 78 L.Ed. 655 (1934), on remand 68 F.2d 993 (9th Cir.1934). Compare the standard of materiality in Restatement, Second, Torts § 538, dealing with monetary relief to the relying party, which requires that the matter represented be such that a reasonable person would view it as important, or that the maker know or have reason to know that the matter will be so viewed by the recipient of the representation. See also Restatement, Second, Contracts §§ 162, 164, positing a similar standard but also permitting rescission based on a fraudulent but non-material misrepresentation. On the requirement that the representation substantially influence the purchasing decision, see the similar rules in Restatement, Second, Torts § 546, Comment *b*; Restatement, Second, Contracts § 167, Comment *a*.

Comment c. Several decisions interpreting § 43(a) of the Lanham Act require that the misrepresentation concern an "inherent quality or characteristic" of the actor's goods or services. This limitation was invoked in Sheldon Friedlich Marketing Corp. v. Carol Wright Sales, Inc., 219 U.S.P.Q. 883 (S.D.N.Y.1983), to justify a refusal to enjoin the misrepresentation "patent applied for"; it was invoked in Abernathy & Closther, Ltd. v. E & M Advertising, Inc., 553 F.Supp. 834 (E.D.N.Y.1982), in connection with the false representation that a television promotion was an "exclusive T.V. offer" made "for the first time on T.V." The "inherent quality or characteristic" standard has been recited in several decisions of the Second Circuit. See, e.g., National Ass'n of Pharmaceutical Mfrs., Inc. v. Ayerst Laboratories, 850 F.2d 904 (2d Cir.1988); Coca-Cola Co. v. Tropicana Products, Inc., 690 F.2d 312 (2d Cir.1982). The apparent origin of the limitation is Fur Information and Fashion Council, Inc. v. E.F. Timme & Son, Inc., 501 F.2d 1048 (2d Cir.), cert. denied 419 U.S. 1022, 95 S.Ct. 498, 42 L.Ed.2d 296 (1974). The "inherent quality or characteristic" standard appears inconsistent with the results of numerous decisions under § 43(a). The boundaries of the limitation are ill-defined, see Illustration 2, and it has been criticized by several commentators. See, e.g., Keller, How Do You Spell Relief? Private Regulation of Advertising Under Section 43(a) of the Lanham Act, 75 Trademark Rep. 227, 237–39 (1985); Bauer, A Federal Law of Unfair Competition: What Should be the Reach of Section 43(a) of the Lanham Act?, 31 U.C.L.A. L.Rev. 671, 742 (1984). The 1988 revision of § 43(a) now expressly encompasses misrepresentations relating to the actor's "commercial activities" in addition to misrepresentations relating to the actor's "goods" or "services."

Illustration 1 is based on the facts of Scotch Whiskey Ass'n v. Barton Distilling Co., 489 F.2d 809 (7th Cir. 1973). See Bohsei Enterprises Co. v. Porteous Fastener Co., 441 F.Supp. 162 (C.D.Cal.1977), holding that failure to disclose the foreign manufacture of screws and bolts was a material misrepresentation. See also Black Hills Jewelry Mfg. Co. v. Gold Rush, Inc., 633 F.2d 746 (8th Cir. 1980), enjoining the use of "Black Hills Gold" in connection with jewelry manufactured outside the Black Hills of South Dakota, noting that the quality of the defendants' jewelry "is not of dispositional significance," quoting Truck Equipment Service Co. v. Fruehauf Corp., 536 F.2d 1210, 1216 (8th Cir.), cert. denied 429 U.S. 861, 97 S.Ct. 164, 50 L.Ed.2d 139 (1976). Misrepresentations of geographic origin were among the first to be actionable as false advertising at common law. See § 2, Comment *b*; see also § 43(a) of the Lanham Act, specifically applicable to misrepresentations of "geographic origin."

Illustration 2 is based on Vidal Sassoon, Inc. v. Bristol–Myers Co., 661 F.2d 272 (2d Cir.1981). The case also illustrates the limited utility of the "inherent quality or characteristic" standard; the court concluded that "the intent and total effect of the advertisements were to lead consumers into believing that Body on Tap was competitively superior, surely a representation regarding its 'inherent quality.'" 661 F.2d at 278. In Thompson Medical Co. v. Hall's Albany Drug Corp., 158 U.S.P.Q. 193 (S.D.N.Y.1968), the court found material a false representation that defendant's appetite control gum had been "clinically tested."

Illustration 3 is suggested by the reasoning in John Wright, Inc. v. Casper Corp., 419 F.Supp. 292 (E.D.Pa.1976), modified on other grounds 587 F.2d 602 (3d Cir.1978), in which the court held that false claims of patent protection for reproductions of penny banks violated § 43(a). See also Upjohn Co. v. Riahom Corp., 641 F.Supp. 1209 (D.Del. 1986). Compare Chromium Industries, Inc. v. Mirror Polishing & Plating Co., 448 F.Supp. 544 (N.D.Ill. 1978). In *Sheldon Friedlich Marketing Corp., supra*, relief was denied in connection with the false representation "patent applied for" on the basis of the "inherent quality or characteristic" standard. The fraudulent use of a copyright notice has been held to violate § 43(a) because of the likelihood that it would mislead consumers as to the nature or quality of the work. Eden Toys, Inc. v. Florelee Undergarment Co., 697 F.2d 27 (2d

Cir.1982). See also Sunset Lamp Corp. v. Alsy Corp., 698 F.Supp. 1146 (S.D.N.Y.1988). But cf. Kregos v. Associated Press, 937 F.2d 700 (2d Cir.1991) (rejecting the argument that use of a copyright notice on an infringing work violates § 43(a)). Relief against a false representation of trademark registration was denied in Universal Athletic Sales Co. v. American Gym, Recreational & Athletic Equipment Corp., 397 F.Supp. 1063 (W.D.Pa.1975), vacated on other grounds 546 F.2d 530 (3d Cir.1976), cert. denied 430 U.S. 984, 97 S.Ct. 1681, 52 L.Ed.2d 378 (1977). The court concluded that the misrepresentation would have no effect on prospective purchasers. For statutory prohibitions against false claims of patent or copyright, see 35 U.S.C.A. § 292 and 17 U.S.C.A. § 506(c).

Illustration 4 is based on In re Uranium Antitrust Litigation, 473 F.Supp. 393 (N.D.Ill.1979).

Illustration 5 is based on Borden, Inc. v. Kraft, Inc., 224 U.S.P.Q. 811 (N.D.Ill.1984). In Parkway Baking Co. v. Freihofer Baking Co., 255 F.2d 641, 648 (3d Cir.1958), a misrepresentation of the licensee-baker's identity on a bread wrapper was held immaterial, there being "no evidence that anyone who purchased 'Hollywood' bread with the false designation on the wrapper did so because of the false wrapper, nor is there any evidence that anyone would have refused to purchase this bread had they known of the fallacious label."

Comment d. On "puffing" as it relates to a seller's liability for disparagement, see Restatement, Second, Torts § 649. On its relevance in actions by purchasers, see *id.* § 539, 542; Restatement, Second, Contracts §§ 168–169. See also Article 2 of the Uniform Commercial Code, which adopts the rule that "an affirmation merely of the value of the goods or a statement purporting to be merely the seller's opinion or commendation of the goods does not create a warranty." U.C.C. § 2–313(2).

On the significance of the actor's intent, see U–Haul International, Inc. v. Jartran, Inc., 522 F.Supp. 1238, 1253 (D.Ariz.1981), affirmed 681 F.2d 1159 (9th Cir.1982).

Illustration 6 is taken from Restatement, Second, Torts § 542, Comment *e*. Compare Cook, Perkiss and Liehe, Inc. v. Northern California Collection Service Inc., 911 F.2d 242 (9th Cir.1990) ("we're the low cost commercial collection experts" held to be mere puffery) with Castrol Inc. v. Pennzoil Co., 987 F.2d 939 (3d Cir. 1993) (claim of better protection against engine wear held not merely a general claim of superiority and actionable under § 43(a)).

Illustration 7 is based on the facts in Data Cash Systems, Inc. v. JS & A Group, Inc., 223 U.S.P.Q. 865 (N.D.Ill.1984).

Illustration 8 is taken from Restatement, Second, Torts § 542, Comment *f.*

Illustration 9 is suggested by Restatement, Second, Contracts § 168, Illustration 5. Cf. Milkovich v. Lorain Journal Co., 497 U.S. 1, 110 S.Ct. 2695, 111 L.Ed.2d 1 (1990) (statement of opinion can be actionable in defamation if the statement implies defamatory facts).

Comment e. Under § 43(a) of the Lanham Act, a person engaged in deceptive marketing is subject to liability to "any person who believes that he or she is or is likely to be damaged." "The statute demands only proof providing a reasonable basis for the belief that the plaintiff is likely to be damaged as a result of the false advertising." Johnson & Johnson v. Carter–Wallace, Inc., 631 F.2d 186, 190 (2d Cir.1980).

Section 3 of the Uniform Deceptive Trade Practices Act affords injunctive relief to a "person likely to be damaged by a deceptive trade practice of another." The Comment to § 3 of the Act states that deceptive conduct may be enjoined "provided that there is a reasonable probability that the complainant will otherwise incur actual damage."

Comment f. Trade associations with a pecuniary interest in the sale of goods that compete with those of the actor have standing to challenge deceptive representations under § 43(a), Potato Chip Institute v. General Mills, Inc., 333 F.Supp. 173 (D.Neb.1971), affirmed 461 F.2d 1088 (8th Cir.1972); Mutation Mink Breeders Ass'n v. Lou Nierenberg Corp., 23 F.R.D. 155 (S.D.N.Y.1959), and may also have standing in their representative capacity to sue on behalf of their members. National Ass'n of Pharmaceutical Mfrs., Inc. v. Ayerst Laboratories, 850 F.2d 904 (2d Cir. 1988); Camel Hair and Cashmere Institute, Inc. v. Associated Dry Goods Corp., 799 F.2d 6 (1st Cir.1986).

In determining whether an asserted injury is sufficiently direct to justify the imposition of liability, the Supreme Court's analysis of similar issues under federal antitrust law may offer a useful analogy. See Associated General Contractors, Inc. v. California State Council of Carpenters, 459 U.S. 519, 103 S.Ct. 897, 74 L.Ed.2d 723 (1983). The absence of a less remote party with an interest in challenging the false representation may account for the Third Circuit's decision in Thorn v. Reliance Van Co., 736 F.2d 929 (3d Cir.1984), holding that an investor in a bankrupt motor carrier had standing under § 43(a) to seek redress for the false advertising of a competing carrier. See Serbin v. Ziebart Int'l Corp., 11 F.3d 1163 (3d Cir.1993) (quoting Restatement Third, Unfair Competition § 3, Reporters' Note to Comment *f* (Tent. Draft No. 1 (1988))).

Traditional statements of the elements of a cause of action for deceptive marketing under § 43(a) emphasize that protection is not limited to the redress of direct diversions of trade. "[P]laintiff has been or is likely to be injured * * * either by direct diversion of sales from itself to defendant, or by lessening of the goodwill which its products enjoy with the buying public." Skil Corp. v. Rockwell International Corp., 375 F.Supp. 777 (N.D.Ill.1974). Professor Callmann's summary of the issue continues to be cited with approval: "The dispositive question should be whether plaintiff has a reasonable interest to be protected against false advertising." Callmann, Unfair Competition, Trademarks & Monopolies § 5.04 (4th ed.).

Nonprofit organizations are eligible for protection against unfair competition. See, e.g., Birthright v. Birthright, Inc., 827 F.Supp. 1114 (D.N.J. 1993) (misleading fundraising letters sent by a former affiliate of a nonprofit organization held actionable by the parent organization under § 43(a)); Athens Lodge No. 70 v. Wilson, 117 Cal.App.2d 322, 255 P.2d 482 (1953). The actions of nonprofit organizations can also subject such entities to liability for unfair competition. See Birthright, *supra* ; National Artists Management Co. v. Weaving, 769 F.Supp. 1224 (S.D.N.Y.1991) (dictum that promotional activities by nonprofit entities fall within the scope of § 43(a)).

Illustration 10 is based on Illustration 9, Restatement, Second, Torts § 712 (Tent. Draft No.8 1963).

Illustration 11 is based on Johnson & Johnson v. Carter–Wallace, Inc., 631 F.2d 186 (2d Cir.1980).

Illustration 12 is based on Illustration 8, Restatement, Second, Torts § 712 (Tent. Draft No.8 1963).

Illustration 13 is derived from Norman M. Morris Corp. v. Weinstein, 466 F.2d 137 (5th Cir.1972). See also Quabaug Rubber Co. v. Fabiano Shoe Co., 567 F.2d 154 (1st Cir.1977) (nonexclusive licensee has standing under § 43(a) of the Lanham Act).

Illustration 14 is based on Amana Refrigeration, Inc. v. Consumers Union of United States, Inc., 431 F.Supp. 324 (N.D.Iowa 1977). On the necessity of establishing falsity, see Consumers Union of United States, Inc. v. General Signal Corp., 724 F.2d 1044 (2d Cir.1983), rehearing denied 730 F.2d 47 (2d Cir.), cert. denied 469 U.S. 823, 105 S.Ct. 100, 83 L.Ed.2d 45 (1984).

Illustration 15 is derived from the facts of PPX Enterprises, Inc. v. Audiofidelity, Inc., 746 F.2d 120 (2d Cir. 1984) and Rich v. RCA Corp., 390 F.Supp. 530 (S.D.N.Y.1975). See Rosenfeld v. W.B. Saunders, 728 F.Supp. 236 (S.D.N.Y.), affirmed 923 F.2d 845 (2d Cir.1990) (holder of royalty interest has standing under § 43(a) with respect to the marketing of a competing work).

§ 4. Misrepresentations Relating to Source: Passing Off

One is subject to liability to another under the rule stated in § 2 if, in connection with the marketing of goods or services, the actor makes a representation likely to deceive or mislead prospective purchasers by causing the mistaken belief that the actor's business is the business of the other, or that the actor is the agent, affiliate, or associate of the other, or that the goods or services that the actor markets are produced, sponsored, or approved by the other.

Comment:

a. Rationale. This Section is a specific application of the general principle stated in § 2. The misrepresentations that are proscribed by this Section cause prospective purchasers to believe that another person is associated with the actor or with the goods or services marketed by the actor, thus placing the other's reputation at risk and diverting to the actor the benefit of the other's good will. Since such misrepresentations necessarily threaten harm to the commercial interests of the person falsely associated with the actor or with the actor's products, independent proof of likely commercial detriment as required under the general rule stated in § 2 is unnecessary in order to establish liability under this Section.

The prohibition against passing off serves many interests. Early case law, viewing the conduct as a form of fraud, emphasized the immorality and the unfairness to consumers and competitors inherent in the actor's deception. Contemporary analysis also emphasizes the function of the rule in protecting and encouraging investments in good will. Since passing off interferes with the opportunity to reap the benefits of a favorable reputation, investments in quality, service, and promotion are undermined by misrepresentations of source. Passing off also deprives purchasers of the opportunity to distinguish among the goods and services of competing sellers. The rule stated in this Section, although not applicable to actions by deceived purchasers, thus also serves as a form of consumer protection.

The policies underlying this Section also provide the basis for the rules governing the protection of trademarks, and much of the commentary in Chapter Three is therefore also relevant to the rule stated here.

b. Relation to trademark infringement and false advertising. The rules stated in this Chapter and in the following Chapter on the law of trademarks developed largely from English and American common law decisions imposing liability on a seller who diverted trade from another by fraudulently misrepresenting that the goods had been produced by the other. Liability was originally imposed in an action variously denominated an "action in the nature of an action for deceit," an "action on the case for a deceit," or simply an "action for deceit." The fraudulent conduct was frequently described as "passing off" or "palming off." These terms are now often used more broadly, however, to describe any situation in which the conduct of a seller creates a likelihood that prospective purchasers will be confused with respect to the source of goods or services, regardless of the actor's intent.

The "passing off" held actionable at common law was frequently accomplished through the use of confusingly similar trade symbols, and during the 19th century this general principle of liability served as the genesis of the technical rules governing the validity and infringement of trademarks and the recognition of secondary meaning. See § 9, Comment *d*. The law of trademarks is discussed in Chapter Three. If a misrepresentation of source or sponsorship arises solely from the unauthorized use of a trademark or other indicia of identification, relief must be sought under the rules stated in that Chapter.

The proscription against passing off also served as the genesis of the common law rules relating to false advertising and their subsequent expansion through state and federal legislation. See § 2, Comment *b*. Thus, the rule stated in this Section historically preceded the general prohibition against the use of deceptive representations in the marketing of goods and services now embodied in § 2. This Section, however, can be viewed as a specific application of that principle to misrepresentations relating to source, and the Comments to § 2 are therefore generally applicable to the rule stated here.

Passing off of goods and services is also prohibited under state and federal legislation. Section 2(a) of the Uniform Deceptive Trade Practices Act (see § 2, Comment *b*) imposes liability upon any person or commercial entity that "passes off goods or services as those of another," or "causes likelihood of confusion or of misunderstanding as to the source, sponsorship, approval, or certification of goods or services." Passing off is also prohibited under the various Unfair Trade Practices and Consumer Protection Acts. See § 1, Comment *g*. Section 43(a) of the Lanham Act similarly prohibits false or misleading representations that are likely to cause confusion "as to the affiliation, connection, or association" between the actor and another or as to the "origin, sponsorship, or approval" of the actor's goods, services, or commercial activities.

c. Likelihood of deception. In order to subject the actor to liability, the representation must create a likelihood that a significant portion of the audience will be deceived or misled with respect to the identity or commercial affiliation of the actor or the source or sponsorship of the actor's goods or services. See § 2, Comment *d*. Proof of actual deception is not required. The issuance of an injunction upon proof that deception is likely serves to safeguard the expectations of consumers and protects the other party from harm that may be impossible to quantify for purposes of monetary relief. Complainants seeking a monetary recovery, however, must establish entitlement to such relief under the rules stated in §§ 36 and 37, which generally require proof of actual deception resulting in demonstrable pecuniary loss to the complainant or demonstrable pecuniary gain to the actor.

d. Intent. Liability for passing off was originally imposed through the common law action for deceit, and thus proof of the actor's fraudulent intent was an essential element of the plaintiff's case. Subsequent developments, however, eroded the emphasis on the actor's subjective state of mind. The requirement of fraud was first discarded in connection with misrepresentations of source accomplished through the infringement of fanciful or arbitrary trademarks. It was later abandoned in cases involving the unauthorized use of other designations that had acquired source significance. See § 9, Comment *d*. State and federal legislation, including § 43(a) of the Lanham Act and the Uniform Deceptive Trade Practices Act, have also dispensed with the necessity of establishing an intent to deceive in connection with misrepresentations of source or other misrepresentations concerning the actor's goods or services. See § 2, Comment *f*. Liability under this Section is determined by an evaluation of the probable consequences of the actor's conduct and does not depend upon the actor's subjective intent.

Although an intent to deceive is not an element of the cause of action under this Section, evidence that the representation was in fact intended to mislead prospective purchasers with respect to the identity of the actor or the source, sponsorship, or approval of the goods or services may justify an inference that deception is likely. When such evidence is adduced, the burden may properly shift to the actor to demonstrate that deception is unlikely despite the attempt to deceive. The subjective intent of the actor is also relevant to an award of monetary relief under the rules stated in §§ 36 and 37.

Illustrations:

1. *A* and *B* are plumbing firms. *A* has a contract to provide plumbing services to the University of Nebraska. *B* falsely represents to prospective customers that it is the firm that does the plumbing work for the University. *B* is subject to liability to *A*.

2. *A*, a cereal company, manufactures by means of a patented process a breakfast cereal that it sells under the generic name "shredded wheat." Upon expiration of the patent, *B* begins to manufacture the same product, which it sells in packages similar in appearance to *A* 's and which prominently display the words "The Original Shredded Wheat." *B* is subject to liability to *A*.

3. *A* designs dresses and sells the designs to dress manufacturers. *B*, a dress manufacturer, *C*, a wholesaler, and *D*, a retailer, sell dresses to their respective customers with the false representation that the dresses were designed by *A*. *B*, *C*, and *D* are subject to liability to *A*.

4. The facts being otherwise as stated in Illustration 3, the evidence establishes that *D* was unaware that the dresses were not in fact designed by *A*. *D* is nevertheless subject to liability to *A*, although the remedy may properly be limited to injunctive relief. See §§ 36 and 37.

5. *A* manufactures baseball gloves. In its advertising, *A* uses without consent a photograph of *B*, a famous baseball player, in a manner that falsely implies that *B* endorses *A* 's product. *A* is subject to liability to *B* under the rule stated in this Section. *A* is also subject to liability to *B* for infringement of *B* 's right of publicity under the rule stated in § 46.

e. Form of representation. A misrepresentation of source actionable under this Section can be made in any manner sufficient to communicate the misrepresentation to prospective purchasers. Thus, the misrepresentation may appear on labels or packaging, or it may be communicated through advertising or by assertions made at the point of sale. The misrepresentation can also be implied from conduct, as when a seller in response to a buyer's request for goods from one producer substitutes without notice goods from a different producer.

Illustration:

6. *A* operates a restaurant. In response to a request by a customer for a particular brand of soft drink manufactured by *B*, *A*, without notifying the customer, substitutes a soft drink manufactured by *C*. *A* is subject to liability to *B*.

f. Scope of liability. This Section affords protection against both direct diversions of trade and harm to reputation and good will. If the person falsely associated with the actor or with the actor's goods or services is in competition with the actor, reliance on the misrepresentation by prospective purchasers may divert trade from that person to the actor. Subsequent dissatisfaction with the actor's goods or services may also result in harm to the other's reputation and good will. Misrepresentations relating to source pose a similar threat to reputation and good will even when the actor's goods or services do not compete with those of the person seeking relief. The quality of the actor's goods or services, although sometimes relevant in determining an appropriate remedy, does not affect the determination of liability under this Section. There is no assurance that any particular level of quality will be maintained by the actor in the future, and a misrepresentation of source in any event interferes with the opportunity of consumers to discriminate among sellers on the basis of factors unrelated to product quality.

The protection of reputational interests is of particular importance in the arts and entertainment industries. The rule of this Section operates to prevent false attributions of authorship. It thus affords protection analogous to some aspects of the paternity right recognized under civil law as an element of an author's moral right, or *droit moral*. See also § 5, Comment *c*; § 24, Comment *d*.

Under the rule stated in this Section, a person who falsely represents that the business is that of another, or that the goods or services are produced, sponsored, or approved by another, is subject to liability to that other but not to third persons who may be injured by the actor's conduct. Thus, employees or suppliers of the other or retailers who sell the other's goods are not within the scope of this

Section. If a misrepresentation of source is to the likely commercial detriment of persons in addition to the person falsely represented to be the source of the goods or services, such as licensees or distributors, the actor may be subject to liability to such persons under the rule stated in § 2. See § 3, Illustration 13.

Illustrations:

7. *A* is a record company. *B* is a well-known band leader and musician. *A* hires an orchestra and records a number of works using musical arrangements made popular by *B*. *A* advertises the recordings as "*B* 's Versions of Swing Era Classics." If a significant number of prospective purchasers are likely to believe that the recordings were made by *B*, *A* is subject to liability to *B*.

8. *A* manufactures spark plugs. *B* sells other spark plugs with the misrepresentation that they are *A* 's plugs. *B* is subject to liability to *A*, whether *B* is a manufacturer, distributor, wholesaler, or retailer. *B* 's liability to other persons who sell *A* 's spark plugs is determined under the rule stated in § 2.

REPORTERS' NOTE

This Section applies the general principles of liability discussed in the two preceding sections to misrepresentations relating to source. The former rule in Restatement of Torts § 712 required proof of fraudulent intent, but that requirement is not carried forward here.

Comment a. The early emphasis on the prevention of fraud is illustrated by the following remarks of Justice Chitty in upholding an injunction against passing off in Lever v. Goodwin, 36 Ch.Div. 1, 2–3 (1887):

> The law applicable to the case is plain; it is founded on fraud. * * * Then comes the case where the manufacturer, by devices which are to accompany the goods on their sale in the market, gets them up in such a form as to be calculated to deceive the ultimate buyer into the belief that the goods which he, the manufacturer, is putting on the market are the goods of some other maker. Here, generally speaking, a double fraud is committed; first, there is the fraud which is perpetrated on the ultimate buyer; and, secondly, there is the fraud perpetrated on the other manufacturer, who loses part of his trade.

Modern decisions imposing liability for misrepresentations of source frequently appeal to the public interest in promoting investment in good will. See, e.g., SK & F, Co. v. Premo Pharmaceutical Laboratories, Inc., 625 F.2d 1055, 1067 (3d Cir.1980) ("Permitting a business climate in which substitutions of products over which the first manufacturer has no quality control in the long run can only discourage the effort to compete on the basis of reputation for quality."). See also Inwood Laboratories,

Inc. v. Ives Laboratories, Inc., 456 U.S. 844, 854 n.14, 102 S.Ct. 2182, 2188 n.14, 72 L.Ed.2d 606 (1982) ("[T]he infringer deprives the owner of the goodwill which he spent energy, time, and money to obtain. * * * At the same time, the infringer deprives consumers of their ability to distinguish among the goods of competing manufacturers.").

Comment b. On the development of the common law rules proscribing passing off and their relationship to the law of trademarks, see F. Schechter, Historical Foundations of Trade–Mark Law (1925); Burrell, Two Hundred Years of English Trade Mark Law, and Pattishall, Two Hundred Years of American Trademark Law, in ABA Section of Patent, Trademark and Copyright Law, Two Hundred Years of English and American Patent, Trademark and Copyright Law (1977); McClure, Trademarks and Unfair Competition: A Critical History of Legal Thought, 69 Trademark Rep. 305 (1979). The relationship between passing off and false advertising is evident in Judge Learned Hand's opinion in Ely–Norris Safe Co. v. Mosler Safe Co., 7 F.2d 603 (2d Cir.1925), reversed on other grounds 273 U.S. 132, 47 S.Ct. 314, 71 L.Ed. 578 (1927).

The Comment to § 2 of the Uniform Deceptive Trade Practices Act describes passing off as "a convenient name for the doctrine that no one should be allowed to sell his goods as those of another," quoting Vogue Co. v. Thompson–Hudson Co., 300 Fed. 509, 511 (6th Cir.1924), cert. denied 273 U.S. 706, 47 S.Ct. 98, 71 L.Ed. 850 (1926). The "unfair methods of competition and unfair or deceptive acts or practices" condemned under state Unfair Trade Practices and Consumer Protection Acts encompass passing off. See Polo Fashions, Inc. v. Craftex, Inc., 816 F.2d 145 (4th Cir.1987). Passing off is also proscribed under § 43(a) of the Lanham Act. See, e.g., American Ventures, Inc. v. Post, Buckley, Schuh & Jernigan, Inc., 27 U.S.P.Q.2d 1587 (W.D.Wash.1993) (summary judgment granted against defendant's misrepresentation to a prospective client that plaintiff was a consultant to the defendant); Raffoler, Ltd. v. Peabody & Wright, Ltd., 671 F.Supp. 947 (E.D.N.Y.1987) (denying a motion to dismiss a claim under § 43(a) based on the defendant's use of advertisements confusingly similar to those used by the plaintiff); Popeil Bros., Inc. v. Morris, 176 U.S.P.Q. 353 (D.N.J.1972) (false representation that defendant's product was the item advertised on television).

Comment c. "Thus, in modern law, emphasis is placed on the objective facts of likely confusion rather than upon the subjective mental state of the infringer." McCarthy, Trademarks and Unfair Competition § 23.-30.

Comment d. Restatement of Torts § 717 extended the principle that fraud is not an essential element in an action for the infringement of arbitrary or "technical" trademarks to the infringement of other marks that have acquired significance as an indication of source. This Section further extends that principle to all misrepresentations relating to source, however communicated, and thus abandons the requirement of a fraudulent misrepresentation in Restatement of Torts § 712. This extension is an aspect of the general elimination of fraud as a necessary element in the imposition of liability for deceptive marketing. See § 2, Comment *f.*

Illustration 1 is based on Illustration 13 to Restatement of Torts § 712.

Illustration 2 is suggested by Kellogg Co. v. National Biscuit Co., 305 U.S. 111, 59 S.Ct. 109, 83 L.Ed. 73 (1938). See King–Seeley Thermos Co. v. Aladdin Industries, Inc., 321 F.2d 577 (2d Cir.1963), affirming an injunction against defendant's use of the words "original" or "genuine" after holding plaintiff's THERMOS mark generic. See also Blinded Veterans Association v. Blinded American Veterans Foundation, 872 F.2d 1035 (D.C.Cir.1989); Murphy Door Bed Co. v. Interior Sleep Systems, Inc., 874 F.2d 95 (2d Cir.1989).

Illustration 3 is based on Illustration 6 to Restatement of Torts § 712.

Illustration 4 is supported by the result in Polo Fashions, Inc. v. Clothes Encounters, 227 U.S.P.Q. 327 (N.D.Ill.1985).

In connection with Illustration 5, see Waits v. Frito–Lay, Inc., 978 F.2d 1093 (9th Cir.1992), cert. denied ___ U.S. ___, 113 S.Ct. 1047, 122 L.Ed.2d 355 (1993) (misrepresentation of endorsement through the use of an imitation of the plaintiff's voice in defendant's commercial); Prudhomme v. Procter & Gamble Co., 800 F.Supp. 390 (E.D.La.1992) (denying a motion to dismiss a claim alleging the use of look-alikes in a television commercial); Tin Pan Apple, Inc. v. Miller Brewing Co., 737 F.Supp. 826 (S.D.N.Y.1990) (same); Allen v. National Video, Inc., 610 F.Supp. 612 (S.D.N.Y.1985) (recognizing a claim under § 43(a) by Woody Allen against an impersonator in advertisements that falsely implied Allen's endorsement of the advertised services); National Bank of Commerce v. Shaklee Corp., 503 F.Supp. 533 (W.D.Tex. 1980) (misrepresentation of endorsement through the use of plaintiff's book in defendant's promotional activities).

Comment e. Illustration 6 is based on Coca–Cola Co. v. Overland, Inc., 692 F.2d 1250 (9th Cir.1982). See also PIC Design Corp. v. Bearings Specialty Co., 436 F.2d 804 (1st Cir.1971); Restatement of Torts § 712, Comment *d.* In the product substitution cases, the seller makes an implicit representation that the product is the brand requested by the purchaser, and the activity thus also constitutes trademark infringement. See § 20, Comment *b.*

Comment f. A person other than the one falsely represented to be the source of the actor's goods or services can subject the actor to liability only under the rule stated in § 2. In particular, that person must establish that the misrepresentation of source is to its likely commercial detriment. See, e.g., Quabaug Rubber Co. v. Fabiano Shoe Co., 567 F.2d 154 (1st Cir.1977) (licensee); Norman M. Morris Corp. v. Weinstein, 466 F.2d 137 (5th Cir.1972) (exclusive distributor); D.M. & Antique Import Corp. v. Royal Saxe Corp., 311 F.Supp. 1261 (S.D.N.Y.1969) (same).

Illustration 7 is based on Shaw v. Time–Life Records, 38 N.Y.2d 201, 379 N.Y.S.2d 390, 341 N.E.2d 817 (1975) (affirming a denial of defendant's motion for summary judgment on a common law unfair competition count). Section 43(a) of the Lanham Act was utilized in Follett v. New American Library, Inc., 497 F.Supp. 304 (S.D.N.Y.1980), to enjoin a false attribution of authorship in connection with a nonfiction work that the plaintiff had merely edited. See also, e.g., King v. Innovation Books, 976

F.2d 824 (2d Cir.1992) (false representation of the plaintiff's connection with the defendant's motion picture); Benson v. Paul Winley Record Sales Corp., 452 F.Supp. 516 (S.D.N.Y. 1978) (misrepresentation by recording company relating to the contribution of the named artist). In another action involving musical recordings, in which the defendant overdubbed words and music onto the performance of the named musicians, relief was granted on a passing off theory under the Uniform Deceptive Trade Practices Act. Bonner v. Westbound Records, Inc., 49 Ill.App.3d 543, 7 Ill.Dec. 409, 364 N.E.2d 570 (1977). Such cases may be seen as misrepresentations relating to source actionable under the rule of this Section or misrepresentations relating to the quality or characteristics of the goods actionable under § 2. See § 2, Illustration 4. For an introduction to the civil law concept of "moral rights" and its common law analogues, see Nimmer & Nimmer on Copyright § 8.21. See also 17 U.S.C.A. § 106A(a), recognizing an author's right "to prevent the use of his or her name as the author of any work of visual art which he or she did not create" or with "a distortion, mutilation, or other modification" of the author's work of visual art "which would be prejudicial to his or her honor or reputation."

Illustration 8 is based on Illustration 10 to Restatement of Torts § 712.

§ 5. Misrepresentations Relating to Source: Reverse Passing Off

One is subject to liability to another under the rule stated in § 2 if, in marketing goods or services manufactured, produced, or supplied by the other, the actor makes a representation likely to deceive or mislead prospective purchasers by causing the mistaken belief that the actor or a third person is the manufacturer, producer, or supplier of the goods or services if the representation is to the likely commercial detriment of the other under the rule stated in § 3.

Comment:

a. Scope. The misrepresentations of source that are the subject of this Section differ from those described in the preceding Section in that they result in the passing off, not of the actor's goods as those of another, but of another's goods as those of the actor. This form of misrepresentation is sometimes referred to as "reverse passing off." This Section, like § 4, is a specific application of the general principles stated in § 2.

Although all forms of passing off involve the creation of confusion with respect to the source of goods or services, the threat of harm to the commercial interests of others is less immediate in the case of reverse passing off. Unlike the misrepresentations of source described in § 4, reverse passing off does not directly threaten the reputation of another since by definition the misrepresentation acts to sever the actual producer's association with the goods or services marketed by the actor. Similarly, it cannot be said that the actual producer is subject to a direct diversion of trade in the usual sense since it has already sold the very goods at issue. Reverse passing off, however, may sometimes misrepresent the relative capabilities or accomplishments of the parties, thus creating the likelihood of a future diversion of trade to the actor. This Section subjects the actor to liability only if the actual producer can establish both the fact of a misrepresentation and a likelihood of harm to its commercial relations.

The misrepresentations that are the subject of this Section should be distinguished from those that may result from the use of goods produced by another, or a photograph of such goods, as a sample or illustration of proffered goods actually produced by the actor or obtained from third persons. Such conduct may result in confusion of source in the traditional sense, see § 16, Comment *a*, or in a misrepresentation of the qualities or characteristics of the actor's goods, see § 2, Illustration 8. However, such conduct is not within the scope of this Section.

b. Likelihood of deception. A misrepresentation can be actionable under this Section if it is likely to deceive or mislead a significant portion of its audience. See § 2, Comment *d*. Proof of an intent to deceive or actual deception is not required.

The actor's representation may be expressed in words or implied by other conduct, but the complainant bears the burden of proving that deception is likely. In particular, proof that the actor has removed the trade name or trademark of the original manufacturer, producer, or other supplier and replaced it with its own name or mark does not in itself establish a likelihood of deception. The circumstances must indicate that prospective purchasers are likely to view the presence of the actor's name or mark as a representation that the actor is the manufacturer, producer, or supplier and not merely the marketer of the goods. In the absence of an express or implied misrepresentation relating to source, the sale of goods from which the manufacturer's name or mark has been removed or replaced by the seller's name or mark amounts to a mere non-disclosure for which the seller is not subject to liability under the rule stated in this Section. See § 2, Comment *e*.

Illustration:

1. *A* operates a restaurant and purchases candies sold by *B* in boxes bearing *B*'s trademark. *A* removes the candies and individually wraps them in paper bearing the name of *A*'s restau-

rant and serves them to its customers. In the absence of evidence indicating that the customers are likely to believe that the candies were manufactured by *A*, *A* has not made a representation likely to deceive or mislead under the rule stated in this Section.

c. Likely commercial detriment. In traditional passing off, the misrepresentation of source ordinarily threatens a diversion of trade or harm to reputation and good will and is thus to the likely commercial detriment of the person falsely represented as the source of the goods or services. The misrepresentations that are the subject of this Section, however, are less clearly injurious to the interests of the other, and that person therefore bears the burden of proving that harm to its commercial relations is in fact likely under the rule stated in § 3.

In many circumstances the physical source of the goods or services is likely to be a matter of indifference to prospective purchasers, who instead choose to rely on the reputation or expertise of the seller with whom they deal. In such instances a misrepresentation of the type described in this Section is not material, and the seller is not subject to liability. The seller is also not subject to liability if the manufacturer has expressly or implicitly consented to sales under the seller's trade name or trademark. In other cases, however, the misrepresentation may be likely to induce prospective purchasers to buy additional goods or services from the actor, resulting in a diversion of trade from the person seeking relief. In these or other circumstances in which the misrepresentation is likely to cause harm to the trade or good will of the complainant, the actor is subject to liability.

The likelihood of harm through reverse passing off is particularly acute in the arts and entertainment industries, in which the marketability of a person's goods or services is in large measure dependent upon recognition for past achievements. The rule of this Section can operate to prevent the misappropriation of credit properly owed to the original creator or performer, thus offering protection analogous in some respects to the "paternity" right recognized in favor of authors and artists under Civil Law. See also § 4, Comment *f*; § 24, Comment *d*.

Illustrations:

2. *A* manufactures precision machine parts. *B*, a former distributor of *A*'s products, is in the process of constructing its own manufacturing facility for the production of similar parts. *B* relabels its remaining supply of *A*'s parts to misrepresent that

the parts were manufactured by *B*. *B* sells the parts to customers and solicits orders for the manufacture of additional parts. The misrepresentation is to the likely commercial detriment of *A* since it threatens to divert future trade from *A* to *B*. *B* is subject to liability to *A*.

3. *A* manufactures jet engine parts sold in domestic and foreign markets. The parts carry a designation indicating that they have been approved for United States military procurement. *B*, a competitor of *A*, sells surplus parts manufactured by *A*, falsely representing that the parts were manufactured by *B*. The evidence indicates that the misrepresentation is likely to cause prospective purchasers to believe that *B* has been approved as a source of supply for United States military procurement. The misrepresentation is to the likely commercial detriment of *A* since it threatens to divert future trade from *A* to *B*. *B* is subject to liability to *A*.

4. *A*, an actor, appears as a principal performer in a movie produced by *B*. *C*, a distributor of the film, removes *A* 's name from the film credits and accompanying advertising and falsely attributes *A* 's performance to another actor. The misrepresentation is to the likely commercial detriment of *A* since it threatens to deprive *A* of future business opportunities. *C* is subject to liability to *A*.

REPORTERS' NOTE

This Section applies the principles developed in §§ 2 and 3 to situations in which an actor falsely represents itself to be the manufacturer or supplier of goods or services that in fact originate from another. It has no antecedent in the Restatement of Torts.

Comment a. The term "reverse passing off" is sometimes used to describe cases in which the seller is not in fact marketing the goods of another, but rather has used those goods as a sample or illustration of its own product. See, e.g., John Wright, Inc. v. Casper Corp., 419 F.Supp. 292, 325 (E.D.Pa.1976), affirmed sub nom. Donsco, Inc. v. Casper Corp., 587 F.2d 602 (3d Cir.1978). See also Smith v. Montoro, 648 F.2d 602 (9th Cir.1981). Although such conduct may subject the seller to liability under the rules stated in § 2 or § 20, this Section applies only when a seller actually markets goods produced by another. Also to be distinguished are cases involving "reverse confusion," in which the infringement of *A* 's mark by *B* creates confusion among prospective purchasers as to the source of *A* 's goods. See § 20, Comment *f*.

For a discussion of the economic consequences of reverse passing off, see Borchard, Reverse Passing Off—Commercial Robbery or Permissible Competition?, 67 Trademark Rep. 1 (1977), arguing for greater protection of the advertising value inherent in the appearance of the original manufacturer's trade name or trademark on the goods.

Comment b. The case law does not recognize an affirmative duty on the part of a seller to disclose the identity of the manufacturer or producer of goods offered for sale; liability is imposed only on the basis of an express or implied misrepresentation that the goods have been produced by the actor or a third person. Cf. Vargas v. Esquire, Inc., 164 F.2d 522 (7th Cir.1947) (refusing to recognize an obligation to credit plaintiff as the creator of drawings published in defendant's magazine).

In connection with Illustration 1, see PIC Design Corp. v. Sterling Precision Corp., 231 F.Supp. 106 (S.D.N.Y.1964), declining to impose liability on a seller who removed the plaintiff's name from a gear purchased through an intermediary and resold it in a box marked with its own name, since the evidence did not establish that the defendant had misrepresented itself as the manufacturer of the product. "To hold otherwise would be to forbid any repackaging, resale, or reshipment of any item not manufactured by the shipper but sold under his name." *Id.* at 115. See also Commodore Import Corp. v. Hiraoka & Co., 422 F.Supp. 628 (S.D.N.Y.1976). Cf. Roho, Inc. v. Marquis, 902 F.2d 356 (5th Cir.1990) (use of plaintiff's product as a component of a new product sold under the defendant's name is not actionable as reverse passing off); Shaw v. Lindheim, 919 F.2d 1353 (9th Cir.1990), on remand, 809 F.Supp. 1393 (C.D.Cal.1992) (sale under defendant's name of television script taken in part from plaintiff's work is not actionable as reverse passing off).

Comment c. Illustration 2 is suggested by the result in Arrow United Industries, Inc. v. Hugh Richards, Inc., 678 F.2d 410 (2d Cir.1982). See Pioneer Hi-Bred Int'l v. Holden Foundation Seeds, Inc., 35 F.3d 1226 (8th Cir.1994) (liability under § 43 (a)); Web Printing Controls Co. v. Oxy–Dry Corp., 906 F.2d 1202 (7th Cir.1990); Whitney, Atwood, Norcross Associates, Inc. v. Architects Collaborative, Inc., 18 U.S.P.Q.2d 1243 (D.Mass.1991) (common law); R.H. Donnelley Corp. v. Illinois Bell Telephone Co., 595 F.Supp. 1202 (N.D.Ill.1984); FRA S.p.A. v. Surg–O–Flex of America, Inc., 415 F.Supp. 421 (S.D.N.Y.1976).

Illustration 3 is taken from the facts of Williams v. Curtiss–Wright Corp., 691 F.2d 168 (3d Cir.1982) (dictum recognizing claim under § 43(a)).

Illustration 4 is based on Smith v. Montoro, 648 F.2d 602 (9th Cir.1981) (reversing the dismissal of a claim under § 43(a)). See also Lamothe v. Atlantic Recording Corp., 847 F.2d 1403 (9th Cir.1988). In C.M. Paula Co. v. Logan, 355 F.Supp. 189 (N.D.Tex.1973), the defendant purchased greeting cards produced by plaintiff and transferred the art work onto ceramic plaques. In order to avoid confusion as to the source of the defendant's product, the court ordered an attribution of authorship. See also Marling v. Ellison, 218 U.S.P.Q. 702 (S.D.Fla.1982), imposing liability under § 43(a) in connection with defendant's false representation of authorship. Cf. Bajpayee v. Rothermich, 53 Ohio App.2d 117, 372 N.E.2d 817 (1977) (reversing summary judgment entered under state law against a medical researcher who alleged that the director of the laboratory had presented plaintiff's discovery to a scientific society as his own).

§ 6. Misrepresentations in Marketing the Goods or Services of Another

One is subject to liability to another under the rule stated in § 2 if, in marketing goods or services of which the other is truthfully identified as the manufacturer, producer, or supplier, the actor makes a representation relating to those goods or services that is likely to deceive or mislead prospective purchasers to the likely commercial detriment of the other under the rule stated in § 3.

Comment:

a. Scope. This Section applies the general principle stated in § 2 to situations in which the representation relates to goods or services truthfully identified as originating from another. In the typical case, the misrepresentation concerns goods marketed under the other's trademark, but the other's association with the goods or services may also be communicated to prospective purchasers in any manner. Liability for the misrepresentations that are within the scope of this Section has long been recognized at common law and has also been imposed under § 43(a) of the Lanham Act and under state statutes including the Uniform Deceptive Trade Practices Act. One who sells repackaged, rebottled, altered, or used goods under the trademark of another, in circumstances in which prospective purchasers are likely to regard them as new goods in their original form, may be subject to liability for trademark infringement under the rule stated in § 24. If the other is falsely represented to be the source of goods or services that it did not in fact produce, the rule stated in this Section is inapplicable and liability is determined under the rules relating to misrepresentations of source in § 4 or the infringement of trademarks in Chapter Three.

b. Types of misrepresentations. There are no technical limitations as to the nature or form of the misrepresentations actionable under this Section. However, the representation must be likely to deceive or mislead prospective purchasers with respect to a matter that relates to goods or services marketed by the actor and truthfully identified as originating from the person seeking relief. It is sufficient if the representation is likely to deceive or mislead a significant portion of its audience. See § 2, Comment *d.* The misrepresentation may be express or implied, and proof of actual deception or of an intention to deceive is not required.

The misrepresentations described in this Section are typically made in an attempt to sell goods that the actor has on hand and are thus generally laudatory rather than derogatory. A seller may assert, for example, that the goods are fresh when in fact they are stale or deteriorated, that they are the manufacturer's latest style or highest quality when in fact they are outdated or seconds, or that they are warranted by the manufacturer in respects that exceed the manufacturer's actual undertaking. If the misrepresentation is derogatory, as is the case in "bait and switch" advertising, the actor may also be subject to liability for product disparagement under the rule stated in Restatement, Second, Torts § 626.

c. Likely commercial detriment. Although proof of actual harm is not required, the original manufacturer, producer, or supplier of the goods or services bears the burden of proving that the misrepresentation is to its likely commercial detriment under the rule stated in § 3. Commercial detriment to the person identified as the source of the goods or services is likely if the misrepresentation threatens to divert trade from that person to the actor, such as a misrepresentation by a seller that its used goods manufactured or supplied by the other are new. A misrepresentation is also to the likely commercial detriment of the manufacturer or supplier if it is likely to tarnish the reputation of the goods among prospective purchasers. Indeed, the other's good will may sometimes suffer even among prospective customers who do not purchase the goods from the actor, but who instead inspect and reject them under the false impression that they represent the manufacturer's current output or highest quality merchandise.

Illustrations:

1. *A* manufactures instant-developing photographic film that is sold in packets identifying the film as *A* 's product. Since the developing chemicals contained in the film packets deteriorate over time, *A* places an expiration date on each packet. *B*, a distributor, alters the expiration date on outdated film and sells the packets to retailers and consumers. The misrepresentation is to the likely commercial detriment of *A* since it threatens to injure *A* 's good will. *B* is subject to liability to *A*.

2. *A* manufactures and sells electrical relays. The relays bear *A* 's trademark and are labeled with model numbers corresponding to the classification system used in *A* 's catalogs. *B* purchases government surplus relays manufactured by *A* bearing model numbers no longer in use and offers them for sale after replacing the numbers with the model numbers used by *A* to designate its new models. The misrepresentation is to the likely

commercial detriment of *A* since it threatens to divert trade from *A* to *B* and to injure *A* 's good will. *B* is subject to liability to *A*.

3. *A* manufactures and sells under its trademark a variety of electronic products through both company-owned stores and authorized dealers. *B*, an authorized dealer, falsely represents in its advertising that *A* 's warranty will be honored wherever *A* 's goods are sold, when in fact authorized dealers are not obligated to honor the warranty on goods sold by others. The misrepresentation is to the likely commercial detriment of *A* since it threatens to injure *A* 's good will. *B* is subject to liability to *A*.

REPORTERS' NOTE

This Section combines the substantive principles in §§ 714 and 760 of the Restatement of Torts. However, unlike the former rule, it does not require proof of fraudulent intent or knowledge that harm to the commercial interests of others is likely.

Comment a. This Section is an application of the general principle of liability stated in § 2, and the Comments to that Section are generally applicable to the rule stated here.

Comment b. For an early case indicating that intent to deceive is not a necessary element of liability at common law, see Thomas G. Plant Co. v. May Mercantile Co., 153 Fed. 229 (C.C.Mo.1907), enjoining defendant from selling the plaintiff's lower quality shoes under a trademark reserved for plaintiff's superior grade.

On liability at common law to the manufacturer of goods used as "bait" in "bait and switch" advertising, see Electrolux Corp. v. Val–Worth, Inc., 6 N.Y.2d 556, 190 N.Y.S.2d 977, 161 N.E.2d 197 (1959). See also Uniform Deceptive Trade Practices Act § 2(a)(9), (10).

Comment c. Illustration 1 is based on Polaroid Corp. v. Blue Dot Corp., 214 U.S.P.Q. 192 (D.N.J.1981), imposing liability under § 43(a) of the Lanham Act. In Adolph Coors Co. v. A. Genderson & Sons, Inc., 486 F.Supp. 131, 134 (D.Colo.1980), the court held that the sale of plaintiff's beer beyond its expiration date by an unauthorized distributor constituted "a representation that the beer distributed and sold by [defendant] and its customers has been subjected to the same high quality and freshness standards ordinarily specified by [plaintiff] * * *." The court found both trademark infringement and common law unfair competition.

Illustration 2 is taken from Cutler–Hammer, Inc. v. Universal Relay Corp., 285 F.Supp. 636 (S.D.N.Y. 1968). The plaintiff was not required to prove that the old design failed to meet current standards. "Defendant is not entitled to have [plaintiff's] reputation bear the burden of defendant's own conclusions as to the fitness of the old relays under the new specifications." *Id.* at 639. See also Burlington Mills Corp. v. Roy Fabrics, 91 F.Supp. 39 (S.D.N.Y.), affirmed 182 F.2d 1020 (2d Cir.1950) (falsely representing plaintiff's seconds as first quality goods is actionable under § 43(a)); Cheney Bros. v. Gimbel Bros., 280 Fed. 746 (S.D.N.Y. 1922) (enjoining at common law a false representation that silks offered by the defendant were the plaintiff's current style). The proscription against misrepresenting one model or grade of goods as another was invoked in Clairol, Inc. v. Boston Discount Center, Inc., 608 F.2d 1114 (6th Cir.1979), to enjoin defendant's retail sales of plaintiff's professional salon product. The court concluded that consumers would mistakenly believe that they were purchasing plaintiff's retail product which, unlike the salon product, was packaged to reduce long-term deterioration and contained detailed warnings and instructions for home use. See also § 2(a)(6) and (7) of the Uniform Deceptive Trade Practices Act.

Illustration 3 is based on Tandy Corp. v. Marymac Industries, Inc., 213 U.S.P.Q. 702 (S.D.Tex.1981).

§ 7. Contributory Liability of Printers, Publishers, and Other Suppliers

(1) One who, by supplying materials or rendering services to a third person, directly and substantially assists the third person in making a representation that subjects the third person to liability to another for deceptive marketing under the rules stated in §§ 2–6 is subject to liability to that other for contributory deceptive marketing.

(2) If an actor subject to contributory liability under the rule stated in Subsection (1) acted without knowledge that the actor was assisting the third person in making a representation likely to deceive or mislead, the actor is subject only to appropriate injunctive relief.

Comment:

a. Scope. This Section subjects to liability those who directly and substantially assist another in misrepresenting goods or services in a manner actionable under the rules stated in this Chapter. Persons subject to liability include those who design or supply materials communicating the misrepresentation such as labels, packaging, printed advertisements, and commercials, and those who disseminate the misrepresentation by publication, broadcast, or other means. Liability under this Section does not extend to those who supply basic materials or services only incidentally related to the misrepresentation. In determining whether a person has directly and substantially assisted in making a misrepresentation, a relevant factor is whether the imposition of a remedy against that person is necessary to fully protect the interests of the complainant and the public.

The relief granted against one who is subject to liability under the rule stated in this Section may differ from that granted against the maker of the representation. In particular, under Subsection (2) a person who acts without knowledge that it is assisting in making a representation likely to deceive or mislead is subject only to injunctive relief.

Amendments to the Lanham Act effective in 1989 expressly limit the relief available under the Act against an "innocent" printer of false or misleading representations produced on behalf of another to an injunction against future printing. When the representations appear in newspaper, magazine, or broadcast advertisements, relief against an "innocent" publisher is limited to an injunction against presentation of the matter in future issues or broadcasts. Even this latter relief is unavailable if the injunction would delay a particular issue or broadcast beyond its scheduled time. 15 U.S.C.A. § 32(2). Similar limitations are appropriate at common law. As a practical matter, however, it is ordinarily unnecessary to pursue a remedy against such parties because an injunction issued against the maker of the representation will upon notice bind others acting in active concert with it. See Fed.R.Civ.P. 65(d); Restatement, Second, Judgments § 63.

If a person knows that the material it is supplying or disseminating is likely to deceive or mislead, it is subject to the remedies appropriate under the rules stated in §§ 35–37. The extent of a person's liability under this Section will thus generally be determined by the nature of the business relationship between it and the maker of the representation and the knowledge attributable to it on the basis of that relationship.

b. Application to the media. Contributory liability under this Section extends to persons who directly and substantially assist in communicating the misrepresentation to the public. Liability is limited, however, to representations actionable under the rules stated in §§ 2–6, and thus the imposition of contributory liability on the media is confined to the dissemination of false, deceptive, or misleading commercial speech. The traditional restrictions against prior restraints have not been applied to commercial speech. The exclusion of monetary relief under Subsection (2) in the absence of actual knowledge of the deception is consistent with the constitutional limitations on liability recognized by the Supreme Court even in cases involving noncommercial speech. Nevertheless, the full extent of the protection available to the media under the first amendment remains unsettled and any application to the media of the rule stated in this Section must take account of the evolving constitutional standards.

Illustrations:

1. The facts being otherwise as stated in Illustration 12 to § 3, *D*, a printer, supplies *C* with packaging and tags stating that

the sweaters are a product of Ireland. *D* is subject to liability to *A* and *B*, but in the absence of proof that *D* knew that the materials supplied to *C* were likely to deceive or mislead, the remedy will be limited to an injunction against the future printing of such materials for *C*.

2. *A*, an appliance repair company, places in a telephone directory published by *B* an advertisement falsely representing that *A* is an authorized agent of *C*, an appliance manufacturer. Both *A* and *B* are subject to liability to *C*, but in the absence of proof that *B* knew that the representation was likely to deceive or mislead, the remedy against it will be limited to an injunction against publication of the advertisement in future directories.

REPORTERS' NOTE

The rules stated in this Section are analogous to those applicable to contributory liability for trademark infringement under § 26 and the Comments and Reporters' Note to that Section are also relevant here.

Comment a. It is not uncommon for advertising agencies to be named as defendants in deceptive advertising actions under § 43(a) of the Lanham Act. See, e.g., U–Haul International, Inc. v. Jartran, Inc., 601 F.Supp. 1140 (D.Ariz.1984), modified on other grounds 793 F.2d 1034 (9th Cir.1986) (settlement agreement with advertising agency); Eastern Air Lines, Inc. v. New York Air Lines, Inc., 559 F.Supp. 1270 (S.D.N.Y.1983) (moot by termination of advertising agency contract); American Brands, Inc. v. R.J. Reynolds Tobacco Co., 413 F.Supp. 1352 (S.D.N.Y.1976).

Fed.R.Civ.P. 65(d) provides that an injunction binds not only the parties and their officers, agents, and employees, but also "those persons in active concert or participation with them who receive actual notice of the order by personal service or otherwise." It is thus often unnecessary to join as parties all persons potentially liable under the rule stated in this Section. See South Central Bell Tel. Co. v. Constant Inc., 304 F.Supp. 732 (E.D.La.1969), affirmed 437 F.2d 1207 (5th Cir.1971), indicating that a telephone company would be in violation of an injunction issued against a trademark infringer if the telephone company knowingly permitted the infringer to use the company's services to continue the infringing conduct. See also Vuitton et fils S.A. v. Carousel Handbags, 592 F.2d 126 (2d Cir.1979); Eastern Air Lines, Inc. v. New York Air Lines, Inc., 565 F.Supp. 800 (S.D.N.Y.1983) (advertising agency).

Comment b. Cases invoking the standards governing commercial speech in cases involving the media include United States v. Edge Broadcasting Company, ___ U.S. ___, 113 S.Ct. 2696, 125 L.Ed.2d 345 (1993); Pittsburgh Press Co. v. Pittsburgh Com. on Human Relations, 413 U.S. 376, 93 S.Ct. 2553, 37 L.Ed.2d 669 (1973); Ragin v. New York Times Co., 923 F.2d 995 (2d Cir.), cert. denied ___ U.S. ___, 112 S.Ct. 81, 116 L.Ed.2d 54 (1991). The rule prohibiting prior restraints is not necessarily applicable to commercial speech. See

Central Hudson Gas & Electric Corp. v. Public Service Com., 447 U.S. 557, 571 n.13, 100 S.Ct. 2343, 2354 n.13, 65 L.Ed.2d 341 (1980); Virginia State Bd. of Pharmacy v. Virginia Citizens Consumer Council, Inc., 425 U.S. 748, 771–72 n.24, 96 S.Ct. 1817, 1830 n.24, 48 L.Ed.2d 346 (1976). It has been held that the prior restraint doctrine does not require alteration of the normal standard for a preliminary injunction in a suit against an advertiser under § 43(a) of the Lanham Act. Vidal Sassoon, Inc. v. Bristol–Myers Co., 661 F.2d 272, 276 n.8 (2d Cir. 1981).

The case law does not impose a duty of investigation on the publisher of advertisements. Goldstein v. Garlick, 65 Misc.2d 538, 318 N.Y.S.2d 370 (Sup.Ct.1971). See, e.g., Pittman v. Dow Jones & Co., 662 F.Supp. 921 (E.D.La.), affirmed 834 F.2d 1171 (5th Cir.1987) (summary judgment against deceived purchaser); Yuhas v. Mudge, 129 N.J.Super. 207, 322 A.2d 824 (1974) (same). Cf. Braun v. Soldier of Fortune Magazine, Inc., 968 F.2d 1110 (11th Cir.1992), cert. denied ___ U.S. ___, 113 S.Ct. 1028, 122 L.Ed.2d 173 (1993), and Eimann v. Soldier of Fortune Magazine, Inc., 880 F.2d 830 (5th Cir.1989), cert. denied 493 U.S. 1024, 110 S.Ct. 729, 107 L.Ed.2d 748 (1990) (both declining to recognize a duty to investigate in negligence actions against the publisher of alleged criminal solicitations).

The 1988 amendments to the Lanham Act made the remedial provisions of the statute expressly applicable to violations of the Act's prohibition against false or misleading representations in § 43(a). The legislative history of the amendments indicates that the limitations on the relief available against "innocent" printers and publishers are intended to implement the constitutional standards embodied in New York Times Co. v. Sullivan, 376 U.S. 254, 84 S.Ct. 710, 11 L.Ed.2d 686 (1964). See the Reporters' Note to § 26. Section 4(a) of the Uniform Deceptive Trade Practices Act (see the Statutory Note accompanying § 2) includes an exclusion for publishers, broadcasters, and printers who disseminate or reproduce material without knowledge of its deceptive character.

Illustration 1 is supported by the result in Polo Fashions, Inc. v. Ontario Printers, Inc., 601 F.Supp. 402 (N.D.Ohio 1984). Cases imposing liability on a supplier who knowingly assists another in misrepresenting goods or services include Grant Airmass Corp. v. Gaymar Industries, Inc., 645 F.Supp. 1507 (S.D.N.Y.1986) (denying summary judgment to a research firm that allegedly provided a false research report used in advertising by a competitor of the plaintiff); Cantrell & Cochrane, Ltd. v. United Bottle Co., 2 F.Supp. 22 (S.D.N.Y.1921); Hennessy v. Herrmann, 89 Fed. 669 (C.C.Cal.1898); Cuervo v. Jacob Henkell Co., 50 Fed. 471 (C.C.N.Y.1892). See also, e.g., Noone v. Banner Talent Associates, Inc., 398 F.Supp. 260 (S.D.N.Y.1975) (booking services provided to performers engaged in passing off held sufficient to subject the booking agent to liability under § 43(a)).

Illustration 2 is based on Hoover Co. v. Groger, 12 Cal.App.2d 417, 55 P.2d 529 (1936). See Union Tank Car Co. v. Lindsay Soft Water Corp., 257 F.Supp. 510 (D.Neb.1966), affirmed sub nom. Heaton Distributing Co. v. Union Tank Car Co., 387 F.2d 477 (8th Cir.1967); Mr. Rooter Corp. v. Morris, 188 U.S.P.Q. 392 (E.D.La. 1975).

§ 8. Contributory Liability of Manufacturers and Distributors

One who markets goods or services to a third person who further markets the goods or services in a manner that subjects the third person to liability to another for deceptive marketing under the rules stated in §§ 2–6 is subject to liability to that other for contributory deceptive marketing if:

(a) the actor intentionally induces the third person to engage in such conduct; or

(b) the actor fails to take reasonable precautions against the occurrence of the third person's conduct in circumstances in which that conduct can be reasonably anticipated.

Comment:

a. Scope. As illustrated in the preceding Section, liability for deceptive marketing may extend beyond those who actually misrepresent goods or services in the marketplace. This Section is an application of that principle to situations in which goods or services provided by the actor are misrepresented to subsequent purchasers by others. Even if the actor does not directly control other persons in the chain of distribution, under certain circumstances the actor may be held responsible for their misrepresentations under the principles of contributory liability. This Section imposes such liability on an actor who intentionally induces others to misrepresent the actor's goods or services or who accepts the benefits of such misconduct by failing to make reasonable efforts to prevent its occurrence.

The situations in which contributory liability is imposed under this Section typically involve misrepresentations relating to source that are actionable under § 4. If the other person's conduct constitutes trademark infringement, contributory liability may be imposed under the rule stated in § 27. However, liability under this Section is not limited to misrepresentations relating to source, and an actor may be subject to contributory liability in connection with any misrepresentation actionable under the rules stated in this Chapter.

A person may be subject to liability under the rule stated in § 2 if the person makes a representation likely to deceive or mislead prospective purchasers, including prospective purchasers from others to whom it markets the goods. A manufacturer who supplies mislabeled goods to a retailer, for example, may be subject to liability under § 2 even if the retailer itself is not deceived. Liability in such circumstances, however, is direct, and application of the rule stated in this Section is therefore unnecessary.

b. Inducing deceptive representations. If a manufacturer or distributor seeks to further its economic interests by inducing others to market its goods or services in a manner proscribed by the rules stated in this Chapter, it is subject to liability under this Section. The inducement may take the form of an express suggestion that the other pass off the goods as those of a third person or otherwise misrepresent the qualities or characteristics of the goods to subsequent purchasers. It may also consist of other conduct sufficient to indicate the actor's desire to encourage such behavior on the part of others to whom it markets the goods. The appearance of the goods or the manner in which they are marketed by the actor, for example, may communicate the actor's message as effectively as an express proposition.

Illustrations:

1. *A*, a pharmaceutical company, manufactures a liquid quinine preparation that it sells to pharmacists. *B* manufactures a similar product. *B* urges pharmacists to dispense its product to customers who request *A* 's product, and a number of pharmacists in fact pass off *B* 's product as *A* 's. *B* is subject to liability to *A*.

2. *A* is a manufacturer of mattresses and foundations. *B*, a manufacturer and distributor of similar products, sells to retailers bed sets consisting of a mattress manufactured by *A* and a foundation manufactured by *B*. The foundations carry no identifying labels and are covered in fabric matching that used by *A*. *B* also furnishes advertising displays used by the retailers that describe the sets as "*A* 's mattress and matching foundation." If prospective purchasers are likely to believe that both the mattresses and the foundations are manufactured by *A*, *B* is subject to liability to *A*.

c. Failure to take reasonable precautions. A seller may also be subject to liability under this Section if it facilitates the wrongful conduct of others by failing to take reasonable precautions against the making of misrepresentations by those who market its goods or services. The duty to take reasonable precautions arises when the actor has reason to anticipate that some substantial degree of passing off or other actionable misrepresentation is likely.

Failure to take reasonable precautions in the face of a known risk of deception may indicate an intention on the part of the actor to encourage others to misrepresent its goods. Some courts have held that the actor's inaction in such circumstances constitutes an inducement to fraud actionable under the rule stated in Subsection (a). Under the rule as stated in Subsection (b), however, liability is determined by an objective evaluation of the actor's conduct without the necessity of inferring intent.

A manufacturer or other seller of goods who has reason to anticipate subsequent misrepresentations by others is required to take only those precautions that are reasonable under the circumstances. The reasonableness of the actor's precautions must be evaluated in light of the actor's own legitimate interests, the quantum of unlawful conduct that can reasonably be anticipated, and the effectiveness of the actor's response. In particular, an actor who has otherwise taken reasonable precautions is not required to forgo the duplication of functional elements of another's product in order to reduce the risk that others may pass off its goods as those of the other. See § 17. An actor who has taken reasonable precautions is not subject to liability despite the fact that others continue to misrepresent the actor's products.

Illustrations:

3. *A* manufactures a cola beverage. *B* also manufactures a cola beverage that it sells under a trademark that is not confusingly similar to *A*'s. Investigations by *A* reveal that some taverns and restaurants on occasion substitute *B*'s product in response to a request for *A*'s beverage. In the absence of evidence indicating that *B* has intentionally induced the substitutions or has otherwise failed to take reasonable precautions to prevent such conduct, *B* is not subject to liability to *A*.

4. *A*, a pharmaceutical company, manufactures a prescription drug in capsules bearing a particular combination of colors. The drug is sold to pharmacists under *A*'s trademark. *B* manufactures a generic equivalent of *A*'s product in capsules identical to *A*'s and sells the drug to pharmacists at a lower price. Because of its experience with other generic drugs, *B* has reason to anticipate that a substantial amount of passing off is likely. In the absence of evidence justifying *B*'s use of identical capsules under the rule stated in § 17, a court may properly conclude that *B* has failed to take reasonable precautions against the passing off and that *B* is subject to liability to *A*.

5. The facts being otherwise as stated in Illustration 4, the court finds that the color combination used on *A*'s capsules is functional under the rule stated in § 17 in that it indicates to pharmacists and patients the type and dosage of the drug. *B* also

places its own trademark on each of its capsules. *B* is not subject to liability to *A*.

d. Sales to particular purchasers. A specific application of the rule stated in Subsection (b) arises when a manufacturer or other supplier learns that a particular retailer or distributor is passing off or otherwise deceptively marketing the manufacturer's goods. If the manufacturer has reason to anticipate that the other person will continue in its course of conduct, the manufacturer is under a duty to take reasonable precautions to prevent further misrepresentations.

The reasonableness of the actor's precautions should be determined primarily by their effect in deterring the other's conduct. If, as a result of its precautions, the actor no longer has reason to anticipate that the misrepresentations will continue, the actor is not subject to liability. However, if the actor later learns that the other is continuing in its course of conduct, the actor is obligated to take any additional precautions that are reasonable under the circumstances.

In many instances the actor may be justified in relying initially upon direct requests to cease the misrepresentations or upon assurances from the other person that it will do so. In some circumstances further precautions such as alterations in labeling may be necessary. In extreme cases of persistent misconduct, judicial proceedings aimed at enjoining the misrepresentations or a refusal to supply further goods may be the only reasonable precautions.

Illustrations:

6. The facts being otherwise as stated in Illustration 5, *B* knows that a particular pharmacist consistently passes off the drug as *A* 's product. *B* continues to supply the pharmacist with its product and takes no action to deter the passing off. *B* is subject to liability to *A*.

7. *A* is a manufacturer and distributor of whisky made in Scotland. *B* is in the business of marketing alcoholic beverages and sells to *C*, its licensee, imported Scotch whisky together with labels that bear *B* 's trademark and also include the words "Product of Scotland." *B* knows that *C* blends the whisky with domestic spirits before offering the product for sale under the labels provided by *B*. Both *B* and *C* are subject to liability to *A*.

REPORTERS' NOTE

This Section is an elaboration of the former rule on contributory liability for misrepresentations of source in Restatement of Torts § 713 (1938).

The scope of the rule is expanded to include other misrepresentations actionable under the rules of this Chapter.

Comment a. On the distinction between contributory liability for the misrepresentations of another and direct liability for a misrepresentation by the actor, see Inwood Laboratories, Inc. v. Ives Laboratories, Inc., 456 U.S. 844, 863–64, 102 S.Ct. 2182, 2193–94, 72 L.Ed.2d 606 (1982) (White, J., concurring). See also Ciba–Geigy Corp. v. Bolar Pharmaceutical Co., 547 F.Supp. 1095 (D.N.J. 1982), affirmed 719 F.2d 56 (3d Cir. 1983), cert. denied 465 U.S. 1080, 104 S.Ct. 1444, 79 L.Ed.2d 763 (1984).

The Supreme Court in *Ives, supra,* 456 U.S. at 854, 102 S.Ct. at 2188, stated the rule on contributory liability for trademark infringement as follows:

> Thus, if a manufacturer or distributor intentionally induces another to infringe a trademark, or if it continues to supply its product to one whom it knows or has reason to know is engaging in trademark infringement, the manufacturer or distributor is contributorily responsible for any harm done as a result of the deceit.

The circumstances in which contributory liability may be imposed on the manufacturer of a product were considered in Coca–Cola Co. v. Snow Crest Beverages, 64 F.Supp. 980 (D.Mass.1946), affirmed 162 F.2d 280 (1st Cir.), cert. denied 332 U.S. 809, 68 S.Ct. 110, 92 L.Ed. 386 (1947). Judge Wyzanski's opinion is discussed in *Ives, supra.* See generally Symposium: The *Ives* Case, 72 Trademark Rep. 1 (1982).

Comment b. Illustration 1 is based on Illustration 1 to Restatement of Torts § 713, which was derived from William R. Warner & Co. v. Eli Lilly & Co., 265 U.S. 526, 44 S.Ct. 615, 68 L.Ed. 1161 (1924). See also Upjohn Co. v. Schwartz, 246 F.2d 254 (2d Cir.1957).

Illustration 2 is based on Sealy, Inc. v. Easy Living, Inc., 743 F.2d 1378 (9th Cir.1984). See American Philatelic Soc. v. Claibourne, 3 Cal.2d 689, 46 P.2d 135 (1935), overruling defendant's demurrer to a complaint brought by stamp dealers alleging that defendant altered postage stamps to resemble more valuable stamps and induced unscrupulous dealers to sell the counterfeits to the public.

Comment c. Supplying goods to another in a form that facilitates passing off is often viewed as an implicit inducement to misrepresent the source of the goods to purchasers. See, e.g., Ciba–Geigy Corp. v. Bolar Pharmaceutical Co., 547 F.Supp. 1095 (D.N.J.1982), affirmed 719 F.2d 56 (3d Cir.1983), cert. denied 465 U.S. 1080, 104 S.Ct. 1444, 79 L.Ed.2d 763 (1984). The rule as formulated in Subsection (b), although not intended to increase the scope of liability, eliminates the necessity of finding an intent on the part of the actor to induce such misconduct.

Subsection (b) emphasizes an important limitation on the imposition of contributing liability that is sometimes overlooked in judicial formulations of the rule. A number of cases recite that a manufacturer is subject to contributory liability if it can reasonably anticipate that the form in which it sells its goods will enable others to pass off the goods as those of a third person. E.g., SK & F, Co. v. Premo Pharmaceutical Laboratories, Inc., 625 F.2d 1055, 1062 (3d Cir.1980); Merrell–National Laboratories, Inc. v. Zenith Laboratories, Inc., 194 U.S.P.Q. 157, 160 (D.N.J. 1977). See Mershon Co. v. Pachmayr, 220 F.2d 879, 884 n.3 (9th Cir.), cert. denied 350 U.S. 885, 76 S.Ct. 139, 100 L.Ed. 780 (1955) ("A manufacturer who puts in the hands of his immediate vendee the means of deceiving the consumer, is chargeable with unfair competition," quoting Nims, Unfair Competition and Trade Marks 1214 (1947)); Reid, Murdoch & Co. v. H.P. Coffee Co., 48 F.2d 817, 819 (8th Cir.), cert. denied 284 U.S. 621, 52 S.Ct. 9, 76 L.Ed. 529 (1931) ("furnished the merchants with the means or tools of committing a fraud upon the public"). The Supreme Court in Inwood Laboratories, Inc. v. Ives Laboratories, Inc., 456 U.S. 844, 102 S.Ct. 2182, 72 L.Ed.2d 606 (1982), rejected the "reasonably anticipate" standard in connection with a claim of contributory trademark infringement under § 32 of the Lanham Act, see 456 U.S. at 854 n.13, 102 S.Ct. at 2188 n.13, but the decision has not been interpreted to preclude reliance on that standard at common law. See Ciba–Geigy Corp., *supra* (declining to apply *Ives* to claims arising under state law and § 43(a) of the Lanham Act). This Section rejects the stated rationale although not necessarily the results of those decisions that impose liability on the basis of the actor's "reasonable anticipation" alone. Under the rule stated in Subsection (b), an actor is not subject to liability if it has taken precautions against the other person's misrepresentations that are reasonable under the circumstances; liability may be imposed only upon a showing of both reasonable anticipation and a failure to take reasonable precautions. Cases emphasizing the relevance of the manufacturer's precautionary measures include Smith v. Chanel, Inc., 402 F.2d 562, 570 (9th Cir.1968) ("But where, as here, the appellants have done all that could reasonably be expected to avoid confusion, the speculative possibility of deliberate fraud by third parties is not a sufficient basis for injunctive relief."); Upjohn Co. v. Schwartz, 246 F.2d 254, 256 (2d Cir. 1957) (no liability if defendant undertook "adequate precautions"). See Sealy, Inc. v. Easy Living, Inc., 743 F.2d 1378, 1382 (9th Cir.1984) (finding "that the defendants' remedial measures were inadequate"). If the other person's conduct could not be reasonably anticipated, the manufacturer is not subject to liability. Mattel, Inc. v. Goldberger Doll Mfg. Co., 200 F.Supp. 517 (E.D.N.Y.1961).

Illustration 3 is based on the facts of Coca–Cola Co. v. Snow Crest Beverages, Inc., 64 F.Supp. 980 (D.Mass. 1946), affirmed 162 F.2d 280 (1st Cir.), cert. denied 332 U.S. 809, 68 S.Ct. 110, 92 L.Ed. 386 (1947). See also Nugrape Co. of America v. Glazier, 22 F.2d 596 (5th Cir.1927).

Illustrations 4 and 5 are suggested by the Supreme Court's reasoning in *Ives, supra.*

Comment d. Traditional formulations of the scope of contributory liability expressly encompass the situations described in Comment *d.* However, the rule as stated here emphasizes that the manufacturer or supplier need not terminate its business relationship with the other person if it reasonably believes that less drastic precautions will be sufficient to deter the misrepresentations. As a practical matter, the rule will frequently permit the continuation of business between the parties unless the actor learns that the attempts to discourage the other's misrepresentations have failed.

Illustration 6 is suggested by the Supreme Court's reasoning in Inwood Laboratories, Inc. v. Ives Laboratories, Inc., 456 U.S. 844, 102 S.Ct. 2182, 72 L.Ed.2d 606 (1982). See also Power Test Petroleum Distributors, Inc. v. Manhattan & Queens Fuel Corp., 556 F.Supp. 392 (E.D.N.Y.1982), denying a motion to dismiss made by a defendant allegedly supplying petroleum products to service stations operating under another's trademark. Cf. Nike, Inc. v. Rubber Mfrs. Ass'n, 509 F.Supp. 919 (S.D.N.Y.1981), in which a shoe manufacturer was held liable under § 43(a) based on its knowledge that professional athletes under contract to the manufacturer were altering shoes made by the manufacturer's competitors in order to falsely represent that they were wearing shoes made by the defendant. The standards governing the contributory liability of manufacturers announced in *Ives, supra,* were invoked by analogy to determine the contributory liability of a franchisor for the trademark infringement of a franchisee in Mini Maid Services Co. v. Maid Brigade Systems, Inc., 967 F.2d 1516 (11th Cir.1992).

Illustration 7 is based on Scotch Whiskey Ass'n v. Barton Distilling Co., 338 F.Supp. 595 (N.D.Ill.1971), affirmed 489 F.2d 809 (7th Cir.1973).

CHAPTER THREE

THE LAW OF TRADEMARKS

Introductory Note: This Chapter addresses the rules governing the protection of trademarks and other indicia of origin or association. Rights in trademarks and related trade symbols are recognized at common law and under federal and state trademark registration statutes. The statutory protection of trademarks is largely a codification of the common law, and except as otherwise noted the rules stated in this Chapter are applicable to both common law and statutory actions.

Topic 1 treats the subject matter of trademark law, including the requirement of distinctiveness. Also included in Topic 1 are the rules governing the recognition of trademark rights in packaging and product designs. Topic 2 states the rules governing acquisition and priority of rights. Topic 3 addresses the scope of trademark protection, including the "likelihood of confusion" standard of liability and the protection afforded to trademarks under the antidilution statutes. Topic 4 treats the rules relating to defenses and limitations on relief. Topic 5 states the rules governing the licensing and assignment of trademark rights. Rules relating to remedies are considered in Topic 6.

TOPIC 1. SUBJECT MATTER OF TRADEMARK LAW

---

§ 9. Definitions of Trademark and Service Mark

A trademark is a word, name, symbol, device, or other designation, or a combination of such designations, that

is distinctive of a person's goods or services and that is used in a manner that identifies those goods or services and distinguishes them from the goods or services of others. A service mark is a trademark that is used in connection with services.

Comment:

a. Relation to other rules. The term "designation" as used in this Chapter subsumes all subject matter eligible for protection as a trademark. See Comment *g*. The requirement that the designation is "distinctive" is discussed in § 13. The process by which rights are acquired in a designation is described in § 18. The special issues presented by designations that consist of product or packaging features are considered in §§ 16 and 17.

b. Historical origins of trademarks. The use of identifying marks on goods dates to antiquity. The original purpose of such marks was to indicate ownership. With the development of commercial trade the marks came to serve a different function—identification of the source of goods offered for sale in the marketplace.

The use of trademarks was well-known in Roman times, although it was apparently left to the defrauded purchaser to bring an action against a trademark infringer. The guild system of medieval England produced the first widespread use of trademarks. Distinctive production marks were required on goods manufactured by the local guilds. The purpose of such compulsory marking was primarily regulatory since the marks fixed responsibility for defective merchandise and facilitated enforcement of the territorial monopolies enjoyed by the guilds. The geographic expansion of markets and the development of more complex distribution systems eventually resulted in a new function for production marks. The marks served to identify the source of the goods to prospective purchasers who could then make their selections based upon the reputation, not merely of the immediate vendor, but also of the manufacturer. Manufacturers began to adopt marks expressly for the purpose of identifying their goods to prospective customers. The medieval production mark thus evolved into the modern trademark used by manufacturers, distributors, and other sellers to identify their goods and services in the marketplace.

c. Rationale for protection. The protection of trademarks has been justified on numerous grounds. Early case law emphasized the unfairness inherent in a diversion of trade from the owner of the mark through a fraudulent use of the trademark. Liability for trademark infringement also served to remedy the unjust enrichment resulting from the infringer's appropriation of benefits attributable to the good will of the trademark owner. The rules prohibiting trademark infringement were seen as part of a general attempt to implement standards of commercial morality and fair dealing in the market.

Modern economic analysis emphasizes additional interests underlying the protection of trademarks. The public benefits afforded by competitive markets cannot be fully realized unless prospective consumers can differentiate the products of competing sellers. In the absence of effective trademark protection, individual sellers gain little from improvements in product quality or service since they cannot easily recapture the benefits of a favorable consumer response. The protection of trademarks thus encourages investment in quality and service by securing to the trademark owner the benefits of a favorable reputation. Nonprofit enterprises such as charitable, educational, governmental, fraternal, and religious organizations have analogous interests in protecting their good will, and the designations adopted by such enterprises to identify their goods or services are similarly eligible for protection as trademarks.

As the geographic scope of markets expanded and systems of distribution became increasingly complex, trademarks came to function as an important instrument of advertising. Trademarks serve as a means of communication between otherwise unknown or anonymous producers and their prospective customers. If the trademark owner succeeds in creating a favorable image for its trademark in the marketplace, the mark itself can become a significant factor in stimulating sales. This ability of a mark to generate good will through advertising has also gained recognition under the law of trademarks.

The protection of trademarks also functions as an indirect form of consumer protection. In some cases a trademark may specifically identify the manufacturer of the goods or services, thus enabling consumers to base their purchasing decisions on the reputation of the business identified by the mark. Even when the trademark does not identify a particular business entity known to consumers, it can nevertheless indicate that the product emanates from the same source as other goods or services that bear the mark. The trademark thus informs consumers that the product shares a common even if anonymous source with other goods with which they may be familiar. Similarly, the presence of a trademark can signify that the goods or services are sponsored or approved by a particular business. In all these circumstances the trademark functions as an indication of consistent and predictable quality. Trademark infringement increases the cost of acquiring knowledge about goods and services by undermining the capacity of trademarks to communicate useful, reliable information. For consumers who are deceived by an unauthorized use of the mark, trademark infringement can result in improvident expenditures and unfulfilled expectations.

The economic analysis that has been invoked to support a vigorous system of trademark protection has not gone unquestioned. Some argue that strong trademarks act as barriers to the entry of new competitors and also enable trademark owners to escape the full rigors of competition through product differentiation and irrational brand loyalty sustained by advertising. Recognition of trademark rights in words and symbols can also inhibit the communication of useful information by other sellers in the market. The extension of trademark protection to packaging and product features can undermine the freedom to copy successful products unprotected by patent or copyright. Such encroachments on the public domain can result in higher prices and decreased access to goods and services. Although these criticisms have not undermined the basic commitment to the protection of trademarks, their influence is evident in the continuing effort to delineate the appropriate scope of protection.

d. Doctrinal development. The earliest cases involving trademarks were actions on the case in the nature of deceit. The issue in each case was whether the defendant had imitated the plaintiff's mark for the purpose of misrepresenting the defendant's goods as those of the plaintiff. These actions eventually evolved into a distinct tort of "passing off," or "unfair competition" as it came to be known in the United States. The gravamen of the tort was fraud; proof of the defendant's intent to deceive prospective consumers was an essential element of the plaintiff's case. Equity jurisdiction was exercised only in aid of this legal right. Cases decided during this formative period of trademark law thus emphasized the character of the defendant's conduct rather than the nature of the plaintiff's rights in the mark.

The conception of trademarks as property first emerged in the mid–19th century when English courts of equity began to grant injunctive relief against the unauthorized use of trademarks without requiring proof of an intent to deceive. Since equity jurisdiction emphasized the protection of "property," the plaintiff's interest in the trademark came to be characterized as a property right arising from the adoption and use of the mark. By 1879, the United States Supreme Court saw "[t]he whole system of trade-mark" as founded on the concept of "a property right." Trade–Mark Cases, 100 U.S. (10 Otto) 82, 92, 25 L.Ed. 550 (1879).

In both England and the United States, however, the property conception of trademark rights extended only to certain designations. When the defendant imitated a designation that was clearly distinctive of the plaintiff's goods, the natural inference that the defendant intended to deceive prospective purchasers eventually led to a conclusive presumption of fraud. Thus, in the case of words or other symbols invented by the plaintiff or arbitrary designations that had no apparent relation to the plaintiff's goods except as an indication of source, the courts began to protect the plaintiff's "property" interest in the mark without regard to the presence of any fraudulent intent. Such marks were characterized as "trademarks," and cases involving the unauthorized use of these marks were designated as actions for "trademark infringement." The focus of the inquiry thus shifted from an analysis of the defendant's conduct to a consideration of the nature of the plaintiff's right. Less distinctive marks that had nevertheless come to be recognized by prospective consumers as indications of source were called "trade names." Although not recognized as "property" in the same sense as technical "trademarks," protection for "trade names" remained available through the action for "unfair competition," with its historical emphasis on the fraudulent character of the defendant's conduct.

The property rationale for trademark protection was limited from its inception by a recognition of the symbolic nature of a trademark. The Supreme Court emphasized that there is "no such thing as property in a trade-mark except as a right appurtenant to an established business," United Drug Co. v. Theodore Rectanus Co., 248 U.S. 90, 97, 39 S.Ct. 48, 50, 63 L.Ed. 141, 145 (1918), and that trademarks were to be classed among property rights "only in the sense that a man's right to the continued enjoyment of his trade reputation and the good-will that flows from it, free from unwarranted interference by others, is a property right, for the protection of which a trade-mark is an instrumentality." Hanover Star Milling Co. v. Metcalf, 240 U.S. 403, 413, 36 S.Ct. 357, 360, 60 L.Ed. 713, 718 (1916). The conception of trademarks as property thus did not yield a general right to exclude others; protection was ordinarily limited to cases involving a threatened appropriation of good will arising from consumer confusion. In a few areas, such as the attempt to gain protection against uses that dilute or tarnish the value of the mark (see § 25), the property conception continues to influence the substantive scope of trademark rights.

The initial emphasis on fraud and property rights has generally given way to a more explicit analysis of the propriety of the defendant's conduct as a means of competition, and the technical distinctions between the actions for trademark infringement and unfair competition have now been abandoned. Economic analysis of trademark issues and sophisticated techniques for measuring consumer perceptions have become increasingly influential. The substantive scope of trademark rights now reflects the recognition of numerous interests, including the trademark owner's claim to the benefits of its good will, the interest of consumers in reliable indicia of source and sponsorship, and the right of other sellers to compete vigorously with the trademark owner in the marketplace.

e. Trademark legislation. The federal government and each of the states have enacted legislation protecting trademarks. The statutes generally provide a mechanism for the registration of trademarks, describe the types of marks that may be registered, and specify the procedural and substantive advantages afforded to the owner of a trademark registration. The statutes, however, do not ordinarily preempt the protection of trademarks at common law.

Although several states had earlier enacted legislation to prevent the fraudulent use of trademarks, the first federal trademark statute was not enacted until 1870. This initial attempt at federal protection proved short-lived, however, when in 1879 the Supreme Court in the Trade–Mark Cases, 100 U.S. (10 Otto) 82, 25 L.Ed. 550 (1879), held that the statute had been unconstitutionally grounded on the patent and copyright clause of the Constitution. A second federal statute was enacted in 1881, but in reaction to the Trade–Mark Cases, registration under the act was limited to marks used in commerce with foreign nations and the Indian tribes. The first modern federal trademark registration statute was the Trademark Act of 1905, grounded on the commerce clause. In a continuation of the distinction that had developed at common law between technical "trademarks" and "trade names," see Comment *d*, the Act of 1905 limited registration to fanciful and arbitrary marks, except for marks that had been in actual use for 10 years preceding passage of the statute.

To clarify and strengthen the rights of trademark owners, the Act of 1905 was replaced by the Trademark Act of 1946 (effective July 5, 1947), 15 U.S.C.A. §§ 1051–1127, commonly known as the Lanham Act. The Lanham Act is generally declarative of existing law, incorporating the principal features of common law trademark protection. However, among the major innovations of the Lanham Act were the adoption of a constructive notice rule that effectively expanded the geographic scope of trademark rights, see § 19, Comment *e*, and an attempt to provide a measure of security to trademark owners in the form of "incontestable" rights in certain trademarks. See § 13, Comment *a*. The Lanham Act in § 43(a) also added a general proscription against false designations and representations that has come to serve as a federal law of deceptive marketing. See § 2, Comment *b*.

Statutes in every state also provide for the registration of trademarks. In 1949 the United States (now International) Trademark

Association prepared a Model State Trademark Bill patterned after the federal registration system. The Model Bill, revised in 1964 and 1992, provides the basis for much of the current state legislation. State trademark registration acts are cited in the Statutory Note following this Section.

f. "Trademark"; "Trade name"; "Service mark". The term "trademark" as originally employed at common law described only inherently-distinctive designations such as fanciful or arbitrary marks. The term "trade name" was used to denote other designations such as descriptive terms or personal names that through use had come to identify the goods of a particular seller. During the first half of the 20th century the substantive rules governing the protection of "trademarks" and "trade names" became essentially identical, and the significance of the distinction diminished. Passage of the Lanham Act in 1946 hastened the abandonment of the former terminology. The statutory definition of "trademark" subsumes all designations that are distinctive of the user's goods. The term "trade name" as defined in the Lanham Act denotes the name of a business or other enterprise. See § 12. The Model State Trademark Bill incorporates similar definitions, and modern common law usage now reflects these statutory formulations. The definition of "trademark" adopted in this Section thus includes all designations that identify the source of goods or services. The requirement of distinctiveness as elaborated in § 13 preserves the substantive distinction between inherently-distinctive marks and other potential trademarks.

The Lanham Act and the Model State Trademark Bill limit the term "trademark" to marks used to identify the source of goods. A mark used to identify the source of services is denominated a "service mark." The substantive rules applicable to both types of marks are fundamentally identical, however, and the term "trademark" is generally understood to include marks used in the marketing of either goods or services. The definitions in this Section adopt this convenient usage. The term "service mark" as defined here thus denotes a specific type of trademark.

g. Subject matter. The subject matter of trademark law was initially limited to fanciful or arbitrary words and symbols. This limitation excluded not only descriptive words and symbols, but also other devices that could identify the source of goods, such as the physical appearance of the goods or the appearance of labels, wrappers, containers, or advertising materials that accompany the goods in the marketplace. When such features in fact served to distinguish the goods of a particular producer, they were protected, together with descriptive marks, in an action for unfair competition. As the distinctions between the actions for trademark infringement and unfair competition diminished, the law of trademarks eventually subsumed descriptive designations that had acquired significance as indications of source. Although the protection of product and packaging designs that are indicative of source remains subject to special limitations not applicable to other marks, they too have now been subsumed under the law of trademarks. See §§ 16 and 17.

The definition of "trademark" adopted in this Section does not incorporate any technical limitations on the nature of the subject matter that may qualify for protection. Words remain the most common type of trademark, such as the word FORD used in connection with the sale of automobiles or KODAK used in connection with cameras. Numbers, letters, and slogans are also eligible for protection as trademarks, as are pictures, symbols, characters, sounds, graphic designs, product and packaging features, and other matter capable of identifying and distinguishing the goods or services of the user. See §§ 13 and 14. Limitations on the recognition of trademark rights in "functional" subject matter are considered in § 17. For other public policy limitations, see § 32.

STATUTORY NOTE

Every state has enacted legislation providing for the registration and protection of trademarks. All but a few of these statutes are derived from the Model State Trademark Bill drafted by the United States Trademark Association in 1949, as revised in 1964 and 1992. The Model Bill or an analogous statute is in effect as follows:

Alabama .... ALA. C. § 8–12–6 et seq.
Alaska.............. ALASKA S. § 45.50.010 et seq.
Arizona............. ARIZ. R.S. § 44–1441 et seq.
Arkansas .... ARK. C.A. § 4–71–101 et seq.
California .... CAL. Bus. & Prof.C. § 14200 et seq.
Colorado............ COLO. R.S. § 7–70–102 et seq.
Connecticut .... CONN. G.S. § 35–11a et seq.; § 35–18a et seq.
Delaware .... DEL. C., tit. 6, § 3301 et seq.
Florida .... FLA. S. § 495.011 et seq.
Georgia............. GA C.A. § 10–1–440 et seq.
Hawaii .... HAW. R.S. § 482–1 et seq.
Idaho .... IDAHO C. § 48–501 et seq.
Illinois.............. ILL. C.S., ch. 765, § 1035/0.01 et seq.
Indiana .... IND. C. § 24–2–1–1 et seq.
Iowa .... IOWA C. § 548.1 et seq.
Kansas .... KAN. S.A. § 81–111 et seq.
Kentucky .... KY. R.S. § 365.560 et seq.

Louisiana .... LA. R.S.A. § 51:211 et seq.
Maine .... ME. R.S.A., tit. 10, § 1521 et seq.
Maryland .... MD. Bus.Reg.C.A. § 1–401 et seq.
Massachusetts .... MASS. G.L.A. ch. 110B, § 1 et seq.
Michigan .... MICH. C.L.A. § 429.31 et seq.
Minnesota .... MINN. S.A. § 333.001 et seq.
Mississippi .... MISS. C.A. § 75–25–1 et seq.
Missouri .... MO. R.S. § 417.005 et seq.
Montana .... MONT. C.A. § 30–13–301 et seq.
Nebraska .... NEB. R.S. § 87–101 et seq.
Nevada .... NEV. R.S.A. § 600.240 et seq.
New Hampshire ..... N.H. R.S.A. § 350–A
New Jersey .... N.J. S.A. § 56:3–13.1 et seq.
New Mexico .... N.M. S.A. § 57–3–1 et seq.
New York .... N.Y. Gen.Bus.L. § 360 et seq.
North Carolina ...... N.C. G.S. § 80–1 et seq.
North Dakota .... N.D. Cent.C. § 47–22–01 et seq.
Ohio .... OHIO R.C. § 1329.54 et seq.
Oklahoma .... OKLA. S.A., tit. 78, § 21 et seq.
Oregon .... OR. R.S. § 647.005 et seq.
Pennsylvania .... PA. S.A., tit. 54, § 1101 et seq.
Puerto Rico .... P.R. L.A., tit. 10, § 171 et seq.
Rhode Island .... R.I. G.L.A. § 6–2–1 et seq.
South Carolina ...... S.C. C.A. § 39–15–120 et seq.
South Dakota .... S.D. Comp.L.A. § 37–6
Tennessee .... TENN. C.A. § 47–25–501 et seq.
Texas .... TEX. Bus. & Com.C. § 16.01 et seq.
Utah .... UTAH C.A. § 70–3–1 et seq.
Vermont .... VT. S.A. tit. 9, § 2521 et seq.
Virginia .... VA. C.A. § 59.1–77 et seq.
Washington .... WASH. R.C.A. § 19.77.010 et seq.
West Virginia .... W.VA. C.A. § 47–2–1 et seq.
Wisconsin .... WIS. S. § 132.01 et seq.
Wyoming .... WYO. S.A. § 40–1–101 et seq.

REPORTERS' NOTE

The primary treatises on the law of trademarks are Callmann, Unfair Competition, Trademarks and Monopolies; Gilson, Trademark Protection and Practice; McCarthy, Trademarks and Unfair Competition. State statutory provisions relevant to the subject matter of this Chapter are collected in International Trademark Association, State Trademark and Unfair Competition Law.

This topic was originally treated in Restatement of Torts, Chapter 35—Confusion of Source (1939).

Comment b. The historical origins of trademarks are described in Schechter, The Historical Foundations of the Law Relating to Trade-Marks (1925). See also Diamond, The Historical Development of Trademarks, 65 Trademark Rep. 265 (1975).

Comment c. The initial emphasis on deceit is evident in the early trademark cases discussed in Burrell, Two Hundred Years of English Trade Mark Law, in ABA, Two Hundred Years of English and American Patent, Trademark and Copyright Law 35 (1977).

The competitive rationale for the protection of trademarks was stressed by the Senate Committee on Patents in its Report on the Lanham Act:

> Trade-marks, indeed, are the essence of competition, because they make possible a choice between competing articles by enabling the buyer to distinguish one from the other. Trade-marks encourage the maintenance of quality by securing to the producer the benefit of the good reputation which excellence creates. To protect trade-marks, therefore, is to protect the public from deceit, to foster fair competition, and to secure to the business community the advantages of reputation and good will by preventing their diversion from those who have created them to those who have not.

S.Rep.No. 1333, 79th Cong., 2d Sess. 4 (1946), reprinted in 1946 U.S. Code Cong. & Admin. News 1274, 1275. The Report also emphasized the significance of trademark law as an instrument of consumer protection:

> The purpose underlying any trade-mark statute is twofold. One is to protect the public so that it may be confident that, in purchasing a product bearing a particular trade-mark which it favorably knows, it will get the product which it asks for and wants to get. Secondly, where the owner of a trade-mark has spent energy, time, and money in presenting to the public the product, he is protected in his investment from its misappropriation by pirates and cheats. This is the well-established rule of law protecting both the public and the trade-mark owner.

Id. at 3; 1946 U.S. Code Cong. & Admin. News at 1274. See also, e.g., Kenner Parker Toys Inc. v. Rose Art Industries, Inc., 963 F.2d 350, 353–54 (Fed.Cir.), cert. denied ___ U.S. ___, 113 S.Ct. 181, 121 L.Ed.2d 126 (1992); Durango Herald, Inc. v. Riddle, 719 F.Supp. 941, 948 (D.Colo.1988).

The first influential analysis of the advertising value of trademarks appeared in Schechter, The Rational Basis of Trade–Mark Protection, 40 Harv.L.Rev. 813 (1927). See also Justice Frankfurter's description of the psychological effect of trademarks in Mishawaka Rubber & Woolen Mfg. Co. v. S.S. Kresge Co., 316 U.S. 203, 205, 62 S.Ct. 1022, 1024, 86 L.Ed. 1381, 1384 (1942). The protection afforded by the law of trademarks extends to designations that identify the goods and services of nonprofit organizations. See, e.g., Birthright v. Birthright, Inc., 827 F.Supp. 1114 (D.N.J.1993); Healing the Children, Inc. v. Heal the Children, Inc., 786 F.Supp. 1209 (W.D.Pa. 1992).

The disputes relating to the economic effects of modern trademarks are briefly surveyed in McClure, Trademarks and Unfair Competition: A Critical History of Legal Thought, 69 Trademark Rep. 305 (1979). Overviews of the economics of trademark law are offered in Kratzke, Normative Economic Analysis of Trademark Law, 21 Memphis St. U.L.Rev. 199 (1991); Landes and Posner, Trademark Law: An Economic Perspective, 30 J.Law & Econ. 265 (1987).

Comment d. The doctrinal development of the law of trademarks is summarized in McClure, *supra.* The property conception is often traced to Millington v. Fox, 3 My. & Cr. 338 (1838), in which the Court of Chancery held that it was unnecessary to establish an intent to deceive on the part of an infringer. Justice Holmes later wrote that "in a qualified sense the mark is property, protected and alienable, although as with other property its outline is shown only by the law of torts, of which the right is a prophetic summary." Beech–Nut Packing Co. v. P. Lorillard Co., 273 U.S. 629, 632, 47 S.Ct. 481, 482, 71 L.Ed. 810, 814 (1927). The former distinctions between "trademarks" and "trade names" were critically examined in an influential article by Handler and Pickett, Trade-marks and Trade Names—An Analysis and Synthesis: I & II, 30 Colum.L.Rev. 168 and 759 (1930).

Comment e. The history of federal trademark legislation is reviewed in Pattishall, Two Hundred Years of American Trademark Law, in ABA, Two Hundred Years of English and American Patent, Trademark and Copyright Law 51 (1977), reprinted in 68 Trademark Rep. 121 (1978). Much of the legislative history of the Lanham Act is conveniently collected in Gilson, *supra.*

The Model State Trademark Bill is reprinted in Gilson, *supra,* § 10.03; McCarthy, *supra,* § 22.04. State trademark registration acts are collected in International Trademark Association, State Trademark and Unfair Competition Law. The limited impact of the state acts is described in Seasonwein, The Effect of State Trademark Registration, 61 Trademark Rep. 457 (1971).

Comment f. The former treatment of this topic, although narrowing the substantive distinctions between "trademarks" and "trade names," adhered to the now obsolete terminology. See Restatement of Torts §§ 715 and 716. The modern definitions appear in the Lanham Act at 15 U.S.C.A. § 1127.

Comment g. Examples of trademark subject matter are collected in McCarthy, *supra,* ch.7. See also the Reporters' Note accompanying § 13, Comment *d.* The Restatement of Torts treated the protection of product and packaging designs under separate rules distinct from those applicable to trademarks. See Restatement of Torts §§ 741–743. Under the definition adopted in this Section, that subject matter is now subsumed under the general rules relating to the protection of trademarks. See § 16.

§ 10. Definition of Collective Mark

A collective mark is a word, name, symbol, device, or other designation, or a combination of such designations, that is distinctive of a cooperative, association, organization, or other collective group and that is used by members of the collective group in a manner that:

(a) identifies the goods or services of members and distinguishes them from the goods or services of nonmembers; or

(b) indicates membership in the collective group.

Comment:

a. Nature of collective marks. A collective mark that is used in connection with the sale of goods or services to indicate that the goods or services originate from a member of the collective group is called a "collective trademark." See Comment *b*. A collective mark that is used to indicate that a person or entity is a member of the collective group is called a "collective membership mark." See Comment *c*. Although collective marks are used by the members of an organization to indicate a connection with the collective group, the organization, by virtue of its control over the use of the mark through its power to determine membership, is ordinarily the owner of the collective mark.

The group or organization to which a collective mark refers may be any group of persons or entities brought together in an organized manner. The sole requirement is that the group functions or exists as a collective body of individual members. The organization may be commercial in nature, such as a business cooperative, trade association, or labor union. It may also be noncommercial, such as a fraternal organization, service club, or other organized social group.

A designation that is used by the collective organization itself to identify goods or services produced or rendered by the organization, as distinguished from its individual members, is not a collective mark under the rule stated in this Section. Such a designation is instead eligible for protection as a trademark under the rule stated in § 9. On the distinction between collective marks and certification marks, see § 11, Comment *a*. Although the characterization of a designation as a trademark, trade name, collective mark, or certification mark is legally significant in connection with registration of the mark under the Lanham Act, rights at common law may exist whenever a designation is used in a manner consistent with any of the various categories of marks protected under the rules in this Chapter.

The general requirements applicable to the protection of trademarks, including the rules relating to distinctiveness (see § 13) and acquisition of rights (see § 18), also apply to collective marks, although application of these criteria must take account of the special function of a collective mark. The principles of law governing trademark infringement are similarly applicable to collective marks. See § 20. On the federal registration of collective marks, see § 4 of the Lanham Act, 15 U.S.C.A. § 1054.

b. Collective trademarks. When a collective mark is used by members to identify their goods or services, the mark indicates source in a manner analogous to a trademark. Such "collective trademarks," however, signify that the goods or services originate with a member of the group rather than with a specific individual. The rationales justifying the protection of trademarks (see § 9, Comment *c*) also apply to the protection of collective trademarks.

Illustrations:

1. *A* is an unincorporated association consisting of numerous independent bus companies. Members of the association use the designation BYWAYS to indicate to prospective customers that their transportation services are rendered by a member of the association. The designation is a collective trademark under the rule stated in this Section.

2. *A* is a membership corporation incorporated under the name "Sunshine Inns United." *A* derives its revenue from dues paid by members who operate motels throughout the United States. *A* prepares and distributes guidebooks listing the names of motels operated by its members and engages in other advertising and promotional activities. To identify their lodging services as those of a member of *A*, individual members prominently display the designation SUNSHINE INN at each motel. The designation is a collective trademark under the rule stated in this Section.

c. Collective membership marks. A collective mark may be used by a person to indicate membership in an organization. The mark may be used, for example, on membership cards, plaques, certificates, or jewelry. Trade and professional associations, cooperatives, and labor unions are typical owners of "collective membership marks." Such marks are also employed by noncommercial entities such as fraternal, religious, and educational organizations. Unlike a collective trademark, a mark used as a collective membership mark is not analogous to a trademark in that it does not indicate the source or sponsorship of goods or services. Membership marks do, however, identify members of the organization and distinguish them from nonmembers. The inclusion of such marks within the scope of trademark law affords protection to organizations that do not use their insignia or symbols on goods or services but that wish to prevent unauthorized use by nonmembers. On the infringement of collective membership marks, including issues relating to noncommercial use, see § 20, Comment *e*.

Illustrations:

3. *A*, a fraternal organization, adopts as a symbol of membership an emblem that consists of a representation of clasped

hands together with geometric designs and letters. The emblem is used by members of *A* on jewelry, certificates, and other items to indicate membership in the organization. The designation is a collective membership mark under the rule stated in this Section.

4. *A* manufactures aircraft escape equipment including ejection seats and parachutes. *A* forms a club, called "The Grasshopper Club," consisting of pilots who have successfully utilized *A* 's equipment. The words GRASSHOPPER CLUB are used on membership cards and pins. The designation is a collective membership mark under the rule stated in this Section.

5. *A* is an association of businesses and individuals active in the electronics industry that operates under the name "Electronics Group." Members of the association are given plaques bearing a distinctive design consisting of the letters EG against a background depicting electron orbits in order to indicate their membership in the association. The designation is a collective membership mark under the rule stated in this Section.

REPORTERS' NOTE

This Section is derived from the definition of "collective mark" in § 45 of the Lanham Act, 15 U.S.C. § 1127. See also 15 U.S.C.A. § 1054. See generally Patent and Trademark Office, Trademark Manual of Examining Procedure §§ 1303–04; McCarthy, Trademarks and Unfair Competition § 19.34.

Comment a. On the distinction between "collective trademarks" and "collective membership marks," see, e.g., Aloe Creme Laboratories, Inc. v. American Soc. for Aesthetic Plastic Surgery, Inc., 192 U.S.P.Q. 170 (Tm. Tr.App.Bd.1976). See also the definition of "collective mark" at 15 U.S.C.A. § 1127. Ownership of a collective mark resides in the organization that controls the use of the mark and not in the individual members. 15 U.S.C.A. § 1054. See, e.g., F.R. Lepage Bakery, Inc. v. Roush Bakery Products Co., 851 F.2d 351 (Fed.Cir.), modified 863 F.2d 43 (Fed.Cir.1988). On the requirement of control, compare In re Stencel Aero Engineering Corp., 170 U.S.P.Q. 292 (Tm.Tr.App. Bd.1971) (summarized in Illustration 4) with Constitution Party of Texas v. Constitution Association USA, 152 U.S.P.Q. 443 (Tm.Tr.App.Bd.1966) (cancellation of a collective mark registration because use was not controlled by the registrant). The distinction between trademark use of a designation by the collective organization itself and use as a collective trademark by members is drawn in, e.g., Seven–Up Bottling Co. v. Seven–Up Co., 561 F.2d 1275 (8th Cir.1977); Quality Courts United, Inc. v. Quality Courts, Inc., 140 F.Supp. 341 (M.D.Pa.1956); Aloe Creme Laboratories, Inc., *supra.* See Trademark Manual of Examining Procedure, *supra,* § 104.

The criteria for the protection of trademarks also apply to collective marks. See, e.g., American Speech–Language–Hearing Ass'n v. National Hearing Aid Soc., 224 U.S.P.Q. 798

(Tm.Tr.App.Bd.1984) (registration of deceptive collective mark canceled); In re Int'l Ass'n for Enterostomal Therapy, Inc., 218 U.S.P.Q. 343 (Tm. Tr.App.Bd.1983) (collective mark held generic). The traditional standard of infringement is also applicable. See, e.g., Supreme Assembly, Order of Rainbow for Girls v. J.H. Ray Jewelry Co., 676 F.2d 1079 (5th Cir.1982); cf. Allstate Life Insurance Co. v. Cuna International, Inc., 169 U.S.P.Q. 313 (Tm.Tr.App.Bd.1971), affirmed 487 F.2d 1407 (C.C.P.A.1973) (registration refused because of likelihood of confusion with an existing mark); Boise Cascade Corp. v. Mississippi Pine Mfrs. Ass'n, 164 U.S.P.Q. 364 (Tm.Tr.App.Bd.1969) (same).

In addition to the protection afforded under the Lanham Act, collective marks are also protected against infringement at common law. See, e.g., Professional Golfers Association v. Bankers Life & Casualty Co., 514 F.2d 665 (5th Cir.1975); National Trailways Bus System v. Trailway Van Lines, Inc., 269 F.Supp. 352 (E.D.N.Y.1965); Quality Courts United, Inc. v. Quality Courts, Inc., 140 F.Supp. 341 (M.D.Pa.1956); cf. Supreme Assembly, Order of Rainbow for Girls, *supra* (common law claim failed for lack of proof). See also Schroeder v. Lotito, 577 F.Supp. 708 (D.R.I.1983), affirmed 747 F.2d 801 (1st Cir.1984) (unauthorized use of labor union mark actionable as common law false advertising). But see Huber Baking Co. v. Stroehmann Brothers Co., 252 F.2d 945 (2d Cir.), cert. denied 358 U.S. 829, 79 S.Ct. 50, 3 L.Ed.2d 69 (1958) (collective mark "unknown to the common law") (dictum). Collective marks also receive indirect protection through the recognition of common law rights in the trade names of both commercial and noncommercial organizations. See § 12.

Comment b. Although some older cases recite, as a matter of definition, that the collective organization itself may not use the collective trademark to identify its own goods or services, see, e.g., Seven–Up Bottling Co. v. Seven–Up Co., 561 F.2d 1275 (8th Cir.1977); Huber Baking Co. v. Stroehmann Brothers Co., 252 F.2d 945 (2d Cir.), cert. denied 358 U.S. 829, 79 S.Ct. 50, 3 L.Ed.2d 69 (1958), a 1988 amendment to § 4 of the Lanham Act, 15 U.S.C.A. § 1054, clarified that the prohibition against use by the owner that is applicable to certification marks (see § 11, Comment *a*) does not apply to collective marks. See McCarthy, *supra*, § 19.34[1][b]. However, if a mark is primarily understood by prospective purchasers as indicating origin in the organization itself, it is more properly viewed as a trademark and use of the mark by members may then be subject to the traditional rules governing trademark licensing described in § 33. See Seven–Up Bottling Co., *supra*. Cf. Callmann, § 17.18 (distinguishing the "control" required over users of collective marks and trademark licensees).

Illustration 1 is based on the facts in National Trailways Bus System v. Trailway Van Lines, Inc., 269 F.Supp. 352 (E.D.N.Y.1965). See, e.g., Professional Golfers Association v. Bankers Life & Casualty Co., 514 F.2d 665 (5th Cir.1975) (PGA as collective service mark for golf instruction and exhibitions furnished by members).

Illustration 2 is based on the facts in Quality Courts United, Inc. v. Quality Courts, Inc., 140 F.Supp. 341 (M.D.Pa.1956) and Lyon v. Quality Courts United, Inc., 249 F.2d 790 (6th Cir.1957).

Comment c. The rationale for the protection of collective membership marks is discussed in In re Supreme Shrine of the Order of the White Shrine of Jerusalem, 109 U.S.P.Q. 248 (Comm'r Pat.1956). On the manner of use sufficient to establish rights in a collective membership mark, see Trademark Manual of Examining Procedure, *supra*, § 1304.09(c).

Illustration 3 is derived from the facts of Supreme Assembly, Order of Rainbow for Girls v. J.H. Ray Jewelry Co., 676 F.2d 1079 (5th Cir.1982), also discussing the scope of protection available under the rules relating to infringement. See § 20, Comment *e.*

Illustration 4 is based on In re Stencel Aero Engineering Corp., 170 U.S.P.Q. 292 (Tm.Tr.App.Bd.1971), illustrating that the owner of the mark need not be the collective organization itself.

Illustration 5 is suggested by the facts in In re Electronic Representatives Ass'n, 150 U.S.P.Q. 476 (Tm.Tr.App.Bd.1966).

§ 11. Definition of Certification Mark

A certification mark is a word, name, symbol, device, or other designation, or a combination of such designations, that is distinctive of goods or services certified by a person but produced and marketed by others and that is used by the others in a manner that certifies regional origin, composition, quality, method of manufacture, or other characteristics of the goods or services.

Comment:

a. Nature of certification marks. Certification marks are designations that are used to certify specific characteristics of the goods or services on which they appear. Unlike trademarks and collective marks, certification marks do not identify the source or sponsor of goods or services. Certification marks indicate that a person other than the producer or seller of the goods or services certifies that the product meets the criteria established for authorized use of the certification mark. The certifying party, by virtue of its control over the use of the designation, is the owner of the certification mark. Recognition of exclusive rights in certification marks protects the good will associated with the owner's certification program and also protects the public from confusion and deception. Certification marks include designations adopted by testing laboratories and rating services for use on qualifying products, insignia authorized by labor unions to appear on goods produced by union labor, and geographic designations adopted by governmental and other entities to certify the geographic origin of goods.

To insure objectivity in the application of the criteria for certification, the owner of a certification mark registered under the Lanham

Act is precluded from certifying its own goods or services. The Lanham Act also provides for cancellation of a certification mark registration if the owner fails to exercise control over the use of the mark or improperly discriminates by refusing to certify goods or services that meet the standards or conditions certified by the mark. Section 14(5), 15 U.S.C.A. § 1064(5). Although these statutory restrictions have not been explicitly incorporated into the common law, the use of a certification mark by the owner in a manner that is likely to deceive prospective purchasers with respect to the impartiality of the certification may limit or preclude protection of the mark under the rules relating to unclean hands as stated in § 32. Such use may also subject the user to liability for deceptive marketing under the rule stated in § 2.

If the owner of a certification mark uses the same designation as a trademark to identify its own goods or services, prospective purchasers may be unable to distinguish the goods or services of the owner from the certified goods or services of others, thus destroying the distinctiveness of the mark as an indication of certification. However, the rule precluding simultaneous trademark and certification use does not prevent the use of related marks for trademark and certification purposes, provided that the marks are sufficiently different to enable purchasers to distinguish the certified goods from the goods marketed by the owner of the marks.

Both collective trademarks (see § 10, Comment *b*) and certification marks are used by persons other than the owner of the mark. Collective trademarks indicate that the goods or services originate from a member of a group, while certification marks certify characteristics of the product itself, regardless of source. The practical significance of the distinction diminishes, however, when membership in the group is determined by standards relating to the characteristics of the members' goods or services. The distinction remains important, however, in the application of the rules restricting use and discrimination by the owner of a registered certification mark. Also distinguishable from certification marks are trademarks licensed by the owner for use by other producers. Use of a mark to identify goods or services produced by licensees under the control and supervision of the owner of the mark is a trademark rather than a certification use. See § 33. Although proper characterization of a mark is not necessary for protection at common law, the evidence must establish use in a manner consistent with the requirements relating to one of the categories of marks protected under the rules stated in this Chapter.

Certification marks are subject to the general criteria for protection applicable to other marks, including the requirements relating to distinctiveness (see Comment *b*) and acquisition of rights (see § 18).

The principles governing trademark infringement are also applicable to the infringement of certification marks. See § 20.

Illustrations:

1. *A* is a non-profit testing laboratory engaged in examining and testing electrical equipment for fire and other hazards. *A* performs its activities under contracts with manufacturers and governmental agencies. Products approved by *A* are entitled to display a designation consisting of *A* 's corporate initials enclosed in a set of concentric circles. The designation is a certification mark under the rule stated in this Section.

2. *A* produces a chemical wood preservative that it markets to manufacturers under the trademark NAILS. *A* also operates a program certifying retail products constructed of wood treated with *A* 's preservative. The certified products are marked with a designation consisting of a scroll bearing the words, "Made to Last with NAILS Preservative." The designation is a certification mark under the rule stated in this Section.

3. *A* is a federation consisting of several hundred automobile clubs located throughout the United States. As a service to the members of its affiliated clubs, *A* inspects motels and similar lodging facilities. Establishments that meet the standards prescribed by *A* are entitled to display a designation consisting of *A* 's name and the word "Approved" enclosed in an oval design. The designation is a certification mark under the rule stated in this Section. Compare § 10, Illustration 2.

b. Requirement of distinctiveness. The concept of "distinctiveness" as applied to certification marks differs from its traditional meaning in the law of trademarks. In the context of trademarks (§ 9), collective marks (§ 10), and trade names (§ 12), distinctiveness refers to the ability of a designation to identify the goods, services, or business of a particular entity or group. See § 13. The distinctiveness of a certification mark refers instead to the ability of the designation to indicate that a particular person has certified some fact concerning the goods or services on which the designation appears. With this difference in mind, however, the rules and commentary relating to the requirement of distinctiveness in §§ 13–14 are also applicable to certification marks.

A certification mark is distinctive if prospective purchasers recognize the mark as an indication that a particular person, whether known or anonymous, has certified that the goods or services meet the standards established for authorized use of the mark. Many certification marks expressly indicate both the fact of certification and the identity of the certifying party. Such marks are inherently distinctive under the rule stated in § 13(a). Terms such as "certified," "inspected by," or "approved by," however, are not essential to the validity of a certification mark. Indeed, a mark consisting of a description of the relevant product characteristics joined with a distinctive graphic design also may qualify as an inherently distinctive certification mark. See § 13, Comment *d*. If a designation is likely to be perceived as mere ornamentation, however, or as merely descriptive of the goods or services, the designation is eligible for protection only upon proof that through use it has acquired significance as a certification mark. See § 13, Comment *e*. The Lanham Act recognizes an exception to the requirement of acquired distinctiveness for geographically descriptive certification marks, and there is no indication of a different rule at common law. See 15 U.S.C.A. § 1052(e)(2). Such marks typically are claimed by governmental entities capable of insuring access to the designation by all eligible producers.

If a designation is perceived as the generic name of the goods or service with which it is used, it cannot be protected as a certification mark. See § 15.

Illustrations:

4. *A* owns a patent for a process of preserving food products through irradiation with high-energy electrons. *A* authorizes food producers using *A* 's process to identify their irradiated goods with the word "Electronized." Because the designation is descriptive (see § 14), in the absence of evidence establishing that it has acquired distinctiveness as an indication of certification (see § 13), the designation is not protectable as a certification mark.

5. *A*, a municipality in France, is well-known for the production of cheese. *A* permits the use of its name only on cheese made by local manufacturers adhering to the traditional methods of production. Although the use of the name is geographically descriptive (see § 14), the designation is a certification mark under the rule stated in this Section.

REPORTERS' NOTE

This Section is derived from the definition of "certification mark" in § 45 of the Lanham Act. 15 U.S.C.A. § 1127. On the registration of certification marks, see §§ 4, 14(5); 15 U.S.C.A. §§ 1054, 1064(5). For general discussions, see Patent and Trademark Office, Trademark Manual of Examining Procedure § 1306; McCarthy, Trademarks and Unfair Competition § 19.32.

Comment a. Well-known certification marks include the Good

Housekeeping Seal and the Underwriters Laboratories designation. On the use of labor union insignia as certification marks, see Trademark Manual of Examining Procedures, *supra*, § 1306.03. Cf. Schroeder v. Lotito, 577 F.Supp. 708 (D.R.I.1983), affirmed 747 F.2d 801 (1st Cir.1984) (analyzing such use as a collective mark).

Simultaneous use of a designation as a trademark and certification mark is prohibited under § 14(5) of the Lanham Act. 15 U.S.C.A. § 1064(5). See, e.g., In re Monsanto Co., 201 U.S.P.Q. 864 (Tm.Tr.App.Bd.1978). The prohibition is said to apply even to trademark use on goods or services different in kind from the certified goods or services in order to avoid confusion as to the scope of the owner's certification program. See In re Florida Citrus Commission, 160 U.S.P.Q. 495 (Tm.Tr.App.Bd.1968). The owner is also precluded from using the mark to certify its own goods or services. See Black Hills Jewelry Mfg. Co. v. Gold Rush, Inc., 633 F.2d 746 (8th Cir.1980) (refusing to protect a common law certification mark used on goods marketed by the parties claiming ownership). Use of the certification mark by the owner in promotional or informational materials, however, is permissible. Underwriters Laboratories, Inc. v. United Laboratories, Inc., 203 U.S.P.Q. 180 (N.D.Ill.1978).

On the requirement of control over the use of a certification mark imposed by § 14(5) of the Lanham Act, 15 U.S.C.A. § 1064(5), see Midwest Plastic Fabricators, Inc. v. Underwriters Laboratories Inc., 906 F.2d 1568, 1572 (Fed.Cir.1990) ("owner must take reasonable steps, under all the circumstances of the case, to prevent the public from being deceived").

The distinction between collective trademarks and certification marks becomes problematic when membership in the collective group denotes a particular standard of quality with respect to the goods or services offered by members. Opticians Ass'n v. Independent Opticians, 920 F.2d 187 (3d Cir.1990). Compare, e.g., Professional Golfers Ass'n v. Bankers Life & Casualty Co., 514 F.2d 665 (5th Cir.1975) (collective service mark serves "to guarantee the quality of service provided by members") with In re National Institute for Automotive Service Excellence, 218 U.S.P.Q. 744 (Tm.Tr.App.Bd.1983) (certification marks include designations used to certify that labor has been performed by a member of a union or other organization). See also In re Institute of Certified Professional Business Consultants, 216 U.S.P.Q. 338 (Tm.Tr.App.Bd.1982) (certification mark use includes use to indicate that services are rendered by a member meeting specific standards). The distinction retains significance, however, in connection with the statutory rules prohibiting use and discrimination by the owner of a certification mark. Cf. American Speech–Language–Hearing Ass'n v. National Hearing Aid Soc., 224 U.S.P.Q. 798 (Tm.Tr.App.Bd.1984) (cancellation of collective mark registration because of certification use). On the distinction between certification marks and trademarks used by licensees of a trademark owner, see, e.g., In re Monsanto Co., 201 U.S.P.Q. 864 (Tm.Tr.App.Bd.1978); In re Celanese Corp. of America, 136 U.S.P.Q. 86 (Tm.Tr.App.Bd.1962); Red Dot Foods, Inc. v. Lanning, 102 U.S.P.Q. 310 (Comm'r Patents 1954).

If a designation is likely to be perceived only as a title or degree that has been conferred on the user, the use is insufficient to establish the distinctiveness of the designation as a certification of services rendered by the recipient. E.g., In re National Association of Legal Secretaries (International), 221 U.S.P.Q. 50 (Tm.Tr. App.Bd.1983); In re Institute of Certified Professional Business Consultants, *supra* ; In re Professional Photographers of Ohio, Inc., 149 U.S.P.Q. 857 (Tm.Tr.App.Bd.1966). Compare In re National Institute for Automotive Service Excellence, *supra.*

Common law protection for certification marks was recognized in Florida v. Real Juices, Inc., 330 F.Supp. 428 (M.D.Fla.1971) (also recognizing a claim under § 43(a) of the Lanham Act). See Stabilisierrungsfonds fur Wein v. Zimmermann–Graeff KG, 199 U.S.P.Q. 488 (Tm.Tr.App.Bd.1978) (common law rights recognized in an opposition proceeding). Cf. Black Hills Jewelry Mfg. Co. v. Gold Rush, Inc., 633 F.2d 746 (8th Cir.1980) (expressing no opinion on the protection of certification marks under § 43(a), but granting relief on a false advertising theory). The creation of confusion as to the certification of goods or services is also actionable under the Uniform Deceptive Trade Practices Act, § 2(a)(2)-(3). In an infringement action the owner of the certification mark serves as a representative of the sellers who use the mark, and likelihood of confusion is measured with respect to the users' goods and services. E.I. Dupont De Nemours and Co. v. Yoshida Int'l, Inc., 393 F.Supp. 502 (E.D.N.Y.1975). The general principles of trademark infringement are otherwise applicable. See, e.g., Community of Roquefort v. William Faehndrich, Inc., 303 F.2d 494 (2d Cir.1962); Underwriters Laboratories, Inc. v. United Laboratories, Inc., 203 U.S.P.Q. 180 (N.D.Ill.1978). Cf. In re Sharfman, 156 U.S.P.Q. 412 (Tm.Tr.App.Bd.1967) and Chemek Corp. v. Nebraska Fertilizer Institute, 122 U.S.P.Q. 343 (Tm.Tr.App. Bd.1959), both applying the likelihood of confusion standard in opposition proceedings under the Lanham Act.

Illustration 1 is based on the facts in *Underwriters Laboratories, Inc., supra.*

In connection with Illustration 2, see, e.g., E.I. Dupont De Nemours and Co., *supra.* Also illustrative is the trademark of GOOD HOUSEKEEPING magazine and its related certification seal. Compare In re Monsanto Co., 201 U.S.P.Q. 864 (Tm. Tr.App.Bd.1978). See also Trademark Manual of Examining Procedure, *supra,* § 1306.05(a).

Illustration 3 is derived from the facts of American Automobile Ass'n v. National Automobile Ass'n, 127 U.S.P.Q. 423 (Tm.Tr.App.Bd.1960).

Comment b. On the general requirement of distinctiveness as applicable to certification marks, see § 4 of the Lanham Act, 15 U.S.C.A. § 1054; Trademark Manual of Examining Procedure, *supra,* § 1306.05; McCarthy, *supra,* § 19.32[5]. A defense based on the alleged generic significance of a certification mark was rejected on the facts in Community of Roquefort v. William Faehndrich, Inc., 303 F.2d 494 (2d Cir.1962) (ROQUEFORT used to certify regional origin of cheese not shown to be generic). Compare In re Cooperativa Produttori Latte E Fontina Valle D'Acosta, 230 U.S.P.Q. 131 (Tm. Tr.App.Bd.1986) (requiring disclaimer of "FONTINA" from certification mark because of its generic significance). Cf. In re National Ass'n of Legal Secretaries (International), 221

U.S.P.Q. 50 (Tm.Tr.App.Bd.1983) (PROFESSIONAL LEGAL SECRETARY), and In re Professional Photographers of Ohio, Inc., 149 U.S.P.Q. 857 (Tm.Tr.App.Bd.1966) (CERTIFIED PROFESSIONAL PHOTOGRAPHER), both indicating that the claimed certification mark might be "incapable" of certification significance. See § 15, Comment *b*.

Illustration 4 is based on In re Electronized Chemicals Corp., 111 U.S.P.Q. 190 (Comm'r Patents 1956). See In re University of Mississippi, 1 U.S.P.Q.2d 1909 (Tm.Tr.App.Bd.1987) (requiring proof of acquired distinctiveness); In re National Ass'n of Purchasing Management, 228 U.S.P.Q. 768, 769 n.3 (Tm.Tr.App.Bd. 1986) (acquired distinctiveness established). Compare In re National Institute for Automotive Service Excellence, 218 U.S.P.Q. 744 (Tm.Tr.App. Bd.1983) (finding gear design at most suggestive).

Illustration 5 is based on *Community of Roquefort, supra.* See also the examples of registered certification marks in Hawes, Trademark Registration Practice § 10.01 (BADEN for wines from the Baden region of Germany and COLOMBIAN for coffee from Columbia). The exception to the requirement of distinctiveness for marks certifying regional origin appears in § 2(e) of the Lanham Act, 15 U.S.C.A. § 1052(e). See Trademark Manual of Examining Procedure, *supra*, § 1306.02. "About the only substantive basis for a refusal to register other marks which is not applicable to certification marks is the ground of geographical descriptiveness specified in § 2(e)(2) of the Act * * *." Hawes, *supra*, § 10.04.

§ 12. Definition of Trade Name

A trade name is a word, name, symbol, device, or other designation, or a combination of such designations, that is distinctive of a person's business or other enterprise and that is used in a manner that identifies that business or enterprise and distinguishes it from the businesses or enterprises of others.

Comment:

a. Subject matter. A "trademark" as defined in § 9 identifies and distinguishes goods or services; a "trade name" as defined in this Section identifies and distinguishes businesses or other enterprises. A trade name may be the real name of the entity operating the business, such as a corporate or personal name. It may also be an assumed name under which business is conducted, such as a name adopted by a sole proprietorship or partnership. The only requirement is that the designation identify the business or other enterprise and distinguish it from the businesses or enterprises of others. See Comment *b*.

Before the enactment of the Lanham Act, the term "trade name" was also used to denote descriptive marks and other non-inherently distinctive designations that had through use acquired significance as indications of the source or sponsorship of goods or services. See § 9,

Comment *f.* This Section follows the modern usage adopted in the Lanham Act and the Model State Trademark Bill and confines the term "trade name" to designations used to identify businesses or other enterprises.

Trade names are not limited to designations adopted by commercial entities. A designation that identifies an enterprise conducted by a nonprofit organization is also eligible for protection. Thus, names adopted by charitable, educational, governmental, fraternal, and religious organizations are included within the definition in this Section. These organizations have the same interest in protecting their identities and good will as do profit-seeking enterprises. The public interest in preventing consumer confusion is similarly applicable to nonprofit organizations.

b. Infringement of rights. The rationales justifying the protection of trade names are analogous to those underlying the protection of trademarks. The protection of trade names prevents an unfair diversion of trade to an infringer who seeks to appropriate the identity and good will of another. Even if the parties are not direct competitors, such an appropriation threatens the legitimate interests of the business identified by the trade name by putting its reputation at risk. The protection of trade names also encourages investment in quality, service, and other activities that generate good will by insuring the opportunity to recapture the benefits of a favorable reputation. As in the case of trademarks, the protection of trade names also serves as an indirect form of consumer protection.

A designation is protectable as a trade name only if it symbolizes the identity and good will of a particular enterprise. The common law has long required as a condition of protection that the trade name distinguish the business of the user from businesses operated by others. This requirement of distinctiveness is analogous to the rule applicable to trademarks. See § 13. On the requirements for the acquisition of rights in a trade name, see § 18.

The standard of trade name infringement is analogous to that applicable to trademarks, and the provisions of this Chapter relating to infringement expressly encompass trade names. Protection against the use of confusingly similar trade names has been recognized at common law and under § 43(a) of the Lanham Act as well as under state statutes such as the Uniform Deceptive Trade Practices Act (see the Statutory Note following § 2) and the Unfair Trade Practices and Consumer Protection Act (see the Statutory Note following § 1). Rights in a trade name can also be infringed by its unauthorized use as a trademark, just as a trademark can be infringed by unauthorized adoption as a trade name. See § 20.

c. Legislation affecting trade names. Business Corporation Acts typically preclude incorporation under a name that is "deceptively similar" to that of an existing domestic corporation or a foreign corporation authorized to transact business in the state. Such restrictions offer an indirect measure of protection to the first person to incorporate under a particular name by preventing others from incorporating under deceptively similar names. Incorporation under a name, however, does not in itself create substantive rights in the name. Substantive rights in a trade name derive from public use, see § 18, and the right of a corporation to obtain relief against the use of a similar trade name by another is determined under the rules in this Chapter relating to infringement. Similarly, in permitting incorporation under a particular name, the state does not pass upon the applicant's right to use the name in business. Thus, the fact of incorporation under the name is not a defense if the corporation's use of the name otherwise subjects it to liability for infringement. Because administrative determinations of deceptive similarity for purposes of incorporation cannot take account of the multitude of factors relevant to the likelihood of confusion (see § 21), administrative acceptance of a corporate name is generally entitled to little or no weight in subsequent infringement litigation.

Many states require the registration of assumed or fictitious names under which individuals or commercial entities conduct business. (See the Statutory Note following this Section.) The primary purpose of these statutes is to assist others in identifying the owners of the businesses with whom they deal. In several states these trade name acts forbid the registration of names that are deceptively similar to a previously-registered name, thus providing a degree of administrative protection to the initial registrant. In the absence of a specific statutory grant of substantive rights, however, registration of a trade name does not expand the registrant's right to prevent use of the name by others. Similarly, registration is not a defense to an infringement claim brought against the registrant by another user. Trade name registration statutes in a few states, however, specifically grant the registrant the right to enjoin the use of the name by another, although some expressly preserve rights previously acquired by others at common law. In addition, the antidilution provisions that are part of many state trademark registration acts often extend protection to trade names as well as trademarks. See § 25.

Trade names are not eligible for registration under the Lanham Act. Rights previously established in a trade name, however, can prevent registration by another of a confusingly similar trademark. 15 U.S.C.A. § 1052(d). If a trade name is also used as a trademark, it is on that basis eligible for registration under the Act.

Illustrations:

1. *A* is a business incorporated under the name "Lawyer's Title Guaranty Company." Although it uses this name for internal purposes, it conducts all its public business under another name. *B*, a foreign corporation, begins to conduct business in *A* 's locality under a name that is similar to *A* 's corporate name. Because *A* 's corporate name has not been "used" as a trade name under the rule stated in § 18, *A* has not acquired rights in the trade name despite incorporation under the name. *B* is thus not subject to liability for infringement.

2. *A* is a domestic corporation incorporated under the name "Indian Oil Company." *B* is a foreign corporation that has previously used a similar designation as its trade name. In an infringement action brought by *B*, *A* 's incorporation under the name does not prevent the imposition of injunctive or monetary relief against *A* if *A* is otherwise subject to liability for infringement of *B* 's trade name under the rules stated in this Chapter.

3. *A* is a charitable organization operating under the name "Cancer Research Institute." *A* 's principal activity is raising funds to support research in the prevention and treatment of cancer. Because of *A* 's extensive activities, the name "Cancer Research Institute" is understood by the public to identify *A* 's organization. *B* begins to solicit contributions for medical research through an organization that uses the name "Cancer Research Society." If the evidence establishes that *B* 's use of the name is likely to cause prospective contributors to confuse the two organizations, *B* is subject to liability for infringement of *A* 's trade name under the rules stated in this Chapter.

STATUTORY NOTE

Trade name registration statutes of general applicability include the following:

Alabama .... ALA. C. § 8–12–6 et seq.
Alaska .... ALASKA S. § 10.35
Arizona .... ARIZ. R.S.A. § 10–108(3); § 44–1460 et seq.
Arkansas .... ARK. C.A. § 4–70–201 et seq.
California .... CAL. Bus. & Prof.C. § 17900 et seq.
Colorado .... COLO. R.S.A. § 24–35–301
Connecticut .... CONN. G.S.A. § 35–1
Delaware .... DEL. C., tit. 6, § 3101 et seq.
Florida .... FLA. S.A. § 865.09
Georgia .... GA. C.A. § 10–1–490(a)
Hawaii .... HAW. R.S. § 482

Idaho .... IDAHO C.A. § 53–501 et seq.
Illinois.............. ILL. C.S., ch. 805, § 405/0.01 et seq.
Indiana .... IND. C. § 23–15–1–1 et seq.
Iowa .... IOWA C.A. § 547.1 et seq.
Kentucky .... KY. R.S. § 365.015
Louisiana .... LA. R.S.A. § 51:211 et seq.
Maine .... ME. R.S.A., tit. 31, § 2
Maryland .... MD. Corps. & Ass'ns C. § 1–406
Massachusetts .... MASS. G.L.A., ch. 110, § 5
Michigan .... MICH. C.L.A. § 445.1 et seq.; § 450.1217
Minnesota .... MINN. S.A. § 333.001 et seq.
Missouri .... MO. R.S. § 417.200
Montana .... MONT. C.A. § 30–13–203
Nebraska .... NEB. R.S. § 87–201 et seq.
Nevada .... NEV. R.S.A. § 600.240 et seq.; § 602.010 et seq.
New Hampshire ..... N.H. R.S.A. § 349
New Jersey .... N.J. S.A. § 56:1–1 et seq.
New York .... N.Y. Gen.Bus.L. § 130
North Carolina ...... N.C. G.S. § 66–68 et seq.
North Dakota .... N.D. Cent.C. § 47–25–01 et seq.
Ohio .... OHIO R.C. § 1329.01 et seq.
Oklahoma .... OKLA. S.A., tit. 18, § 1140
Oregon .... OR. R.S. § 648.005 et seq.
Pennsylvania .... PA. S.A., tit. 54, § 302 et seq.
Puerto Rico .... P.R. S.A., tit. 10, § 225 et seq.
Rhode Island .... R.I. G.L.A. § 6–1–1 et seq.; § 7–1.1–7.1
South Carolina ...... S.C. C.A. § 33–15–106
South Dakota .... S.D. Comp.L. § 37–11–1 et seq.
Tennessee .... TENN. C.A. § 48–14–101
Texas .... TEX. Bus. & Com.C. § 36.11
Utah .... UTAH C.A. § 42–2–5 et seq.
Vermont .... VT. S.A., tit. 11, §§ 1621, 1623
Virginia .... VA. C.A. § 59.1–69 et seq.
Washington .... WASH. R.C.A. § 19.80.001 et seq.
West Virginia .... W.VA. C.A. § 47–8–2 et seq.
Wisconsin .... WIS. S.A. § 134.17 et seq.
Wyoming .... WYO. S.A. § 40–2–101 et seq.

REPORTERS' NOTE

This Section abandons the former definition of "trade name" in Restatement of Torts § 716 (1938) and adopts the modern statutory and common law usage. On the protection of trade names, see generally Gilson, Trademark Protection and Practice § 2.15; McCarthy, Trademarks and Unfair Competition §§ 9.01–06, discussing both commercial and noncommercial trade names.

Comment a. For examples of state statutory provisions protecting noncommercial names, see, e.g., Cal.

Bus. & Prof.C. §§ 14492–95; Mass. Gen.L.Ann. ch. 266, § 71A; N.Y. Gen.Bus.L. §§ 135, 397. State statutes that are applicable to the trade names of specific categories of businesses and organizations are collected in International Trademark Association, State Trademark and Unfair Competition Law.

Comment b. Trade names receive protection under the same principles applicable to trademarks. See, e.g., American Steel Foundries v. Robertson, 269 U.S. 372, 46 S.Ct. 160, 70 L.Ed. 317 (1926).

On the requirement of distinctiveness as applied to trade names, compare President and Trustees of Colby College v. Colby College—New Hampshire, 508 F.2d 804 (1st Cir. 1975) (secondary meaning found for COLBY COLLEGE); Powder River Oil Co. v. Powder River Petroleum Corp., 830 P.2d 403 (Wyo.1992) (same as to POWDER RIVER OIL COMPANY); and Reis v. Ralls, 250 Ga. 721, 301 S.E.2d 40 (1983) (same as to ATLANTA REFRIGERATION SERVICE COMPANY), with Boston Beer Co. L.P. v. Slesar Bros. Brewing Co., 9 F.3d 175 (1st Cir.1993) (no secondary meaning shown for BOSTON BEER COMPANY); Vision Center v. Opticks, Inc., 596 F.2d 111 (5th Cir.1979), cert. denied, 444 U.S. 1016, 100 S.Ct. 668, 62 L.Ed.2d 646 (1980) (VISION CENTER descriptive and without secondary meaning); and George v. Peterson, 671 P.2d 208 (Utah 1983) (same as to HIGH COUNTRY). See Great Southern Bank v. First Southern Bank, 625 So.2d 463 (Fla.1993) (FIRST SOUTHERN BANK is protectable only upon proof of secondary meaning); Two Way Radio Service, Inc. v. Two Way Radio of Carolina, Inc., 322 N.C. 809, 370 S.E.2d 408 (1988) (TWO WAY RADIO descriptive); North Star State Bank v. North Star Bank, 361 N.W.2d 889 (Minn.App. 1985) (NORTH STAR is an arbitrary name and proof of secondary meaning is unnecessary). See generally § 13.

The likelihood of confusion standard described in § 20 applies to the infringement of trade names at common law, see, e.g., Communications Satellite Corp. v. Comcet, Inc., 429 F.2d 1245 (4th Cir.), cert. denied 400 U.S. 942, 91 S.Ct. 240, 27 L.Ed.2d 245 (1970), and under § 43(a) of the Lanham Act. See, e.g., Metric & Multistandard Components Corp. v. Metric's, Inc., 635 F.2d 710 (8th Cir.1980). The standard is also applicable under state statutes such as the Uniform Deceptive Trade Practices Act § 2(a)(3), see, e.g., Giant Mart Corp. v. Giant Discount Foods, Inc., 247 Ga. 775, 279 S.E.2d 683 (1981), and the Unfair Trade Practices and Consumer Protection Act, see Nordstrom, Inc. v. Tampourlos, 107 Wash.2d 735, 733 P.2d 208 (1987). (See the Statutory Notes following §§ 1 and 2 of this Restatement.)

Comment c. Illustration 1 is based on Lawyers Title Ins. Co. v. Lawyers Title Ins. Corp., 109 F.2d 35 (D.C.Cir.1939), cert. denied 309 U.S. 684, 60 S.Ct. 806, 84 L.Ed. 1028 (1940). See Galt House, Inc. v. Home Supply Co., 483 S.W.2d 107 (Ky.1972) (mere incorporation creates no protectable rights in the name). See also, e.g., Two Way Radio Service, Inc. v. Two Way Radio, Inc., 322 N.C. 809, 370 S.E.2d 408 (1988) (descriptive corporate name lacking secondary meaning held unprotectable); Cornucopia, Inc. v. Wagman, 710 S.W.2d 882 (Mo.App.1986) (same). Cf. Cal. Bus. & Prof.C. § 14415, creating a rebuttable presumption of an exclusive right to use the corporate name. The administrative protection afforded prior incorporators by statutory prohibitions against the registration of deceptively similar corporate names is analyzed in Guilbert, Corporate Names and Assumed Business Names: "Deceptively Similar" Creates a Likelihood of Confusion, 62 Or.L.Rev. 151 (1983). The practical effect of the prohibition is augmented in some states by provisions authorizing affected parties to seek injunctions against violations of the statutory standard. See, e.g., Me.R.S.A. tit. 13–A, § 301(2); N.C.G.S. § 55–12(j); N.D.Cent.C. § 10–19.1–13(5); Pa.S.A. tit. 15, § 1202(D).

In the absence of specific statutory rights, registration under a state trade name registration act creates no substantive rights in the name. E.g., Vision Center v. Opticks, Inc., 596 F.2d 111 (5th Cir.1979), cert. denied 444 U.S. 1016, 100 S.Ct. 668, 62 L.Ed.2d 646 (1980); Photo & Sound Co. v. Corvallis, 291 Or. 105, 628 P.2d 733 (1981). Trade name acts in several states, however, recognize a right in the registrant to proceed under the statute against other users of the same or similar names. See, e.g., Alaska Stat. § 10.35.040; Neb.Rev. Stat. § 87–216; N.H.Rev.Stat.Ann. § 349:10; N.D.Cent.C. § 47–25–01. Cf. Cal. Bus. & Prof.C. § 14411 (rebuttable presumption of exclusive right). Some of these statutes expressly preserve existing common law rights. See Neb.Rev.Stat. § 87–218; N.H.Rev.Stat.Ann. § 349:11.

Illustration 2 is based on Indian Territory Oil & Gas Co. v. Indian Territory Illuminating Oil Co., 95 F.2d 711 (10th Cir.), cert. denied 305 U.S. 607, 59 S.Ct. 67, 83 L.Ed. 386 (1938). Accord Hulburt Oil & Grease Co. v. Hulburt Oil & Grease Co., 371 F.2d 251 (7th Cir.1966), cert. denied 386 U.S. 1032, 87 S.Ct. 1482, 18 L.Ed.2d 594 (1967); American United Life Insurance Co. v. American United Insurance Co., 731 F.Supp. 480 (S.D.Fla.1990); American Kennel Club v. American Kennel Club, Inc., 216 F.Supp. 267 (E.D.La.1963); Powder River Oil Co v. Powder River Petroleum Corp., 830 P.2d 403 (Wyo. 1992).

Determinations of the deceptive similarity of proposed corporate names under state business corporation acts are ordinarily based solely on the submitted name and the described nature of the business and thus cannot take into account the various factual elements relevant to the issue of infringement under the rules stated in §§ 21–23. The same administrative limitations exist in jurisdictions that preclude registration of deceptively similar trade names under a state trade name registration statute. See, e.g., Alaska Stat. § 10.35.040; Neb.Rev.Stat. § 87–209; N.D.Cent.C. § 47–25–03. The disparities between the administrative and tort standards are examined in Gilson, Trade Name Infringement, Trap for the Unwary Corporation, 59 Trademark Rep. 582 (1969). See also Guilbert, *supra*. The Revised Model Business Corporation Act (1984) abandons the "deceptively similar" standard that had appeared in earlier versions of the Act and requires instead under § 4.01(b) that "a corporate name must be distinguishable upon the records of the secretary of state" from other registered names. The Official Comment recognizes that "[p]rinciples of unfair competition, not the business corporation act, provide the limits on the competitive use of similar names."

Trade names are not eligible for registration under the Lanham Act. Prior use of a designation as a trade name, however, can prevent the registration of a confusingly similar trademark. 15 U.S.C.A. § 1052(d). See also the analogous proscription in § 2(f) of the Model State Trademark Bill (1992). If a trade name is also used as a trademark for goods or services, it is on that basis eligible for federal trademark registration. Practical guidelines for establishing trademark rights in a trade name are offered in Gilson, Trademark Protection and Practice § 2.14[1]. Compare In re Walker Process Equipment, Inc., 233 F.2d 329 (C.C.P.A.1956), with In re Texaco Inc., 143 U.S.P.Q. 364 (Tm.Tr.App.Bd.1964). See Communications Satellite Corp. v. Comcet, Inc., 429 F.2d 1245 (4th Cir.), cert. denied 400 U.S. 942, 91 S.Ct. 240, 27 L.Ed.2d 245 (1970) (infringement of COMSAT as a trade name and service mark).

Cases affording protection to trade names under state antidilution statutes include Hyatt Corp. v. Hyatt Legal Services, 736 F.2d 1153 (7th Cir.), cert. denied 469 U.S. 1019, 105 S.Ct. 434, 83 L.Ed.2d 361 (1984); Wedgwood Homes, Inc. v. Lund, 294 Or. 493, 659 P.2d 377 (1983); Marks v. Cayo Hueso, Ltd., 437 So.2d 775 (Fla.App.1983). See § 25.

Illustration 3 is based on Cancer Research Institute, Inc. v. Cancer Research Society, Inc., 694 F.Supp. 1051 (S.D.N.Y.1988).

§ 13. Distinctiveness; Secondary Meaning

A word, name, symbol, device, or other designation, or a combination of such designations, is "distinctive" under the rules stated in §§ 9–12 if:

(a) the designation is "inherently distinctive," in that, because of the nature of the designation and the context in which it is used, prospective purchasers are likely to perceive it as a designation that, in the case of a trademark, identifies goods or services produced or sponsored by a particular person, whether known or anonymous, or in the case of a trade name, identifies the business or other enterprise of a particular person, whether known or anonymous, or in the case of a collective mark, identifies members of the collective group or goods or services produced or sponsored by members, or in the case of a certification mark, identifies the certified goods or services; or

(b) the designation, although not "inherently distinctive," has become distinctive, in that, as a result of its use, prospective purchasers have come to perceive it as a designation that identifies goods, services, businesses, or members in the manner described in

Subsection (a). Such acquired distinctiveness is commonly referred to as "secondary meaning."

Comment:

a. Requirement of distinctiveness. Under the rules stated in §§ 9–12, a designation is protectable as a trademark, trade name, collective mark, or certification mark only if the designation is "distinctive." This Section states the criteria governing that requirement. On the distinctiveness of descriptive, geographic, and personal name designations, see § 14. On generic designations, see § 15.

A designation is distinctive only if it functions as a symbol of identification. To be eligible for protection as a trademark or trade name, the designation must identify the goods, services, or business of the person asserting rights in the designation. See § 9, Comment *f*; § 12, Comment *b*. Collective marks must identify the members of the collective group or the goods or services of members, and certification marks must identify the certified goods or services. See § 10, Comment *a*; § 11, Comment *b*.

The person claiming rights in a mark or name bears the burden of proving that the designation is inherently distinctive or that it has become distinctive by acquiring secondary meaning. A trademark registration on the principal register of the Lanham Act is prima facie evidence of the validity of the registered mark. 15 U.S.C.A. §§ 1057(b), 1115(a). This has been interpreted as creating a rebuttable presumption of either inherent distinctiveness or secondary meaning, depending upon the basis of the registration. If the registration has become "incontestable" under the provisions of 15 U.S.C.A. § 1065 applicable to marks in continuous use for five years subsequent to registration, the presumption is conclusive and the mark cannot be challenged as a descriptive designation lacking secondary meaning. See 15 U.S.C.A. § 1115.

b. Inherently distinctive designations. Certain designations by their nature are likely to be perceived by prospective purchasers as symbols of identification that indicate an association with a particular source. These designations are "inherently distinctive." A word with no existing meaning coined to identify the products of a particular manufacturer, for example, is inherently distinctive because its lack of lexicographic significance makes it likely that the designation will be perceived as a symbol of identification. See Comment *c*. If the recognition of trademark rights in a particular designation is likely to diminish the ability of other sellers to communicate information about their own goods or services or is otherwise likely to undermine a legitimate interest in unrestricted access to the designation, it will not ordinarily be considered inherently distinctive.

Inherently distinctive designations are eligible for protection immediately upon use. See § 18. They are also eligible for registration under state and federal trademark statutes without further evidence of distinctiveness.

c. Fanciful, arbitrary, and suggestive terms. Fanciful terms that are coined by a user to identify itself or its goods or services are inherently distinctive. Because a fanciful term has no meaning other than as an identifying symbol, prospective purchasers can be expected to view it as an indication of source or other association with a particular user. In addition, the recognition of trademark rights in fanciful terms does not diminish the vocabulary available to other sellers of similar products.

A designation that consists of an existing word whose lexicographic meaning has no apparent application to the particular product or business with which it is used, such as SHELL used in connection with petroleum products, is also inherently distinctive. Prospective purchasers are likely to perceive such "arbitrary" designations as symbols of identification. Restrictions on the use of arbitrary designations are also unlikely to hinder communication by competitors.

Both the likely reaction of prospective purchasers and the potential impact on other sellers are less certain when the ordinary lexicographic meaning of a designation is relevant to the specific goods, services, or business to which it is applied. If the ordinary meaning of the word only indirectly or tangentially applies to the product or business, consumers remain likely to place primary emphasis on its identifying rather than its lexicographic significance. Restrictions on the use of terms that are only marginally related to the goods, service, or business with which they are used are also unlikely to interfere with the ability of other sellers to convey information about competing products. Thus, words that are merely suggestive of the nature or characteristics of the product or business are also considered inherently distinctive and eligible for protection without additional proof of distinctiveness. As the designation becomes more clearly descriptive of the goods, service, or business, however, it is more likely to be perceived by consumers in its ordinary lexicographic sense rather than as a symbol of identification. Recognition of trademark rights in descriptive terms also presents a more substantial threat to the legitimate interests of competitors in accurately and prominently describing their own products or business. Thus, if the designation is not merely suggestive but actually describes the nature or characteristics of the product or business of the user, the recognition of trademark rights requires proof of actual distinctiveness under the rule stated in Subsection (b). The distinction between "suggestive" and "descriptive" terms is considered in § 14, Comment *b*.

Illustrations:

1. *A*, a manufacturer of steel girders, prominently places the coined word TRAQ on its goods as an indication of source. The designation is a fanciful term that is inherently distinctive.

2. The facts being otherwise as stated in Illustration 1, *A* instead places the word LION on its girders. The designation is an arbitrary term that is inherently distinctive.

3. The facts again being otherwise as stated in Illustration 1, *A* instead places the word HERCULES on its girders. The designation is a suggestive term that is inherently distinctive.

4. The facts again being otherwise as stated in Illustration 1, *A* instead places the word RIGID on its girders. The designation is a descriptive term that is not inherently distinctive. See § 14.

d. Symbols, graphic designs, and colors. Symbols and graphic designs are eligible for protection as trademarks under the same principles applicable to other designations. Inherently distinctive symbols and graphic designs are protectable as trademarks under the rule stated in Subsection (a); other symbols and graphic designs are protectable only if the user establishes that the designation has become distinctive of its goods or services under the rule stated in Subsection (b).

A symbol or graphic design is not inherently distinctive unless the nature of the designation and the manner of its use make it likely that prospective purchasers will perceive the designation as an indication of source. Commonplace symbols and designs are not inherently distinctive since their appearance on numerous products makes it unlikely that consumers will view them as distinctive of the goods or services of a particular seller. Thus, unless the symbol or design is striking, unusual, or otherwise likely to differentiate the products of a particular producer, the designation is not inherently distinctive. Recognition of exclusive rights in symbols or designs that are inherently distinctive is also unlikely to inhibit the legitimate activities of competitors.

The manner in which a symbol or design is used also is relevant to the likelihood that it will be perceived as an indication of source. In some instances a design is likely to be viewed as mere ornamentation rather than as a symbol of identification. Colored stripes on socks, for example, or a floral design on cookware may be seen merely as ornamental features of the product and not as the trademark of a particular manufacturer. Similarly, a series of white concentric rings applied to automobile tires might be seen merely as a pleasing variation of the standard white-wall tire. Protection is available in such cases only upon proof that, in addition to its ornamental significance, the design has acquired secondary meaning as an indication of source.

A background design used in connection with other trademarks can be protected as a separate mark only if the design functions independently as a trademark. Thus, unless the design creates a separate and distinctive impression on prospective purchasers, it will not be recognized as an independent trademark.

Color can be protected as an element of a trademark when used as part of a design, pattern, or combination of colors that as a whole is inherently distinctive or has acquired secondary meaning. Thus, a seller may acquire trademark rights in a yellow octagonal design placed on shoe soles or in a particular combination of colors used on a toy puzzle. Some cases have also recognized trademark rights in a product's color per se.

On the application of the doctrine of functionality to graphic designs and colors, see § 17, Comment *c*. On the protection of distinctive packaging and product features, see § 16.

e. Secondary meaning. A designation that is not inherently distinctive, such as a word that describes the nature of the product on which it appears, nevertheless may become, as a result of its use by a specific person, uniquely associated with that person's goods, services, or business. Such acquired distinctiveness is called "secondary meaning." Secondary meaning does not connote a subordinate or rare meaning. It refers instead to a subsequent significance added to the original meaning of the term. Secondary meaning exists only if a significant number of prospective purchasers understand the term, when used in connection with a particular kind of good, service, or business, not merely in its lexicographic sense, but also as an indication of association with a particular, even if anonymous, entity. The concept of secondary meaning is also applicable to designations such as graphic designs, symbols, packaging features, and product designs. In these contexts secondary meaning denotes that the feature, although not inherently distinctive, has come through use to be uniquely associated with a particular source. A designation that has acquired secondary meaning thus distinguishes the goods, services, or business of one person from those of others.

When a designation has become distinctive through the acquisition of secondary meaning, it is protected under the same principles applicable to inherently distinctive designations. Protection extends, however, only to the secondary meaning that has attached to the designation. The trademark owner acquires no exclusive right to the use of the term in its original, lexicographic sense. See § 28. On secondary meaning as it relates to the "strength" of a mark and hence to its scope of protection, see § 21, Comment *i*.

The doctrine of secondary meaning is applicable both at common law and under the various state and federal trademark registration statutes. A designation that is not inherently distinctive is registrable under the Lanham Act and under the Model State Trademark Bill only if it "has become distinctive" of the applicant's goods or services. The doctrine is also applicable to actions for the infringement of unregistered designations under § 43(a) of the Lanham Act.

The existence of secondary meaning is a question of fact, with the burden of proof on the person claiming rights in the designation. See Comment *a*. The sufficiency of the evidence offered to prove secondary meaning should be evaluated in light of the nature of the designation. Highly descriptive terms, for example, are less likely to be perceived as trademarks and more likely to be useful to competing sellers than are less descriptive terms. More substantial evidence of secondary meaning thus will ordinarily be required to establish their distinctiveness. Indeed, some designations may be incapable of acquiring distinctiveness. See § 15. Personal names, on the other hand, although subject to the requirement of secondary meaning (see § 14, Comment *e*), are frequently adopted as trademarks and readily recognized as such by consumers. Their prima facie lack of distinctiveness may thus be overcome more easily than in the case of descriptive terms.

Secondary meaning may be established by either direct or circumstantial evidence. Testimony from individual consumers is clearly relevant to the existence of secondary meaning, but the lack of a representative sample of consumers often undermines its probative value. Surveys of prospective purchasers, if properly formulated and conducted, can be particularly persuasive. Proof of actual consumer confusion caused by another's use of the designation is also evidence of secondary meaning, since if the designation is not distinctive, use by another will not result in confusion.

The required association between the designation and the user may also be established by circumstantial evidence. Secondary meaning may be inferred, for example, from evidence relating to the nature and extent of the public exposure achieved by the designation. Thus, evidence of the volume of sales made under the designation is relevant, particularly for designations such as personal names and marginally descriptive terms that are more likely to be perceived as trademarks than more clearly descriptive designations or ornamental designs. The length of time the designation has been in use is also relevant. Although secondary meaning may sometimes be inferred from evidence of long and continuous use, no particular length of use is required. In some cases distinctiveness is not acquired even after an extended period of time; in others it may be acquired soon after adoption. Section 2(f) of the Lanham Act, 15 U.S.C.A. § 1052(f), permits but does not require the Patent and Trademark Office to accept as prima facie evidence of distinctiveness proof of "substantially exclusive and continuous use" for five years. Advertising and other promotional efforts resulting in increased public exposure for the designation may also support an inference of secondary meaning. It is the likely effect rather than the effort invested in such activities, however, that is determinative, and the expenditure of substantial sums in advertising does not in itself create protectable rights. Advertisements that emphasize the source significance of the designation through prominent use of the term or symbol or that invite consumers to "look for" the designation when selecting goods, for example, are more likely to generate secondary meaning than are more descriptive advertising uses.

The physical manner in which the designation is used with the goods, services, or business can also affect the likelihood that the designation will acquire secondary meaning. A designation that is relatively inconspicuous or that is used only in conjunction with other trademarks may be less likely to acquire secondary meaning than a more prominently displayed designation. Similarly, prominent use of a designation in the manner typical of a trade name, such as its appearance on signs or correspondence, can emphasize its association with the particular business more clearly than less conspicuous uses.

Concurrent use of a term by competitors is relevant as tending to negate the existence of secondary meaning. If the term has been used in a descriptive sense or as part of a trademark or trade name by numerous sellers in the market, it is unlikely to become associated exclusively with a single producer.

The significance of the designation to prospective purchasers may also be demonstrated by the nature of its use in newspapers, popular magazines, or dictionaries, at least when the product is marketed to the general public. The significance of the term to professionals in the trade such as dealers or retailers is also relevant, although it may not be accorded substantial weight if the goods or services are marketed primarily to nonprofessionals.

Proof that a competing seller has intentionally copied a designation previously used by another is often accepted as evidence of secondary meaning on the theory that the copying was motivated by a desire to benefit from confusion with the prior user. The strength of the inference may be diminished, however, by other credible motives for the copying. Thus, if the designation is plainly descriptive and equally applicable to the products of both sellers, or consists of a feature that is functional (see § 17) or that otherwise enhances the value of the product for reasons unrelated to any alleged source significance, evidence of intentional copying may carry little weight on the issue of secondary meaning. See also § 22.

A person attempting to prove the existence of secondary meaning is not required to establish that the designation is recognized as distinctive by all prospective purchasers in the relevant market, nor even by a majority of them. It is sufficient if the designation is distinctive to a significant number of prospective purchasers, taking into account the interest of the user in preventing a misappropriation of its good will, the harm to consumers from potential confusion, and the interest in permitting access to the particular designation by competing sellers.

On the geographic scope of secondary meaning as it relates to issues of priority and infringement, see § 19, Comment *b*; § 21, Comment *l*.

Illustration:

5. The facts being otherwise as stated in Illustration 4, the evidence establishes that as a result of *A* 's use of the designation prospective purchasers have come to perceive the term RIGID when displayed on steel girders as a designation that identifies girders manufactured by *A*. The designation has become distinctive through the acquisition of secondary meaning.

REPORTERS' NOTE

The requirement of distinctiveness appeared in the former treatment of this subject as part of the now obsolete distinction between "trademarks" and "trade names." See Restatement of Torts §§ 715 and 716 (1938). For general discussions of the requirement, see Gilson, Trademark Protection and Practice § 2.01; McCarthy, Trademarks and Unfair Competition §§ 11.01–02. On "secondary meaning," see Gilson, *supra*, § 2.09; McCarthy, *supra*, §§ 15.01–27.

Comment a. The requirement of distinctiveness is fundamental to the nature of a trademark. "The general rule regarding distinctiveness is clear: an identifying mark is distinctive and capable of being protected if it *either* (1) is inherently distinctive *or* (2) has acquired distinctiveness through secondary meaning." Two Pesos, Inc. v. Taco Cabana, Inc., ___ U.S. ___, 112 S.Ct. 2753, 2758, 120 L.Ed.2d 615, 625 (1992) (citing Restatement Third, Unfair Competition § 13 (Tent. Draft No.2 (1990))). See, e.g., Estate of P.D. Beckwith, Inc. v. Commissioner of Patents, 252 U.S. 538, 543, 40 S.Ct. 414, 416, 64 L.Ed. 705, 707 (1920) (inherently distinctive mark) ("the function of a trade-mark is to point distinctively, either by its own meaning or by association, to the origin or ownership of the wares to which it is applied"); Armstrong Paint & Varnish Works v. Nu–Enamel Corp., 305 U.S. 315, 336, 59 S.Ct. 191, 201, 83 L.Ed. 195, 207 (1938) (descriptive term with secondary meaning) (the designation "has come to indicate that the goods in connection with which it is used are the goods manufactured by the respondent. When a name is endowed with this quality, it becomes a mark, entitled to protection."). Section 2 of the Lanham Act provides for the registration of marks "by which the goods of the applicant may be distinguished from the goods of others." 15 U.S.C.A. § 1052.

On the general burden of proving distinctiveness, see, e.g., Anheuser–Busch Inc. v. Stroh Brewery Co., 750 F.2d 631 (8th Cir.1984); National Conference of Bar Examiners v. Multistate Legal Studies, Inc., 692 F.2d 478 (7th Cir.1982), cert. denied 464 U.S. 814, 104 S.Ct. 69, 78 L.Ed.2d 83 (1983); Reese Publishing Co. v. Hampton Int'l Communications, Inc., 620 F.2d 7 (2d Cir.1980). A federal trademark registration is prima facie evidence of the validity of the registered mark, 15 U.S.C.A. §§ 1057(b), 1115(a). A registration granted without proof of secondary meaning has been interpreted as creating a rebuttable presumption that the mark is inherently distinctive. E.g., Pizzeria Uno Corp. v. Temple, 747 F.2d 1522 (4th Cir.1984); McGregor–Doniger Inc. v. Drizzle Inc., 599 F.2d 1126 (2d Cir.1979). A registration granted on the basis of acquired distinctiveness has been interpreted as creating a rebuttable presumption of secondary meaning. E.g., Boden Products, Inc. v. Doric Foods Corp., 552 F.Supp. 493 (N.D.Ill.1982); Evelyn Wood Reading Dynamics Institutes, Inc. v. Zimmerman, 134 U.S.P.Q. 475 (N.D.Cal.1962). The registration is said to shift the burden of proof to the party challenging the validity of the trademark, who must establish invalidity by a preponderance of the evidence. See, e.g., Pizzeria Uno Corp., *supra* ; Vuitton et fils S.A. v. J. Young Enterprises, Inc., 644 F.2d 769 (9th Cir.1981); Keebler Co. v. Rovira Biscuit Corp., 624 F.2d 366 (1st Cir.1980). If the registration has become incontestable, the mark cannot be challenged as descriptive and lacking secondary meaning. 15 U.S.C.A. § 1115(b); Park 'N Fly, Inc. v. Dollar Park and Fly, Inc., 469 U.S. 189, 105 S.Ct. 658, 83 L.Ed.2d 582 (1985). Trademark rights are lost, however, if the mark becomes generic. See § 15.

Comment b. On the principle of inherent distinctiveness, see, e.g., Blisscraft of Hollywood v. United Plastics Co., 294 F.2d 694, 700 (2d Cir.1961) ("The presumption that a fanciful word or mark becomes distinctive and identifies the source of goods on which it is used immediately after adoption and *bona fide* first use is basic in trademark law."). See also Gilson, *supra,* § 2.09 ("The public is presumed to regard [inherently distinctive marks] on first encounter as designating the origin of the products and distinguishing them from the products of others."); McCarthy, *supra*, § 15.01 ("In a sense, [inherently distinctive marks] are irrebuttably presumed to have achieved customer recognition and association immediately upon adoption and use.").

Distinctiveness is commonly analyzed in terms of a spectrum reflecting degrees of inherent distinctiveness. The traditional categories are generic designations, which cannot be distinctive (see § 15); descriptive designations, which are not distinctive absent proof of secondary meaning (see § 14); and suggestive, arbitrary, and fanciful designations, which are considered inherently distinctive. See Comment *c*. The spectrum is delineated in, e.g., Zatarains, Inc. v. Oak Grove Smokehouse, Inc., 698 F.2d 786 (5th Cir.1983); Abercrombie & Fitch Co. v. Hunting World, Inc., 537 F.2d 4 (2d Cir.1976); Great Southern Bank v. First Southern Bank, 625 So.2d 463 (Fla.1993) (citing Restatement Third, Unfair Competition §§ 13–15 (Tent. Draft No.2 (1990))). A similar analysis is applicable to graphic designations. See, e.g., Wiley v. American Greetings Corp., 762 F.2d 139 (1st Cir. 1985); Chevron Chemical Co. v. Voluntary Purchasing Groups, Inc., 659 F.2d 695 (5th Cir.1981), cert. denied, 457 U.S. 1126, 102 S.Ct. 2947, 73 L.Ed.2d 1342 (1982). See also Comment *d*; § 14, Comment *f*. The classification of a designation is a question of fact. E.g., Bristol–Myers Squibb Co. v. McNeil–P.P.C., Inc., 973 F.2d 1033 (2d Cir.1992); Investacorp, Inc. v. Arabian Investment Banking Corp., 931 F.2d 1519 (11th Cir.), cert. denied ___ U.S. ___, 112 S.Ct. 639, 116 L.Ed.2d 657 (1991); Forum Corp. v. Forum, Ltd., 903 F.2d 434 (7th Cir.1990).

Comment c. Examples of fanciful marks include, e.g., Polaroid Corp. v. Polaraid, Inc., 319 F.2d 830 (7th Cir.1963) (POLAROID "is a coined or invented word"); Kotabs, Inc. v. Kotex Co., 50 F.2d 810 (3d Cir.), cert. denied 284 U.S. 665, 52 S.Ct. 41, 76 L.Ed. 563 (1931) (KOTEX "is a coined word, arbitrary in the extreme"); Clorox Chemical Co. v. Chlorit Mfg. Corp., 25 F.Supp. 702 (E.D.N.Y.1938) (CLOROX "is a fanciful word, arbitrarily selected").

Examples of arbitrary marks include, e.g., Stork Restaurant v. Sahati, 166 F.2d 348 (9th Cir.1948) (THE STORK CLUB for a night club); WGBH Educational Foundation, Inc. v. Penthouse International Ltd., 453 F.Supp. 1347 (S.D.N.Y.1978), affirmed 598 F.2d 610 (2d Cir.1979) (NOVA for a television science program); Borden, Inc. v. Topps Chewing Gum, Inc., 173 U.S.P.Q. 447 (Tm. Tr.App.Bd.1972) (ICE CREAM for chewing gum).

Examples of suggestive marks include, e.g., Hindu Incense v. Meadows, 692 F.2d 1048 (6th Cir.1982) (GENIE on incense); American Home Products Corp. v. Johnson Chemical Co., 589 F.2d 103 (2d Cir. 1978) (ROACH MOTEL on insect trap); Norwich Pharmacal Co. v. Chas. Pfizer & Co., 165 U.S.P.Q. 644 (Tm.Tr.App.Bd.1970) (UNBURN on sunburn remedy). See also § 14, Comment *b*.

Comment d. In determining that a stylized leaf design used with other trademarks on frozen food was not inherently distinctive, the Court of Customs and Patent Appeals (predecessor to the Court of Appeals for the Federal Circuit) summarized its case law on inherent distinctiveness:

> In determining whether a design is arbitrary or distinctive this court has looked to whether it was a "common" basic shape or design, whether it was unique or unusual in a particular field, whether it was a mere refinement of a commonly-adopted and well-known form of ornamentation for a particular class of goods viewed by the public as a dress or ornamentation for the goods, or whether it was capable of creating a commercial impression distinct from the accompanying words.

Seabrook Foods, Inc. v. Bar–Well Foods Ltd., 568 F.2d 1342, 1344 (C.C.P.A.1977) (footnotes omitted). Accord Tone Bros., Inc. v. Sysco Corp., 28 F.3d 1192 (Fed.Cir.1994). The criteria were applied in Brooks Shoe Mfg. Co. v. Suave Shoe Corp., 716 F.2d 854 (11th Cir.1983) ("V" design on athletic shoes not inherently distinctive and insufficient proof of secondary meaning). See, e.g., In re Swift & Co., 223 F.2d 950, 955 (C.C.P.A.1955) (polka dot design in red with white dots used as background on a cleanser label creating "definite and lasting impression * * * pointing distinctly to the commercial origin" held inherently distinctive); In re Interstate Bakeries Corp., 153 U.S.P.Q. 488 (Tm.Tr.App. Bd.1967) (checkered gingham design on bakery products held inherently distinctive as "arbitrary and eye catching" and not "commonplace in the bakery field"). Examples of designs accepted for registration under the Lanham Act without proof of secondary meaning include In re W.B. Roddenbery Co., 135 U.S.P.Q. 215 (Tm.Tr.App.Bd.1962) ("representation of gold coin in association with varied colored panels"); In re Dairy Queen of Georgia, Inc., 134 U.S.P.Q. 136 (Tm.Tr.App.Bd.1962) (crooked star and face); In re Sunbeam Corp., 120 U.S.P.Q. 304 (Tm.Tr.App.Bd. 1959) ("fanciful" geometric design).

Designs recognized as trademarks upon proof of secondary meaning include Beconta, Inc. v. Larson Industries, Inc., 330 F.Supp. 116 (N.D.Ill. 1971) (zebra-striped skis); Federal Glass Co. v. Corning Glass Works, 162 U.S.P.Q. 279 (Tm.Tr.App.Bd. 1969) (blue cornflower design on cookware). On the relevance of advertising that calls attention to the design, see, e.g., In re Data Packaging Corp., 453 F.2d 1300 (C.C.P.A. 1972) (advertisements emphasizing the identification function of the design supported a finding of secondary meaning); Seabrook Foods, Inc., *supra* (noting the absence of such advertising).

Designs found to be merely ornamental and lacking secondary meaning include Wiley v. American Greetings Corp., 762 F.2d 139 (1st Cir. 1985) (red heart on a teddy bear); In re General Tire & Rubber Co., 404 F.2d 1396 (C.C.P.A.1969) (three concentric rings on automobile tires); In re David Crystal, Inc., 296 F.2d 771 (C.C.P.A.1961) (two-colored stripes on socks). See In re Swift & Co., *supra*, holding that the decorative nature of a design does not preclude simultaneous trademark significance.

On the recognition of independent trademark rights in background designs used with other marks, in addition to In re Swift & Co., *supra*, see, e.g., In re Hehr Mfg. Co., 279 F.2d 526 (C.C.P.A.1960) (secondary meaning found for red square background); In re Wendy's International, Inc., 227 U.S.P.Q. 884 (Tm.Tr.App.

Bd.1985) (background for signs not inherently distinctive and no proof of secondary meaning); In re Servotronics, Inc., 156 U.S.P.Q. 592 (Tm. Tr.App.Bd.1968) (globe and airplane background design held inherently distinctive).

The example of the octagonal yellow mark on shoe soles is taken from Quabaug Rubber Co. v. Fabiano Shoe Co., 567 F.2d 154 (1st Cir.1977); the toy puzzle example is from Ideal Toy Corp. v. Plawner Toy Mfg. Corp., 685 F.2d 78 (3d Cir.1982). See also, e.g., Transportation, Inc. v. Mayflower Services, Inc., 769 F.2d 952 (4th Cir. 1985) (red and black color scheme on taxicabs protected); Chevron Chemical Co. v. Voluntary Purchasing Groups, Inc., 659 F.2d 695 (5th Cir. 1981), cert. denied 457 U.S. 1126, 102 S.Ct. 2947, 73 L.Ed.2d 1342 (1982) (combination of colors arranged in a particular pattern protected); In re Eagle Fence Rentals, Inc., 231 U.S.P.Q. 228 (Tm.Tr.App.Bd.1986) (pattern of wire colors in a chain link fence registered as a service mark for fence rentals). On the "color depletion" rationale for denying exclusive rights in color per se, see, e.g., Diamond Match Co. v. Saginaw Match Co., 142 Fed. 727 (6th Cir.), cert. denied 203 U.S. 589, 27 S.Ct. 776, 51 L.Ed. 330 (1906); Campbell Soup Co. v. Armour & Co., 175 F.2d 795 (3d Cir.), cert. denied 338 U.S. 847, 70 S.Ct. 88, 94 L.Ed. 518 (1949). The rationale was rejected and registration allowed upon proof of secondary meaning for the color pink used on residential insulation in In re Owens–Corning Fiberglas Corp., 774 F.2d 1116 (Fed.Cir.1985). The court found no competitive need for the color, relying in part on evidence that other manufacturers did not color their products. See also Master Distributors, Inc. v. Pako Corp., 986 F.2d 219 (8th Cir.1993) (there is no per se rule precluding colors as trademarks). Contra, NutraSweet Co. v. Stadt Corp., 917 F.2d 1024 (7th Cir.1990), cert. denied 499 U.S. 983, 111 S.Ct. 1640, 113 L.Ed. 735 (1991) (rejecting *Owens–Corning*). See, Qualitex Co. v. Jacobson Products Co., 13 F.3d 1297 (9th Cir.), cert. granted ___ U.S. ___, 115 S.Ct. 40, ___ L.Ed.2d ___ (1994).

For other examples of subject matter protectable upon proof of secondary meaning, see In re Clarke, 17 U.S.P.Q.2d 1238 (Tm.Tr.App.Bd.1990) (fragrance registered as trademark for yarn); In re General Electric Broadcasting Co., 199 U.S.P.Q. 560 (Tm.Tr.App.Bd.1978) (ship's bell sound eligible for registration as a service mark for broadcasting services).

Comment e. The explanation of secondary meaning offered by Judge Denison in G. & C. Merriam Co. v. Saalfield, 198 Fed. 369, 373 (6th Cir. 1912), is frequently recited:

> It contemplates that a word or phrase originally, and in that sense primarily, incapable of exclusive appropriation with reference to an article on the market, because geographically or otherwise descriptive, might nevertheless have been used so long and so exclusively by one producer with reference to his article that, in that trade and to that branch of the purchasing public, the word or phrase had come to mean that the article was his product; in other words, had come to be, to them, his trade-mark. So it was said that the word had come to have a secondary meaning * * *.

The phrase "secondary meaning" apparently was first used in Wotherspoon v. Currie, 5 L.R.-E. & I. App. 508 (1872). The doctrine remains essentially unchanged. "Secondary meaning is the connection in the consumer's mind between the mark and the product's producer, whether the producer is known or unknown." AmBrit, Inc. v. Kraft, Inc., 812 F.2d 1531, 1536 n.14 (11th Cir.1986), cert. denied 481 U.S. 1041, 107 S.Ct. 1983, 95 L.Ed.2d 822 (1987). Judge Learned Hand emphasized that knowledge of the identity of the producer is unnecessary. "It is, of course, not necessary that he should be known as the maker; on the contrary, it will suffice if the article be known as coming from a single, though anonymous, source." Coty, Inc. v. Le Blume Import Co., 292 Fed. 264, 267–68 (S.D.N.Y.), affirmed 293 Fed. 344 (2d Cir.1923). Accord, e.g., Tone Bros., Inc. v. Sysco Corp., 28 F.3d 1192 (Fed.Cir.1994); Union Carbide Corp. v. Ever–Ready Inc., 531 F.2d 366, 380 (7th Cir.), cert. denied 429 U.S. 830, 97 S.Ct. 91, 50 L.Ed.2d 94 (1976). See also the definitions of "trademark" and "service mark" in the Lanham Act, 15 U.S.C.A. § 45 ("even if that source is unknown"). Descriptive terms that have acquired secondary meaning are protected according to the same principles applicable to inherently distinctive marks. PaperCutter, Inc. v. Fay's Drug Co., 900 F.2d 558 (2d Cir.1990) (citing Restatement Third, Unfair Competition § 13, Comment *e* (Tent. Draft No.2 (1990))).

Although the Lanham Act in § 2(f), 15 U.S.C.A. § 1052(f), employs the phrase "become distinctive of the applicant's goods," in construing the Act both the Patent and Trademark Office and the courts regularly speak of "secondary meaning." See, e.g., Park 'N Fly, Inc. v. Dollar Park and Fly, Inc., 469 U.S. 189, 105 S.Ct. 658, 83 L.Ed.2d 582 (1985). The doctrine also applies in actions under § 43(a) of the Lanham Act. See, e.g., University of Georgia Athletic Association v. Laite, 756 F.2d 1535 (11th Cir.1985) (depiction of the "Georgia Bulldog"); Thompson Medical Co. v. Pfizer Inc., 753 F.2d 208 (2d Cir.1985) (SPORTSCREME).

It is sometimes said that under New York law proof of secondary meaning is not a prerequisite for protection even if the designation is not inherently distinctive. See, e.g., Norwich Pharmacal Co. v. Sterling Drug, Inc., 271 F.2d 569 (2d Cir.1959), cert. denied 362 U.S. 919, 80 S.Ct. 671, 4 L.Ed.2d 739 (1960). Many of the cases reciting this principle, however, involve the application of doctrines outside the law of trademarks, such as the general proscription against passing off, see § 4, or the concept of misappropriation. See § 38. See, e.g., Flexitized, Inc. v. National Flexitized Corp., 335 F.2d 774 (2d Cir. 1964), cert. denied 380 U.S. 913, 85 S.Ct. 899, 13 L.Ed.2d 799 (1965) (misappropriation); Upjohn Co. v. Schwartz, 246 F.2d 254 (2d Cir.1957) (contributory passing off). Other cases can be understood as resting on an inference of secondary meaning arising, for example, from evidence of intentional copying. See, e.g., Lincoln Restaurant Corp. v. Wolfies Rest. Inc., 291 F.2d 302 (2d Cir.), cert. denied 368 U.S. 889, 82 S.Ct. 143, 7 L.Ed.2d 88 (1961) (intentional attempt to trade on the plaintiff's mark). The "New York rule" is criticized in McCarthy, *supra*, §§ 15.04–05. The rule has been invoked most often in connection with the protection of trade dress. See § 16.

Several decisions in the Southern District of New York indicated, primarily in dicta, that protection might be accorded to a designation that is in the *process* of acquiring secondary meaning. See, e.g., Metro Kane Imports, Ltd. v. Federated Department Stores Inc., 625 F.Supp. 313, 316 (S.D.N.Y.1985), affirmed without op., 800 F.2d 1128 (2d Cir.1986) (citing prior cases). This "secondary meaning in the making" doctrine, however, was generally raised in cases in which secondary meaning already existed or in which an inference of secondary meaning based on intentional copying could be drawn. The doctrine, if taken literally, is inimical to the purpose of the secondary meaning requirement. It has been rejected in a number of cases, see, e.g., Laureyssens v. Idea Group, Inc., 964 F.2d 131 (2d Cir.1992) (citing Restatement Third, Unfair Competition § 13, Reporters' Note to Comment *e* (Tent. Draft No.2 (1990))); Cicena Ltd. v. Columbia Telecommunications Group, 900 F.2d 1546 (Fed.Cir.1990) (applying Second Circuit law); Black & Decker Manufacturing Co. v. Ever–Ready Appliance Mfg. Co., 684 F.2d 546, 550 (8th Cir.1982); A.J. Canfield Co. v. Concord Beverage Co., 629 F.Supp. 200, 211–12 (E.D.Pa.1985), affirmed on other grounds 808 F.2d 291 (3d Cir. 1986). The doctrine is criticized in McCarthy, *supra*, § 15:21 and Scagnelli, Dawn of a New Doctrine? Trademark Protection for Incipient Secondary Meaning, 71 Trademark Rep. 527 (1981).

On secondary meaning as a question of fact, see, e.g., Bristol–Myers Squibb Co. v. McNeil–P.P.C., Inc., 973 F.2d 1033 (2d Cir.1992) (finding of secondary meaning is reversed only if clearly erroneous); In re Loew's Theatres, Inc., 769 F.2d 764 (Fed.Cir.1985). The relationship between the degree of apparent descriptiveness and the quantum of proof required to establish secondary meaning is frequently evident in the case law. See, e.g., Yamaha International Corp. v. Hoshino Gakki Co., 840 F.2d 1572 (Fed.Cir.1988) (the greater the descriptiveness, the heavier the evidentiary burden, citing Gilson, *supra*, § 2.09 and McCarthy, *supra*, § 15.10); American Heritage Life Insurance Co. v. Heritage Life Insurance Co., 494 F.2d 3, 12 (5th Cir.1974) (HERITAGE for insurance services) ("We agree that the evidentiary burden necessary to establish secondary meaning is substantial where the proposed mark's original or primary meaning suggests the basic nature of the service to be rendered."); Supreme Wine Co. v. American Distilling Co., 310 F.2d 888, 889 (2d Cir.1962) (SUPREME for vodka) ("We hold that the word 'supreme' is so totally lacking in distinctiveness, originality and uniqueness that, in the absence of compelling proof that it has acquired a secondary meaning to the buying public, it is not entitled to trademark protection."). See also In re Synergistics Research Corp., 218 U.S.P.Q. 165 (Tm.Tr.App. Bd.1983) (BALL DARTS for target game) (the five-year presumption of distinctiveness under § 2(f) of the Lanham Act is insufficient for "highly descriptive" terms). The trend is particularly apparent when the designation approaches the generic category. See, e.g., Aloe Creme Laboratories, Inc. v. Milsan, Inc., 423 F.2d 845, 850 (5th Cir.), cert. denied 398 U.S. 928, 90 S.Ct. 1818, 26 L.Ed.2d 90 (1970) ("substantial" evidentiary burden with respect to ALO on products containing extract from the aloe vera plant).

Descriptions of the required extent of secondary meaning include, e.g., President and Trustees of Colby College v. Colby College—New Hampshire, 508 F.2d 804 (1st Cir.1975) ("significant quantity of the consuming public"); Food Fair Stores, Inc. v. Lakeland Grocery Corp., 301 F.2d 156 (4th Cir.), cert. denied 371 U.S. 817, 83 S.Ct. 31, 9 L.Ed.2d 58 (1962) ("substantial number of present or prospective customers"); Roselux Chemical Co. v. Parsons Ammonia Co., 299 F.2d 855 (C.C.P.A.1962) (more than a "relatively small number"); North Carolina Dairy Foundation, Inc. v. Foremost–McKesson, Inc., 92 Cal.App.3d 98, 154 Cal.Rptr. 794 (1979) ("substantial segment of the buying population").

On the evidence relevant to the existence of secondary meaning, see, e.g., Ford Motor Co. v. Summit Motor Products, Inc., 930 F.2d 277 (3d Cir.), cert. denied ___ U.S. ___, 112 S.Ct. 373, 116 L.Ed.2d 324 (1991) (extent of sales and advertising, length of use, exclusivity of use, copying by another, customer surveys, customer testimony, use in trade journals, size of the company, number of sales, number of customers, and actual confusion); Bristol–Myers, *supra* (advertising expenditures, consumer studies, sales success, media coverage, attempts to plagiarize, and length and exclusivity of use); Perini Corp. v. Perini Construction, Inc., 915 F.2d 121 (4th Cir.1990) (same).

The shortcomings of direct consumer testimony are noted in Premier–Pabst Corp. v. Elm City Brewing Co., 9 F.Supp. 754 (D.Conn.1935). See Hot Shoppes, Inc. v. Hot Shoppe, Inc., 203 F.Supp. 777 (M.D.N.C.1962) ("some weight" given to the testimony of witnesses that they did not attach source significance to the designation). On the use of consumer surveys, see, e.g., Brooks Shoe Mfg. Co. v. Suave Shoe Corp., 716 F.2d 854 (11th Cir.1983) (defendant's survey universe found more appropriate than the plaintiff's); Zatarains, Inc. v. Oak Grove Smokehouse, Inc., 698 F.2d 786 (5th Cir.1983). Cf. Toys "R" Us, Inc. v. Canarsie Kiddie Shop, Inc., 559 F.Supp. 1189 (E.D.N.Y.1983) (survey excluded). See generally Manual for Complex Litigation, Second, § 21.484 (1985); Gilson, *supra*, § 8.11; McCarthy, *supra*, §§ 32.46–55. On the relevance of evidence indicating actual confusion, see, e.g., American Scientific Chemical, Inc. v. American Hospital Supply Corp., 690 F.2d 791 (9th Cir.1982); Union Carbide Corp. v. Ever–Ready Inc., 531 F.2d 366 (7th Cir.), cert. denied 429 U.S. 830, 97 S.Ct. 91, 50 L.Ed.2d 94 (1976); Little Tavern Shops, Inc. v. Davis, 116 F.2d 903 (4th Cir.1941).

The use of circumstantial evidence of secondary meaning is considered in, e.g., Yamaha International Corp. v. Hoshino Gakki Co., 840 F.2d 1572 (Fed.Cir.1988) (direct evidence of consumer perceptions is not required); Fund of Funds, Ltd. v. First American Fund of Funds, 274 F.Supp. 517 (S.D.N.Y.1967); Premier–Pabst Corp., *supra*. Sales figures were admitted in, e.g., Turner v. HMH Pub. Co., 380 F.2d 224 (5th Cir.), cert. denied 389 U.S. 1006, 88 S.Ct. 566, 19 L.Ed.2d 601 (1967); Family Record Plan, Inc. v. Mitchell, 172 Cal.App.2d 235, 342 P.2d 10 (1959); Great Scott Food Market, Inc. v. Sunderland Wonder Inc., 348 Mass. 320, 203 N.E.2d 376 (1965). Cases noting the length of use include, e.g., Co–Rect Products, Inc. v. Marvy! Advertising Photography,

Inc., 780 F.2d 1324 (8th Cir.1985) (no secondary meaning after 10 months); Trak Inc. v. Benner Ski KG, 475 F.Supp. 1076 (D.Mass.1979) (exclusive use for six years taken as evidence of secondary meaning); Atlantic Monthly Co. v. Frederick Ungar Publishing Co., 197 F.Supp. 524 (S.D.N.Y.1961) (secondary meaning of ATLANTIC on magazines found "firmly embedded" by 100 years of use). The possibility of rapidly-acquired secondary meaning is discussed in Speedry Products, Inc. v. Dri Mark Products, Inc., 271 F.2d 646 (2d Cir.1959). See, e.g., Karen Industries, Inc. v. Chiaverotti, 181 F.Supp. 827 (E.D.Wis.1960) (secondary meaning for trade dress acquired in several months); Jackson v. Universal International Pictures, Inc., 36 Cal.2d 116, 222 P.2d 433 (1950) (preproduction publicity and 22 performances sufficient to create secondary meaning in a play title).

Guidelines appearing in Patent and Trademark Office, Trademark Manual of Examining Procedure § 1212.05 indicate that under § 2(f) of the Lanham Act proof of substantially exclusive and continuous use for five years will generally suffice to establish secondary meaning for surnames and marks that are not highly descriptive; it is not sufficient for highly descriptive terms, container shapes, or ornamentation.

Use of the mark in advertising was emphasized in, e.g., In re Owens–Corning Fiberglas Corp., 774 F.2d 1116 (Fed.Cir.1985); Carling Brewing Co. v. Philip Morris Inc., 297 F.Supp. 1330 (N.D.Ga.1968). Substantial promotional expenditures were found insufficient in, e.g., American Footwear Corp. v. General Footwear Co., 609 F.2d 655 (2d Cir.1979), cert. denied 445 U.S. 951, 100 S.Ct. 1601, 63 L.Ed.2d 787 (1980); Aloe Creme Laboratories, Inc. v. Milsan, Inc., 423 F.2d 845 (5th Cir.), cert. denied 398 U.S. 928, 90 S.Ct. 1818, 26 L.Ed.2d 90 (1970). On the nature of the advertising use, compare In re Data Packaging Corp., 453 F.2d 1300 (C.C.P.A. 1972) ("look for" promotion) and In re Swift & Co., 223 F.2d 950 (C.C.P.A. 1955) (same) with First Brands Corp. v. Fred Meyer, Inc., 809 F.2d 1378 (9th Cir.1987) (designation was not emphasized) and Loctite Corp. v. National Starch and Chemical Corp., 516 F.Supp. 190 (S.D.N.Y.1981) (descriptive use).

Cases noting the inconspicuousness of the use or the presence of more recognizable marks include, e.g., Walt–West Enterprises, Inc. v. Gannett Co., 695 F.2d 1050 (7th Cir.1982); Norm Thompson Outfitters, Inc. v. General Motors Corp., 448 F.2d 1293 (9th Cir.1971); Wilhartz v. Turco Products, Inc., 164 F.2d 731 (7th Cir. 1947). Cf. In re Int'l Spike, Inc., 196 U.S.P.Q. 447 (Tm.Tr.App.Bd.1977) (illustration appeared only on the back of the carton).

Descriptive use of the term by third persons is often invoked as a factor weighing against a finding of secondary meaning. See, e.g., American Heritage Life Insurance Co. v. Heritage Life Insurance Co., 494 F.2d 3 (5th Cir.1974); Quaker State Oil Refining Corp. v. Quaker Oil Corp., 453 F.2d 1296 (C.C.P.A.1972); Carter–Wallace, Inc. v. Procter & Gamble Co., 434 F.2d 794 (9th Cir. 1970). Similar principles apply to graphic designations. See, e.g., Sweetheart Plastics, Inc. v. Detroit Forming, Inc., 743 F.2d 1039 (4th Cir.1984) (dish designs); Levi Strauss & Co. v. Genesco, Inc., 742 F.2d 1401 (Fed.Cir.1984) (placement of tab); Mennen Co. v. Gillette Co., 565

F.Supp. 648 (S.D.N.Y.1983), affirmed 742 F.2d 1437 (2d Cir.1984) (diagonal stripes). The use by the person claiming secondary meaning, however, need not be exclusive. E.g., President and Trustees of Colby College v. Colby College—New Hampshire, 508 F.2d 804 (1st Cir.1975); Goodyear Tire & Rubber Co. v. H. Rosenthal Co., 246 F.Supp. 724 (D.Minn. 1965). Use of the term by others on unrelated goods is generally given little weight. See, e.g., W.E. Bassett Co. v. Revlon, Inc., 435 F.2d 656 (2d Cir.1970); Time, Inc. v. Life Television Corp., 123 F.Supp. 470 (D.Minn. 1954).

Acknowledgment of trademark or trade name significance in newspaper and magazine references was held insufficient to prove secondary meaning in *American Heritage Life Insurance Co., supra*, and *Aloe Creme Laboratories, supra.* Affidavits from persons engaged in the trade were used to support an inference of secondary meaning among prospective purchasers in In re Hollywood Brands, Inc., 214 F.2d 139 (C.C.P.A.1954); similar affidavits were held insufficient in In re Meyer & Wenthe, Inc., 267 F.2d 945 (C.C.P.A.1959) and In re Duvernoy & Sons, Inc., 212 F.2d 202 (C.C.P.A.1954).

Cases relying on evidence of intentional copying include, e.g., Harlequin Enterprises Ltd. v. Gulf & Western Corp., 644 F.2d 946 (2d Cir.1981); RJR Foods, Inc. v. White Rock Corp., 603 F.2d 1058 (2d Cir.1979). Cf. Co–Rect Products, Inc. v. Marvy! Advertising Photography, Inc., 780 F.2d 1324 (8th Cir.1985) (copying relevant but overcome by other evidence). Some decisions hold that deliberate copying creates a prima facie case of secondary meaning. See, e.g., M. Kramer Manufacturing Co. v. Andrews, 783 F.2d 421 (4th Cir.1986); Audio Fidelity, Inc. v. High Fidelity Recordings, Inc., 283 F.2d 551 (9th Cir.1960). Cf. Vaughan Mfg. Co. v. Brikam Int'l, Inc., 814 F.2d 346 (7th Cir.1987) (copying probative, but reserving decision on the appropriateness of a "presumption"). Cases emphasizing the possibility of legitimate motives for copying include, e.g., Blau Plumbing, Inc. v. S.O.S. Fix–It, Inc., 781 F.2d 604 (7th Cir.1986); Brooks Shoe Mfg. Co. v. Suave Shoe Corp., 716 F.2d 854 (11th Cir.1983). See Laureyssens v. Idea Group, Inc., 964 F.2d 131 (2d Cir.1992) (intentional copying supports an inference of secondary meaning if the circumstances show an intent to benefit from the prior user's good will, citing Restatement Third, Unfair Competition § 16, Comment *b* (Tent. Draft No.2 (1990))).

§ 14. Descriptive, Geographic, and Personal Name Designations

A designation that is likely to be perceived by prospective purchasers as merely descriptive of the nature, qualities, or other characteristics of the goods, services, or business with which it is used, or as merely geographically descriptive of their origin or location, or as the personal name of a person connected with the goods, services, or business, is not inherently distinctive under the rule stated in § 13(a). Such a designation is distinctive only if it

has acquired secondary meaning under the rule stated in § 13(b).

Comment:

a. Descriptive terms. A person cannot, by mere adoption and use, obtain exclusive rights in words that describe the attributes of the goods, services, or business to which the words are applied. Prospective purchasers are likely to understand such words in their descriptive sense rather than as indications of source. Appropriation of descriptive words can also limit the ability of other sellers to emphasize the characteristics of their own goods, services, or business by restricting the manner in which the descriptive term can be used. Over time, however, the descriptive meaning of a word may become subordinate and the word may become instead primarily a symbol of identification. The threat of confusion or deception resulting from the use of the word by others will then ordinarily outweigh the costs of restricted access, particularly in light of the right of competitors to make "fair use" of the word in its original descriptive sense. See § 28. Protection for descriptive designations is therefore available upon proof that the designation has become distinctive of the goods, services, or business of the user under the rule stated in § 13(b). On the proof of such "secondary meaning," see § 13, Comment *e*.

In general, if a word directly conveys information about the product or business with which it is used, other than information relating to source or association with a particular entity, the word is "descriptive." Thus, words that describe the characteristics of the goods, services, or business are descriptive. So too are words describing the purpose or function of a product, the effect of its use, or the class of intended purchasers. Indications of size, quantity, or capacity are also descriptive, as are laudatory terms such as "premium" or "superior."

Determinations of descriptiveness must be made with reference to the specific goods, services, or business with which the designation is used. The term TRIM may be descriptive when used in connection with hedge clippers, clothing, or hair styling services but arbitrary when used as a trademark for toothpaste, cement, or brokerage services. Thus, CAR–FRESHNER is descriptive of an auto deodorizer, VISION CENTER of an optical clinic, RICH 'N CHIPS of chocolate-chip cookies, and HOMEMAKERS of housekeeping services. Similarly, slogans adopted by sellers to identify their goods and services may be descriptive of the products to which they relate. The slogan EXTRA STRENGTH PAIN RELIEVER used in connection with the marketing of an analgesic, for example, is descriptive and therefore unprotectable as a trademark absent proof of secondary meaning.

Designations adopted by a seller merely to distinguish the various styles, grades, or models of its goods are also descriptive. Even when the lexicographic meaning of the term is "arbitrary" with respect to the goods, its use to describe a particular style or model of the seller's goods undermines the likelihood that the designation will also serve to indicate source. Thus, unless such designations are used in a manner that also emphasizes their source significance, style and model names such as alphanumeric symbols used to denominate machine parts, terms used to designate the colors of cosmetics, and names indicating the patterns on china are descriptive and hence unprotectable absent proof that they have acquired secondary meaning.

Descriptiveness is determined by the commercial impression created by the mark as a whole. A designation consisting of a combination of elements may be inherently distinctive even if some or all of the individual elements are descriptive. Recognition of rights in the composite will not deprive competitors of access to the descriptive components. The combination of a descriptive word with a distinctive design or picture, for example, may produce a composite that is inherently distinctive. Similarly, the combination of two or more words, each of which is descriptive, may result in a composite that is fanciful, arbitrary, or suggestive.

The misspelling or corruption of an otherwise descriptive word will not ordinarily alter the descriptive character of the designation. In many instances the contrivance will not overcome the ordinary meaning of the term, and prospective purchasers will thus continue to understand the designation in a purely descriptive sense. Indeed, in some instances the alteration may go entirely unnoticed by a significant number of consumers. If the altered form is phonetically equivalent to the original word, its aural significance will also remain merely descriptive. Recognition of exclusive rights in variants and corruptions of descriptive words also imposes a risk of liability on subsequent users of the original words. See § 21, Comment *c*. Thus, unless the alteration is sufficient to avoid encumbering use of the original word, the variation remains descriptive. If the term FLEXIBLE is descriptive of a particular product, for example, so too is the term FLEXITIZED. Similarly, if the designation STEAM is descriptive, the requirement of secondary meaning cannot be avoided by substituting STEEM. Abbreviations recognized as shorthand forms of descriptive terms are also descriptive.

If the descriptive meaning of a designation is generally unknown in the marketplace, it is likely to be perceived as an indication of source. A word is therefore descriptive only if a significant number of prospective purchasers are likely to understand its descriptive connotations. In many instances dictionary definitions are sufficient to establish descriptiveness, but they are not always conclusive. If the descriptive meaning of a term is obsolete or known only to lexicographers or other select groups, the designation is ordinarily not descriptive. The mark L'ORIGAN is thus not necessarily descriptive of a perfume despite the fact that origan is an aromatic mint.

Similar rules apply to words in a foreign language. If a descriptive foreign word is similar to its English equivalent, prospective purchasers are likely to understand the word in its descriptive sense, and proof of secondary meaning is therefore required to establish trademark rights. Thus, OPTIQUE for eyeglasses and SELECTA as the Spanish equivalent of "select" for beer are descriptive. The same is true for foreign words generally understood by English-speaking consumers, such as BLANC used on white wine. For other foreign words, the test remains whether a significant number of prospective purchasers are likely to understand the word merely in its descriptive sense. The multilingual character of the purchasing public and the increasing exposure to foreign terms on imported goods justify general adherence to the "doctrine of foreign equivalents" under which the descriptiveness of a foreign word is determined according to its English translation. The doctrine applies to words from major foreign languages and to other foreign words used on products marketed to groups familiar with the language from which the word is taken. A word from a little-known or dead language, however, although literally descriptive, will typically be perceived by consumers as fanciful and thus protectable without proof of secondary meaning.

Illustrations:

1. *A*, a manufacturer of audio equipment, displays on its products a designation consisting of the words "Stereo–Fidelity" and a stylized depiction of two stereo speakers connected by lines representing sound waves bounded by a hyperbola. The composite mark is inherently distinctive because taken as a whole it is not merely descriptive of the goods.

2. *A* markets pasta and meats under the designation SAPORITO, which in Italian means "tasty" or "delicious." Because a significant number of prospective purchasers of the goods are likely to perceive the designation as describing the attributes of the products, the designation is descriptive and thus not distinctive absent proof of secondary meaning.

b. Suggestive versus descriptive terms. Terms that are descriptive of the nature, qualities, or other characteristics of the goods, services, or business with which they are used were not historically protected as trademarks at common law even if they had acquired secondary meaning. Relief against the unauthorized use of such designations was available only through an action for "unfair competition" rather than through the less onerous action for "trademark infringement" available for inherently distinctive marks. See § 9, Comment *d.* Registration under federal law also was generally unavailable for descriptive marks prior to the enactment of the Lanham Act. Judicial attempts to expand the common law and statutory protection of trademarks eventually resulted in a distinction between terms that are directly descriptive and terms that instead merely *suggest* some quality or characteristic of the goods, services, or business with which they are used. These "suggestive" marks were not classified as "descriptive" and thus were protected under the same rules applicable to fanciful and arbitrary marks. The distinction retains significance under modern law since unlike descriptive designations, suggestive designations are registrable and protectable without proof of secondary meaning. See § 13, Comment *c.*

The distinction between suggestive and descriptive designations is an aspect of the more general distinction between designations treated as inherently distinctive of source and designations for which actual proof of source significance is required. See § 13. The classification of a designation as either suggestive or descriptive thus depends upon both the likelihood that prospective purchasers will perceive it as an indication of source and the potential effect on competitors of its appropriation as a trademark by a particular seller. Both factors are often evaluated indirectly by considering the degree of imagination required to extract from the designation information concerning the nature, qualities, or other characteristics of the product or business. If the lexicographic meaning of the term is only remotely or subtly related to the product or business with which it is used, consumers are unlikely to view the designation as a mere description, and the designation is also unlikely to be needed by other merchants selling similar products. Thus, COPPERTONE is merely suggestive of a tanning lotion, CYCLONE of wire fencing, WRANGLER of jeans, and GOBBLE GOBBLE of turkey meat. Such suggestive terms are considered to be inherently distinctive. If the term is more directly informative, consumers are more likely to perceive it solely in a descriptive sense and it is also more likely to be useful to other sellers marketing similar goods or services. It is also appropriate to consider the extent to which the same or similar terms have been used by others in connection with comparable goods. If the term has been frequently employed by other sellers, an inference of descriptiveness may be justified.

c. Misdescriptive and deceptive terms. The issue in determining descriptiveness is whether the designation is likely to be perceived as descriptive by prospective purchasers, not whether the perceived description is factually accurate. Thus, a person claiming rights in a descriptive designation cannot avoid the necessity of proving secondary meaning by arguing that the description is inaccurate. "Misdescriptive" designations are therefore subject to the same rules applicable to other descriptive terms. G.I. used on gun-cleaning equipment, for example, is descriptive if the equipment is in fact government issue and misdescriptive if it is not; in neither case is the designation inherently distinctive.

The perceptions of prospective purchasers determine whether a designation that literally misdescribes the goods, services, or business is in fact "misdescriptive." If, for example, the descriptive connotations of the term are clearly inapplicable to the product, purchasers will likely view the designation as arbitrary or suggestive rather than as a description of the goods. This point is emphasized by the terminology in the Lanham Act and the Model State Trademark Bill, which require proof of secondary meaning only when the designation is "deceptively misdescriptive." The designations AUTOMATIC RADIO as a trademark for air conditioners, ICE CREAM for chewing gum, and GEORGE WASHINGTON ATE HERE for a modern restaurant in Indiana, for example, are not misdescriptive because purchasers are unlikely to understand the designations in a descriptive sense. As a general matter, unless a significant number of prospective purchasers are likely to perceive the designation as a description of the goods, service, or business, the designation is not descriptive or misdescriptive.

If the inaccurate information conveyed by a misdescriptive designation is likely to influence the purchasing decisions of a significant number of prospective consumers, the designation is also "deceptive." The distinction between designations that are merely "misdescriptive" ("deceptively misdescriptive" in the statutory terminology) and those that are also "deceptive" thus turns on the materiality of the misrepresentation. Deceptive marks are ineligible for registration under the Lanham Act and the Model State Trademark Bill. Deceptive marks can also be denied protection against infringement at common law under the doctrine of unclean hands as described in § 32. A person using a deceptive mark also may be subject to liability to other sellers for deceptive marketing under the rule stated in § 2. See § 2, Illustration 7.

Illustration:

3. *A* markets a glass and metal cleaner under the designation GLASS WAX. The cleaner contains no wax. If prospective purchasers are likely to understand the designation as indicating that the product contains wax, the designation is misdescriptive and thus not distinctive absent proof of secondary meaning. If the evidence further establishes that the misrepresentation is likely to influence the purchasing decisions of a significant number of prospective purchasers, the designation is also deceptive and relief against infringement may be barred in whole or in part under the rule stated in § 32.

d. Geographic terms. A geographic term is any word or symbol that designates a geographic location. Such terms include the names of countries and their political or territorial subdivisions, the names of portions of the globe such as Europe or the Orient, and the names of geographical features such as lakes, rivers, and mountains. Also included are maps as well as nicknames and abbreviations of geographic locations such as Frisco or USA.

The distinctiveness of geographic designations is determined according to the same principles applicable to other designations. If prospective purchasers are likely to understand a designation as describing the geographic origin of the goods or services, or the location of the business with which it is used, the designation is geographically descriptive. Such designations are not inherently distinctive and are thus protectable only upon proof of distinctiveness under the rule stated in § 13(b).

The rationale for the requirement of secondary meaning for geographically descriptive terms is analogous to that applicable to other descriptive designations. Consumers may perceive the designation only in its geographically descriptive sense rather than as a symbol of source or other association with a particular person. In addition, the recognition of exclusive rights in geographic terms can interfere with the ability of others to emphasize the location or origin of their own products or business. Because the range of terms available to designate a particular location often is limited, the appropriation of geographic designations can have a more substantial impact than the appropriation of other descriptive designations. That a watch is Swiss, that wine is from California, that maple syrup is from Vermont, or that a dress has been designed in New York or Paris are facts in which consumers are interested and which sellers therefore wish to disclose in a prominent manner. While not all locales are of special importance to consumers, merchants should remain free to indicate the location of their place of business or the geographic origin of their goods without unnecessary risk of infringement.

The requirement of secondary meaning is applicable only when the geographic designation is likely to be understood by prospective purchasers as descriptive of the geographic location or origin of the product or business. If the designation is instead perceived as arbitrary or suggestive, consumers are likely to view the term as a symbol of identification. The latter designations are also unlikely to be needed by other sellers seeking to communicate information relating to location or origin. However, it is often difficult to determine whether a particular designation is likely to be perceived by consumers as geographically descriptive. If the locale is known to lack commercial activity or if the designation is so all-inclusive that it does not indicate a specific location, the use will be understood as arbitrary or suggestive. NORTH POLE as a trademark for ice cream or WORLD as a service mark for dry cleaning will not be taken as descriptive and thus will not require proof of secondary meaning. The same is true of designations whose geographic significance is either unknown to prospective purchasers or is subordinate to other meanings of the term. The mark COLUMBIA on books, for example, is unlikely to be understood in its geographic sense. In each case, however, the issue is whether a significant number of prospective purchasers are likely to understand the term as descriptive of geographic origin or location. If the place is noted for the goods on which the term is used, consumers can be expected to view the designation descriptively. Thus, FRANCE on wine and FLORIDA on grapefruit are clearly descriptive. Terms designating locations that are not generally connected with the relevant goods or services, however, may also be taken in a descriptive sense, particularly when the term has no other apparent connotations that would account for its use. While EUROPEAN used as a mark on health clubs may be viewed by prospective purchasers as suggesting sophistication rather than geographic origin, CHICAGO on shirts is more likely to be taken in a geographically descriptive sense. The fact that goods of the type sold under the designation are produced in the named locality is also relevant to the public's likely perception of the term as geographically descriptive. In such instances the potential impact on other sellers further supports a finding of descriptiveness.

If a geographic designation that is perceived by prospective purchasers as descriptive is in fact inaccurate, the designation is geographically misdescriptive. Like other misdescriptive designations, see Comment *c*, such terms have traditionally been protected only upon proof of secondary meaning. See Model State Trademark Bill § 2(e) (1992). Thus, if the designation MANHATTAN when used on cookies is likely to be taken in a descriptive sense by prospective purchasers, the designation is descriptive if the cookies originate in Manhattan and misdescriptive if they do not. In either case, the designation is not protectable as a trademark unless it has acquired secondary meaning as an indication of source. Under a 1993 amendment to the Lanham Act, however, geographically misdescriptive designations are ineligible for registration without regard to the existence of secondary meaning unless the mark had become distinctive of the applicant's goods prior to the effective date of the amendment. See 15 U.S.C.A. § 1052.

If the misrepresentation conveyed by a geographically misdescriptive mark is material, the designation is also deceptive. See Comment *c*. This is particularly likely when the location falsely indicated by the designation is noted for the goods on which the term is used. Thus, if MAID IN PARIS used as a trademark on perfume manufactured in the United States is perceived as geographically descriptive despite its double meaning, the designation is also deceptive. Deceptive marks are ineligible for federal and state registration and they may be denied protection at common law regardless of secondary meaning. See § 32. Their use also may subject the user to liability for deceptive marketing. See § 2.

Geographic terms can also become part of the generic designation of a product or service. Thus, "Swiss" cannot be appropriated as a trademark for cheese nor "Worcestershire" for sauce. See § 15.

On the extent of permissible "fair use" of geographic designations that have acquired secondary meaning, see § 28.

e. Personal names. Personal names, including both first names and surnames, are not considered to be inherently distinctive and are therefore protectable as trademarks or trade names only upon proof of secondary meaning. Thus, the first person who adopts a particular personal name to identify the person's goods, services, or business obtains no rights in the designation unless consumers have in fact come to recognize the name as a symbol that distinguishes the products or business of that person from those of others.

The rationale for requiring proof of secondary meaning for personal names is somewhat analogous to that applicable to descriptive terms. The known multiplicity of similar personal names may make consumers hesitant to assume a common source for products bearing a particular name. The name will therefore not function as a trademark or trade name unless, through use, it has become accepted by prospective purchasers as an indication of source or association with a particular person. Because trademark rights in personal names limit the opportunity for similarly-named persons to exploit their name in business, protection is extended to a prior user only upon proof that the recognition of trademark rights is necessary to prevent the misappropriation of good will and the deception of consumers. Indeed, at early common law, the recognition of an unencumbered right to use one's name in trade effectively precluded the existence of trademark or trade name rights in personal names despite the possibility of confusion. Although it eventually became settled that the doctrine of secondary meaning can operate to create trademark rights in personal names, the interest of others in the good faith use of their own name retains appropriate influence in the formulation of relief. See § 35, Comment *d*.

Proof of secondary meaning is required for protection only if the primary significance of the designation to prospective purchasers is as a personal name. If a term has a common lexicographic meaning, for example, it ordinarily will not be perceived as a personal name unless the manner of use enhances its surname significance. Thus, in most instances the mark KING, although a common surname, will be understood in its ordinary lexicographic sense by consumers. In such cases, unless the mark otherwise describes the goods or services with which it is used, it will be considered an arbitrary or suggestive term eligible for protection as an inherently distinctive designation. Use of the mark KING in connection with titles such as Mr. or Miss, or with a first name or initial, however, will ordinarily render its surname significance predominant.

If a term has no common meaning other than its significance as a recognizable name, such as "James" and "Mary" or "Higgins" and "Reeves," it is likely to be perceived as a personal name and protection will thus depend upon proof of secondary meaning. The rarity of the name can also be relevant to the likely significance of the designation. Designations such as EXXON or KODAK are likely to be seen as fanciful designations even if they are also in rare use as surnames. Other names, however, although rare, are recognizable as such, as with "Seidenberg," for example.

Although the requirement of secondary meaning applies at common law to any personal name, registration under the Lanham Act and the Model State Trademark Bill is available without proof of distinctiveness unless the designation is "primarily merely a surname." See 15 U.S.C.A. § 1052(e); Model State Trademark Bill § 2(e) (1992).

If a mark consists of the name of an historical figure or other noted person and is likely to be recognized as such by prospective purchasers, secondary meaning ordinarily will not be required. Unless consumers are likely to believe that the named person is connected with the goods, services, or business, the use will be understood as arbitrary or suggestive. DA VINCI on jewelry, for example, is an inherently distinctive designation. However, if the use of a well-known name as a trademark falsely suggests to prospective purchasers that a particular person is associated with the product or business, protection for the designation may be denied on the grounds that the mark is deceptive or that its use violates that person's privacy or publicity rights. See § 32, Comments *b* and *c*. The designation will also be unregistrable under state and federal law. See 15 U.S.C.A. § 1052(a), (c); Model State Trademark Bill § 2(b), (d) (1992). Unauthorized use of a personal name recognized as identifying a particular individual may also subject the user to liability to the named person under the rules relating to the right of publicity as stated in §§ 46–49.

On the issues relating to assignments of personal name marks, see § 34, Comment *g*.

Illustration:

4. *A*, a business incorporated under the name "Singleton Packing Corporation," markets processed seafood products to large food-service customers. The labels on its products prominently display the term SINGLETON. As a result of *A*'s use and promotion of the term, prospective purchasers have come to associate seafood products bearing the name SINGLETON with *A*'s business. The designation is distinctive under the rule stated in § 13(b).

f. Pictures and illustrations. The distinctiveness of pictures and illustrations is determined according to the same principles applicable to marks consisting of words. If the picture or illustration has only a fanciful, arbitrary, or suggestive significance in relation to the goods or services, its appropriation will not interfere with the marketing efforts of others selling similar products. Such pictures or illustrations are also likely to be perceived by consumers as indications of source. These designations are thus inherently distinctive. However, if the picture or illustration is descriptive of the nature, uses, or results produced by the goods or services, other sellers have an interest in access to similar depictions and prospective purchasers are more likely to view the designation as merely illustrative of the product. Such designations are not presumed to be distinctive and are protectable only upon proof that they have through use become identified with the goods or services of a particular seller.

Even when a picture or illustration conveys information about the product, its overall appearance may be sufficiently unusual or unique to justify a conclusion of inherent distinctiveness. Thus, although a mere representation of a peanut is not an inherently distinctive designation when used in connection with salted nuts, a "humanized" peanut wearing a monocle, spats, and top hat is likely to be perceived as a trademark. The recognition of exclusive rights in such a depiction does not undermine the ability of other peanut producers to depict their own goods, and the designation will be considered inherently distinctive. The same reasoning applies to any product depiction that, because of its fanciful or stylized nature, is likely to be seen as more than a mere representation of the goods. Similarly, because the distinctiveness of a designation is determined on the basis of the mark as a whole, the combination of a product depiction with additional arbitrary features may result in a composite mark that is inherently distinctive. In each instance the characterization of the designation depends upon its likely effect on prospective purchasers and the potential impact of its appropriation on other sellers of similar products.

A picture or illustration that merely depicts the nature, uses, or results of the goods or services is descriptive. Trademark protection is therefore unavailable absent proof that the material has acquired secondary meaning. If the designation in which trademark rights are claimed consists merely of an accurate depiction of the product without additional distinguishing elements, it may be considered a generic designation of the good and thus ineligible for protection as a trademark under the rule stated in § 15.

REPORTERS' NOTE

This Section combines the rules formerly appearing in Restatement of Torts §§ 720–725 (1938). General discussions of this subject matter can be found in Gilson, Trademark Protection and Practice §§ 2.03–12; McCarthy, Trademarks and Unfair Competition §§ 11.05–19, 13.01–12, 14.01–13.

Comment a. Both the Lanham Act and the Model State Trademark Bill preclude the registration of a designation that is "merely descriptive" unless it has "become distinctive" of the applicant's goods or services. 15 U.S.C.A. § 1052(d), (f); Model Bill § 2(e) (1992). On the rationale for the exclusion of descriptive terms, see, e.g., Estate of P.D. Beckwith, Inc. v. Commissioner of Patents, 252 U.S. 538, 40 S.Ct. 414, 64 L.Ed. 705 (1920), emphasizing both the lack of distinctiveness and the interest in unrestricted access. See also Armstrong Paint & Varnish Works v. Nu–Enamel Corp., 305 U.S. 315, 59 S.Ct. 191, 83 L.Ed. 195 (1938) (protection for a descriptive designation that has acquired secondary meaning). On the standard for descriptiveness, see, e.g., 20th Century Wear, Inc. v. Sanmark–Stardust Inc., 747 F.2d 81, 88 (2d Cir.1984), cert. denied 470 U.S. 1052, 105 S.Ct. 1755, 84 L.Ed.2d 818 (1985) (mark is descriptive if it describes the "qualities, ingredients, effects or other features of the product," the "problem or condition" to be remedied by the product, "the use to which the product or service is put," or "the effect that the product or service" produces, citing Callmann, Unfair Competition, Trademarks and Monopolies § 18.05); Zatarains, Inc. v. Oak Grove Smokehouse, Inc., 698 F.2d 786, 792 (5th Cir.1983) (descriptive "of the qualities, characteristics, effect, purpose, or ingredients of a product or service"). The interpretation of the designation by prospective purchasers in the context of its use in the marketplace is controlling. See, e.g., G. Heileman Brewing Co. v. Anheuser–Busch, Inc., 873 F.2d 985 (7th Cir. 1989); In re Abcor Development Corp., 588 F.2d 811 (C.C.P.A.1978); Educational Development Corp. v. Economy Co., 562 F.2d 26 (10th Cir. 1977).

The examples of descriptive designations appearing in the Comment are taken from W.E. Bassett Co. v. Revlon, Inc., 354 F.2d 868 (2d Cir. 1966) (TRIM on manicuring implements); Car–Freshner Corp. v. Auto Aid Mfg. Corp., 461 F.Supp. 1055 (N.D.N.Y.1978) (CAR–FRESHNER); Vision Center v. Opticks, Inc., 596 F.2d 111 (5th Cir.1979), cert. denied 444 U.S. 1016, 100 S.Ct. 668, 62 L.Ed.2d 646 (1980) (VISION CENTER); In re Keebler Co., 479 F.2d 1405 (C.C.P.A.1973) (RICH 'N CHIPS); Homemakers Home & Health Care Services, Inc. v. Chicago Home for the Friendless, 484 F.2d 625 (7th Cir.1973) (HOMEMAKERS).

Slogans found to be descriptive and thus unprotectable absent proof of secondary meaning include, e.g., Norm Thompson Outfitters, Inc. v. General Motors Corp., 448 F.2d 1293 (9th Cir.1971) (ESCAPE FROM THE ORDINARY for clothing held descriptive and lacking secondary meaning); Roux Laboratories, Inc. v. Clairol, Inc., 427 F.2d 823 (C.C.P.A. 1970) (HAIR COLOR SO NATURAL ONLY HER HAIRDRESSER KNOWS FOR SURE descriptive of hair coloring but secondary meaning established). The example in the Comment is taken from Bristol–Myers Co. v. Approved Pharmaceutical Corp., 149 U.S.P.Q. 896 (N.Y.Sup. Ct.1966) (EXTRA STRENGTH PAIN RELIEVER found to have acquired secondary meaning). Slogans found to be suggestive rather than descriptive include, e.g., In re Marriott Corp., 517 F.2d 1364 (C.C.P.A. 1975) (WE SMILE MORE for hotel services); In re Wilderness Group, Inc., 189 U.S.P.Q. 44 (Tm.Tr.App.Bd. 1975) (LET YOUR HIPS SHOULDER THE LOAD on hiking equipment); In re Lincoln Park Van Lines, 149 U.S.P.Q. 313 (Tm.Tr.App.Bd. 1966) (FROM MAINE'S COOL BREEZE TO THE FLORIDA KEYS for moving services).

Titles used to designate a series of literary or similar works, such as the names of newspapers, periodicals, and television programs, can function as trademarks by identifying works that share a common source. Such titles are eligible for protection and registration under the general rules applicable to other trademarks. If the series title is fanciful, arbitrary, or suggestive with respect to the subject matter of the series, it is inherently distinctive; if the title is descriptive, it is protectable only if it has acquired secondary meaning as an indication of source. Series titles found to be inherently distinctive include, e.g., C.L.A.S.S. Promotions, Inc. v. D.S. Magazines, Inc., 753 F.2d 14 (2d Cir.1985) (CLASS on a magazine); Giannini Controls Corp. v. Litton Precision Products, Inc., 150 U.S.P.Q. 387 (Tm.Tr.App.Bd.1966) (POTPOURRI on employee newsletter). Series titles found descriptive of the contents of the works include, e.g., Walt Disney Co. v. Cable News Network, Inc., 231 U.S.P.Q. 235 (C.D.Cal.1986) (BUSINESS DAY on financial news television programs; secondary meaning found); Eirinberg v. CBS Inc., 521 F.Supp. 450 (N.D.Ill. 1981) (YOUR DOLLAR'S WORTH on radio programs intended for consumers); American Ass'n for the Advancement of Science v. Hearst Corp., 498 F.Supp. 244 (D.D.C.1980) (SCIENCE on a science magazine; secondary meaning found); MacPhail v. Stevens, 41 Colo.App. 99, 586 P.2d 1339 (1978) (DENVER MAGAZINE on a magazine relating to Denver). Titles of individual works such as books, motion pictures, plays, and songs, however, have long been subject to special rules that are only partially consistent with general trademark principles. Such titles have been denied registration under the Lanham Act, apparently on the grounds that they are the generic designations of the works, see In re Cooper, 254 F.2d 611 (C.C.P.A.), cert. denied 358 U.S. 840, 79 S.Ct. 63, 3 L.Ed.2d 75 (1958), although this per se rule appears inconsistent with the statutory acknowledgement that a mark is not generic merely because it is "used as a name of or to identify a unique product or service." 15 U.S.C.A. § 1064(3). See § 15, Comment *c*. At common law, titles of individual works have been treated instead as descriptive and thus protectable upon proof that the public associates the title with the work of a particular, even if anonymous, source. In a departure from traditional principles, however, the requirement of secondary meaning is imposed even when the title is fanciful, arbitrary, or suggestive with respect to the contents of the work. Although this result has been criticized, see, e.g., Callmann, *supra*, § 17.23; McCarthy, *supra*, § 10.02, the cases are virtually unanimous in requiring secondary meaning. See e.g., Twin Peaks Prods., Inc. v. Publications Int'l, Ltd., 996 F.2d 1366 (2d Cir.1993) (noting the special rule applied to titles); Int'l Film Service Co. v. Associated Producers, Inc., 273 Fed. 585, 587 (S.D.N.Y.1921) (L. Hand, J.) ("The plaintiff succeeds as soon as he shows an audience educated to understand that the title means his play."); Jackson v. Universal International Pictures, Inc., 36 Cal.2d 116, 222 P.2d 433 (1950); Gotham Music Service, Inc. v. Denton & Haskins Music Pub. Co., 259 N.Y. 86, 181 N.E. 57 (1932) (Pound, J.) (the "name describes the song" and is unprotected "unless it is identified with the source or origin of production").

For an early application of the rule relating to grade and style designations, see Amoskeag Manufacturing Co. v. Trainer, 101 U.S. (11 Otto) 51, 25 L.Ed. 993 (1880). Even "arbitrary" designations that are used merely to distinguish one of the user's products from another are unprotectable absent proof that they have acquired secondary meaning as an indication of source. See, e.g., J.M. Huber Corp. v. Lowery Wellheads, Inc., 778 F.2d 1467 (10th Cir. 1985) (alphanumeric symbols used to designate product models); Ideal Industries, Inc. v. Gardner Bender, Inc., 612 F.2d 1018 (7th Cir.1979), cert. denied 447 U.S. 924, 100 S.Ct. 3016, 65 L.Ed.2d 1116 (1980) (alphanumeric symbols indicating size). See also C.B. Sports v. Gaechter–Haber & Associates, Inc., 210

U.S.P.Q. 597, 602 (D.Vt.1981) ("the court should not assume that fanciful or arbitrary style names automatically have a secondary meaning"). Cf. Dayton Progress Corp. v. Lane Punch Corp., 917 F.2d 836 (4th Cir. 1990) (secondary meaning found for descriptive product designation codes). Cases applying the rule to names designating shades or colors include, e.g., Clairol Inc. v. Gillette Co., 389 F.2d 264 (2d Cir.1968); Stagelight Cosmetics, Ltd. v. Revlon, Inc., 218 U.S.P.Q. 500 (S.D.N.Y.1982). If an arbitrary term is used both as a model designation and as a trademark, however, the presumption of distinctiveness applies. See, e.g., In re Clairol Inc., 457 F.2d 509 (C.C.P.A. 1972) (SWEDISH CRYSTAL used both as a color designation and trademark); Kiekhaefer Corp. v. Willys–Overland Motors, Inc., 236 F.2d 423 (C.C.P.A.1956) (HURRICANE used both as a model designation and trademark). Compare In re Castleton China, Inc., 151 U.S.P.Q. 744 (Tm.Tr.App.Bd.1966) (name of dinnerware pattern also used as a trademark) and In re Shenango Ceramics, Inc., 151 U.S.P.Q. 746 (Tm.Tr.App. Bd.1966) (same), with In re Oneida Ltd., 135 U.S.P.Q. 164 (Tm.Tr.App. Bd.1962) (pattern names were used only to denote styles).

The distinctiveness of a combination of words depends on the distinctiveness of the composite as a whole. See, e.g., Minnesota Mining and Manufacturing Co. v. Johnson & Johnson, 454 F.2d 1179 (C.C.P.A.1972) (SKIN-VISIBLE not merely descriptive of transparent medical tape); Aluminum Fabricating Co. v. Season–All Window Corp., 259 F.2d 314 (2d Cir.1958) (SEASON–ALL on storm windows not descriptive); W.G. Reardon Laboratories, Inc. v. B. & B. Exterminators, Inc., 71 F.2d 515 (4th Cir.1934) (MOUSE SEED on rodent poison not descriptive); In re Hester Industries, Inc., 230 U.S.P.Q. 797 (Tm.Tr.App. Bd.1986) (THIGHSTIX suggestive and not descriptive of boneless chicken parts). If the composite as a whole is descriptive, the designation is not inherently distinctive. See, e.g., In re Quik–Print Copy Shops, Inc., 616 F.2d 523 (C.C.P.A.1980) (QUIK–PRINT merely descriptive of printing services); General Foods Corp. v. Ralston Purina Co., 220 U.S.P.Q. 990 (Tm.Tr.App.Bd.1984) (ORIGINAL BLEND merely descriptive of cat food); In re Uniroyal, Inc., 215 U.S.P.Q. 716 (Tm.Tr.App. Bd.1982) (STEELGLAS descriptive of steel and glass belted tires). Cf. In re Certified Burglar Alarm Systems, 191 U.S.P.Q. 47 (Tm.Tr.App. Bd.1976) ("Certified" with seal design held merely descriptive of guarantee).

Illustration 1 is based on In re Miller International Co., 312 F.2d 819 (C.C.P.A.1963). See, e.g., Estate of P.D. Beckwith, Inc. v. Commissioner of Patents, 252 U.S. 538, 40 S.Ct. 414, 64 L.Ed. 705 (1920) ("Moistair Heating System" combined with a design held not merely descriptive of heaters); In re Clutter Control Inc., 231 U.S.P.Q. 588 (Tm.Tr.App.Bd.1986) ("Construct–A–Closet" with tube-like rendition of a double "C" distinctive for shelf components). Cf. Judson Dunaway Corp. v. Hygienic Products Co., 178 F.2d 461 (1st Cir.1949), cert. denied 339 U.S. 948, 70 S.Ct. 802, 94 L.Ed. 1362 (1950) (descriptive and arbitrary pictorial elements resulting in an arbitrary composite).

A designation that evokes two connotations, only one of which is descriptive, is less likely to be perceived as a mere description of the goods than is a designation that is solely descriptive. The Lanham Act and the Model State Trademark Bill thus require proof of secondary meaning only when the designation is "merely" descriptive. See, e.g., In re Colonial Stores, Inc., 394 F.2d 549 (C.C.P.A. 1968) (SUGAR & SPICE as a trademark for bakery products is not merely descriptive if it also evokes an association with the nursery rhyme "Sugar and Spice and Everything Nice"). See also Big O Tire Dealers, Inc. v. Goodyear Tire & Rubber Co., 561 F.2d 1365 (10th Cir.1977), cert. dismissed 434 U.S. 1052, 98 S.Ct. 905, 54 L.Ed.2d 805 (1978) (BIG FOOT not merely descriptive of tires in also evoking the image of the Sasquatch monster); Blisscraft v. United Plastics Co., 294 F.2d 694 (2d Cir.1961) (POLY PITCHER on polyethylene pitchers held non-descriptive, noting suggestion to Molly Pitcher). Cf. Minnesota Mining and Manufacturing Co., *supra* (Baldwin, J., concurring) (SKINVISIBLE not merely descriptive of transparent medical tape, noting the word play on "skin" and "invisible").

Misspelling was found insufficient to overcome descriptiveness in Standard Paint Co. v. Trinidad Asphalt Manufacturing Co., 220 U.S. 446, 31 S.Ct. 456, 55 L.Ed. 536 (1911) (RUBEROID on flexible roofing materials). Application of the rule turns on both the distinctiveness of the altered form and the extent to which the remaining visual or aural similarities with the word as correctly spelled create a risk of infringement for others using the original term. Discussions of the rationale appear in, e.g., Armour and Co. v. Organon, Inc., 245 F.2d 495 (C.C.P.A.1957) (CORTROPHIN not descriptive of the drug corticotrophin); Oakland Chemical Co. v. Bookman, 22 F.2d 930 (2d Cir. 1927) (L. Hand, J.) (DIOXOGEN descriptive of hydrogen dioxide); In re State Chemical Manufacturing Co., 225 U.S.P.Q. 687 (Tm.Tr.App.Bd. 1985) (FOM in lettering having the appearance of foam descriptive of a foam rug cleaner). Cases holding corruptions distinctive include, e.g., Armour and Co., *supra* ; Clairol Inc. v. Roux Laboratories, Inc., 442 F.2d 980 (C.C.P.A.1971) (LEKTRONIC on electric shavers); Venetianaire Corp. v. A & P Import Co., 302 F.Supp. 156 (S.D.N.Y.1969), affirmed 429 F.2d 1079 (2d Cir.1970) (HYGIENT on plastic mattress covers). The examples in the Comment are taken from Flexitized, Inc. v. National Flexitized Corp., 335 F.2d 774 (2d Cir.1964), cert. denied 380 U.S. 913, 85 S.Ct. 899, 13 L.Ed.2d 799 (1965) and Steem–Electric Corp. v. Herzfeld–Phillipson Co., 118 F.2d 122 (7th Cir. 1940).

Abbreviations held descriptive include, e.g., FS Services, Inc. v. Custom Farm Services, Inc., 471 F.2d 671 (7th Cir.1972) (FS, recognized as "farm service," descriptive of a farm cooperative); Martell & Co. v. Societe Anonyme De La Benedictine, Etc., 116 F.2d 516 (C.C.P.A.1941) ("B and B" recognized as "Benedictine and brandy"). Abbreviations found distinctive include, e.g., Modern Optics, Inc. v. Univis Lens Co., 234 F.2d 504 (C.C.P.A.1956) (CV on lenses not recognized as denoting "continuous vision"). In Anheuser–Busch Inc. v. Stroh Brewery Co., 750 F.2d 631 (8th Cir.1984), the Eighth Circuit found that LA on beer was distinctive because consumers did not generally recognize the designation as denoting "low alcohol"; the Seventh Circuit in G. Heileman Brewing Co. v. Anheuser–Busch, Inc., 873 F.2d 985, 994 (7th Cir.1989), imposing "a heavy burden on a trademark claimant seeking to show an independent meaning of initials apart from the descriptive words which are their source," found the same designation to be merely descriptive.

On the use of dictionaries as evidence of descriptiveness, see, e.g., Zatarains, Inc. v. Oak Grove Smokehouse, Inc., 698 F.2d 786 (5th Cir. 1983); Telemed Corp. v. Tel–Med, Inc., 588 F.2d 213 (7th Cir.1978). Cf. Blisscraft v. United Plastics Co., 294 F.2d 694 (2d Cir.1961) (noting the absence of a dictionary entry for the descriptive meaning); Stix Products, Inc. v. United Merchants & Mfrs., Inc., 295 F.Supp. 479 (S.D.N.Y.1968) (same). The L'ORIGAN example in the Comment is taken from Le Blume Import Co. v. Coty, 293 Fed. 344 (2d Cir.1923). See Blisscraft of Hollywood, *supra* (no evidence that "prospective purchasers of the article" understood "poly" in POLY PITCHER to mean polyethylene).

The OPTIQUE and SELECTA examples in the Comment are taken from In re Optica International, 196 U.S.P.Q. 775 (Tm.Tr.App.Bd.1977) and In re San Miguel Corp., 229 U.S.P.Q. 617 (Tm.Tr.App.Bd.1986). See, e.g., In re Jacqueline Cochran, Inc., 196 U.S.P.Q. 715 (Tm.Tr.App. Bd.1977) (AIROMATIQUE descriptive of toilet water). The BLANC example is from In re California Growers Winery, Inc., 195 U.S.P.Q. 130 (Tm.Tr.App.Bd.1977). See also In re Champion Int'l Corp., 183 U.S.P.Q. 318 (Tm.Tr.App.Bd.1974) (BLANCO descriptive of plywood color). On the doctrine of foreign equivalents, compare In re Garcia, 175 U.S.P.Q. 732 (Tm.Tr.App.Bd.1972) (MUSICA LATINA descriptive of music distribution services) and In re Bagel Nosh, Inc., 193 U.S.P.Q. 316 (Tm.Tr.App.Bd.1976) (BAGEL NOSH descriptive of sandwiches) with Pizzeria Uno Corp. v. Temple, 747 F.2d 1522 (4th Cir.1984) (PIZZERIA UNO merely suggestive based on the Italian meaning) and In re Sweet Victory, Inc., 228 U.S.P.Q. 959 (Tm.Tr.App.Bd.1986) (finding juxtaposition of the French GLACE (ice) and the English LITE not merely descriptive of ice cream). The doctrine should not generally apply to words from obscure languages. See In re Northern Paper Mills, 64 F.2d 998 (C.C.P.A.1933) (dictum); McKesson & Robbins, Inc. v. Charles H. Phillips Chemical Co., 53 F.2d 1011 (2d Cir.1931) (dictum). On the doctrine as applicable to the issue of infringement, see § 21, Comment *e*. As in other contexts, descriptiveness is determined with reference to the intended purchasers. See, e.g., In re Oriental Daily News, Inc., 230 U.S.P.Q. 637 (Tm.Tr.App.Bd.1986) (Chinese characters translated as "Oriental Daily News" descriptive of a Chinese language newspaper); In re Organon Teknika Corp., 216 U.S.P.Q. 935 (Tm.Tr.App.Bd.1983) (NEPHROSS as equivalent of Greek "nephros" meaning "kidney" likely to be understood by the medical profession as descriptive of a dialyzer).

Illustration 2 is derived from In re Geo. A. Hormel & Co., 227 U.S.P.Q. 813 (Tm.Tr.App.Bd.1985).

Comment b. The limited scope of the Trade–Mark Act of 1905 is illustrated by Judge Learned Hand's decision in Franklin Knitting Mills, Inc. v. Fashionit Sweater Mills, Inc., 297 Fed. 247, 248 (S.D.N.Y.1923), affirmed 4 F.2d 1018 (2d Cir.1925), holding the designation FASHION-KNIT descriptive as applied to neckties and thus outside the protection of the 1905 Act despite the likely presence of secondary meaning. "It is quite impossible to get any rule out of the cases beyond this: That the validity of the mark ends where suggestion ends and description begins."

An early application of the "imagination" test to distinguish suggestive from descriptive designations appears in General Shoe Corp. v. Rosen, 111 F.2d 95 (4th Cir.1940) (FRIENDLY on shoes held suggestive). See, e.g., Security Center, Ltd. v. First National Security Centers, 750 F.2d 1295 (5th Cir.1985) (SECURITY CENTER for storage services held descriptive); Zatarains, Inc. v. Oak Grove Smokehouse, Inc., 698 F.2d 786 (5th Cir.1983) (FISH–FRI on fish batter held descriptive); Stix Products, Inc. v. United Merchants & Mfrs., Inc., 295 F.Supp. 479 (S.D.N.Y. 1968) (CON–TACT on self-adhesive plastic held suggestive). The interest of competitors in access to the term is explicitly considered in, e.g., Paper-Cutter, Inc. v. Fay's Drug Co., 900 F.2d 558 (2d Cir.1990) (PAPERCUTTER on paper ornaments is descriptive, citing Restatement Third, Unfair Competition § 14, Comment *b* (Tent. Draft No. 2 (1990))); Security Center, Ltd., *supra*; Zatarains, Inc., *supra*; Vision Center v. Opticks, Inc., 596 F.2d 111 (5th Cir.1979), cert. denied 444 U.S. 1016, 100 S.Ct. 668, 62 L.Ed.2d 646 (1980) (VISION CENTER held descriptive of optical services); Educational Development Corp. v. Economy Co., 562 F.2d 26 (10th Cir.1977) (CONTINUOUS PROGRESS for educational materials held descriptive); Contemporary Restaurant Concepts, Ltd. v. Las Tapas–Jacksonville, Inc., 753 F.Supp. 1560 (M.D.Fla.1991) (LONG HORN as service mark for restaurant found descriptive); Great Southern Bank v. First Southern Bank, 625 So.2d 463 (Fla.1993) (FIRST SOUTHERN BANK is descriptive). Use of the term by other sellers marketing similar products is evidence that the designation is descriptive rather than suggestive. See, e.g., Investacorp, Inc. v. Arabian Investment Banking Corp., 931 F.2d 1519 (11th Cir.), cert. denied ___ U.S. ___, 112 S.Ct. 639, 116 L.Ed.2d 657 (1991) (INVESTACORP as service mark for financial services is descriptive); Zatarains, Inc., *supra*; Vision Center, *supra*. Cf. A.J. Canfield Co. v. Honickman, 808 F.2d 291 (3d Cir.1986) (CHOCOLATE FUDGE on soda held generic and not suggestive); Great Southern Bank, *supra*. See also Union Nat. Bank v. Union Nat. Bank, 909 F.2d 839 (5th Cir.1990) (listing as relevant to the classification of a designation the dictionary meaning, consumer surveys, the imagination test, the needs of competitors, and use by others). The classification of a designation is a question of fact. E.g., Bristol–Myers Squibb Co. v. McNeil–P.P.C., Inc., 973 F.2d 1033 (2d Cir. 1992); Investacorp, *supra*; Forum Corp. v. Forum, Ltd., 903 F.2d 434 (7th Cir.1990).

The COPPERTONE example is taken from Douglas Laboratories Corp. v. Copper Tan, Inc., 210 F.2d 453 (2d Cir.), cert. denied 347 U.S. 968, 74 S.Ct. 779, 98 L.Ed. 1109 (1954); CYCLONE is taken from Hancock v. American Steel & Wire Co., 203 F.2d 737 (C.C.P.A.1953); WRANGLER is taken from Blue Bell, Inc. v. Ruesman, 335 F.Supp. 236 (N.D.Ga.1971); GOBBLE–GOBBLE is taken from Louis Rich, Inc. v. Horace W. Longacre, Inc., 423 F.Supp. 1327 (E.D.Pa.1976).

Comment c. "Deceptively misdescriptive" marks are registrable under the Lanham Act and the Model

State Trademark Bill only upon proof of secondary meaning. 15 U.S.C.A. § 1052(e), (f); Model State Trademark Bill § 2(e) (1992). "Deceptive" marks are ineligible for registration. 15 U.S.C.A. § 1052(a); Model State Trademark Bill § 2(a) (1992).

The examples appearing in the Comment are taken from In re Ox–Yoke Originals, Inc., 222 U.S.P.Q. 352 (Tm.Tr.App.Bd.1983) (G.I.); In re Automatic Radio Manufacturing Co., 404 F.2d 1391 (C.C.P.A.1969) (AUTOMATIC RADIO); Borden, Inc. v. Topps Chewing Gum, Inc., 173 U.S.P.Q. 447 (Tm.Tr.App.Bd.1972) (ICE CREAM); In re George Washington Ate Here, Inc., 167 U.S.P.Q. 702 (Tm.Tr.App.Bd.1970) (GEORGE WASHINGTON ATE HERE).

Illustration 3 is based on Gold Seal Co. v. Weeks, 129 F.Supp. 928 (D.D.C.1955), affirmed 230 F.2d 832 (D.C.Cir.), cert. denied 352 U.S. 829, 77 S.Ct. 41, 1 L.Ed.2d 50 (1956). On the materiality standard, see, e.g., In re Budge Manufacturing Co., 857 F.2d 773 (Fed.Cir.1988) (LOVEE LAMB on synthetic seat covers held deceptive); In re Shapely, Inc., 231 U.S.P.Q. 72 (Tm.Tr.App.Bd.1986) (SILKEASE on polyester blouses held deceptive). Designations found to be deceptive include, e.g., R. Neumann & Co. v. Overseas Shipments, Inc., 326 F.2d 786 (C.C.P.A.1964) (DURA–HYDE for plastic material with the appearance of leather); American Speech–Language–Hearing Ass'n v. National Hearing Aid Soc., 224 U.S.P.Q. 798 (Tm.Tr.App.Bd. 1984) (CERTIFIED HEARING AID AUDIOLOGIST as collective mark for organization whose members are not audiologists); Evans Products Co. v. Boise Cascade Corp., 218 U.S.P.Q. 160 (Tm.Tr.App.Bd.1983) (CEDAR RIDGE on siding not made of cedar). On the distinction between "deceptively misdescriptive" and "deceptive," see generally Germain, Trademark Registration Under Sections 2(a) and 2(e) of the Lanham Act: The Deception Decision, 44 Fordham L.Rev. 249 (1975); McCarthy, *supra*, § 11.19; Hawes, Trademark Registration Practice §§ 7.05, 8.04.

Comment d. The rationale for limiting exclusive rights in geographically descriptive designations was succinctly stated by the Supreme Court in the "Lackawanna Coal" case: "Their nature is such that they cannot point to the origin (personal origin) or ownership of the articles of trade to which they may be applied. They point only at the place of production, not to the producer, and could they be appropriated exclusively, the appropriation would result in mischievous monopolies." Delaware & Hudson Canal Co. v. Clark, 80 U.S. (13 Wall.) 311, 324, 20 L.Ed. 581 (1872). The classic case recognizing secondary meaning in geographic designations is the decision by Judge Holmes in American Waltham Watch Co. v. United States Watch Co., 173 Mass. 85, 53 N.E. 141 (1899) (WALTHAM as a trademark for watches).

Cases finding geographic designations arbitrary or suggestive include World Carpets, Inc. v. Dick Littrell's New World Carpets, 438 F.2d 482 (5th Cir.1971) (WORLD on carpets); Spice Islands Co. v. Spice Land Products, Inc., 262 F.2d 356 (2d Cir.1959) (SPICE ISLANDS on spices); National Lead Co. v. Wolfe, 223 F.2d 195 (9th Cir.), cert. denied 350 U.S. 883, 76 S.Ct. 135, 100 L.Ed. 778 (1955) (DUTCH and DUTCH BOY on paint); Health Industries, Inc. v. European Health Spas, 489 F.Supp. 860 (D.S.D.1980) (EUROPEAN on health club). See also In re Nantucket, Inc., 677 F.2d 95 (C.C.P.A.1982) (NANTUCKET on shirts, emphasizing that the fact a term has a readily recognizable geographic meaning does not render it geographically descriptive or misdescriptive unless purchasers are likely to believe the goods originate from that locality). If the geographic significance of the designation is unknown to prospective consumers, the use is arbitrary. See, e.g., LaTouraine Coffee Co. v. Lorraine Coffee Co., 157 F.2d 115 (2d Cir.), cert. denied 329 U.S. 771, 67 S.Ct. 189, 91 L.Ed. 663 (1946) (LaTOURAINE not indicative of the ancient French province of Touraine). The rule has been applied even when the goods originate from the named location. See In re Societe Generale Des Eaux Minerales De Vittel, S.A., 824 F.2d 957 (Fed.Cir.1987) (VITTEL on cosmetics not perceived as geographically descriptive although the goods originate in the French town of Vittel).

For illustrations of geographically descriptive designations, see, e.g., Boston Beer Co. L.P. v. Slesar Bros. Brewing Co., 9 F.3d 175 (1st Cir. 1993) (BOSTON BEER COMPANY descriptive and lacking secondary meaning); Bank of Texas v. Commerce Southwest, Inc., 741 F.2d 785 (5th Cir.1984) (same as to BANK OF TEXAS); In re Canada Dry Ginger Ale, Inc., 86 F.2d 830 (C.C.P.A.1936) (map of Canada geographically descriptive); Warwood v. Hubbard, 218 Mont. 438, 709 P.2d 637 (1985) (YELLOWSTONE OUTFITTERS descriptive and lacking secondary meaning); In re Cambridge Digital Systems, 1 U.S.P.Q.2d 1659 (Tm.Tr. App.Bd.1986) (CAMBRIDGE DIGITAL on computers descriptive of origin in Cambridge, Mass.). The CHICAGO example discussed in the Comment is taken from Judge Nies's concurring opinion in *In re Nantucket, supra*, which also emphasizes that descriptiveness is not limited to terms designating locations noted for the goods at issue.

Examples of geographically misdescriptive designations include In re Loew's Theatres, Inc., 769 F.2d 764 (Fed.Cir.1985) (DURANGO misdescriptive of chewing tobacco not produced in Durango, Mexico, pointing out that if the locale is noted for the goods, the misdescription is also likely to be deceptive); In re Jack's Hi–Grade Foods, Inc., 226 U.S.P.Q. 1028 (Tm.Tr.App.Bd.1985) (NEAPOLITAN misdescriptive of sausage made in Florida). The MANHATTAN example discussed in the Comment is based on In re Cookie Kitchen, Inc., 228 U.S.P.Q. 873 (Tm.Tr.App.Bd. 1986), holding the mark geographically misdescriptive. The MAID IN PARIS example is taken from In re Richmond, 131 U.S.P.Q. 441 (Tm.Tr. App.Bd.1961). See In re Jacques Bernier, Inc., 894 F.2d 389 (Fed.Cir. 1990) (RODEO DRIVE on perfume is not geographically misdescriptive since consumers will not think that the goods are actually associated with that location). A 1993 amendment to the Lanham Act precludes registration of geographically misdescriptive designations, with an exemption for marks that had acquired secondary meaning prior to the amendment. See 15 U.S.C.A. § 1052.

On the materiality standard for deceptiveness, see Institut National Des Appellations D'Origine v. Vintners International Co., 958 F.2d 1574 (Fed.Cir.1992); In re House of Windsor, Inc., 221 U.S.P.Q. 53 (Tm.Tr. App.Bd.1983), reconsideration denied 223 U.S.P.Q. 191 (Tm.Tr.App.Bd.

1984) (holding BAHIA on cigars deceptive because Bahia is a Brazilian tobacco-growing state). Misrepresentations of geographic origin are also actionable as false advertising under § 43(a) of the Lanham Act. 15 U.S.C.A. § 1125(a).

Comment e. On the shift from an absolute right to use one's name in business to the recognition of secondary meaning arising from prior use of a personal name by another, compare Howe Scale Co. v. Wyckoff, Seamans & Benedict, 198 U.S. 118, 25 S.Ct. 609, 49 L.Ed. 972 (1905) with L.E. Waterman Co. v. Modern Pen Co., 235 U.S. 88, 35 S.Ct. 91, 59 L.Ed. 142 (1914). See also David B. Findlay, Inc. v. Findlay, 18 N.Y.2d 12, 271 N.Y.S.2d 652, 218 N.E.2d 531, cert. denied 385 U.S. 930, 87 S.Ct. 289, 17 L.Ed.2d 212 (1966).

"Personal names used as trademarks are generally treated as descriptive terms, since a name might be regarded as a convenient description of the fact that the individual was affiliated with the firm." Pirone v. MacMillan, Inc., 894 F.2d 579, 583 (2d Cir.1990).

Illustration 4 is based on Conagra, Inc. v. Singleton, 743 F.2d 1508 (11th Cir.1984). See, e.g., Scott Paper Co. v. Scott's Liquid Gold, Inc., 589 F.2d 1225 (3d Cir.1978) (secondary meaning but no infringement of SCOTT on paper products); Taylor Wine Co. v. Bully Hill Vineyards, Inc., 569 F.2d 731 (2d Cir.1978) (infringement of TAYLOR on wines). The secondary meaning requirement also applies to first names. See, e.g., Perini Corp. v. Perini Construction, Inc., 915 F.2d 121 (4th Cir.1990); Creager v. Russ Togs, Inc., 218 U.S.P.Q. 582 (C.D.Cal. 1982) (no secondary meaning shown for VICTORIA on women's clothing).

On the "primary significance" standard, see In re Rivera Watch Corp., 106 U.S.P.Q. 145 (Comm'r Pat.1955) (RIVERA on watches not primarily merely a surname). The *Rivera* test was applied in In re Kahan & Weisz Jewelry Mfg. Corp., 508 F.2d 831 (C.C.P.A.1975). The KING, HIGGINS and REEVES examples discussed in the Comment are taken from Commissioner Leed's opinion in *Rivera.* On the relevance of the manner of use, see In re Etablissements Darty et Fils, 759 F.2d 15 (Fed.Cir.1985) (use of "Darty et Fils" emphasizes surname significance of DARTY). The SEIDENBERG example is based on In re I. Lewis Cigar Mfg. Co., 205 F.2d 204 (C.C.P.A.1953) (S. SEIDENBERG & CO'S. held primarily merely a surname). The addition of other matter to the surname can produce a composite mark that is inherently distinctive. See In re Hutchinson Technology Inc., 852 F.2d 552 (Fed.Cir.1988).

Cases concluding that a surname combined with initials remains "primarily merely a surname" requiring secondary meaning for registration under the Lanham Act include I. Lewis Cigar Mfg. Co., *supra*; In re Piquet, 5 U.S.P.Q.2d 1367 (Tm.Tr. App.Bd.1987); In re Taverniti, SARL, 225 U.S.P.Q. 1263 (Tm.Tr. App.Bd.1985). The opinion by the Court of Customs and Patent Appeals in *Lewis Cigar* implies that designations consisting of full names also require proof of secondary meaning for registration under the Lanham Act. But see Jack Winter, Inc. v. Langer of California, Inc., 183 U.S.P.Q. 445 (Tm.Tr.App.Bd.1974).

The DA VINCI illustration is based on Lucien Piccard Watch Corp. v. Since 1868 Crescent Corp., 314 F.Supp. 329 (S.D.N.Y.1970). See

Goldstein v. Whelan, 62 Fed. 124 (C.C.N.Y.1894) (NAPOLEON on cigars). Compare In re Pickett Hotel Co., 229 U.S.P.Q. 760 (Tm.Tr.App.Bd. 1986) (PICKETT on a hotel recognized only as a surname and not as an arbitrary use of the Confederate general's name).

On the requirement of written assent for registration of names that identify particular individuals, see Martin v. Carter Hawley Hale Stores, Inc., 206 U.S.P.Q. 931 (Tm.Tr.App. Bd.1979), dismissing an opposition by Neil F. Martin to the registration of NEIL MARTIN for men's shirts because of insufficient evidence that the public would associate the mark with the opposer.

Comment f. The "Mr. Peanut" example is taken from Planters Nut & Chocolate Co. v. Crown Nut Co., 305 F.2d 916 (C.C.P.A.1962). Cases distinguishing fanciful from descriptive representations are collected in In re LRC Products, Ltd., 223 U.S.P.Q. 1250 (Tm.Tr.App.Bd.1984). "The cases wherein registration of this kind of subject matter has been granted involve fanciful characterizations rather than representations of the goods, or where matter has been added to the depiction which renders the subject matter distinctive of source." In re Underwater Connections, Inc., 221 U.S.P.Q. 95, 96 (Tm. Tr.App.Bd.1983) (footnotes omitted) (representation of a scuba tank descriptive of underwater diving services). See also In re American Red Magen David for Israel, 222 U.S.P.Q. 266 (Tm.Tr.App.Bd.1984) (Red Star of David suggestive rather than merely descriptive of fund-raising services for Israeli medical supplies). On the addition of arbitrary features to form a composite representation that is not merely descriptive, see, e.g., Judson Dunaway Corp. v. Hygienic Products Co., 178 F.2d 461 (1st Cir.1949), cert. denied 339 U.S. 948, 70 S.Ct. 802, 94 L.Ed. 1362 (1950) (representation of a woman pouring toilet cleaner into the bowl found not descriptive but not infringed by a similar illustration); Jantzen Knitting Mills v. West Coast Knitting Mills, 46 F.2d 182 (C.C.P.A.1931) (trademark for swimwear consisting of an illustration of a female diver held distinctive). The likely impact of trademark rights on competitors is considered in, e.g., In re DC Comics, Inc., 689 F.2d 1042 (C.C.P.A.1982); In re Curtiss–Wright Corp., 183 U.S.P.Q. 621 (Tm.Tr.App.Bd.1974) ("registration would not prohibit other manufacturers from illustrating" similar products).

Illustrations found descriptive include, e.g., In re Harry N. Abrams, Inc., 223 U.S.P.Q. 832 (Tm.Tr.App. Bd.1984) (illustration of jewelry); In re Frederick Warne & Co., 218 U.S.P.Q. 345 (Tm.Tr.App.Bd.1983) (book cover illustration depicting fictional character); In re Eight Ball, Inc., 217 U.S.P.Q. 1183 (Tm.Tr.App. Bd.1983) (cue stick and ball descriptive of billiard services); In re Int'l Spike, Inc., 196 U.S.P.Q. 447 (Tm.Tr. App.Bd.1977) (illustration of product use).

Several decisions suggest, through analogies to the doctrine prohibiting protection for generic words (see § 15) and the concept of functionality (see § 17), that a mere representation of a product in the form in which it typically appears is ineligible for protection as a trademark. See, e.g., Chun King Sales, Inc. v. Oriental Foods, Inc., 136 F.Supp. 659 (S.D.Cal. 1955), affirmed 244 F.2d 909 (9th Cir. 1957) (pictures of Chinese cooking); Thomas J. Lipton, Inc. v. Borden

Inc., 72 Misc.2d 757, 340 N.Y.S.2d 328 (1972) (photograph of clear glass cup containing instant soup being filled with hot water); In re Frederick Warne, *supra* (dictum); Textron Inc. v. Pilling Chain Co., 175 U.S.P.Q. 621 (Tm.Tr.App.Bd.1972) (illustration of a zipper). Cf. In re DC Comics, *supra* (rejecting the proposition that a depiction of the product can never function as a trademark).

§ 15. Generic Designations

(1) A designation that is understood by prospective purchasers to denominate the general category, type, or class of the goods, services, or business with which it is used is a generic designation. A user cannot acquire rights in a generic designation as a trademark, trade name, collective mark, or certification mark.

(2) If prospective purchasers have come to perceive a trademark, trade name, collective mark, or certification mark primarily as a generic designation for the category, type, or class of the goods, services, or business with which it is used, the designation is no longer eligible for protection as a trademark, trade name, collective mark, or certification mark.

Comment:

a. Rationale. A generic designation is a term that denominates a general type or class of goods, services, or business. Thus, "camera" is a generic designation for a type of good, "computer programming" for a type of service, and "bank" for a type of business. A term that denominates a subcategory of a more general class, such as "light" used with beer or "diet" with cola, is also generic. As in the case of descriptive designations, abbreviations or misspellings that are recognized as shorthand or corrupted forms of generic words retain the character of the original term, and words in foreign languages are generally characterized according to their English translations. See § 14, Comment *a*. Generic designations are not subject to appropriation as trademarks at common law and are ineligible for registration under federal and state trademark registration statutes.

The recognition of trademark rights in generic designations could significantly impede competition in the market for the goods or services denominated by the generic term. Competitors denied access to a term that denominates the goods or services to prospective purchasers would be at a distinct disadvantage in communicating information regarding the nature or characteristics of their product. Consumers would be forced either to expend additional time and money investigating the characteristics of competing goods or to pay a premium price to the seller with trademark rights in the accepted generic term.

The rule stated in this Section prohibits the recognition of exclusive rights in generic designations. See Comment *b.* It also prohibits the continued recognition of rights in formerly distinctive designations that have become generic. See Comment *c.* Thus, use of a generic term will not subject a subsequent user to liability for trademark infringement. However, this Section does not preclude relief under other rules relating to misrepresentations of source or deceptive advertising. See Comment *d.*

b. Existing generic designations. No seller can acquire trademark rights in an existing generic term used in connection with the goods, services, or business that the term denominates. A seller thus cannot remove a generic term from the public domain and cast upon competitors the burden of using an alternative name. Success in achieving an association between a generic term and a particular user will not overcome the prohibition against the recognition of trademark rights. In some instances, for example, the public may come to associate a particular product, and hence the name of that product, with its sole or principal producer. Evidence of such an association does not establish source significance for the term itself and will not support an assertion of trademark rights. In other instances, extensive promotion and commercial success may result in the creation of secondary meaning for a term that formerly had only generic significance. Prospective purchasers may come to understand the term, at least in some contexts, as an indication of source, and for some consumers its generic significance may become subordinate. The existence of such de facto secondary meaning, however, does not result in the acquisition of trademark rights. Although the beneficiary of such secondary meaning may be entitled to relief against misrepresentations of source (see Comment *d*), the public interest in maintaining access to generic terms precludes the recognition of trademark rights. Thus, unless the generic significance of the designation has become virtually obsolete, proof of secondary meaning will not establish trademark rights in a generic term.

Any evidence that is probative of the significance of the designation to prospective purchasers is relevant in determining whether a designation is generic. Prior use of the term in a generic sense by other sellers and generic usage in textbooks, newspapers, and magazines are evidence that the term is generic. Consumer surveys are also relevant. Dictionary definitions may be particularly persuasive evidence that the designation is a generic term ineligible for appropriation as a trademark.

The person asserting trademark rights bears the burden of proving that a term challenged as generic is in fact eligible for protection as a trademark. However, registration on the principal register of the Lanham Act, which is prima facie evidence of the validity of the registered mark, 15 U.S.C.A. §§ 1057(b), 1115(a), has been interpreted to shift the burden of proof to the person challenging the mark as a generic designation.

The rule precluding the recognition of trademark rights in existing generic terms is sometimes applied to new designations that have not previously been used as generic names. To preclude the establishment of trademark rights in terms that are likely to be needed by competitors, designations found to be particularly apt or appropriate means of identifying a new product category are sometimes treated as generic *ab initio*. TURBODIESEL as applied to a new engine design combining a diesel engine and exhaust turbine, and CHOCOLATE FUDGE as used on a new diet soda, for example, have been treated as generic designations despite the lack of prior use as generic names for the relevant goods. Cases characterizing such newly-adopted terms as generic typically rely on dictionary definitions of the component elements of the designation and the relationship between those definitions and the nature and characteristics of the new product category. Use of the term in a generic sense by the person asserting trademark rights will also contribute to a finding of genericness.

Application of the rule precluding protection for generic terms to designations that have not previously been used as a generic name creates in effect a conclusive presumption that the term will become a generic designation for the new product. Although the presumption insures access to the designation by competitors, it precludes the protection of secondary meaning. The presumption is justified only when the interest in access clearly outweighs the potential harm resulting from confusion of source. In this limited context the existence of alternative terms that are equally useful in denominating the new product category may be sufficient to overcome the presumption of inherent genericness. The status of the designation will then be determined by the actual understanding of prospective purchasers. The designation will thus be protectable as a trademark upon proof that the term has become distinctive of the goods or services of the user, although the highly descriptive nature of a designation may justify insistence upon substantial proof of secondary meaning. See § 13, Comment *e*. If the term in fact comes to be perceived as a generic designation by prospective purchasers, any trademark rights acquired by the initial user will no longer be recognized. See Comment *c*.

Illustrations:

1. *A* adopts the designation BUNDT for a cake mix used in the preparation of a "ring cake." Evidence in the form of recipes and newspaper articles establishes prior and continuing use of the term as a generic name for a ring-shaped cake. A survey conducted by *A*, however, shows that a majority of prospective purchasers recognize the designation as indicating that *A* is the source of the cake mix. Because the evidence establishes that the original generic meaning has not become obsolete, *A* cannot acquire trademark rights in the designation. Whether in a particular case *A* is entitled to other relief is determined by the principles discussed in Comment *d*.

2. *A* develops a new method of processing chickens. *A* 's product cooks in less time than conventional chickens. *A* markets its product as FAST FRYER brand quick-cooking chicken. Because of the absence of prior generic usage and the availability of alternative terms to denominate the new product category, a court may conclude that the designation FAST FRYER, although highly descriptive, is not inherently generic. Protection of the designation will then depend upon proof of distinctiveness under the rule stated in § 13. However, if the designation in fact comes to be understood by consumers as a generic name for the new product category, trademark rights will no longer be recognized. See Comment *c*.

c. Loss of distinctiveness. The rule precluding protection for generic terms also applies to designations originally perceived as indications of source or sponsorship but that later come to be understood by prospective purchasers as generic. A designation formerly distinctive of the goods or services of a particular seller may lose its significance as a trademark and become instead the generic name applied to a particular product category regardless of source. This loss of distinctiveness occurs most frequently in connection with trademarks used on new categories of goods initially available only from a single source. A designation adopted as a trademark for such a product may become incorporated into the language as the generic name for the product itself. "Aspirin," for example, although initially a fanciful term applied to the product of a single manufacturer, came instead to be understood by prospective purchasers as the generic name for a type of medicine. The principle is applicable, however, to any trademark ultimately adopted by consumers as a generic term. Other designations found to have lost their distinctiveness as indications of source include "cellophane," "escalator," and "thermos." In addition to the loss of common law rights, a registration under the

Lanham Act is subject to cancellation if the mark becomes a generic term for the goods or services. If a designation used on several different products becomes a generic name for only one of the products, trademark rights are not lost in connection with its use on the remaining products.

The rule in Subsection (1) prohibiting the acquisition of trademark rights in existing generic terms operates against users who have chosen to adopt as a mark a term that may already be generic. The risk created by such a choice is appropriately borne by the user, and evidence of any significant generic usage is sufficient to preclude the recognition of trademark rights. See Comment *b*. Equity and public policy dictate a more cautious approach in the case of a valid trademark that is alleged to have become a generic term. The public interest in access to generic terms will outweigh the residual good will associated with the designation and its value to consumers as an indication of source only if the designation has acquired substantial generic significance. Under the rule stated in Subsection (2), trademark rights are not lost unless the generic meaning becomes the primary or principal significance of the designation to prospective purchasers. The burden of proof may be properly placed on the person alleging such a loss of distinctiveness. Although the difficulties of quantitative measurement and the possibility of multiple meanings often preclude analysis in terms of percentages, if majority usage is established as a fact, it will generally be determinative of the designation's primary significance.

The fact that a trademark is used by consumers as the name of a product does not necessarily establish that the designation has become generic. In the case of products advertised as unique or otherwise distinguishable from competing goods, it is customary to adopt the trademark as the name for the product itself. Thus, a consumer may state that he drives a FORD, drinks COCA–COLA, or washes laundry with TIDE. Use of a designation to denominate only the product of a specific manufacturer, whether known or anonymous, is not a generic use. A designation is used generically only if it is used to denominate a type of good or service irrespective of source.

Consumers who are aware of the trademark significance of a designation may nevertheless use it on occasion in a purely generic sense. A person who understands the designation DICTAPHONE as the trademark of a particular manufacturer, for example, may nevertheless employ it in a generic sense in casual conversation. It is the use and understanding of the term in the context of purchasing decisions, however, that determines the primary significance of a designation.

A designation challenged as generic will often have significance as a trademark to some prospective purchasers and significance as a generic term to other prospective purchasers. The status of the designation as a trademark is determined by the primary or principal significance in the market as a whole. Although surveys can provide important evidence of the significance of a designation to prospective purchasers, the nature of the relevant factual inquiry creates difficult problems of formulation and interpretation. Survey questions focusing on use of the designation as the name of a product, for example, must be sufficiently sophisticated to distinguish use to denominate only the goods of a specific producer from truly generic usage. Questions emphasizing an association between the designation and a single source must permit a distinction between true trademark significance and the mere association of a generic term with a sole or principal producer of that type of product.

The primary significance of a designation also may be established by indirect evidence of the understanding of prospective purchasers. The manner in which the designation has been used by the person claiming trademark rights, for example, is evidence of the likely significance of the designation to consumers. A pattern of use that emphasizes the source significance of the term may support an inference that the designation has not become generic. Use of the designation with accompanying generic terms or with indications of trademark status such as the prescribed notice of federal registration or the notations "TM" or "brand" is thus evidence of continuing distinctiveness. Consistent use of the term by the claimant to denominate the product itself, however, may support an inference that the public perceives the designation as a generic name for the goods, particularly when the product has no other well-known generic name.

The manner in which the term is used by third persons in publications likely to reflect or influence the understanding of the relevant consumers, such as magazine and newspaper articles or technical journals and texts, also is probative of the current status of the designation. Dictionary entries, although relevant, must be discounted to the extent that they reflect the protective efforts of trademark owners rather than the independent judgment of lexicographers. Substantial policing efforts undertaken to preserve distinctiveness such as infringement actions, letters to the media regarding improper use, and educational advertising are themselves some evidence that the designation retains its source significance.

The effect on competition resulting from the continued recognition of trademark rights in the designation is also relevant in determining genericness, particularly if the primary significance of the designation to prospective purchasers is unclear. If alternative generic designations for the product are well-known to consumers, or if the nature of the product permits a simple investigation of its characteristics, the harm to competition from the recognition of trademark rights in the disputed designation may be relatively minor. The risk of confusion and the threatened loss of good will may then justify continued protection. Even when trademark rights persist, however, others remain free to employ the mark in a non-infringing manner such as use in comparative advertising. See § 20, Illustration 3.

Illustration:

3. *A* develops a new toy consisting of a ball containing weights that cause the ball to curve when thrown through the air. *A* markets the product in packages that prominently display the phrase "WHIZ BALL." When *B*, a competing toy manufacturer, begins to market a similar product in boxes bearing the words "whiz ball," *A* commences an action against *B* for trademark infringement. Surveys introduced by *B* establish that a majority of prospective purchasers understand the term "whiz ball" to denominate any curving ball regardless of source. *A* cannot prevent the use of the term by *B*. Whether *A* is entitled to other relief is determined by the principles discussed in Comment *d*.

d. Misrepresentations of source. A designation determined to be generic under the rules stated in this Section is not protectable as a trademark, trade name, collective mark, or certification mark. Subsequent users of such designations are thus not subject to liability for infringement under the rules stated in this Chapter. Use of a generic term in a manner likely to deceive or mislead a significant number of prospective purchasers as to the source of the goods or services, however, may subject the user to liability under the general rule proscribing misrepresentations of source stated in § 4. Subsequent users, although protected in their right to use a generic term, may thus be required to take reasonable precautions to avoid a likelihood of confusion. This principle is frequently invoked in connection with the use of designations no longer protectable as trademarks due to a loss of distinctiveness. Although its primary significance may be generic, a designation may retain significance as a trademark to some prospective purchasers. Use of the designation by a subsequent seller without an accompanying indication of source, or use in a distinctive script identified with another, or use in conjunction with words such as "original" or "genuine," for example, may create a likelihood of deception sufficient to subject the user to liability under the rule stated in § 4. See § 4, Illustration 2.

Relief is also available when a misrepresentation of source arises through the use of a designation that is generic *ab initio*. An existing generic term may not be appropriated as a trademark even if the designation becomes associated with a particular producer. See Comment *b*. The existence of such de facto secondary meaning, however, creates a potential for confusion when the designation is used by others. A subsequent user who fails to take reasonable precautions to prevent confusion may thus be subject to liability under § 4.

REPORTERS' NOTE

This Section treats the subject matter formerly appearing in Restatement of Torts §§ 721, 735 (1938). See generally Gilson, Trademark Protection and Practice § 2.02; McCarthy, Trademarks and Unfair Competition §§ 12.01–18.

Comment a. "A generic term is one that refers to the genus of which the particular product is a species." Park 'N Fly, Inc. v. Dollar Park and Fly, Inc., 469 U.S. 189, 194, 105 S.Ct. 658, 661, 83 L.Ed.2d 582, 587 (1985). The rule precluding trademark protection for generic designations also applies to service marks, see, e.g., Eastern Air Lines, Inc. v. New York Air Lines, Inc., 559 F.Supp. 1270 (S.D.N.Y.1983) (AIR SHUTTLE held generic), certification marks, see Community of Roquefort v. William Faehndrich, Inc., 303 F.2d 494 (2d Cir.1962) (evidence insufficient to prove ROQUEFORT generic for cheese), and trade names, see, e.g., S.S. Kresge Co. v. United Factory Outlet, Inc., 598 F.2d 694 (1st Cir. 1979) (THE MART held generic); Imported Auto Parts Corp. v. R.B. Shaller & Sons, Inc., 258 N.W.2d 797 (Minn.1977) (IMPORTED AUTO PARTS held generic).

On abbreviations of generic terms, compare National Conference of Bar Examiners v. Multistate Legal Studies, Inc., 692 F.2d 478 (7th Cir.1982), cert. denied 464 U.S. 814, 104 S.Ct. 69, 78 L.Ed.2d 83 (1983) (holding both MULTISTATE BAR EXAMINATION and MBE generic), with Anheuser–Busch Inc. v. Stroh Brewery Co., 750 F.2d 631 (8th Cir.1984) (LA not generally recognized as equivalent of "low alcohol" on beer). On misspellings, see, e.g., Miller Brewing Co. v. G. Heileman Brewing Co., 561 F.2d 75 (7th Cir.1977), cert. denied 434 U.S. 1025, 98 S.Ct. 751, 54 L.Ed.2d 772 (1978) (LITE on beer generic as phonetic equivalent of "light"); American Aloe Corp. v. Aloe Creme Laboratories, Inc., 420 F.2d 1248 (7th Cir.), cert. denied 398 U.S. 929, 90 S.Ct. 1820, 26 L.Ed.2d 91 (1970) (ALO on cosmetics generic equivalent of "aloe"). See also Surgicenters of America, Inc. v. Medical Dental Surgeries Co., 601 F.2d 1011 (9th Cir.1979) (SURGICENTER equivalent of "surgical center"); Monarch Licensing, Ltd. v. Ritam Int'l Ltd., 24 U.S.P.Q.2d 1456 (S.D.N.Y.1992) (OOZ treated as the equivalent of ooze, citing Restatement Third, Unfair Competition § 15, Comment *a* (Tent. Draft No. 2 (1990))). Generic terms from foreign languages are also ineligible for protection. See, e.g., Weiss Noodle Co. v. Golden Cracknel & Specialty Co., 290 F.2d 845 (C.C.P.A.1961) (HA–LUSH–KA refused registration as the phonetic equivalent of Hungarian "haluska" meaning noodles). The rule permits the free flow of foreign goods under their customary designations. See In re Le Sorbet, Inc., 228 U.S.P.Q. 27 (Tm.Tr.App.Bd.1985).

The importance of defining the relevant consumer universe in determining genericness is illustrated by Ross–Whitney Corp. v. Smith Kline & French Laboratories, 207 F.2d 190 (9th Cir.1953) (genericness of a designation used on a prescription drug is determined by the understanding of physicians rather than patients). See also, e.g., W.R. Grace & Co. v. Union Carbide Corp., 581 F.Supp. 148 (S.D.N.Y.1983) (relevant consumers of meat packaging bags are meat wholesalers). The distinction between generic and merely descriptive designations is discussed in Henri's Food Products Co. v. Tasty Snacks, Inc., 817 F.2d 1303 (7th Cir.1987), holding TAS–TEE on salad dressing merely descriptive. The economic implications of recognizing trademark rights in generic terms are analyzed in Folsom and Teply, Trademarked Generic Words, 89 Yale L.J. 1323 (1980).

Comment b. Generic terms are not registrable under the Lanham Act—a result supported in some cases by reference to the general requirement that a trademark must distinguish the goods of the applicant, see 15 U.S.C.A. §§ 1052, 1127, and in others by holding that generic terms are descriptive and incapable of acquiring de jure secondary meaning, see 15 U.S.C.A. § 1052(e), (f). Compare San Francisco Arts & Athletics, Inc. v. United States Olympic Committee, 483 U.S. 522, 532 n.7, 107 S.Ct. 2971, 2978 n.7, 97 L.Ed.2d 427, 445 n.7 (1987), with H. Marvin Ginn Corp. v. Int'l Ass'n of Fire Chiefs, Inc., 782 F.2d 987 (Fed.Cir.1986). See In re Northland Aluminum Products, Inc., 777 F.2d 1556 (Fed.Cir. 1985).

Evidence of existing generic use by competitors was relied on in Miller Brewing Co. v. G. Heileman Brewing Co., 561 F.2d 75 (7th Cir.1977), cert. denied 434 U.S. 1025, 98 S.Ct. 751, 54 L.Ed.2d 772 (1978) (LITE beer generic). See S.S. Kresge Co. v. United Factory Outlet, Inc., 598 F.2d 694 (1st Cir.1979) (THE MART held generic, noting prior use in numerous trade names and trademarks). Other types of evidence include, e.g., Loglan Institute, Inc. v. Logical Language Group, Inc., 962 F.2d 1038 (Fed.Cir. 1992) (generic use by the person claiming trademark rights); Liquid Controls Corp. v. Liquid Control Corp., 802 F.2d 934 (7th Cir.1986) (generic use of LIQUID CONTROLS in patent applications); Loctite Corp. v. National Starch & Chemical Corp., 516 F.Supp. 190 (S.D.N.Y.1981) (generic use of SUPER GLUE in newspapers). See also In re Johanna Farms, Inc., 8 U.S.P.Q.2d 1408 (Tm. Tr.App.Bd.1988) (relying on a survey and letters from consumers to overturn a finding of genericness). Cf. Gimix, Inc. v. JS & A Group, Inc., 699 F.2d 901 (7th Cir.1983) and Miller Brewing Co. v. Jos. Schlitz Brewing Co., 605 F.2d 990 (7th Cir.1979), cert. denied 444 U.S. 1102, 100 S.Ct. 1067, 62 L.Ed.2d 787 (1980), both emphasizing the limited utility of surveys to establish an existing generic meaning, distinguishing the loss of distinctiveness cases discussed in Comment *c*. Primary reliance is often placed on dictionary definitions in determining whether a designation is generic *ab initio*. See, e.g., Liquid Controls Corp., *supra*; S.S. Kresge Co., *supra*; Miller Brewing Co. v. G. Heileman Brewing Co., *supra.* See also Gimix, Inc., *supra,* using dictionary definitions to support a finding that AUTO PAGE is not a generic designation for an automatic telephone dialing device. Goods or services may have several generic names, and thus the existence of other generic designations does not preclude a finding of genericness. See, e.g., Loctite Corp., *supra.* On the burden of proof, compare Technical Pub. Co. v. Lebhar–Friedman, Inc., 729 F.2d 1136 (7th Cir.1984) and Reese Pub. Co. v. Hampton Int'l Communications, Inc., 620 F.2d 7 (2d Cir.1980) (burden is on the trademark owner in the case of an unregistered mark), with Liquid Controls Corp., *supra,* and WSM, Inc. v. Hilton, 724 F.2d 1320 (8th Cir.1984) (federal registration shifts the burden of establishing genericness to the subsequent user).

The principle that secondary meaning cannot establish trademark rights in a term that retains its original generic significance has been forcefully reiterated in numerous decisions. "[N]o matter how much money and effort the user of a generic term has poured into promoting the sale of its merchandise and what success it has achieved in securing public identification, it cannot deprive competing manufacturers of the product of the right to call an article by its name." Abercrombie & Fitch Co. v. Hunting World, Inc., 537 F.2d 4, 9 (2d Cir.1976). "[N]o matter what the market situation may have been as to indication of origin or secondary meaning, the common descriptive name of the product cannot become a trademark * * *." Weiss Noodle Co. v. Golden Cracknel & Specialty Co., 290 F.2d 845, 847–48 (C.C.P.A.1961). Accord, A.J. Canfield Co. v. Honickman, 808 F.2d 291, 297 (3d Cir.1986) ("evidence of secondary meaning is not even relevant"); Technical Pub. Co., *supra* ("even when a generic term has developed a secondary meaning it is unprotectable as a trademark"). Other decisions relying on the principle include, e.g., Clipper Cruise Line, Inc. v. Star Clippers, Inc., 952 F.2d 1046 (8th Cir.1992); Blinded Veterans Ass'n v. Blinded American Veterans Foundation, 872 F.2d 1035 (D.C.Cir.1989); In re Northland Aluminum Products, *supra*; WSM, Inc., *supra*; National Conference of Bar Examiners v. Multistate Legal Studies, Inc., 692 F.2d 478 (7th Cir.1982), cert. denied 464 U.S. 814, 104 S.Ct. 69, 78 L.Ed.2d 83 (1983); S.S. Kresge Co. v. United Factory Outlet, Inc., 634 F.2d 1 (1st Cir.1980); Reese Pub. Co. v. Hampton Int'l Communications, Inc., 620 F.2d 7 (2d Cir.1980); Miller Brewing Co. v. Jos. Schlitz Brewing Co., *supra*; CES Pub. Corp. v. St. Regis Publications, Inc., 531 F.2d 11 (2d Cir.1975); J. Kohnstam, Ltd. v. Louis Marx & Co., 280 F.2d 437 (C.C.P.A. 1960); Expoconsul Int'l, Inc. v. A/E Systems, Inc., 755 F.Supp. 1237 (S.D.N.Y.1991) (citing Restatement Third, Unfair Competition § 15, Comment *b* (Tent. Draft No.2 (1990))). Cf. In re Miller Brewing Co., 226 U.S.P.Q. 666 (Tm.Tr.App.Bd. 1985), permitting registration of stylized lettering for the term LITE on beer (with a disclaimer of rights in the word itself) upon proof that the design identifies the applicant's goods. See also In re Johanna Farms, Inc., *supra* (combination of French article with English generic term in LA YOGURT held not generic).

The TURBODIESEL example is taken from Cummins Engine Co. v. Continental Motors Corp., 359 F.2d

892 (C.C.P.A.1966). The CHOCOLATE FUDGE example is taken from the Third Circuit's decision in A.J. Canfield Co. v. Honickman, 808 F.2d 291 (3d Cir.1986). The Seventh Circuit, which had earlier affirmed a preliminary injunction against a competitor's use of the CHOCOLATE FUDGE designation, A.J. Canfield Co. v. Vess Beverages, Inc., 796 F.2d 903 (7th Cir.1986), ultimately held that collateral estoppel precluded relitigation of the Third Circuit's finding of genericness. See 859 F.2d 36 (7th Cir.1988). Other decisions finding designations generic *ab initio* despite the absence of significant prior generic usage include, e.g., Liquid Controls Corp., *supra* (LIQUID CONTROLS for flow meters); National Conference of Bar Examiners, *supra* (MULTISTATE BAR EXAMINATION for bar examination); In re Institutional Investor, Inc., 229 U.S.P.Q. 614 (Tm.Tr.App.Bd.1986) (INTERNATIONAL BANKING INSTITUTE for banking seminars); In re Bausch & Lomb, Inc., 206 U.S.P.Q. 534 (Tm.Tr.App.Bd.1979) (ZOOM TRANSFER SCOPE for tracing instrument). Cases applying the principle to magazine titles include Technical Pub. Co., *supra* (SOFTWARE NEWS generic); Reese Pub. Co., *supra* (VIDEO BUYER'S GUIDE generic); CES Pub. Corp., *supra* (CONSUMER ELECTRONICS MONTHLY generic). Compare H. Marvin Ginn Corp. v. Int'l Ass'n of Fire Chiefs, Inc., 782 F.2d 987 (Fed. Cir.1986) (FIRE CHIEF for magazine on fire fighting held not generic). The lack of alternative generic designations was emphasized in, e.g., A.J. Canfield Co., *supra*, 808 F.2d at 306, and CES Publishing Corp., *supra*.

The principle that a new designation may be inherently generic and thus incapable of functioning as a trademark is not generally applied to designations used in connection with existing products that have other well-established generic names. See, e.g., In re Ideal Industries, Inc., 508 F.2d 1336 (C.C.P.A.1975) (WING–NUT not generic for electrical connectors); Maremont Corp. v. Air Lift Co., 463 F.2d 1114 (C.C.P.A.1972) (LOAD–CARRIER not generic for shock absorbers); Salton Inc. v. Cornwall Corp., 477 F.Supp. 975 (D.N.J.1979) (HOTRAY not generic for a food warmer). The concept of inherent genericness has been the subject of judicial and scholarly criticism. See, e.g., Henri's Food Products Co. v. Tasty Snacks, Inc., 817 F.2d 1303 (7th Cir.1987); In re Seats, Inc., 757 F.2d 274 (Fed.Cir.1985). See also Greenbaum, Ginsburg and Weinberg, A Proposal for Evaluating Genericism After "Anti–Monopoly," 73 Trademark Rep. 101 (1983).

On the increased burden of proving secondary meaning for "highly descriptive" designations, see, e.g., In re Seats, Inc., *supra*; Aloe Creme Laboratories, Inc. v. Milsan, Inc., 423 F.2d 845 (5th Cir.), cert. denied 398 U.S. 928, 90 S.Ct. 1818, 26 L.Ed.2d 90 (1970); American Aloe Corp. v. Aloe Creme Laboratories, Inc., 420 F.2d 1248 (7th Cir.), cert. denied 398 U.S. 929, 90 S.Ct. 1820, 26 L.Ed.2d 91 (1970).

Illustration 1 is taken from In re Northland Aluminum Products, Inc., 777 F.2d 1556 (Fed.Cir.1985). Illustration 2 is based on an example in Greenbaum, et al., *supra*.

Comment c. The "aspirin" example is taken from Bayer Co. v. United Drug Co., 272 Fed. 505 (S.D.N.Y.1921). Judge Learned Hand's formulation of the issue continues to be quoted with approval:

"The single question, as I view it, in all these cases, is merely one of fact: What do the buyers understand by the word for whose use the parties are contending?" *Id.* at 509.

The product monopoly that is present in many of the loss-of-distinctiveness cases typically rests on the existence of a patent, and dicta in several older opinions relate the loss of trademark rights to the expiration of the patent. See, e.g., Singer Mfg. Co. v. June Mfg. Co., 163 U.S. 169, 16 S.Ct. 1002, 41 L.Ed. 118 (1896); Kellogg Co. v. National Biscuit Co., 305 U.S. 111, 59 S.Ct. 109, 83 L.Ed. 73 (1938). A monopoly over production may encourage an association between the trademark of the single producer and the product itself, thus resulting in a loss of distinctiveness. It is the significance of the designation to the public, however, and not the existence or expiration of a patent that determines the status of the designation. There is no rule that a trademark used in connection with a patented product falls into the public domain when the patent expires.

The "cellophane," "escalator," and "thermos" examples are from DuPont Cellophane Co. v. Waxed Products Co., 85 F.2d 75 (2d Cir.), cert. denied 299 U.S. 601, 57 S.Ct. 194, 81 L.Ed. 443 (1936); Haughton Elevator Co. v. Seeberger, 85 U.S.P.Q. 80 (Comm'r Pat.1950); and King–Seeley Thermos Co. v. Aladdin Industries, Inc., 321 F.2d 577 (2d Cir.1963). Cases involving personal name trademarks that later became generic include Murphy Door Bed Co. v. Interior Sleep Systems, Inc., 874 F.2d 95 (2d Cir.1989) ("Murphy" bed); Dresser Industries, Inc. v. Heraeus Engelhard Vacuum, Inc., 395 F.2d 457 (3d Cir.), cert. denied 393 U.S. 934, 89 S.Ct. 293, 21 L.Ed.2d 270 (1968) ("Roots" is a generic designation for one type of pump but not for other products sold under the mark); Ludlow Valve Mfg. Co. v. Pittsburgh Mfg. Co., 166 Fed. 26 (3d Cir.1908) ("Ludlow" is a generic designation for a type of valve).

The Lanham Act provides for the cancellation of a trademark registration at any time if the mark becomes "the generic name for the goods or services, or a portion thereof." 15 U.S.C.A. § 1064(3). The "incontestability" provisions of the statute are also inapplicable to generic designations. 15 U.S.C.A. § 1065.

Cases distinguishing the standard used to determine if a designation is generic *ab initio* from that used to determine a loss of distinctiveness include, e.g., Gimix, Inc. v. JS & A Group, Inc., 699 F.2d 901 (7th Cir. 1983); Miller Brewing Co. v. Jos. Schlitz Brewing Co., 605 F.2d 990 (7th Cir.1979), cert. denied 444 U.S. 1102, 100 S.Ct. 1067, 62 L.Ed.2d 787 (1980); First Nat. Bank & Trust Co. v. First Nationwide Bank, 15 U.S.P.Q.2d 1457 (W.D.Mo.1990); Christian Science Bd. of Directors of First Church of Christ, Scientist v. Evans, 105 N.J. 297, 520 A.2d 1347 (1987). But see Berner Int'l Corp. v. Mars Sales Co., 987 F.2d 975 (3d Cir.1993) (applying the primary significance test). See McCarthy, *supra*, § 12.02[6]. In *Murphy Door Bed Co., supra*, the Second Circuit, distinguishing the generic *ab initio* cases with respect to the burden of proof, held that in a loss of distinctiveness case the burden of proving genericness is on the person challenging the validity of the mark.

The "primary significance" standard is often traced to the Supreme Court's decision in *Kellogg Co., supra*, although the phrase there appears in the context of a discussion of secondary meaning. On the application of the standard, see, e.g., King–Seeley Thermos Co., *supra.* The standard was explicitly incorporated into the Lanham Act, see 15 U.S.C.A. § 1064(3), in response to the Ninth Circuit's emphasis on consumer motivation in Anti–Monopoly, Inc. v. General Mills Fun Group, Inc., 684 F.2d 1316 (9th Cir.1982), cert. denied 459 U.S. 1227, 103 S.Ct. 1234, 75 L.Ed.2d 468 (1983). It has also been applied under § 43(a) of the Lanham Act in cases involving unregistered marks. See A.J. Canfield Co. v. Honickman, 808 F.2d 291 (3d Cir.1986). The standard is often interpreted as a rule of majority usage. See McCarthy, *supra,* § 12.02[3]; Gilson, *supra,* § 2.02[1].

Although the distinction has sometimes been overlooked, even the early case law recognized that use of a trademark by consumers as the name of a product manufactured by a specific source is not a generic use. Judge Learned Hand in *Bayer Co., supra,* said: "So here the question is whether the buyers merely understood that the word 'Aspirin' meant this kind of drug, or whether it meant that and more than that; i.e., that it came from the same single, though, if one please anonymous, source from which they had got it before." 272 Fed. at 509. For a more recent articulation of the principle, see In re DC Comics, Inc., 689 F.2d 1042 (C.C.P.A. 1982) (Nies, J., concurring). The point was reinforced after the decision in *Anti–Monopoly, Inc., supra,* by the addition of language to the Lanham Act stating, "A registered mark shall not be deemed to be the generic name of goods or services solely because such mark is also used as a name of or to identify a unique product or service." 15 U.S.C.A. § 1064(3). See In re Montrachet S.A., 878 F.2d 375 (Fed.Cir.1989).

The DICTAPHONE example discussed in the Comment is taken from Dictaphone Corp. v. Dictamatic Corp., 199 U.S.P.Q. 437 (D.Or.1978). See Folsom and Teply, Surveying "Genericness" in Trademark Litigation, 78 Trademark Rep. 1, 6–8 (1988).

Critiques of survey evidence often proceed through reference to the "Thermos" survey described in American Thermos Products Co. v. Aladdin Industries, Inc., 207 F.Supp. 9 (D.Conn.1962), affirmed 321 F.2d 577 (2d Cir.1963), which inquired into the terms used by consumers to denominate the product, and the "Teflon" survey described in E.I. DuPont de Nemours & Co. v. Yoshida Int'l, Inc., 393 F.Supp. 502 (E.D.N.Y.1975), which probed the association between the designation and a particular source through analogies to well-known trademarks. On the general admissibility of surveys relating to genericness, see the discussion in Nestle Co. v. Chester's Market, Inc., 571 F.Supp. 763 (D.Conn.1983), vacated on settlement 756 F.2d 280 (2d Cir.1985). The difficulties inherent in the formulation and interpretation of surveys and their relationship to the divergent substantive perspectives are illustrated by the analyses offered in Folsom and Teply, Surveying "Genericness" in Trademark Litigation, 78 Trademark Rep. 1 (1988); Swann and Palladino, Surveying "Genericness": A Critique of Folsom and Teply, *id.* at 179; Folsom and Teply, A Reply to Swann and Palladino's Critique of Folsom and Teply's Model Survey, *id.* at 197.

The manner of use by the trademark owner was cited as a factor contributing to the loss of distinctiveness in, e.g., King–Seeley Thermos Co. v. Aladdin Industries, Inc., 321 F.2d 577 (2d Cir.1963) (thermos); DuPont Cellophane Co. v. Waxed Products Co., 85 F.2d 75 (2d Cir.), cert. denied 299 U.S. 601, 57 S.Ct. 194, 81 L.Ed. 443 (1936) (cellophane); Nestle Co., *supra* (toll house cookies). Compare E.I. DuPont de Nemours & Co. v. Yoshida Int'l, *supra* (noting use of accompanying generic designation with TEFLON trademark). On evidence of media usage, see, e.g., Murphy Door Bed Co. v. Interior Sleep Systems, Inc., 874 F.2d 95 (2d Cir. 1989) (generic use of "Murphy bed" in newspapers and magazines); American Thermos Products Co. v. Aladdin Industries, Inc., 207 F.Supp. 9 (D.Conn.1962), affirmed 321 F.2d 577 (2d Cir.1963); DuPont Cellophane Co., *supra*; Nestle Co., *supra*. The influence of the Trademark Usage Committee (formerly the Dictionary Listings Committee) of the International Trademark Association on dictionary entries for words claimed as trademarks is described in Trademarks in Dictionaries, 59 Trademark Rep. 735 (1969).

Evidence of extensive policing efforts was recited in support of a finding in *E.I. DuPont de Nemours & Co.*, *supra*, that TEFLON had not lost its distinctiveness as a trademark. In addition to policing against improper use, trademark owners often take affirmative steps to emphasize the source significance of a designation. Common techniques include accompanying the designation with the word "brand" and a generic designation for the product, as in "SCOTCH brand cellophane tape," and use of the designation on a variety of different goods. See, e.g., King–Seeley Thermos Co., *supra*. Suggested practices are summarized in Gilson, *supra*, § 2.02[7]. The significance of the designation to prospective purchasers, however, remains controlling. "It, therefore, makes no difference what efforts or money the DuPont Company expended in order to persuade the public that 'cellophane' means an article of DuPont manufacture. So far as it did not succeed in actually converting the world to its gospel it can have no relief." DuPont Cellophane Co., *supra*, 85 F.2d at 81.

Comment d. For examples of limitations imposed on the use by others of former trademarks found to have become generic, see, e.g., Singer Mfg. Co. v. Bent, 163 U.S. 205, 16 S.Ct. 1016, 41 L.Ed. 131 (1896); King–Seeley Thermos Co. v. Aladdin Industries, Inc., 321 F.2d 577 (2d Cir. 1963); DuPont Cellophane Co. v. Waxed Products Co., 85 F.2d 75 (2d Cir.), cert. denied 299 U.S. 601, 57 S.Ct. 194, 81 L.Ed. 443 (1936). See also Murphy Door Bed Co. v. Interior Sleep Systems, Inc., 874 F.2d 95 (2d Cir.1989), awarding damages for the deceptive use of a former trademark. If the remaining source significance is confined to a separately identifiable market, trademark rights may be recognized with respect to sales in that market even when the designation has become generic in other markets. See Bayer Co. v. United Drug Co., 272 Fed. 505 (S.D.N.Y.1921) (enjoining a competitor's use of "aspirin" in sales to physicians but holding the designation generic with respect to consumers). On the recognition of trademark rights in a particular configuration of a generic designation, see King–Seeley Thermos Co., *supra*; In re Miller Brewing Co., 226 U.S.P.Q. 666 (Tm.Tr.App.Bd.1985).

Liability for the deceptive use of a designation found to be generic *ab initio* was considered in Kellogg Co. v. National Biscuit Co., 305 U.S. 111, 59 S.Ct. 109, 83 L.Ed. 73 (1938). After finding the term "shredded wheat" generic, the Court recognized an obligation on the part of subsequent users "to use every reasonable means to prevent confusion," although not to the point of refraining from use. See, e.g., Forschner Group, Inc. v. Arrow Trading Co., 30 F.3d 348 (2d Cir.1994) (citing Restatement Third, Unfair Competition § 15, Comment *d* (Tent.Draft No. 2 (1990))). Blinded Veterans Association v. Blinded American Veterans Foundation, 872 F.2d 1035, 1045 n.22 (D.C.Cir.1989) ("generic term with de facto secondary meaning may be protected against passing off, e.g., by requiring fair notice that a newcomer's product or service does not come from the original source"); Imported Auto Parts Corp. v. R.B. Shaller & Sons, Inc., 258 N.W.2d 797 (Minn. 1977) ("doctrine of unfair competition requires that subsequent use of the term be fair"). Cf. Expoconsul Int'l, Inc. v. A/E Systems, Inc., 755 F.Supp. 1237 (S.D.N.Y.1991) (suggesting that certain conduct involving generic terms may constitute a misrepresentation of source). See also WSM, Inc. v. Hilton, 724 F.2d 1320 (8th Cir.1984) (generic designations may be protected against unfair use under § 43(a) of the Lanham Act). Language in other cases indicating that generic terms are not protectable under § 43(a), see, e.g., Miller Brewing Co. v. Falstaff Brewing Corp., 655 F.2d 5 (1st Cir.1981), can be interpreted merely to preclude the recognition of exclusive rights in the term. See Technical Pub. Co. v. Lebhar–Friedman, Inc., 729 F.2d 1136 (7th Cir.1984) (distinguishing protection as a trademark from other remedies under § 43(a)). But cf. Liquid Controls Corp. v. Liquid Control Corp., 802 F.2d 934 (7th Cir.1986) (confusion arising merely from the use of the generic designation is not actionable under § 43(a), distinguishing the loss of distinctiveness cases).

Use of a generic term in a manner that misrepresents the nature or characteristics of the goods or services may be actionable as deceptive marketing under the rule stated in § 2. See Eastern Air Lines, Inc. v. New York Air Lines, Inc., 559 F.Supp. 1270 (S.D.N.Y.1983).

§ 16. Configurations of Packaging and Products: Trade Dress and Product Designs

The design of elements that constitute the appearance or image of goods or services as presented to prospective purchasers, including the design of packaging, labels, containers, displays, decor, or the design of a product, a product feature, or a combination of product features, is eligible for protection as a mark under the rules stated in this Chapter if:

(a) the design is distinctive under the rule stated in § 13; and

(b) the design is not functional under the rule stated in § 17.

Comment:

a. Scope. The freedom to engage in business and to compete for the patronage of prospective purchasers generally includes, in the absence of a patent or copyright, the freedom to copy the goods and marketing methods of others. However, the freedom to copy is qualified by the law of trademarks to the extent necessary to prevent confusion as to the source or sponsorship of goods or services.

The law of trademarks deals primarily with designations consisting of words or other symbols used to indicate the source of goods or services. However, the manner in which the goods or services are presented to prospective purchasers, or the physical features of the product itself, may also serve as an indication of source. Source significance may attach, for example, to the overall appearance of a product or its packaging, or to some specific element or aspect of that appearance. The appearance then functions as a trademark, distinguishing the goods or services of one seller from those of others.

The term "trade dress" is often used to describe the overall appearance or image of goods or services as offered for sale in the marketplace. "Trade dress" traditionally includes the appearance of labels, wrappers, and containers used in packaging a product as well as displays and other materials used in presenting the product to prospective purchasers. The design features of the product itself are also sometimes included within the meaning of "trade dress," although the substantive rules applicable to the protection of product designs differ in some respects from those applicable to packaging and related subject matter. See Comments *b* and *c*.

Although not originally classified as "trademarks," distinctive packaging and product designs were afforded protection through the common law action for "unfair competition." See § 9, Comment *d*. With the abandonment of the distinction between technical "trademarks" and other indicia of source, the protection of distinctive packaging and product designs has been incorporated into the general law of trademarks. A nonfunctional design feature of a product or its packaging that is identified with a particular source is thus protectable as a trademark under the rules stated in this Chapter. Nonfunctional packaging and product features are eligible for registration as trademarks under the Lanham Act, and unregistered features are protectable under § 43(a) of the Act. The recognition of trademark rights in packaging and product features under state law is discussed in Comment *c*.

The scope of the rights recognized in packaging features and product designs protected under the rule in this Section is determined according to the general principles relating to infringement as stated in § 20. Thus, if another seller markets a product incorporating a protected packaging or product feature in a manner that is likely to cause confusion as to the source of the product, the seller is subject to liability for trademark infringement. Similarly, use of the protected feature by another in advertising or samples can subject the user to liability if the use is likely to confuse prospective purchasers as to the source of the product offered for sale. At least with respect to product designs, however, the public interest in access may in some cases influence the choice of appropriate relief by encouraging consideration of alternatives to an injunction against imitation, such as mandatory labeling or other precautionary measures. See § 35, Comment *d*.

b. Distinctiveness. The freedom to copy product and packaging features is limited by the law of trademarks only when the copying is likely to confuse prospective purchasers as to the source or sponsorship of goods or services. The imitation or even complete duplication of another's product or packaging will not create a risk of confusion unless some aspect of the duplicated appearance is identified with a particular source. Thus, unless a feature is distinctive under the rule stated in § 13, it is ineligible for protection as a trademark. A further restriction that prohibits protection for functional features is discussed in Comment *d* and in § 17. Rigorous application of the requirements of distinctiveness and nonfunctionality is necessary in order to avoid undermining the carefully circumscribed statutory regimes for the protection of useful and ornamental designs under federal patent and copyright law.

Many of the cases adjudicating trademark rights in product and packaging designs recite that proof of secondary meaning is a prerequisite for protection. At least with respect to packaging and related features, however, it is now recognized that trade dress can be inherently distinctive. This Section, through reference to the rules stated in § 13, recognizes both inherent and acquired distinctiveness, thus assimilating trade dress within the general rules applicable to other trademarks. If the trade dress used by a particular seller differs in significant respects from that employed by others, consumers may be expected to utilize the trade dress as an indication of source. The wide range of designs available for labels and packaging generally permits the recognition of exclusive rights without significantly hindering competition. Trade dress that is unique and prominent can thus be inherently distinctive. If the trade dress is descriptive (see § 14), or inconspicuous, or not sufficiently different from that used by others to justify a conclusion of inherent distinctiveness, trademark rights will depend upon proof of distinctiveness through evidence of secondary meaning.

This Section is also applicable to the recognition of trademark rights in the distinctive design features of the goods themselves. As a practical matter, however, it is less common for consumers to recognize the design of a product or product feature as an indication of source. Product designs are more likely to be seen merely as utilitarian or ornamental aspects of the goods. In addition, the competitive interest in copying product designs is more substantial than in the case of packaging, containers, labels, and related subject matter. Product designs are therefore not ordinarily considered inherently distinctive and are thus normally protected only upon proof of secondary meaning.

The methods of proving secondary meaning for words and symbols (see § 13, Comment *e*) are also applicable to packaging and product designs. Thus, length and exclusivity of use, sales volume, and promotional efforts that focus on the source significance of the design are relevant, as is direct evidence of consumer recognition through surveys or testimony from prospective purchasers. The source significance, however, must attach to the design feature itself, independent of other trademarks that may accompany the product in the marketplace. Evidence that the packaging or product design was intentionally copied by a competitor can support an inference of secondary meaning if the circumstances indicate an intent to benefit from the good will of the prior user through confusion. An inference of secondary meaning may not be justified, however, if the descriptiveness or other inherent value of the design affords an alternative explanation for the copying. See also § 22.

Illustrations:

1. *A* manufactures ice cream products. One of *A* 's products is a square, chocolate-covered ice cream bar. Each bar is wrapped in pebbled foil with a silver background featuring a white polar bear and a sunburst design outlined in blue. The trademark KLONDIKE appears below the design. The bars are sold in six-packs consisting of a double layer of three bars wrapped in clear plastic. At the time *A* adopted the wrapper design, no other manufacturer used a similar design. A court may properly conclude that *A* 's wrapper design is inherently distinctive and protectable as a trademark apart from *A* 's independent rights in the KLONDIKE trademark.

2. *A* produces wine that it sells in a glass decanter. Although designed by *A*, the appearance of the decanter is not

sufficiently different from that used by other producers to qualify as inherently distinctive. *A* offers no evidence that wine consumers identify the decanter design with wine produced by *A*. Since the decanter design is not distinctive under the rules stated in § 13, the design is not protectable as a trademark.

3. *A* manufactures a liquid drain opener. The product is marketed in a unique and eye-catching container formed in the shape of the pipe trap commonly found below household sinks. A court may properly conclude that the container shape is inherently distinctive.

4. *A*, a manufacturer of prestige automobiles, has for more than 50 years incorporated into its product a square-framed, vertically-louvered front grill. As a result of long use and extensive publicity, the appearance of the grill has come to be identified with automobiles manufactured by *A*. The design of the grill is distinctive under the rules stated in § 13 and it is protectable as a trademark unless it is determined to be functional under the rule stated in § 17.

5. *A* has for many years manufactured steel vacuum bottles. The exterior of the cylindrical bottle is made of stainless steel, with an additional encircling ring of steel at the top and bottom. A steel cup lined with black plastic screws onto the upper portion of the bottle. *A*'s trademark appears on both the bottle and the carton in which it is sold. Although the product has been commercially successful, the appearance of the bottle, apart from the accompanying trademark, is not recognized by consumers as an indication of source. Since the design of the bottle is not distinctive under the rules stated in § 13, the design is not protectable as a trademark.

c. Protection under state law. In the 1964 companion cases of Sears, Roebuck & Co. v. Stiffel Co., 376 U.S. 225, 84 S.Ct. 784, 11 L.Ed.2d 661 (1964) and Compco Corp. v. Day–Brite Lighting, Inc., 376 U.S. 234, 84 S.Ct. 779, 11 L.Ed.2d 669 (1964), the Supreme Court broadly declared that state law could not, consistent with the supremacy clause, forbid the copying of articles that are unprotected by federal patent and copyright law. Although *Sears* could be read to preclude only state law prohibitions against copying per se, the Court in *Compco* adhered to its preemption analysis despite lower court findings of secondary meaning, nonfunctionality, and a likelihood of confusion. Both decisions, however, carefully reaffirmed the validity of state protection for distinctive trade symbols and trade dress, as well as state doctrines requiring labeling and other precautionary measures designed to minimize confusion. Thus, after *Sears* and *Compco*, labels, wrappers, and other packaging elements, presumably including container designs, remained protectable under traditional principles of state unfair competition law, but the recognition of trademark rights in the distinctive design features of the product itself was apparently preempted.

The preemption analysis propounded in *Sears* and *Compco* was not directly applicable to *federal* trademark protection. Decisions under the Lanham Act quickly reaffirmed the continued availability of trademark registration for distinctive product designs. Protection also remained available under federal law even for unregistered product designs through the application of § 43(a) of the Lanham Act.

The Supreme Court's preemption analysis was refined in a series of subsequent decisions beginning with Goldstein v. California, 412 U.S. 546, 93 S.Ct. 2303, 37 L.Ed.2d 163 (1973). In *Goldstein,* the Court held that the preemptive effect of federal patent and copyright law did not extend to subject matter left "unattended" by federal law. Because product features are clearly within the subject matter of federal patent law, however, the decision did not undercut the holdings of *Sears* and *Compco,* which were expressly reaffirmed. In Kewanee Oil Co. v. Bicron Corp., 416 U.S. 470, 94 S.Ct. 1879, 40 L.Ed.2d 315 (1974), an injunction under state law against the unauthorized use of trade secrets was upheld on the rationale that it did not conflict with the federal policy of unrestricted access to material in the public domain upon which *Sears* and *Compco* rested.

Sears and *Compco,* to the extent that they undertook to define the preemptive effect of federal copyright law, were supplemented by the explicit Congressional delineation of preemption in the Copyright Act of 1976. Section 301 of the Act, 17 U.S.C.A. § 301, states an intention to preempt only state laws affording rights "equivalent" to copyright in subject matter within the scope of the Act. Case law indicates that rights against deception and passing off are not equivalent to the exclusive reproduction right embodied in the federal copyright statute.

Perhaps emboldened by the more circumspect view of preemption evident in *Goldstein* and *Kewanee* and the Congressional tolerance of state deceptive trade practice doctrines under § 301 of the Copyright Act, a number of courts persisted in the recognition of state trademark protection for distinctive, nonfunctional product designs. Other courts, however, adhered to the broader preemption analysis in *Sears* and *Compco.*

The preemptive scope of federal patent law was again before the Supreme Court in Bonito Boats, Inc. v. Thunder Craft Boats, Inc., 489 U.S. 141, 109 S.Ct. 971, 103 L.Ed.2d 118 (1989), when *Sears* and *Compco* were invoked against a Florida statute that prohibited the use of a direct molding process to duplicate boat hulls. The Court distinguished both the Florida statute and the Illinois common law held preempted in *Sears* and *Compco* from the limited protection available to distinctive, nonfunctional product designs under traditional principles of unfair competition. The "patent-like" protection afforded under the Florida statute and under Justice O'Connor's interpretation of the Illinois law at issue in *Sears* and *Compco* is preempted by federal patent law. In contrast, the Court noted that the protection available under unfair competition law for nonfunctional product designs that have acquired secondary meaning is "limited to the one context where consumer confusion is likely to result; the design 'idea' itself may be freely exploited in all other contexts." In dictum citing § 43(a) of the Lanham Act, Justice O'Connor concluded that "there are affirmative indications from Congress that both the law of unfair competition and trade secret protection are consistent with the balance struck by the patent laws," and "the application of *Sears* and *Compco* to nonfunctional aspects of a product which have been shown to identify source must take account of competing federal policies in this regard."

The full implications of the Supreme Court's opinion in *Bonito Boats* remain unclear. The Court's distinction between state laws such as the preempted Florida statute that provide rights "similar in scope and operation to the rights accorded a federal patentee" and state laws "limited to protection against copying of nonfunctional aspects of consumer products which have acquired secondary meaning" suggests that the preemptive effect of federal patent law is determined by an equivalency test similar to that adopted by Congress in § 301 of the Copyright Act. The recognition of state trademark rights in distinctive, nonfunctional product features may therefore be permissible notwithstanding the contrary conclusion in *Compco*. Thus, the black-letter rule of this Section is not restricted to the recognition of *federal* trademark rights in product features, but its application to claims arising under *state* law must take account of any further clarification of the preemptive effect of federal copyright and patent law.

d. Functional designs. A packaging or product feature found to be functional under the rule stated in § 17 is ineligible for trademark protection. Secondary meaning does not create exclusive rights in functional designs, and use by others is therefore not actionable under the rules relating to trademark infringement. The copying of functional designs that have acquired secondary meaning, however, may cause a likelihood of confusion among prospective purchasers as to the source of the goods or services. Although the possibility or even certainty of such confusion will not deprive competitors of their right to copy functional designs, the general proscription against misrepresentations of source may require subsequent users of functional but distinctive designs to take reasonable precautions to minimize the risk of confusion. A likelihood of confusion resulting from a failure to take such precautions may thus subject the user to liability under the rule stated in § 4. Whether a particular precaution is required depends upon the circumstances of the case, including the extent of the confusion otherwise likely to occur, the probable effectiveness of the precaution, and the costs of its implementation. In most instances, the prominent appearance of the user's name or trademark will suffice. In others, additional labeling may be required. In cases in which substantial confusion is otherwise likely, the user may be required to adopt its own distinctive packaging or to employ a different arrangement of nonfunctional features to reduce the likelihood of confusion. If the implementation of a particular precaution would significantly hinder competition or effectively preclude the use of the functional feature, however, the precaution is not required.

Illustration:

6. *A*, using a patented machine, manufactures a breakfast cereal consisting of strands of wheat formed into pillow-shaped biscuits. Upon the expiration of the patent, *B* begins to manufacture a similar product. In a suit brought by *A*, the pillow shape is shown to have acquired a secondary meaning indicating to prospective purchasers a product made by *A*. If the pillow shape is determined to be functional under the rule stated in § 17 because, for example, it is significantly less expensive to produce, the shape is not protectable as a trademark and *B* is not subject to liability for trademark infringement. However, if *B* fails to identify itself in a prominent manner as the source of its cereal or otherwise fails to take reasonable precautions to prevent confusion, *B* may be subject to liability to *A* under the rule stated in § 4.

REPORTERS' NOTE

The former treatment of this topic analyzed the protection of distinctive product and packaging features as an independent aspect of the law of unfair competition. See Restatement of Torts §§ 741–743 (1938). This Section, although stating similar substantive principles, subsumes this subject within the general law of trademarks. The Section is thus an elaboration of the subject matter of trademark law described in § 9. For general discussions, see Gilson, Trademark Protection and Practice §§ 2.13–14; McCarthy, Trademarks and Unfair Competition §§ 7.23–33, 8.01–07.

Comment a. On the meaning of "trade dress", see, e.g., Two Pesos,

Inc. v. Taco Cabana, Inc., ___ U.S. ___, ___ n.1, 112 S.Ct. 2753, 2755 n.1, 120 L.Ed.2d 615, 621 n.1 (1992) (trade dress is the total image of a product, citing Restatement Third, Unfair Competition § 16, Comment *a* (Tent. Draft No.2 (1990))); L.A. Gear, Inc. v. Thom McAn Shoe Co., 988 F.2d 1117, 1129 (Fed.Cir.), cert. denied ___ U.S. ___, 114 S.Ct. 291, 126 L.Ed.2d 240 (1993) ("overall combination and arrangement of design elements into the total image by which the product is perceived by the consuming public"); Blau Plumbing, Inc. v. S.O.S. Fix–It, Inc., 781 F.2d 604, 608 (7th Cir.1986) (trade dress "denotes the form in which a producer presents his brand to the market"); Falcon Rice Mill, Inc. v. Community Rice Mill, Inc., 725 F.2d 336, 337 n.1 (5th Cir. 1984) (trade dress "embraces the total image of a given product, including advertising materials and marketing techniques"); John H. Harland Co. v. Clarke Checks, Inc., 711 F.2d 966, 980 (11th Cir.1983) (trade dress includes "features such as size, shape, color or color combinations, texture, graphics, or even particular sales techniques"). Although sales techniques that contribute to the "image" of a product are sometimes protected as trade dress, courts do not permit the monopolization of general marketing schemes. Compare Computer Care v. Service Systems Enterprises, Inc., 982 F.2d 1063 (7th Cir.1992) (sales brochures, letters, and reports are protectable trade dress of a service firm) and Original Appalachian Artworks, Inc. v. Toy Loft, Inc., 684 F.2d 821 (11th Cir.1982) (birth certificate and adoption procedures used by doll maker protected as trade dress), with Woodsmith Pub. Co. v. Meredith Corp., 904 F.2d 1244 (8th Cir.1990) (no protectable interest will be recognized in "the mere style of doing business"); Prufrock Ltd. v. Lasater, 781 F.2d 129 (8th Cir.1986) ("down home country cooking" atmosphere of restaurant not protectable); and Haagen–Dazs, Inc. v. Frusen Gladje Ltd., 493 F.Supp. 73 (S.D.N.Y.1980) (marketing of premium ice cream with Scandinavian flair not protectable). See § 17, Comment *b*. Trade dress typically indicates the source of goods, but it can also function as a mark for services. See, e.g., Two Pesos, *supra* (restaurant decor); Computer Care, *supra* ; Dallas Cowboys Cheerleaders, Inc. v. Pussycat Cinema, Ltd., 604 F.2d 200 (2d Cir. 1979) (appearance of uniforms protected under § 43(a)); Warehouse Restaurant, Inc. v. Customs House Restaurant, Inc., 217 U.S.P.Q. 411 (N.D.Cal.1982) (restaurant decor protected under § 43(a)); In re Eagle Fence Rentals, Inc., 231 U.S.P.Q. 228 (Tm.Tr.App.Bd.1986) (fence design registered as service mark for fence rentals). See also Fuddruckers, Inc. v. Doc's B.R. Others, Inc., 826 F.2d 837 (9th Cir.1987).

Cases analyzing the protection of product designs as "trade dress" include, e.g., Ferrari S.p.A. Esercizio Fabriche Automobili E Corse v. Roberts, 944 F.2d 1235 (6th Cir.1991), cert. denied ___ U.S. ___, 112 S.Ct. 3028, 120 L.Ed.2d 899 (1992); Coach Leatherware Co. v. AnnTaylor, Inc., 933 F.2d 162 (2d Cir.1991); Roulo v. Russ Berrie & Co., 886 F.2d 931 (7th Cir.1989), cert. denied 493 U.S. 1075, 110 S.Ct. 1124, 107 L.Ed.2d 1030 (1990); Hartford House, Ltd. v. Hallmark Cards, Inc., 846 F.2d 1268 (10th Cir.), cert. denied 488 U.S. 908, 109 S.Ct. 260, 102 L.Ed.2d 248 (1988); Brunswick Corp. v. Spinit Reel Co., 832 F.2d 513 (10th Cir.1987); LeSportsac, Inc. v. K Mart Corp., 754

F.2d 71 (2d Cir.1985); John H. Harland Co. v. Clarke Checks, Inc., 711 F.2d 966 (11th Cir.1983); Ideal Toy Corp. v. Plawner Toy Mfg. Corp., 685 F.2d 78 (3d Cir.1982). The designation of product designs as "trade dress" does not alter the applicable substantive rules. See Comments *b* and *c*.

The view of trade dress as a species of trademark is persuasively articulated in *Blau Plumbing, supra.* See also Two Pesos, *supra* ("§ 43(a) provides no basis for distinguishing between trademark and trade dress"); Vaughan Manufacturing Co. v. Brikam International, Inc., 814 F.2d 346 (7th Cir.1987). Other cases simply refer to trade dress as an "unregistered trademark." See, e.g., Hartford House, Ltd., *supra* ; Brunswick Corp., *supra* ; LeSportsac, Inc., *supra* ; Morex S.p.A. v. Design Institute America, Inc., 779 F.2d 799 (2d Cir.1985) (product features as "unregistered trademarks"); Union Manufacturing Co. v. Han Baek Trading Co., 763 F.2d 42 (2d Cir. 1985) (same). See also Aromatique, Inc. v. Gold Seal, Inc., 28 F.3d 863, 868 (8th Cir.1994) ("The difference between trade dress and trademark is no longer of importance in determining whether trade dress is protected by federal law."); Petersen Mfg. Co. v. Central Purchasing, Inc., 740 F.2d 1541 (Fed.Cir.1984) ("a potential trademark may be found in a product shape"). On trade dress considered as a composite trademark, see, e.g., Blau Plumbing, Inc., *supra* ; AmBrit, Inc. v. Kraft, Inc., 812 F.2d 1531 (11th Cir.1986), cert. denied 481 U.S. 1041, 107 S.Ct. 1983, 95 L.Ed.2d 822 (1987); Chevron Chemical Co. v. Voluntary Purchasing Groups, Inc., 659 F.2d 695 (5th Cir.1981), cert. denied 457 U.S. 1126, 102 S.Ct. 2947, 73 L.Ed.2d 1342 (1982).

Packaging designs and other elements of trade dress have been registered as trademarks under the Lanham Act. See, e.g., In re World's Finest Chocolate, Inc., 474 F.2d 1012 (C.C.P.A.1973) (design and shape of candy packaging); In re Swift & Co., 223 F.2d 950 (C.C.P.A.1955) (label design); In re McIlhenny Co., 152 U.S.P.Q. 716 (Tm.Tr.App.Bd.1967) (carton layout). On container shapes, see, e.g., In re Chesebrough–Pond's, Inc., 224 U.S.P.Q. 967 (Tm.Tr.App. Bd.1984) (petroleum jelly jar); In re Haig & Haig, Ltd., 118 U.S.P.Q. 229 (Comm'r Pat.1958) (whisky bottle). See also In re Mogen David Wine Corp., 328 F.2d 925 (C.C.P.A.1964). On the registration of product designs, see, e.g., Kohler Co. v. Moen Inc., 12 F.3d 632 (7th Cir.1993) (faucet design); In re Ovation Instruments, Inc., 201 U.S.P.Q. 116 (Tm.Tr. App.Bd.1978) (guitar shape); In re Jockey Int'l, Inc., 192 U.S.P.Q. 579 (Tm.Tr.App.Bd.1976) (garment features).

If a seller's goods incorporate packaging or product features protected as a trademark, use of the goods by a competitor as a sample or illustration of its own merchandise can constitute infringement. See Accurate Leather & Novelty Co. v. LTD Commodities Inc., 18 U.S.P.Q.2d 1327 (N.D.Ill.1990) (use of a photograph of the distinctive product of another can create confusion of source). Such conduct can also constitute a misrepresentation of the qualities or characteristics of the goods offered for sale. See § 2, Illustration 8.

Comment b. Cases that have recited a requirement of secondary meaning for the protection of product and packaging designs include, e.g.,

Union Manufacturing Co. v. Han Baek Trading Co., 763 F.2d 42 (2d Cir.1985) (§ 43(a)); Vibrant Sales, Inc. v. New Body Boutique, Inc., 652 F.2d 299 (2d Cir.1981), cert. denied 455 U.S. 909, 102 S.Ct. 1257, 71 L.Ed.2d 448 (1982) (same); Tas–T–Nut Co. v. Variety Nut & Date Co., 245 F.2d 3 (6th Cir.1957) (common law); Filter Dynamics International, Inc. v. Astron Battery, Inc., 19 Ill. App.3d 299, 311 N.E.2d 386 (1974) (state Deceptive Trade Practices Act); Mr. Gasket Co. v. Travis, 35 Ohio App.2d 65, 299 N.E.2d 906 (1973) (same). However, in Two Pesos, Inc. v. Taco Cabana, Inc., ___ U.S. ___, 112 S.Ct. 2753, 120 L.Ed.2d 615 (1992), the Supreme Court held that inherently distinctive trade dress was protectable under § 43(a) of the Lanham Act without proof of secondary meaning. Earlier cases indicating that trade dress may sometimes qualify as inherently distinctive include, e.g., Roulo v. Russ Berrie & Co., 886 F.2d 931 (7th Cir.1989), cert. denied 493 U.S. 1075, 110 S.Ct. 1124, 107 L.Ed.2d 1030 (1990); AmBrit, Inc. v. Kraft, Inc., 812 F.2d 1531 (11th Cir.1986), cert. denied 481 U.S. 1041, 107 S.Ct. 1983, 95 L.Ed.2d 822 (1987); Sno–Wizard Manufacturing, Inc. v. Eisemann Products Co., 791 F.2d 423 (5th Cir.1986); M. Kramer Manufacturing Co. v. Andrews, 783 F.2d 421 (4th Cir.1986); Blau Plumbing, Inc. v. S.O.S. Fix–It, Inc., 781 F.2d 604 (7th Cir.1986); Sicilia Di R. Biebow & Co. v. Cox, 732 F.2d 417 (5th Cir.1984); In re Morton–Norwich Products, Inc., 671 F.2d 1332 (C.C.P.A.1982); Chevron Chemical Co. v. Voluntary Purchasing Groups, Inc., 659 F.2d 695 (5th Cir.1981), cert. denied 457 U.S. 1126, 102 S.Ct. 2947, 73 L.Ed.2d 1342 (1982); In re Soccer Sport Supply Co., 507 F.2d 1400 (C.C.P.A.1975).

Cases discussing the protection of trade dress under New York law sometimes state that proof of secondary meaning is unnecessary. Some of these cases limit the exception to instances of deliberate copying and can thus be seen as resting on an inference of secondary meaning. See, e.g., Morex S.p.A. v. Design Institute America, Inc., 779 F.2d 799 (2d Cir.1985); Harlequin Enterprises Ltd. v. Gulf & Western Corp., 644 F.2d 946 (2d Cir.1981). Others involve the application of other doctrines such as passing off actionable under the rule stated in § 4. See Upjohn Co. v. Schwartz, 246 F.2d 254 (2d Cir.1957). See also Norwich Pharmacal Co. v. Sterling Drug, Inc., 271 F.2d 569 (2d Cir.1959), cert. denied 362 U.S. 919, 80 S.Ct. 671, 4 L.Ed.2d 739 (1960). In 20th Century Wear, Inc. v. Sanmark–Stardust, Inc., 815 F.2d 8 (2d Cir.1987), the New York rule was limited to "distinctive" dress. See also Perfect Fit Industries, Inc. v. Acme Quilting Co., 618 F.2d 950 (2d Cir.1980), appeal after remand 646 F.2d 800 (2d Cir.1981) (secondary meaning is not required but noting that the trade dress was "distinctive and memorable"). This interpretation of the exception to the secondary meaning requirement brings the New York rule into essential agreement with the rule recognizing inherent as well as acquired distinctiveness for trade dress. Application of the New York rule to protect product features that are not distinctive may be preempted under the analysis in Bonito Boats, Inc. v. Thunder Craft Boats, Inc., 489 U.S. 141, 109 S.Ct. 971, 103 L.Ed.2d 118 (1989). See PAF S.r.l. v. Lisa Lighting Co., 712 F.Supp. 394, 412 n.19 (S.D.N.Y.1989).

On the distinction between product and packaging designs with respect to the application of the distinctiveness criteria, see Kohler Co. v. Moen Inc., 12 F.3d 632, 641 n.11 (7th Cir. 1993) (product shapes are not inherently distinctive); In re DC Comics, Inc., 689 F.2d 1042 (C.C.P.A.1982) (Nies, J., concurring); Devan Designs Inc. v. Palliser Furniture Corp., 25 U.S.P.Q.2d 1991 (M.D.N.C.1992), affirmed 27 U.S.P.Q.2d 1399 (4th Cir. 1993) (product features are less likely than packaging features to function as indications of source, citing Restatement Third, Unfair Competition § 16, Comment *b* (Tent. Draft No.2 (1990))). See also Sicilia Di R. Biebow & Co. v. Cox, 732 F.2d 417, 426 n.7 (5th Cir.1984); Tas–T–Nut Co. v. Variety Nut & Date Co., 245 F.2d 3, 6 (6th Cir.1957).

Older decisions sometimes required, in addition to proof of distinctiveness, evidence that purchasers were motivated to buy in part by the source of the product. See, e.g., Hygienic Specialties Co. v. H.G. Salzman, Inc., 302 F.2d 614 (2d Cir. 1962); Zippo Manufacturing Co. v. Rogers Imports, Inc., 216 F.Supp. 670 (S.D.N.Y.1963). The motivation requirement can be traced to Learned Hand's articulation of the secondary meaning doctrine in Crescent Tool Co. v. Kilborn & Bishop Co., 247 Fed. 299 (2d Cir.1917). The requirement has not been carried forward in more recent formulations. See, e.g., Warner Bros., Inc. v. Gay Toys, Inc., 724 F.2d 327 (2d Cir.1983). Inquiry into consumer motivation was also expressly repudiated under the Lanham Act in connection with the issue of genericness. See 15 U.S.C.A. §§ 1064(3), 1127.

Decisions discussing the distinctiveness of product and packaging designs typically denote the acquisition of source significance as "secondary meaning," although unlike descriptive words, visual design features generally have no "primary" meaning. Union Manufacturing Co. v. Han Baek Trading Co., 763 F.2d 42, 48 (2d Cir. 1985). See In re Soccer Sport Supply Co., 507 F.2d 1400, 1403 n.3 (C.C.P.A.1975), noting the application to design features of the Lanham Act's codification of secondary meaning in § 2(f), 15 U.S.C.A. § 1052(f). For an illustration of descriptive trade dress, see Blau Plumbing, Inc. v. S.O.S. Fix–It, Inc., 781 F.2d 604 (7th Cir.1986) ("location box" format used in yellow pages advertisement).

On the type of evidence probative of secondary meaning, see, e.g., PAF S.r.l., *supra* (secondary meaning of a lamp design shown by sales success, advertising expenditures, media coverage, consumers surveys, intentional copying, and length and exclusivity of use); Mark Charcoal Co. v. Almarc Manufacturing, Inc., 215 U.S.P.Q. 1076, 1077 (N.D.Ill.1981) ("amount and manner of advertising, volume of sales, length and manner of use, direct consumer testimony and consumer surveys"). On the significance of advertising that emphasizes the design feature for which protection is sought, compare In re Swift & Co., 223 F.2d 950 (C.C.P.A.1955) ("look for" promotion), with Aromatique, Inc. v. Gold Seal, Inc., 28 F.3d 863 (8th Cir.1994) (advertisements did not separate the claimed dress from other identifying marks), and First Brands Corp. v. Fred Meyer, Inc., 809 F.2d 1378 (9th Cir.1987) (trade dress was not emphasized). The use of similar dress by others makes the acquisition of source significance unlikely. See, e.g., T.G.I. Friday's, Inc. v. Int'l Restaurant Group, Inc., 569

F.2d 895 (5th Cir.1978) (common restaurant decor). The use of numerous variations of the design by the person seeking to establish trademark rights also decreases the likelihood of acquiring secondary meaning. In re Schaefer Marine, Inc., 223 U.S.P.Q. 170 (Tm.Tr.App.Bd.1984). The necessity of establishing secondary meaning for the specific design feature claimed as the trademark is emphasized in, e.g., In re Mogen David Wine Corp., 372 F.2d 539 (C.C.P.A. 1967) and In re McIlhenny Co., 278 F.2d 953 (C.C.P.A.1960), both finding that the bottle shapes at issue were not recognized as indications of source independent of the trademarks that appeared on the labels.

Numerous trade dress cases hold that proof of deliberate copying supports an inference of secondary meaning. See, e.g., Osem Food Industries Ltd. v. Sherwood Foods, Inc., 917 F.2d 161 (4th Cir.1990) (intentional copying of trade dress creates a presumption of secondary meaning); M. Kramer Manufacturing Co. v. Andrews, 783 F.2d 421 (4th Cir.1986) (intentional copying establishes a prima facie case of secondary meaning); Harlequin Enterprises Ltd. v. Gulf & Western Corp., 644 F.2d 946 (2d Cir.1981) (copying is significant evidence of secondary meaning); RJR Foods, Inc. v. White Rock Corp., 603 F.2d 1058 (2d Cir. 1979) (copying supports argument for consumer recognition). The case law also recognizes, however, that such evidence is often ambiguous because copying does not necessarily imply an intent to pass off, particularly when the trade dress is descriptive or otherwise useful apart from any alleged source significance. Laureyssens v. Idea Group, Inc., 964 F.2d 131 (2d Cir.1992) (intentional copying supports an inference of secondary meaning if the circumstances show an intent to benefit from the prior user's good will, citing Restatement Third, Unfair Competition § 16, Comment *b* (Tent. Draft No.2 (1990))); Blau Plumbing, Inc. v. S.O.S. Fix–It, Inc., 781 F.2d 604 (7th Cir.1986); see Aromatique, Inc. v. Gold Seal, Inc., 28 F.3d 863 (8th Cir.1994) (conspicuous use of defendant's own mark overcame inference based on copying); Brooks Shoe Manufacturing Co. v. Suave Shoe Corp., 716 F.2d 854 (11th Cir.1983) (copying probative but not conclusive because of other possible motivations).

Illustration 1 is based on AmBrit, Inc. v. Kraft, Inc., 812 F.2d 1531 (11th Cir.1986), cert. denied 481 U.S. 1041, 107 S.Ct. 1983, 95 L.Ed.2d 822 (1987). See Chevron Chemical Co. v. Voluntary Purchasing Groups, Inc., 659 F.2d 695 (5th Cir.1981), cert. denied 457 U.S. 1126, 102 S.Ct. 2947, 73 L.Ed.2d 1342 (1982). Compare Blau Plumbing, *supra* ; In re Soccer Sport Supply Co., 507 F.2d 1400 (C.C.P.A. 1975).

Illustration 2 is based on In re Mogen David Wine Corp., 372 F.2d 539 (C.C.P.A.1967). See First Brands Corp., *supra* (PRESTONE antifreeze container); In re McIlhenny Co., 152 U.S.P.Q. 716 (Tm.Tr.App. Bd.1967) (TABASCO bottle). Compare Source Perrier, S.A. v. Waters of Saratoga Springs, Inc., 217 U.S.P.Q. 617 (S.D.N.Y.1982) (secondary meaning found for the shape of the PERRIER bottle).

Illustration 3 is based on In re Days–Ease Home Products Corp., 197 U.S.P.Q. 566 (Tm.Tr.App.Bd. 1977). "The question of 'inherently distinctive' obviously must be determined in relation to the goods for which registration is sought, the uniqueness of the container's configuration in this field, which would condition the reaction of purchasers to the shape, and what would be the anticipated reaction of the average purchaser to this shape." *Id.* at 568. See Tone Bros., Inc. v. Sysco Corp., 28 F.3d 1192, 1206 (Fed.Cir.1994) ("[T]he focus of the inquiry is whether or not the trade dress is of such a design that a buyer will immediately rely on it to differentiate the product from those of competing manufacturers; if so, it is inherently distinctive."); Paddington Corp. v. Attiki Importers & Distributors, Inc., 996 F.2d 577 (2d Cir.1993) (trade dress of a liquor bottle found inherently distinctive); Sicilia Di R. Biebow & Co. v. Cox, 732 F.2d 417 (5th Cir.1984) (remanding for a determination of inherent distinctiveness of a "tear-shape-on-a-pedestal" container for lemon juice); In re International Playtex Corp., 153 U.S.P.Q. 377 (Tm. Tr.App.Bd.1967) (ice cream cone shape for diaper packaging found inherently distinctive). Compare Turtle Wax, Inc. v. First Brands Corp., 781 F.Supp. 1314 (N.D.Ill.1991) (trade dress of car wax was not inherently distinctive); In re Semel, 189 U.S.P.Q. 285 (Tm.Tr.App.Bd.1975) (rocket-shaped container for fireworks was not inherently distinctive).

Illustration 4 is based on Rolls–Royce Motors Ltd. v. A. & A. Fiberglass, Inc., 428 F.Supp. 689 (N.D.Ga. 1976). See also Rolls–Royce Motors Ltd. v. Custom Cloud Motors, Inc., 190 U.S.P.Q. 80 (S.D.N.Y.1976).

Illustration 5 is based on Union Manufacturing Co. v. Han Baek Trading Co., 763 F.2d 42 (2d Cir. 1985). See, e.g., Vibrant Sales, Inc. v. New Body Boutique, Inc., 652 F.2d 299 (2d Cir.1981), cert. denied 455 U.S. 909, 102 S.Ct. 1257, 71 L.Ed.2d 448 (1982); West Point Manufacturing Co. v. Detroit Stamping Co., 222 F.2d 581 (6th Cir.), cert. denied 350 U.S. 840, 76 S.Ct. 80, 100 L.Ed. 749 (1955). Compare, e.g., Vaughan Manufacturing Co. v. Brikam International, Inc., 814 F.2d 346 (7th Cir. 1987); LeSportsac, Inc. v. K Mart Corp., 754 F.2d 71 (2d Cir.1985); John H. Harland Co. v. Clarke Checks, Inc., 711 F.2d 966 (11th Cir. 1983).

Comment c. The breadth of the Supreme Court's opinions in *Sears* and *Compco* is evident from Justice Black's summation in *Compco*, 376 U.S. at 238, 84 S.Ct. at 782:

> That an article copied from an unpatented article could be made in some other way, that the design is "nonfunctional" and not essential to the use of either article, that the configuration of the article copied may have a "secondary meaning" which identifies the maker to the trade, or that there may be "confusion" among purchasers as to which article is which or as to who is the maker, may be relevant evidence in applying a State's law requiring such precautions as labeling; however, and regardless of the copier's motives, neither these facts nor any others can furnish a basis for imposing liability for or prohibiting the actual acts of copying and selling.

Although both decisions made reference to Patent and Copyright Clause of the United States Constitution empowering Congress to enact patent and copyright legislation, Art. I, § 8, cl. 8, the Supreme Court later held that the federal power to protect "Writings and Discoveries" is not exclusive and that the *Sears* and *Comp-*

co decisions rest solely on the Supremacy Clause. Goldstein v. California, 412 U.S. 546, 93 S.Ct. 2303, 37 L.Ed.2d 163 (1973); Kewanee Oil Co. v. Bicron Corp., 416 U.S. 470, 94 S.Ct. 1879, 40 L.Ed.2d 315 (1974). See also Aronson v. Quick Point Pencil Co., 440 U.S. 257, 99 S.Ct. 1096, 59 L.Ed.2d 296 (1979).

Twenty-five years later the Supreme Court proffered a different view of the preemptive scope of federal patent law in its unanimous opinion in *Bonito Boats,* 489 U.S. at 166:

> Both the law of unfair competition and state trade secret law have co-existed harmoniously with federal patent protection for almost 200 years, and Congress has given no indication that their operation is inconsistent with the operation of the federal patent laws.

On the continued registrability of product designs under the Lanham Act following *Sears* and *Compco,* see, e.g., Kohler Co. v. Moen Inc., 12 F.3d 632 (7th Cir.1993); In re Teledyne Industries, Inc., 696 F.2d 968 (Fed. Cir.1982); In re Honeywell, Inc., 497 F.2d 1344 (C.C.P.A.), cert. denied 419 U.S. 1080, 95 S.Ct. 669, 42 L.Ed.2d 674 (1974); In re Mogen David Wine Corp., 372 F.2d 539 (C.C.P.A.1967) (Smith, J., concurring). In addition, § 43(a) of the Lanham Act remained available to protect unregistered product designs. See, e.g., Ferrari S.p.A. Esercizio Fabriche Automobili E Corse v. Roberts, 944 F.2d 1235 (6th Cir.1991), cert. denied ___ U.S. ___, 112 S.Ct. 3028, 120 L.Ed.2d 899 (1992) (availability of design patent does not preclude a § 43(a) claim); Keene Corp. v. Paraflex Industries, Inc., 653 F.2d 822 (3d Cir.1981); SK & F, Co. v. Premo Pharmaceutical Laboratories, Inc., 625 F.2d 1055 (3d Cir.1980); Inwood Laboratories, Inc. v. Ives Laboratories, Inc., 456 U.S. 844, 863, 102 S.Ct. 2182, 2193, 72 L.Ed.2d 606, 621 (1982) ("The use of a product or package design that is so similar to that of another producer that it is likely to confuse purchasers as to the product's source may constitute 'false designation of origin' within the meaning of the Act." (White, J., concurring)); Truck Equipment Service Co. v. Fruehauf Corp., 536 F.2d 1210 (8th Cir.), cert. denied 429 U.S. 861, 97 S.Ct. 164, 50 L.Ed.2d 139 (1976).

Cases holding that protection against confusion and passing off is not "equivalent" to copyright and therefore not preempted under § 301 of the Copyright Act include, e.g., Donald Frederick Evans and Associates, Inc. v. Continental Homes, Inc., 785 F.2d 897 (11th Cir.1986); Warner Bros. Inc. v. American Broadcasting Cos., 720 F.2d 231 (2d Cir.1983); John H. Harland Co. v. Clarke Checks, Inc., 207 U.S.P.Q. 664 (N.D.Ga.1980), affirmed 711 F.2d 966 (11th Cir.1983).

The decisions recognizing the continued viability of state protection for distinctive product designs after *Sears* and *Compco* rely on a variety of rationales. Most decisions emphasize the distinctions between patent and trademark rights in order to demonstrate the basic consistency of state and federal policy, thus effectively rearguing the preemption issue on the merits. See, e.g., Truck Equipment Service Co., *supra* (dictum in action under § 43(a)); Black & Decker, Inc. v. North American Philips Corp., 632 F.Supp. 185 (D.Conn.1986); Vermont Castings, Inc. v. Evans Products Co., 215 U.S.P.Q. 758 (D.Vt.1981); Rolls–Royce Motors Ltd. v. A. & A. Fiberglass, Inc., 428 F.Supp. 689 (N.D.Ga.

1976); Time Mechanisms, Inc. v. Qonaar Corp., 422 F.Supp. 905 (D.N.J.1976). See also 20th Century Wear, Inc. v. Sanmark–Stardust Inc., 747 F.2d 81 (2d Cir.1984), cert. denied 470 U.S. 1052, 105 S.Ct. 1755, 84 L.Ed.2d 818 (1985) (packaging); Dallas Cowboys Cheerleaders, Inc. v. Pussycat Cinema, Ltd., 604 F.2d 200 (2d Cir.1979) (cheerleaders' uniform); Duo–Tint Bulb & Battery Co. v. Moline Supply Co., 46 Ill.App.3d 145, 4 Ill.Dec. 685, 360 N.E.2d 798 (1977) (container). Cf. Kohler Co., *supra* (distinguishing patent and trademark rights to justify federal trademark registration of product configurations); In re Honeywell, Inc., 497 F.2d 1344 (C.C.P.A.), cert. denied 419 U.S. 1080, 95 S.Ct. 669, 42 L.Ed.2d 674 (1974) (same); In re Mogen David Wine Corp., 372 F.2d 539 (C.C.P.A.1967) (Smith, J., concurring) (same). This is the also the premise adopted by the Supreme Court in its subsequent dictum in Bonito Boats, Inc. v. Thunder Craft Boats, Inc., 489 U.S. 141, 109 S.Ct. 971, 103 L.Ed.2d 118 (1989). Other decisions rely on the Supreme Court's opinions in *Goldstein* and *Kewanee*. See SK & F, Co. v. Premo Pharmaceutical Laboratories, Inc., 625 F.2d 1055 (3d Cir. 1980); Howw Mfg., Inc. v. Formac, Inc., 213 U.S.P.Q. 793 (N.D.Ill.1981). Still others rely on the Court's references in *Sears* to state protection for "trademarks" and "distinctive dress." See, e.g., Brunswick Corp. v. Spinit Reel Co., 832 F.2d 513 (10th Cir. 1987); Ideal Toy Corp. v. Plawner Toy Mfg. Corp., 685 F.2d 78 (3d Cir. 1982).

While many decisions accorded only marginal deference to *Sears* and *Compco*, others adhered to the full implications of Justice Black's opinions. See, e.g., Litton Systems, Inc. v. Whirlpool Corp., 728 F.2d 1423 (Fed.Cir.1984); North Shore Laboratories Corp. v. Cohen, 721 F.2d 514 (5th Cir.1983); Tveter v. AB Turn–O–Matic, 633 F.2d 831 (9th Cir.1980), cert. denied 451 U.S. 911, 101 S.Ct. 1983, 68 L.Ed.2d 300 (1981); Classic Instruments, Inc. v. VDO–Argo Instruments, Inc., 73 Or.App. 732, 700 P.2d 677 (1985); Kaibab Shop v. Desert Son, Inc., 135 Ariz. 487, 662 P.2d 452 (App.1982). The *Litton* decision was questioned in Cable Electric Products, Inc. v. Genmark, Inc., 770 F.2d 1015 (Fed.Cir.1985), which held that preemption issues in the Federal Circuit should be determined under the law of the originating circuit. But cf. Gemveto Jewelry Co. v. Jeff Cooper Inc., 800 F.2d 256 (Fed.Cir. 1986) (adhering to *Sears* and *Compco* without reference to Second Circuit precedents).

Comment d. The duty to take reasonable precautions against confusion in connection with the use of functional designs is retained from the former statement of the rule in Restatement of Torts § 741. The duty is similar to that imposed on subsequent users of generic designations that have acquired or retain de facto secondary meaning. See § 15, Comment *d.* The duty has been recognized under § 43(a) of the Lanham Act, see, e.g., American Greetings Corp. v. Dan–Dee Imports, Inc., 807 F.2d 1136 (3d Cir.1986); Keene Corp. v. Paraflex Industries, Inc., 653 F.2d 822 (3d Cir.1981), and under the common law of unfair competition. See, e.g., Kellogg Co. v. National Biscuit Co., 305 U.S. 111, 59 S.Ct. 109, 83 L.Ed. 73 (1938); General Radio Co. v. Superior Electric Co., 321 F.2d 857 (3d Cir.1963), cert. denied 376 U.S. 938, 84 S.Ct. 793, 11 L.Ed.2d 659 (1964); Modern Aids, Inc. v. R.H.

Macy & Co., 264 F.2d 93 (2d Cir. 1959); Sylvania Electric Products, Inc. v. Dura Electric Lamp Co., 247 F.2d 730 (3d Cir.1957); Zippo Mfg. Co. v. Rogers Imports, Inc., 216 F.Supp. 670 (S.D.N.Y.1963); Kaibab Shop v. Desert Son, Inc., 135 Ariz. 487, 662 P.2d 452 (App.1982); Pocket Books, Inc. v. Meyers, 292 N.Y. 58, 54 N.E.2d 6 (1944). See also Duo–Tint Bulb & Battery Co. v. Moline Supply Co., 46 Ill.App.3d 145, 4 Ill.Dec. 685, 360 N.E.2d 798 (1977) (Uniform Deceptive Trade Practices Act). Cf. § 8, Illustration 5 (precautions relevant to contributory liability). The duty extends only to precautions that are reasonable under the circumstances and does not require steps that would interfere with the user's underlying right to copy the functional design. See, e.g., American Greetings Corp., *supra* ; Vaughan Novelty Mfg. Co. v. G.G. Greene Mfg. Corp., 202 F.2d 172 (3d Cir.), cert. denied 346 U.S. 820, 74 S.Ct. 34, 98 L.Ed. 346 (1953); Shredded Wheat Co. v. Humphrey Cornell Co., 250 Fed. 960 (2d Cir.1918) (L. Hand, J.).

A likelihood of confusion resulting from similarities in product or packaging designs can sometimes be overcome through labeling. Thus, the prominent appearance of the subsequent user's name or trademark may in some cases be sufficient to avoid liability. See, e.g., Fisher Stoves, Inc. v. All Nighter Stove Works, Inc., 626 F.2d 193 (1st Cir.1980); Vaughan Novelty Mfg. Co., *supra* ; J.C. Penney Co. v. H.D. Lee Mercantile Co., 120 F.2d 949 (8th Cir.1941); Duo–Tint Bulb & Battery Co., *supra* ; Pocket Books, Inc., *supra*. In some cases disclaimers may be necessary. See Keene Corp., *supra* ; Zippo Mfg. Co., *supra*. In others, changes in packaging or other nonfunctional features may be required. See American Greetings Corp., *supra*.

Illustration 6 is taken from the facts in Kellogg Co. v. National Biscuit Co., 305 U.S. 111, 59 S.Ct. 109, 83 L.Ed. 73 (1938). See also § 4, Illustration 2.

§ 17. Functional Designs

A design is "functional" for purposes of the rule stated in § 16 if the design affords benefits in the manufacturing, marketing, or use of the goods or services with which the design is used, apart from any benefits attributable to the design's significance as an indication of source, that are important to effective competition by others and that are not practically available through the use of alternative designs.

Comment:

a. Exclusion from trademark protection. The freedom to copy goods and services that have proven successful in the marketplace is fundamental to the operation of a competitive economy. When the public interest in permitting copying is outweighed by the need to insure adequate incentive for investments in innovation, the freedom to copy may be temporarily interrupted by a federal patent or copyright. In other instances the public interest in copying may conflict with the interest in preventing confusion as to the source or sponsorship of goods and services. The rule excluding functional designs from the subject matter of trademark law is an attempt to identify situations in which the public and private interest in avoiding confusion is outweighed by the anticompetitive consequences of trademark protection. Thus, in determining whether a particular design is "functional" and therefore ineligible for protection as a trademark, the ultimate inquiry is whether a prohibition against copying will significantly hinder competition by others.

If a design is functional under the rule stated in this Section, it is ineligible for protection regardless of its inherent or acquired distinctiveness. Competitors thus remain free, in the absence of a patent or copyright, to copy functional designs regardless of any association with a particular source. The public interest in avoiding confusion must then be pursued through requirements relating to labeling and other precautionary measures (see § 16, Comment *d*) rather than through prohibitions against copying.

b. Functionality. A packaging or product feature is not functional merely because the feature serves a utilitarian purpose. The recognition of trademark rights is precluded only when the particular design affords benefits that are not practically available through alternative designs. A bottle, for example, is a utilitarian element of the packaging for wine, but the design of a particular wine bottle is not functional under the rule of this Section unless the shape or other aspects of the bottle provide significant benefits that are not practically obtainable through the use of alternative bottle designs.

In general, a functional design is one that is costly to do without. Thus, the benefits afforded by a particular design do not themselves determine whether that design is functional; a design is functional only if those benefits cannot practically be duplicated through the use of other designs. The availability of alternative designs that satisfy the utilitarian requirements or that otherwise afford similar advantages is therefore decisive in determining functionality. If a particular design affords benefits that are superior to those of any practical alternative design, it is functional if the benefits are important to effective competition.

The exclusion of functional designs from the subject matter of trademark law is intended to insure effective competition, not just by the defendant, but also by other existing and potential competitors. Thus, a design may be functional if it is one of a limited number of superior designs. The range of alternative designs sufficient to preclude a finding of functionality depends on the particular facts of each case.

The benefit conferred by a particular packaging or product design may take various forms. The benefit may lie, for example, in greater economy in manufacturing, shipping, or handling, in increased utility or durability, or in enhanced effectiveness or ease of use. (On aesthetic benefits, see Comment *c*.) If the benefit afforded by the design resides solely in its association with a particular source, however, the design is not functional; the extent to which others may use such a design is determined by the rules of this Chapter governing trademark infringement. See § 20.

Any evidence that relates to the advantages inherent in a particular design is relevant to the issue of functionality. Functionality may thus be inferred from evidence of advertising or other promotional efforts by the plaintiff that emphasize the benefits of the design. Benefits claimed in pursuit of a utility patent may be particularly persuasive evidence of functionality. Discussions of the design in textbooks or trade literature and engineering analysis of its utilitarian aspects are also relevant. The fact that other manufacturers familiar with the design have rejected it in favor of other designs is evidence that the design is not functional.

When the matter claimed as a trademark consists of the overall design of a product or its packaging, or the design of a combination or arrangement of features, eligibility for trademark protection is determined by the functionality of the claimed design as a whole. The fact that the overall design or combination contains individual features that are themselves functional does not preclude protection for the composite. The issue is whether trademark protection should be recognized in the particular combination or arrangement of features, and the functionality of the combination or arrangement as a whole is determinative. If the overall shape of a bottle is distinctive and nonfunctional, for example, the shape may be protected as a trademark despite the inclusion of a top that is functionally configured to accept a standard bottle cap. Protection of the overall design, however, will not preclude others from adopting the functional constituents. If the overall design of a product or package is otherwise functional, however, the addition of minor nonfunctional elements will not render the overall design protectable; trademark rights will be limited to only the nonfunctional elements.

A design that is nonfunctional may be protected as a trademark upon proof that it is distinctive under the rule stated in § 13. Possible limitations on the protection of product features under state law are discussed in § 16, Comment *c*.

Illustrations:

1. *A* manufactures china plates intended for commercial use. The undersides of *A* 's plates have a circular rib located midway between the rim and base of the plate. When the product was first introduced *A* obtained a now-expired utility patent on the rib design, citing as advantages of the design its ability to reduce breakage by evenly distributing vibrational stress and its contribution to ease of handling by providing a finger hold on the underside of the plate. The rib design is functional under the rule stated in this Section.

2. *A* manufactures a breakfast cereal consisting of strands of wheat formed into pillow-shaped biscuits. The evidence establishes that the cost of producing the biscuits would increase and their quality would decrease if another form was substituted for the pillow shape. The pillow-shape design is functional under the rule stated in this Section. See § 16, Illustration 6.

3. *A*, a fishing reel manufacturer, markets a spin-cast reel with a front cover in the shape of a 40-degree cone ending in a fishing-line guide at its narrow front end. The evidence establishes that various shapes can accommodate the utilitarian functions performed by the cover and that numerous other shapes are used by competing manufacturers. In the absence of other evidence relating to the benefits of the cover shape, the design is not functional under the rule stated in this Section, and it is protectable as a trademark if the design is distinctive under the rules stated in § 13.

4. *A* manufactures chocolate candy in the form of a six-sided bar with sloping ends. The bars are wrapped with an inner layer of silver foil covered by an outer white paper wrapper that leaves a significant portion of the foil visible at both ends of the bar. The packaging retains the shape of the enclosed chocolate bar. The evidence establishes that chocolate bars can be shaped and wrapped in a variety of forms and styles. In the absence of evidence indicating that *A* 's overall design affords benefits not practically available through the use of other designs, the design is not functional under the rule stated in this Section, and it is protectable as a trademark if the design is distinctive under the rules stated in § 13.

c. "Aesthetic" functionality. When aesthetic considerations play an important role in the purchasing decisions of prospective consumers, a design feature that substantially contributes to the aesthetic appeal of a product may qualify as "functional." As with utilitarian design features, however, the fact that the design performs a function by contributing to the aesthetic value of the product does not in itself render the design ineligible for protection as a trademark. A manufacturer thus does not forfeit trademark rights simply because prospective purchasers find the design aesthetically pleasing. A design is functional because of its aesthetic value only if it confers a significant benefit that cannot practically be duplicated by the use of alternative designs. Because of the difficulties inherent in evaluating the aesthetic superiority of a particular design, a finding of aesthetic functionality ordinarily will be made only when objective evidence indicates a lack of adequate alternative designs. Such evidence typically is available only when the range of alternative designs is limited either by the nature of the design feature or by the basis of its aesthetic appeal. The ultimate test of aesthetic functionality, as with utilitarian functionality, is whether the recognition of trademark rights would significantly hinder competition.

Illustrations:

5. *A* manufactures a line of lightweight luggage. Each bag is made of parachute nylon trimmed with matching cotton tape and matching straps of cotton webbing. The bags have zippers with hollow rectangular metal pulls that are similarly color coordinated. Each bag is covered with the repetitive printing of *A* 's logo enclosed in a small ellipse. The background within the ellipse contrasts with the color of the bag. The evidence establishes that although *A* 's bags are aesthetically attractive to prospective purchasers, the number of alternative designs is virtually unlimited. In the absence of evidence establishing that similarly attractive designs are unavailable to competing manufacturers, the overall design of *A* 's luggage is not functional under the rule stated in this Section, and it is protectable as a trademark if the design is distinctive under the rules stated in § 13.

6. *A* manufactures china. Among the products marketed by *A* is a set of china bearing a particular floral pattern covering the entire surface of each plate. Evidence establishes that aesthetic factors play an important role in the purchase of china, that *A* 's design is attractive to a significant number of consumers, and that the number of alternative floral patterns for china is virtually unlimited. In the absence of evidence establishing that similarly attractive patterns are unavailable to competing manufacturers, *A* 's design is not functional under the rule stated in this Section,

and it is protectable as a trademark if the design is distinctive under the rules stated in § 13.

7. The facts being otherwise as stated in Illustration 6, *A* 's design consists solely of the placement of various gemstones around the rim of each plate. Evidence establishes that the rim design is attractive to a significant number of consumers. Because of the limited number of alternative designs available to satisfy the aesthetic desires of these prospective purchasers, a court may properly conclude that the design is functional under the rule stated in this Section.

8. *A* is the first seller to market candy intended for Valentine's Day in heart-shaped boxes. Evidence establishes that the shape of the box is an important factor in the appeal of the product to a significant number of consumers. Because there are no alternative designs capable of satisfying the aesthetic desires of these prospective purchasers, the design of the box is functional under the rule stated in this Section.

9. *A* manufactures outdoor lighting fixtures intended for mounting on the walls of commercial buildings to illuminate adjacent areas. The evidence establishes that architectural compatibility with the building is an important factor in the purchase of such fixtures and that A's product is considered to be aesthetically compatible with contemporary architecture. The evidence also establishes that only a limited number of designs are considered compatible with the type of buildings on which A's product is used. Because of the limited range of alternative designs available to competitors, a court may properly conclude that the design of the lighting fixture is functional under the rule stated in this Section.

REPORTERS' NOTE

This Section defines the scope of the exclusion in § 16(b), which precludes the recognition of trademark rights in functional designs. The Section clarifies the former statement of the rule in Restatement of Torts § 742 (1938). See generally McCarthy, Trademarks and Unfair Competition §§ 7.26–29.

Comment a. Cases resting the functionality doctrine on the public interest in competition include, e.g., Two Pesos, Inc. v. Taco Cabana, Inc., ___ U.S. ___, ___, 112 S.Ct. 2753, 2760–61, 120 L.Ed.2d 615, 628 (1992) (the doctrine "serves to assure that competitors will not be stifled by the exhaustion of a limited number of trade dresses") (dictum in an action under § 43(a) of the Lanham Act); Textron, Inc. v. U.S. Int'l Trade Com., 753 F.2d 1019 (Fed.Cir.1985); Warner Bros. Inc. v. Gay Toys, Inc., 724 F.2d 327 (2d Cir.1983); In re

Morton–Norwich Products, Inc., 671 F.2d 1332 (C.C.P.A.1982); Keene Corp. v. Paraflex Industries, Inc., 653 F.2d 822 (3d Cir.1981); In re Deister Concentrator Co., 289 F.2d 496 (C.C.P.A.1961); Classic Instruments, Inc. v. VDO–Argo Instruments, Inc., 73 Or.App. 732, 700 P.2d 677 (1985). That proof of de facto secondary meaning is insufficient to establish trademark rights in a functional design, see, e.g., In re Water Gremlin Co., 635 F.2d 841 (C.C.P.A.1980); In re Deister Concentrator Co., *supra*; In re North American Phillips Corp., 217 U.S.P.Q. 926 (Tm.Tr.App.Bd. 1983) ("extremely high public recognition and association with applicant" was insufficient to obtain a trademark registration for the functional design of a triple-headed electric shaver).

Comment b. Functionality is frequently measured by whether the recognition of trademark rights would "hinder competition or impinge upon the rights of others to compete effectively in the sale of the goods." In re Morton–Norwich Products, Inc., 671 F.2d 1332, 1342 (C.C.P.A.1982). Accord, Woodsmith Pub. Co. v. Meredith Corp., 904 F.2d 1244 (8th Cir. 1990); Hartford House, Ltd. v. Hallmark Cards, Inc., 846 F.2d 1268, 1274 (10th Cir.), cert. denied 488 U.S. 908, 109 S.Ct. 260, 102 L.Ed.2d 248 (1988); Brunswick Corp. v. Spinit Reel Co., 832 F.2d 513, 519 (10th Cir.1987); Stormy Clime, Ltd. v. ProGroup, Inc., 809 F.2d 971, 977 (2d Cir.1987); Sno–Wizard Manufacturing, Inc. v. Eisemann Products Co., 791 F.2d 423, 426 n.3 (5th Cir.1986); Sicilia Di R. Biebow & Co. v. Cox, 732 F.2d 417, 429 (5th Cir.1984). Other decisions emphasizing the potential hindrance to competition include, e.g., Abbott Laboratories v. Mead Johnson & Co., 971 F.2d 6 (7th Cir.1992); Clamp Manufacturing Co. v. Enco Manufacturing Co., 870 F.2d 512, 516 (9th Cir.), cert. denied 493 U.S. 872, 110 S.Ct. 202, 107 L.Ed.2d 155 (1989); Vaughan Manufacturing Co. v. Brikam Int'l, Inc., 814 F.2d 346, 349 (7th Cir.1987); Prufrock Ltd. v. Lasater, 781 F.2d 129, 133 (8th Cir.1986); W.T. Rogers Co. v. Keene, 778 F.2d 334, 343 (7th Cir.1985); In re Teledyne Industries, Inc., 696 F.2d 968, 970 (Fed.Cir.1982); Truck Equipment Service Co. v. Fruehauf Corp., 536 F.2d 1210, 1218 (8th Cir.), cert. denied 429 U.S. 861, 97 S.Ct. 164, 50 L.Ed.2d 139 (1976); In re Mogen David Wine Corp., 328 F.2d 925, 933 (C.C.P.A.1964) (Rich, J., concurring).

Cases emphasizing that the utility of a design feature does not in itself justify a finding of functionality include, e.g., In re Morton–Norwich Products, Inc., *supra*; In re Mogen David Wine Corp., *supra*; Classic Instruments, Inc. v. VDO–Argo Instruments, Inc., 73 Or.App. 732, 700 P.2d 677 (1985). It is the availability of alternative designs offering similar benefits that is generally determinative. See, e.g., Clamp Manufacturing Co., *supra*; Hartford House, Ltd., *supra*; Brunswick Corp., *supra*; W.T. Rogers Co., *supra*; Sicilia Di R. Biebow & Co., *supra*; Ideal Toy Corp. v. Plawner Toy Mfg. Corp., 685 F.2d 78 (3d Cir.1982); Keene Corp. v. Paraflex Industries, Inc., 653 F.2d 822 (3d Cir.1981). A design is generally held to be functional if it is one of a few superior choices for the purpose. See, e.g., In re Bose Corp., 772 F.2d 866 (Fed.Cir.1985); In re Honeywell, Inc., 532 F.2d 180 (C.C.P.A.1976).

Descriptions of the types of benefits relevant to a finding of functionality appear in, e.g., Sicilia Di R. Biebow & Co., *supra*; Zippo Manufacturing Co. v. Rogers Imports, Inc., 216 F.Supp. 670 (S.D.N.Y.1963); Duo–Tint Bulb & Battery Co. v. Moline Supply Co., 46 Ill.App.3d 145, 4 Ill.Dec. 685, 360 N.E.2d 798 (1977). Cf. Inwood Laboratories, Inc. v. Ives Laboratories, Inc., 456 U.S. 844, 850 n.10, 102 S.Ct. 2182, 2187 n.10, 72 L.Ed.2d 606, 613 n.10 (1982) ("In general terms, a product feature is functional if it is essential to the use or purpose of the article or if it affects the cost or quality of the article.") (dictum).

General marketing schemes and other merchandising concepts claimed as trademarks on the basis of acquired distinctiveness may be denied protection as functional. See Duo–Tint Bulb & Battery Co., *supra*, finding a system of selling replacement bulbs in self-contained displays that facilitated reordering "functional" and hence unprotectable. See also Woodsmith, *supra* (protection for "the mere method and style of doing business" would be inconsistent with the free enterprise system); Hartford House, Ltd., *supra* ("concept of emotionally expressive non-occasion greeting cards" not protected); Prufrock Ltd., *supra* ("down home country cooking" concept not protected). Cf. Schwinn Bicycle Co. v. Diversified Products Corp., 740 F.Supp. 517 (N.D.Ill.1990) (general association between a manufacturer and a type of product is not sufficient to exclude new entrants based on a trade dress claim); Haagen–Dazs, Inc. v. Frusen Gladje Ltd., 493 F.Supp. 73 (S.D.N.Y. 1980) ("unique Scandinavian marketing scheme" not protected).

In some instances the color of a design feature may offer utilitarian advantages sufficient to support a finding of functionality. See, e.g., Transgo, Inc. v. Ajac Transmission Parts Corp., 768 F.2d 1001 (9th Cir. 1985), cert. denied 474 U.S. 1059, 106 S.Ct. 802, 88 L.Ed.2d 778 (1986) (colors of transmission springs were functional as indicative of proper location); Norwich Pharmacal Co. v. Sterling Drug, Inc., 271 F.2d 569 (2d Cir.1959), cert. denied 362 U.S. 919, 80 S.Ct. 671, 4 L.Ed.2d 739 (1960) (suggesting that pink color of medicine may have psychosomatic effect); U.S. Electric Mfg. Corp. v. Bright Star Battery Co., 6 N.Y.S.2d 690 (1938) (red lens on a flashlight was functional because of its utility as a warning beacon). The functionality of color combinations used on prescription drug capsules was discussed by the Supreme Court in Inwood Laboratories, Inc. v. Ives Laboratories, Inc., 456 U.S. 844, 102 S.Ct. 2182, 72 L.Ed.2d 606 (1982), in which the Court held that the court of appeals erred by failing to apply the "clearly erroneous" standard in setting aside findings of fact, including the trial court's finding of functionality. The district court had found that the capsule colors assisted patients in identifying the medication and reduced the anxiety that might result from a switch to generic equivalents. See Ives Laboratories, Inc. v. Darby Drug Co., 488 F.Supp. 394, 398–99 (E.D.N.Y.1980), reversed 638 F.2d 538 (2d Cir.1981), reversed 456 U.S. 844, 102 S.Ct. 2182, 72 L.Ed.2d 606 (1982). A similar functionality argument was rejected in, e.g., Ciba–Geigy Corp. v. Bolar Pharmaceutical Co., 747 F.2d 844 (3d Cir.1984), cert. denied 471 U.S. 1137, 105 S.Ct. 2678, 86 L.Ed.2d 696 (1985); SK & F, Co. v. Premo Pharmaceutical Laboratories, Inc., 625 F.2d 1055 (3d Cir.1980). But see Upjohn Co. v. Schwartz, 246 F.2d 254 (2d Cir.1957). Cf. § 8, Illustration 5. See also, e.g., Vision

Sports, Inc. v. Melville Corp., 888 F.2d 609 (9th Cir.1989) (functionality is a question of fact).

If the advantage of a particular design lies solely in its association with a specific source, the design is not "functional" under the rule stated in this Section. See, e.g., Warner Bros. Inc. v. Gay Toys, Inc., 724 F.2d 327 (2d Cir.1983); Vuitton et fils S.A. v. J. Young Enterprises, Inc., 644 F.2d 769 (9th Cir.1981); Boston Professional Hockey Ass'n v. Dallas Cap & Emblem Mfg., Inc., 510 F.2d 1004 (5th Cir.), cert. denied 423 U.S. 868, 96 S.Ct. 132, 46 L.Ed.2d 98 (1975). A few cases, however, invoke the doctrine of functionality to permit the use of another's trademark as ornamentation on goods such as jewelry and clothing, arguing that in such contexts the mark is an important functional component of the goods. See, e.g., International Order of Job's Daughters v. Lindeburg and Co., 633 F.2d 912 (9th Cir.1980), cert. denied 452 U.S. 941, 101 S.Ct. 3086, 69 L.Ed.2d 956 (1981); Plasticolor Molded Products v. Ford Motor Co., 713 F.Supp. 1329 (C.D.Cal.1989), vacated 767 F.Supp. 1036 (C.D.Cal.1991); University of Pittsburgh v. Champion Products, Inc., 566 F.Supp. 711 (W.D.Pa.1983). The issue in such cases, however, is not the eligibility of the design for protection as a trademark, but rather the scope of permissible use of a trademark by another. Thus, the rule stated in this Section is inapplicable, and liability is determined under the rules governing trademark infringement. See § 20, Comment *e*.

Advertising and promotional claims made by the plaintiff can sometimes justify a finding of functionality. See, e.g., In re Bose Corp., 772 F.2d 866 (Fed.Cir.1985); Fisher Stoves, Inc. v. All Nighter Stove Works, Inc., 626 F.2d 193 (1st Cir.1980); In re Deister Concentrator Co., 289 F.2d 496 (C.C.P.A.1961). On the use of analyses in trade journals and texts, see, e.g., In re Hollaender Mfg. Co., 511 F.2d 1186 (C.C.P.A.1975); In re Deister Concentrator Co., *supra*; see also Truck Equipment Service Co. v. Fruehauf Corp., 536 F.2d 1210 (8th Cir.), cert. denied 429 U.S. 861, 97 S.Ct. 164, 50 L.Ed.2d 139 (1976) (engineering analysis used to establish nonfunctionality). Functional advantages claimed in utility patents were cited in, e.g., In re Bose Corp., *supra*; New England Butt Co. v. Int'l Trade Com., 756 F.2d 874 (Fed.Cir. 1985); In re Hollaender Mfg. Co., *supra*; In re Shenango Ceramics, Inc., 362 F.2d 287 (C.C.P.A.1966). See also Cable Electric Products, Inc. v. Genmark, Inc., 770 F.2d 1015 (Fed. Cir.1985), emphasizing that it is the functionality of the product design as marketed, not as depicted in the patent, that is determinative, and Best Lock Corp. v. Schlage Lock Co., 413 F.2d 1195 (C.C.P.A.1969), noting that a utility patent is not evidence of functionality with respect to arbitrary design features only incidentally disclosed in the patent. Because design patents are available only for "ornamental" designs (see 35 U.S.C.A. § 171), a design patent is not incompatible with the recognition of trademark rights. See, e.g., In re Honeywell, Inc., 497 F.2d 1344 (C.C.P.A.), cert. denied 419 U.S. 1080, 95 S.Ct. 669, 42 L.Ed.2d 674 (1974); In re World's Finest Chocolate, Inc., 474 F.2d 1012 (C.C.P.A.1973); In re Mogen David Wine Corp., 328 F.2d 925 (C.C.P.A.1964). Indeed, the existence of a design patent may be evidence that the design is not functional in a utilitarian sense. See In re Morton–Norwich Products, Inc., 671 F.2d 1332 (C.C.P.A.1982).

There is as yet no consensus with respect to the burden of proof on the issue of functionality. Cases viewing functionality as a defense, with the burden of proof on the subsequent user, include, e.g., Badger Meter, Inc. v. Grinnell Corp., 13 F.3d 1145 (7th Cir.1994) ("affirmative defense"); Hartford House, Ltd. v. Hallmark Cards, Inc., 846 F.2d 1268 (10th Cir.), cert. denied 488 U.S. 908, 109 S.Ct. 260, 102 L.Ed.2d 248 (1988); Brunswick Corp. v. Spinit Reel Co., 832 F.2d 513 (10th Cir.1987); Stormy Clime, Ltd. v. ProGroup, Inc., 809 F.2d 971 (2d Cir.1987); LeSportsac, Inc. v. K Mart Corp., 754 F.2d 71 (2d Cir.1985) (noting the public interest in preventing confusion); see Inwood Laboratories, Inc. v. Ives Laboratories, Inc., 456 U.S. 844, 863, 102 S.Ct. 2182, 2193, 72 L.Ed.2d 606, 621 (1982) ("functionality is a defense to a suit under § 43(a)") (White, J., concurring). Other cases indicate that the burden of proof may be on the person asserting exclusive rights. See, e.g., Merchant & Evans, Inc. v. Roosevelt Building Products Co., 963 F.2d 628 (3d Cir.1992) (noting the split among the circuits); Clamp Manufacturing Co. v. Enco Manufacturing Co., 870 F.2d 512 (9th Cir.), cert. denied 493 U.S. 872, 110 S.Ct. 202, 107 L.Ed.2d 155 (1989); Fisher Stoves, Inc. v. All Nighter Stove Works, Inc., 626 F.2d 193 (1st Cir.1980) (dictum); Duo–Tint Bulb & Battery Co. v. Moline Supply Co., 46 Ill.App.3d 145, 4 Ill.Dec. 685, 360 N.E.2d 798 (1977). See also John H. Harland Co. v. Clarke Checks, Inc., 711 F.2d 966 (11th Cir.1983) (commenting on the divergent conclusions). In view of the threat of confusion established by plaintiff's proof of distinctiveness and subsequent use by the defendant, it may be appropriate to place upon the defendant at least the initial burden of producing evidence of functionality, regardless of the allocation of the ultimate burden of persuasion. A design will be denied registration as a trademark under the Lanham Act if the Patent and Trademark Office establishes a prima facie case of functionality that is not rebutted by the applicant. See, e.g., In re Teledyne Industries, Inc., 696 F.2d 968 (Fed.Cir.1982). Registration is prima facie evidence of the validity of the mark, 15 U.S.C.A. § 1057(b), which has been interpreted to place upon the person challenging a registered mark the burden of proving functionality by a preponderance of the evidence. See Vuitton et fils S.A. v. J. Young Enterprises, Inc., 644 F.2d 769 (9th Cir.1981). If the registration has become incontestable under 15 U.S.C.A. § 1065, it may be immune from challenges alleging functionality. Shakespeare Co. v. Silstar Corp., 9 F.3d 1091 (4th Cir. 1993), cert. denied ___ U.S. ___, 114 S.Ct. 2134, 128 L.Ed.2d 864 (1994).

Several decisions emphasize that when a design consists of a combination of elements, the functionality of the design as a whole and not that of the individual components determines its eligibility for protection. See, e.g., Hartford House, Ltd., *supra*; Fuddruckers, Inc. v. Doc's B.R. Others, Inc., 826 F.2d 837 (9th Cir.1987); Vaughan Manufacturing Co. v. Brikam Int'l, Inc., 814 F.2d 346 (7th Cir.1987); Stormy Clime, Ltd., *supra*; American Greetings Corp. v. Dan–Dee Imports, Inc., 807 F.2d 1136 (3d Cir.1986); AmBrit, Inc. v. Kraft, Inc., 812 F.2d 1531 (11th Cir. 1986), cert. denied 481 U.S. 1041, 107 S.Ct. 1983, 95 L.Ed.2d 822 (1987); CPG Products Corp. v. Pegasus Luggage, Inc., 776 F.2d 1007 (Fed.Cir. 1985); LeSportsac, Inc., *supra*; John H. Harland Co., *supra*. The availability of alternative arrangements and combinations of the individual elements was considered in, e.g., Stormy Clime, Ltd., *supra*; American Greetings Corp., *supra*; LeSportsac, Inc., *supra*. When the overall design is dominated by functional features, however, trademark rights may be limited to the nonfunctional elements. See Textron, Inc. v. U.S. Int'l Trade Com., 753 F.2d 1019 (Fed.Cir.1985); Petersen Mfg. Co. v. Central Purchasing, Inc., 740 F.2d 1541 (Fed.Cir.1984).

Illustration 1 is based on In re Shenango Ceramics, Inc., 362 F.2d 287 (C.C.P.A.1966). Compare Illustrations 6 and 7.

Illustration 2 is based on Kellogg Co. v. National Biscuit Co., 305 U.S. 111, 59 S.Ct. 109, 83 L.Ed. 73 (1938). See Shredded Wheat Co. v. Humphrey Cornell Co., 250 Fed. 960 (2d Cir.1918). See also § 16, Illustration 6.

Illustration 3 is based on Brunswick Corp. v. Spinit Reel Co., 832 F.2d 513 (10th Cir.1987).

Illustration 4 is based on In re World's Finest Chocolate, Inc., 474 F.2d 1012 (C.C.P.A.1973). See In re Bachman Chocolate Manufacturing Co., 153 U.S.P.Q. 753 (Tm.Tr.App.Bd. 1967).

Comment c. The concept of aesthetic functionality is sometimes said to apply if the aesthetic feature "is an important ingredient in the commercial success of the product." E.g., Prufrock Ltd. v. Lasater, 781 F.2d 129 (8th Cir.1986); Industria Arredamenti Fratelli Saporiti v. Charles Craig, Ltd., 725 F.2d 18 (2d Cir.1984). This standard was initially formulated in Pagliero v. Wallace China Co., 198 F.2d 339 (9th Cir. 1952). The rule stated in this Section, however, follows the numerous decisions that reject the view that aesthetic appeal alone is sufficient to establish functionality. See, e.g., Wallace Int'l Silversmiths, Inc. v. Godinger Silver Art Co., 916 F.2d 76 (2d Cir.1990), cert. denied 499 U.S. 976, 111 S.Ct. 1622, 413 L.Ed.2d 720 (1991) (citing Restatement Third, Unfair Competition § 17 (Tent. Draft No.2 (1990))); Brunswick Corp. v. Spinit Reel Co., 832 F.2d 513 (10th Cir.1987); Stormy Clime Ltd. v. ProGroup, Inc., 809 F.2d 971 (2d Cir. 1987); American Greetings Corp. v. Dan–Dee Imports, Inc., 807 F.2d 1136 (3d Cir.1986); LeSportsac, Inc. v. K Mart Corp., 754 F.2d 71 (2d Cir.1985); Sicilia Di R. Biebow & Co. v. Cox, 732 F.2d 417 (5th Cir.1984); Fabrica Inc. v. El Dorado Corp., 697 F.2d 890 (9th Cir.1983); In re DC Comics, Inc., 689 F.2d 1042 (C.C.P.A. 1982); Keene Corp. v. Paraflex Industries, Inc., 653 F.2d 822 (3d Cir. 1981); Vuitton et fils S.A. v. J. Young Enterprises, Inc., 644 F.2d 769 (9th Cir.1981). The analysis adopted here takes account of the available alternatives—a proposition expressly rejected in *Pagliero, supra*. See, e.g., Villeroy & Boch Keramische Werke K.G. v. THC Systems, Inc., 999 F.2d 619 (2d Cir.1993) (citing Restatement Third, Unfair Competition § 17, Comment *c* (Tent. Draft No.2 (1990))); Wallace Int'l, *supra*; Hartford House, Ltd. v. Hallmark Cards, Inc., 846 F.2d 1268 (10th Cir.), cert. denied 488 U.S. 908, 109 S.Ct. 260, 102 L.Ed.2d 248 (1988); Brunswick Corp., *supra*; Stormy Clime, Ltd., *supra*; American Greetings Corp., *supra*; W.T. Rogers Co. v. Keene, 778 F.2d 334 (7th Cir.1985); LeSportsac, Inc., *supra*; Keene Corp., *supra*; Lon Tai Shing Co. v. Koch + Lowy, 19 U.S.P.Q.2d 1081 (S.D.N.Y. 1991) (citing Restatement Third, Unfair Competition § 17, Comment *c* (Tent. Draft No.2 (1990))). Some decisions also express concern about the disincentives created by a rule that would exclude all attractive designs from the scope of trademark protection. See LeSportsac, Inc., *supra* ; Keene Corp., *supra* ; cf. In re DC Comics, Inc., *supra* (Nies, J., concurring) (interest in encouraging diversity of designs). As with utilitarian design features, the potential effect on competition that would result from a recognition of trademark rights remains the central inquiry. See, e.g., W.T. Rogers Co., *supra* ; LeSportsac, Inc., *supra* ; Keene Corp., *supra*.

Several decisions invoke the concept of aesthetic functionality to justify a denial of protection to ornamental features that are not distinctive of source. See, e.g., Damn I'm Good, Inc. v. Sakowitz, Inc., 514 F.Supp. 1357 (S.D.N.Y.1981); PPS, Inc. v. Jewelry Sales Representatives, Inc., 392 F.Supp. 375 (S.D.N.Y.1975); cf. In re DC Comics, *supra* (Rich, J., concurring) (limiting aesthetic functionality to non-distinctive designs). Similarly, other decisions loosely define functional designs as those that "connote other than a trademark purpose." E.g., Vuitton et fils S.A., *supra*, and Truck Equipment Service Co. v. Fruehauf Corp., 536 F.2d 1210 (8th Cir.), cert. denied 429 U.S. 861, 97 S.Ct. 164, 50 L.Ed.2d 139 (1976), both citing *Pagliero, supra*. If the design is not distinctive, however, it is unnecessary to consider functionality. See, e.g., In re Morton–Norwich Products, Inc., 671 F.2d 1332 (C.C.P.A.1982); Keene Corp., *supra* ; In re Deister Concentrator Co., 289 F.2d 496 (C.C.P.A.1961).

Illustration 5 is based on *LeSportsac, supra.*

Illustration 6 is based on the facts but not the result in *Pagliero, supra.* Compare the result in Illustration 7. See Villeroy & Boch, *supra* (china pattern was not functional, citing Restatement Third, Unfair Competition § 17, Comment *c* (Tent. Draft No.2 (1990))).

Illustration 8 is taken from the former discussion of the rule in Restatement of Torts § 742, Comment *a*.

Illustration 9 is based on *Keene Corp., supra.* Compare Lon Tai Shing Co., *supra* (lamp design was not aesthetically functional, noting the absence of evidence indicating a lack of alternative designs, citing Restatement Third, Unfair Competition § 17, Comment *c* (Tent. Draft No.2 (1990))). See Aromatique, Inc. v. Gold Seal, Inc., 28 F.3d 863 (8th Cir. 1994) (red and green cord held functional on packaging for a Christmas product); Deere & Co. v. Farmhand, Inc., 560 F.Supp. 85 (S.D.Iowa 1982), affirmed 721 F.2d 253 (8th Cir.1983), holding "John Deere green" aesthetically functional as used on farm loaders because farmers prefer to match the color of their loaders and tractors; Brunswick Corp. v. British Seagull Ltd., 35 F.3d 1527 (Fed.Cir.1994) (black color on outboard motors was functional because it is compatible with a wide variety of boat colors and makes the motor appear smaller).

TOPIC 2. ACQUISITION AND PRIORITY OF RIGHTS

---

§ 18. Acquisition of Rights

Rights can be acquired in a designation only when the designation has been actually used as a trademark, trade name, collective mark, or certification mark as defined in §§ 9–12, or when an applicable statutory provision recognizes a protectable interest in the designation prior to actual use. A designation is "used" as a trademark, trade name, collective trademark, or certification mark when the designation is displayed or otherwise made known to prospective purchasers in the ordinary course of business in a manner that associates the designation with the goods, services, or business of the user or, in the case of a certification mark, with the certified goods or services. A designation is "used" as a collective membership mark when the designation is displayed or otherwise made known in a manner that signifies membership in the collective group.

Comment:

a. Requirement of "use." The definitions of "trademark," "collective mark," "certification mark," and "trade name" in §§ 9–12 describe designations "used" to identify and distinguish goods, services, or businesses. The rule stated in this Section determines when a designation has been "used" within the meaning of those definitions. The nature of the rights that are acquired through "use" is determined by the rules relating to priority and infringement as specified in §§ 19–25. On the abandonment of acquired rights, see § 30.

Until a designation has been actually used as a symbol of identification, its use by others creates no risk of confusion. Actual use by the claimant also furnishes public notice of the user's potential rights in the designation. Thus, in the absence of an applicable statutory provision of the kind described in Comment *b*, no rights arise in trademarks or other designations eligible for protection under the rules in this Chapter until the designation is in actual use. To be protectable as a trademark, collective mark, certification mark, or trade name the designation must also be "distinctive" as defined in § 13. If a designation is inherently distinctive under the rule in § 13(a), it can be protected immediately upon actual use as defined in this Section. Designations that are not inherently distinctive, however, are not protected until the designation has achieved the required secondary meaning under the rule stated in § 13(b). See also § 19, Comment *b*. On the ownership of a designation as between a manufacturer and an exclusive distributor, see § 34, Comment *d*.

b. Statutory rights preceding "use." The rule recognizing the acquisition of rights in a designation upon actual use, although sufficient to preclude subsequent appropriations of good will, affords no security for preparatory investments undertaken prior to actual use. Thus, the expenditures required to introduce a new mark or name in the marketplace remain at risk of the designation's prior adoption by another. Until 1988, the federal trademark statute, like the common law, made actual use a prerequisite to protection. In an acknowledged effort to afford a measure of security for preparatory investments, however, it became settled that even a use of the mark made outside the ordinary course of business and primarily for the purpose of establishing trademark rights could be sufficient to support a federal registration, at least if the circumstances indicated an intent to commence bona fide commercial use of the mark within a reasonable time. Administrative and judicial decisions upheld federal registrations founded on such "token use" even when the use occurred months before the initiation of significant marketing under the trademark. Registration based on token use provided public notice of the registrant's claim to the designation and under federal law afforded priority against others who might subsequently adopt it. This liberal interpretation of the use requirement, however, was invoked only in connection with the right to register the mark under the Lanham Act; such "registration use" was often distinguished from the more stringent use requirement applicable to the acquisition of rights at common law.

The first explicit recognition of trademark rights prior to actual use appeared in the 1988 amendments to the Lanham Act. An application for federal registration may be filed by any "person who has a bona fide intention, under circumstances showing the good faith of such person, to use a trademark in commerce." 15 U.S.C.A. § 1051(b). The filing of an application for registration constitutes "constructive use" of the mark, 15 U.S.C.A. § 1057(c), conferring nationwide priority against all persons except prior users and prior applicants for registration. The advantages of "constructive use," however, are contingent on the issuance of the registration, which in turn is contingent on the applicant's actual use of the designation in commerce within the statutory period specified in the Act. 15 U.S.C.A. § 1051(d). Token use is no longer sufficient to establish actual use; the Lanham Act as amended requires "the bona fide use of a mark in the ordinary course of trade, and not made merely to reserve a right in a mark." 15 U.S.C.A. § 1127. The intent-to-use provisions of the Lanham Act are also applicable to service marks (see § 9), collective marks (see § 10), and certification marks (see § 11).

c. Use in the ordinary course of business. Common law rights in a designation can be acquired only when the user commences use of the mark in the ordinary course of business. The same principle now governs the requirement of "use" under the Lanham Act. See Comment *b*. No specific quantum of use is required. The bona fide nature of the use rather than its extent or frequency is determinative. A single use can be sufficient if it marks the beginning of commercial exploitation of the designation, while multiple uses made solely for the purpose of establishing trademark rights will not suffice.

The requirement that the use be in the ordinary course of business is intended to distinguish bona fide commercial use from uses made merely to reserve rights in the designation. The commencement of bona fide commercial use must be determined in light of all the circumstances surrounding the use. The initial use of a designation can be sufficient to constitute bona fide commercial use if the circumstances indicate an intention to continue use in the ordinary course of business. Subsequent activity involving the mark can confirm that an earlier use initiated bona fide commercial use. Sham transactions and limited-volume token sales made solely to acquire trademark rights are not sufficient. Similarly, use of the designation on a product other than that for which it is ultimately intended may also indicate that the use is not in the ordinary course of business.

Use in the ordinary course of business includes uses that are typical in the particular market or trade in which the mark is used. Thus, for example, it might be in the ordinary course of business for sellers of expensive or seasonal products to make infrequent sales or for sellers of certain goods to engage in test marketing in confined geographic areas. Even a use that is unusual in the particular trade may be in the ordinary course of business if it is motivated by commercial considerations unrelated to the acquisition of trademark rights in the designation.

Good faith is also relevant in determining whether a use is in the ordinary course of business. Use of a designation merely to frustrate the marketing plans of another seller who is preparing to use a similar mark is not a use in the ordinary course of business. The same is true of small-scale use intended merely to foreclose expansion by a competitor who has established rights in the mark in another geographic area. See § 19, Comment *d*.

Illustrations:

1. In April, *A* begins the manufacture of a novel pencil box for which it adopts the name VIRGIL. *A* attaches to each box a label prominently bearing that designation. On May 20, *A* makes a small sale to a local distributor. Other small sales to the distributor follow in June and July. On August 1, *A* makes a large sale in anticipation of the new school year. In the absence of evidence to the contrary, *A* 's use on May 20 is a use in the ordinary course of business.

2. The facts being otherwise as stated in Illustration 1, *A* decides in April to postpone marketing the new pencil boxes until August. On May 1, solely in order to establish trademark rights in the designation, *A* sells one carton of the pencil boxes to the distributor who has agreed to market the product beginning in August. No further use of the designation is made until a large shipment is delivered to the distributor on August 1. A court may properly conclude that the use of the designation on May 1 was not a use in the ordinary course of business and that *A* did not use the designation in the ordinary course of business until August 1.

3. *A* manufactures video games. *B*, a competitor, learns that *A* is about to introduce a new game under the name GEMINI. In an attempt to prevent *A* from acquiring rights in the name, *B* places that designation over the existing name on a few games in its inventory and makes several sales prior to the introduction of *A* 's new game. A court may properly conclude that *B* 's use is not a use in the ordinary course of business.

d. Manner of use. A designation is used as a trademark, trade name, collective mark, or certification mark under the rule stated in this Section only if the designation is employed as a symbol of identification. Thus, the manner of use must be calculated to cause prospective purchasers to associate the designation with the goods, services, or business of the user. Intra-company sales, transient use in shipping or storage, or other transactions that do not put the designation before prospective purchasers will not support a claim to trademark rights. Similarly, the manner of use must project to prospective purchasers the significance of the designation as an identifying symbol. Although there are no technical requirements as to the size or prominence of the use, the designation must create a separate commercial impression, distinct from that created by other accompanying marks, that signifies the designation's function as a symbol of identification. Use of the designation in a location or size that is not likely to attract the attention of prospective purchasers, for example, or use in textual material in a manner that does not create a distinct impression as an identifying symbol will not suffice. If the manner of use is not in itself sufficient to establish that the designation has been used as an identifying symbol, the requirement of use may be satisfied by proof that the designation is in fact perceived by prospective purchasers as an indication of source or other association with the user. The proof of secondary meaning that is required under the rule stated in § 13(b) for designations that are not inherently distinctive thus also satisfies the use requirement imposed under this Section.

The law of trademarks originally recognized as "use" only the direct physical affixation of the designation to the goods marketed by the person claiming trademark rights. A designation that was not physically affixed to the goods could not be protected as a technical "trademark" in an action for trademark infringement. See § 9, Comment *d*. In part the reason was historical, since trademarks developed from medieval production marks that were affixed to goods manufactured by the local guilds. *Id.*, Comment *b*. The requirement of physical affixation also served to facilitate proof of use by minimizing disputed issues of fact. A designation that was not protectable as a technical "trademark" because of the affixation requirement, however, could be protected in an action for unfair competition upon proof that it had become associated with the goods or services of the person seeking relief. *Id.*, Comment *d*.

Changes in commercial practices eventually made the requirement of physical affixation impractical. Designations adopted to indicate the source of services, for example, achieved protection at common law and under the federal trademark statute despite the impossibility of physical affixation. Modern marketing techniques also rendered the affixation requirement obsolete with respect to trademarks for goods. Use of a designation in the various advertising media can now establish the designation's significance as an identifying symbol as surely as its appearance on packaging or labels. Although physical affixation remains a common method of trademark use, the rule stated in this Section recognizes any manner of use that is sufficient to create an association between the designation and the user's goods or services. Common forms of trademark use on goods include placement of the mark on labels, tags, containers, or other packaging for the goods or the imprinting or similar affixation of the mark on the goods themselves. Under the rule as stated in this Section, use of a mark on point of sale displays, price lists, menus, or mail solicitations can also constitute use as a trademark, as can other advertising uses calculated to inform prospective purchasers of the association between the designation and the user or the user's goods and services.

In the case of goods, trademark claims based on a use of the mark in advertising are typically raised in an attempt to establish rights prior to the initiation of actual sales. The use of a designation in pre-sales solicitations, presentations, or other advertising can result in the creation of good will symbolized by the designation even before any actual sales. The case law, although not always denominating the user's interest a trademark, frequently recognizes in such circumstances the user's right to protection against unfair competition resulting from a use of the designation by another. Under the rule as stated in this Section, such pre-sales activity can qualify as a trademark use if the use is calculated to produce the required association between the mark and the user's goods and is done in the user's ordinary course of business.

The physical nature of the use necessary to support registration of a trademark for goods under the Lanham Act is more circumscribed that the rules described here. The statute requires use on the goods or on their containers or labels, or on displays associated with the goods, or if such use is impracticable, on documents associated with the goods. 15 U.S.C.A. § 1127. The breadth of activities sufficient to constitute use on "associated" displays, however, continues to expand, thus bringing the requirements for registration closer to the rule stated in this Section. The displays, for example, need not be in close physical association with the goods. Use of a mark on a menu can be sufficient to register a trademark for sandwiches, and use of a mark in taking orders at a trade fair can be sufficient for registration even if the goods are not physically present at the point of sale. Further, methods of use that do not fulfill the statutory requirements for registration can be "tacked" onto subsequent qualifying uses in order to establish priority of use over others. Use in any manner sufficient to acquire rights under the rule stated in this Section will thus preserve the user's right to register the designation against subsequent users if such use is followed by use in the manner required under the Lanham Act.

Rights can be acquired in a service mark under both the common law and the Lanham Act through use of the mark in the sale or rendering of the service, such as the presence of the mark on vehicles, equipment, or documents associated with the service, and also through use of the mark in advertisements for the service, whether at the point of sale or elsewhere.

Trade names identify businesses and similar enterprises. § 12. The mere adoption of a trade name, including incorporation under the name, does not constitute use as a trade name under this Section. See § 12, Illustration 1. The name must be used in a manner that creates a public association between the designation and the particular business or enterprise. Although trade names often appear on the goods sold by the business or with the services rendered by the business, such use is not required. The necessary use of a trade name may also be established by its appearance on signs, documents employed in conducting business, mail solicitations, or advertising. If a trade name in whole or in part is used to identify the goods or services of the business, it is also protectable as a trademark.

Collective trademarks are trademarks used by members of a collective group. They must be used in a manner analogous to other trademarks. See § 10, Illustrations 1 and 2. Collective membership marks identify the members of a collective group rather than the goods or services of members. A designation is used as a collective membership mark when it is publicly used to indicate the fact of membership through its appearance on membership cards or certificates, pins, plaques, letterhead, or other materials signifying that the user is a member of the collective group. See § 10, Comment *c*, Illustrations 3–5. Depending on the nature of the use, a designation intended for use as a collective membership mark may also be protectable as a trade name or trademark of the collective organization even before the commencement of use as a membership mark by the members of the organization.

Certification marks are used to certify the qualities or characteristics of goods and services. A designation is used as a certification mark when it is used in connection with the goods or services of others, in a manner analogous to a trademark, for the purpose of identifying the certified goods or services. See § 11, Illustrations 1–3.

Illustrations:

4. *A* manufacturers fertilizer spikes used for feeding trees and shrubs. *A* places the designation SUN in large letters on the front of each package to identify the goods as its own. The packages are then sold to retailers of garden supplies. Because *A* has used the designation in a manner likely to cause prospective purchasers to associate the designation with goods produced by *A*, the designation has been used as a trademark under the rule stated in this Section.

5. The facts being otherwise as stated in Illustration 4, *A* also places on the back of each package a small stylized drawing of a bending man hammering a fertilizer spike into the ground. Because *A* has not used the illustration in a manner likely to cause prospective purchasers to associate the illustration with goods produced by *A*, *A* can establish that it has used the

illustration as a trademark only through proof that prospective purchasers in fact associate the illustration with *A* 's goods.

6. *A*, a manufacturer of chemicals sold in bulk to industrial customers, adopts the designation IMAGINATIVE SOLUTIONS to identify its products. The designation is prominently displayed on the booth at which *A* takes orders for the chemicals at trade fairs. Because *A* has used the designation in a manner likely to cause prospective purchasers to associate the designation with goods produced by *A*, the designation has been used as a trademark under the rule stated in this Section.

7. *A*, a publishing company, adopts the designation NEW WORLD for a magazine that it plans to introduce within several months. *A* sends a mockup of an issue of NEW WORLD magazine with sample advertising and editorial copy to a number of advertising agencies. After a press release announcing the intended publication of NEW WORLD, *A* sends to prospective subscribers direct mail solicitations with an exemplar cover of the magazine bearing the NEW WORLD designation. Although *A* has not yet begun publication of the magazine, its use of the NEW WORLD mark is in the ordinary course of business. Because *A* has used the designation in a manner likely to cause prospective purchasers to associate the designation with goods produced by *A*, the designation has been used as a trademark under the rule stated in this Section.

8. *A* operates an unincorporated retail bakery. *A* uses the trade name STARLITE on signs and in newspaper advertising to identify its business. Because *A* has used the designation in a manner likely to cause prospective purchasers to associate the designation with *A* 's business, the designation has been used as a trade name under the rule stated in this Section.

REPORTERS' NOTE

The subject matter of this Section was originally treated in Restatement of Torts §§ 718–719 (1938). This Section retains the substance of the use requirement stated in § 719, but it does not carry forward the requirement of physical affixation formerly applicable to trademarks under § 718.

Comment a. For general discussions of the "use" requirement, see Gilson, Trademark Protection and Practice § 3.02; McCarthy, Trademarks and Unfair Competition §§ 16.01–12, 19.36–39. See, e.g., Zazu Designs v. L'Oreal, S.A., 979 F.2d 499, 503 (7th Cir.1992) (the use requirement "prevents entrepreneurs from reserving brand names in order to make their rivals' marketing more costly" and lets "others know that they should not invest resources to develop a mark similar to one already used in the trade").

Comment b. Cases that recognized token use as sufficient for federal registration prior to the 1988 intent-to-use amendments to the Lanham Act include Int'l Mobile Machines Corp. v. Int'l Tel. & Tel. Corp., 800 F.2d 1118 (Fed.Cir.1986); Ralston Purina Co. v. On–Cor Frozen Foods, Inc., 746 F.2d 801 (Fed.Cir. 1984); Fort Howard Paper Co. v. Kimberly–Clark Corp., 390 F.2d 1015 (C.C.P.A.), cert. denied 393 U.S. 831, 89 S.Ct. 99, 21 L.Ed.2d 101 (1968); Ginseng–Up Corp. v. American Ginseng Co., 215 U.S.P.Q. 471 (S.D.N.Y. 1981); Standard Pressed Steel Co. v. Midwest Chrome Process Co., 183 U.S.P.Q. 758 (Tm.Tr.App.Bd.1974). Cf. Procter & Gamble Co. v. Johnson & Johnson Inc., 485 F.Supp. 1185 (S.D.N.Y.1979), affirmed without op., 636 F.2d 1203 (2d Cir.1980), refusing to recognize registration rights based on token use in the absence of a present intention to develop trade under the designation. The distinction between "registration use" and use sufficient to acquire rights at common law was emphasized in Blue Bell, Inc. v. Farah Mfg. Co., 508 F.2d 1260 (5th Cir.1975). See also Zazu Designs v. L'Oreal, S.A., 979 F.2d 499 (7th Cir. 1992) (the distinction is justified since registration itself satisfies the notice function of the use requirement). On the requirement under the Lanham Act that the use be "in commerce," see Gilson, *supra* § 3.02; McCarthy, *supra* §§ 19.36–38.

The Senate Report accompanying the Trademark Law Revision Act of 1988, discussing the "bona fide intention" to use necessary to support an intent-to-use application, states that the requirement "should be read to mean a fair, objective determination of the applicant's intent based on all the circumstances." S.Rep.No. 515, 100th Cong., 2d Sess. 24 (1988). In some instances multiple intent-to-use applications may themselves cast doubt on the bona fide nature of the applicant's intent. *Id.* at 23–24. On the intent-to-use provisions, see Leeds, Intent to Use—Its Time Has Come, 79 Trademark Rep. 269 (1989). See generally Gilson, *supra*, § 3.04[2]; McCarthy, *supra*, §§ 19.-07–08.

Comment c. Judge Friendly summarized the rule on acquisition of trademark rights in La Societe Anonyme des Parfums le Galion v. Jean Patou, Inc., 495 F.2d 1265, 1271 (2d Cir.1974): "The user who first appropriates the mark obtains an enforceable right to exclude others from using it, as long as the initial appropriation and use are accompanied by an intention to continue exploiting the mark commercially." See, e.g., Blue Bell, Inc. v. Farah Mfg. Co., 508 F.2d 1260, 1265 (5th Cir.1975) ("[E]ven a single use in trade may sustain trademark rights if followed by continuous commercial utilization."). Compare Zazu Designs v. L'Oreal, S.A., 979 F.2d 499 (7th Cir.1992), finding a small number of sales insufficient under the facts to establish trademark rights.

The House Report accompanying the Trademark Law Revision Act of 1988, H.R.Rep.No. 1028, 100th Cong., 2d Sess. 15 (1988), emphasizes that the interpretation of use "in the ordinary course of trade" may vary by industry, but token use for the purpose of reserving a mark is not sufficient. See Gilson, *supra*, § 3.02[8]; McCarthy, *supra*, § 19.37[1].

Illustrations 1 and 2 are based on Illustrations 1 and 2 to Restatement of Torts § 719 (1938).

Illustration 3 is based on Stern Electronics, Inc. v. Kaufman, 669 F.2d 852 (2d Cir.1982). Cf. Blue Bell, Inc., *supra* (adding a designation intended for use on a new product to old goods already ordered by customers under an existing mark is not a bona fide use). See also La Societe Anonyme, *supra* (small-scale use intended to bar imports by a foreign user does not constitute "good faith commercial exploitation").

In Erva Pharmaceuticals, Inc. v. American Cyanamid Co., 755 F.Supp. 36 (D.P.R.1991), the court held that the use of a mark on a drug sold in violation of federal labelling laws was not a lawful use that could establish trademark rights. On the effect of "unlawful" use on applications for registration under the Lanham Act, see Kellogg Co. v. New Generation Foods, Inc., 6 U.S.P.Q.2d 2045 (Tm. Tr.App.Bd.1988); McCarthy, *supra*, § 19.39. See also § 32, Comment *d.*

Comment d. On the necessity of public use, see e.g., Blue Bell, Inc. v. Farah Mfg. Co., 508 F.2d 1260 (5th Cir.1975) (no rights acquired through sales to regional managers of the user); In re Lyndale Farm, 186 F.2d 723 (C.C.P.A.1951) (use on shipping crates for cattle insufficient because the designation would not come to the attention of wholesale or retail purchasers). Sales made under the mark to independent distributors can be sufficient to constitute trademark use. E.g., Raintree Publishers, Inc. v. Brewer, 218 U.S.P.Q. 272 (Tm.Tr. App.Bd.1983).

The former common law requirement of affixation stated in Restatement of Torts § 718 was abandoned in a Tentative Draft of this topic prepared in 1963 in connection with the Restatement, Second, of Torts. See Tent. Draft No.8 § 719 (1963). See also Gilson, *supra*, § 3.02[6] ("The overall trend appears to be away from strict affixation and in the direction of legal protection more in keeping with modern business practices and realities."); McCarthy, *supra*, § 16.09 ("Such a rigid test of priority is no longer in keeping with modern advertising methods where media advertising may make a greater impression on buyers than symbols physically imprinted on a package or label.").

Illustrations 4 and 5 are suggested by the facts in In re Int'l Spike, Inc., 196 U.S.P.Q. 447 (Tm.Tr.App.Bd. 1977), which held that the drawing was not used as a trademark and that it was also descriptive, thus requiring proof of secondary meaning. Compare In re Morganroth, 208 U.S.P.Q. 284 (Tm.Tr.App.Bd.1980) (slogan used in advertising did not create a separate impression as an indication of the source of the advertised services), with In re First Union National Bank, 223 U.S.P.Q. 278 (Tm.Tr.App. Bd.1984) (reaching the opposite conclusion on the facts).

Illustration 6 is based on In re Shipley Co., 230 U.S.P.Q. 691 (Tm.Tr. App.Bd.1986). Non-affixed uses held sufficient under the Lanham Act to support federal registration of a trademark for goods usually involve point of sale displays. But cf. In re Griffin Pollution Control Corp., 517 F.2d 1356 (C.C.P.A.1975) (descriptive material distributed to the public could be "displays associated with the goods") (dictum); Lands' End, Inc. v. Manbeck, 797 F.Supp. 511 (E.D.Va. 1992) (use of a mark by a mail order business in a catalog was sufficient for registration since the use was in effect a point of sale display). Other uses held sufficient to constitute trademark use despite a lack of physical affixation to the goods include use on menus, In re Marriott Corp., 459 F.2d 525 (C.C.P.A.1972), sales solicitations, New West Corp. v. NYM Co., 595 F.2d 1194 (9th Cir.1979), and delivery trucks, In re E.A. Miller & Sons Packing Co., 225 U.S.P.Q. 592 (Tm.Tr.App.Bd.1985). Cf. Malcolm Nicol & Co. v. Witco Corp., 881 F.2d 1063 (Fed.Cir.1989) (use in advertising can be sufficient to create an association with the designation for purposes of cancelling another's registration). On the right to "tack" use that does not meet the statutory requirements for registration onto the first qualifying use for purposes of establishing priority under the Lanham Act, see Dynamet Technology, Inc. v. Dynamet Inc., 593 F.2d 1007 (C.C.P.A.1979) (trade name use); Oromeccanica, Inc. v. Ottmar Botzenhardt G.m.b.H. & Co. KG, 223 U.S.P.Q. 59, 64 (Tm.Tr.App.Bd.1983) (for priority, it is sufficient to have made "use 'analogous to' trademark (or service mark) use such as use in advertising, as a trade name, or grade mark, or in a promotional sense, etc."). Illustration 7 is based on *New West Corp., supra.* See, e.g., Marvel Comics Ltd. v. Defiant, Ltd., 28 U.S.P.Q.2d 1794 (S.D.N.Y.1993) (pre-publication promotion of a comic book series can create trademark rights in the title); Maryland Stadium Authority v. Becker, 806 F.Supp. 1236 (D.Md.1992) (promotion of new stadium created rights in the name prior to actual sales of goods or services); Geo. Washington Mint, Inc. v. Washington Mint Inc., 349 F.Supp. 255 (S.D.N.Y.1972) (priority based on use in pre-sales solicitations). See also Sunbeam Corp. v. Merit Enterprises, Inc., 451 F.Supp. 571 (S.D.N.Y.1978) (first use found in pre-sale presentation of product with designation affixed). Cf. Stabilisierungsfonds fur Wein v. Zimmermann–Graeff KG, 206 U.S.P.Q. 934 (Tm.Tr.App.Bd.1979) (suggesting that rights in a certification mark might be acquired prior to its actual use on the certified goods if the mark has already become known). On the requirement that the pre-sales activity be in the ordinary course of business, see, e.g., Evans Chemetics, Inc. v. Chemetics Int'l Ltd., 207 U.S.P.Q. 695, 700 (Tm.Tr.App.Bd.1980), requiring, in order to establish service mark use through pre-sales advertising, that "the services were actually rendered or available for performance soon enough after the initial advertising campaign to preclude a finding that the advertising was merely an attempt to preempt a mark for use at an indefinite future date." See also Metro–Goldwyn Mayer, Inc. v. Lee, 212 Cal.App.2d 23, 27 Cal.Rptr. 833 (1963) (noting, in upholding pre-release rights in a movie title, the "economic necessity" of pre-release publicity in the film industry).

Compare Illustration 8 with Illustration 1 to § 12.

§ 19. Priority of Rights

One who has used a designation as a trademark, trade name, collective mark, or certification mark under the rule stated in § 18 has priority in the use of the designation over another user:

(a) in any geographic area in which the actor has used the designation in good faith or in which the

designation has become associated with the actor as a result of good faith use before the designation is used in good faith by, or becomes associated with, the other; and

(b) in any additional geographic area in which the actor has priority over the other under an applicable statutory provision.

Comment:

a. Priority of appropriation. The priority of rights in a designation is generally determined by the priority of appropriation. The priority extends, however, only to the geographic areas described in this Section. Subsection (a) describes the geographic scope of rights recognized at common law and in actions for the infringement of unregistered marks under § 43(a) of the Lanham Act. Subsection (b) refers to the more expansive protection available through federal registration. See Comment *e*. If a person has priority over another in the use of a designation in the relevant geographic area, the other will be subject to liability for infringement for uses that result in a likelihood of confusion. See § 20.

The rules in this Section establish the relative priority of the parties' rights in particular geographic areas. It is sufficient for a plaintiff seeking relief under the rule stated in § 20 to establish that its rights have priority over those of the defendant in the relevant area, regardless of whether the plaintiff's rights are also superior to those of third persons. However, if plaintiff's own use of the mark infringes the rights of a third person, the plaintiff's relief against the defendant may be limited under the rule stated in § 32. If, because of a third person's prior use, the designation is not in fact distinctive of the goods, services, or business of the plaintiff, the defendant is not subject to liability to the plaintiff since the plaintiff has not acquired rights in the designation. See § 18, Comment *a*.

b. Areas of use and reputation. A person who has used a designation in good faith as a trademark, trade name, collective mark, or certification mark has priority over a subsequent user in those geographic areas in which the prior user has used the designation or in which the designation has become associated with the prior user before the commencement of use in that area by the subsequent user. Thus, the prior user has priority in areas in which a subsequent use of the designation by another would be likely to confuse prospective purchasers.

To establish prior use of a mark in a particular area, a prior user must, at a minimum, prove a level of use in the ordinary course of business in that area that is sufficient to acquire rights in the mark under the rule stated in § 18. As against a subsequent user who has invested in the designation without knowledge of the prior use, some courts, in weighing the respective equities, require more substantial use by the prior user in order to establish priority in the area of concurrent use. Small or sporadic use has sometimes been dismissed as de minimis. In determining the prior user's area of use, the number and dollar value of sales in the area, the number of customers, and the pattern of sales over time, among other factors, are relevant.

The geographic scope of priority extends beyond the area in which the prior user has actually used the mark if the user's association with the mark is known to prospective purchasers in other areas. Advertising, for example, may carry the reputation of the mark beyond the geographic market in which the trademark owner conducts business. Similarly, if goods bearing the trademark are transported by purchasers to other areas, or if the business attracts customers from distant locations, as in the case of a hotel, the designation may become known in areas far removed from the user's immediate location or actual area of sales. Thus, evidence relating to the nature and extent of the user's advertising and other promotional activities, the geographic distribution of catalogs and solicitations, the geographic origin of orders and inquiries from consumers, the geographic distribution of goods bearing the user's mark, the ambulatory character of the user's customers, and surveys and testimony from prospective purchasers residing in the area are all relevant to a determination of the geographic scope of a prior user's priority.

The rules recognizing priority in areas in which the mark or trade name is used or associated with the prior user are equally applicable to inherently distinctive designations and designations that require proof of distinctiveness under the rule stated in § 13(b). However, the latter designations are not protectable as trademarks, trade names, collective marks, or certifications marks until they have acquired the necessary secondary meaning. Thus, for purposes of the rule stated here, such designations are used or known as a mark or trade name in a particular area only when they have acquired secondary meaning in that area. If the prior user's designation has not yet acquired secondary meaning in the relevant area, the prior user does not have priority over a subsequent good faith user who adopts the designation in that area.

Illustrations:

1. *A* operates a hotel in New York under the trade name MERCURY SUITES. *A* makes substantial expenditures on na-

tionwide advertising for the hotel in magazines and newspapers. *A* 's hotel is also mentioned in numerous articles and news stories in the national media. *A* has priority in the use of the name against all subsequent users because the name has become associated with *A* 's business throughout the country.

2. *A* operates several discount stores in the Midwest under the trade name SHOPPERS FAIR. Advertising for each store is confined to the local media in the city in which the store is located. The name SHOPPERS FAIR has become distinctive of *A* 's business in each of these cities. *B*, without knowledge of *A* 's use, opens a similar store in Boston under the trade name *B* 's SHOPPERS FAIR. *A* does not have priority over *B* in the use of the name in Boston unless *A* can establish that the name has become distinctive of *A* 's business in Boston.

c. Zone of probable expansion. In an effort to preserve the prior user's opportunity for geographic expansion under its trademark or trade name, a number of decisions purport to extend the scope of priority beyond areas of current use or reputation to the prior user's "zone of probable or natural expansion." This extension of the prior user's priority is theoretically independent of the knowledge or good faith of subsequent users. Under this doctrine, a prior user who can prove neither use nor current association with the mark in the disputed area can nevertheless prevail over a subsequent good faith user by establishing that the area is within the zone of the prior user's natural expansion.

The doctrine of natural expansion has rarely been decisive in determining priority. Many of the opinions in which the doctrine is invoked also find that the prior user's mark was already known in the relevant area, thus permitting relief under the rule discussed in the preceding Comment. The factual indeterminacy of the "zone of natural expansion" also invites implicit consideration of other equities. When raised against a subsequent good faith user, the doctrine typically has been rejected on the facts. Some recent decisions go further, explicitly repudiating the doctrine as an independent basis of priority.

The policy justification for the zone of natural expansion doctrine as developed at common law has also been eroded by the statutory doctrines of constructive notice and constructive use available to federally registered marks. As described in Comment *e*, these statutory mechanisms afford a prior user the opportunity to insure priority over subsequent users in remote areas, while also providing an accessible public record of the prior user's claim. A person who forgoes the territorial advantages of registration under the Lanham Act thus can no longer raise the equitable claim to protection against good faith remote users that served as the genesis of the natural expansion doctrine.

The rule stated in this Section does not recognize a claim to priority based solely on a right to natural expansion. However, if a subsequent user adopts the mark in a particular area with knowledge of the prior user's likely expansion into that area, the subsequent use is not in good faith. See Comment *d*.

d. Good faith use in remote areas. A subsequent user who has used the designation in good faith in a remote area where the prior user's mark is neither used nor known acquires priority in that area over the prior user. Each party then has priority over the other in its respective area for purposes of determining infringement under the rule stated in § 20. However, if the adoption of the mark by the subsequent user, although remote, is in bad faith, the subsequent user remains subject to the rights of the prior user.

Knowledge of another's prior use of the designation is a critical factor in evaluating good faith. If, at the time a subsequent user commences use of the mark, the user has no actual knowledge of the prior use by another, the use is in good faith, at least absent evidence indicating a bad faith attempt to avoid the acquisition of such knowledge. Use of a designation with knowledge of its previous use on similar goods, services, or businesses by another, however, raises an inference of bad faith. Some cases elevate this inference to a rule of law precluding a remote subsequent user with knowledge of the prior use from claiming use in good faith. Other cases, although recognizing the relevance of such knowledge, evaluate the subsequent user's good faith based upon the totality of circumstances surrounding the use of the mark. The rule as stated in Subsection (a) does not accord conclusive significance to the subsequent user's knowledge of the prior use.

Adoption of a mark or name already in use by another is not in good faith if the subsequent user intends or expects that its use will create, either immediately or in the future, a likelihood of confusion with the goods, services, or business of the prior user. The same is true if the designation is adopted by the subsequent user for the purpose or with the expectation of forestalling expansion under the mark by the prior user or causing injury to the prior user's reputation or good will. Evidence indicating that the subsequent user knowingly adopted the mark on goods or services similar to those of the prior user in an area of likely expansion by the prior user or in an area in which the mark is likely to become associated with the prior user can be sufficient to establish bad faith. In addition to evidence relating to the nature and extent of the subsequent user's knowledge, the factors listed in § 21 relating to the likelihood of confusion are also relevant in evaluating the subsequent user's good faith, including the degree of similarity between the respective marks, the nature of the respective goods, services, or businesses, the similarity of marketing channels and methods, the distinctiveness of the prior user's mark, and the proximity of the respective areas of use. Good faith reliance by the subsequent user on an opinion of counsel is also relevant. If the mark is highly distinctive, evidence of the subsequent user's adoption with knowledge of the other's prior use on similar products may itself justify an inference of bad faith.

Priority in areas into which a remote good faith user later expands is also determined by the rules stated in this Section. Thus, the subsequent user cannot acquire priority through expansion into areas where the prior user's mark is already used or known. Expansion into other remote areas remains subject to the requirement of good faith, evaluated on the basis of the subsequent user's current knowledge and the equities created by the subsequent user's good faith investment in the designation. On the effect of federal registration by the prior user, see Comment *e*.

The recognition of concurrent rights in the same or similar designations can require a delicate balancing of interests, particularly when expansion results in use by the parties in contiguous areas. Each user enjoys a right to protection against both direct and reverse confusion (see § 20, Comment *f*) within its area of priority, but the enforcement of that right should not invade the concomitant right of each party to exploit the mark within its own area of priority. In such circumstances some residual confusion may be inevitable. A national user that is subject to the prior rights of another in a local area, for example, is not obliged to forgo the use of national advertising media if it has taken reasonable precautions to minimize the impact on the local market. Some of the remedial problems inherent in the recognition of concurrent rights are considered in § 35, Comment *f*.

Illustrations:

3. *A* has operated a small restaurant in San Diego under the designation BURGERS & BREW since 1975. *B* became acquainted with *A* 's restaurant during a brief visit to San Diego in 1983. In 1990, after an investigation reveals no use of a similar name in Washington, *B* opens a restaurant in Seattle under that name. In the absence of evidence that *B* 's use is likely to cause present or future confusion or prevent likely expansion under the name by *A*, a court may properly conclude that *B* 's use of the name is in good

faith and that *B* thus has priority over *A* in the use of the name in *B* 's area of use and reputation.

4. The facts being otherwise as stated in Illustration 3, *A* begins to license the use of the name to franchisees in 1985. During the next four years, ten licensed BURGERS & BREW restaurants are opened, including franchises in Los Angeles, San Francisco, and Portland, Oregon. *B* has knowledge of these franchises prior to opening its Seattle restaurant. Because *B* could reasonably foresee that its use of the name is likely to cause present or future confusion or prevent likely expansion under the name by *A*, *B* 's use of the name is not in good faith. *B* thus does not have priority over *A* in the use of the name in the Seattle area.

e. Priority under federal and state statutes. The system of federal trademark registration implemented in the Lanham Act promotes a policy of national trademark protection by limiting instances of territorial fragmentation and concurrent rights. The enhanced geographic priority available under the Act is a primary incentive to federal registration.

Section 22 of the Lanham Act, 15 U.S.C.A. § 1072, provides that registration of a mark on the principal register shall be "constructive notice" of the registrant's claim of ownership. This provision has been interpreted to preclude others from acquiring priority over the registrant in remote areas through subsequent use of the mark. The owner of a federal registration thus enjoys priority in the use of the designation against all persons who commence use after the date of registration.

Amendments to the Lanham Act effective in 1989 expand the geographic scope of priority for registered marks through the concept of "constructive use." Section 7(c), 15 U.S.C.A. § 1057(c), provides that, contingent upon ultimate registration, the filing of an application for registration on the principal register constitutes "constructive use of the mark, conferring a right of priority, nationwide in effect," against others who have not previously used the mark or filed an application for its registration. The filing of an application for registration is thus equivalent to nationwide use, thereby preventing third persons from acquiring rights in the mark through commencement of use after the registrant's filing date. Constructive use applies to all applications for registration, whether founded on the applicant's intent-to-use or actual use of the designation. Its practical effect is to move the date after which others can no longer acquire priority in the designation from the date of registration to the date of filing. Although both constructive notice under § 22 and constructive use under

§ 7(c) operate to insure the registrant's priority over subsequent users in remote areas, the registrant is not entitled to remedies for infringement unless the subsequent use creates a likelihood of confusion.

Neither "constructive notice" nor "constructive use" undermines existing rights previously acquired by others under the common law rules described in the preceding Comments. The "constructive notice" provision in § 22, however, has been interpreted to preclude a subsequent user who has acquired concurrent common law rights in a designation from extending its priority over the registrant through expansion occurring after the prior user's registration. Registration by the prior user thus effectively freezes the geographic scope of the subsequent user's priority. If the registration has become incontestable under § 15 of the Lanham Act, 15 U.S.C.A. § 1065, a similar result is explicit in § 33(b)(5), 15 U.S.C.A. § 1115(b)(5), which limits the subsequent user's defense to the area of its continuous use prior to the registrant's filing or registration date. A subsequent user with priority over the registrant in a remote area may obtain the advantages of federal registration through a geographically restricted concurrent registration under § 2(d) of the Lanham Act, 15 U.S.C.A. § 1052(d), thus limiting the geographic scope of the prior user's registration.

State trademark registration statutes have not generally been interpreted to confer priority in the use of the registered mark beyond the area of the registrant's common law rights. Application of state registration statutes in a manner that conflicts with the geographic scope of a federal registrant's priority under the Lanham Act is preempted.

Illustrations:

5. *A* files an intent-to-use application under the Lanham Act on June 1, 1990, to register the mark BRAVO for cheese. On July 1, 1990, *B* commences use of the mark BRAVO on yogurt. *A* begins shipping BRAVO cheese in commercial quantities to brokers and retailers in several states on November 1, 1990, and ultimately obtains a registration on the principal register. *A* has nationwide priority over *B* in the use of the designation because *B* did not commence use of the mark until after *A* 's June 1, 1990, date of nationwide "constructive use."

6. In 1983, *A* begins to use the designation KING as a service mark in connection with a chain of Florida restaurants. In 1984, *B* adopts the same designation for use with a restaurant in Illinois without knowledge of *A* 's prior use. In 1985, *A* files an application to register the mark under the Lanham Act. The registration is issued in 1986. *B*, in 1987, begins use of the

designation on another restaurant located in Ohio. In 1991, *A* 's registration becomes incontestable. *A* has priority over *B* in the use of the designation in all areas except in the area of *B* 's use in connection with the Illinois restaurant because *B* acquired priority over *A* only in that area prior to *A* 's federal registration.

REPORTERS' NOTE

This Section combines the rules on priority formerly stated in Restatement of Torts §§ 732–733 (1938). In addition to the prior user's area of trade protected under the former rule, this Section recognizes priority in other areas in which the mark is associated with the prior user. This Section also encompasses the rules governing the geographic priority of trademarks registered under the Lanham Act.

For general discussions of the geographic scope of trademark rights, see McCarthy, Trademarks and Unfair Competition §§ 26.01–19; Alexander and Coil, Geographic Rights in Trademarks and Service Marks, 68 Trademark Rep. 101 (1978).

Comment a. On the general rule of priority of rights, see, e.g., Columbia Mill Co. v. Alcorn, 150 U.S. 460, 463–64, 14 S.Ct. 151, 152, 37 L.Ed. 1144, 1146 (1893), reciting among its "general propositions" of trademark law "[t]hat the exclusive right to the use of the mark or device claimed as a trade-mark is founded on priority of appropriation." The principle cases recognizing territorial limits on the scope of trademark rights are Hanover Star Milling Co. v. Metcalf, 240 U.S. 403, 36 S.Ct. 357, 60 L.Ed. 713 (1916) and United Drug Co. v. Theodore Rectanus Co., 248 U.S. 90, 39 S.Ct. 48, 63 L.Ed. 141 (1918).

For cases indicating that relative and not absolute priority is sufficient for the imposition of liability, see, e.g., Specialty Measurements, Inc. v. Measurement Systems, Inc., 763 F.Supp. 91 (D.N.J.1991); Marshak v. Sheppard, 666 F.Supp. 590 (S.D.N.Y. 1987); Eagle Snacks, Inc. v. Nabisco Brands, Inc., 625 F.Supp. 571 (D.N.J. 1985); Bulk Mfg. Co. v. Schoenbach Products Co., 208 U.S.P.Q. 664 (S.D.N.Y.1980). See also Stock Pot Restaurant, Inc. v. Stockpot, Inc., 737 F.2d 1576 (Fed.Cir.1984) (applying a similar rule to cancellation proceedings under the Lanham Act). See generally McCarthy, *supra*, § 31.39.

Comment b. Priority in areas of use and reputation was recognized by the Supreme Court in Hanover Star Milling Co. v. Metcalf, 240 U.S. 403, 415–16, 36 S.Ct. 357, 361–62, 60 L.Ed. 713, 719 (1916) ("Into whatever markets the use of a trade-mark has extended, or its meaning has become known, there will the manufacturer or trader whose trade is pirated by an infringing use be entitled to protection and redress."). The Eighth Circuit, in a frequently cited analysis of the extent of a prior user's market area, instructed the trial court to "weigh all the factors including plaintiff's dollar value of sales at the time defendants entered the market, number of customers compared to the population of the state, relative and potential growth of sales, and length of time since significant sales." Sweetarts v. Sunline, Inc., 380 F.2d 923, 929 (8th Cir.1967). See also the later opinion at 436 F.2d 705 (8th Cir.1971) (reiterating that "the market penetration must be 'significant enough to pose the real likelihood of confusion among the consumers in that area' "). See, e.g., Charles Jacquin Et Cie, Inc. v. Destileria Serralles, Inc., 921 F.2d 467 (3d Cir. 1990), on remand 784 F.Supp. 231 (E.D.Pa.1992); Wrist–Rocket Manufacturing Co. v. Saunders Archery Co., 578 F.2d 727 (8th Cir.1978); ACCU Personnel, Inc. v. AccuStaff, Inc., 846 F.Supp. 1191 (D.Del.1994). Compare Sweet Sixteen Co. v. Sweet "16" Shop, Inc., 15 F.2d 920 (8th Cir. 1926), adopting, against a subsequent user with knowledge of the prior use, a test of market penetration by the prior user requiring only use analogous to that necessary to establish use as a trademark as described in § 18.

On Illustration 1, see Stork Restaurant, Inc. v. Sahati, 166 F.2d 348 (9th Cir.1948) (granting the owner of a New York night club an injunction against use of the name STORK CLUB on a San Francisco tavern). See, e.g., Tisch Hotels, Inc. v. Americana Inn, Inc., 350 F.2d 609 (7th Cir. 1965) (enjoining use of AMERICANA from plaintiff's Miami hotel on defendant's motel in Chicago). Other examples of injunctions against subsequent use in areas where the plaintiff's mark is already known are collected in McCarthy, *supra*, § 26.07.

Illustration 2 is suggested by the facts in Shoppers Fair, Inc. v. Sanders Co., 328 F.2d 496 (8th Cir.1964). Other cases requiring the prior user of a descriptive mark to prove secondary meaning in the disputed territory include, e.g., Bank of Texas v. Commerce Southwest, Inc., 741 F.2d 785 (5th Cir.1984); Home Savings of America v. Home Savings Ass'n, 219 U.S.P.Q. 157 (S.D.Tex.1982); Buscemi's Inc. v. Anthony Buscemi Delicatessen & Party Store, Inc., 96 Mich. App. 714, 294 N.W.2d 218 (1980) (for non-distinctive designations, "rights in the mark extend only so far as it is shown that secondary meaning extends"). The party seeking relief is ordinarily required to establish the existence of secondary meaning at the time of the commencement of use by the other party. "Priority depends not upon which mark succeeds in first obtaining secondary meaning but upon whether the plaintiff can prove by a preponderance of the evidence that his mark possessed secondary meaning at the time the defendant commenced his use of the mark." Saratoga Vichy Spring Co. v. Lehman, 625 F.2d 1037, 1043 (2d Cir. 1980) (quoting Scott Paper Co. v. Scott's Liquid Gold, Inc., 589 F.2d 1225, 1231 (3d Cir.1978)). See, e.g., Tone Bros., Inc. v. Sysco Corp., 28 F.3d 1192 (Fed.Cir.1994); Investacorp, Inc. v. Arabian Investment Banking Corp., 931 F.2d 1519 (11th Cir.), cert. denied ___ U.S. ___, 112 S.Ct. 639, 116 L.Ed.2d 657 (1991); Perini Corp. v. Perini Construction, Inc., 915 F.2d 121 (4th Cir.1990). Cf. Towers v. Advent Software, Inc., 913 F.2d 942 (Fed.Cir.1990) (party seeking to oppose or cancel another's trademark registration on grounds of confusing similarity must prove that the prior mark is distinctive).

Comment c. The doctrine recognizing priority in the user's "zone of natural expansion" is often traced to dictum in Hanover Star Milling Co. v. Metcalf, 240 U.S. 403, 420, 36 S.Ct. 357, 363, 60 L.Ed. 713, 721 (1916) ("We are not dealing with a case where the junior appropriator of a trade-mark is occupying territory that would probably be reached by the prior user in the natural expansion of his trade, and need pass no judgment upon such a case."). Cases invoking the doctrine in dicta despite findings of existing good will in the disputed area that make application of the doctrine unnecessary include, e.g., Food Fair Stores, Inc. v. Lakeland Grocery Corp., 301 F.2d 156 (4th Cir.), cert. denied 371 U.S. 817, 83 S.Ct. 31, 9 L.Ed.2d 58 (1962); Pedi–Care, Inc. v. Pedi–A–Care Nursing, Inc., 656 F.Supp. 449 (D.N.J.1987). "As may be seen by close examination of the leading zone of expansion cases, each rests upon a finding of secondary meaning or bad faith, or both." beef & brew, inc. v. Beef & Brew, Inc., 389 F.Supp. 179, 185–86 (D.Or.1974). See also Tally–Ho, Inc. v. Coast Community College Dist., 889 F.2d 1018 (11th Cir.1989) (the doctrine has been narrowly defined and is usually rejected on the facts).

The leading case rejecting an independent doctrine of natural expansion is Raxton Corp. v. Anania Associates, Inc., 635 F.2d 924 (1st Cir.1980), appeal after remand 668 F.2d 622 (1st Cir.1982). In addition to finding the doctrine unnecessary in light of the availability of statutory protection under the Lanham Act, the court noted "that in none of the cases cited by the parties before this court has a court applied the 'natural expansion' doctrine to bar a party from adopting a trademark in good faith merely on the ground that that user lay in the 'natural expansion path' of a prior appropriator from a remote area." *Id.* at 930. Other cases relating the doctrine to the good faith of the subsequent user include, e.g., Shoppers Fair, Inc. v. Sanders Co., 328 F.2d 496 (8th Cir.1964); beef & brew, inc., *supra*; Burger King of Florida, Inc. v. Brewer, 244 F.Supp. 293 (W.D.Tenn.1965); Buscemi's Inc. v. Anthony Buscemi Delicatessen & Party Store, Inc., 96 Mich.App. 714, 294 N.W.2d 218 (1980). See generally McCarthy, *supra*, §§ 26.08–09, noting that in most cases the zone of natural expansion doctrine has been rejected on the facts.

Comment d. The principal cases establishing the right of concurrent use at common law are Hanover Star Milling Co. v. Metcalf, 240 U.S. 403, 36 S.Ct. 357, 60 L.Ed. 713 (1916) and United Drug Co. v. Theodore Rectanus Co., 248 U.S. 90, 39 S.Ct. 48, 63 L.Ed. 141 (1918). These decisions may be responsible for the uncertainty regarding the effect of the subsequent user's knowledge of the prior use. Both decisions found that the remote subsequent use was made in good faith and without knowledge of the earlier use. Statements of the applicable principle in both opinions, however, suggest that mere knowledge may not necessarily defeat the subsequent user's claim to priority. Justice Pitney summarized the rule in *Hanover:*

> But where two parties independently are employing the same mark upon goods of the same class, but in separate markets wholly remote the one from the other, the question of prior appropriation is legally insignificant, unless at least it appear that the second adopter has selected the mark with some design inimical to the interests of the first user, such as to take the benefit of the reputation of his goods, to forestall the extension of his trade, or the like.

240 U.S. at 415, 36 S.Ct. at 361. *United Drug*, after quoting his previous reference to inimical designs, Justice Pitney found "no suggestion of a sinister purpose" in the subse-

quent user's adoption of the mark. 248 U.S. at 101, 39 S.Ct. at 52.

Cases equating good faith with an absence of knowledge of the prior use include, e.g., Money Store v. Harriscorp Finance, Inc., 689 F.2d 666 (7th Cir.1982); Phoenix Mfg. Co. v. Plymouth Mfg. Co., 286 F.Supp. 324 (D.Mass.1968); Cesare v. Work, 36 Ohio App.3d 26, 520 N.E.2d 586 (1987). See also Person's Co. v. Christman, 900 F.2d 1565 (Fed.Cir. 1990) (concurrent use registrations are not available to subsequent users who adopt with knowledge, since their knowledge justifies a presumption of customer confusion) (dictum); Woman's World Shops Inc. v. Lane Bryant Inc., 5 U.S.P.Q.2d 1985 (Tm. Tr.App.Bd.1988) (same). Cases indicating that the subsequent user's knowledge is not necessarily disqualifying include, e.g., GTE Corp. v. Williams, 904 F.2d 536, 541 (10th Cir.), cert. denied 498 U.S. 998, 111 S.Ct. 557, 112 L.Ed.2d 564 (1990) ("The ultimate focus is on whether the second user had the intent to benefit from the reputation or goodwill of the first user."); El Chico, Inc. v. El Chico Cafe, 214 F.2d 721 (5th Cir.1954); ACCU Personnel, Inc. v. AccuStaff, Inc., 846 F.Supp. 1191 (D.Del.1994) (junior user's knowledge is probative but not dispositive, citing Restatement Third, Unfair Competition § 19, Comment *d* (Tent. Draft No. 2 (1990))); Big O Tire Dealers, Inc. v. Goodyear Tire & Rubber Co., 408 F.Supp. 1219 (D.Colo.1976), modified 561 F.2d 1365 (10th Cir.1977), cert. dismissed 434 U.S. 1052, 98 S.Ct. 905, 54 L.Ed.2d 805 (1978); beef & brew, Inc. v. Beef & Brew, Inc., 389 F.Supp. 179 (D.Or.1974). See White Tower System, inc. v. White Castle System of Eating Houses Corp., 90 F.2d 67 (6th Cir.), cert. denied 302 U.S. 720, 58 S.Ct. 41, 82 L.Ed. 556 (1937) (emphasizing the reference to an "inimical" design in *Hanover*). See also, e.g., Value House v. Phillips Mercantile Co., 523 F.2d 424 (10th Cir.1975) (recognizing a subsequent user's priority despite knowledge of third-party uses); Sweetarts v. Sunline, Inc., 380 F.2d 923 (8th Cir.1967), on remand 299 F.Supp. 572 (E.D.Mo.1969), affirmed in part, reversed in part 436 F.2d 705 (8th Cir.1971) (finding good faith despite knowledge of the prior user's use on other products). Cf. Zazu Designs v. L'Oreal, S.A., 979 F.2d 499 (7th Cir.1992) (knowledge of another's intent to use a mark in the future is irrelevant, since otherwise investigation would be discouraged). The broader view of good faith adopted in this Section is also suggested in Myers, Conflicting Rights in the Same Trademark in Different Geographic Areas: Should Knowledge of Prior Use Amount to Bad Faith?, 37 Fed.B.J. (No.4) 82 (1978). The divergent authority is reviewed in McCarthy, *supra*, § 26.03. In some instances knowledge by the subsequent user may indicate that the prior user's mark is already known to consumers in the relevant area, thus establishing the prior user's priority under the rules described in Comment *b*. Cf. Person's Co., *supra* (adopting a presumption of confusion) (dictum). For cases indicating that adoption with knowledge in the prior user's zone of natural expansion constitutes bad faith, see the decisions cited in the Reporters' Note to Comment *c*.

The requirement of good faith by the subsequent user is applicable even when the prior user's trademark is not inherently distinctive. See, e.g., Fuddruckers, Inc. v. Doc's B.R. Others, Inc., 826 F.2d 837 (9th Cir.

1987); Katz Drug Co. v. Katz, 188 F.2d 696 (8th Cir.1951); beef & brew, inc., *supra*.

The principal case applying the good faith criteria in the context of subsequent expansion by a good faith remote user is Weiner King, Inc. v. Wiener King Corp., 615 F.2d 512 (C.C.P.A.1980), distinguishing expansion with knowledge of the prior use from initial adoption with knowledge and finding no intent on the part of the subsequent user to pass off or "box in" the prior user. See also Noah's, Inc. v. Nark, Inc., 560 F.Supp. 1253 (E.D.Mo.1983), affirmed 728 F.2d 410 (8th Cir.1984).

Illustration 3 is suggested by the facts in *beef & brew, inc., supra.* See, e.g., El Chico, Inc., *supra.* See also the illustration offered in Myers, *supra,* 37 Fed.B.J. (No.4) at 87–88.

Illustration 4 is supported by the results in, e.g., Burger King of Florida, Inc. v. Brewer, 244 F.Supp. 293 (W.D.Tenn.1965). Cf. Big O Tire Dealers, Inc. v. Goodyear Tire & Rubber Co., 408 F.Supp. 1219 (D.Colo.1976), modified 561 F.2d 1365 (10th Cir.1977), cert. dismissed 434 U.S. 1052, 98 S.Ct. 905, 54 L.Ed.2d 805 (1978) (finding bad faith in the subsequent user's decision to adopt the mark with knowledge that the use was likely to destroy the value of the mark to the prior user).

Comment e. Cases that interpret constructive notice of the prior use under § 22 of the Lanham Act, 15 U.S.C.A. § 1072, as barring claims of subsequent good faith adoption include, e.g., In re Beatrice Foods Co., 429 F.2d 466 (C.C.P.A.1970); John R. Thompson Co. v. Holloway, 366 F.2d 108 (5th Cir.1966); Dawn Donut Co. v. Hart's Food Stores, Inc., 267 F.2d 358 (2d Cir.1959).

Constructive notice was interpreted to freeze a good faith subsequent user's area of priority as of the date of the prior user's registration in, e.g., Thrifty Rent-A-Car System, Inc. v. Thrift Cars, Inc., 831 F.2d 1177 (1st Cir.1987); Old Dutch Foods, Inc. v. Dan Dee Pretzel & Potato Chip Co., 477 F.2d 150 (6th Cir.1973); Burger King of Florida, Inc. v. Hoots, 403 F.2d 904 (7th Cir. 1968). See Leeds, Intent to Use—Its Time Has Come, 79 Trademark Rep. 269, 281–82; McCarthy, *supra,* § 26.-18[2].

The concept of "constructive use" under § 7(c) of the Lanham Act, 15 U.S.C.A. § 1057(c), is described in United States Trademark Association Trademark Review Commission, Report and Recommendations on the United States Trademark System and the Lanham Act, 77 Trademark Rep. 375, 397–99 (1987). See also Leeds, *supra,* at 278–82; Gilson, Trademark Protection and Practice § 3.03[3].

The rule precluding remedies for infringement until the use by the subordinate user creates a present likelihood of confusion is usually traced to *Dawn Donut Co., supra.* See also, e.g., Pizzeria Uno Corp. v. Temple, 747 F.2d 1522 (4th Cir.1984); John R. Thompson Co., *supra.* See generally McCarthy, *supra,* § 26.14.

Registration under a state trademark registration statute generally does not in itself confer statewide priority. E.g., Abeyta v. State, 592 P.2d 705 (Wyo.1979); Abner's Beef House Corp. v. Abner's Int'l, Inc., 227 So.2d 865 (Fla.1969). Contra, Kirk v. Big Apple Supermarket, 42 Tenn. App. 502, 304 S.W.2d 511 (1957). See, e.g., Tally-Ho, Inc. v. Coast Community College Dist., 889 F.2d 1018 (11th Cir.1989) (state registration rights are subject to common law rights acquired by others). Federal law preempts an attempt under state trademark law to reduce the geographic priority of a federal registrant. E.g., Spartan Food Systems, Inc. v. HFS Corp., 813 F.2d 1279 (4th Cir.1987); Burger King, *supra.*

Illustration 5 is based on an Illustration appearing in the Report of the United States Trademark Association Trademark Review Commission, *supra,* at 398–99.

Illustration 6 is suggested by *Burger King, supra.* The boundaries of the non-registrant's area of priority are determined by principles analogous to those described in Comment *b.* See Natural Footwear Ltd. v. Hart, Schaffner & Marx, 760 F.2d 1383 (3d Cir.), cert. denied 474 U.S. 920, 106 S.Ct. 249, 88 L.Ed.2d 257 (1985) (adopting the factors listed in Sweetarts v. Sunline, Inc., 380 F.2d 923 (8th Cir.1967), discussed in the Reporters' Note accompanying Comment *b*). In the case of concurrent registrations, the prior user's rights arising from an incontestable registration are restricted to the geographic area encompassed in the concurrent registration. See § 33(b), 15 U.S.C.A. § 1115(b).

If it is the subsequent user who first obtains a federal registration, there is authority for restricting a later concurrent registration issued to the prior user to the prior user's area of actual use, with all remaining territory subsumed in the subsequent user's registration. See, e.g., Weiner King, Inc. v. Wiener King Corp., 615 F.2d 512 (C.C.P.A.1980) (rejecting a "mechanical approach" to determining the territorial extent of concurrent registrations); Architemps, Inc. v. Architemps, Ltd., 11 U.S.P.Q.2d 1885 (S.D.N.Y.1989). If the subsequent user's registration has become incontestable, this result is supported by the statutory delineation of incontestability in 15 U.S.C.A. § 1065. See also Noah's, Inc. v. Nark, Inc., 560 F.Supp. 1253 (E.D.Mo.1983), affirmed 728 F.2d 410 (8th Cir.1984) (restricting, in a case of co-pending applications, the concurrent registration of a static prior user to the area of its actual use). See generally McCarthy, *supra,* § 26.19.

On the priority of rights afforded pursuant to international conventions, see § 44 of the Lanham Act, 15 U.S.C.A. § 1126.

TOPIC 3. INFRINGEMENT OF RIGHTS

Section

§ 20. Standard of Infringement

(1) One is subject to liability for infringement of another's trademark, trade name, collective mark, or certification mark if the other's use has priority under the rules stated in § 19 and in identifying the actor's business or in marketing the actor's goods or services the actor uses a designation that causes a likelihood of confusion:

(a) that the actor's business is the business of the other or is associated or otherwise connected with the other; or

(b) that the goods or services marketed by the actor are produced, sponsored, certified, or approved by the other; or

(c) that the goods or services marketed by the other are produced, sponsored, certified, or approved by the actor.

(2) One is also subject to liability for infringement of another's collective membership mark if the other's use has priority under the rules stated in § 19 and the actor uses a designation that causes a likelihood of confusion that the actor is a member of or otherwise associated with the collective group.

Comment:

a. Cross-references. The rule stated in this Section applies to the infringement of any designation that is protected as a trademark, trade name, collective mark, or certification mark as defined in §§ 9–12, whether the designation is inherently distinctive or has become distinctive through the acquisition of secondary meaning. See § 13. Sections 21–23 enumerate factors relevant in proving a likelihood of confusion. The priority of use required under this Section in order to subject another to liability for infringement is determined under the rules stated in §§ 18 and 19. Defenses and limitations on the scope of relief are treated in §§ 28–32. Remedies for infringement are treated in §§ 35–37.

b. Scope. Early decisions suggested substantive differences between the protection accorded inherently distinctive marks and other designations. See § 9, Comment *d.* Inherently distinctive trademarks were eligible for the protection afforded through the action of trademark infringement; narrower protection through the action of unfair competition was available for other trade symbols including trade names. Proof of fraud was generally required as an element of unfair competition but not trademark infringement, although it is now no longer required for either. Notwithstanding some residual use of the archaic nomenclature, modern cases no longer draw a substantive distinction between the protection of inherently distinctive marks and the protection of marks that have acquired secondary meaning, or between trademarks and trade names. Trademarks identify goods and services and trade names identify businesses, but the standard of infringement is the same, and the rules stated in this and the following Sections on proof of likelihood of confusion are applicable to both types of designations.

This Section is also applicable to the infringement of collective and certification marks. Certification marks identify goods or services certified by the owner of the mark. See § 11. Collective trademarks identify goods or services produced or sponsored by a member of a collective group. Collective membership marks identify members of the collective group. See § 10. Collective membership marks can thus be infringed by a use that is likely to cause confusion as to membership as stated in Subsection (2).

The rule stated in this Section protects the right of the owner of a designation to identify its goods, services, or business and prevents the misappropriation of good will through the use of confusingly similar designations by others. The rule also protects the interests of prospective purchasers who rely on the information conveyed by trademarks and other identifying symbols in making their purchasing decisions. Liability for trademark infringement can extend to anyone who uses an infringing designation in the marketing of goods or services, including manufacturers who apply an infringing mark to their goods and distributors or retailers who market the goods under the infringing mark. Although trademark infringement arises most frequently in a commercial context, the rule stated here also protects the designations used by charitable, educational, governmental, fraternal, religious, and other nonprofit organizations to identify themselves or their goods, services, or members.

An actor is subject to liability for infringement only if it uses another's mark or name in identifying the actor's own goods, services, or business, or in representing the actor's membership in a collective group. This Section does not apply to the use of another's protected designation for other purposes. Thus, the use of a term, not as a trademark, but solely to describe the actor's goods or services is not an infringement of any trademark rights in the term. See § 28. Nor does this Section subject to liability one who uses another's protected designation to refer to the other or the other's goods, services, or business, since such use does not create a likelihood of confusion. For example, use of another's trademark in comparative advertising, even if the comparison is unfavorable to the other, does not subject the actor to liability under this Section. A false comparison, however, may subject the actor to liability under the rule stated in § 2 or under the rules relating to liability for product disparagement as stated in Restatement, Second, Torts §§ 623A–652. As a further example, see the rule permitting use of another's trademark on genuine goods stated in § 24.

Whether an actor has used another's trademark to indicate the source or sponsorship of the actor's own goods or services or has instead used the mark merely to refer to the trademark owner is not always clear, particularly when the mark is used in an expressive manner on articles such as T-shirts or posters. The perception of prospective purchasers and not the intent of the actor is determinative. If prospective purchasers falsely believe that the trademark owner is the source or sponsor of the merchandise, there is a likelihood of confusion actionable under the rule stated here. On the other hand, if the use merely causes prospective purchasers to recognize the mark as a reference to the trademark owner, the use is not an infringement. Some uses of another's mark on posters, T-shirts, or other vehicles of expression may also implicate the public and constitutional interests in free expression, and courts may thus properly demand more substantial evidence of likely confusion to support a finding of infringement.

To be actionable under this Section, the confusion must threaten the commercial interests of the owner of the mark, but it is not limited to the confusion of persons doing business directly with the actor. An actor who sells goods bearing the trademark of another to retailers or distributors for resale to consumers is subject to liability despite the fact that the actor's immediate purchasers are not confused. Similarly, although the purchaser of a counterfeit watch from a street vendor may know that the watch is a counterfeit, the commercial interests of the trademark owner may be threatened by the potential confusion of third persons. The good will of the genuine product, for example, may be harmed among prospective purchasers who examine the inferior counterfeit or who conclude that the genuine product has now become too commonplace. On the other hand, not every instance of potential confusion by third persons sufficiently threatens the commercial interests of the trademark owner to constitute an infringement. The confusion must present a significant risk to the sales or good will of the trademark owner.

Confusion that threatens a nonprofit organization's interest in avoiding harm to reputation and diversion of potential members, donors, or sponsors is also actionable under this Section.

The use of another's mark need not be explicit in order to subject the user to liability under this Section. A seller who responds to a request for trademarked goods by substituting different goods without the knowledge of the purchaser makes an implicit representation that the offered goods are those identified by the trademark and is thus subject to liability for infringement.

Illustrations:

1. Although two competing manufacturers of printing presses use similar trademarks, persons in the printing industry can easily distinguish them. Visitors touring printing facilities, however, are confused into believing that both presses originate from the same source. Neither manufacturer is subject to liability for infringement because the confusion does not threaten the commercial interests of the trademark owners.

2. In the course of a theater production, an actor drinks from a bottle bearing the trademark of a well-known soft drink and refers to the drink by its trademark. The bottle in fact contains colored water. The actor is not subject to liability for infringement.

3. *A* markets ROSE perfume. *B* promotes its own PETUNIA perfume with the phrase, "Smells just like ROSE at half the price." *B* is not subject to liability for infringement because *A* 's mark is used by *B* merely to identify *A* 's goods. If PETUNIA does not in fact smell like ROSE, *B* may be subject to liability to *A* for deceptive marketing under the rule stated in § 2.

c. Intent. Intent to deceive or confuse is not required for the imposition of liability under this Section. The likelihood of confusion standard focuses on the consequences of the defendant's conduct, not on the defendant's motives. Although early cases of trademark infringement were brought as actions at law for deceit, the element of fraud was later presumed, and eventually eliminated. See § 9, Comment *d.* Now even an innocent seller of infringing goods is subject to liability, although the remedy may be limited. See §§ 36 and 37. Nonetheless, the intent of the defendant continues to play a significant role in infringement actions. Evidence of an intent to deceive can create an inference that the prior user's mark is distinctive and that the defendant's use creates a likelihood of confusion. See § 13, Comment *e*; § 22. Defenses may be nullified by an intent to deceive, see §§ 28, 31–32, and the scope of relief may be more extensive when there has been an intentional appropriation of good will. See §§ 35–37.

d. Type of confusion prohibited. The term "likelihood of confusion" has long been used to describe the standard of liability for trademark infringement in actions at common law and under federal and state trademark and unfair competition statutes. The types of confusion actionable as trademark infringement, however, has expanded in response to changing market conditions. Early trademarks identified the manufacturer of the goods, who typically sold directly to the ultimate consumer. In such cases, confusion of "source" or "origin" meant confusion as to the identity of the manufacturer. Later cases and statutes recognized that the "source" identified by a mark can be a distributor or retailer who plays no part in manufacturing the goods but who assures the quality and consistency of the product. The trademark may also identify an entity outside the chain of distribution that controls the quality of the goods or services that are authorized to carry the mark. Courts sometimes use the term "confusion of sponsorship" to describe confusion relating to these less direct relationships between the goods or services and the owner of the mark. Whatever the terminology, it is now recognized that the good will associated with a designation can be jeopardized whenever prospective purchasers incorrectly attribute their experience with the goods or services to the owner of the designation, and in all such instances trademark law affords a remedy for the infringement. Thus, the rule stated in this Section applies to all forms of confusion, including the false belief that the owner of the mark has formally certified the goods as meeting particular standards, as in the case of a certification mark, the false belief that the subsequent user of the mark is affiliated with the owner as a franchisee, agent, or distributor, or the false belief that the subsequent user has the approval of the owner in manufacturing or marketing goods under the mark.

In some cases, such as those involving prescription drugs, the risk of physical injury created by confusingly similar trademarks has led courts to emphasize protection against confusion of products in addition to confusion of source or sponsorship. These cases, although sometimes used to illustrate an exception to normal trademark rules, in fact fit comfortably within traditional doctrine, and the attempt to recognize a separate confusion of product doctrine is unnecessary. A finding that a confusingly similar trademark is likely to cause patients, physicians, or pharmacists to select one drug in a mistaken attempt to select another, for example, is sufficient for the imposition of liability under the traditional rules relating to confusion of source. Courts are likely, however, to require less rigorous proof of likelihood of confusion when the consequences of confusion include the possibility of serious physical harm.

Although trademarks serve to identify goods or services that share a common source or sponsor, the identity of the source or sponsor may remain anonymous. It is universally recognized that a likelihood of confusion sufficient to establish infringement may exist regardless of whether prospective purchasers know the specific identity of the trademark owner.

The rules protecting against confusion of source or sponsorship are equally applicable to the unauthorized use of trademarks, trade names, collective marks, and certification marks. The use of another's trademark as the actor's trade name, for example, or the use of another's certification mark as a trademark for the actor's goods can subject the actor to liability under this Section. The question in each case is whether the actor's use of the mark is likely to cause confusion regarding the association between the actor's goods, services, or business and the goods, services, or business of the owner of the mark.

Illustrations:

4. *A* publishes SIXTEEN, a magazine that features articles on fashions and carries substantial advertising for clothing directed at the teenage audience. *B* uses the title of the magazine as a trademark for teenage clothing. Although prospective purchasers are not likely to believe that the magazine publisher is the manufacturer of the clothing, *B* is subject to liability under this Section if the use of the trademark is likely to confuse prospective purchasers regarding *A* 's sponsorship or approval of *B* 's clothing.

5. *A* manufactures and sells vegetable juice under the trademark V–12. *B* begins to sell vitamin tablets using the same trademark. *B* is subject to liability under this Section if prospective purchasers are likely to believe either that *A* is the manufacturer or distributor of the vitamin tablets or that *A* endorses or is otherwise associated with *B* 's goods.

e. Collective membership marks and ornamental use. A collective membership mark, frequently an insignia, emblem, or organization name, is used to identify the members of a collective group. See § 10, Comment *c.* It can be infringed by an unauthorized use that is likely to cause confusion as to the organization's sponsorship or approval of goods or services, or, as stated in Subsection (2), by a use that is likely to cause others to believe that the user is a member of the organization. Thus, the display of a collective membership mark by an individual or a firm to indicate falsely that the user is a member of the organization is an infringement. However, it is sometimes difficult, particularly in a noncommercial setting, to determine whether the display of a membership mark is in fact a claim of membership or merely an indication of the user's support for the organization. The noncommercial display of a membership mark by an individual is also unlikely to cause harm to the sales or good will of the organization and may also implicate the free speech rights of the user. The absence of any case law suggests that individuals who display in a noncommercial setting the membership mark of a group to which they do not belong are not subject to liability for infringement. The deceptive use of another's membership mark for the purpose of causing harm to the owner of the mark, however, may subject the user to liability for injurious falsehood under the rule stated in Restatement, Second, Torts § 623A.

Several decisions allow the unauthorized sale of goods such as jewelry and clothing bearing another's collective membership mark by finding that in such contexts the mark is functional and thus unprotectable. See § 17. The proper inquiry, however, is what the unauthorized use of the mark signifies to prospective purchasers. If purchasers believe that the organization has authorized or approved the sale of the merchandise bearing the mark, the mark serves a trademark function and the unauthorized use is an infringement. On the other hand, if the appearance of the mark on the merchandise is perceived by prospective purchasers merely as a means for them to use the goods to indicate membership or support for the organization, the use of the mark creates no likelihood of confusion and is not an infringement. Cases involving the unauthorized sale of goods bearing school or athletic team names or emblems are best resolved through a similar inquiry. See Comment *b*.

Illustrations:

6. *A*, without authorization, sells sweatshirts bearing the emblem of *B* fraternity. *C*, who is not a member of *B*, purchases and wears one of *A* 's sweatshirts. *A* is subject to liability to *B* if prospective purchasers are likely to believe that the sweatshirts are sponsored or approved by *B*. *C* is not subject to liability to *B* under the rule stated in this Section.

7. The facts being otherwise as stated in Illustration 6, *A* markets the sweatshirts in packages bearing the notation "Official *B* Clothing." *A* is subject to liability to *B* because prospective purchasers are likely to believe that the sweatshirts are sponsored or approved by *B*.

f. Reverse confusion. In the typical case of trademark infringement, consumers are led to believe that the goods sold by the subsequent user of the mark are associated in some manner with the trademark owner. However, in some cases the subsequent user's promotion of the mark may so overwhelm the use by the prior user that most purchasers come to associate the mark with the subsequent user. This can result in reverse confusion—purchasers are likely to believe that the goods sold by the prior user are actually those of the subsequent user. Reverse confusion is actionable under the rule stated in clause (c) of Subsection (1). Reverse confusion should be distinguished from reverse passing off, which involves an actor's passing off of goods made by another as the actor's own goods. See § 5.

The injury to the trademark owner caused by a likelihood of reverse confusion is more subtle than that resulting from direct confusion. Reverse confusion does not ordinarily threaten a direct diversion of trade from the trademark owner; indeed, the owner's sales may benefit to some extent from the infringer's promotion of the mark. On the other hand, because of the infringer's concurrent use of the mark, the reputation of the trademark owner's goods or services among prospective purchasers is no longer within the owner's exclusive control. Failure to protect against reverse confusion would also permit large subsequent users to undermine by extensive advertising the investments of smaller firms in their trade symbols. Because these potential injuries result from a likelihood of confusion as to the source of goods or services, the creation of reverse confusion falls within the traditional rules governing the infringement of trademarks.

Illustration:

8. *A*, a small tire manufacturer, sells BIGTRACK tires in a regional market. Consumers in that market associate BIGTRACK with *A*. *B*, a prominent tire manufacturer, subsequently begins selling BIGTRACK tires and engages in an extensive promotional campaign on national television. *B* 's advertising overwhelms *A* 's promotional efforts with the result that consumers encountering *A* 's tires now think that the tires are actually produced by *B*. *B* is subject to liability to *A* under the rule stated in this Section.

g. Extent of confusion required. Establishing a likelihood of confusion can pose difficult evidentiary problems because the proof relates not to a past event but rather to the likelihood of a present or future state of mind. In a dispersed and impersonal marketplace, direct proof of the quantum of actual purchaser confusion is often unavailable. Because consumer behavior is animated by a variety of factors, it is also difficult to determine the extent of actual confusion from evidence relating to the conduct of consumers. Thus, in many instances the likelihood of confusion must be determined without direct evidence of actual confusion, and conclusions must instead be drawn about the understanding of hypothetical purchasers operating in the market context in which the designations are used.

Except in the most egregious cases of trademark counterfeiting, an unauthorized use is unlikely to confuse all prospective purchasers. At the same time, some residual confusion exists in most markets, and a few particularly undiscerning persons may make purchasing decisions under a wide range of misconceptions. An actor is subject to liability for infringement only if the actor's use of another's designation is likely to confuse a significant number of prospective purchasers. What is a "significant number" depends on the context of the case. The likely confusion of even a few individuals, for example, may be significant if they represent a substantial proportion of the potential market.

Whether a particular use of another's trademark creates a likelihood of confusion sufficient to subject the user to liability is often determined by considering the effect of the use on a reasonably prudent purchaser of the goods or services. Proof that a particular use is likely to confuse a reasonably prudent purchaser is ordinarily sufficient to establish infringement because it is assumed that such a hypothetical purchaser reflects the behavior of a significant number of actual purchasers. However, when direct evidence of actual confusion or survey evidence of the likelihood of confusion is available, the court must determine whether the evidence taken as a whole is sufficient to establish that significant confusion is likely. An actor is liable under the rule in this Section for creating a likelihood of confusion among a significant number of prospective purchasers, regardless of whether such confusion is "reasonable."

Courts have not expressed the test for trademark infringement in terms of a specific percentage of prospective purchasers likely to be confused. Accurate quantification of the extent of likely confusion is usually impossible. Evidence of actual confusion, typically consisting of the testimony of a number of confused purchasers or instances of misdirected letters or telephone calls, is often insufficient to permit accurate generalizations. Similarly, no consumer survey can precisely replicate actual market conditions. Margins of error can arise because of the nature of the sampling techniques, the structure and use of the survey instrument, and the inherent difference between what consumers report they think and do and what they actually think and do. Thus, the extent of confusion indicated by a survey must be considered in light of the credibility of the survey and any other evidence bearing on the likelihood of confusion. Courts have given weight to survey results showing confusion among 25 percent or more of those surveyed even when the survey was partially flawed. Similarly, surveys without obvious defects indicating confusion of seven percent to 15 percent of the sample have been held adequate, when supported by other evidence, to prove a likelihood of confusion. The weight to be accorded a specific survey depends on the facts and circumstances of each case. The fact that a particular percentage is held sufficient to establish infringement in one case thus does not necessarily indicate that it is sufficient to establish infringement in other cases.

In some circumstances courts may tolerate a greater likelihood of confusion than in others, particularly if the subsequent user has a legitimate interest in the use of the designation. For example, the interest in using one's own name in business may prompt a court to accept a higher risk of confusion than in the case of an arbitrary mark. Similarly, in some cases descriptive marks may require more substantial evidence of a likelihood of confusion because of the interest in maintaining access to descriptive terms. When protected trade dress consists of a particular combination of both functional and non-functional elements, later users may be unable to avoid all confusion without compromising access to the functional elements of the trade dress. In such circumstances some confusion may be an acceptable cost of preserving competition. On the other hand, when the potential harm to confused purchasers is great, the court may be unwilling to permit even a relatively small degree of confusion. See Comment *d.* In the last analysis, whether the extent of likely confusion is significant is a judgment to be made based on all the circumstances of the case.

h. Reasonably prudent purchaser. The reasonably prudent purchaser often invoked in determining likelihood of confusion is the ordinary purchaser of the goods or services buying with ordinary care. As with the standard of the reasonable person in negligence cases, the discernment exercised by a reasonably prudent purchaser varies with the circumstances. One can expect, for example, more careful inquiry in purchases of expensive rather than inexpensive items. Some courts have announced a "reasonable discriminating purchaser" standard in cases involving expensive goods, but this is more appropriately viewed as a recognition of the degree of care likely to be exercised by a reasonable purchaser under the circumstances. Other courts have observed that the law protects not only the expert and wise, but also the "ignorant, the unthinking and the credulous," although such statements are typically found in contexts in which a reasonably prudent purchaser is unlikely to exercise considerable care. Similarly, the degree of expected care will depend upon the class of prospective purchasers. The care expected of children, for example, will differ from the care expected from adults or from professional buyers.

REPORTERS' NOTE

The standards governing trademark infringement were formerly treated in Restatement of Torts § 717 (1938). See generally, McCarthy, Trademarks and Unfair Competition ch. 23; Gilson, Trademark Protection and Practice ch. 5.

Comment b. The United States Supreme Court has noted that the protection accorded trademarks and trade names is based on the "same fundamental principles." American Steel Foundries v. Robertson, 269 U.S. 372, 46 S.Ct. 160, 70 L.Ed. 317 (1926). See Lawyers Title Ins. Co. v. Lawyers Title Ins. Corp., 109 F.2d 35, 41 (D.C.Cir.1939), cert. denied 309 U.S. 684, 60 S.Ct. 806, 84 L.Ed. 1028 (1940) ("[R]elief is granted under circumstances, upon considerations and subject to limitations equally applicable either to trade-marks or to trade names."). See also, e.g., Lang v. Retirement Living Pub. Co., 949 F.2d 576 (2d Cir.1991) (the issue in trade name infringement, as in trademark infringement, is the likelihood of confusion, citing Restatement Third, Unfair Competition § 20 (Tent. Draft No.2 (1990))); Accuride Int'l, Inc. v. Accuride Corp., 871 F.2d 1531 (9th Cir.1989) (applying the same multifactor analysis used in trademark cases to determine likelihood of confusion in a trade name case). In some cases the same designation may function as both a trademark and a trade name. See, e.g., Communications Satellite Corp. v. Comcet, Inc., 429 F.2d 1245 (4th Cir.), cert. denied 400 U.S. 942, 91 S.Ct. 240, 27 L.Ed.2d 245 (1970). Use of another's trademark as the actor's trade name or use of another's trade name as the actor's trademark can be actionable. See, e.g., Safeway Stores, Inc. v. Safeway Properties, Inc., 307 F.2d 495 (2d Cir.1962) (trademark of grocery chain used in defendant's trade name); John Roberts Mfg. Co. v. University of Notre Dame Du Lac, 258 F.2d 256 (7th Cir.1958) (trade name of a university used by defendant as a trademark on class rings).

A common law certification mark was protected against infringement in Florida v. Real Juices, Inc., 330 F.Supp. 428 (M.D.Fla.1971). Infringement of a common law collective service mark was enjoined in National Trailways Bus System v. Trailway Van Lines, Inc., 269 F.Supp. 352 (E.D.N.Y.1965). See also Quality Courts United, Inc. v. Quality Courts, Inc., 140 F.Supp. 341 (M.D.Pa.1956) (infringement of a registered collective service mark). Cases illustrating infringement of collective membership marks are cited in the Reporters' Note accompanying Comment *e*.

Liability for trademark infringement extends to any person who markets goods or services under the infringing designation. See, e.g., Grocers Baking Co. v. Sigler, 132 F.2d 498 (6th Cir.1942) (manufacturer and distributor are joint tortfeasors); Estee Lauder, Inc. v. Watsky, 323 F.Supp. 1064 (S.D.N.Y.1970) (retailer).

The courts have not adopted a consistent approach to cases involving the use of another's mark in an expressive manner on goods such as posters or T-shirts. Some decisions emphasize the requirement of a likelihood of confusion and thus demand proof that prospective purchasers are likely to believe that the trademark owner is the source or sponsor of the merchandise. See, e.g., Nike, Inc. v. "Just Did It" Enterprises, 6 F.3d 1225 (7th Cir.1993); Anheuser–

Busch, Inc. v. L & L Wings, Inc., 962 F.2d 316 (4th Cir.), cert. denied ___ U.S. ___, 113 S.Ct. 206, 121 L.Ed.2d 147 (1992); Eveready Battery Co. v. Adolph Coors Co., 765 F.Supp. 440 (N.D.Ill.1991); Stop the Olympic Prison v. United States Olympic Committee, 489 F.Supp. 1112 (S.D.N.Y.1980); Girl Scouts of the United States v. Personality Posters Mfg. Co., 304 F.Supp. 1228 (S.D.N.Y. 1969). Other cases, although employing the likelihood of confusion test, seemingly require little evidence of confusion. See, e.g., Mutual of Omaha Ins. Co. v. Novak, 836 F.2d 397 (8th Cir.1987), cert. denied 488 U.S. 933, 109 S.Ct. 326, 102 L.Ed.2d 344 (1988). Others, although finding confusion, emphasize the disparaging associations created by the defendant's use of the plaintiff's mark. See, e.g., Hard Rock Cafe Licensing Corp. v. Pacific Graphics, Inc., 776 F.Supp. 1454 (W.D.Wash.1991); Coca–Cola Co. v. Gemini Rising, Inc., 346 F.Supp. 1183 (E.D.N.Y.1972). Still other cases emphasize an appropriation of the selling power of the mark. See Boston Athletic Ass'n v. Sullivan, 867 F.2d 22 (1st Cir.1989) (proof that consumers were likely to purchase the defendant's T-shirts because the goods displayed the plaintiff's mark justified a presumption of confusion); Boston Professional Hockey Ass'n v. Dallas Cap & Emblem Mfg., Inc., 510 F.2d 1004 (5th Cir.), cert. denied 423 U.S. 868, 96 S.Ct. 132, 46 L.Ed.2d 312 (1975) (knowledge by consumers that the marks displayed on the defendant's patches belonged to the plaintiffs was sufficient to find confusion). Traditional principles of trademark law as reiterated in this Section, however, require a likelihood of confusion. It has long been the rule that the trademark owner is not protected against uses that merely bring to mind its mark without creating confusion. See Toho Co. v. Sears, Roebuck & Co., 645 F.2d 788 (9th Cir. 1981); In re Ferrero, 479 F.2d 1395 (C.C.P.A.1973). In addition, many of these cases involve expressions of noncommercial speech entitled to broad constitutional protection, and although parody is not in itself a defense to trademark infringement, see, e.g., Nike, Inc., *supra*; Hard Rock Cafe, *supra*, it has been recognized that in the context of expressive uses a court may require more substantial evidence of confusion. Cliffs Notes, Inc. v. Bantam Doubleday Dell Pub. Group, Inc., 886 F.2d 490 (2d Cir. 1989) (substantial evidence of confusion required to enjoin use in a parody); Yankee Pub. Inc. v. News America Pub., Inc., 809 F.Supp. 267 (S.D.N.Y.1992) (use of a trademark in the communication of an expressive message requires a balancing of the trademark owner's rights and the free speech rights of the user, citing Restatement Third, Unfair Competition § 20, Comment *b* (Tent. Draft No.2 (1990))); Girl Scouts v. Bantam Doubleday Dell Pub. Group, 808 F.Supp. 1112 (S.D.N.Y.1992), affirmed 996 F.2d 1477 (2d Cir.1993); Ocean Bio–Chem, Inc. v. Turner Network Television, Inc., 741 F.Supp. 1546 (S.D.Fla.1990) (Lanham Act must be narrowly construed in light of the first amendment interests implicated by the use of a trademark in a fictional movie); Lucasfilm Ltd. v. High Frontier, 622 F.Supp. 931 (D.D.C.1985) (use of "Star Wars" by opponents of the strategic defense initiative did not infringe the STAR

WARS trademark for motion pictures). Cf. Anheuser-Busch, Inc. v. Balducci Pub., 28 F.3d 769 (8th Cir. 1994) (concluding that the balance favored the trademark owner since the extent of confusion was greater than necessary for defendant's purpose).

Use of another's trademark merely to refer to the trademark owner or its products is not an infringement. See, e.g., WCVB–TV v. Boston Athletic Ass'n, 926 F.2d 42 (1st Cir.1991); Hypertherm, Inc. v. Precision Products, Inc., 832 F.2d 697 (1st Cir.1987); Volkswagenwerk Aktiengesellschaft v. Church, 411 F.2d 350 (9th Cir. 1969); Yankee Pub., *supra* (citing Restatement Third, Unfair Competition § 20, Comment *b* (Tent. Draft No.2 (1990))). American law does not prohibit a competitor from using another's trademark in comparative advertising. See, e.g., G.D. Searle & Co. v. Hudson Pharmaceutical Corp., 715 F.2d 837, 843 (3d Cir.1983) ("In short, whether one is entitled to refer to a competitor's trademark depends not on where the reference appears but on whether the reference is truthful."); Smith v. Chanel, Inc., 402 F.2d 562 (9th Cir.1968). It is reported that some countries regard any reference to a competitor's trademark as an infringement. Robin & Barnaby, Comparative Advertising: A Skeptical View, 67 Trademark Rep. 358 (1977). False product comparisons, however, can be actionable under § 43(a) of the Lanham Act and the common law of disparagement. See, e.g., American Home Products Corp. v. Johnson & Johnson, 577 F.2d 160 (2d Cir.1978) (§ 43(a)). See § 2, Comment *c*.

For cases involving post-sale confusion of persons other than the actual purchaser, see, e.g., Payless Shoesource, Inc. v. Reebok Int'l Ltd., 998 F.2d 985 (Fed.Cir.1993); Ferrari S.P.A. Esercizio Fabriche Automobili E Corse v. Roberts, 944 F.2d 1235 (6th Cir.1991), cert. denied ___ U.S. ___, 112 S.Ct. 3028, 120 L.Ed.2d 899 (1992) (the reputation of the trademark owner can be damaged by post-sale confusion of third persons); Keds Corp. v. Renee Int'l Trading Corp., 888 F.2d 215 (1st Cir.1989); Polo Fashions, Inc. v. Craftex, Inc., 816 F.2d 145 (4th Cir.1987); Lois Sportswear, U.S.A., Inc. v. Levi Strauss & Co., 799 F.2d 867 (2d Cir. 1986) (infringement of a stitching design on pants was likely to confuse persons who observed purchasers wearing the defendant's pants and thus might influence potential customers of the plaintiff); Levi Strauss & Co. v. Blue Bell, Inc., 632 F.2d 817 (9th Cir.1980) (similar conclusion with respect to pocket tab label); Nabisco Brands, Inc. v. Conusa Corp., 722 F.Supp. 1287 (M.D.N.C.1989); Rolex Watch U.S.A., Inc. v. Canner, 645 F.Supp. 484 (S.D.Fla.1986) (counterfeit watches). See also Mastercrafters Clock & Radio Co. v. Vacheron & Constantin–LeCoultre Watches, Inc., 221 F.2d 464 (2d Cir.), cert. denied 350 U.S. 832, 76 S.Ct. 67, 100 L.Ed. 743 (1955), in which Judge Frank upheld liability for the sale of a counterfeit "Atmos" clock because a "visitor would be likely to assume that the clock was an Atmos clock." Cf. American Cyanamid Co. v. United States Rubber Co., 356 F.2d 1008 (C.C.P.A.1966) (potential confusion of employees of the purchasers of farm chemicals). Confusion of persons other than the actual purchaser is actionable, however, only if it is likely to cause harm to the commercial interests of the trademark owner. See, e.g., Electronic Design & Sales, Inc. v. Electronic Data Systems Corp., 954 F.2d 713 (Fed.Cir.1992) (the confusion cognizable in a registration proceeding is confusion of "relevant persons," usually actual or potential purchasers); Lang v. Retirement Living Pub. Co., 949 F.2d 576 (2d

Cir.1991) (trademark infringement protects against mistaken purchasing decisions and not against confusion generally, citing Restatement Third, Unfair Competition § 20, Reporters' Note to Comment *b* (Tent. Draft No.2 (1990))); Perini Corp. v. Perini Construction, Inc., 915 F.2d 121 (4th Cir. 1990) (confusion among non-purchasers is relevant if it affects the trademark owner's reputation among the groups with whom it interacts); Beneficial Corp. v. Beneficial Capital Corp., 529 F.Supp. 445 (S.D.N.Y. 1982) (protection is available against confusion in purchasing, not against confusion generally).

On the infringement of marks used by non-profit organizations, see, e.g., Birthright v. Birthright, Inc., 827 F.Supp. 1114 (D.N.J.1993) (confusion of potential donors); Healing the Children, Inc. v. Heal the Children, Inc., 786 F.Supp. 1209 (W.D.Pa.1992) (infringement of a service mark used by a medical service organization was likely to confuse doctors, hospitals, and patients).

When a purchaser orders goods by their trademark, the substitution without notice of different goods is an infringement. Coca–Cola Co. v. Overland, Inc., 692 F.2d 1250 (9th Cir. 1982); Heaton Distributing Co. v. Union Tank Car Co., 387 F.2d 477 (8th Cir.1967); Singer Mfg. Co. v. Golden, 171 F.2d 266 (7th Cir.1948).

Illustration 3 is based on Smith v. Chanel, *supra*.

Comment c. For cases relating to the significance of intent in trademark infringement actions, see the Reporters' Note accompanying § 22.

Comment d. The evolution of the concept of likelihood of confusion from confusion of source to the broader perspective of quality assurance is traced in McCarthy, *supra*, ch. 3; Gilson, *supra*, § 1.03. An early case recognizing trademark rights in a distributor who did not manufacture the goods sold under the mark is Menendez v. Holt, 128 U.S. 514, 9 S.Ct. 143, 32 L.Ed. 526 (1888). The modern view is reflected in Victor Tool & Machine Corp. v. Sun Control Awnings, Inc., 299 F.Supp. 868, 874 (E.D.Mich.1968), affirmed 411 F.2d 792 (6th Cir.1969):

> The use of a trademark, however, does not necessarily and as a matter of law impart that the articles on which it is used are manufactured by its user. It is enough that they are manufactured for him, that he controls their production, or that they pass through his hands in the course of trade and that he gives to them the benefit of his reputation or of his name and business style.

Although trademarks serve as symbols of identification, the trademark need not identify a specific source known to the purchaser. "[Indication of source] means only that a trademark indicates that the goods in connection with which it is used come from a common source, whether the source is known or anonymous * * *." Restatement of Torts § 715, Comment *b* (1938). See also Mastercrafters Clock & Radio Co. v. Vacheron & Constantin–LeCoultre Watches, Inc., 221 F.2d 464 (2d Cir.), cert. denied 350 U.S. 832, 76 S.Ct. 67, 100 L.Ed. 743 (1955).

The Lanham Act as originally enacted defined infringement as a use "likely to cause confusion or mistake or to deceive purchasers as to the source of origin of such goods or services." 60 Stat. 437 (1946). Subsequent amendment eliminated the language after the word "deceive" to recognize a broader scope of potential confusion. 15 U.S.C.A. § 1114(1).

Confusion of sponsorship, as distinct from confusion of source, is also actionable as an infringement. See, e.g., Fuddruckers, Inc. v. Doc's B.R. Others, Inc., 826 F.2d 837 (9th Cir. 1987); Lindy Pen Co. v. Bic Pen Corp., 725 F.2d 1240 (9th Cir.1984), cert. denied 469 U.S. 1188, 105 S.Ct. 955, 83 L.Ed.2d 962 (1985). Confusion of sponsorship may arise in a variety of contexts. For example, use of a magazine's trademark on goods of the type advertised in the magazine has been found to be an infringement because consumers are likely to believe that the magazine sponsors or approves the goods. See, e.g., HMH Pub. Co. v. Brincat, 504 F.2d 713 (9th Cir.1974) (PLAYBOY on automobile products found likely to create confusion of sponsorship with the magazine of that name); Triangle Pub., Inc. v. Rohrlich, 167 F.2d 969 (2d Cir.1948). Although businesses that specialize in selling or servicing a certain brand of product may advertise that fact to consumers, they may not do so in a manner likely to create the belief that they are affiliated with or approved by the manufacturer of the goods. Compare, e.g., Volkswagenwerk Aktiengesellschaft v. Church, 411 F.2d 350 (9th Cir. 1969), with Volkswagenwerk, G.M.B.H. v. Frank, 198 F.Supp. 916 (D.Colo.1961). See, e.g., Trail Chevrolet, Inc. v. General Motors Corp., 381 F.2d 353 (5th Cir.1967). Similarly, a major issue in cases involving the unauthorized use of membership insignia or athletic team emblems is whether prospective purchasers are likely to believe that the organization or team has sponsored or licensed the use of its mark on the goods. See, e.g., University of Georgia Athletic Ass'n v. Laite, 756 F.2d 1535 (11th Cir.1985); National Football League Properties, Inc. v. Wichita Falls Sportswear, Inc., 532 F.Supp. 651 (W.D.Wash.1982). See Comment *b*.

Morgenstern Chemical Co. v. G.D. Searle & Co., 253 F.2d 390 (3d Cir.), cert. denied 358 U.S. 816, 79 S.Ct. 25, 3 L.Ed.2d 58 (1958), is often cited as the leading case affording greater protection to trademarks for prescription drugs. The case concerned MICTURIN as a trademark for a drug to relieve urinary tract infections and MICTINE for diuretic therapy. The lower court found no likelihood of confusion because the drugs were not intended for the same symptoms. The appellate court reversed, holding, "If there is any possibility of such confusion in the case of medicines public policy requires that the use of the confusingly similar name be enjoined." 253 F.2d at 394. A distinction between confusion of product and confusion of source was stated with no apparent effect on the outcome in Syntex Laboratories, Inc. v. Norwich Pharmacal Co., 437 F.2d 566 (2d Cir.1971), in which VAGESTROL for a vaginal suppository was held to infringe VAGETROL for a vaginal cream. The "stricter standard" was found inapplicable in Schering Corp. v. Thompson Medical Co., 209 U.S.P.Q. 72 (S.D.N.Y.1979), since the risk of product confusion between PROLAMINE for a nonprescription appetite suppressant and POLARAMINE for a prescription antihistamine was de minimis.

Several cases suggest that pre-sale confusion of source or association that is likely to harm the commercial interests of the trademark owner is actionable as an infringement even if the confusion is dispelled before the actual purchase. See, e.g., Mobil Oil

Corp. v. Pegasus Petroleum Corp., 818 F.2d 254 (2d Cir.1987); Grotrian, Helfferich, Schulz, Th. Steinweg Nachf. v. Steinway & Sons, 523 F.2d 1331 (2d Cir.1975); Dreyfus Fund, Inc. v. Royal Bank of Canada, 525 F.Supp. 1108 (S.D.N.Y.1981); Koppers Co. v. Krupp–Koppers GmbH, 517 F.Supp. 836 (W.D.Pa.1981). Cf. Astra Pharmaceutical Products, Inc. v. Beckman Instruments, Inc., 718 F.2d 1201 (1st Cir.1983) (no evidence that minimal temporary confusion had any effect on purchasing decisions).

Illustration 4 is based on *Triangle Publications, Inc., supra.* Illustration 5 is based on Standard Brands, Inc. v. Smidler, 151 F.2d 34 (2d Cir. 1945).

Comment e. Infringement of collective membership marks has been found in cases in which a local chapter disaffiliates from its national organization but continues to use the national name and insignia. See Kappa Sigma Fraternity v. Kappa Sigma Gamma Fraternity, 654 F.Supp. 1095 (D.N.H.1987); United States Jaycees v. San Francisco Junior Chamber of Commerce, 354 F.Supp. 61 (N.D.Cal.1972), affirmed 513 F.2d 1226 (9th Cir.1975); National Bd. of Y.W.C.A. v. Y.W.C.A. of Charleston, 335 F.Supp. 615 (D.S.C. 1971).

The fact that the defendant was not using the plaintiff's insignia to indicate source or sponsorship prevented an organization from enjoining the unauthorized manufacture and sale of jewelry bearing its insignia in Supreme Assembly, Order of Rainbow for Girls v. J.H. Ray Jewelry Co., 676 F.2d 1079 (5th Cir.1982). See also International Order of Job's Daughters v. Lindeburg & Co., 633 F.2d 912 (9th Cir.1980), cert. denied 452 U.S. 941, 101 S.Ct. 3086, 69 L.Ed.2d 956 (1981).

Some cases have invoked the functionality doctrine to deny relief against ornamental use, see, e.g., International Order of Job's Daughters, *supra* ; see also University of Pittsburgh v. Champion Products, Inc., 566 F.Supp. 711 (W.D.Pa.1983) (college insignia), although functionality addresses the eligibility of a designation for protection as a trademark rather than the scope of a trademark owner's rights against unauthorized use. See the Reporters' Note accompanying § 17, Comment *b.*

Illustrations 6 and 7 reflect the results of the cases cited above. No case has been found in which a collective membership mark has been protected against an individual wearing or otherwise displaying the mark without authorization in a noncommercial context.

Comment f. The leading case on infringement through reverse confusion is Big O Tire Dealers, Inc. v. Goodyear Tire & Rubber Co., 561 F.2d 1365 (10th Cir.1977), cert. dismissed 434 U.S. 1052, 98 S.Ct. 905, 54 L.Ed.2d 805 (1978). The doctrine has been adopted in numerous decisions. See, e.g., In re Shell Oil Co., 992 F.2d 1204 (Fed.Cir.1993) (reverse confusion is cognizable in registration proceedings under the Lanham Act); Sands, Taylor & Wood Co. v. Quaker Oats Co., 978 F.2d 947 (7th Cir.1992), cert. denied ___ U.S. ___, 113 S.Ct. 1879, 123 L.Ed.2d 497 (1993); Banff, Ltd. v. Federated Dept. Stores, Inc., 841 F.2d 486 (2d Cir.1988) (reverse confusion under § 43(a)); Ameritech, Inc. v. American Information Technologies Corp., 811 F.2d 960 (6th Cir. 1987) (Ohio law); Fuji Photo Film Co. v. Shinohara Shoji Kabushiki Kaisha, 754 F.2d 591 (5th Cir.1985) (reverse confusion is actionable under § 32 of the Lanham Act); Capital Films Corp. v. Charles Fries Productions, Inc., 628 F.2d 387 (5th Cir. 1980) (Texas law). Contra, Westward Coach Mfg. Co. v. Ford Motor Co., 388 F.2d 627 (7th Cir.), cert. denied 392 U.S. 927, 88 S.Ct. 2286, 20 L.Ed.2d 1386 (1968) (reverse confusion held not actionable under Indiana law). Reverse confusion is demonstrated by evidence relating to the understanding of the senior user's customers. Sterling Drug, Inc. v. Bayer AG, 14 F.3d 733 (2d Cir.1994).

The *Big O Tire* case, *supra*, also imposed liability for "trademark disparagement" in connection with an advertisement by the subsequent user claiming that it was the only legitimate source of the trademarked goods. Although not a necessary consequence of reverse confusion, if some purchasers come to believe that the prior user is an infringer, the defendant's conduct may be actionable as defamation or disparagement. See DeCosta v. Viacom Int'l, Inc., 981 F.2d 602 (1st Cir.1992), cert. denied ___ U.S. ___, 113 S.Ct. 3039, 125 L.Ed.2d 725 (1993) (inducing the false belief that the prior user is an infringer may be actionable as disparagement) (dictum). Although language in some opinions suggests that liability for trademark infringement through reverse confusion extends to subsequent uses that induce consumers into believing that the prior user is an infringer, see W.W.W. Pharmaceutical Co. v. Gillette Co., 984 F.2d 567 (2d Cir.1993); Banff Ltd., *supra*, if consumers are not in fact confused about the source of the parties goods or services, the subsequent use, even if actionable on other grounds, does not constitute trademark infringement. See DeCosta, *supra*.

Illustration 8 is based on the *Big O Tire* case, *supra*.

Comment g. In Mushroom Makers, Inc. v. R.G. Barry Corp., 580 F.2d 44, 47 (2d Cir.1978), cert. denied 439 U.S. 1116, 99 S.Ct. 1022, 59 L.Ed.2d 75 (1979), the court stated the standard for likelihood of confusion as "whether there is any likelihood that an appreciable number of ordinarily prudent purchasers are likely to be misled, or indeed simply confused, as to the source of the goods in question." Accord, Perini Corp. v. Perini Construction, Inc., 915 F.2d 121 (4th Cir.1990). See also, e.g., Indianapolis Colts, Inc. v. Metropolitan Baltimore Football Club Ltd., 34 F.3d 410, 414 (7th Cir.1994) ("it would be undesirable to impoverish the lexicon of trade names merely to protect the most gullible fringe of the consuming public."); American Ass'n for Advancement of Science v. Hearst Corp., 498 F.Supp. 244 (D.D.C.1980) (an "appreciable" number can be less than a majority).

Courts have evaluated both the credibility of the survey and the market factors relating to the defendant's use in deciding whether the percentage of consumers shown by the survey to be confused is sufficient. See, e.g., Miles Laboratories, Inc. v. Naturally Vitamin Supplements, Inc. 1 U.S.P.Q.2d 1445, 1457 (Tm.Tr.App. Bd.1986) ("percentages may be deceiving since the probative value of results must be considered in light of an evaluation of the survey itself"); Selchow & Righter Co. v. Decipher, Inc., 598 F.Supp. 1489, 1502 (E.D.Va. 1984) ("It must be recognized that no survey is perfect."). Cases relying on survey evidence include James Burrough Ltd. v. Sign of Beefeater, Inc., 540 F.2d 266 (7th Cir.1976), appeal after remand 572 F.2d 574 (7th Cir. 1978) (15% confusion is not de minimis); Humble Oil & Ref. Co. v. American Oil Co., 405 F.2d 803 (8th Cir.), cert. denied 395 U.S. 905, 89 S.Ct.

1745, 23 L.Ed.2d 218 (1969) (11% to 49%); McDonald's Corp. v. McBagel's, Inc., 649 F.Supp. 1268 (S.D.N.Y.1986) (24% of a national sample and 36% of a local sample was sufficient despite imperfections in the survey); Wendy's Int'l, Inc. v. Big Bite, Inc., 576 F.Supp. 816 (S.D.Ohio 1983) (7% to 21% confusion in two surveys was sufficient); Grotrian, Helfferich, Schulz, Th. Steinweg Nachf. v. Steinway & Sons, 365 F.Supp. 707 (S.D.N.Y.1973), affirmed 523 F.2d 1331 (2d Cir.1975) (7.7% found sufficient in conjunction with other evidence). Cases finding survey evidence insufficient to support a finding of infringement include Universal City Studios, Inc. v. Nintendo Co., 746 F.2d 112 (2d Cir.1984) (18% in a flawed survey); Henri's Food Prods. Co. v. Kraft, Inc., 717 F.2d 352 (7th Cir.1983) (7.6% survey result weighed against a finding of infringement). Wuv's Int'l, Inc. v. Love's Enterprises, Inc., 208 U.S.P.Q. 736 (D.Colo.1980) (9% was insufficient to establish infringement).

Comment h. Numerous cases utilize the "reasonably prudent purchaser" or "ordinary consumer using ordinary care" as the standard against which to evaluate the likelihood of confusion. See, e.g., McLean v. Fleming, 96 U.S. 245, 24 L.Ed. 828 (1878); Plus Products v. Plus Discount Foods, Inc., 722 F.2d 999 (2d Cir.1983); New West Corp. v. NYM Co., 595 F.2d 1194 (9th Cir.1979); Mushroom Makers, Inc. v. R.G. Barry Corp., 580 F.2d 44 (2d Cir.1978), cert. denied 439 U.S. 1116, 99 S.Ct. 1022, 59 L.Ed.2d 75 (1979); David Sherman Corp. v. Heublein, Inc., 340 F.2d 377 (8th Cir.1965). Although some courts have attempted to ascribe universal characteristics to this hypothetical consumer, see, e.g., Stork Restaurant v. Sahati, 166 F.2d 348 (9th Cir.1948) (trademark law protects the "ignorant, the inexperienced, and the gullible"), the attributes should reflect the particular market in which the case arises. It is widely recognized that consumers are usually more discerning when buying expensive merchandise than when making an inexpensive, impulsive purchase. See McGregor–Doniger, Inc. v. Drizzle Inc., 599 F.2d 1126 (2d Cir.1979); AMF Inc. v. Sleekcraft Boats, 599 F.2d 341 (9th Cir.1979). The standard of the reasonable consumer is thus defined by the market context in which the trademark is encountered. Similarly, the nature of the prospective consumers must be considered in defining the care exercised by a reasonable purchaser. See Oreck Corp. v. U.S. Floor Systems, Inc., 803 F.2d 166 (5th Cir.1986), cert. denied 481 U.S. 1069, 107 S.Ct. 2462, 95 L.Ed.2d 871 (1987) (building service contractors and purchasers of professional cleaning services are more likely to be deliberative than purchasers of consumer goods). Numerous cases recognize that professional or expert buyers are less easily confused. See, e.g., Perini Corp. v. Perini Construction, Inc., 915 F.2d 121 (4th Cir.1990) (construction services); Clark Equipment Co. v. Baker–Lull Corp., 288 F.2d 926 (C.C.P.A. 1961) (purchasers of fork-lift trucks).

§ 21. Proof of Likelihood of Confusion: Market Factors

Whether an actor's use of a designation causes a likelihood of confusion with the use of a trademark, trade name, collective mark, or certification mark by another

under the rule stated in § 20 is determined by a consideration of all the circumstances involved in the marketing of the respective goods or services or in the operation of the respective businesses. In making that determination the following market factors, among others, may be important:

(a) the degree of similarity between the respective designations, including a comparison of

(i) the overall impression created by the designations as they are used in marketing the respective goods or services or in identifying the respective businesses;

(ii) the pronunciation of the designations;

(iii) the translation of any foreign words contained in the designations;

(iv) the verbal translation of any pictures, illustrations, or designs contained in the designations;

(v) the suggestions, connotations, or meanings of the designations;

(b) the degree of similarity in the marketing methods and channels of distribution used for the respective goods or services;

(c) the characteristics of the prospective purchasers of the goods or services and the degree of care they are likely to exercise in making purchasing decisions;

(d) the degree of distinctiveness of the other's designation;

(e) when the goods, services, or business of the actor differ in kind from those of the other, the likelihood that the actor's prospective purchasers would expect a person in the position of the other to expand its marketing or sponsorship into the product, service, or business market of the actor;

(f) when the actor and the other sell their goods or services or carry on their businesses in different geographic markets, the extent to which the other's designation is identified with the other in the geographic market of the actor.

Comment:

a. General. The test for infringement is whether the actor's use of a designation as a trademark, trade name, collective mark, or certification mark creates a likelihood of confusion as described in § 20. The likelihood of confusion standard applies in infringement actions at common law as well as in actions arising under the Lanham Act and under state trademark registration and unfair competition statutes. Whether the use of a particular designation causes a likelihood of confusion must be evaluated in light of the overall market context in which the designation is used. This Section addresses several market factors that are important in many cases. The factors listed in this Section are not exhaustive of the relevant circumstances, however, and any factor that is likely to influence the impression conveyed to prospective purchasers by the actor's use of the designation is relevant is assessing the likelihood of confusion. No mechanistic formula or list can set forth in advance the variety of factors that may contribute to the particular marketing context of an actor's use. Not all the factors listed here will be applicable in every case, nor can the factors be applied independently. The likelihood of confusion depends on the interplay of all the factors that constitute the marketing environment in which the designation is used. The relevance of the actor's intent to the likelihood of confusion is considered in § 22, and the significance of proof of actual confusion is considered in § 23. The relative importance of any factor, including intent or actual confusion, depends on the facts of the particular case.

Some cases, in an effort to weigh the equities created by each party's use of its designation, include as part of an analysis of the likelihood of confusion additional factors such as the likelihood of harm to the reputation of the prior user's goods or whether the prior user is likely to "bridge the gap" and expand into the subsequent user's product market. These factors, however, are not relevant to whether prospective purchasers are likely to be confused, but rather to the likely consequences of confusion and hence to the nature of the relief that is appropriate if confusion is likely. See §§ 35 and 36.

b. Historical development. The oldest and simplest form of trademark infringement occurs when a seller identifies its goods by a designation that is identical to a designation previously used by a competitor marketing similar goods. The subsequent use is likely to divert trade from the prior user to the actor as consumers mistakenly purchase the actor's goods in the belief that the goods are those of the trademark owner. The emergence of more impersonal markets, the development of more aggressive and more extensive advertising, and the tendency of manufacturers to diversify created more subtle opportunities for confusion of prospective purchasers and injury to trademark owners. The use of another's trademark on goods of a different type than those marketed by the trademark owner cannot result in a direct diversion of trade, but the use may permit the imitator to appropriate the good will associated with the trademark and may also place the reputation of the trademark owner at risk. Thus, if *B* begins to sell suits under a designation identical to that used by *A*, who sells only coats, the use is unlikely to confuse a purchaser interested in buying a coat from *A* into buying instead a suit from *B*. Although diversion of trade from *A* to *B* is therefore unlikely, *A* may nevertheless suffer harm to its business. Persons previously satisfied with *A* 's coats may have an unsatisfactory experience with *B* 's suits and consequently cease to buy from *A* in the mistaken belief that *A* is responsible for both goods. Persons who have no previous experience with *A* 's goods may for the same reason decline to purchase a coat from *A*. Trade symbols thus came to be protected against imitation, not only on competing goods, but also on other goods sufficiently related to those of the prior user to pose a threat to the prior user's reputation and good will. At first, designations were protected against unauthorized use only on a narrow range of goods closely related to those of the prior user. Ultimately, both statutory and common law protection came to encompass any use of a designation that falsely suggests an association or connection between the actor and the trademark owner. It is sufficient if the actor's use is likely to create the impression that the goods are produced by the trademark owner, or that the trademark owner sponsors or certifies the actor's goods, or that the actor and the trademark owner are otherwise affiliated.

When the goods of the actor and the trademark owner directly compete, the similarity of the respective designations may dominate the likelihood of confusion analysis. If the actor uses an identical or nearly identical mark on directly competing goods, there is ordinarily a likelihood of confusion. As the similarity between the actor's designation and that of the trademark owner decreases, other factors such as a comparison of the respective marketing methods and the degree of care exercised by purchasers assume greater importance. In competing goods cases courts sometimes describe the inquiry as a determination of whether the designations are "confusingly similar." Properly understood, this standard includes considerations in addition to a physical comparison of the two designations.

For cases in which the designation is used by an actor on goods that do not directly compete with those of the trademark owner, various courts developed lists of contextual factors to be considered in determining the likelihood of confusion. Although in some jurisdictions trial courts may be obligated to make specific factual findings with respect to each of a list of enumerated factors, determinations of the likelihood of confusion cannot be made in a mechanical fashion. Findings as to individual factors are merely discrete aspects of a comprehensive analysis intended to achieve a practical evaluation of what consumers are likely to believe when they encounter the competing designations in the marketplace. Precedent from prior cases is frequently of little assistance.

An analysis of the market context of the use is appropriate in cases involving either competing or non-competing goods, and the rules stated in this Section are applicable to all forms of infringement. Some factors will be more or less important depending on the facts of the particular case. A court may properly decide, for example, that in a case in which the two marks are identical and are used on directly competing goods in the same geographic market, the inference of likelihood of confusion is sufficiently strong that an evaluation of other factors is unnecessary. The factor listed in clause (e) is relevant only when the goods or services of the actor do not directly compete with the goods or services of the trademark owner; clause (f) is relevant only when the marks are used in different geographic areas.

Comment on Clause (a):

c. Comparison of designations. The starting point in any infringement case is a comparison of the actor's designation with the trademark, trade name, collective mark, or certification mark of the prior user. The use of an identical designation on goods similar to those of the prior user is strong evidence of a likelihood of confusion. Differences in details will not be sufficient to avoid infringement if prospective purchasers are unlikely to distinguish the two designations. Even if prospective purchasers recognize that the two designations are distinct, confusion may result if purchasers are likely to assume that the similarities in the designations indicate a connection between the two users. The relevant inquiry is whether, under the circumstances of the use, the two designations are sufficiently similar that prospective purchasers are likely to believe that the prior user is associated in some manner with the goods, services, or business of the actor.

Whether the similarity between two designations is likely to cause confusion depends on the conditions under which the designations are encountered by prospective purchasers, and any comparison should thus be based on the marks as they appear in the marketplace and not as they may appear in the artificial context of a courtroom. A side-by-side comparison of two designations may not be useful if the goods on which they are used do not appear side by side in the market. Two marks may appear similar when viewed together but may be distinguishable in their market context, and two marks that are distinguishable when viewed side by side may create a likelihood of confusion when consumers must instead rely only on their memories of the marks.

The similarity between two designations is judged by the total impression created by the designations and not by a comparison of individual features. Although individual features may be dissimilar, the total effect of the two designations may be similar. In other cases, the total impressions may be dissimilar despite similarities in individual features. Although an analysis of the individual elements that comprise the designations may sometimes assist in predicting the likely consumer reaction, such as by distinguishing the dominant features of the marks from features that are likely to have only a marginal influence on purchasers, a dissection and comparison of individual details will not generally reflect the perceptions of consumers in the marketplace.

When a trademark or trade name consists of a combination of several elements, some of which are individually unprotectable as generic, functional, or merely descriptive, the comparison between the actor's designation and the trademark owner's protectable combination should take into account the actor's right to utilize the unprotected elements. Similarities that are attributable to the use of only unprotected elements will not support a finding of infringement. The emphasis is therefore properly on the protectable elements or combination of elements. However, the relevant comparison is with the overall impression created by the actor's designation, and the presence of similar generic, functional, or descriptive elements in the marks may increase the likelihood that similarities in protected elements will result in confusion. For example, when one element of a two-element trademark is generic or descriptive, a subsequent user who includes that unprotected element in a trademark may be required to depart substantially from the protected element of the prior mark in order to avoid a likelihood of confusion.

Evaluation of the overall impression created by a designation must also take account of the presence of other trademarks, disclaimers, or clarifying material that may reduce the risk of confusion. In some circumstances, for example, the presence of an additional trademark recognized as the actor's may be sufficient to avoid a likelihood of confusion. In other cases, however, the presence of the actor's mark may only aggravate the confusion by causing prospective purchasers to believe that the actor is licensed or otherwise associated with the prior user. The use of disclaimers such as "not associated with * * * " has generally been found insufficient to avoid a finding of infringement in the absence of a strong justification for the actor's use of a designation similar to that of the trademark owner.

Liability for trademark infringement ultimately depends upon proof of a likelihood of confusion and not on proof of any particular degree of similarity between the designations. Although the marks must be sufficiently similar to create the potential for confusion, whether the similarity is sufficient to subject the subsequent user to liability depends on the market context in which the marks are used, including the relationship between the respective goods or services, the distinctiveness of the prior user's trademark, the manner in which the goods or services are sold, and the care likely to be exercised by prospective purchasers.

d. Similarity in pronunciation. Similarity in pronunciation may contribute to consumer confusion despite differences in the spelling or appearance of the marks. Similar pronunciation may be a significant factor when the marks are used in connection with goods that are frequently ordered orally, but may be insignificant when used, for example, on goods sold exclusively through self-service outlets. The comparison of pronunciations should relate to the pronunciations likely to take place in the marketplace, which may differ from the correct pronunciation.

e. Translations. Words or pictures that are dissimilar in appearance may nevertheless be similar in translation. A foreign word, for example, may be confusingly similar to an existing trademark that is its English translation, and a picture may be confusingly similar to its verbal translation. Thus, the designation EL TORO may lead to confusion when used in competition with either a picture of a bull or the word BULL. The translation, however, must be one that is likely to be made by a significant number of prospective purchasers.

f. Similarity of meaning or connotation. Two designations may be dissimilar in appearance yet create the same mental impression because they share the same meaning or connotation. To the extent that the similarity of mental impression predominates over the dissimilarities in appearance, a likelihood of confusion may result.

Illustration:

1. *A* markets wire fencing with the trademark CYCLONE. *B* begins to market wire fencing using the designation TORNADO. Although the two designations are dissimilar in appearance and pronunciation, the similar mental image evoked by the two marks may contribute to a likelihood of confusion.

Comment on Clause (b):

g. Marketing methods. The likelihood that confusion will result from the concurrent use of similar designations may depend on the marketing methods and channels of distribution used by the respective sellers. If similar marks are used on goods sold through the same marketing channels, the probability of confusion may be higher than if the goods are marketed through separate channels. Thus, similar marks used on goods sold through single-brand distributors may be less confusing than when used on goods sold through multi-brand outlets, and goods sold only at discount outlets might not be confused with goods sold only in specialty shops.

If similar marks are used on goods or services that are marketed to the same prospective purchasers, the likelihood of confusion is greater than if there are few common purchasers. Use of a mark in advertisements appearing only in trade journals directed at professional buyers, for example, may be unlikely to cause confusion with a similar mark used in advertising directed to the general public. Men's suits and are men's ties bearing similar marks are more likely to be associated with a common source than are men's suits and women's shoes, in part because the latter kinds of goods are normally sold in different stores or departments and are purchased by different consumers.

Comment on Clause (c):

h. Care exercised by purchasers. The buying habits of purchasers of the relevant goods or services and the degree of care they are likely to exercise in making their purchases can be important factors in determining whether two similar designations are likely to cause confusion. If the goods or services are normally purchased only after considerable attention and inspection, greater similarity between the designations may be permitted than when the goods or services are purchased casually or impulsively. It is generally thought that professional purchasers are more discerning and less easily confused than casual purchasers, and that most purchasers exercise greater care when buying expensive items, but such assumptions must be evaluated in the context of the particular case.

Comment on Clause (d):

i. Distinctiveness or "strength" of the mark. The distinctiveness or "strength" of a mark measures its capacity to indicate the source of the goods or services with which it is used. The greater the distinctiveness of the mark, the greater the likelihood that prospective purchasers will associate the same or a similar designation found on other goods, services, or businesses with the prior user. "Strong" marks that have a high degree of distinctiveness are thus protected against the use of similar marks on a wider range of goods or services than are "weak" designations that have less distinctiveness or market recognition. See also § 28 on the "fair use" of descriptive terms.

As a general rule, trademarks that are fanciful or arbitrary tend to be stronger than those that are suggestive, and suggestive marks tend to be stronger than those that are descriptive, geographically descriptive, or are personal names. Such classifications are not conclusive of "strength," however, since the issue ultimately depends on the degree to which the designation is associated by prospective purchasers with a particular source. Thus, a descriptive mark through vigorous promotion can become a strong mark, and an arbitrary mark that is not well known in the market can be a weak mark.

The strength of a mark is related to the concept of secondary meaning described in § 13. For designations that are not inherently distinctive, proof of distinctiveness in the form of secondary meaning is required in order to establish the validity of the mark. The strength of a mark measures the degree of distinctiveness for the purpose of determining the likelihood of confusion resulting from another's use of a similar mark. Evidentiary factors relevant to the proof of secondary meaning are therefore also relevant in assessing the strength of the mark. See § 13, Comment *e*. An examination of these factors, although unnecessary to establish the validity of an inherently distinctive mark, is relevant to show the strength of the mark for purposes of determining its scope of protection.

Comment on Clause (e):

j. Competitive proximity of the goods. When the designations are used on competing goods, services, or businesses, the likelihood of confusion will depend largely on a comparison of the similarities between the two designations as used in the marketplace. See Comment *b*. When the actor uses a similar designation on different goods, services, or businesses, the likelihood of confusion will also depend on the relationship between the goods, services, or businesses of the respective users. The issue in each case is whether the goods, services, or businesses of the actor and of the trademark owner are sufficiently related that prospective purchasers are likely to perceive the similar designations as indicating a common source or other association. For example, the use of similar designations on goods that are used together, or that perform the same function, or that are of the same general class, is more likely to cause confusion than is a use in connection with goods used for different purposes, or in different contexts, or by different purchasers. Thus, if pancake syrup is marketed under a designation substantially similar to a trademark for pancake flour, the market reputation of the flour will be subjected to the hazards of the market reputation of the syrup since purchasers are likely to believe there is a connection between the two products. On the other hand, if lipstick is marketed under a designation substantially similar to one used on steam shovels, it is unlikely that consumers will assume a common source or other connection between the goods or their producers. Between these extremes, the courts must weigh the relationship between the respective goods, services, or businesses in the context of the other relevant market factors.

Consumer impressions of the tendency of particular types of businesses to diversify can influence the likelihood that different goods bearing similar marks will be associated with a common source. Some cases purport to protect the prior user of a mark with respect to use on goods or services falling within its "natural expansion" by finding that the prior user is likely to "bridge the gap" between its current product market and that of the subsequent user. If consumers believe, even though falsely, that the natural tendency of producers of the type of goods marketed by the prior user is to expand into the market for the type of goods marketed by the subsequent user, confusion may be likely. On the other hand, the actual intentions of the prior user with respect to future expansion will not ordinarily affect the likelihood that prospective purchasers are confused.

Intent to expand or the level of investment made in contemplation of expansion may be a factor in measuring the harm to a prior user resulting from a confusing use by another, and hence may be relevant in fashioning appropriate relief. See §§ 35 and 36. Adoption of a mark that is similar to another's with knowledge of the other's intent to expand can also be evidence of bad faith. See § 18, Comment *c*. But the relevant inquiry is whether consumers are likely to associate the respective goods, services, or businesses of the parties by assuming that the prior user has expanded into the other market, not whether the prior user in fact intends to do so. The rule stated in § 20 does not protect the interest of a business in future product expansion in the absence of a likelihood of confusion. A prior user who intends to expand into a new product market may insure its priority in that market by filing an application for federal registration based upon its intended use on the new product prior to the commencement of use in that market by another.

In any particular case there may be uncertainty regarding the likelihood of confusion. The divergent case law in the area of noncompeting goods also may be due in part, however, to the tension between the perception of trademarks and their associated good will as property to be protected from appropriation by others and the concern that expansive trademark protection may create excessive market power in trademark owners. Nonetheless, the courts agree that likelihood of confusion remains the applicable standard. On the protection of trademarks in the absence of a likelihood of confusion under state antidilution statutes, see § 25.

k. Quality of the actor's goods or services. The quality of the actor's goods or services may be relevant in assessing the likelihood of confusion. For purposes of determining whether confusion is likely, the relevant factor is the extent of the difference in quality between the goods or services of the subsequent user and those of the trademark owner. Markedly different quality may suggest that the goods are sold to different purchasers or in different market channels, or that the products are unlikely to be associated with a common source. On the other hand, if the subsequent user's goods are inferior to those of the prior user and confusion does occur, the threat to the reputation of the prior user is particularly acute. Although courts sometimes require less evidence of confusion when the subsequent use is on inferior goods, evidence of inferior quality is more properly relevant to fashioning appropriate relief if a likelihood of confusion is otherwise established. See §§ 35 and 36.

Comment on Clause (f):

l. Different geographic markets. The use of another's designation in a geographic area outside the marketing area of the prior user can cause confusion only if the designation already identifies the prior user in that territory. In such cases the prior user has priority in that area under the rule stated in § 19, and the subsequent user is thus subject to liability if the use is likely to cause confusion. If the prior user's mark is not already known in the area, the subsequent user may be entitled to priority under § 19 as the first user in a remote territory. Factors to be considered in determining whether a designation is already associated with a prior user in a particular area are discussed in § 19, Comment *b*.

Registration under the Lanham Act provides nationwide priority over subsequent users regardless of the geographic scope of the prior user's actual use or reputation. Thus, a registrant, although the second to use a designation in a particular area, may have priority through registration over an earlier user in that territory. Similarly, at common law, if a subsequent user commences use of a mark in a remote area in bad faith, it does not acquire priority in that territory over the prior user even if the prior user has not yet used the mark in that territory. See § 19, Comment *d*. In either case, however, the subordinate user is not subject to liability until its use creates a likelihood of confusion. Such confusion will arise only when the priority user commences use of the mark in that area or when the mark otherwise becomes associated in that area with the priority user.

Illustration:

2. *A* uses the mark SUNSET for baked goods in Florida and registers the mark under the Lanham Act. *B* subsequently uses SUNSET for baked goods in Georgia. Although *A* has priority over *B* in the use of the mark in Georgia by virtue of the federal registration, *B* is not subject to liability to *A* unless *A* can establish that *B* 's use of the mark in Georgia causes a likelihood of confusion.

m. Question of law or fact. Although the cases are not unanimous, whether the defendant's use of a trademark creates a likelihood of confusion is properly regarded as a question of fact. In jury trials the issue is submitted to the jury with appropriate instructions and the jury's determination is entitled to the usual deference accorded jury verdicts. In non-jury cases the findings of the trial judge concerning the likelihood of confusion should be subject to reversal only if clearly erroneous. Some courts have held that while findings relating to the relevant factors described in this Section present questions of fact subject to a clearly erroneous standard of review, the balancing of those factors to determine the ultimate issue of likelihood of confusion is a question of law subject to de novo review. However, the likelihood of confusion is determined by the totality of the circumstances rather than the summation of discrete factors, and the better view, adopted by the majority of courts, regards likelihood of confusion as a question of fact subject to the clearly erroneous rule. The interpretation of the factors listed in this Section, such as the meaning of "strength" and its substantive relevance to the likelihood of confusion, remain issues of law.

REPORTERS' NOTE

Likelihood of confusion is the standard of trademark infringement at common law, under the Lanham Act, and under most state statutory provisions. See, e.g., Century 21 Real Estate Corp. v. Sandlin, 846 F.2d 1175 (9th Cir.1988) (likelihood of confusion required under the Lanham Act, California statutory trademark law, and California law of unfair competition); Sno–Wizard Mfg., Inc. v. Eisemann Products Co., 791 F.2d 423 (5th Cir. 1986) (§ 43(a) of the Lanham Act); Dawn Donut Co. v. Hart's Food Stores, Inc., 267 F.2d 358 (2d Cir.

1959) (infringement of a registered mark under the Lanham Act). See also Model State Trademark Bill § 12 (1992).

Factors relevant in determining infringement were listed in Restatement of Torts §§ 729, 731 (1938). On proof of likelihood of confusion, see generally McCarthy, Trademarks and Unfair Competition, chs. 23–24; Gilson, Trademark Protection and Practice, ch. 5.

Comment b. Many courts initially framed the likelihood of confusion analysis in different terms depending on whether the designations were used on directly competing goods. In competing goods cases, the test was said to be whether the subsequent user's mark was "confusingly similar" to the mark of the prior user, and the major focus was on a comparison of the two designations within the market context of their use. When the goods of the subsequent user did not compete directly with those of the prior user, additional factors were recited as relevant.

The evolving views of the Second Circuit have been influential in the approach adopted by most courts to the likelihood of confusion issue. A few early cases, emphasizing the property interest of the trademark owner, afforded protection whenever the goods were sufficiently related to place the owner's reputation in the hands of the subsequent user. See, e.g., Aunt Jemima Mills Co. v. Rigney & Co., 247 Fed. 407 (2d Cir.1917), cert. denied 245 U.S. 672, 38 S.Ct. 222, 62 L.Ed. 540 (1918). The property perspective was enhanced by publication of an influential article by Schechter, The Rational Basis of Trademark Protection, 40 Harv. L.Rev. 813 (1927). See § 25, Comment *b*. However, later decisions sometimes required specific proof that the prior user's interest in its reputation or in expanding into new product markets was in fact threatened by the subsequent use. See, e.g., S.C. Johnson & Son, Inc. v. Johnson, 116 F.2d 427 (2d Cir.1940).

The federal Trademark Act of 1905 provided protection against the use of registered marks on goods of "substantially the same descriptive properties." Act of February 20, 1905, ch. 592, 33 Stat. 728, § 16. The statutory focus on the physical characteristics of the goods limited the scope of protection against noncompeting goods. However, the Lanham Act as enacted in 1946 required only proof that the subsequent use was "likely to cause confusion or mistake or to deceive purchasers as to the source of origin of such goods or services." Lanham Act, ch. 540, 60 Stat. 437, § 32(1). Although the provision was initially interpreted as codifying a narrow scope of protection, see, e.g., S.C. Johnson & Son, Inc. v. Johnson, 175 F.2d 176 (2d Cir.), cert. denied 338 U.S. 860, 70 S.Ct. 103, 94 L.Ed. 527 (1949), a more flexible approach to the noncompeting goods cases was ultimately adopted by the Second Circuit in Polaroid Corp. v. Polarad Electronics Corp., 287 F.2d 492, 495 (2d Cir.), cert. denied 368 U.S. 820, 82 S.Ct. 36, 7 L.Ed.2d 25 (1961):

> Where the products are different, the prior owner's chance of success is a function of many variables: the strength of his mark, the degree of similarity between the two marks, the proximity of the products, the likelihood that the prior owner will bridge the gap, actual confusion, and the reciprocal of defendant's good faith in adopting its own mark, the quality of defendant's product, and the sophistication of

the buyers. Even this extensive catalogue does not exhaust the possibilities—the court may have to take still other variables into account.

In Triumph Hosiery Mills, Inc. v. Triumph Int'l Corp., 308 F.2d 196 (2d Cir.1962), the court held that the absence of proof of present injury to the prior user's interests was not fatal to an infringement claim if confusion from the concurrent use of the marks was likely. The Lanham Act was also amended to delete the references to purchasers and source of origin. See 15 U.S.C.A. § 1114(1). These developments led to an emphasis on likelihood of confusion, determined through an analysis of all the facts of the case. The history of the Second Circuit cases is reviewed in Goldberg & Borchard, Related Goods Trademark Cases in the Second Circuit, 70 Trademark Rep. 287 (1980).

The fact-oriented approach adopted in *Polaroid* has been followed by other courts, although the enumeration of the relevant factors varies among jurisdictions. See, e.g., Piper Aircraft Corp. v. Wag–Aero, Inc., 741 F.2d 925, 934 (7th Cir.1984) (degree of similarity between the marks in appearance and suggestion, the similarity of the products, the area and manner of concurrent use, the degree of care likely to be exercised by consumers, the strength of the mark, actual confusion, and an intent on the part of the alleged infringer to palm off the goods as those of another); Falcon Rice Mill, Inc. v. Community Rice Mill, Inc., 725 F.2d 336, 345 (5th Cir.1984) (similarity of products, identity of retail outlets and purchasers, identity of advertising media, type or strength of trademark or trade dress, defendant's intent, similarity of design, and actual confusion); Frisch's Restaurants, Inc. v. Elby's Big Boy, Inc., 670 F.2d 642, 648 (6th Cir.), cert. denied 459 U.S. 916, 103 S.Ct. 231, 74 L.Ed.2d 182 (1982) (strength of the mark, relatedness of the goods, similarity of the marks, actual confusion, similarity of marketing channels, likely degree of purchaser care, defendant's intent, and the likelihood of expansion of product lines). Not all factors may be relevant in a particular case, see Eclipse Associates Ltd. v. Data General Corp., 894 F.2d 1114 (9th Cir.1990) (no set formulation of factors must be applied); Ocean Bio–Chem, Inc. v. Turner Network Television, Inc., 741 F.Supp. 1546 (S.D.Fla.1990), and in some circumstances a single factor may be dispositive. See, e.g., Kellogg Co. v. Pack'em Enterprises, Inc., 951 F.2d 330 (Fed.Cir.1991). But cf. Keds Corp. v. Renee Int'l Trading Corp., 888 F.2d 215 (1st Cir.1989) (each factor must be considered).

The likelihood of confusion standard is also applicable under § 2(d) of the Lanham Act, which prohibits registration of a mark likely to cause confusion with a mark previously used or registered, and the same multifactor analysis has been employed. See, e.g., In re E.I. DuPont deNemours & Co., 476 F.2d 1357 (C.C.P.A. 1973).

In Thompson Medical Co. v. Pfizer Inc., 753 F.2d 208 (2d Cir.1985), the court held that the *Polaroid* analysis was not limited to concurrent use on noncompeting goods but rather applied in all infringement cases. Other decisions have also recognized that in competing goods cases factors beyond the resemblance of the two marks may be relevant to the likelihood of confusion. See, e.g., J.B. Williams Co. v. Le Conte Cosmetics, Inc., 523 F.2d 187, 192 (9th Cir.1975), cert. denied 424 U.S. 913, 96 S.Ct. 1110, 47 L.Ed.2d 317 (1976):

> Viewing the foundational question as one of "confusing similarity" is improper because it merges analysis of one of the preliminary inquiries [similarity of marks] with the conceptually distinct step of applying the statutory standard [likelihood of confusion]. The marks may be similar in appearance (foundational fact) yet not likely to cause confusion as to their source, particularly when all the factors are considered.

However, when the defendant's goods or services directly compete with those of the plaintiff, the similarity of the marks is often the predominate factor. Bell Pub. Corp. v. Bantam Doubleday Dell Pub. Group, Inc., 17 U.S.P.Q.2d 1634 (E.D.Pa.1990). This Section offers a unified approach for all trademark infringement cases and enumerates a single set of factors, not intended to be exhaustive, for determining the likelihood of confusion.

Comment c. The factors enumerated in clause (a) of this Section are derived from Restatement of Torts § 729 (1938) and are known as the "sound, sight, and meaning" trilogy. See AMF Inc. v. Sleekcraft Boats, 599 F.2d 341 (9th Cir.1979); McCarthy, *supra*, § 23.04.

A designation need not be identical to the prior user's mark in order to constitute infringement, nor is a close similarity between two marks necessarily dispositive. The question is not the degree of similarity but rather whether confusion is likely. McGregor–Doniger Inc. v. Drizzle Inc., 599 F.2d 1126 (2d Cir.1979).

The comparison of the designations should replicate the market conditions under which the marks will be encountered by prospective purchasers. See, e.g., Wynn Oil Co. v. Thomas, 839 F.2d 1183 (6th Cir.1988); Calvin Klein Cosmetics Corp. v. Lenox Laboratories, Inc., 815 F.2d 500 (8th Cir.1987). Thus, a side-by-side comparison is proper if the products are seen by prospective purchasers side by side in the marketplace, Lever Bros. Co. v. Winzer Co., 326 F.2d 817 (C.C.P.A.1964), but is otherwise improper. See, e.g., Levi Strauss & Co. v. Blue Bell, Inc., 632 F.2d 817 (9th Cir.1980); James Burrough Ltd. v. Sign of Beefeater, Inc., 540 F.2d 266 (7th Cir.1976), appeal after remand 572 F.2d 574 (7th Cir.1978).

The similarity of appearance between two designations must necessarily be determined on a subjective basis. McCarthy, *supra*, § 23.07. The proper comparison is between the overall impressions likely to be perceived by prospective purchasers. Sun–Fun Products, Inc. v. Suntan Research & Development, Inc., 656 F.2d 186 (5th Cir.1981); Dreyfus Fund, Inc. v. Royal Bank of Canada, 525 F.Supp. 1108 (S.D.N.Y.1981). A comparison based on a dissection of the designations is normally improper. Chevron Chemical Co. v. Voluntary Purchasing Groups, Inc., 659 F.2d 695 (5th Cir.1981), cert. denied 457 U.S. 1126, 102 S.Ct. 2947, 73 L.Ed.2d 1342 (1982). However, the overall impression may be strongly influenced by the dominant elements of a mark. See, e.g., Burger Chef Systems, Inc. v. Sandwich Chef, Inc., 608 F.2d 875 (C.C.P.A.1979); Standard Oil Co. v. Standard Oil Co., 56 F.2d 973 (10th Cir.1932) (STANDARD OIL CO. OF NEW MEXICO confusingly similar to STANDARD OIL CO. OF CALIFORNIA). See also, e.g., J & J Snack Foods Corp. v.

McDonald's Corp., 932 F.2d 1460 (Fed.Cir.1991) (a common characteristic of a family of marks used by the plaintiff may itself become associated with the trademark owner; McPRETZEL created a likelihood of confusion with the McDONALD'S family of trademarks).

The presence of the subsequent user's own mark is one of the elements affecting the overall impression created by the use. Fuddruckers, Inc. v. Doc's B.R. Others, Inc., 826 F.2d 837 (9th Cir.1987). Particularly when the distinctiveness of the other's designation is weak, the addition of the defendant's house mark may avoid confusion. See L.A. Gear, Inc. v. Thom McAn Shoe Co., 988 F.2d 1117 (Fed.Cir.), cert. denied ___ U.S. ___, 114 S.Ct. 291, 126 L.Ed.2d 240 (1993); Bristol–Myers Squibb Co. v. McNeil–P.P.C., Inc., 973 F.2d 1033 (2d Cir.1992); General Mills, Inc. v. Kellogg Co., 824 F.2d 622 (8th Cir. 1987). However, in some circumstances the use of a house mark may not alleviate the likelihood of confusion. See, e.g., Menendez v. Holt, 128 U.S. 514, 9 S.Ct. 143, 32 L.Ed. 526 (1888); Banff, Ltd. v. Federated Department Stores, Inc., 638 F.Supp. 652 (S.D.N.Y.1986), affirmed 841 F.2d 486 (2d Cir.1988). Thus, the addition of a prominent label bearing the user's name or mark may or may not prevent confusion from similar trade dress. See Badger Meter, Inc. v. Grinnell Corp., 13 F.3d 1145 (7th Cir. 1994) (since the defendant was known to sell goods manufactured by others, the presence of the defendant's own trademark would not prevent confusion of association resulting from the similarity of trade dress); Litton Systems, Inc. v. Whirlpool Corp., 728 F.2d 1423 (Fed.Cir.1984) (prominent labelling prevented confusion between similar microwave ovens); Source Perrier S.A. v. Waters of Saratoga Springs, Inc., 217 U.S.P.Q. 617 (S.D.N.Y.1982) (label was insufficient to prevent confusion resulting from the use of a distinctive bottle shape). Although in theory a prominent disclaimer of association with the prior user can reduce or eliminate the likelihood of confusion, the courts have ordinarily found the use of disclaimers insufficient to avoid liability for infringement. See, e.g., Int'l Kennel Club, Inc. v. Mighty Star, Inc., 846 F.2d 1079 (7th Cir.1988); Home Box Office, Inc. v. Showtime/The Movie Channel, Inc., 832 F.2d 1311 (2d Cir. 1987); Weight Watchers Int'l, Inc. v. Stouffer Corp., 744 F.Supp. 1259 (S.D.N.Y.1990); Paramount Pictures Corp. v. Worldwide Entertainment Corp., 195 U.S.P.Q. 539 (S.D.N.Y. 1977). Disclaimers are occasionally ordered as a remedy for infringement. See § 35, Comment *d.*

When an element of a composite mark is generic or functional, the determination of infringement must take into account the right of others to employ the generic or functional element. See, e.g., Dranoff–Perlstein Associates v. Sklar, 967 F.2d 852 (3d Cir.1992) (likelihood of confusion test must emphasize the non-generic components); Fuddruckers, Inc., *supra;* American Cyanamid Corp. v. Connaught Laboratories, Inc., 800 F.2d 306 (2d Cir.1986) (infringement cannot rest on use of the same generic term alone if other elements are dissimilar); Expoconsul Int'l, Inc. v. A/E Systems, Inc., 755 F.Supp. 1237 (S.D.N.Y.1991) (same). Cf. Banff, Ltd. v. Federated Dept. Stores, Inc., 841 F.2d 486 (2d Cir.1988) (must compare non-generic elements "in the context of the overall composite mark").

Comment d. Phonetic similarity can be significant in determining the likelihood of confusion, G.D. Searle & Co. v. Charles Pfizer & Co., 265 F.2d 385 (7th Cir.), cert. denied 361 U.S. 819, 80 S.Ct. 64, 4 L.Ed.2d 65 (1959) (BONAMINE similar to DRAMAMINE), but it is not controlling when other factors minimize the potential confusion, LeBow Bros., Inc. v. Lebole Euroconf S.P.A., 503 F.Supp. 209 (E.D.Pa.1980) (LEBOW clothing was not confusingly similar to LEBOLE clothing). The relevant comparison is not between the proper pronunciations but rather how prospective purchasers are likely to hear or use the words. *Id.* See also Mead Data Central, Inc. v. Toyota Motor Sales, Inc., 875 F.2d 1026 (2d Cir.1989).

Comment e. A word mark and a graphic mark may cause a likelihood of confusion if both create the same mental impression. Mobil Oil Corp. v. Pegasus Petroleum Corp., 818 F.2d 254 (2d Cir.1987) (PEGASUS is likely to cause confusion with a flying horse symbol when both are used in the petroleum industry); Beer Nuts, Inc. v. King Nut Co., 477 F.2d 326 (6th Cir.), cert. denied 414 U.S. 858, 94 S.Ct. 66, 38 L.Ed.2d 108 (1973) (picture of a beer stein containing nuts infringes BEER NUTS). Similarly, a foreign word may be confused with its English translation. In re Maclin–Zimmer–McGill Tobacco Co., 262 Fed. 635 (D.C.Cir.1920) (EL GALLO confusingly similar to THE ROOSTER).

Comment f. If the meanings or connotations of the respective designations are similar, confusion may result. See, e.g., Beer Nuts, Inc. v. Clover Club Foods Co., 805 F.2d 920 (10th Cir.1986) (BEER NUTS confusingly similar to BREW NUTS). A difference in meaning can also produce a different overall impression and thus reduce the likelihood of confusion. Ross Bicycles, Inc. v. Cycles USA, Inc., 765 F.2d 1502 (11th Cir. 1985), cert. denied 475 U.S. 1013, 106 S.Ct. 1190, 89 L.Ed.2d 306 (1986) (ROSS bicycles and BOSS CRUISER bicycles).

Illustration 1 is based on Hancock v. American Steel & Wire Co., 203 F.2d 737 (C.C.P.A.1953).

Comment g. See Interpace Corp. v. Lapp, Inc., 721 F.2d 460 (3d Cir.1983) (similar sales contexts can enhance the likelihood of confusion). See also, e.g., Boston Athletic Ass'n v. Sullivan, 867 F.2d 22 (1st Cir.1989) (identical nature of sales outlets and advertising methods supported a finding of infringement). Different retailing strategies or advertising media may not reduce confusion if they are directed at the same prospective purchasers. Dieter v. B & H Industries, Inc., 880 F.2d 322 (11th Cir. 1989), cert. denied 498 U.S. 950, 111 S.Ct. 369, 112 L.Ed.2d 332 (1990) (outlets and home sales). Even when the marks are used in the same stores, the fact that the goods are sold in different departments and targeted at different purchasers may reduce the likelihood of confusion. Vitarroz Corp. v. Borden, Inc., 644 F.2d 960 (2d Cir.1981).

Comment h. Proof that purchasers normally inspect the goods with care will reduce the likelihood of confusion, Blue Bell Bio–Medical v. Cin–Bad, Inc., 864 F.2d 1253 (5th Cir. 1989) (medical professionals purchasing expensive medical goods), and sophisticated consumers may be less easily confused than the general population. See, e.g., Perini Corp. v. Perini Construction, Inc., 915 F.2d

121 (4th Cir.1990); Astra Pharmaceutical Products, Inc. v. Beckman Instruments, Inc., 718 F.2d 1201 (1st Cir.1983). On the other hand, well-educated and technically-trained persons may or may not be more discerning in their purchasing decisions, depending on the circumstances. Fuji Photo Film Co. v. Shinohara Shoji Kabushiki Kaisha, 754 F.2d 591 (5th Cir.1985) (busy printers may not carefully investigate the source of inexpensive printing supplies). See also Koppers Co. v. Krupp–Koppers GmbH, 517 F.Supp. 836 (W.D.Pa. 1981) (collecting instances of confusion by sophisticated purchasers buying expensive goods). Concurrent use of similar designations on goods targeted to children may be especially likely to create confusion. Blake Publishing Corp. v. O'Quinn Studios, Inc., 202 U.S.P.Q. 848 (S.D.N.Y.1979).

Comment i. The "strength" of a mark depends on its distinctiveness to prospective purchasers. "The strength of a particular mark or dress is measured by its distinctiveness or the degree to which it indicates the source or origin of the product." Bristol–Myers Squibb Co. v. McNeil–P.P.C., Inc., 973 F.2d 1033, 1045 (2d Cir.1992). The strength of a mark is determined not only by its conceptual strength, i.e., whether the mark is arbitrary or descriptive, but also by the mark's actual strength in the marketplace. Thus, inherently distinctive marks, if not widely promoted, may be "weak" marks, and descriptive marks may through extensive advertising become "strong" marks. See, e.g., John H. Harland Co. v. Clarke Checks, Inc., 711 F.2d 966 (11th Cir.1983); Sun Banks of Florida, Inc. v. Sun Federal Savings & Loan Ass'n, 651 F.2d 311 (5th Cir. 1981); McGregor–Doniger Inc. v. Drizzle Inc., 599 F.2d 1126 (2d Cir. 1979); McCarthy, *supra,* § 11.25. Contra, Paddington Corp. v. Attiki Importers & Distributors, Inc., 996 F.2d 577 (2d Cir.1993) (suggesting that trade dress, if inherently distinctive, is strong "whether or not the consumer is familiar with the mark or knows the source").

Factors held relevant to the strength of a mark include the length of use, the exclusivity of use within the particular product market, and the extent of promotion. See, e.g., Lang v. Retirement Living Pub. Co., 949 F.2d 576 (2d Cir.1991) (third-party use weighs against strength, citing Restatement Third, Unfair Competition § 13, Comment *e* (Tent. Draft No.2 (1990))); Western Pub. Co. v. Rose Art Industries, Inc., 910 F.2d 57 (2d Cir.1990); Boston Athletic Ass'n v. Sullivan, 867 F.2d 22 (1st Cir.1989). The market factors used to prove secondary meaning, see § 13, Comment *e*, are generally relevant in determining the strength of a mark. See McGregor–Doniger, *supra.*

A mark registered under the Lanham Act for five years may become "incontestable," 15 U.S.C.A. § 1065, and cannot then be challenged as descriptive and lacking secondary meaning. A few cases suggest that an incontestable mark is "strong" for purposes of the likelihood of confusion analysis, see, e.g., Wynn Oil Co. v. Thomas, 839 F.2d 1183 (6th Cir. 1988) (see also Wynn Oil Co. v. American Way Service Corp., 943 F.2d 595 (6th Cir.1991)), or at least that incontestability is a factor to be considered in assessing the strength of a mark. Dieter v. B & H Industries, Inc., 880 F.2d 322 (11th Cir.1989), cert. denied 498 U.S. 950, 111 S.Ct. 369, 112 L.Ed.2d 332 (1990). However, the test for likelihood of confusion is based on the perceptions of consumers in the marketplace, which are ordinarily unaffected by the status of a mark's registration. Munters Corp. v. Matsui America, Inc., 909 F.2d 250 (7th Cir.), cert. denied 498 U.S. 1016, 111 S.Ct. 591, 112 L.Ed.2d 595 (1990); Miss World (UK) Ltd. v. Mrs. America Pageants, Inc., 856 F.2d 1445 (9th Cir.1988); Source Services Corp. v. Chicagoland JobSource, Inc., 643 F.Supp. 1523 (N.D.Ill.1986); Source Services Corp. v. Source Telecomputing Corp., 635 F.Supp. 600 (N.D.Ill. 1986). Cf. DeCosta v. Viacom Int'l, Inc., 981 F.2d 602 (1st Cir.1992), cert. denied ___ U.S. ___, 113 S.Ct. 3039, 125 L.Ed.2d 725 (1993) (fact of registration does not affect the proof of confusion). See McCarthy, *supra*, § 11.25[1][c].

Comment j. The nature of the goods with which the designations are used is an important factor in determining whether confusion is likely. When the respective products are related in function there is a greater likelihood of confusion. In Wynn Oil Co. v. Thomas, 839 F.2d 1183 (6th Cir.1988), it was held that use of the mark CLASSIC for car care products might be confused with the same designation as a service mark on car washing services. Dissimilarity in function may be unimportant, however, if the goods or services are otherwise related. See, e.g., Int'l Kennel Club, Inc. v. Mighty Star, Inc., 846 F.2d 1079 (7th Cir.1988) (INTERNATIONAL KENNEL CLUB as a sponsor of dog shows infringed by use as a trademark on toy dogs). Confusion is also more likely if the respective goods are normally used together. Aunt Jemima Mills Co. v. Rigney & Co., 247 Fed. 407 (2d Cir. 1917), cert. denied 245 U.S. 672, 38 S.Ct. 222, 62 L.Ed. 540 (1918) (pancake flour and pancake syrup); Lambda Electronics Corp. v. Lambda Technology, Inc., 515 F.Supp. 915 (S.D.N.Y.1981) (computer software and computer hardware).

The fact that many companies are known to diversify their product lines was recognized as increasing the likelihood that prospective purchasers may associate noncompeting goods with a common source in, e.g., Armco, Inc. v. Armco Burglar Alarm Co., 693 F.2d 1155 (5th Cir.1982).

Language in some cases suggests that the intent of the prior user to "bridge the gap" and expand into the product line of the subsequent user is relevant in establishing infringement. See, e.g., Wynn Oil Co. v. American Way Service Corp., 943 F.2d 595 (6th Cir.1991); McGregor–Doniger Inc. v. Drizzle Inc., 599 F.2d 1126 (2d Cir. 1979). However, unless the expansion is so imminent as to create a present likelihood of confusion, the intent of the prior user to expand or its activity in preparation to do so, unless known by prospective purchasers, does not affect the likelihood of confusion. Lang v. Retirement Living Pub. Co., 949 F.2d 576 (2d Cir. 1991) (citing Restatement Third, Unfair Competition § 21, Reporters' Note to Comment *j* (Tent. Draft No.2 (1990))); Nikon, Inc. v. Ikon Corp., 803 F.Supp. 910 (S.D.N.Y.1992) (same); Universal Money Centers, Inc. v. American Tel. & Tel. Co., 797 F.Supp. 891 (D.Kan.1992) (same). The relevant inquiry is whether prospective purchasers believe that such expansion by the prior user has in fact occurred. See, e.g., Private Eyes Sunglass Corp. v. Private Eye Vision Center, 25 U.S.P.Q.2d 1709 (D.Conn.1992) (citing Restatement Third, Unfair Competition § 21, Reporters' Note to Comment *j* (Tent.

Draft No.2 (1990))); E.I. Dupont de Nemours & Co. v. Yoshida International, Inc., 393 F.Supp. 502 (E.D.N.Y.1975).

Comment k. Cases recognizing that a distinct difference in the quality of the goods concurrently sold under the mark can decrease the likelihood of confusion include Hasbro, Inc. v. Lanard Toys, Ltd., 858 F.2d 70 (2d Cir.1988) (use of another's mark on inferior goods increases the potential harm to the senior user's reputation if purchasers are confused but may decrease the likelihood of such confusion); Plus Products v. Plus Discount Foods, Inc., 722 F.2d 999 (2d Cir.1983); Lenox Inc. v. Ranmaru U.S.A. Corp., 17 U.S.P.Q.2d 1696 (S.D.N.Y.1990).

Comment l. The rules establishing priority of use are stated in § 19. The second user in a particular territory may have priority in that area by operation of the constructive use and notice provisions of the Lanham Act, 15 U.S.C.A. §§ 1057(c), 1072, or because the first user of the mark in that area adopted it in bad faith. See, e.g., Hanover Star Milling Co. v. Metcalf, 240 U.S. 403, 36 S.Ct. 357, 60 L.Ed. 713 (1916). See § 19, Comment *d.* However, even if the first user in the area does not have priority, its use of the mark does not infringe until confusion is likely. See, e.g., Dawn Donut Co. v. Hart's Food Stores, Inc., 267 F.2d 358 (2d Cir. 1959). A likelihood of confusion will arise if the priority user commences use of the mark on its own goods or services in that area, or in the absence of actual use, if the mark comes to be associated with the priority user's goods or services in that area. Cases relating to proof of use or association in an area are collected in the Reporters' Note accompanying § 19.

Comment m. In jury trials the issue of likelihood of confusion is determined by the jury. See, e.g., Roulo v. Russ Berrie & Co., 886 F.2d 931 (7th Cir.1989), cert. denied 493 U.S. 1075, 110 S.Ct. 1124, 107 L.Ed.2d 1030 (1990); Fuddruckers, Inc. v. Doc's B.R. Others, Inc., 826 F.2d 837 (9th Cir.1987); Oreck Corp. v. U.S. Floor Systems, Inc., 803 F.2d 166 (5th Cir.1986), cert. denied 481 U.S. 1069, 107 S.Ct. 2462, 95 L.Ed.2d 871 (1987); W.W.W. Pharmaceutical Co. v. Gillette Co., 14 U.S.P.Q.2d 1333 (S.D.N.Y.1989). Jury findings are preserved on appeal if supported by substantial evidence. See, e.g., Fuddruckers, Inc., *supra* (citing Sarkisian v. Winn–Proof Corp., 688 F.2d 647 (9th Cir.1982), cert. denied 460 U.S. 1052, 103 S.Ct. 1499, 75 L.Ed.2d 930 (1983)); Oreck Corp., *supra* ; John H. Harland Co. v. Clarke Checks, Inc., 711 F.2d 966 (11th Cir.1983).

State appellate courts have generally considered the issue of likelihood of confusion to be one of fact. See McCarthy, *supra,* § 23.22[3]. In most federal circuits, likelihood of confusion is similarly regarded as a question of fact subject to a clearly erroneous standard of review under Fed.R.Civ.Pro. 52(a). See, e.g., ConAgra, Inc. v. George A. Hormel & Co., 990 F.2d 368 (8th Cir.1993); Moore Business Forms, Inc. v. Ryu, 960 F.2d 486 (5th Cir.1992); Purolator, Inc. v. EFRA Distributors, Inc., 687 F.2d 554 (1st Cir.1982) (clearly erroneous standard applies even if the decision of the trial judge is based solely on documentary evidence and product comparisons); Safeway Stores, Inc. v. Safeway Discount Drugs, Inc., 675 F.2d 1160 (11th Cir.1982). Cf. Inwood Laboratories, Inc. v. Ives Laboratories, Inc., 456 U.S. 844, 102 S.Ct. 2182, 72

L.Ed.2d 606 (1982) (reversing an appellate court's rejection in a trademark case of findings of fact that were not determined to be clearly erroneous). See generally McCarthy, *supra*, § 23.22; Comment, Clearly Erroneous Review of Mixed Questions of Law and Fact: The Likelihood of Confusion Determination in Trademark Law, 59 U.Chi.L.Rev. 1291 (1992); Rubin, The Role of the Clearly Erroneous Standard of Federal Rule of Civil Procedure 52(a) in Reviewing Trial Court Determinations of Likelihood or No Likelihood of Confusion, 74 Trademark Rep. 20 (1984). Two circuits that had earlier indicated that likelihood of confusion presents a question of law later rejected those decisions and held the issue to be one of fact. See Eclipse Associates, Ltd. v. Data General Corp., 894 F.2d 1114 (9th Cir.1990), reaffirming Levi Strauss & Co. v. Blue Bell, Inc., 778 F.2d 1352 (9th Cir.1985) (en banc), which had rejected a line of decisions based on J.B. Williams Co. v. Le Conte Cosmetics, Inc., 523 F.2d 187 (9th Cir.1975), cert. denied 424 U.S. 913, 96 S.Ct. 1110, 47 L.Ed.2d 317 (1976) (holding that likelihood of confusion is a question of law); Scandia Down Corp. v. Euroquilt, Inc., 772 F.2d 1423 (7th Cir. 1985), cert. denied 475 U.S. 1147, 106 S.Ct. 1801, 90 L.Ed.2d 346 (1986) (likelihood of confusion is a question of fact, explicitly rejecting a contrary suggestion in Union Carbide Corp. v. Ever–Ready, Inc., 531 F.2d 366 (7th Cir.), cert. denied 429 U.S. 830, 97 S.Ct. 91, 50 L.Ed.2d 94 (1976) (de novo review of a decision founded solely on the similarity of marks)). See also Forum Corp. v. Forum, Ltd., 903 F.2d 434 (7th Cir.1990).

Several circuits, however, continue to hold that the determination of likelihood of confusion is a question of law subject to de novo review. See Bristol–Myers Squibb Co. v. McNeil–P.P.C., Inc., 973 F.2d 1033 (2d Cir. 1992) (findings as to the relevant factors are factual but the balancing of factors to determine the likelihood of confusion is a legal issue); Western Pub. Co. v. Rose Art Industries, Inc., 910 F.2d 57 (2d Cir.1990); In re Shell Oil Co., 992 F.2d 1204 (Fed.Cir.1993); Nina Ricci, S.A.R.L. v. E.T.F. Enterprises, Inc., 889 F.2d 1070 (Fed.Cir. 1989); Wynn Oil Co. v. American Way Service Corp., 943 F.2d 595 (6th Cir.1991); Frisch's Restaurants, Inc. v. Elby's Big Boy, Inc., 670 F.2d 642 (6th Cir.), cert. denied 459 U.S. 916, 103 S.Ct. 231, 74 L.Ed.2d 182 (1982). It is not clear, however, that these courts would substitute their judgment for a jury verdict on the likelihood of confusion.

The suggestion that an appellate court can substitute its judgment for that of the trial judge when the decision is based exclusively on a comparison of the competing designations is traceable to Judge Frank's decision in Eastern Wine Corp. v. Winslow–Warren, Ltd., 137 F.2d 955 (2d Cir.), cert. denied 320 U.S. 758, 64 S.Ct. 65, 88 L.Ed. 452 (1943). But see Anderson v. Bessemer City, 470 U.S. 564, 105 S.Ct. 1504, 84 L.Ed.2d 518 (1985). Fed.R.Civ.Pro. 52(a) was amended in 1985 to emphasize that the clearly erroneous standard of review applies to factual findings "whether based on oral or documentary evidence." For an argument that the earlier version of Fed.R.Civ. Pro. 52(a) also required the application of the clearly erroneous standard to factual findings of the trial judge even when based solely on documentary evidence, see Wright, Law of Federal Courts § 96 (4th ed.1983).

§ 22. Proof of Likelihood of Confusion: Intent of the Actor

(1) A likelihood of confusion may be inferred from proof that the actor used a designation resembling another's trademark, trade name, collective mark, or certification mark with the intent to cause confusion or to deceive.

(2) A likelihood of confusion should not be inferred from proof that the actor intentionally copied the other's designation if the actor acted in good faith under circumstances that do not otherwise indicate an intent to cause confusion or to deceive.

Comment:

a. Scope. This Section describes the role of the actor's intent in determining whether the use of a designation creates a likelihood of confusion under the rule stated in § 20. The intent of the actor may also be relevant in determining priority, see § 19, and in fashioning appropriate relief, see §§ 35–37.

b. Relation to other factors. Use of a designation that is likely to cause confusion with another's trademark, trade name, collective mark, or certification mark is an infringement regardless of whether the actor knows of the other's prior use or intends to confuse prospective purchasers. Thus, proof of an intent to deceive is not required in order to subject the actor to liability. However, in deciding whether a use is likely to cause confusion, the intent of the subsequent user is widely regarded as relevant and is often included in the enumeration of factors that determine the likelihood of confusion. Intent differs, however, from the factors listed in § 21, which relate to the market context in which the designations are used. The similarity of the competing marks, the methods by which the goods or services are marketed, the distinctiveness of the prior user's mark, the care likely to be exercised by purchasers, and the relationship of the parties' goods or services all contribute to the manner in which the subsequent user's mark is likely to be perceived by prospective purchasers. The subsequent user's intent, on the other hand, does not itself affect the impression created by the use of the designation since the user's intent is generally unknown to prospective purchasers.

c. Intent as proof of likelihood of confusion. Although the actor's intent does not affect the perceptions of prospective purchasers, it may be appropriate to assume that an actor who intends to cause confusion will be successful in doing so. Proof of an intent to confuse may thus create an inference that confusion is likely, although the inference can be overcome by other evidence indicating that, notwithstanding such an intent, consumers are unlikely to be widow confused.

It is the intent to cause confusion or to deceive that may justify an inference that confusion is likely. Proof that the actor adopted a similar designation with knowledge of the other's prior use, or even that the actor intentionally copied all or part of the other's designation, is not necessarily sufficient to establish an intent to confuse. For example, if the actor reasonably believes that the other's designation is functional or that the actor's use is on goods sufficiently unrelated to the other's goods that confusion is unlikely, proof that the actor intentionally copied the other's designation does not justify an inference of confusion. Copying another's trademark for the purpose of parody or for use as ornamentation on goods such as clothing or jewelry also does not in itself support an inference that confusion is likely. The issue in such cases is whether the actor's use in fact creates a likelihood of confusion, and resolution of that issue is not affected by the existence of intentional copying. On the other hand, if there is proof of intentional copying with no alternative explanation, an intent to benefit from the other's good will through confusion may be inferred.

Even if an actor believes in good faith that the copying of another's designation is justified, an inference that confusion is likely may arise from other circumstances that suggest an intent to confuse, such as a failure to take reasonable steps to minimize the risk of confusion. For example, although the actor may reasonably believe that the copied element is functional and therefore unprotectable, an intent to confuse may be inferred if the actor fails to label or otherwise distinguish its goods or services from those of the other. See § 16, Comment *d*. What steps are reasonable will depend upon the circumstances of each case, and there may be situations in which no reasonable precautions against confusion are available. The issue is whether the actor's failure to take precautions fairly demonstrates an intent to confuse.

Illustrations:

1. *A* sells lawn chemicals using a distinctive trade dress consisting of bottles with labels that prominently display a particular pattern of red and yellow stripes. *B*, knowing of *A*'s prior use, begins to sell similar products in bottles with labels bearing the same pattern and colors but with a different brand name. There is evidence that *B* instructed its marketing staff to "get as close to *A*'s label as the law allows." In the absence of any

alternative explanation for the copying of *A* 's distinctive trade dress, a likelihood of confusion may be inferred.

2. *A*, a credit card company, has acquired trademark rights in the overall appearance of its credit card. As a parody of *A* 's slogan, "Don't leave home without it," *B* manufacturers and sells packages of condoms that closely resemble *A* 's credit card. The intentional copying by *B* does not necessarily indicate an intent to confuse and thus does not justify an inference that confusion is likely.

3. *A* uses a printed advertisement for its plumbing service that includes a map of the city divided into service areas in order to assist consumers in locating the service center nearest to their home or business. The advertisement has become distinctive of *A* 's business under the rule stated in § 13. *B* begins to use an advertisement for its competing business that includes a map copied from *A* 's advertisement. If *B* in good faith believed that the map is functional under the rule stated in § 17, *B* 's intentional copying does not justify an inference that confusion is likely unless *B* has failed to take reasonable steps to minimize the risk of confusion.

REPORTERS' NOTE

The relevance of the actor's intent is analyzed in McCarthy, Trademarks and Unfair Competition §§ 23.30–35; Gilson, Trademark Practice and Procedure § 5.07. See also Pattishall, The Impact of Intent in Trade Identity Cases, 65 Nw.U.L.Rev. 421 (1970).

Comment b. Good faith is not a defense to trademark infringement. E.g., Fuji Photo Film Co. v. Shinohara Shoji Kabushiki Kaisha, 754 F.2d 591 (5th Cir.1985); Pizzeria Uno Corp. v. Temple, 747 F.2d 1522 (4th Cir.1984); President and Trustees of Colby College v. Colby College—New Hampshire, 508 F.2d 804 (1st Cir. 1975); Best & Co. v. Miller, 167 F.2d 374 (2d Cir.), cert. denied 335 U.S. 818, 69 S.Ct. 39, 93 L.Ed. 373 (1948). On the other hand, courts regularly include intent as one of the factors to be considered in evaluating the likelihood of confusion. See, e.g., Sno–Wizard Mfg., Inc. v. Eisemann Products Co., 791 F.2d 423 (5th Cir.1986) (intent alone is sufficient to support a finding of likelihood of confusion); Golden Door, Inc. v. Odisho, 646 F.2d 347 (9th Cir.1980) (intent is entitled to great weight); Polaroid Corp. v. Polarad Electronics Corp., 287 F.2d 492 (2d Cir.), cert. denied 368 U.S. 820, 82 S.Ct. 36, 7 L.Ed.2d 25 (1961) ("reciprocal of defendant's good faith"). See also Restatement of Torts § 729 (1938).

Comment c. Some courts have held that the adoption of a mark with an intent to confuse prospective purchasers raises a presumption that confusion is likely, thus shifting the burden to the defendant to prove that there is no likelihood of confusion. E.g., Osem Food Industries Ltd. v. Sherwood Foods, Inc., 917 F.2d 161

(4th Cir.1990); Mobil Oil Corp. v. Pegasus Petroleum Corp., 818 F.2d 254 (2d Cir.1987); My–T Fine Corp. v. Samuels, 69 F.2d 76 (2d Cir.1934). Cf. Resource Developers, Inc. v. Statue of Liberty–Ellis Island Foundation, Inc., 926 F.2d 134 (2d Cir.1991) (intent to deceive creates a presumption of actual confusion for the purpose of proving damages, citing Restatement Third, Unfair Competition § 22 (Tent. Draft No.2 (1990))) (dictum). Other courts view an intent to confuse merely as a factor that may justify an inference that confusion is likely. E.g., Computer Care v. Service Systems Enterprises, Inc., 982 F.2d 1063 (7th Cir.); American Home Products Corp. v. Barr Laboratories, Inc., 834 F.2d 368 (3d Cir.1987); Restatement of Torts § 729, Comment *f* (1938). However, an intent to copy or imitate another's mark does not necessarily establish an intent to confuse. See, e.g., American Home Products, *supra* ; Sno–Wizard Mfg., Inc. v. Eisemann Products Co., 791 F.2d 423 (5th Cir.1986); Blau Plumbing, Inc. v. S.O.S. Fix–It, Inc., 781 F.2d 604 (7th Cir.1986); Devan Designs, Inc. v. Palliser Furniture Corp., 25 U.S.P.Q.2d 1991 (M.D.N.C. 1992), affirmed 998 F.2d 1008 (4th Cir.1993) (citing Restatement Third, Unfair Competition § 22 (Tent. Draft No.2 (1990))). See also Nike, Inc. v. "Just Did It" Enterprises, 6 F.3d 1225 (7th Cir.1993) (distinguishing an intent to parody from an intent to confuse); Anheuser–Busch, Inc. v. L & L Wings, Inc., 962 F.2d 316 (4th Cir.), cert. denied ___ U.S. ___, 113 S.Ct. 206, 121 L.Ed.2d 147 (1992) (same); Jordache Enterprises, Inc. v. Hogg Wyld, Ltd., 828 F.2d 1482 (10th Cir.1987) (same); American Express Co. v. Vibra Approved Laboratories Corp., 10 U.S.P.Q.2d 2006 (S.D.N.Y. 1989); Tetley, Inc. v. Topps Chewing Gum, Inc., 556 F.Supp. 785 (E.D.N.Y. 1983). On the other hand, an intent to cause confusion may be inferred from intentional copying if there is no other plausible explanation for the copying. See Chevron Chemical Co. v. Voluntary Purchasing Groups, Inc., 659 F.2d 695 (5th Cir.1981), cert. denied 457 U.S. 1126, 102 S.Ct. 2947, 73 L.Ed.2d 1342 (1982).

Illustration 1 is based on *Chevron Chemical Co., supra.*

Illustration 2 is based on *American Express Co., supra.*

Illustration 3 is suggested by the facts in *Blau Plumbing, supra.*

§ 23. Proof of Likelihood of Confusion: Evidence of Actual Confusion

(1) A likelihood of confusion may be inferred from proof of actual confusion.

(2) An absence of likelihood of confusion may be inferred from the absence of proof of actual confusion if the actor and the other have made significant use of their respective designations in the same geographic market for

a substantial period of time, and any resulting confusion would ordinarily be manifested by provable facts.

Comment:

a. Scope. This Section describes the role of proof of actual confusion in determining the likelihood of confusion under the rule stated in § 20. Evidence of actual confusion can also be relevant in determining appropriate relief under the rules stated in §§ 35–37.

b. Relevance of actual confusion. Evidence of actual confusion is not necessary in order to prove infringement, but the existence of actual confusion is frequently included in judicial enumerations of the factors to be considered in determining the likelihood of confusion. However, like the actor's intent (see § 22), proof of actual confusion differs from the factors listed in § 21 because it does not relate to the marketing circumstances that influence the manner in which the designation is perceived by prospective purchasers. Rather, the existence of actual confusion is direct evidence that in the market context of their actual use the similarities between the two designations are sufficient to create confusion. Thus, actual confusion, or the absence of actual confusion, can confirm or discredit inferences drawn from the market factors in § 21.

All courts recognize the relevance of proof of actual confusion in determining whether there is a likelihood of confusion, and convincing evidence of substantial actual confusion is ordinarily decisive. Courts occasionally suggest that proof of actual confusion is necessary if the evidence relating to market factors fails to establish a likelihood of confusion, but these statements merely recognize that such proof can overcome a contrary inference arising from the marketing context of the use.

c. Proof of actual confusion. Actual confusion can be established through the direct testimony of consumers. It can also be shown through evidence of conduct probative of confusion such as misdirected letters and telephone calls. Evidence of inquiries by customers as to whether the plaintiff and the defendant are associated, however, may not establish the existence of actual confusion if the nature of the inquiries indicates that consumers perceive a difference between the designations and are skeptical of the existence of a connection between the users. Evidence of confusion arising in circumstances that differ from those in which the designations are encountered by prospective purchasers may be entitled to little weight. Proof of only a few instances of actual confusion may also be insufficient to support an inference that a significant number of prospective purchasers are likely to be confused. See § 20, Comment *g*.

Consumer surveys can be helpful in establishing whether confusion is likely. Although no survey can duplicate perfectly the marketing circumstances of the use, a survey that reasonably reflects the state of mind of prospective purchasers as they encounter the designations in the marketplace is admissible evidence of the likelihood of confusion. The reliability of a survey depends on the construction of the survey instrument, the validity of the sample, and the manner in which the survey is conducted. A survey that is substantially flawed on any of these grounds may be so unreliable as to be inadmissible. Less substantial flaws may be considered in assessing the appropriate weight to be accorded to the survey's findings. See § 20, Comment *g*.

Although surveys can be helpful in resolving the issue of infringement, they can also add significantly to the cost of trademark litigation. While some courts have drawn adverse inferences against parties who fail to introduce a consumer survey, such an approach attributes too much importance to survey evidence. Surveys are useful but not indispensable evidence of the likelihood of confusion, and no inference on that issue should be drawn from a mere failure to offer survey evidence.

d. Absence of actual confusion. A trademark owner need not prove actual confusion in order to prove a likelihood of confusion, and ordinarily the absence of proof of actual confusion is not significant. In an impersonal marketplace, instances of actual confusion may not be readily discoverable because consumers do not typically disclose their state of mind when making purchases. However, when the parties have made significant use of their respective designations in the same geographic market for a substantial period of time, the absence of any evidence of actual confusion may in some cases justify an inference that the actor's use does not create a likelihood of confusion. Whether such an inference is justified depends upon the likelihood that any actual confusion of prospective purchasers would be manifested by provable facts.

REPORTERS' NOTE

The relevance of evidence of actual confusion is discussed in McCarthy, Trademarks and Unfair Competition § 23.02.

Comment b. Evidence of actual confusion is not necessary in order to prove a likelihood of confusion. See Wynn Oil Co. v. Thomas, 839 F.2d 1183 (6th Cir.1988); Lois Sportswear, U.S.A., Inc. v. Levi Strauss & Co., 799 F.2d 867 (2d Cir.1986); Chevron Chemical Co. v. Voluntary Purchasing Groups, Inc., 659 F.2d 695 (5th Cir.1981), cert. denied 457 U.S. 1126, 102 S.Ct. 2947, 73 L.Ed.2d 1342 (1982) (actual confusion may be difficult to detect when the goods are relatively inexpensive). However, proof of actual confusion is strong evidence of a likelihood of confusion and in some cases may be sufficient to prove infringement. See, e.g.,

Fuddruckers, Inc. v. Doc's B.R. Others, Inc., 826 F.2d 837 (9th Cir.1987); Fuji Photo Film Co. v. Shinohara Shoji Kabushiki Kaisha, 754 F.2d 591 (5th Cir.1985).

Actual confusion is generally enumerated as a factor to be considered in evaluating the likelihood of confusion. See, e.g., Falcon Rice Mill, Inc. v. Community Rice Mill, Inc., 725 F.2d 336 (5th Cir.1984); Frisch's Restaurants, Inc. v. Elby's Big Boy, Inc., 670 F.2d 642 (6th Cir.), cert. denied 459 U.S. 916, 103 S.Ct. 231, 74 L.Ed.2d 182 (1982); Helene Curtis Industries, Inc. v. Church & Dwight Co., 560 F.2d 1325 (7th Cir.1977), cert. denied 434 U.S. 1070, 98 S.Ct. 1252, 55 L.Ed.2d 772 (1978); Polaroid Corp. v. Polarad Electronics Corp., 287 F.2d 492 (2d Cir.), cert. denied 368 U.S. 820, 82 S.Ct. 36, 7 L.Ed.2d 25 (1961). In *Falcon Rice Mill, supra*, it was recognized that if other factors indicate only a marginal risk of confusion, proof of actual confusion may be necessary as a practical matter to establish infringement.

Comment c. Actual confusion can be proved by the direct testimony of confused purchasers, see AmBrit, Inc. v. Kraft, Inc., 812 F.2d 1531 (11th Cir.1986), cert. denied 481 U.S. 1041, 107 S.Ct. 1983, 95 L.Ed.2d 822 (1987), but is more often proved by testimony concerning the receipt by the trademark owner of misdirected letters or telephone calls. See, e.g., Int'l Kennel Club, Inc. v. Mighty Star, Inc., 846 F.2d 1079 (7th Cir. 1988); Armco, Inc. v. Armco Burglar Alarm Co., 693 F.2d 1155 (5th Cir. 1982). Proof that distributors, retailers, or sales clerks are confused permits but does not require the inference that prospective purchasers are also likely to be confused. See Fuji Photo Film Co. v. Shinohara Shoji Kabushiki Kaisha, 754 F.2d 591 (5th Cir.1985); Union Carbide Corp. v. Ever-Ready, Inc., 531 F.2d 366 (7th Cir.), cert. denied 429 U.S. 830, 97 S.Ct. 91, 50 L.Ed. 94 (1976); Polo Fashions, Inc. v. Extra Special Products, Inc., 451 F.Supp. 555 (S.D.N.Y. 1978).

Evidence of only occasional instances of actual confusion may be inadequate to establish infringement. See Nutri/System, Inc. v. Con-Stan Industries, Inc., 809 F.2d 601 (9th Cir.1987) (several misdirected letters insufficient in light of sales volume); Amstar Corp. v. Domino's Pizza, Inc., 615 F.2d 252 (5th Cir.), cert. denied 449 U.S. 899, 101 S.Ct. 268, 66 L.Ed.2d 129 (1980) (two verbal inquires and one misdirected letter found insufficient); Scott Paper Co. v. Scott's Liquid Gold, Inc., 589 F.2d 1225 (3d Cir.1978) (19 misdirected letters in four years was insufficient). But see AmBrit, Inc., *supra* (four instances of confusion given weight); Jellibeans, Inc. v. Skating Clubs of Georgia, Inc., 716 F.2d 833 (11th Cir. 1983) (three instances of confusion); Safeway Stores, Inc. v. Safeway Discount Drugs, Inc., 675 F.2d 1160 (11th Cir.1982) (two instances of confusion).

Inquiries from consumers concerning the relationship between the trademark owner and the subsequent user are generally considered to be only weak evidence of confusion. See Jordache Enterprises, Inc. v. Hogg Wyld, Ltd., 828 F.2d 1482 (10th Cir. 1987); Pignons S.A. de Mecanique de Precision v. Polaroid Corp., 657 F.2d 482 (1st Cir.1981).

Survey evidence in trademark cases is discussed in McCarthy, *supra*, §§ 32.46–55; Gilson, Trademark Protection and Practice § 8.11. See also Symposium, The Structure and

Uses of Survey Evidence in Trademark Cases, 67 Trademark Rep. 97 (1977). The reliability of a survey generally goes to its evidentiary weight rather than to admissibility. E. & J. Gallo Winery v. Gallo Cattle Co., 967 F.2d 1280 (9th Cir.1992). Cf. Weight Watchers Int'l, Inc. v. Stouffer Corp., 744 F.Supp. 1259 (S.D.N.Y. 1990) (no weight given to a seriously flawed survey). A few cases suggest that a trademark owner's failure to introduce survey evidence can justify an adverse inference, but for the most part such cases involve substantial concurrent use in which some evidence of actual confusion may be necessary to prevent an inference that there is no likelihood of confusion under the rule stated in Subsection (2). See, e.g., Mushroom Makers, Inc. v. R.G. Barry Corp., 441 F.Supp. 1220 (S.D.N.Y.1977), affirmed 580 F.2d 44 (2d Cir.1978), cert. denied 439 U.S. 1116, 99 S.Ct. 1022, 59 L.Ed.2d 75 (1979). Cf. Eagle Snacks, Inc. v. Nabisco Brands, Inc., 625 F.Supp. 571 (D.N.J.1985) (the absence of survey evidence by the plaintiff was relevant to the argument that the results of the defendant's survey would have been different if the survey had followed plaintiff's suggested methodology). That there is no general requirement of survey evidence in order to establish a likelihood of confusion, see, e.g., Charles Jacquin Et Cie, Inc. v. Destileria Serralles, Inc., 921 F.2d 467 (3d Cir.1990); Woodsmith Pub. Co. v. Meredith Corp., 904 F.2d 1244 (8th Cir.1990) (dictum).

Comment d. Several cases have held that when there is longstanding concurrent use of the designations, an absence of actual confusion may be evidence of an absence of the likelihood of confusion. Homeowners Group, Inc. v. Home Marketing Specialists, Inc., 931 F.2d 1100 (6th Cir. 1991); Oreck Corp. v. U.S. Floor Systems, Inc., 803 F.2d 166 (5th Cir. 1986), cert. denied 481 U.S. 1069, 107 S.Ct. 2462, 95 L.Ed.2d 871 (1987) (no actual confusion after 17 months of concurrent use is evidence that confusion is unlikely); Plus Products v. Plus Discount Foods, Inc., 722 F.2d 999 (2d Cir.1983); Amstar Corp. v. Domino's Pizza, Inc., 615 F.2d 252 (5th Cir.), cert. denied 449 U.S. 899, 101 S.Ct. 268, 66 L.Ed.2d 129 (1980) (three instances of actual confusion in 15 years of concurrent use raises a presumption that there is no likelihood of confusion).

§ 24. Use of Another's Trademark on Genuine Goods

One is not subject to liability under the rule stated in § 20 for using another's trademark, trade name, collective mark, or certification mark in marketing genuine goods or services the source, sponsorship, or certification of which is accurately identified by the mark unless:

(a) the other uses a different mark for different types or grades of goods or services and the actor markets one of the types or grades under a mark used for another type or grade; or

(b) the actor markets under the mark genuine goods of the other that have been repaired, recondi-

tioned, altered, or used, or genuine services that do not conform to the standards imposed by the other, and the actor's use of the mark causes a likelihood of confusion that the goods are new or unaltered or that the repair, reconditioning, or alteration was performed, authorized, or certified by the other, or that the services conform to the other's standards.

Comment:

a. Scope. The rules stated in this Section determine whether the use of another's mark on genuine goods or services constitutes an infringement under the rule stated in § 20. The rules are also applicable in determining whether the importation and sale of genuine goods made abroad is an infringement of the trademark rights of the domestic trademark owner. See Comments *e* and *f*.

b. General rule. The rules governing the protection of trademarks are intended to prevent the diversion of trade or harm to reputation that is likely to result if consumers are confused as to the source or sponsorship of goods and services. Confusion does not occur, however, when a trademark is used to identify genuine goods marketed under that mark by the trademark owner. Thus, the trademark owner cannot ordinarily prevent or control the sale of goods bearing the mark once the owner has permitted those goods to enter commerce. It can be said that the rights of the trademark owner are exhausted once the owner authorizes the initial sale of the product under the trademark or that the owner implicitly licenses others to further market the goods under the mark. Thus, no infringement occurs when the use of a mark properly identifies the source, sponsorship, or certification of the goods or services, even if the owner of the mark objects to the use.

c. Genuine goods. The rule stated in this Section applies only to genuine goods that can be properly marketed under the trademark because the trademark owner has approved their initial sale under the mark. The test of genuineness does not involve an evaluation of the quality or characteristics of the goods. The rule stated in this Section does not authorize the use of the trademark owner's mark on another's goods that imitate, even perfectly, the goods of the trademark owner.

Trademarked goods produced by a manufacturer under a contract with the trademark owner should not be considered genuine goods until sale of the goods under the mark has been authorized by the trademark owner. Thus, if the trademark owner rejects the goods, the manufacturer may not use the mark in reselling the goods to others. This principle should apply without regard to whether the rejection constitutes a breach of contract by the trademark owner. Although it can be argued that a manufacturer of wrongfully rejected goods should be permitted to resell the goods under the trademark of the breaching buyer, ordinarily the propriety of the rejection by the trademark owner will not be determined until after resale of the goods. Because a trademark owner who wrongfully rejects trademarked goods will be liable for any reduction in resale value caused by removal of the mark, the better policy is to protect consumers from the confusion that results if unauthorized goods are sold under the mark of the trademark owner. The trademark owner by contract, however, may waive the right to object to the sale of rejected goods under the mark, and the owner is then precluded from claiming infringement.

In order to use another's mark on genuine goods without liability for infringement, the goods must be those that the trademark owner sells under that mark in the marketplace. It is not sufficient that the goods come from the source identified by the trademark if the trademark owner has not authorized the use of the mark on those particular goods. Thus, although the goods are in fact made by the trademark owner, it is an infringement if the actor uses the owner's mark on goods that have been sold by the trademark owner under a different mark.

Illustrations:

1. *A* markets SWEETSOUND compact discs. *A* refuses to sell the recordings to *B*, a retailer. *B* obtains a number of SWEETSOUND compact discs from various persons who had purchased the goods directly or indirectly from *A*. *B* advertises the recordings for sale as SWEETSOUND compact discs. *B* has not infringed *A* 's trademark.

2. *B* operates a fast-food restaurant under a franchise agreement with *A*, the franchisor, that authorizes *B* to use *A* 's trademark. After the expiration of the franchise agreement, *B* continues to use *A* 's trademark. *B* is subject to liability for the infringement of *A* 's trademark even if *B* continues to utilize *A* 's recipes and in every other manner continues to comply with the requirements of the expired franchise agreement.

3. *A* contracts with *B* for the production of shirts made according to *A* 's specifications for sale by *A* under *A* 's trademark. Pursuant to the contract, *B* manufactures the shirts, attaches *A* 's label, and packages the shirts in bags bearing *A* 's trademark. *A* rejects delivery of the shirts as not being timely. *B* sells the shirts to *C*, a discounter, who markets the shirts under

A 's trademark. *B* and *C* are subject to liability for the infringement of *A* 's mark because *A* did not authorize sale of the shirts under the trademark.

4. *A* manufacturers two grades of automobile tires, one marketed to independent retailers and the other marketed through its own retail outlets. The tires marketed through *A* 's own retail outlets bear the trademark FLY; those marketed to independent retailers bear the trademark OX or no trademark at all. *B* buys a quantity of *A* 's unmarked tires and advertises them for sale as FLY tires. *B* is subject to liability for the infringement of *A* 's trademark.

d. Used, repaired, reconditioned, or altered goods. One may use another's mark in marketing genuine goods that are used, repaired, reconditioned, or altered if consumers are not likely to be confused into believing that the goods are new or in their original form or that the alterations were performed or approved by the trademark owner. Whether there is a likelihood of such confusion often depends on the assumptions made by consumers regarding the operation of the market for the particular goods. It is unlikely, for example, that consumers buying a used automobile bearing its original trademark will believe that the automobile is unaltered from its original condition or that all repairs and reconditioning were performed by the original manufacturer. On the other hand, sale of reconditioned automobile engine parts under their original trademark may cause confusion or deception absent an adequate explanatory disclaimer. Thus, although use of another's mark to indicate the original source of the goods is permitted, accompanying material communicating the fact and source of any alterations may sometimes be required in order to avoid infringement. In some contexts, however, use of the original trademark on altered goods may be likely to cause confusion despite the presence of a disclaimer. For example, it is an infringement to emphasize the original trademark in a manner that confuses purchasers as to the source of the alterations. Similarly, in some instances the repair or reconditioning of the original product may be so extensive that it is deceptive to continue to associate the product with the trademark owner.

The rule stated in this Section is also applicable to the unauthorized sale of deteriorated or out-of-date merchandise under the original trademark. Use of the original mark is permitted only if prospective purchasers are adequately informed about the condition of the goods.

If genuine goods when sold by the actor are not accompanied by the same warranty, rebate, or other incidents of sale that consumers associate with the goods sold under the trademark, an actor who fails to disclose such departures may be subject to liability either for trademark infringement or for deceptive marketing actionable under § 2 of this Restatement. Such goods can be regarded as "altered" when sold without an expected warranty or rebate, thus subjecting the actor to liability under this Section. The actor's use of the original trademark may also be regarded as an implied misrepresentation concerning the accompanying incidents of sale actionable under § 2. The remedy awarded under either cause of action may, if appropriate, permit the continued use of the trademark to describe accurately the original source of the goods if the use is accompanied by adequate disclosures.

Manufacturers sometimes sell materially different goods or services under the same mark to different classes of purchasers or in separate geographic markets. Both goods are genuine under the rule stated in this Section, and the unauthorized sale of goods designed for one market in the other market is thus not in itself an infringement. However, as in the case of altered or repaired goods, the seller may be required to disclose the nature of the goods and the circumstances relating to the departure from the expectations created by the presence of the mark. For example, a manufacturer of hair coloring may sell different formulations of the product under the same trademark in separate retail and professional markets. Unauthorized sales of the professional product to retail buyers is not an infringement if the nature of the goods and the circumstances of their sale are adequately disclosed to the retail purchasers.

Artists and performers have an analogous interest in protecting the integrity of their work and avoiding a false association with works or performances that do not accurately reflect their achievements. The unauthorized use of an artist's or performer's name or trademark in association with a substantially edited or altered version of a work may thus be actionable by analogy to the rule stated in this Section.

Illustrations:

5. *A* manufactures and sells face powder under the trademark ANGEL. *B* purchases ANGEL face powder in bulk, adds a binder to give it coherence, and sells the powder in metal compacts using the trademark ANGEL with no accompanying disclosures. *B* is subject to liability for the infringement of *A*'s trademark.

6. The facts being otherwise as stated in Illustration 5, *B* markets its compacts with a label that prominently states, "This compact of face powder was independently compounded by *B*

from ANGEL loose powder and our own binder." *B* has not infringed *A* 's trademark.

e. Import restrictions on gray market goods. Gray market goods are goods produced abroad under a trademark that properly identifies the source of the goods in the country of origin, but which are subsequently marketed in this country without the consent of the owner of the trademark in the United States. A gray market can result from various marketing arrangements. A domestic company may purchase exclusive United States distribution and trademark rights from a foreign manufacturer, for example, or a foreign manufacturer may form a domestic subsidiary to which it grants the exclusive right to market goods under the trademark in this country. Similarly, a domestic trademark owner may retain exclusive rights in the United States but license the use of the mark to a foreign company for sales abroad. In these and other situations, a gray market develops when a third person purchases foreign-made goods bearing the trademark and imports them into the United States for sale in competition with the United States trademark owner.

Federal law prohibits the importation of merchandise bearing a trademark registered in the United States without the consent of the United States trademark owner. See § 526 of the Tariff Act, 19 U.S.C.A. § 1526, and § 42 of the Lanham Act, 15 U.S.C.A. § 1124. The United States Customs Service is authorized to issue regulations enforcing these legislative restrictions. Although the statutes appear to provide a total ban against such imports in all situations, the Customs Service historically permitted the importation of genuine foreign-made goods when the foreign and United States trademarks were owned by the same person or when the foreign producer and the United States trademark owner were under common control, as when one was a parent or subsidiary of the other, or when the use of the trademark, although not the importation, had been authorized by the domestic trademark owner. After inconsistent rulings in the lower courts, the United States Supreme Court in K Mart Corp. v. Cartier, Inc., 486 U.S. 281, 108 S.Ct. 1811, 100 L.Ed.2d 313 (1988), upheld the common ownership and control exceptions but not the authorized use exception.

The question of whether or under what circumstances the United States Customs Service should protect domestic trademark owners by barring the importation of gray market goods is a distinct question from whether or under what circumstances the sale of such goods infringes the rights of a domestic trademark owner. The former question is outside the scope of this Restatement. The issue of infringement is considered in Comment *f.*

f. Gray market goods and trademark infringement. Several early decisions adopted a "universality" principle of trademark rights under which goods lawfully made under a trademark in one country could be imported and sold in another country without infringing the rights of the domestic trademark owner. Under this view, the source of the goods identified by a trademark is thought to be the original manufacturer, and thus no confusion can arise when genuine goods bearing the mark are imported into the United States. However, in A. Bourjois & Co. v. Katzel, 260 U.S. 689, 43 S.Ct. 244, 67 L.Ed. 464 (1923), the United States Supreme Court ruled in favor of a plaintiff who had purchased the domestic business, good will, and trademark registrations of the French manufacturer of JAVA face powder and later sued a defendant who imported for sale genuine JAVA powder purchased in France. The Supreme Court rejected the "universality" principle in favor of a "territoriality" principle that recognizes a separate legal existence for a trademark in each country whose laws afford protection to the mark. Under this view, the trademark does not necessarily identify to purchasers in a particular country the original manufacturer of the goods, but may instead identify the company that owns exclusive trademark rights within that country.

The scope and meaning of the territoriality principle announced in *Katzel* remain unclear. The broadest interpretation recognizes independent trademark rights in the domestic owner by operation of law, and any importation and sale of gray market goods without the domestic owner's consent would thus be an infringement. This view gives primacy to the domestic law of registration and ownership without regard to the actual significance of the trademark in the marketplace. Some cases, limiting the *Katzel* decision more closely to its facts, have held instead that when the domestic trademark owner and the foreign manufacturer are affiliated, gray market sales do not infringe.

The most appropriate view applies to gray market goods the traditional rules relating to the use of trademarks on genuine goods stated in this Section. The premise of the universality principle that trademarks necessarily identify the original manufacturer has been rejected in our domestic law. The "source" indicated by a trademark may instead be the company perceived by consumers as assuring the consistent quality of the goods. In gray market contexts, a factual question thus exists as to whether the trademark identifies the domestic trademark owner or the foreign manufacturer. To the extent that the trademark identifies to prospective purchasers the domestic owner as distinguished from the foreign manufacturer, imported gray market goods are not goods the source of which is accurately identified by the trademark as required under the rule stated in this Section. The sale of such goods under the trademark is therefore an infringement. The proper inquiry is whether the use of the trademark on the gray market goods is likely to confuse prospective purchasers, and the issue must be resolved on the basis of the particular circumstances of the case. For example, if the domestic and foreign companies are entirely separate entities and their respective goods are independently produced and marketed, the good will identified by the mark in the United States will be that of the domestic trademark owner. On the other hand, the nature of any on-going relationship between the foreign and domestic companies can affect whether consumers understand the mark to identify the domestic trademark owner as distinguished from the foreign manufacturer. Thus, it may be difficult for a wholly-owned subsidiary of a foreign manufacturer to develop a good will represented by the trademark that is distinct from that of its foreign parent company. However, an independent domestic company that owns exclusive United States distribution and trademark rights may by actively promoting and servicing the goods acquire a good will symbolized by the mark that is distinct from that of the foreign manufacturer. The wide range of possible relationships between the domestic trademark owner and the foreign manufacturer, however, cautions against the formulation of a rule based solely on affiliation. The issue is whether the domestic trademark owner can establish that the presence of the trademark on the imported goods creates a likelihood of confusion because the mark identifies to prospective purchasers the good will of the domestic owner.

A variation of the gray market problem arises from the importation and sale under a trademark of foreign goods that are materially different from those sold under the mark by the domestic trademark owner. The foreign goods, for example, may be separately formulated to account for differing national tastes or conditions, or the foreign producer may sell a different grade in the foreign market, or the foreign goods may not carry the same warranty, rebate, or other incidents of sale commonly expected by domestic purchasers. The fact that the domestic and foreign goods are materially different demonstrates a good will in the domestic trademark owner that is distinct from that of the foreign producer. The importation and sale of such gray market goods thus infringes the rights of the domestic trademark owner.

Illustrations:

7. *A*, a domestic company, has exclusive distribution and trademark rights in the United States for camera equipment manufactured by *B*, a foreign manufacturer. *B* owns 40 percent of *A* 's stock. *A* extensively advertises *B* 's cameras in the United

States and prospective purchasers in this country associate the trademark with cameras sold and serviced by *A*. *C* acquires genuine cameras produced abroad by *B* and sells them in the United States. Since *A* has developed an independent good will under the mark in the United States, *C* is subject to liability to *A* for the infringement of *A* 's trademark.

8. *A* manufactures SHIELD soap for sale in Great Britain. *B*, a company affiliated with *A*, manufactures SHIELD soap for the United States market and owns the exclusive United States distribution and trademark rights. The soap for each market is manufactured according to materially different formulas to respond to different national tastes and customs, including the preference for showers rather than baths in the United States. *C* purchases SHIELD soap in Great Britain and imports and sells the soap in the United States. *C* is subject to liability to *B* for the infringement of *B* 's trademark.

REPORTERS' NOTE

This Section combines the rules governing the use of another's trademark on genuine goods originally stated in Restatement of Torts §§ 736–737 (1938). See generally, McCarthy, Trademarks and Unfair Competition §§ 25.08–11.

Comment b. The right to use another's trademark on genuine goods originally sold under the mark is widely-recognized. As Justice Holmes observed in Prestonettes, Inc. v. Coty, 264 U.S. 359, 368, 44 S.Ct. 350, 351, 68 L.Ed. 731, 742 (1924), "When the mark is used in a way that does not deceive the public we see no such sanctity in the word as to prevent its being used to tell the truth. It is not taboo."

Comment c. The Second Circuit has held that goods made to the trademark owner's order but then rejected cannot be resold under the trademark. El Greco Leather Products Co. v. Shoe World, Inc., 806 F.2d 392, 395–96 (2d Cir.1986), cert. denied 484 U.S. 817, 108 S.Ct. 71, 98 L.Ed.2d 34 (1987) ("The mere act of ordering a product to be labeled with a trademark does not deprive its holder of the right to control the product and the trademark."). Contra, Monte Carlo Shirt, Inc. v. Daewoo International (America) Corp., 707 F.2d 1054 (9th Cir.1983). If the trademark owner's refusal to accept the goods is unjustified, the seller may resell the goods under § 2–706 of the Uniform Commercial Code and recover from the breaching buyer the difference between the resale price and the contract price. In a case of wrongful rejection, any loss on resale caused by the removal of the mark will thus ultimately fall on the trademark owner. See Burberrys (Wholesale) Ltd. v. After Six Inc., 122 Misc.2d 561, 471 N.Y.S.2d 235 (1984) (§ 2–706 does not authorize the seller to infringe the buyer's trademark). The trademark owner, however, can waive the right to control the use of the trademark on rejected goods. See Diamond Supply Co. v. Prudential Paper Products Co., 589 F.Supp. 470 (S.D.N.Y.

1984) (trademark owner indicated he "did not care" how the defendant disposed of the goods). Cf. Puritan Sportswear Corp. v. Shure, 307 F.Supp. 377 (W.D.Pa.1969) (trademark owner did not remove the mark or restrict the manner of disposal prior to the return of the goods).

Illustration 1 is taken from Illustration 1 to Restatement of Torts § 736 (1938).

Illustration 2 is supported by, e.g., Burger King Corp. v. Mason, 710 F.2d 1480 (11th Cir.1983), cert. denied 465 U.S. 1102, 104 S.Ct. 1599, 80 L.Ed.2d 130 (1984). See also, e.g., S & R Corp. v. Jiffy Lube Int'l, Inc., 968 F.2d 371 (3d Cir.1992) (injunction issued against continued use of the mark by a franchisee after termination for non-payment of royalties).

Illustration 3 is taken from the facts although not the result in *Monte Carlo Shirt, supra.* Compare El Greco Leather Products Co., *supra.*

Illustration 4 is taken from Illustration 5 to Restatement of Torts § 736 (1938). See Intel Corp. v. Terabyte Int'l, Inc., 6 F.3d 614 (9th Cir. 1993) (distributor held liable for altering the model designation on plaintiff's product).

Comment d. The classic cases on repackaged and reconditioned goods are Prestonettes, Inc. v. Coty, 264 U.S. 359, 44 S.Ct. 350, 68 L.Ed. 731 (1924) (use of the original trademark with an explanatory disclaimer on rebottled and repackaged goods permitted) and Champion Spark Plug Co. v. Sanders, 331 U.S. 125, 67 S.Ct. 1136, 91 L.Ed. 1386 (1947) (use of the original trademark on reconditioned spark plugs with an explanatory disclaimer permitted). See, e.g., Major League Baseball Players Ass'n v. Dad's Kid Corp., 806 F.Supp. 458 (S.D.N.Y.1992); Brandtjen & Kluge, Inc. v. Prudhomme, 765 F.Supp. 1551 (N.D.Tex.1991). See also William Grant & Sons Ltd. v. European Beverages Co., 668 F.Supp. 1421 (C.D.Cal.1987) (truthful use of the trademark of an ingredient used in blended scotch whiskey permitted with a disclaimer provided that the trademark is not unduly emphasized).

Some states have criminal prohibitions against selling rebottled or repackaged merchandise under the mark of the original owner. See, e.g., N.Y. Arts & Cult.Aff.L. § 33.09(6). These statutes have been interpreted to permit injunctions against the sale of rebottled merchandise even when the name of the rebottler is prominently displayed. See Lanvin Parfums, Inc. v. Le Dans, Ltd., 9 N.Y.2d 516, 215 N.Y.S.2d 257, 174 N.E.2d 920, cert. denied 368 U.S. 834, 82 S.Ct. 58, 7 L.Ed.2d 35 (1961).

Justice Douglas observed in *Champion Spark Plug Co., supra,* that "[c]ases may be imagined where the reconditioning or repair would be so extensive or so basic that it would be a misnomer to call the article by its original name, even though the words 'used' or 'repaired' were added." 331 U.S. at 129, 67 S.Ct. at 1138. See also By–Rite Distributing, Inc. v. Coca–Cola Co., 577 F.Supp. 530 (D.Utah 1983) (use of the original trademark prohibited when the rebottling may result in a reduction in quality).

The unauthorized sale of deteriorated or out-of-date merchandise without adequate disclosure has been held to be an infringement. Polaroid Corp. v. Blue Dot Corp., 214 U.S.P.Q. 192 (D.N.J.1981) (film sold after its expiration date); Adolph Coors Co. v. A. Genderson & Sons, Inc., 486 F.Supp. 131 (D.Colo.1980) (unauthorized distribution of deteriorated beer under the original trademark). See also J.C. Penney Co. v. Charbeth's Little General Store, 185 U.S.P.Q. 254 (E.D.N.Y.1975) (unauthorized sale of old or discontinued merchandise without removing the trademark is an infringement). Cf. Shell Oil Co. v. Commercial Petroleum, Inc., 928 F.2d 104 (4th Cir.1991) (goods originating with the trademark owner are not genuine goods if the goods are not marketed under the trademark owner's quality control standards).

Whether the sale in one market of genuine goods designed for another market is an infringement depends upon whether there is a likelihood of confusion. See Matrix Essentials, Inc. v. Emporium Drug Mart, Inc., 988 F.2d 587 (5th Cir.1993) (sale of products directly to consumers in violation of the trademark owner's policy of selling only through professional cosmetologists was not an infringement); Clairol, Inc. v. Cody's Cosmetics, Inc., 353 Mass. 385, 231 N.E.2d 912 (1967) (sale of "professional use only" products to consumers permitted if the seller makes a full disclosure). Confusion may arise, however, if the product is sold without the attributes expected by retail consumers. See Clairol, Inc. v. Boston Discount Center, Inc., 608 F.2d 1114 (6th Cir.1979) (sale of "professional use only" products to consumers without the warnings and instructions normally included with the retail product). See also Polymer Technology Corp. v. Mimran, 975 F.2d 58 (2d Cir.1992) (unauthorized sales in the consumer market constitute infringement if confusion results). Illustrations 5 and 6 are taken from Prestonettes, Inc., *supra.* Cf. Gilliam v. American Broadcasting Cos., 538 F.2d 14 (2d Cir.1976) (unauthorized broadcast of an altered version of a television program attributed to the plaintiffs was actionable under § 43(a) of the Lanham Act).

Comment e. Section 526 of the Tariff Act, 19 U.S.C.A. § 1526, prohibits the importation without written consent of foreign manufactured merchandise that "bears a trademark owned by a citizen [of the United States] and registered in the Patent and Trademark Office." Section 42 of the Lanham Act, 15 U.S.C.A. § 1124, prohibits the importation of merchandise that "shall copy or simulate a trademark registered" under the Act. The United States Customs Service promulgated regulations that exempted foreign goods from the import restrictions when (1) the foreign and domestic trademark or trade name are "owned by" the same person, or (2) the foreign and domestic trademark owners are "parent and subsidiary companies or are otherwise subject to common ownership or control," or (3) the foreign use of the trademark is authorized by the domestic trademark owner. 19 C.F.R. § 133.21 (1989). The Custom Service regulations are thought to have been influenced by United States v. Guerlain, Inc., 155 F.Supp. 77 (S.D.N.Y. 1957), vacated 358 U.S. 915, 79 S.Ct. 285, 3 L.Ed.2d 236 (1958), in which the district court held that attempts by a domestic company affiliated with the foreign manufacturer to ban imports of genuine goods were a violation of the antitrust laws. Inconsistent rulings on the validity of the regulations were resolved by the United States Supreme Court in K Mart Corp. v. Cartier, Inc., 486 U.S. 281, 108 S.Ct. 1811, 100 L.Ed.2d 313 (1988). See McCarthy, *supra,* §§ 29.11–17.

Comment f. Until A. Bourjois & Co. v. Katzel, 260 U.S. 689, 43 S.Ct. 244, 67 L.Ed. 464 (1923), some courts held that the use of a trademark on genuine imported goods could not be an infringement. See, e.g., Apollinaris Co. v. Scherer, 27 Fed. 18 (C.C.N.Y.1886). In Roger & Gallet v. Janmarie, Inc., 245 F.2d 505 (C.C.P.A.1957), the court interpreted *Katzel* to authorize an infringement action by the domestic trademark owner as a matter of law, regardless of the actual significance of the mark to consumers. Other courts interpreted *Katzel* to require a factual showing that the trademark identifies the domestic owner rather than the foreign manufacturer. See Bell & Howell: Mamiya Co. v. Masel Supply Co., 548 F.Supp. 1063 (E.D.N.Y. 1982), vacated 719 F.2d 42 (2d Cir. 1983) (the district court granted a preliminary injunction to the United States trademark owner; the decision was reversed in the absence of a factual basis for finding a likelihood of confusion); Osawa & Co. v. B & H Photo, 589 F.Supp. 1163 (S.D.N.Y. 1984) (United States trademark owner showed a "separate, factually independent goodwill" within the United States). The finding of a separate good will was also critical in Int'l Armament Corp. v. Matra Manurhin Int'l, Inc., 630 F.Supp. 741 (E.D.Va. 1986). See also Weil Ceramics and Glass, Inc. v. Dash, 878 F.2d 659 (3d Cir.), cert. denied 493 U.S. 853, 110 S.Ct. 156, 107 L.Ed.2d 114 (1989) (Becker, J., concurring). Some courts have found *Katzel* inapplicable when the domestic trademark owner is affiliated with the foreign manufacturer. Weil Ceramics and Glass, *supra* ; NEC Electronics v. Cal Circuit Abco, 810 F.2d 1506 (9th Cir.), cert. denied 484 U.S. 851, 108 S.Ct. 152, 98 L.Ed.2d 108 (1987).

Sales of imported genuine goods without disclosing that the goods were not covered by the manufacturer's warranty was held to violate § 43(a) of the Lanham Act in Seiko Time Corp. v. Alexander's, Inc., 218 U.S.P.Q. 560 (S.D.N.Y.1982). Cases finding infringement when the imported goods are genuine but materially different from those sold by the United States trademark owner include Societe Des Produits Nestle, S.A. v. Casa Helvetia, Inc., 982 F.2d 633 (1st Cir.1992); Original Appalachian Artworks, Inc. v. Granada Electronics, Inc., 816 F.2d 68 (2d Cir.), cert. denied 484 U.S. 847, 108 S.Ct. 143, 98 L.Ed.2d 99 (1987); Ferrero U.S.A., Inc. v. Ozak Trading, Inc., 753 F.Supp. 1240 (D.N.J.), affirmed 935 F.2d 1281 (3d Cir.1991). See also Lever Bros. Co. v. United States, 981 F.2d 1330 (D.C.Cir.1993) (§ 42 of the Lanham Act precludes the application of the Customs Service affiliate exception to the import prohibition if the goods are materially different). But see Becker, J., concurring in Weil Ceramics and Glass, *supra* (a wholly-owned subsidiary is not injured by the importation of different goods because the parent could stop marketing different goods under the same mark).

Illustration 7 is based on *Bell & Howell: Mamiya Co., supra.* Illustration 8 is based on *Lever Brothers Co., supra.*

The gray market problem is reviewed in Davis, Lever Bros. v. United States and the Legality of Gray Market Imports, 28 Wake Forest L.Rev. 571 (1993). See also McCarthy, *supra*, §§ 29.18–19.

§ 25. Liability Without Proof of Confusion: Dilution and Tarnishment

(1) One may be subject to liability under the law of trademarks for the use of a designation that resembles the trademark, trade name, collective mark, or certification mark of another without proof of a likelihood of confusion only under an applicable antidilution statute. An actor is subject to liability under an antidilution statute if the actor uses such a designation in a manner that is likely to associate the other's mark with the goods, services, or business of the actor and:

(a) the other's mark is highly distinctive and the association of the mark with the actor's goods, services, or business is likely to cause a reduction in that distinctiveness; or

(b) the association of the other's mark with the actor's goods, services, or business, or the nature of the actor's use, is likely to disparage the other's goods, services, or business or tarnish the images associated with the other's mark.

(2) One who uses a designation that resembles the trademark, trade name, collective mark, or certification mark of another, not in a manner that is likely to associate the other's mark with the goods, services, or business of the actor, but rather to comment on, criticize, ridicule, parody, or disparage the other or the other's goods, services, business, or mark, is subject to liability without proof of a likelihood of confusion only if the actor's conduct meets the requirements of a cause of action for defamation, invasion of privacy, or injurious falsehood.

Comment:

a. Scope and applicability. The rules stated in § 20 governing liability for trademark infringement require proof that the actor's use causes a likelihood of confusion. A number of states, however, have created a statutory cause of action for trademark "dilution"—a theory of liability that does not require proof of a likelihood of confusion. These "antidilution" statutes protect the commercial value or "selling power" of a mark by prohibiting uses that dilute the distinctiveness of the mark or tarnish the associations evoked by the mark. Subsection (1) states the rules applicable to actions brought under these statutory provisions. There is no comparable cause of action for trademark dilution at common law.

The rules stated in Subsection (1) apply only when the actor uses the other's mark as a means of identification for the actor's own goods, services, or business. However, the value of a trademark can also be damaged by an actor's use of the mark other than as a symbol of identification for the actor's own products or business, such as use of the trademark as the subject of a parody. Subsection (2) states the rule applicable to injuries occurring from such nontrademark use by the actor.

b. History. Liability for trademark infringement, with its requirement of a likelihood of confusion, protects the prior user of a mark from the potential diversion of trade or harm to reputation that results when purchasers are confused as to the source or sponsorship of goods or services bearing the mark. Courts and legislatures were initially reluctant to impose liability for trademark infringement in connection with a use by the actor on goods that did not compete with those of the trademark owner. A new rationale for trademark protection was then advanced that viewed as the primary value of trade symbols their power to generate sales. Accordingly, it was urged that legal protection was appropriate to protect against the "gradual whittling away or dispersion of the identity and hold upon the public mind of the mark or name by its use upon non-competing goods." Schechter, The Rational Basis of Trademark Protection, 40 Harvard Law Review 813, 825 (1927). This new rationale required neither consumer confusion nor competition between the users' goods or services. Although a few decisions acknowledged the interest of a trademark owner in protecting a mark from a dilution of the mark's distinctiveness and commercial value, for the most part the common law cases reflected a more modest extension of trademark protection to noncompeting goods through an expansion of the confusion rationale.

Beginning with Massachusetts in 1947, a number of states enacted statutes that offered protection against a dilution of the distinctive quality of a trademark. At first the courts applied the statutes reluctantly, if at all. In many cases dilution claims were denied because the plaintiff failed to prove a likelihood of confusion, notwithstanding the clear language of the statutes eliminating confusion as an element of the cause of action. Some courts, and numerous commentators, expressed fear that the uncertain limits of the antidilution cause of action would unduly expand the ability of trademark owners to monopolize language and inhibit free competition. A broad antidilution theory also has the potential to render superfluous the traditional likelihood of confusion standard of liability. It was further suggested that a state cause of action for dilution might interfere with the federal policy of uniform, national trademark protection implemented under the Lanham Act, although only isolated cases supported this preemption theory. Other commentators, however, continued to urge protection for the selling power of well-known trademarks. After the New York Court of Appeals in Allied Maintenance Corp. v. Allied Mechanical Trades, Inc., 42 N.Y.2d 538, 399 N.Y.S.2d 628, 369 N.E.2d 1162 (1977), expressed the need for protection against the "cancer-like growth of dissimilar products or services which feeds upon the business reputation of an established distinctive trade-mark or name," judicial acceptance of the antidilution statutes increased. Nonetheless, in apparent recognition that broad interpretation of the statutes would undermine the balance between private and public rights reflected in the traditional limits of trademark protection, the courts have continued to confine the cause of action for dilution to cases in which the protectable interest is clear and the threat of interference is substantial.

c. Interests protected. The antidilution statutes have been invoked against two distinct threats to the interests of a trademark owner. First, a mark may be so highly distinctive and so well advertised that it acts as a powerful selling tool. Such a mark may evoke among prospective purchasers a positive response that is associated exclusively with the goods or services of the trademark owner. To the extent that others use the trademark to identify different goods, services, or businesses, a dissonance occurs that blurs this stimulant effect of the mark. The antidilution statutes protect against this dilution of the distinctiveness and selling power of the mark.

The selling power of a trademark also can be undermined by a use of the mark with goods or services such as illicit drugs or pornography that "tarnish" the mark's image through inherently negative or unsavory associations, or with goods or services that produce a negative response when linked in the minds of prospective purchasers with the goods or services of the prior user, such as the use on insecticide of a trademark similar to one previously used by another on food products.

Tarnishment and dilution of distinctiveness, although conceptually distinct, both undermine the selling power of a mark, the latter by disturbing the conditioned association of the mark with the prior user and the former by displacing positive with negative associations. Thus, tarnishment and dilution of distinctiveness reduce the value of the mark to the trademark owner.

The rule stated in this Section distinguishes between those cases in which the actor uses another's designation to identify the actor's own goods or services and those cases in which the actor uses the other's designation in some other manner. The protection accorded by the law of trademarks is limited to the exploitation of a designation as an identifying symbol. Although the antidilution statutes extend protection to certain nonconfusing uses, they remain part of the general law of trademarks and should be applicable only to disputes involving the concurrent use of similar designations to identify goods, services, or businesses. Subsection (1) states the rules applicable to cases within the scope of the antidilution statutes. Subsection (2) states the rule applicable to cases in which the value of a trademark is undermined by a use other than as an identifying symbol for the actor's own goods, services, or business.

d. Designations protected. The antidilution statutes are applicable to both registered or unregistered marks. Although most of the case law involves word marks, the statutes are also generally applicable to slogans, trade dress, and other symbols that qualify for protection as a trademark. However, the protection of product designs from non-confusing use by others raises special problems in light of the preemptive effect of federal copyright and patent law. Courts have sometimes justified trademark protection for product designs on the rationale that trademark law protects only against confusion and does not create a property interest that competes or interferes with the rights conferred by copyright or patent. See § 16, Comment *c*. Application of the antidilution statutes to prohibit the use of another's product design without proof of a likelihood of confusion may thus be preempted, but a definitive statement of the law is not possible from the existing cases.

Comment on Subsection (1)(a):

e. Highly distinctive. Not all trademarks warrant protection against a dilution of the mark's distinctiveness. In applying the antidilution statutes, most courts require that the mark possess a degree of distinctiveness beyond that needed for the designation to qualify as a valid trademark. As a general matter, a trademark is sufficiently distinctive to be diluted by a nonconfusing use if the mark retains its source significance when encountered outside the context of the goods or services with which the mark is used by the trademark owner. For example, the trademark KODAK evokes an association with the cameras sold under that mark whether the word is displayed with cameras or simply appears alone. On the other hand, the designation ALPHA could become sufficiently distinctive to be protectable as a trademark for cameras, but a use of the term by itself might still evoke a variety of different associations, including nothing more than the first letter of the Greek alphabet. A mark that evokes an association with a specific source only when used in connection with the particular goods or services that it identifies is ordinarily not sufficiently distinctive to be protected against dilution.

A number of factors are relevant to whether a mark has acquired sufficient distinctiveness to be protected from dilution, including the inherent distinctiveness and uniqueness of the mark, the duration and extent of its use, the duration and extent of advertising that emphasizes the mark, and the degree of recognition by prospective purchasers. Third-party use of the mark either as a trade symbol or for other purposes is also an important factor in assessing distinctiveness. Concurrent use by others makes it unlikely that consumers will form a single mental association between the mark and one specific user.

Protection against the dilution of a mark's distinctiveness is not limited to fanciful, arbitrary, or suggestive marks. A descriptive mark may by extensive advertising and long and exclusive use also acquire a sufficiently high degree of distinctiveness to justify protection against dilution. However, competitors and others are entitled to use descriptive terms in their primary, lexicographic sense, and such permissible use makes it less likely that consumers will associate a descriptive term exclusively with the trademark owner.

A mark that is highly distinctive only to a select class or group of purchasers may be protected from diluting uses directed at that particular class or group. For example, a mark may be highly distinctive among purchasers of a specific type of product. In such circumstances, protection against a dilution of the mark's distinctiveness is ordinarily appropriate only against uses specifically directed at that particular class of purchasers; uses of the mark in broader markets, although they may produce an incidental diluting effect in the protected market, are not normally actionable.

Illustrations:

1. *A* provides computerized research services to attorneys under the trademark LEXIT. The trademark is highly distinctive among attorneys but largely unknown outside the legal profession. *B*, an automobile manufacturer, names a new model automobile the LEXIT. *C*, an insurance company, markets a new life insurance policy designed for attorneys under the mark LEXIT–LIFE. *B* is not subject to liability to *A* under an antidilution statute because *A* 's mark is highly distinctive only in a select market and *B* 's use of the mark is not specifically directed to that market. *C* may be subject to liability to *A* under an applicable antidilution statute because *C* 's product is specifically directed at the market in which *A* 's mark is highly distinctive.

If *A* can prove a likelihood of confusion, *B* or *C* may be subject to liability to *A* for trademark infringement under the rule stated in § 20.

2. *A* markets a laundry detergent using the mark BETA. BETA is sufficiently distinctive to identify *A*'s detergent and distinguish it from other detergents, but prospective purchasers do not normally think of *A*'s detergent when they see the word BETA alone or on unrelated products. *B* sells a new laundry bleach under the mark ALPHA–BETA. *B* is not subject to liability to *A* under an antidilution statute because *A*'s mark is not highly distinctive. If *A* can prove a likelihood of confusion, *B* may be subject to liability to *A* for trademark infringement under the rule stated in § 20.

f. Dilution of distinctiveness. Dilution of a mark's distinctiveness blurs the associations evoked by the mark and thus reduces the mark's commercial value to the trademark owner. In order for such dilution to occur, prospective purchasers must make a mental connection between the plaintiff's mark and the designation used by the defendant. The connection, however, is not that which serves as the basis of liability for trademark infringement—the mistaken belief that the plaintiff is in some way associated with defendant's goods—but rather is the accurate recognition that a mark associated with the plaintiff is now also in use as an identifying symbol by another.

Proof of a likelihood of dilution, like that of a likelihood of confusion, requires proof of a likely state of mind on the part of consumers. In most instances this determination must rest on inferences drawn from the market context in which the use occurs. Direct evidence of a dilution of distinctiveness is seldom available because the harm at issue is a blurring of the mental associations evoked by the mark, a phenomenon not easily sampled by consumer surveys and not normally manifested by unambiguous consumer behavior.

Many of the factors enumerated in § 21 as relevant to the likelihood of confusion are also relevant in determining the likelihood of dilution. Use of a designation may create a likelihood of dilution even if the designation is not identical to the protected mark, but the resemblance between the two must be sufficiently close that the subsequent use evokes the requisite mental connection with the prior user's mark. A comparison of marketing methods and channels of distribution is also relevant. If the goods are marketed in different stores to different buyers, for example, a connection between the prior and subsequent use may be unlikely. The nature of the respective goods is also relevant to the likelihood of dilution. The antidilution statutes explicitly recognize that dilution can result from use of another's mark on either competing or noncompeting goods. In some cases, however, the actor's goods may be so far removed from those of the prior user that any mental connection by purchasers between the two uses of the mark is unlikely, thus averting any likelihood of dilution.

The sophistication of purchasers and the care they are likely to exercise in connection with purchasing decisions can also affect the likelihood that a dilution of distinctiveness will occur. Discerning purchasers are more likely to recognize elements that distinguish two similar marks and are thus more likely to retain separate mental associations for each of the designations. The degree of distinctiveness of the prior user's mark is also relevant because it measures the likelihood that the mark evokes the type of exclusive images and associations protected under the antidilution statutes. A very distinctive mark is thus more likely to suffer dilution of distinctiveness than is a less distinctive mark.

Comment on Subsection (1)(b):

g. Tarnishment. The antidilution statutes have also been invoked to protect the positive associations evoked by a mark from subsequent uses that may disparage or tarnish those associations. The rule stated in Subsection (1)(b) applies to cases in which the tarnishment results from a subsequent use of the mark or a substantially similar mark in a manner that associates the mark with different goods, services, or businesses. Use of another's mark by the actor, not as a trademark or trade name, but in other ways that may disparage or tarnish the prior user's goods, services, business, or mark is governed by the rule stated in Subsection (2).

Any designation that is distinctive under the criteria established in § 13 is eligible for protection against disparaging or tarnishing use by others. Whenever the subsequent use brings to mind the goods, services, business, or mark of the prior user, there is a potential for interference with the positive images associated with the mark. To prove a case of tarnishment, the prior user must demonstrate that the subsequent use is likely to come to the attention of the prior user's prospective purchasers and that the use is likely to undermine or damage the positive associations evoked by the mark.

Illustration:

3. *A*, a bank, uses the designation "Cookie Jar" to identify its automatic teller machines. *B* opens a topless bar across the street from *A* under the trade name "Cookie Jar." Although prospective customers of *A* are unlikely to believe that *A* operates

or sponsors the bar, *B* is subject to liability to *A* for tarnishment under an applicable antidilution statute if the customers are likely to associate *A* 's mark or *A* 's business with the images evoked by *B* 's use.

h. Intent. The plaintiff in an antidilution action is not required to prove that the defendant intended to dilute or tarnish the trademark. On the other hand, a likelihood of dilution or tarnishment may be inferred if the actor has intentionally attempted to bring about either result. Intentional copying or mere knowledge of the existence of the plaintiff's mark, however, is not necessarily sufficient to establish an intent to tarnish or dilute the distinctiveness of the mark. The scope of protection afforded under the antidilution statutes is sufficiently unclear that it would be improper in many instances to infer an intent to intrude on the trademark owner's rights from an actor's mere adoption of a mark with knowledge of the mark's prior use on other goods or services.

Comment on Subsection (2):

i. Nontrademark uses. The commercial value of a highly distinctive trade symbol results from the strong association between the designation and the goods, services, or business of a particular user. If the same or a similar designation is later adopted as a symbol of identification by another, the power of the mark to evoke its original association is diluted. Nontrademark uses, because they do not create an association with a different user's goods, services, or business, are unlikely to dilute the distinctiveness of a mark. In most instances such uses are intended to refer back to the original trademark owner and serve to confirm rather than undermine the associational significance of the mark. For example, the use of another's mark in comparative advertising or as mere ornamentation on the subsequent user's goods does not dilute the distinctiveness of the mark by associating the mark as a symbol of identification with different goods or services or with a different business.

The positive images associated with a particular designation can be tarnished by either a trademark or a nontrademark use by the actor. A statement by *B* that "*A* 's brand of beer is contaminated with insecticide" is at least as damaging to the mental images associated with *A* 's mark as is *B* 's adoption of *A* 's mark as the trademark for an insecticide. However, extension of the antidilution statutes to protect against damaging nontrademark uses raises substantial free speech issues and duplicates other potential remedies better suited to balance the relevant interests.

The distinction between the use of another's mark as a trademark for the actor's own goods or services and a nontrademark use of the mark is not always obvious, yet it delimits the proper scope of both the traditional cause of action for trademark infringement as stated in § 20 and the statutory action created by the antidilution statutes. In both contexts the perception of prospective purchasers and not the intent of the user is controlling. See § 20, Comment *b*. In a dilution case, for example, if prospective purchasers interpret the actor's use of the mark as an indication of the source or sponsorship of the actor's goods or services, the use is within the scope of the antidilution statutes. On the other hand, if the use is interpreted merely as a reference to or a comment on the goods, services, business, or mark of the trademark owner, the antidilution statutes should not be applicable.

The Supreme Court has held that the first amendment allows greater latitude for the regulation of commercial as opposed to noncommercial speech. The Court's decisions permit narrowly-tailored restrictions on commercial speech that directly further a substantial state interest. There is no indication that the first amendment limits application of the antidilution statutes in the context of a subsequent use of a mark as a trademark by another. Use of another's trademark, not as a means of identifying the user's own goods or services, but as an incident of speech directed at the trademark owner, however, raises serious free speech concerns that cannot be easily accommodated under traditional trademark doctrine. The expression of an idea by means of the use of another's trademark in a parody, for example, will often lie within the substantial constitutional protection accorded noncommercial speech and may thus be the subject of liability only in the most narrow circumstances. Although such nontrademark uses of another's mark may undermine the reputation and value of the mark, they should not be actionable under the law of trademarks. However, in some instances the imposition of liability may be appropriate under other branches of law. Use or commentary on a trade symbol, for example, may defame the reputation of the trademark owner. Application of the law of defamation, which already recognizes and accommodates the speaker's constitutional interest in freedom of expression, is then appropriate. The Restatement, Second, of Torts in § 623A also states a general rule prohibiting injurious falsehoods—false statements harmful to the pecuniary interests of another—as well as a more specific rule in § 626 prohibiting statements that falsely disparage the quality of another's goods. In some cases the use by the actor of another's trademark may imply facts about the trademark owner's business that are false or may falsely disparage the quality of the trademark owner's products. In such cases the tort of injurious falsehood can provide appropriate relief.

Although in appropriate cases these alternative torts can protect the same interests now sometimes protected under the antidilution statutes, their well-developed limitations can better accommodate the actor's right of free expression. Neither claims for traditional trademark infringement nor claims under the antidilution statutes, for example, require proof that the user acted with intent, recklessness, or negligence, yet in some circumstances such proof may be constitutionally required in order to subject a speaker to liability.

With regard to individuals, the law also recognizes a right of privacy applicable to situations in which an actor places the plaintiff before the public in a false light that would be "highly offensive to a reasonable person" if the actor "had knowledge of or acted in reckless disregard as to the falsity of the publicized matter and the false light in which the other would be placed." Restatement, Second, Torts § 652E. A trade symbol can identify a business just as a personal name identifies an individual, and use of the symbol to place its owner in a false light can produce significant harm to the owner's interests. There is no case law applying the false light branch of the right of privacy to situations involving the use of trade symbols, perhaps because the Restatement, Second, of Torts in § 652I precludes corporations from asserting the false light privacy tort. The rules applicable to individuals, however, may provide a useful analogy for cases involving injuries resulting from the nontrademark use of another's trade symbol, both with respect to the nature of the potential harm and the required accommodation with free speech interests. The false light privacy, defamation, and injurious falsehood torts are more appropriate than an extension of traditional infringement or dilution doctrines as a basis of analysis in cases involving a nontrademark use of another's mark.

Some commentators have suggested that a trademark owner should have a cause of action under the antidilution statutes against others who use the trademark as a generic term and thereby threaten the distinctiveness of the mark, as might occur, for example, if the author of a dictionary defines the designation as a generic term. There are no cases that adopt this view, and an extension of the antidilution statutes to include such nontrademark use would significantly expand the traditional scope of trademark protection. To the extent that the use occurs in a commercial context, normal trademark infringement and dilution doctrines remain applicable. Significant free speech issues are raised, however, if trademark owners can arrest the development of language through lawsuits brought against noncommercial use by members of the general public.

Illustrations:

4. *A*, a well-known brewer, adopts the slogan "Where There's Life, There's Bud" as a trademark for its BUDWEISER brand beer. *B*, the manufacturer of a floor wax that contains insecticide, subsequently markets the product using the slogan "Where There's Life, There's Bugs." A court may properly conclude that *B* is subject to liability to *A* under an applicable antidilution statute because *B* has used a designation that resembles *A* 's trademark in a manner that is likely to create an association between *A* 's mark and *B* 's product and the association tarnishes the images evoked by *A* 's mark.

5. *A* is a well-known mail order company that distributes catalogs nationwide. *B*, a publisher of "adult" magazines, publishes in one of its magazines a parody of *A* 's catalog entitled "*A* 's Back–to–School Sex Catalog" using a facsimile of *A* 's mark. *B* is not subject to liability to *A* for tarnishment under an antidilution statute because *B* has not used *A* 's mark in a manner that is likely to create an association between the mark and *B* 's own goods, services, or business. Whether *B* is subject to liability to *A* under other causes of action such as defamation or injurious falsehood is determined under the rules applicable to those causes of action.

STATUTORY NOTE

State antidilution statutes are in effect as follows:

Alabama .... ALA. C. § 8–12–17
Arkansas .... ARK. C.A. § 4–71–113
California .... CAL. Bus. & Prof.C. § 14330
Connecticut .... CONN. G.S. § 35–11i(c)
Delaware .... DEL. C., tit. 6, § 3313
Florida .... FLA. S. § 495.151
Georgia .... GA. C.A. § 10–1–451(b)
Idaho .... IDAHO C. § 48–512
Illinois .... ILL. C.S., ch. 765, § 1035/15
Iowa .... IOWA C. § 548.11(2)
Louisiana .... LA. R.S.A. § 51:223.1
Maine .... ME. R.S.A., tit. 10, § 1530
Massachusetts .... MASS. G.L.A., ch. 110B, § 12
Missouri .... MO. R.S. § 417.061(1)
Montana .... MONT. C.A. § 30–13–334
Nebraska .... NEB. R.S. § 87–122
New Hampshire ..... N.H. R.S.A. § 350–A:12
New Mexico .... N.M. S.A. § 57–3–10
New York .... N.Y. Gen.Bus.L. § 368–d

Oregon ....OR. R.S. § 647.107
Pennsylvania ....PA. S.A., tit. 54, § 1124
Rhode Island........R.I. G.L.A. § 6–2–12
Tennessee ....TENN. C.A. § 47–25–512
Texas ....TEX. Bus. & Com.C. § 16.29
Washington ....WASH. R.C.A. § 19.77.160

REPORTERS' NOTE

Comment a. Early common law cases sometimes cited as supporting the dilution rationale include Stork Restaurant, Inc. v. Sahati, 166 F.2d 348 (9th Cir.1948); Bulova Watch Co. v. Stolzberg, 69 F.Supp. 543 (D.Mass. 1947); Alfred Dunhill of London, Inc. v. Dunhill Shirt Shop, Inc., 3 F.Supp. 487 (S.D.N.Y.1929); Tiffany & Co. v. Tiffany Productions, Inc., 147 Misc. 679, 264 N.Y.S. 459 (Sup.Ct.), affirmed 237 App.Div. 801, 260 N.Y.S. 821 (1932), affirmed 262 N.Y. 482, 188 N.E. 30 (1933). None of these cases unambiguously adopts the dilution rationale, however, and more recent cases decline to apply the doctrine in the absence of an applicable statute. See, e.g., Texas Dairy Queen Operators Council v. Feed Store, Inc., 1 U.S.P.Q.2d 1804 (N.D.Tex.1986). But see Ameritech Inc. v. American Information Technologies Corp., 811 F.2d 960 (6th Cir.1987), purporting to find a dilution cause of action in Ohio common law based on Ohio decisions that appear to rest instead on confusion of sponsorship. On the interpretation of state antidilution statutes, see generally McCarthy, Trademarks and Unfair Competition §§ 24.13–20; Gilson, Trademark Protection and Practice § 5.05[9].

The infringement standard in § 32 of the Lanham Act, 15 U.S.C.A. § 1114, requires a plaintiff to show that the defendant's use of the mark "is likely to cause confusion, or to cause mistake, or to deceive." Courts have consistently held that this language precludes recognition of the dilution rationale under § 32. E.g., Tiffany & Co. v. National Gypsum Co., 459 F.2d 527 (C.C.P.A.1972) (dilution is not a ground for opposition to registration); Jean Patou, Inc. v. Jacqueline Cochran, Inc., 201 F.Supp. 861 (S.D.N.Y.1962), affirmed on other grounds 312 F.2d 125 (2d Cir.1963). But see Dreyfus Fund, Inc. v. Royal Bank of Canada, 525 F.Supp. 1108 (S.D.N.Y.1981), suggesting that dilution, "which is in fact the product of a form of confusion," might be actionable under the Lanham Act. Section 2(a) of the Act prevents the registration of marks that may "disparage * * * persons, * * * institutions, beliefs, or national symbols," but not trademarks that may disparage other marks.

Comment b. The history of the dilution doctrine is reviewed in Pattishall, Dawning Acceptance of the Dilution Rationale for Trademark–Trade Identity Protection, 74 Trademark Rep. 289 (1984).

The selling power of a trademark was recognized by Justice Frankfurter in Mishawaka Rubber & Woolen Mfg. Co. v. S.S. Kresge Co., 316 U.S. 203, 205, 62 S.Ct. 1022, 1024, 86 L.Ed. 1381 (1942):

> The protection of trade-marks is the law's recognition of the psychological function of symbols. If it is true that we live by symbols, it is

no less true that we purchase goods by them. A trade-mark is a merchandising short-cut which induces a purchaser to select what he wants, or what he has been led to believe he wants. The owner of a mark exploits this human propensity by making every effort to impregnate the atmosphere of the market with the drawing power of a congenial symbol. Whatever the means employed, the aim is the same to convey through the mark, in the minds of potential customers, the desirability of the commodity upon which it appears. Once this is attained, the trade-mark owner has something of value. If another poaches upon the commercial magnetism of the symbol he has created, the owner can obtain legal redress.

The wisdom of protecting trade symbols from dilution has been actively debated in legal commentary. Those advancing arguments in favor of protection include Derenberg, The Problem of Trademark Dilution and the Antidilution Statutes, 44 Calif.L.Rev. 439 (1956); Pattishall, The Dilution Rationale for Trademark—Trade Identity Protection, Its Progress and Prospects, 71 Nw.U.L.Rev. 618 (1976); Pattishall, Dawning Acceptance of the Dilution Rationale for Trademark–Trade Identity Protection, 74 Trademark Rep. 289 (1984). Those urging caution include Brown, Advertising and the Public Interest: Legal Protection of Trade Symbols, 57 Yale L.J. 1165 (1948); Handler, Are the State Antidilution Laws Compatible with the National Protection of Trademarks?, 75 Trademark Rep. 269 (1985); Weehowitz, Reexamining Trademark Dilution, 44 Vand.L.Rev. 531 (1991). See also Toho Co. v. Sears, Roebuck & Co., 645 F.2d 788 (9th Cir.1981); Coffee Dan's, Inc. v. Coffee Don's Charcoal Broiler, 305 F.Supp. 1210 (N.D.Cal. 1969) (the antidilution doctrine should be cautiously applied "lest it swallow up all competition in the claim of protection against trade name infringement").

A few cases, mostly in dicta, suggest that the expansion of trademark protection through state antidilution statutes undermines the national policy of the Lanham Act and thus may be preempted. See United States Jaycees v. Commodities Magazine, Inc., 661 F.Supp. 1360 (N.D.Iowa 1987). Cf. Mortellito v. Nina of California, Inc., 335 F.Supp. 1288 (S.D.N.Y.1972) (dictum noting the preemption issue). See also Handler, *supra*. This view has not attracted wide support. See Nikon Inc. v. Ikon Corp., 987 F.2d 91 (2d Cir.1993); Golden Door, Inc. v. Odisho, 646 F.2d 347 (9th Cir.1980); Plasticolor Molded Products v. Ford Motor Co., 713 F.Supp. 1329 (C.D.Cal.1989), vacated 767 F.Supp. 1036 (C.D.Cal.1991) (state law extending greater protection to trademarks does not interfere with federal policy); Dallas Cowboys Cheerleaders, Inc. v. Pussycat Cinema, Ltd., 467 F.Supp. 366 (S.D.N.Y.), affirmed 604 F.2d 200 (2d Cir.1979). But see Escada AG v. Limited, Inc., 810 F.Supp. 571 (S.D.N.Y.1993) (application of a state antidilution statute to protect trademark rights in a bottle design is preempted since the subject matter is within the scope of federal patent law and the protection goes beyond the prevention of confusion). But cf. Coca–Cola Co. v. Alma–Leo U.S.A., Inc., 719 F.Supp. 725 (N.D.Ill.1989) (applying an antidilution statute to a bottle design). See also § 16, Comment *c*.

Comment c. The purpose of the antidilution statutes and the evil at which they are directed have been variously described. See Holiday Inns, Inc. v. Holiday Out in America, 481 F.2d 445, 450 (5th Cir.1973) (lessening "the uniqueness of the prior user's mark with the possible future result that a strong mark may become a weak mark"); Toys "R" Us, Inc. v. Canarsie Kiddie Shop, Inc., 559 F.Supp. 1189, 1208 (E.D.N.Y. 1983) ("the watering down of the potency of a mark and the gradual debilitation of its selling power"); Stop the Olympic Prison v. United States Olympic Committee, 489 F.Supp. 1112, 1123 (S.D.N.Y.1980) ("weakening of a mark's propensity to bring to mind a particular product, service, or source of either"); Allied Maintenance Corp. v. Allied Mechanical Trades, Inc., 42 N.Y.2d 538, 542, 399 N.Y.S.2d 628, 630, 369 N.E.2d 1162, 1164 (1977) (the "whittling away of an established trademark's selling power and value through its unauthorized use by others upon dissimilar products").

The distinction between dilution of the distinctiveness of a mark and tarnishment is now widely recognized and applied. See, e.g., Mead Data Central, Inc. v. Toyota Motor Sales, Inc., 875 F.2d 1026 (2d Cir.1989); L.L. Bean, Inc. v. Drake Publishers, Inc., 811 F.2d 26 (1st Cir.), cert. denied 483 U.S. 1013, 107 S.Ct. 3254, 97 L.Ed.2d 753 (1987); Sally Gee, Inc. v. Myra Hogan, Inc., 699 F.2d 621 (2d Cir.1983).

Comment d. Many antidilution statutes expressly extend protection to trade names as well as trademarks. But see Model State Trademark Bill § 13 (1992). Some courts have limited application of the statutes to word marks. Walt Disney Productions v. Air Pirates, 581 F.2d 751 (9th Cir.1978), cert. denied 439 U.S. 1132, 99 S.Ct. 1054, 59 L.Ed.2d 94 (1979) (cartoon characters not protected). A few of the antidilution statutes specifically include "labels and forms of advertisements." Fla. Stat.Ann. § 495.151; Ga.Code § 10–1–451(b); 765 Ill.C.S. 1035/15. Courts have occasionally included trade dress and slogans within the scope of the antidilution statutes. See Ringling Brothers—Barnum & Bailey Combined Shows, Inc. v. Celozzi–Ettelson Chevrolet, Inc., 855 F.2d 480 (7th Cir.1988) (slogan); Soft Sheen Products, Inc. v. Revlon, Inc., 675 F.Supp. 408 (N.D.Ill.1987) (bright yellow and red trade dress). See also Academy of Motion Picture Arts & Sciences v. Creative House Promotions, Inc., 944 F.2d 1446 (9th Cir. 1991) (sale of statuettes similar to the "Oscar" violated California antidilution statute); Coca–Cola Co. v. Alma–Leo U.S.A., Inc., 719 F.Supp. 725 (N.D.Ill.1989) (Coca–Cola bottle).

Comment e. It has been argued that protection against the dilution of a mark's distinctiveness should be accorded to every trademark. See Allied Maintenance Corp. v. Allied Mechanical Trades, Inc., 42 N.Y.2d 538, 399 N.Y.S.2d 628, 369 N.E.2d 1162 (1977) (Cooke, J., dissenting); Lunsford, Trademarks: Dilution and Deception, 63 Trademark Rep. 41 (1956). However, the majority of courts recognize that a higher degree of distinctiveness is required to support a dilution claim than is required to establish rights in a mark for purposes of a traditional infringement claim. See, e.g., Fruit of the Loom, Inc. v. Girouard, 994 F.2d 1359 (9th Cir.1993) (mark must be "mature and well-known"); Bristol–Myers Squibb Co. v. McNeil–P.P.C., Inc., 973 F.2d

1033 (2d Cir.1992) (New York antidilution statute "protects only extremely strong marks"); Glen Raven Mills, Inc. v. Ramada Int'l, Inc., 852 F.Supp. 1544 (M.D.Fla.1994) (mark must be "highly distinctive," citing Restatement Third, Unfair Competition § 25, Comment *e* (Tent. Draft No. 2 (1990))); Tower Publications, Inc. v. MTS Inc., 21 U.S.P.Q.2d 1303 (N.D.Ill.1991) (finding TOWER RECORDS not sufficiently strong for dilution protection, citing Restatement Third, Unfair Competition § 25, Comment *e* (Tent. Draft No.2 (1990))); Great Southern Bank v. First Southern Bank, 625 So.2d 463 (Fla.1993) (mark must be "highly distinctive", citing Restatement Third, Unfair Competition § 25, Comment *e* (Tent. Draft No.2 (1990))); Allied Maintenance, *supra*; Model State Trademark Bill § 13 (1992) ("mark which is famous in this state"). See also McCarthy, *supra*, § 24.17. The court in Sally Gee, Inc. v. Myra Hogan, Inc., 699 F.2d 621, 626 (2d Cir. 1983), suggested a standard similar to that described in the Comment: "[The plaintiff] must set forth some proof that its marks conjure up images of its clothing in the minds of the consuming public in order to establish associational qualities entitling it to protection from dilution." See also Wedgwood Homes, Inc. v. Lund, 294 Or. 493, 659 P.2d 377 (1983) (defining the subject matter of the antidilution statutes as a trademark's "power to evoke images of the product, that is, its favorable associational value in the minds of consumers").

Numerous third-party uses were held sufficient to bar a claim for dilution of the distinctiveness of the trademark DOMINO in Amstar Corp. v. Domino's Pizza, Inc., 615 F.2d 252 (5th Cir.), cert. denied 449 U.S. 899, 101 S.Ct. 268, 66 L.Ed.2d 129 (1980). See also Pignons S.A. de Mecanique de Precision v. Polaroid Corp., 657 F.2d 482 (1st Cir.1981).

Although some cases suggest that a mark must be fanciful or arbitrary to be protected from a dilution of the mark's distinctiveness, other courts recognize that it is possible for a descriptive mark to acquire sufficient distinctiveness to warrant protection. See Hyatt Corp. v. Hyatt Legal Services, 736 F.2d 1153 (7th Cir.), cert. denied 469 U.S. 1019, 105 S.Ct. 434, 83 L.Ed.2d 361 (1984) (surname mark eligible for protection if it has acquired sufficient distinctiveness); Allied Maintenance Corp., *supra*; Wedgwood Homes, Inc. *supra*; Model State Trademark Bill § 13 (1992) ("inherent or acquired distinctiveness").

A mark need not have national distinctiveness to be protected from dilution. In *Wedgwood Homes, Inc., supra*, the mark WEDGWOOD HOMES was held sufficiently distinctive in plaintiff's local marketing area to be diluted by the use of WEDGWOOD DOWNS and WEDGWOOD PLACE in the same market. See also Community Federal Savings & Loan Ass'n v. Orondorff, 678 F.2d 1034 (11th Cir.1982); Dreyfus Fund, Inc. v. Royal Bank of Canada, 525 F.Supp. 1108 (S.D.N.Y.1981); Model State Trademark Bill § 13 (1992) ("famous in this state"). One court observed, "if a mark circulates only in a limited market, it is unlikely to be associated generally with the mark for a dissimilar product circulating elsewhere." Mead Data Central, Inc. v. Toyota Motor Sales, Inc., 875 F.2d 1026, 1031 (2d Cir.1989) (LEXIS for computerized legal research distinctive only among lawyers and not diluted by the use of LEXUS on an automobile). Illustration 1 is based on *Mead Data Central, supra.*

Comment f. A few cases appear to hold that a finding of confusion is sufficient to sustain a dilution claim. See Astra Pharmaceutical Products, Inc. v. Beckman Instruments, Inc., 718 F.2d 1201 (1st Cir.1983); PPG Industries, Inc. v. Clinical Data, Inc., 620 F.Supp. 604 (D.Mass.1985); Lambda Electronics Corp. v. Lambda Technology, Inc., 515 F.Supp. 915 (S.D.N.Y.1981). Although in a particular case the use of another's mark may confuse some consumers and dilute the value of the mark in the minds of other consumers, the state of mind required for confusion and dilution are distinct and inconsistent. Confused consumers believe that the actor's use of the mark indicates a connection with the trademark owner, and thus for those consumers the actor's use does not dilute the distinctiveness of the mark.

A multifactor inquiry for determining the likelihood of dilution analogous to that used to prove a likelihood of confusion was suggested in Mead Data Central, Inc. v. Toyota Motor Sales, Inc., 875 F.2d 1026 (2d Cir.1989) (Sweet, J., concurring). See also Roadway Express, Inc. v. Roadway Motor Plazas, Inc., 17 U.S.P.Q.2d 1131 (N.D.N.Y.1990).

Although a literal interpretation of some antidilution statutes might limit their application to the use of an exact reproduction of the prior user's mark, the courts have recognized that the statutes can be applicable to the use of substantially similar marks. See, e.g., Mead Data Central, *supra* ("the similarity must be substantial before the doctrine of dilution may be applied"); Community Federal Savings & Loan Ass'n v. Orondorff, 678 F.2d 1034 (11th Cir.1982); Dreyfus Fund, Inc. v. Royal Bank of Canada, 525 F.Supp. 1108 (S.D.N.Y.1981). Cf. Fruit of the Loom, Inc. v. Girouard, 994 F.2d 1359 (9th Cir.1993) (finding the marks too dissimilar to create the necessary mental association); Girl Scouts v. Bantam Doubleday Dell Pub. Group, 808 F.Supp. 1112 (S.D.N.Y.1992), affirmed 996 F.2d 1477 (2d Cir.1993) (the marks did not possess the "substantial similarity" required for dilution); Eveready Battery Co. v. Adolph Coors Co., 765 F.Supp. 440 (N.D.Ill.1991) (noting the differences between the marks in rejecting a dilution claim). Use of a trademark in a parody is unlikely to cause a dilution of the mark's distinctiveness since the actor's use refers back to the trademark owner. See, e.g., Yankee Pub., Inc. v. News America Pub., Inc., 809 F.Supp. 267 (S.D.N.Y.1992); Eveready Battery, *supra.*

The sophistication of purchasers was held to reduce the likelihood of dilution in *Mead Data Central, Inc., supra; Astra Pharmaceutical Products, supra;* Lenox, Inc. v. Ranmaru U.S.A. Corp., 17 U.S.P.Q.2d 1696 (S.D.N.Y.1990). For the view that differences between the goods can be so substantial that the likelihood of dilution is remote, see Pattishall, Dawning Acceptance of the Dilution Rationale for Trademark–Trade Identity Protection, 74 Trademark Rep. 289, 299 (1984). Cf. Roadway Express, *supra* (the similarity of the products increases the likelihood of dilution).

Some cases hold that a cause of action for dilution is not available when the actor's use is on competing goods. EZ Loader Boat Trailers, Inc. v. Cox Trailers, Inc., 746 F.2d 375 (7th Cir.1984); Filter Dynamics International, Inc. v. Astron Battery,

Inc., 19 Ill.App.3d 299, 311 N.E.2d 386 (1974). Contra, Nikon, Inc. v. Ikon Corp., 987 F.2d 91 (2d Cir.1993). These cases offer no explanation beyond the desire not to duplicate traditional trademark doctrines. See Model State Trademark Bill § 1(k) (1992) (competition does not preclude dilution).

Comment g. Courts have often enjoined the tarnishment of trademarks without carefully exploring the elements of the cause of action. In many cases the tarnishment rationale is buttressed by findings of likelihood of confusion. See, e.g., Chemical Corp. v. Anheuser–Busch, Inc., 306 F.2d 433 (5th Cir.1962), cert. denied 372 U.S. 965, 83 S.Ct. 1089, 10 L.Ed.2d 129 (1963) (plaintiff's slogan "Where there's life, there's Bud" for beer imitated for use with insecticide); Gucci Shops, Inc. v. R.H. Macy & Co., 446 F.Supp. 838 (S.D.N.Y. 1977) (use of "Gucci Goo" and an imitation of plaintiff's distinctive stripes on diaper bags); Coca–Cola Co. v. Gemini Rising, Inc., 346 F.Supp. 1183 (E.D.N.Y.1972) (use of "Enjoy Cocaine" on poster in soft drink maker's distinctive script).

The tarnishment rationale has been applied in cases involving nationally distinctive marks, e.g., Coca–Cola, *supra*, and marks with limited distinctiveness. See Community Federal Savings & Loan Ass'n v. Orondorff, 678 F.2d 1034 (11th Cir.1982) ("Cookie Jar" for automatic teller machine). The tarnishment cases do not require any particular degree of distinctiveness beyond that necessary for prospective purchasers to associate the two uses of the mark. Illustration 3 is based on *Community Federal Savings, supra.*

Although some courts have recognized that the antidilution statutes are properly applicable only when the actor uses the plaintiff's mark as a trademark or trade name to identify the actor's own goods, services, or business, see, e.g., Jordache Enterprises, Inc. v. Hogg Wyld, Ltd., 828 F.2d 1482 (10th Cir.1987); L.L. Bean, Inc. v. Drake Publishers, Inc., 811 F.2d 26 (1st Cir.), cert. denied 483 U.S. 1013, 107 S.Ct. 3254, 97 L.Ed.2d 753 (1987), other courts have ignored the distinction or have adopted a broad view of the required trademark use. See, e.g., Anheuser–Busch, Inc. v. Balducci Pub., 28 F.2d 769 (8th Cir.1994) (use in an advertisement parody); Dallas Cowboys Cheerleaders, Inc. v. Pussycat Cinema, Ltd., 604 F.2d 200 (2d Cir.1979) (movie featuring actresses in sexually explicit performance dressed in plaintiff's distinctive costume); Pillsbury Co. v. Milky Way Productions, Inc., 215 U.S.P.Q. 124 (N.D.Ga.1981) (use in a cartoon). In a number of the latter cases, the plaintiffs' marks were used on posters or T-shirts. See, e.g., Pillsbury, *supra*; Coca–Cola, *supra*. These cases can raise substantial free speech issues, and the line between a tarnishing trademark use and a protected parody is difficult to establish. See Denicola, Trademarks as Speech: Constitutional Implications of the Emerging Rationales for the Protection of Trade Symbols, 1982 Wis. L.Rev. 158; Dorsen, Satiric Appropriation and the Law of Libel, Trademark and Copyright: Remedies Without Wrongs, 65 B.U.L.Rev. 923 (1986); Note, Trademark Parody: A Fair Use and First Amendment Analysis, 72 Va.L.Rev. 1079 (1986).

Comment h. Notwithstanding cases such as Sally Gee, Inc. v. Myra Hogan, Inc., 699 F.2d 621, 626 (2d Cir.1983), the intent of the defendant should not be balanced against factors relating to the market context of the use in order to determine the likelihood of dilution. (Cf. § 22 on the relevance of intent in proving likelihood of confusion.) Rather, an intent to tarnish or to dilute the distinctiveness of another's mark may in some cases justify an inference that the intended harm has in fact occurred. See also Model State Trademark Bill § 13 (1992) (willful intent may be relevant to remedies). A few cases suggest that bad faith is a necessary element of a dilution case, although these decisions may merely reflect the initial judicial reluctance to apply the antidilution statutes according to their terms. See Beneficial Corp. v. Beneficial Capital Corp., 529 F.Supp. 445 (S.D.N.Y.1982) (either likelihood of confusion or bad faith is required for liability under an antidilution statute). But see Eastman Kodak Co. v. Rakow, 739 F.Supp. 116 (W.D.N.Y.1989) (bad faith is relevant but not required); Roadway Express, Inc. v. Roadway Motor Plazas, Inc., 17 U.S.P.Q.2d 1131 (N.D.N.Y.1990) (predatory intent is a relevant factor).

Comment i. The constitutional basis for distinguishing between trademark and nontrademark uses for purpose of both trademark infringement and the antidilution statutes is explored in Denicola, Trademarks as Speech: Constitutional Implications of the Emerging Rationales for the Protection of Trade Symbols, 1982 Wis.L.Rev. 158; McCarthy, *supra*, §§ 31.37–38. Some cases make the distinction explicit. See, e.g., Jordache Enterprises, Inc. v. Hogg Wyld, Ltd., 828 F.2d 1482 (10th Cir. 1987); L.L. Bean, Inc. v. Drake Publishers, Inc., 811 F.2d 26 (1st Cir.), cert. denied 483 U.S. 1013, 107 S.Ct. 3254, 97 L.Ed.2d 753 (1987); Lucasfilm Ltd. v. High Frontier, 622 F.Supp. 931 (D.D.C.1985); Stop the Olympic Prison v. United States Olympic Committee, 489 F.Supp. 1112 (S.D.N.Y.1980). Cf. LightHawk, Environmental Air Force v. Robertson, 812 F.Supp. 1095 (W.D.Wash. 1993) (federal statute granting the Forest Service exclusive use of the SMOKEY BEAR designation held unconstitutional as applied against use in a political advertisement); Yankee Pub., Inc. v. News America Pub., Inc., 809 F.Supp. 267 (S.D.N.Y. 1992) (first amendment is applicable to a dilution claim involving the use of a trademark in a parody); Ocean Bio–Chem, Inc. v. Turner Network Television, Inc., 741 F.Supp. 1546 (S.D.Fla.1990) (dismissing a dilution claim because of the uncertainty as to whether the antidilution statute applies to use in expressive works). Compare San Francisco Arts & Athletics, Inc. v. United States Olympic Committee, 483 U.S. 522, 107 S.Ct. 2971, 97 L.Ed.2d 427 (1987) (upholding a federal statute prohibiting any unauthorized use in trade of the OLYMPIC marks).

Dilution does not prohibit the use of a mark to refer accurately to the goods of the prior user, even after rebottling or repair. See Chanel Inc. v. Casa Flora Co., 100 N.J.Super. 19, 241 A.2d 24 (1968); Clairol, Inc. v. Cody's Cosmetics, Inc., 353 Mass. 385, 231 N.E.2d 912 (1967).

Some courts in tarnishment cases appear to find a likelihood of confusion in order to impose liability even when it is unlikely that the actor's use actually misidentifies the source or sponsorship of the actor's goods or services. See, e.g., Mutual of Omaha Ins. Co. v. Novak, 836 F.2d 397 (8th

Cir.1987), cert. denied 488 U.S. 933, 109 S.Ct. 326, 102 L.Ed.2d 344 (1988) (finding a likelihood of confusion when an anti-nuclear weapons activist sold T-shirts bearing the words "Mutant of Omaha" and a crest similar to the trademark of the plaintiff insurance company); Coca–Cola Co. v. Gemini Rising, Inc., 346 F.Supp. 1183 (E.D.N.Y.1972) ("Enjoy Cocaine" on a poster written in the distinctive script of the Coca–Cola Company held an infringement based on confusion of sponsorship). Indeed, it has been argued that adoption of the dilution rationale might be unnecessary because courts are likely to afford relief in dilution cases through a finding of confusion. Middleton, Some Aspects of Trademark Dilution, 47 Trademark Rep. 1023 (1957). Trademark infringement, however, is not an appropriate doctrine for resolving cases that do not involve the use of a designation as a trademark. Other forms of relief may be appropriate, however, if the audience understands the defendant's use as a serious statement about the trademark owner. Thus, if it could be shown in a case such as Dallas Cowboys Cheerleaders, Inc. v. Pussycat Cinema, Ltd., 467 F.Supp. 366 (S.D.N.Y.), affirmed 604 F.2d 200 (2d Cir.1979), that the use of the plaintiff's distinctive uniform in the defendant's X-rated movie was perceived by viewers as a serious statement about the nature of the plaintiff's organization or the character of its employees, an action for defamation might be appropriate. In other cases, such as *Mutual of Omaha*, *supra*, although the association of the trademark owner with the antiwar movement, even if taken seriously, would not be defamatory, liability might be analyzed under the rules relating to injurious falsehood or false light privacy. See also Anheuser–Busch, Inc. v. Balducci Pub., 28 F.3d 769 (8th Cir.1994) (parody advertisement suggesting that plaintiff's beer contained oil could be actionable as disparagement if understood as a factual assertion).

The difficulty of distinguishing between impermissible appropriation and permissible parody is also apparent under copyright law. The "fair use" defense has been used to balance the competing interests, see Campbell v. Acuff-Rose Music, Inc., ___ U.S. ___, 114 S.Ct. 1164, 127 L.Ed.2d 500 (1994), and it has been suggested that a similar analysis should apply in trademark parody cases. Note, Trademark Parody, 72 Va.L.Rev. 1079 (1986).

The suggestion that a trademark owner should have a cause of action under the antidilution statutes to prevent the mark from being used generically is made in Wolff, Trademark Dilution: The Need for Reform, 74 Trademark Rep. 311 (1984). See McCarthy, *supra*, § 24.13[5].

Illustration 4 is suggested by the facts in Chemical Corp. v. Anheuser–Busch, Inc., 306 F.2d 433 (5th Cir. 1962), cert. denied 372 U.S. 965, 83 S.Ct. 1089, 10 L.Ed.2d 129 (1963). The facts of Illustration 5 are based on L.L. Bean, Inc. v. Drake Publishers, Inc., 811 F.2d 26 (1st Cir.), cert. denied 483 U.S. 1013, 107 S.Ct. 3254, 97 L.Ed.2d 753 (1987). The court refused to apply the antidilution statute to such nontrademark use in light of the first amendment interests implicated by the use. See also, e.g., Anheuser–Busch, Inc. v. Balducci Publications, 814 F.Supp. 791 (E.D.Mo.1993); Yankee Pub. Inc. v. News America Pub. Inc., 809 F.Supp. 267 (S.D.N.Y.1992); Ocean Bio–Chem, Inc. v. Turner Network Television, Inc., 741 F.Supp. 1546 (S.D.Fla.1990). Whether a cause of action exists under other doctrines would depend upon how the defendant's catalog was interpreted by readers. For a communication to be defamatory under Restatement, Second, Torts § 559, it must be either a statement of fact, see § 565, or an expression of opinion that implies a statement of fact, see § 566, Comment *d* (humor may be defamatory only if it implies the existence of a false defamatory fact). A communication may result in liability for injurious falsehood under Restatement, Second, Torts § 623A if the communication is harmful to the interests of another and the maker intended to harm the interests of the other and acted with knowledge that the statement was false or with reckless disregard for its truth or falsity. Thus, unless the catalog in Illustration 4 is interpreted to state or imply false statements of fact about the plaintiff or its goods or services, no liability would attach to its publication.

§ 26. Contributory Infringement by Printers, Publishers, and Other Suppliers

(1) One who, on behalf of a third person, reproduces or imitates the trademark, trade name, collective mark, or certification mark of another on goods, labels, packaging, advertisements, or other materials that are used by the third person in a manner that subjects the third person to liability to the other for infringement under the rule stated in § 20 is subject to liability to that other for contributory infringement.

(2) If an actor subject to contributory liability under the rule stated in Subsection (1) acted without knowledge that the reproduction or imitation was intended by the third person to confuse or deceive, the actor is subject only to appropriate injunctive relief.

Comment:

a. Scope. This Section imposes liability on persons who contribute to the infringement of another's trademark, trade name, collective mark, or certification mark by reproducing the mark or name at the request of a third person on goods, packaging, or advertising. Persons subject to liability under this Section include printers who reproduce the mark on labels, wrappers, tags, or containers, manufacturers who stamp, embroider, or otherwise affix the mark to goods at the request of a customer, and publishers and broadcasters who reproduce the mark in advertisements disseminated on behalf of another. The relief granted against a person liable under the rule stated in this Section, however, may differ from that granted against the direct infringer. For example, under Subsection (2) a supplier or publisher who acts without knowledge that it is assisting in the infringement of another's mark is subject only to injunctive relief.

The relief available under the Lanham Act against an "innocent" printer is limited to an injunction against future printing of the infringing mark. Relief against an "innocent" publisher is limited to an injunction against inclusion of the infringing advertisement in future issues or transmissions. Even the latter relief is unavailable with respect to a particular issue or transmission if the injunction would delay delivery beyond the regularly scheduled time. Section 32(2), 15 U.S.C.A. § 1114(2). Similar limitations are appropriate at common law. However, if the person subject to liability under this Section knows that the reproduction is intended for use in a manner that infringes the mark or trade name of another, liability extends to any remedy appropriate under the rules stated in §§ 35–37. Thus, as in the case of contributory liability for deceptive marketing as described in § 7, the remedies for which a person is liable under the rule stated here depend upon the nature of the business relationship between the person and the direct infringer and the knowledge attributable to the person on the basis of that relationship.

Even without the imposition of contributory liability under this Section, an injunction issued against the direct infringer will upon notice bind those acting in active concert with it. See Fed.R.Civ.P. 65(d); Restatement, Second, Judgments § 63.

b. Application to the media. Contributory liability under this Section extends to publishers and broadcasters who disseminate infringing advertisements. The rule against prior restraints has not been applied to commercial speech, and the exclusion of monetary relief under Subsection (2) in the absence of actual knowledge of the direct infringer's deceptive intent is consistent with the constitutional limitations on liability recognized by the Supreme Court even with respect to noncommercial speech. Nevertheless, as in the case of contributory liability for deceptive marketing under § 7, any application of this Section to publishers and broadcasters must take account of the controlling constitutional standards applicable to the media under the first amendment.

Illustrations:

1. *A* uses as a trademark for clothing a fanciful design consisting of a horse and rider. *B*, another clothing manufacturer, contracts with *C*, a printer, to supply tags bearing an identical design. *B* attaches the tags to its clothing and markets the goods in a manner that infringes *A*'s trademark. Both *B* and *C* are subject to liability to *A*. In the absence of proof that *C* knew that the tags were intended to deceive or confuse *B*'s customers, the

remedy against *C* will be limited to an injunction against the future printing of such materials for *B*.

2. *A* manufactures water-conditioning equipment that it sells through a network of exclusive distributors, including *B*. After *A* terminates *B* 's distributorship and reclaims all unsold equipment, *B* continues to place advertisements displaying *A* 's trademark in *C* 's telephone directory. The advertisements cause prospective purchasers to believe that the equipment now offered for sale by *B* is manufactured by *A*. Both *B* and *C* are subject to liability to *A*. In the absence of proof that *C* knew that the advertisements were intended to deceive or confuse *B* 's customers, the remedy against *C* will be limited to an injunction against publication of the advertisements in future directories.

3. *A* is a manufacturer of cookware. *C*, a glass company, manufactures cookware sets under an order from *B*, a distributor. At *B* 's direction *C* places a stylized flower design on the cookware that is substantially similar to the trademark used by *A*. *C* knows that *B* sells the cookware to retailers with promotional materials intended to assist the retailers in selling the product as *A* 's cookware. Both *B* and *C* are subject to liability to *A* for the remedies appropriate under the rules stated in §§ 35–37.

REPORTERS' NOTE

This Section restates the rule governing liability for contributory trademark infringement in Restatement of Torts § 739 (1938). On the liability of printers and publishers for infringement of marks registered under the Lanham Act, see § 32(1)(b) and § 32(2), 15 U.S.C.A. § 1114(1)(b) and § 1114(2).

The rules stated here are analogous to those stated in § 7, and the Comments and Reporters' Note accompanying that section are also relevant here.

Comment a. Section 32(1)(b) of the Lanham Act imposes liability on any person who without authorization reproduces a registered mark on "labels, signs, prints, packages, wrappers, receptacles or advertisements" intended for use in the sale or advertising of goods or services and likely to cause confusion or to deceive. The section precludes the recovery of profits or damages, however, unless the reproduction was done with knowledge that the imitation was intended to confuse or deceive.

Under Fed.R.Civ.P. 65(d) an injunction against direct infringers will also bind "those persons in active concert or participation with them who receive actual notice of the order by personal service or otherwise." See, e.g., Vuitton et fils S.A. v. Carousel Handbags, 592 F.2d 126 (2d Cir.1979); South Central Bell Tel. Co. v. Constant Inc., 304 F.Supp. 732 (E.D.La.1969), affirmed 437 F.2d 1207 (5th Cir.1971).

Comment b. On the distinction between commercial and noncommercial speech, see, e.g., Board of Trustees v. Fox, 492 U.S. 469, 109 S.Ct. 3028, 106 L.Ed.2d 388 (1989); Bolger v. Youngs Drug Products Corp., 463 U.S. 60, 103 S.Ct. 2875, 77 L.Ed.2d 469 (1983). That a prior restraint on commercial speech may be permissible, see, e.g., Central Hudson Gas & Electric Corp. v. Public Services Com., 447 U.S. 557, 571 n.13, 100 S.Ct. 2343, 2354 n.13, 65 L.Ed.2d 341, 354 n.13 (1980); Virginia State Bd. of Pharmacy v. Virginia Citizens Consumer Council, 425 U.S. 748, 771–72 n.24, 96 S.Ct. 1817, 1830–31 n.24, 48 L.Ed.2d 346, 364 n.24 (1976).

Illustration 1 is based on the facts in Polo Fashions, Inc. v. Ontario Printers, Inc., 601 F.Supp. 402 (N.D.Ohio 1984). See, e.g., Hennessy v. Herrmann, 89 Fed. 669 (C.C.Cal. 1898); New England Awl & Needle Co. v. Marlborough Awl & Needle Co., 168 Mass. 154, 46 N.E. 386 (1897).

Dictum in *Polo Fashions, Inc., supra,* suggests that a printer or manufacturer must make "reasonable inquiry" and that the standard should be "an objective, reasonable business person test and not the subjective state-of-the-mind test." The rule as stated in this Section, however, recognizes liability for remedies other than an injunction only upon proof of actual knowledge. The legislative history of the 1988 amendments to the Lanham Act advises that under § 32(2), which limits relief against "innocent" printers and publishers to an injunction, "[t]he word 'innocent' is intended to encompass the constitutional standards set forth in New York Times Co. v. Sullivan, 376 U.S. 254, 84 S.Ct. 710, 11 L.Ed.2d 686 (1964) and its progeny," thus suggesting that "reckless disregard" for the likelihood of deception may be sufficient for the recovery of monetary relief. 134 Cong.Rec. H10420 (Oct.19, 1988) (statement of Subcommittee Chairman Kastenmeier). Section 32(1) of the Lanham Act, however, expressly prohibits the recovery of profits and damages against printers and publishers unless the acts are committed "with knowledge" of the intent to confuse, and that standard is adopted in the rule as stated here.

Illustration 2 is based on Union Tank Car Co. v. Lindsay Soft Water Corp., 257 F.Supp. 510 (D.Neb.1966), affirmed 387 F.2d 477 (8th Cir.1967). See Mr. Rooter Corp. v. Morris, 188 U.S.P.Q. 392 (E.D.La.1975); Hoover Co. v. Groger, 12 Cal.App.2d 417, 55 P.2d 529 (1936). See also Crazy Eddie, Inc. v. Lois Pitts Gershon, Inc., 600 F.Supp. 537 (S.D.N.Y.1984) (temporary restraining order granted against an advertising agency that produced an infringing commercial). Compare Century 21 Real Estate Corp. v. R.M. Post, Inc., 8 U.S.P.Q.2d 1614 (N.D.Ill.1988) (denying a motion to dismiss a damage claim under § 32 against telephone directory publishers alleged to have published infringing advertisements with knowledge of the infringement). See generally Gilson, Trademark Protection and Practice § 8.09.

Illustration 3 is suggested by Corning Glass Works v. Jeannette Glass Co., 308 F.Supp. 1321 (S.D.N.Y.), affirmed 432 F.2d 784 (2d Cir.1970). See Andrew Jergens Co. v. Bonded Products Corp., 21 F.2d 419 (2d Cir. 1927), cert. denied 275 U.S. 572, 48 S.Ct. 204, 72 L.Ed. 432 (1928) (enjoining a soap manufacturer from placing an infringing mark on goods produced for another).

§ 27. Contributory Infringement by Manufacturers and Distributors

One who markets goods or services to a third person who further markets the goods or services in a manner that subjects the third person to liability to another for infringement under the rule stated in § 20 is subject to liability to that other for contributory infringement if:

(a) the actor intentionally induces the third person to engage in the infringing conduct; or

(b) the actor fails to take reasonable precautions against the occurrence of the third person's infringing conduct in circumstances in which the infringing conduct can be reasonably anticipated.

Comment:

a. Scope. Liability for trademark infringement extends beyond those persons who actually use another's mark in selling their goods or services. If products sold by a manufacturer or distributor are subsequently marketed in a manner that infringes another's trademark, trade name, collective mark, or certification mark, the manufacturer or distributor may in some circumstances be subject to liability for contributory infringement. This Section recognizes such liability when the manufacturer or distributor intentionally induces others in the chain of distribution to engage in the infringing conduct or accepts the benefits of the infringement by failing to take reasonable precautions against its occurrence.

This Section is an application of principles analogous to those governing contributory liability for deceptive marketing as described in § 8. Certain conduct such as a seller's substitution without the buyer's knowledge of goods made by one producer in response to the buyer's request for a brand made by a different producer can be considered either as trademark infringement under § 20 or as a misrepresentation of source under § 4. See § 4, Illustration 6. Contributory liability in connection with such conduct thus may be imposed either under the rules stated in § 8 or the rules stated here.

This Section imposes contributory liability on a manufacturer or distributor for infringing sales made by others. If the manufacturer or distributor itself markets goods or services under a designation that is likely to confuse prospective purchasers, the manufacturer or distributor is subject to liability under the rules stated in § 20 even if the designation does not confuse the retailers or other intermediate purchasers to whom the goods are initially sold. The liability in such cases, however, is direct and application of the rules stated in this Section is unnecessary.

b. Inducing infringement. A manufacturer or distributor who intentionally induces third persons to market its goods or services in a manner that infringes another's trademark is subject to liability under this Section. The inducement may consist of an express suggestion that the third person market the goods or services under another's trademark. The inducement may also be implicit in the actor's conduct. The appearance of the goods or the manner in which they are marketed by the manufacturer or distributor, for example, may be sufficient to indicate an intention to induce infringing sales by others.

Illustration:

1. *A* markets vegetables under the trademark SUNLIGHT. *B* sells similar goods to wholesalers and advises the wholesalers to sell the goods as SUNLIGHT vegetables. Some of the wholesalers subsequently offer *B*'s vegetables for sale under the SUNLIGHT trademark. *B* is subject to liability to *A*.

c. Failure to take reasonable precautions. A manufacturer or distributor who fails to take reasonable precautions to prevent infringing sales of its product by others may be subject to liability for contributory infringement under this Section even in the absence of an intention to induce the infringement. The duty to take reasonable precautions, however, arises only when the manufacturer or distributor has reason to anticipate that some substantial number of infringing sales will otherwise occur.

A failure to take reasonable precautions when there is a known risk of substantial infringement may indicate an intention to induce the infringing conduct, thus subjecting the manufacturer or distributor to liability under clause (a) of this Section. Under the rule stated in clause (b), however, liability may be imposed on the basis of an objective evaluation of the actor's conduct without the necessity of inferring intent. A manufacturer or distributor who has reasonable grounds to anticipate infringing sales of its product by others, however, is obligated to take only those precautions that are reasonable under the circumstances. See § 8, Comment *c*. It is not obliged, for example, to forgo the duplication of features of another's product that are functional under the rule stated in § 17 in order to deter infringement by subsequent sellers. Compare Illustrations 4 and 5 to § 8.

Illustration:

2. *A* markets a popular doll under the trademark BARBARA. *B* manufactures a somewhat similar doll that it sells to distributors under a trademark that is not confusingly similar to *A* 's mark. The packaging of *B* 's doll also differs from that used by *A*. Some retailers have removed *B* 's dolls from their packaging and offered them for sale as BARBARA dolls. In the absence of evidence establishing that *B* intentionally induced the infringement of *A* 's trademark or failed to take reasonable precautions to prevent the infringement, *B* is not subject to liability to *A*.

d. Sales to particular purchasers. A manufacturer or distributor who has reason to anticipate that a particular buyer will resell the goods in a manner that infringes another's trademark is subject to contributory liability under the rule stated in clause (b) if the manufacturer or distributor continues to supply the goods to that buyer without taking reasonable precautions against the infringement. In the case of sales to specific buyers known to be engaged in infringing resales, the reasonableness of the precautions should be evaluated primarily by their effectiveness in preventing the infringement. See § 8, Comment *d.* Although in many instances the manufacturer or distributor may initially be justified in relying upon requests to cease the infringement or assurances from the other that it will do so, in extreme cases of persistent infringement judicial proceedings or a refusal to supply further goods may be the only precautions reasonable under the circumstances.

Illustrations:

3. *A*, an oil company, uses the trademark SWIFT in marketing its gasoline products. *B*, a distributor, sells gasoline produced by another oil company to SWIFT-brand service stations, which dispense the gasoline to customers from pumps bearing the SWIFT trademark. *B* is subject to liability to *A*.

4. *C* purchases goods from *B* and requests *B* to package the goods in containers that *C* supplies bearing a trademark identical to that used by *A* on similar goods. *B* packages the goods as requested and *C* resells the goods in a manner that infringes *A* 's trademark. If *B* knows or has reason to know that *C* is not authorized to use *A* 's mark, *B* is subject to liability to *A*.

REPORTERS' NOTE

This Section amplifies the rule relating to contributory trademark infringement stated in Restatement of

Torts § 738 (1938). See generally McCarthy, Trademarks and Unfair Competition § 25.02.

The rules stated here are analogous to those stated in § 8, and the Comments and Reporters' Note accompanying that Section are also relevant here.

Comment a. Many of the recent cases on contributory trademark infringement concern attempts by the producers of formerly-patented drugs to impose liability on the manufacturers of generic equivalents in connection with sales by pharmacists of the generic products under the trademark of the original producer. The Supreme Court in Inwood Laboratories, Inc. v. Ives Laboratories, Inc., 456 U.S. 844, 854, 102 S.Ct. 2182, 2188, 72 L.Ed.2d 606, 615 (1982), stated that a manufacturer would be contributorily liable if it "intentionally induces another to infringe a trademark, or if it continues to supply its product to one whom it knows or has reason to know is engaging in trademark infringement." The Court's statement of principle was derived from William R. Warner & Co. v. Eli Lilly & Co., 265 U.S. 526, 44 S.Ct. 615, 68 L.Ed. 1161 (1924) and Coca–Cola Co. v. Snow Crest Beverages, Inc., 64 F.Supp. 980 (D.Mass.1946), affirmed 162 F.2d 280 (1st Cir.), cert. denied 332 U.S. 809, 68 S.Ct. 110, 92 L.Ed. 386 (1947). See generally Symposium: The Ives Case, 72 Trademark Rep. 1 (1982). Cf. Hard Rock Cafe Licensing Corp. v. Concession Services, Inc., 955 F.2d 1143 (7th Cir.1992) (applying the *Ives* standard to determine the liability of a landlord for infringing sales made on its premises).

The distinction between contributory liability for another's infringing use of a mark and direct liability for an infringing use by the actor is illustrated in Justice White's concurrence in *Ives*, 456 U.S. at 863–64, 102 S.Ct. at 2193–94, noting the allegation of direct infringement against a generic manufacturer under § 43(a) for the manufacturer's imitation of the capsule colors used by the original producer. See also, e.g., SK & F, Co. v. Premo Pharmaceutical Laboratories, Inc., 625 F.2d 1055 (3d Cir.1980).

Comment b. In Inwood Laboratories, Inc. v. Ives Laboratories, Inc., 456 U.S. 844, 102 S.Ct. 2182, 72 L.Ed.2d 606 (1982), the Supreme Court endorsed the proposition that contributory liability could be imposed if a manufacturer "suggested, even if only by implication," that its retailers sell the goods under another's trademark. The Court also concluded, however, that the fact that a manufacturer "could reasonably anticipate" the infringing conduct was not itself sufficient to establish intentional inducement and hence contributory liability under § 32 of the Lanham Act. 456 U.S. at 854 n.13, 102 S.Ct. at 2188 n.13, 72 L.Ed.2d at 615 n.13. The Court's decision, however, has not been interpreted to preclude reliance on the "reasonably anticipate" standard in actions at common law. See Ciba–Geigy Corp. v. Bolar Pharmaceutical Co., 547 F.Supp. 1095 (D.N.J.1982), affirmed 719 F.2d 56 (3d Cir.1983), cert. denied 465 U.S. 1080, 104 S.Ct. 1444, 79 L.Ed.2d 763 (1984).

Illustration 1 is based on Illustration 1 to Restatement of Torts § 738 (1938). See, e.g., Smith, Kline & French Laboratories v. Clark & Clark, 157 F.2d 725 (3d Cir.), cert. denied 329 U.S. 796, 67 S.Ct. 482, 91 L.Ed. 681 (1946). See also § 8, Illustration 1.

Comment c. If a manufacturer or distributor of goods has no reason to know of the subsequent infringing resales of its product, contributory liability will not be imposed. See, e.g., David Berg & Co. v. Gatto Int'l Trading Co., 884 F.2d 306 (7th Cir. 1989); cf. Mini Maid Services Co. v. Maid Brigade Systems, Inc., 967 F.2d 1516 (11th Cir.1992) (franchisor is liable for infringement by its franchisee only if the franchisor induced or knowingly participated in the infringement).

Several cases recite that a manufacturer or distributor may be subject to contributory liability if it can reasonably anticipate that retailers will sell the goods in a manner that infringes another's trademark. See, e.g., Ciba–Geigy Corp. v. Bolar Pharmaceutical Co., 747 F.2d 844 (3d Cir. 1984), cert. denied 471 U.S. 1137, 105 S.Ct. 2678, 86 L.Ed.2d 696 (1985); SK & F, Co. v. Premo Pharmaceutical Laboratories, Inc., 625 F.2d 1055 (3d Cir.1980); Merrell–National Laboratories, Inc. v. Zenith Laboratories, Inc., 194 U.S.P.Q. 157 (D.N.J.1977). The rule as stated in clause (b) of this Section, however, emphasizes that liability may be imposed upon a manufacturer or distributor who reasonably anticipates infringing sales of its goods by others only if the manufacturer or distributor has failed to take precautions that are reasonable under the circumstances. Cases noting the relevance of precautionary measures include Upjohn Co. v. Schwartz, 246 F.2d 254 (2d Cir.1957); Coca–Cola Co. v. Snow Crest Beverages, Inc., 64 F.Supp. 980 (D.Mass.1946), affirmed 162 F.2d 280 (1st Cir.), cert. denied 332 U.S. 809, 68 S.Ct. 110, 92 L.Ed. 386 (1947). See also, e.g., William R. Warner & Co. v. Eli Lilly & Co., 265 U.S. 526, 44 S.Ct. 615, 68 L.Ed. 1161 (1924); Smith, Kline & French Laboratories v. Clark & Clark, 157 F.2d 725 (3d Cir.), cert. denied 329 U.S. 796, 67 S.Ct. 482, 91 L.Ed. 681 (1946) (remedies in the nature of further precautions). The latter two cases also emphasize that the duty to adopt precautions does not require the manufacturer to refrain from imitating functional features of a competitor's product. See also, e.g., Famolare, Inc. v. Melville Corp., 472 F.Supp. 738 (D.Haw.1979), affirmed without op. 652 F.2d 62 (9th Cir.1981).

Illustration 2 is suggested by Mattel, Inc. v. Goldberger Doll Mfg. Co., 200 F.Supp. 517 (E.D.N.Y.1961). See also § 8, Illustration 3.

Comment d. Sales to known infringers are expressly included within the traditional formulations of the scope of contributory liability. See, e.g., Inwood Laboratories, Inc. v. Ives Laboratories, Inc., discussed in the Reporters' Note accompanying Comment *a*; Coca–Cola Co. v. Snow Crest Beverages, Inc., 64 F.Supp. 980 (D.Mass.1946), affirmed 162 F.2d 280 (1st Cir.), cert. denied 332 U.S. 809, 68 S.Ct. 110, 92 L.Ed. 386 (1947). Under the rule as stated here, however, a manufacturer is not obliged to terminate its business relationship with the infringer if it reasonably believes that less drastic precautions will deter further infringement.

Illustration 3 is based on Getty Petroleum Corp. v. Island Transportation Corp., 862 F.2d 10 (2d Cir.1988), cert. denied 490 U.S. 1006, 109 S.Ct. 1642, 104 L.Ed.2d 157 (1989) and Power Test Petroleum Distributors, Inc. v. Manhattan & Queens Fuel Corp., 556 F.Supp. 392 (E.D.N.Y. 1982). See also § 8, Illustration 6.

Illustration 4 is based on Illustration 2 to Restatement of Torts § 738 (1938). See Stix Products, Inc. v. United Merchants & Mfrs., Inc., 295 F.Supp. 479 (S.D.N.Y.1968), imposing contributory liability on a manufacturer who assembled the product for a buyer with knowledge of the subsequent infringing sales. See also John B. Stetson Co. v. Stephen L. Stetson Co., 85 F.2d 586 (2d Cir.), cert. denied 299 U.S. 605, 57 S.Ct. 232, 81 L.Ed. 446 (1936).

TOPIC 4. DEFENSES AND LIMITATIONS ON RELIEF

Section

---

§ 28. Descriptive Use (Fair Use)

In an action for infringement of a trademark, trade name, collective mark, or certification mark, it is a defense that the term used by the actor is descriptive or geographically descriptive of the actor's goods, services, or business, or is the personal name of the actor or a person connected with the actor, and the actor has used the term fairly and in good faith solely to describe the actor's goods, services, or business or to indicate a connection with the named person.

Comment:

a. Extent of rights in descriptive terms. Section 14 recognizes trademark rights in descriptive and geographically descriptive terms upon proof that the designation has acquired secondary meaning as a symbol of identification. Trademark rights, however, extend only to the source significance that has been acquired by such terms, not to their original descriptive meanings. The owner of a trademark thus cannot deprive others of the use of the term in its original descriptive sense. Reasonable use of a descriptive term by another solely to describe the nature or characteristics of its own goods or services will not subject the user to liability for infringement. An analogous rule is applicable to personal name designations. A subsequent user is not subject to liability if the name is used solely to indicate truthfully the named person's connection with the goods, services, or business.

The defense recognized in this Section is commonly referred to as the "fair use" defense. However, the defense does not represent a general right of reasonable use of another's trademark equivalent to the fair use defense recognized under the law of copyright. See 17 U.S.C.A. § 107. The defense of fair use under the law of trademarks is limited to use of the original descriptive or personal name significance of a term. This limitation on the scope of the fair use doctrine is sometimes described by stating that the doctrine applies only to use "otherwise than as a trademark," or only to "nontrademark use" of another's mark. When the defendant uses a descriptive term that is another's trademark as an element of a trademark for the defendant's own goods or services, the courts generally decline to recognize a fair use defense. In such cases the appropriate balance between the defendant's interest in access to the original lexicographic meaning of the term and the plaintiff's interest in protection against confusion is ordinarily pursued through the application of the likelihood of confusion standard. See § 20. Descriptive trademarks are accorded a narrower scope of protection under the likelihood of confusion analysis than are arbitrary marks, see *id.*, Comment *g*; § 21, Comments *c* and *i*, and the remedies available for infringement of descriptive marks may be similarly limited. See § 35, Comment *d*. However, in some cases it may be difficult to distinguish use as an element of a trademark from a nontrademark use. Thus, there is not always a clear distinction between cases appropriately analyzed under the rule stated in this Section and cases more properly analyzed under the general standard of likelihood of confusion as stated in § 20.

The fair use defense has been recognized with respect to both registered and unregistered trademarks. Section 33(b)(4) of the Lanham Act recognizes as a defense that the name or term is used, not as a trademark, but "fairly and in good faith only to describe" the user's goods or services. 15 U.S.C.A. § 1115(b)(4). The defense has also been recognized at common law and under § 43(a) of the Lanham Act.

Use of another's trademark for the purpose of identifying goods or services that originate from the owner of the trademark is subject to the rules stated in § 24 rather than to the rules stated here. Similarly, use of another's trademark solely as a means of referring to the trademark owner or to the owner's products or business is not within the scope of this Section. See § 20, Comment *b*; § 25, Comment *i*.

b. Relation to likelihood of confusion. Use of another's trademark subjects the user to liability under § 20 only if the use is likely to cause confusion. In the case of a descriptive trademark, the likelihood of confusion will depend in part on whether prospective purchasers are likely to understand the defendant's use of the term as a mere description of the defendant's goods, services, or business rather than as an indication of source or sponsorship. In some cases the manner of the defendant's use may thus justify an inference that confusion is unlikely. Unless this inference is overcome by other evidence, the defendant is not subject to liability—a result sometimes ascribed to the fair use defense. In such cases, however, fair use is a "defense" only in the sense that evidence relating to the manner of use can rebut a necessary element of the plaintiff's case. The burden of proving likelihood of confusion remains on the trademark owner and application of the rule stated here is unnecessary.

The fair use defense recognized in this Section can be applicable even if the trademark owner presents evidence sufficient to prove a likelihood of confusion. If the manner of use by the defendant is reasonable in light of the commercial justification for the use, the possibility or even certainty that some prospective purchasers will perceive the term as an indication of source despite the reasonableness of the defendant's use is not sufficient to deprive the defendant of the right to employ the term in its descriptive sense. Thus, a defendant who uses a descriptive term fairly and in good faith to describe its goods or services is not liable for infringement even if some residual confusion is likely. However, the strength of the plaintiff's mark and the extent of likely or actual confusion are important factors in determining whether a use is fair. Surveys and other evidence relating to the perceptions of prospective purchasers are thus relevant to the application of the defense, and a use that is likely to create substantial confusion will not ordinarily be considered a fair use. The defendant bears the burden of establishing the defense of fair use under this Section.

c. Manner of use. Fair use is a reasonable and good faith use of a descriptive term that is another's trademark to describe rather than to identify the user's goods, services, or business. Use of a descriptive term in textual commentary or instructions, for example, may be unlikely as a practical matter to create a likelihood of confusion, but in any event it is ordinarily a fair use. More prominent use of a descriptive term can also qualify as a fair use. In some instances the presence of the defendant's own trademark in conjunction with the descriptive term can be sufficient to emphasize that the use is merely descriptive. The physical nature of the use in terms of size, location, and other characteristics in comparison with the appearance of other descriptive matter or other trademarks is also relevant to the fairness of the use. The presence or absence of precautionary measures such as labeling or other devices designed to minimize the risk that the term will be understood in its trademark sense are similarly relevant.

Commercial justification is also important in assessing the fairness of the defendant's use. The scope of use permitted under the fair use defense should reflect the degree to which the descriptive meaning of the term is relevant to the goods, services, or business of the subsequent user. If the original meaning of the term is not in fact descriptive of the attributes of the user's goods, services, or business, the defense is not applicable. If the term is only marginally descriptive or descriptive of only a relatively unimportant characteristic, the scope of fair use will be narrower than for terms that directly describe aspects or features of the goods or services that are of importance to prospective purchasers. Similarly, the absence of alternative terms capable of adequately describing the pertinent characteristic is also relevant in assessing the commercial justification for the use and hence the scope of permissible fair use.

Similar principles are applicable to personal name trademarks, particularly in light of the lack of alternative terms available to others with similar names. Factors relevant in accessing whether a subsequent user has made a reasonable descriptive use of a personal name include the relative importance in the particular industry or market of identifying the individuals who are connected with a business, the strength of the plaintiff's personal name mark, the subsequent user's good faith, and the presence or absence of precautionary measures calculated to minimize the risk of confusion.

d. Good faith. The fair use defense is applicable only if the descriptive term has been used in good faith. Knowledge of a prior trademark use of the term does not in itself prove a lack of good faith. However, if the evidence establishes that the subsequent user intends to trade on the good will of the trademark owner by creating confusion as to source or sponsorship, the use is not in good faith.

Use by the actor of the precise form of the descriptive term adopted by the trademark owner can be evidence of bad faith when equally useful alternative forms are available. Indeed, if there are other terms equally suited to the legitimate commercial needs of the subsequent user, the prominent use of any form of the particular term in which trademark rights exist may in some circumstances support an inference of bad faith. Similarly, a shift by the actor from other descriptive words to the trademarked term after another's adoption of the term as a trademark can also indicate bad faith. Copying aspects of another's trademark that are unrelated to its descriptive significance, such as lettering style or color, can indicate bad faith, as does evidence of other similarities in labeling or packaging that contribute to the likelihood that the subsequent use will confuse prospective purchasers. A refusal to take reasonable precautions to reduce the risk of confusion can also indicate that the use is not in good faith.

Illustrations:

1. *A* has acquired trademark rights in the designation NATURALLY for organically grown frozen vegetables. *B* markets organically grown frozen vegetables and other products under the trademark "*B* 's PREMIER." *B* 's trademark prominently appears in stylized script on the packaging of *B* 's goods. Below the trademark is a photograph of the cooked product. Beneath the photograph is a generic description of the product preceded by the words "Naturally Grown," such as "Naturally Grown Baby Lima Beans." In the absence of evidence establishing that *B* has not acted in good faith, *B* 's use of the term "naturally" is a fair use under the rule stated in this Section.

2. The facts being otherwise as stated in Illustration 1, *B* instead markets its products under the trademark FROM *B*, NATURALLY. Below the trademark in smaller letters is a generic description of the product, such as "Lima Beans." A photograph of the cooked product occupies the rest of the package. A court may properly conclude that *B* 's use of the term "naturally" is not a use solely to describe *B* 's product and is thus not a fair use under the rule stated in this Section. *B* is then subject to liability for infringement if *A* establishes that it has priority under the rule stated in § 19 and that, despite the descriptive connotations of the term, *B* 's use creates a likelihood of confusion under the rule stated in § 20.

REPORTERS' NOTE

Restatement of Torts § 740, Comment *a* (1938), recognized that in some circumstances the use of a descriptive term that is another's trademark may be understood only in a descriptive rather than a denominative sense, thus creating no likelihood of confusion. This Section goes further, recognizing such fair use as an independent defense to infringement.

Cases on fair use are collected in McCarthy, Trademarks and Unfair Competition § 11.17.

Comment a. "The purpose of the defense is to prevent the trademark rights of one party from being extended to preclude another party from the description of his product to the public." United States Shoe Corp. v. Brown Group Inc., 740 F.Supp. 196, 198 (S.D.N.Y.), affirmed 923 F.2d 844 (2d Cir.1990). Although the fair use doctrine has sometimes been invoked in connection with the use of another's mark as part of the actor's own trademark, see, e.g., Western Pub. Co. v. Rose Art Industries, Inc., 733 F.Supp. 698 (S.D.N.Y.), affirmed on other grounds 910 F.2d 57 (2d Cir.1990), liability in such cases is typically determined under the rules relating to likelihood of confusion as stated in §§ 20–23. Cf., e.g., White Swan, Ltd. v. Nature Co., 26 U.S.P.Q.2d 1290 (D.Or.1993), finding the designation not used as a trademark, but also concluding that even if the use was as a mark, there was no infringement based on the narrow scope of protection accorded to descriptive designations.

The term "fair use" is also occasionally applied to the use of another's trademark for the purpose of referring to the owner of the mark or to the owner's goods or services. See New Kids on the Block v. New America Pub., Inc., 971 F.2d 302 (9th Cir. 1992). However, such a use does not implicate the private and public interest in preserving access to the original lexicographic meaning of descriptive terms and is not within the scope of this Section.

The fair use defense in § 33(b)(4) of the Lanham Act, 15 U.S.C.A. § 1115(b)(4), together with the other § 33(b) defenses, is technically a "defense" only to the conclusive evidentiary effect of an incontestable trademark registration. An incontestable registration that is subject to one of the defenses enumerated in § 33(b) becomes merely prima facie evidence of the registrant's exclusive right to use the mark, and under § 33(a) is then subject to any legal or equitable defenses applicable to unregistered marks. See Park 'N Fly, Inc. v. Dollar Park and Fly, Inc., 469 U.S. 189, 199 n.6, 105 S.Ct. 658, 664 n.6, 83 L.Ed.2d 582, 591 n.6 (1985). The other § 33(b) defenses are fraud in obtaining a registration, use of the mark to misrepresent source, and use to violate the antitrust laws, § 33(b)(1), (3), (7) (see § 32 of this Chapter); abandonment, § 33(b)(2) (see § 30); prior use, § 33(b)(5), (6) (see § 19); and equitable principles including laches, estoppel, and acquiescence, § 33(b)(8) (see §§ 29, 31).

Cases viewing the statutory formulation of fair use in § 33(b)(4) of the Lanham Act as a codification of analogous common law principles include, e.g., M.B.H. Enterprises, Inc. v. WOKY, Inc., 633 F.2d 50 (7th Cir. 1980); Venetianaire Corp. v. A & P Import Co., 429 F.2d 1079 (2d Cir. 1970). See, e.g., Fund of Funds, Ltd. v. First American Fund of Funds, 274 F.Supp. 517 (S.D.N.Y.1967) (common law). The fair use doctrine is also applicable under § 43(a) of the Lanham Act. E.g., Eli Lilly and Co. v. Revlon, Inc., 577 F.Supp. 477 (S.D.N.Y.1983); Robert B. Vance & Associates, Inc. v. Baronet Corp., 487 F.Supp. 790 (N.D.Ga.1979).

Comment b. The case law reflects substantial uncertainty regarding the nature of the fair use doctrine. Many cases apparently view fair use as relevant only to the likelihood of confusion, thus precluding reliance on the doctrine whenever confusion is likely. See, e.g., Lindy Pen Co. v. Bic Pen Corp., 725 F.2d 1240 (9th Cir.1984), cert. denied 469 U.S. 1188, 105 S.Ct. 955, 83 L.Ed.2d 962 (1985); Zatarains, Inc. v. Oak Grove Smokehouse, Inc., 698 F.2d 786 (5th Cir.1983); Cullman Ventures, Inc. v. Columbian Art Works, Inc., 717 F.Supp. 96, 134 (S.D.N.Y.1989) ("The 'fair use' defense does not encompass use that will lead to consumer confusion as to the source or origin of the goods at issue."); Schering Corp. v. Schering Aktiengesellschaft, 667 F.Supp. 175, 189 (D.N.J.1987) ("[A] confusing use of the name is not a fair use of the name."); Byrnes & Keifer Co. v. Flavoripe Co., 1 U.S.P.Q.2d 1124 (W.D.Pa.1986); Glamorene Products Corp. v. Boyle–Midway, Inc., 188 U.S.P.Q. 145 (S.D.N.Y. 1975). Other cases, however, recognize fair use as an independent defense to infringement. "Moreover, we are convinced that even if there were a likelihood of confusion, the defendant would still be entitled to its fair-use defense, so long as it had met the requirements of § 1115(b)(4). To hold otherwise would effectively eviscerate the fair-use defense." Soweco, Inc. v. Shell Oil Co., 617 F.2d 1178, 1189 n.30 (5th Cir.1980), cert. denied 450 U.S. 981, 101 S.Ct. 1516, 67 L.Ed.2d 816 (1981). See, e.g., Frito–Lay, Inc. v. Bachman Co., 704 F.Supp. 432 (S.D.N.Y.1989) (relief precluded "regardless of likelihood of confusion" if the use is fair); Salton Inc. v. Cornwall Corp., 477 F.Supp. 975 (D.N.J.1979) (fair use defense is "available even if there is a likelihood of confusion"); John O. Butler Co. v. Oral B Co., 185 U.S.P.Q. 594 (N.D.Ill. 1975); Laura Secord Candy Shops Ltd. v. Barton's Candy Corp., 368 F.Supp. 851, 853 (N.D.Ill.1973) (if the term "is used not as a trademark, but fairly and in good faith only to describe the product to purchasers, there is no infringement even if such use results in a likelihood of confusion"). Cf., e.g., Venetianaire Corp. v. A & P Import Co., 429 F.2d 1079 (2d Cir.1970) (evaluating a fair use claim despite a likelihood of confusion); Henry Heide, Inc. v. George Ziegler Co., 354 F.2d 574 (7th Cir. 1965) (same). Compare McCarthy, *supra*, § 11.17 ("The better view is that it is inconsistent to find both likely confusion and a fair use.") with Kane, Trademark Law 173 (1987) ("So long as defendant's use is descriptive, in good faith, and not as a trademark, it will be permitted even if it causes likely confusion."). This Section follows those cases that recognize fair use as an independent defense to infringement.

The defendant bears the burden of proving each of the elements of fair use required under this Section. E.g., Burger King Corp. v. Pilgrim's Pride Corp., 705 F.Supp. 1522 (S.D.Fla.1988), affirmed 894 F.2d 412 (11th Cir.1990); Byrnes & Keifer Co., *supra*; Eli Lilly and Co. v. Revlon, Inc., 577 F.Supp. 477 (S.D.N.Y.1983); Salton Inc., *supra*. See, e.g., Venetianaire Corp., *supra* ("defendant has not been able to establish that such use was nevertheless within the purview of the defense claimed").

Comment c. On the requirement that the term be descriptive of the goods, services, or business of the subsequent user, see, e.g., Zatarains, Inc. v. Oak Grove Smokehouse, Inc., 698 F.2d 786 (5th Cir.1983); Soweco, Inc. v. Shell Oil Co., 617 F.2d 1178 (5th Cir.1980), cert. denied 450 U.S. 981, 101 S.Ct. 1516, 67 L.Ed.2d 816 (1981); Pure Foods, Inc. v. Minute Maid Corp., 214 F.2d 792 (5th Cir.), cert. denied 348 U.S. 888, 75 S.Ct. 208, 99 L.Ed. 697 (1954); Charles of the Ritz Group, Ltd. v. Marcon, Ltd., 635 F.Supp. 158 (S.D.N.Y.1986) ("Silk" is part of the vocabulary of the cosmetics industry).

Use in textual descriptions is ordinarily a fair use. See, e.g., Kiki Undies Corp. v. Alexander's Department Stores, Inc., 390 F.2d 604 (2d Cir. 1968) (description of clothing as "kicky" in newspaper advertising did not infringe KIKI trademark for clothing); United States Shoe Corp. v. Brown Group, Inc., 740 F.Supp. 196 (S.D.N.Y.), affirmed 923 F.2d 844 (2d Cir.1990) (use of a portion of the plaintiff's slogan in text held a fair use); Fund of Funds, Ltd. v. First American Fund of Funds, 274 F.Supp. 517 (S.D.N.Y.1967) (enjoining use of plaintiff's FUND OF FUNDS trade name as part of defendant's trade name, but permitting use in descriptions of defendant's business).

Even a prominent use of a descriptive term that is another's trademark may qualify as a fair use. E.g., WCVB–TV v. Boston Athletic Association, 926 F.2d 42 (1st Cir.1991) (prominent use of plaintiff's BOSTON MARATHON trademark during defendant's unauthorized broadcast of the race held a fair use); Eli Lilly and Co. v. Revlon, Inc., 577 F.Supp. 477, 486 (S.D.N.Y.1983) ("Emphasis of a descriptive term on packaging does not show that the term is being used as a trademark."); see Citrus Group, Inc. v. Cadbury Beverages, Inc., 781 F.Supp. 386 (D.Md.1991) (use to attract public attention is not necessarily use as trademark); Schmid Laboratories v. Youngs Drug Products Corp., 482 F.Supp. 14 (D.N.J.1979) (same). The comparative appearance of the term with other descriptive matter is relevant in determining whether the term has been used descriptively or as a trademark. See, e.g., Beer Nuts, Inc. v. Clover Club Foods Co., 711 F.2d 934 (10th Cir.1983) (noting that the term was visually distinct from the generic description of the product); Tree Tavern Products, Inc. v. Conagra, Inc., 640 F.Supp. 1263 (D.Del.1986); Venetianaire Corp. v. A & P Import Co., 302 F.Supp. 156 (S.D.N.Y.1969), affirmed 429 F.2d 1079 (2d Cir.1970). Cf. Sands, Taylor & Wood Co. v. Quaker Oats Co., 978 F.2d 947 (7th Cir.1992), cert. denied ___ U.S. ___, 113 S.Ct. 1879, 123 L.Ed.2d 497 (1993) (rejecting a fair use defense when the term was used by the defendant as part of "a memorable slogan that is uniquely associated" with the defendant's product).

The prominent display by the defendant of its own trademark may reduce the likelihood that the use of the term will be understood in a denominative rather than a descriptive sense. See, e.g., M.B.H. Enterprises, Inc. v. WOKY, Inc., 633 F.2d 50 (7th Cir.1980); United States Shoe Corp., *supra;* Charles of the Ritz Group, Ltd. v. Marcon, Ltd., 635 F.Supp. 158 (S.D.N.Y.1986); Mem Co. v. Yardley of London, Inc., 212 U.S.P.Q. 280 (S.D.N.Y.1981); Schmid Laboratories, *supra.* But see, e.g., Sands, Taylor & Wood Co., *supra;* Tree Tavern Products, *supra;* and Salton Inc. v. Cornwall Corp., 477 F.Supp. 975 (D.N.J.1979), each finding that the defendant had not made a fair use of plaintiff's descriptive designation despite the prominent use of the defendant's own mark. Cf. Frito–Lay, Inc. v. Bachman Co., 704 F.Supp. 432 (S.D.N.Y.1989) (denying defendant's motion for summary judgment despite the prominent use of its own trademark). Use of another's descriptive trademark as part of the defendant's trade name can constitute an infringing use of the designation. See, e.g., Safeway Stores, Inc. v. Safeway Properties, Inc., 307 F.2d 495 (2d Cir.1962); Fund of Funds, Ltd. v. First American Fund of Funds, 274 F.Supp. 517 (S.D.N.Y. 1967). Even use as part of a trade name, however, has sometimes been held to be a fair use if the term is used merely to describe the nature of the defendant's business. See Leathersmith of London, Ltd. v. Alleyn, 695 F.2d 27 (1st Cir.1982), cert. denied 459 U.S. 1209, 103 S.Ct. 1202, 75 L.Ed.2d 444 (1983) (TANTALUS CUSTOM LEATHERSMITHS &

BOOKBINDERS held fair use of plaintiff's LEATHERSMITH trademark); Coherent, Inc. v. Coherent Technologies, Inc., 736 F.Supp. 1055 (D.Colo.1990), affirmed 935 F.2d 1122 (10th Cir.1991) (COHERENT TECHNOLOGIES found a fair use of defendant's COHERENT trademark); American Olean Tile Co. v. American Marazzi Tile, Inc., 9 U.S.P.Q.2d 1145 (E.D.Pa.1988) (use of plaintiff's AMERICAN trademark in defendant's AMERICAN MARAZZI trade name held to be a descriptive use).

The classic analysis of the limits of trademark rights in geographically descriptive designations is Judge Holmes' opinion in American Waltham Watch Co. v. United States Watch Co., 173 Mass. 85, 86–87, 53 N.E. 141, 142 (1899). "It is desirable that the plaintiff should not lose custom by reason of the public mistaking another manufacturer for it. It is desirable that the defendant should be free to manufacture watches at Waltham, and to tell the world that it does so. The two desiderata cannot both be had to their full extent, and we have to fix the boundaries as best we can." See, e.g., Schafer Co. v. Innco Management Corp., 797 F.Supp. 477 (E.D.N.C.1992), affirmed 995 F.2d 1064 (4th Cir.1993); American Olean Tile, *supra*. Cf. Genadeen Caterers v. Hotel Genadeen, 95 N.Y.S.2d 196 (Sup.), affirmed 277 App.Div. 892, 98 N.Y.S.2d 290 (1950) (use of a hotel name in a business address did not violate an injunction against use of the hotel name as part of defendant's trade name).

On the permissible fair use of personal names to indicate truthfully a connection with the named individual, see, e.g., Taylor Wine Co. v. Bully Hill Vineyards, Inc., 569 F.2d 731 (2d Cir.), appeal after remand 590 F.2d 701 (2d Cir.,1978) (enjoining use as a trademark, but permitting use to show individual's connection with the corporate defendant); Crane Co. v. Crane Heating & Air Conditioning Co., 299 F.2d 577 (6th Cir.1962); Gucci v. Gucci Shops, Inc., 688 F.Supp. 916 (S.D.N.Y.1988) (enjoining trademark use but permitting use to show individual's connection with goods sold under other trademarks). Cf., e.g., Jerrico, Inc. v. Jerry's, Inc., 376 F.Supp. 1079 (S.D.Fla.1974) (defendant's use of the name as a trademark precluded a fair use defense).

Comment d. Knowledge of the prior use does not in itself establish bad faith. See, e.g., M.B.H. Enterprises, Inc. v. WOKY, Inc., 633 F.2d 50 (7th Cir.1980); United States Shoe Corp. v. Brown Group, Inc., 740 F.Supp. 196 (S.D.N.Y.), affirmed 923 F.2d 844 (2d Cir.1990); Wonder Labs, Inc. v. Procter & Gamble Co., 728 F.Supp. 1058 (S.D.N.Y.1990); Schmid Laboratories v. Youngs Drug Products Corp., 482 F.Supp. 14 (D.N.J.1979). But cf. Frito–Lay, Inc. v. Bachman Co., 704 F.Supp. 432 (S.D.N.Y.1989) (knowledge of pre-existing use can raise an inference of bad faith).

Use of an exact copy of a descriptive trademark without commercial justification can indicate an intent to trade on the good will of the prior user. Sierra On–Line, Inc. v. Phoenix Software, Inc., 739 F.2d 1415 (9th Cir.1984) (HI–RES ADVENTURE on computer games). The existence of adequate alternatives to the trademarked term is often cited as a factor supporting rejection of a fair use defense. See, e.g., Frito–Lay, Inc., *supra*; Salton Inc. v. Cornwall Corp., 477 F.Supp. 975 (D.N.J.1979); Glamorene Products Corp. v. Boyle–Midway, Inc., 188 U.S.P.Q. 145 (S.D.N.Y. 1975). The lack of adequate alternatives was cited as a factor favoring a finding of fair use in Mem Co. v. Yardley of London, Inc., 212 U.S.P.Q. 280 (S.D.N.Y.1981) ("leather" scent). Cf. White Swan, Ltd. v. Nature Co., 26 U.S.P.Q.2d 1290 (D.Or.1993) (finding that the terms used by the defendant "are the only words reasonably available to describe defendant's product"). A shift to the trademarked term following its adoption as a mark by another can indicate a lack of good faith. See Burger King Corp. v. Pilgrim's Pride Corp., 705 F.Supp. 1522 (S.D.Fla.1988), affirmed 894 F.2d 412 (11th Cir.1990). Copying the typestyle of plaintiff's trademark or other packaging or labelling features unrelated to the descriptive significance of the designation can also create an inference of bad faith. Compare Venetianaire Corp. v. A & P Import Co., 429 F.2d 1079 (2d Cir. 1970) (duplication of typestyle and packaging) with Andy Warhol Enterprises, Inc. v. Time Inc., 700 F.Supp. 760 (S.D.N.Y.1988) (plaintiff's stylized version of trademark was not copied). Cf., e.g., Zatarains, Inc. v. Oak Grove Smokehouse, Inc., 698 F.2d 786 (5th Cir.1983), noting that differences in packaging and labelling can support a defense of fair use by minimizing the risk of confusion. An attempt by the subsequent user to claim trademark rights in the term indicates that the use is intended to signify source and is thus not merely a descriptive use. Girls Clubs of America, Inc. v. Boys Clubs of America, Inc., 683 F.Supp. 50 (S.D.N.Y.), affirmed 859 F.2d 148 (2d Cir.1988).

Illustrations 1 and 2 are suggested by examples in Tree Tavern Products, Inc. v. Conagra, Inc., 640 F.Supp. 1263 (D.Del.1986).

§ 29. Consent

In an action for infringement of a trademark, trade name, collective mark, or certification mark, it is a defense that the actor's use is within the scope of the owner's consent as manifested by an agreement between the parties or by other conduct from which the owner's consent can reasonably be inferred.

Comment:

a. Nature of consent. Consent is a willingness on the part of a trademark owner for another to make a specific use of the same or a similar designation. Such willingness is normally manifested through an agreement that licenses or assigns the owner's rights, see §§ 33 and 34, or otherwise expresses the owner's consent to the other's use. Consent can also be manifested by other conduct or inaction on the part of the trademark owner such as a failure to object to the other's use of the designation.

Words, conduct, or inaction can be effective as a manifestation of consent even if the trademark owner does not in fact intend to consent to the use if a reasonable person in the position of the other party would understand the owner's conduct to indicate consent and it is in fact so interpreted by the other. Such consent is effective, however, only with respect to uses of which the trademark owner was or should have been aware at the time of the apparent consent.

The consent of the trademark owner precludes the imposition of liability only with respect to uses within the scope of the consent. Whether particular conduct is within the scope of the consent is determined according to the general principles applicable to the interpretation of agreements. See Restatement, Second, Contracts, Chapter 10 (1981). If the consent is restricted to use of the designation in a particular form, or on particular goods or services, or in particular geographic markets, it is effective only within the limits of the restriction. If an actor's use is beyond the scope of the consent given by the trademark owner, the actor may be subject to liability for the harm resulting from the conduct that exceeds the consent. If it is impossible as a practical matter to separate the harm resulting from such conduct from harm caused by the consented use, the actor is subject to liability for the entire harm.

b. Express consent. A trademark owner can consent to the use of its mark by another through an agreement in the form of an assignment, license, or statement of consent to a specified use. Use of the designation within the scope of an enforceable agreement expressing consent does not subject the user to liability for infringement.

An assignment seeks to transfer the trademark owner's rights in the mark to an assignee, thus giving the assignee the benefit of the assignor's priority over third persons in the use of the designation. An assignment is effective to transfer the assignor's priority only if the transaction includes a transfer of the line of business associated with the designation as required under the rule stated in § 34. However, even an assignment that is ineffective to transfer the assignor's priority operates as an expression of consent to the assignee's use of the designation.

A license authorizes the licensee to exploit the good will associated with the designation through a use that prospective purchasers are likely to attribute to the trademark owner. Use of the designation by a licensee accrues to the benefit of the trademark owner only if the owner exercises reasonable control over the licensee's use as required under the rule stated in § 33. However, even in the absence of reasonable control a license to use the designation is effective as an expression of the trademark owner's consent to the licensee's use.

In some instances an agreement, however labelled, is intended merely to resolve a conflict between two users of the same or similar marks by delineating their respective rights. Unlike a license, such a consent agreement does not contemplate that the use of the mark by one party will be attributed by the public to the other. The agreement serves instead to limit the risk of confusion by controlling the manner in which the designation is used by one or both of the parties. Consent agreements provide a useful vehicle for the settlement of existing or potential disputes involving trademark rights. Within broad limits, the parties to such an agreement are free to determine the scope of their respective rights. However, if the use permitted under a consent agreement is likely to cause substantial confusion that threatens significant harm to consumers, the agreement may be unenforceable as a matter of public policy. The agreement will not then preclude the issuance of an injunction against a continuation of the confusing use, although the parties to the agreement may be estopped from obtaining monetary relief for infringement. An agreement consenting to a clearly confusing use may also be interpreted as an unsupervised license or an assignment in gross, thus endangering the continued validity of the trademark under the rules stated in §§ 33 and 34. However, the fact that those most familiar with the significance of the designation in the marketplace have indicated by their consent that the agreed uses are not confusing is itself evidence that substantial confusion is unlikely.

c. Implied consent and relation to laches. The consent of the trademark owner may be expressed in words or inferred from other conduct. In situations in which consent is inferred from conduct, courts sometimes state that the trademark owner is estopped by its "acquiescence" from obtaining relief. When the conduct from which such acquiescence is inferred consists solely of the trademark owner's failure to institute litigation or otherwise object to a known use by the actor, the rule stated in this Section overlaps the principle of laches described in § 31. Some trademark infringement cases thus speak synonymously of "acquiescence" and "laches." However, when acquiescence is inferred instead from affirmative conduct of the trademark owner such as expressions of encouragement to the actor or business proposals fairly implying consent, the actor may have a defense under this Section without regard to the lack of reasonable diligence on the part of the trademark owner necessary to establish laches under § 31. As in the case of laches, however, the public interest in preventing the confusion of prospective purchasers may sometimes preclude recognition of a defense founded on acquiescence, at least with respect to injunctive relief against a continuation of the defendant's confusing use. See Comment *d*.

d. Duration of consent. Consent precludes the imposition of liability for acts occurring while the consent is effective. If the consent is terminated, an actor has no defense with respect to any use of the trademark subsequent to the termination. Consent is terminated when the actor knows or has reason to know that the trademark owner is no longer willing to permit the particular use. The unwillingness may be manifested by words or by conduct inconsistent with continued consent, such as the commencement of an infringement action. However, if the trademark owner is estopped or otherwise precluded from withdrawing its consent, an attempted termination of consent is not effective.

A trademark owner may be precluded from terminating its consent by the express or implied terms of an agreement with the actor. The trademark owner may also be estopped from terminating the consent if the termination would be inequitable because of the actor's reasonable reliance, evaluated in light of the specific terms of any agreement between the parties. In some circumstances termination of consent may also be precluded by statute or case law restricting the termination of franchise licensing agreements in the absence of proper cause.

When consent is based solely on an inference arising from the trademark owner's conduct, the strength of the inference is relevant in determining whether the actor's reliance is sufficient to create an estoppel against subsequent termination of the consent. If the inference of consent rests on mere silence or inaction on the part of the trademark owner, for example, substantial reliance may be necessary to preclude liability for continued use of the designation after an objection by the owner. See also § 31, Comment *b*. The public interest in preventing the deception of consumers is also relevant in determining whether a trademark owner should be estopped from withdrawing its consent. The threat of substantial harm to consumers may outweigh the actor's reliance interest, thus justifying an injunction against the continuation of a confusing use. In such cases the legitimate interests of the actor may sometimes be protected to the extent compatible with the public interest by permitting continued use of the designation with disclaimers or other precautionary measures. See also § 31, Comment *e*.

REPORTERS' NOTE

This Section is an expansion of the former statement of the rule in Restatement of Torts § 754 (1938). On the general concept of consent, see Restatement, Second, Torts §§ 892 and 892A (1979). On consent and acquiescence in trademark law, see Gilson, Trademark Protection and

Practice § 8.12[12][m]; McCarthy, Trademarks and Unfair Competition §§ 18.25, 31.14.

Comment a. On the means by which consent may be manifested, see generally Restatement, Second, Torts § 892. Use beyond the scope of consent can subject the user to liability for infringement. See, e.g., Waukesha Hygeia Mineral Springs Co. v. Hygeia Sparkling Distilled Water Co., 63 Fed. 438 (7th Cir.1894) (violation of consent agreement); Professional Golfers Association v. Bankers Life & Casualty Co., 514 F.2d 665 (5th Cir.1975) (use beyond the term of the license); Franchised Stores, Inc. v. Winter, 394 F.2d 664 (2d Cir. 1968) (use by licensee on unauthorized goods); Baskin–Robbins Ice Cream Co. v. D & L Ice Cream Co., 576 F.Supp. 1055 (E.D.N.Y.1983) (same).

Comment b. In addition to operating as an expression of consent, an assignment that is ineffective to transfer the assignor's priority may nevertheless prevent continued use of the mark by the assignor. See Replogle v. Air–Way Co., 287 Fed. 765 (D.C.Cir.1923); Russia Cement Co. v. Le Page, 147 Mass. 206, 17 N.E. 304 (1888) ("It is not upon the ground of the invasion of the trade-name adopted by another, but by reason of the contract he has made, that he is deprived of the right himself to use his name as all others of the same name may use theirs."). See also McCarthy, *supra*, § 18.04[1].

On the distinction between a license and a mere consent to use, see, e.g., Moore Business Forms, Inc. v. Ryu, 960 F.2d 486 (5th Cir.1992); In re Mastic Inc., 829 F.2d 1114 (Fed. Cir.1987); Waukesha Hygeia Mineral Springs Co. v. Hygeia Sparkling Distilled Water Co., 63 Fed. 438 (7th Cir.1894); Universal City Studios, Inc. v. Nintendo Co., 578 F.Supp. 911 (S.D.N.Y.1983), affirmed on other grounds 746 F.2d 112 (2d Cir.1984) (noting the possibility that a consent agreement could be an uncontrolled license that threatens the continued validity of the mark); McCarthy, *supra*, § 18.25.

Consent agreements have been admitted as evidence that a similar use of the designation by a third person is not likely to cause confusion. See, e.g., Swedish Beer Export Co. Aktiebolag v. Canada Dry Corp., 469 F.2d 1096 (C.C.P.A.1972); Croton Watch Co. v. Laughlin, 208 F.2d 93 (2d Cir. 1953); California Fruit Growers Exchange v. Sunkist Baking Co., 166 F.2d 971 (7th Cir.1947); Universal City Studios, *supra.*

In T & T Manufacturing Co. v. A.T. Cross Co., 449 F.Supp. 813 (D.R.I.), affirmed 587 F.2d 533 (1st Cir.1978), cert. denied 441 U.S. 908, 99 S.Ct. 2000, 60 L.Ed.2d 377 (1979), the court indicated that consent agreements that injure the public by creating confusion may be unenforceable as a matter of public policy, but found on the facts that the actor's reliance interest and the public interest in enforcing contracts outweighed any threatened harm to consumers. See also VISA International Service Association v. Bankcard Holders of America, 784 F.2d 1472 (9th Cir. 1986). Although a consent agreement is evidence of a lack of confusion between the respective uses, it is not conclusive. Compare In re Four Seasons Hotels Ltd., 987 F.2d 1565 (Fed.Cir.1993) and In re E.I. DuPont DeNemours & Co., 476 F.2d 1357 (C.C.P.A.1973) with In re Mastic Inc., 829 F.2d 1114 (Fed.Cir.1987), each indicating that agreements incorporating restrictions designed to avoid confusion are entitled to greater weight than "naked" consents. Similarly, because of the public interest in avoiding confusion, acquiescence will not ordinarily preclude an objection to trademark registration if the likelihood of confusion is clear. Ultra–White Co. v. Johnson Chemical Industries, Inc., 465 F.2d 891 (C.C.P.A. 1972); CBS Inc. v. Man's Day Pub. Co., 205 U.S.P.Q. 470 (Tm.Tr.App.Bd. 1980). Cf. Coach House Restaurant, Inc. v. Coach and Six Restaurants, Inc., 934 F.2d 1551 (11th Cir.1991) (inevitability of public confusion would preclude defendant's estoppel by acquiescence defense to plaintiff's infringement claim).

Comment c. Cases equating laches and acquiescence inferred from a delay in objecting to the defendant's use include, e.g., Menendez v. Holt, 128 U.S. 514, 9 S.Ct. 143, 32 L.Ed. 526 (1888); Conan Properties, Inc. v. Conans Pizza, Inc., 752 F.2d 145 (5th Cir.1985); University of Pittsburgh v. Champion Products Inc., 686 F.2d 1040 (3d Cir.), cert. denied 459 U.S. 1087, 103 S.Ct. 571, 74 L.Ed.2d 933 (1982). "When silence is the basis of alleged acquiescence, the doctrines of 'acquiescence and laches blend together.'" Piper Aircraft Corp. v. Wag–Aero, Inc., 741 F.2d 925, 937 (7th Cir.1984). Other cases maintain a distinction between the doctrines. "As distinguished from laches, acquiescence constitutes a ground for denial of relief only upon a finding of conduct on the plaintiff's part that amounted to an assurance to the defendant, express or implied, that the plaintiff would not assert his trademark rights against the defendant." Carl Zeiss Stiftung v. V.E.B. Carl Zeiss, Jena, 293 F.Supp. 892, 917 (S.D.N.Y.1968), affirmed 433 F.2d 686 (2d Cir.1970), cert. denied 403 U.S. 905, 91 S.Ct. 2205, 29 L.Ed.2d 680 (1971). See, e.g., Elvis Presley Enterprises, Inc. v. Elvisly Yours, Inc., 936 F.2d 889 (6th Cir.1991). The distinction is important when acquiescence is inferred from conduct other than mere silence since such conduct can provide a defense without regard to any delay or lack of diligence on the part of the trademark owner. Consent has been inferred from business proposals and transactions between the parties, National Ass'n for the Advancement of Colored People v. N.A.A.C.P. Legal Defense & Educational Fund, Inc., 753 F.2d 131 (D.C.Cir.), cert. denied 472 U.S. 1021, 105 S.Ct. 3489, 87 L.Ed.2d 623 (1985); Ambrosia Chocolate Co. v. Ambrosia Cake Bakery, Inc., 165 F.2d 693 (4th Cir.1947), cert. denied 333 U.S. 882, 68 S.Ct. 914, 92 L.Ed. 1157 (1948); Dwinell–Wright Co. v. White House Milk Co., 132 F.2d 822 (2d Cir.1943), the discontinuance of litigation, Anheuser–Busch, Inc. v. Du Bois Brewing Co., 175 F.2d 370 (3d Cir.1949), cert. denied 339 U.S. 934, 70 S.Ct. 664, 94 L.Ed. 1353 (1950), and letters of encouragement or good wishes from the trademark owner, Conan Properties, *supra*; Saratoga Vichy Spring Co. v. Lehman, 625 F.2d 1037 (2d Cir.1980).

Comment d. Consent is a defense only with respect to acts undertaken prior to an effective termination of the consent. See, e.g., Menendez v. Holt, 128 U.S. 514, 9 S.Ct. 143, 32 L.Ed. 526 (1888); S & R Corp. v. Jiffy Lube Int'l, Inc., 968 F.2d 371 (3d Cir.1992) (injunction against use by franchisee after termination of the franchise agreement); Conan Properties, Inc. v. Conans Pizza, Inc., 752 F.2d 145 (5th Cir.1985). The actor's reliance on the consent or acquiescence of the trademark owner, however, may create an estoppel precluding an effective termination of the consent. See, e.g., Coach House Restaurant, Inc. v. Coach and Six Restaurants, Inc., 934 F.2d 1551 (11th Cir.1991); Saratoga Vichy Spring Co. v. Lehman, 625 F.2d 1037 (2d Cir.1980); Anheuser-Busch, Inc. v. Du Bois Brewing Co., 175 F.2d 370 (3d Cir.1949), cert. denied 339 U.S. 934, 70 S.Ct. 664, 94 L.Ed. 1353 (1950); Ambrosia Chocolate Co. v. Ambrosia Cake Bakery, Inc., 165 F.2d 693 (4th Cir.1947), cert. denied 333 U.S. 882, 68 S.Ct. 914, 92 L.Ed. 1157 (1948); Dwinell-Wright Co. v. White House Milk Co., 132 F.2d 822 (2d Cir.1943). See also Conan Properties, *supra* (reliance on consent does not preclude injunctive relief outside the geographic scope of the consent); Piper Aircraft Corp. v. Wag-Aero, Inc., 741 F.2d 925 (7th Cir.1984) (actor's reliance must be reasonable).

Decisions in some states limit the ability of a licensor to terminate a franchise agreement in the absence of good cause. See, e.g., Mariniello v. Shell Oil Co., 511 F.2d 853 (3d Cir. 1975). The constitutionality of statutory limitations on franchise terminations has been upheld in several cases. See, e.g., Kealey Pharmacy & Home Care Services, Inc. v. Walgreen Co., 761 F.2d 345 (7th Cir. 1985). The state statutes are collected in International Trademark Association, State Trademark and Unfair Competition Law. For examples of federal statutes restricting the termination of certain franchise relationships, see 15 U.S.C.A. §§ 1221–25 (automobile dealers); 15 U.S.C.A. §§ 2801–06 (petroleum marketing franchises).

§ 30. Abandonment

(1) In an action for infringement of a trademark, trade name, collective mark, or certification mark, it is a defense that the designation was abandoned by the party asserting rights in the designation prior to the commencement of use by the actor.

(2) A trademark, trade name, collective mark, or certification mark is abandoned if:

(a) the party asserting rights in the designation has ceased to use the designation with an intent not to resume use; or

(b) the designation has lost its significance as a trademark, trade name, collective mark, or certification mark as a result of a cessation of use or other acts or omissions by the party asserting rights in the designation.

Comment:

a. Consequences of abandonment. The priority acquired through the use of a designation as a trademark, trade name, collective mark, or certification mark under the rules stated in §§ 18 and 19 is lost if the designation is abandoned. Abandonment is thus a defense to a claim of infringement brought against a use of the designation occurring subsequent to the abandonment by the prior user. The defense is applicable to infringement claims at common law and to claims for the infringement of marks registered under the Lanham Act, even if the federal registration has become incontestable. 15 U.S.C.A. § 1115(b)(2). Abandonment is also grounds for the cancellation of a trademark registration under both the Lanham Act and the Model State Trademark Bill. *Id.* § 1064(3); Model Bill § 9(3)(a) (1992). The party asserting abandonment bears the burden of proving the elements necessary to establish the defense under this Section.

A federal trademark registration provides nationwide priority against subsequent users without regard to the actual geographic scope of the registrant's use. See § 19, Comment *e*. Priority in the use of a trademark registered under the Act is not lost unless the designation is abandoned throughout the nation. Priority at common law, however, extends only to the geographic areas in which the trademark owner uses the designation or in which the designation is associated with the trademark owner. *Id.*, Comment *b*. Common law priority in a particular geographic area is thus lost if the designation has been abandoned by the owner in that geographic area.

If the original owner resumes use of a designation that has been abandoned under the rules stated in this Section, the owner's priority under § 19 is determined solely on the basis of the subsequent use. If another user has acquired rights in the abandoned designation prior to the resumption of use by the original owner, the original owner may thus be subject to liability for infringement under the rule stated in § 20.

Rights may be acquired in an abandoned designation under the same principles applicable to other designations. A subsequent user claiming rights in the designation must therefore satisfy the usual requirements relating to use, see § 18, and distinctiveness, see § 13. Thus, if the designation is inherently distinctive or retains the distinctiveness acquired through its previous use, a subsequent user can acquire rights in the designation upon use in the ordinary course of business. See § 18. If the abandoned designation is a personal name or descriptive designation that has lost its former significance as a trademark, a subsequent user can acquire rights in the designation only upon proof that the designation has again acquired secondary meaning as an indication of source or sponsorship. See § 14.

A designation that has been abandoned under the rule stated in Subsection (2)(a) may for a time retain its significance as an indication of association with the former user. During the period of this residual significance, use of the designation by another is likely to be perceived by prospective purchasers as an indication of association with the former user. Unless the subsequent user adequately distinguishes its use of the designation from the use by the original owner, the subsequent use is likely to deceive prospective purchasers with respect to the source or sponsorship of the goods or services. Rights acquired in the designation by the subsequent user may then be limited under the rules relating to unclean hands as stated in § 32. Although a subsequent user of an abandoned mark will not be subject to liability for trademark infringement, use of an abandoned designation in a manner likely to deceive or mislead a significant number of prospective purchasers may subject the user to liability to the former owner under the general rule proscribing misrepresentations of source stated in § 4. Subsequent users, although free to use the abandoned designation, may thus be required to take precautions necessary to avoid a likelihood of confusion if the designation retains its association with the former owner.

Illustrations:

1. *A* sells wood polish under the trademark SHEILA. For several years *A* sold its product only in California. *A* then opened a distribution facility in Chicago and began to sell the product in Illinois. *A* later closed the Chicago distribution facility and ceased sales in Illinois, and the trademark is no longer associated with *A* in that area. In the absence of rights arising from a federal trademark registration, *A* has abandoned the designation in Illinois and no longer has priority in the use of the designation in that area.

2. *A* used the trademark SMITH on cosmetics. When *A* subsequently changed to another trademark and announced that it did not intend to resume use of the SMITH mark, *B* immediately commenced use of SMITH on its own cosmetics. Despite the abandonment of the designation by *A*, if *B* 's use of the mark is likely to confuse prospective purchasers because of the mark's continuing association with *A*, *B* 's rights in the designation may be limited under the rule relating to unclean hands. See § 32, Comment *b*. *B* may also be subject to liability to *A* for deceptive marketing under the rule stated in § 4.

b. Cessation of use with intent not to resume. A trademark owner has ceased to use a mark under the rule stated in this Section if the owner no longer makes bona fide use of the designation in the ordinary course of business; mere token use made for the purpose of maintaining trademark rights is not sufficient. See § 18, Comment *c*.

Similarly, the intent to resume use necessary to avoid abandonment is an intention to resume bona fide use of the designation in the ordinary course of business.

A change by the trademark owner in the form or appearance of a trademark will not result in abandonment if the new format continues the same commercial impression as the prior format. A change in the kind of goods or services marketed under the trademark is not an abandonment of the trademark owner's priority if the new goods or services are sufficiently related to the original goods or services such that prospective purchasers are likely to perceive the new product as originating from the same source as the original product. Similarly, a cessation of use with an intent to resume use on a related product is not an abandonment. If the trademark owner has used the same mark on unrelated goods or services, a cessation of use on one product with an intent not to resume use will not result in a loss of priority with respect to use on the other products.

Early cases, drawing on an analogy to the abandonment of tangible property, sometimes held that trademark rights were lost as a result of a cessation of use only if the trademark owner intended to abandon its rights. More recent decisions, influenced by the definition of abandonment in § 45 of the Lanham Act, 15 U.S.C.A. § 1127, emphasize that a subjective intent not to abandon ownership is insufficient to preserve trademark rights. Rights in a designation that is no longer in use are lost if the evidence establishes that the trademark owner does not intend to resume use of the mark, notwithstanding an intent or desire by the owner to retain the right to prevent use of the designation by others. If the cessation of use has caused the designation to lose its association with the former user, even an intent to resume use is insufficient to maintain trademark rights. See Comment *c*.

The intent not to resume use of a designation may sometimes be explicit, as in the case of an express announcement of abandonment by the owner of a trademark. More typically, the owner's intentions regarding the resumption of use must be inferred from the circumstances surrounding the cessation of use. A prolonged cessation of use can itself justify an inference that there is no intent to resume use of the designation. The strength of the inference increases with the duration of nonuse. Under the Lanham Act, nonuse for the statutory period specified in § 45 is prima facie evidence of abandonment. 15 U.S.C.A. § 1127. The statutory presumption has been interpreted to shift to the former user the burden of producing evidence of an intent to resume use. The presumption is also sometimes invoked with respect to the abandonment of rights in unregistered marks.

The reason for the cessation of use is relevant in assessing the intentions of the former user. Forced suspensions of use due to temporary factors beyond the control of the trademark owner such as natural disasters, war, or temporary legal prohibitions are ordinarily not sufficient to justify an inference that the owner does not intend to resume use of the designation. Similarly, nonuse caused by a lack of demand for the goods or services ordinarily can be overcome by evidence of continuing marketing efforts on the part of the trademark owner. Other explanations for a cessation of use, such as a suspension of marketing to permit redesign or improvement, also can indicate an intention to resume use.

Trademark rights can be maintained through the use of the designation by licensees or assignees. See §§ 33 and 34. Thus, efforts to license or assign the mark by an owner who has discontinued its own use are evidence of an intent to resume use. In the absence of such efforts, however, evidence that the former user has withdrawn from the business in which the mark was used will ordinarily justify the conclusion that there is no intent to resume use. Similarly, although a failure to object to unauthorized use by others will not necessarily result in abandonment, see Comment *c*, in some circumstances it may indicate that the former user does not intend to resume its own use of the designation.

A trademark may retain significant good will despite a period of nonuse. A finding of abandonment can therefore result in the forfeiture of valuable rights and can also create the potential for confusion as to the source of goods or services by allowing use of the designation by others. Thus, to support a finding of abandonment, a court may properly require clear and convincing evidence of the former user's intent not to resume use of the mark.

Illustration:

3. *A*, a Canadian brewer, sold beer in New England under the trademark SCHOONER. In 1968, *A* modernized its brewery, but the new equipment could not process bottles capable of accommodating the labelling requirements applicable to sales in the United States. *A* then discontinued sales in New England while it sought approval to use its Canadian bottles in the United States. *A* also continued to advertise its beer in travel magazines distributed in New England and on radio stations heard in the area. Because of *A* 's marketing activities, the designation continued to be associated by consumers in New England with *A* 's product. In 1975, *A* resumed sales in New England. A court may properly conclude that the trademark was not abandoned by *A*.

c. Loss of trademark significance. A designation is protectable as a trademark only if it identifies the goods or services of the user. See §§ 9–13. If the trademark owner ceases to use the mark in the ordinary course of business, the required association between the designation and the owner may gradually erode. If the period of nonuse is sufficiently long, the designation may lose its significance as an indication of source or sponsorship. Under the rule stated in Subsection (2)(b), the designation is then abandoned.

When a designation has lost its significance as a trademark because of a cessation of use, abandonment is often found by inferring an intent on the part of the former owner not to resume use. See Comment *b*. Under the rule as stated in this Section, however, abandonment may be found if the designation has lost its significance as a trademark due to a cessation of use without regard to the intentions of the former user. Any facts probative of the continuing significance of the designation in the marketplace, such as the length of nonuse or the willingness of others to purchase rights in the mark, are relevant to a determination of abandonment under Subsection (2)(b).

A trademark owner's failure to take action against the unauthorized use of its trademark by third persons can result in an abandonment of the mark, but only if the unauthorized use is so widespread that the designation loses its significance as an indication of source or sponsorship. More typically, the fact of third-party use is relevant only to the "strength" of the mark, and hence to its appropriate scope of protection. See § 21, Comment *i*.

Other acts or omissions by the trademark owner may also cause the designation to loss its significance as a trademark, thus resulting in abandonment under the rule stated in Subsection (2)(b). On abandonment resulting from uncontrolled licensing, see § 33; on abandonment resulting from an assignment in gross, see § 34. Trademark rights are also lost if the mark becomes the generic name for the goods or services with which it is used. See § 15(2).

Illustration:

4. *A* publishes a magazine entitled INFORMATION PLEASE, but discontinues publication after several issues because of poor sales. For 18 months *A* attempts without success to find new investors in order to resume publication. *B* then adopts the name for a radio program. In subsequent litigation between *A* and *B*, the evidence establishes that at the time *B* commenced use of the name the public no longer associated the designation with *A* or *A* 's magazine. The designation has been abandoned by

A regardless of any intent by *A* to resume use. *B* thus has priority over *A* in the use of the designation.

REPORTERS' NOTE

This Section combines the analysis of abandonment appearing in Restatement of Torts §§ 752–753 (1938). See generally Gilson, Trademark Protection and Practice § 3.06; McCarthy, Trademarks and Unfair Competition §§ 17.01–10.

Comment a. A trademark that is the subject of an incontestable registration under the Lanham Act cannot be challenged on grounds of a lack of distinctiveness, see § 13, Comment *a*, but abandonment, including loss of distinctiveness resulting from the acts or omissions of the trademark owner, remains an available defense. 15 U.S.C.A. § 1115(b)(2).

Abandonment of a mark registered under the Lanham Act occurs "only when the registrant fails to use his mark * * * anywhere in the nation." Dawn Donut Co. v. Hart's Food Stores, Inc., 267 F.2d 358, 363 (2d Cir.1959). But see H.H. Scott, Inc. v. Annapolis Electroacoustic Corp., 195 F.Supp. 208 (D.Md.1961). If the registrant has ceased use in a particular area, however, it will not be entitled to relief against a subsequent user in that area unless there is a present likelihood of confusion. See § 21, Comment *l*. Common law trademark rights, however, can be abandoned in particular geographic areas. Sheila's Shine Products, Inc. v. Sheila Shine, Inc., 486 F.2d 114 (5th Cir.1973).

The priority of a former owner who resumes use of an abandoned mark is determined by the date and areas of its subsequent use. See, e.g., Major League Baseball Properties, Inc. v. Sed Non Olet Denarius, Ltd., 817 F.Supp. 1103 (S.D.N.Y.1993), vacated pursuant to settlement 859 F.Supp. 80 (1994); SODIMA v. Int'l Yogurt Co., 662 F.Supp. 839 (D.Or.1987); Royal Baking Powder Co. v. Raymond, 70 Fed. 376 (C.C.Ill.1895), affirmed 85 Fed. 231 (7th Cir.1898). Cf. AmBrit, Inc. v. Kraft, Inc., 812 F.2d 1531 (11th Cir.1986), cert. denied 481 U.S. 1041, 107 S.Ct. 1983, 95 L.Ed.2d 822 (1987) (an owner's trademark registration for an abandoned mark was subject to cancellation despite the owner's subsequent resumption of use).

There is little precedent on the acquisition of rights in abandoned marks. Some cases suggest that trademark rights are acquired by the first bona fide use after abandonment. See California Cedar Products Co. v. Pine Mountain Corp., 724 F.2d 827 (9th Cir.1984); Manhattan Industries, Inc. v. Sweater Bee by Banff, Ltd., 627 F.2d 628 (2d Cir.1980); Sutton Cosmetics (P.R.), Inc. v. Lander Co., 455 F.2d 285 (2d Cir.1972). However, if the abandoned designation is not inherently distinctive and has lost any acquired distinctiveness created by the former use, proof of secondary meaning arising from the subsequent use should be required in order to establish trademark rights. Some commentators go further, arguing that the subsequent user should not be permitted to rely on any residual secondary meaning retained by the designation from the former use. See Kargen, The First User of an Abandoned Trademark Acquires the Secondary Meaning Associated with the Abandoned Mark by Virtue of His First Use, 64 Trademark Rep. 8

(1974); Atkinson, Appropriation of Expressly Abandoned Trademarks: Caveat Emptor?, 65 Trademark Rep. 1 (1975). See also Sutton Cosmetics, *supra* (Hays, J., dissenting).

Additional complications arise if the abandoned designation retains its original trademark significance. At least for a time, undifferentiated use by a subsequent user is likely to be perceived as an indication of source in the former user. Rights acquired by a subsequent user who fails to distinguish its use of the designation from the use by the former user may thus be subject to the doctrine of unclean hands as stated in § 32. See Interstate Distilleries, Inc. v. Sherwood Distilling & Distributing Co., 173 Md. 173, 195 A. 387 (1937); Sutton Cosmetics, *supra* (Hays, J., dissenting). Cf. Acme Valve & Fittings Co. v. Wayne, 386 F.Supp. 1162 (S.D.Tex. 1974) (subsequent user distinguished its use from that of the former user). A number of decisions also suggest a continuing right in the former user to prevent deceptive use of an abandoned mark that retains trademark significance. See Indianapolis Colts, Inc. v. Metropolitan Baltimore Football Club Ltd., 34 F.3d 410 (7th Cir. 1994); Browning King Co. v. Browning King Co., 176 F.2d 105 (3d Cir. 1949); Interstate Distilleries, *supra*. Cf. Baglin v. Cusenier Co., 221 U.S. 580, 31 S.Ct. 669, 55 L.Ed. 863 (1911) (protecting the association retained by the former trademark). But see Exxon Corp. v. Humble Exploration Co., 695 F.2d 96 (5th Cir.1983) (declining to recognize a claim under § 43(a) of the Lanham Act based on use of an abandoned mark). Protection for the continuing associative significance of an abandoned mark is also advocated in Kargen, *supra*, and Atkinson, *supra*. See also Gilson, *supra*, § 3.06; Restatement of Torts § 752, Comment *b*.

Illustration 1 is suggested by the facts in Sheila's Shine Products, Inc. v. Sheila Shine, Inc., 486 F.2d 114 (5th Cir.1973). Compare Dawn Donut Co. v. Hart's Food Stores, Inc., 267 F.2d 358 (2d Cir.1959).

Illustration 2 is suggested by the facts but not the result in *Sutton Cosmetics, supra.*

Comment b. Under the 1988 amendments to the Lanham Act, the use necessary to avoid abandonment "means the bona fide use of that mark made in the ordinary course of trade, and not made merely to reserve a right in a mark." 15 U.S.C.A. § 1127. See Major League Baseball Properties, Inc. v. Sed Non Olet Denarius, Ltd., 817 F.Supp. 1103 (S.D.N.Y.1993), vacated pursuant to settlement 859 F.Supp. 80 (1994). Similarly, the priority obtained through the filing of an intent-to-use application under the Lanham Act, see § 18, Comment *b*, is lost if bona fide use in the ordinary course of trade is not commenced within the required statutory period. 15 U.S.C.A. § 1051(d). Cases prior to the statutory amendments also generally refused to recognize mere token use as sufficient to maintain trademark rights. See, e.g., Silverman v. CBS Inc., 870 F.2d 40 (2d Cir.), cert. denied 492 U.S. 907, 109 S.Ct. 3219, 106 L.Ed.2d 569 (1989); Exxon Corp. v. Humble Exploration Co., 695 F.2d 96 (5th Cir.1983); SODIMA v. Int'l Yogurt Co., 662 F.Supp. 839 (D.Or.1987).

Cessation of use on a particular product will not result in abandonment if use continues on related products. See, e.g., Lucien Piccard Watch Corp. v. Crescent Corp., 314 F.Supp. 329 (S.D.N.Y.1970); Robinson Co. v. Plastics Research and Development Corp., 264 F.Supp. 852 (W.D.Ark.1967). On the effect of a change in the format of the mark, compare Sands, Taylor & Wood Co. v. Quaker Oats Co., 978 F.2d 947 (7th Cir.1992), cert. denied ___ U.S. ___, 113 S.Ct. 1879, 123 L.Ed.2d 497 (1993); Drexel Enterprises, Inc. v. Richardson, 312 F.2d 525 (10th Cir. 1962); Markel v. Scovill Manufacturing Co., 471 F.Supp. 1244 (W.D.N.Y.), affirmed 610 F.2d 807 (2d Cir.1979); and Humble Oil & Refining Co. v. Sekisui Chemical Co., 165 U.S.P.Q. 597 (Tm.Tr.App.Bd.1970) (all recognizing continuing rights) with Ilco Corp. v. Ideal Security Hardware Corp., 527 F.2d 1221 (C.C.P.A.1976); Lawyers Title Ins. Co. v. Lawyers Title Ins. Corp., 109 F.2d 35 (D.C.Cir. 1939), cert. denied 309 U.S. 684, 60 S.Ct. 806, 84 L.Ed. 1028 (1940); and General Mills, Inc. v. Frito–Lay, Inc., 176 U.S.P.Q. 148 (Tm.Tr.App.Bd. 1972) (all declining to find a continuity of usage). A change in the ingredients or formulation of the product sold under a trademark does not result in abandonment since it is not a cessation of use under Subsection (2)(a) of this Section, nor does it cause the designation to lose its significance as an indication of source under Subsection (2)(b). A substantial change in the formulation of the product, however, may render continued use of the trademark deceptive, resulting in a potential limitation of rights under the doctrine of unclean hands. See § 32, Comment *b*.

The United States Supreme Court, relying on cases involving the abandonment of real property and other tangible assets, held in Saxlehner v. Eisner & Mendelson Co., 179 U.S. 19, 21 S.Ct. 7, 45 L.Ed. 60 (1900), that the defense of abandonment required proof of "an actual intent to abandon," described by the Court as "an intention to give up and relinquish the right claimed." Under § 45 of the Lanham Act, however, a mark is deemed abandoned "[w]hen its use has been discontinued with intent not to resume such use," and case law under the statute emphasizes that the relevant inquiry is thus the intent to resume use rather than the intent to abandon rights. See, e.g., Imperial Tobacco Ltd. v. Philip Morris, Inc., 899 F.2d 1575 (Fed.Cir.1990); Exxon Corp., *supra*; SODIMA, *supra*. The distinction has also been applied in connection with the abandonment of unregistered marks. See, e.g., Silverman, *supra*; Hiland Potato Chip Co. v. Culbro Snack Foods, Inc., 720 F.2d 981 (8th Cir.1983).

For examples of express announcements of trademark abandonment, see, e.g., California Cedar Products Co. v. Pine Mountain Corp., 724 F.2d 827 (9th Cir.1984); Manhattan Industries, Inc. v. Sweater Bee by Banff, Ltd., 627 F.2d 628 (2d Cir.1980); Sutton Cosmetics (P.R.), Inc. v. Lander Co., 455 F.2d 285 (2d Cir.1972).

The definition of abandonment in § 45 of the Lanham Act, 15 U.S.C.A. § 1127, states that "[i]ntent not to resume may be inferred from circumstances." The statutory presumption of abandonment arising from nonuse for the period stated in § 45 generally has been interpreted to shift to the original user the burden of producing evidence of an intent to resume use, while leaving the ultimate burden of proof on the party asserting abandonment. See, e.g., Roulo v. Russ Berrie & Co., 886 F.2d 931 (7th Cir.1989), cert. denied 493 U.S. 1075, 110 S.Ct. 1124, 107 L.Ed.2d 1030 (1990); Lipton Industries, Inc. v. Ralston Purina Co., 670 F.2d 1024 (C.C.P.A.1982); SODIMA, *supra*. But see E. Remy

Martin & Co., S.A. v. Shaw–Ross Int'l Imports, Inc., 756 F.2d 1525 (11th Cir.1985) (shifting "burden of proof"). The statutory presumption is also occasionally applied to the abandonment of unregistered trademarks. See, e.g., Saratoga Vichy Spring Co. v. Lehman, 625 F.2d 1037 (2d Cir. 1980); Miller Brewing Co. v. Oland's Breweries (1971) Ltd., 548 F.2d 349 (C.C.P.A.1976); Kardex Systems, Inc. v. Sistemco N.V., 583 F.Supp. 803 (D.Me.1984). But see Imperial Tobacco Ltd., *supra* (dictum indicating no presumption at common law).

Temporary suspensions of use caused by factors beyond the control of the trademark owner will not ordinarily result in a finding of abandonment. See, e.g., Miller Brewing Co., *supra*; Chandon Champagne Corp. v. San Marino Wine Corp., 335 F.2d 531 (2d Cir.1964). Cf. Baglin v. Cusenier Co., 221 U.S. 580, 31 S.Ct. 669, 55 L.Ed. 863 (1911) (finding no intent to abandon when use was prohibited by a foreign government). Nonuse due to lack of demand will not constitute abandonment if the trademark owner continues its marketing efforts. See, e.g., American Lava Corp. v. Multronics, Inc., 461 F.2d 836 (C.C.P.A.1972); Daybrook–Ottawa Corp. v. F.A.B. Manufacturing Co., 152 U.S.P.Q. 441 (Tm.Tr.App.Bd. 1966). See also, e.g., Field Enterprises Educational Corp. v. Grosset & Dunlap, Inc., 256 F.Supp. 382 (S.D.N.Y.1966) (no abandonment resulted from nonuse during the preparation of a replacement product). Attempts to negotiate a license or sale of the mark are also evidence of an intent to resume use. See, e.g., Sands, Taylor & Wood Co., *supra*; California Cedar Products Co., *supra*; Saratoga Vichy Spring Co., *supra*; Sterling Brewers, Inc. v. Schenley Industries, Inc., 441 F.2d 675 (C.C.P.A.1971); Kardex Systems, *supra*. In the absence of attempts to license or sell the trademark, evidence that the former user has withdrawn from the business ordinarily justifies a finding of abandonment. See, e.g., Uncas Manufacturing Co. v. Clark & Coombs Co., 309 F.2d 818 (1st Cir.1962). Failure to object to subsequent use of the designation by others after a cessation of use by the former user can indicate the absence of an intent to resume use. See, e.g., Uncas Manufacturing Co., *supra*; Sherwood Co. v. Sherwood Distilling Co., 177 Md. 455, 9 A.2d 842 (1939). See also Baglin, *supra* (efforts to prevent use by others are inconsistent with an intent to abandon). In some circumstances the presence of substantial good will retained by the mark may itself be evidence of an intent to continue use. See Ferrari S.p.A. Esercizio Fabbriche Automobili e Corse v. McBurnie, 11 U.S.P.Q.2d 1843 (S.D.Cal.1989).

Cases stressing that abandonment, being in the nature of a forfeiture, must be "strictly" proved by the party asserting it include, e.g., Prudential Insurance Co. v. Gibraltar Financial Corp., 694 F.2d 1150 (9th Cir. 1982), cert. denied 463 U.S. 1208, 103 S.Ct. 3538, 77 L.Ed.2d 1389 (1983); United States Jaycees v. Philadelphia Jaycees, 639 F.2d 134 (3d Cir.1981); Saratoga Vichy Spring Co., *supra*; Kardex Systems, *supra*. See also McCarthy, *supra*, § 17.03. But see Cerveceria Centroamericana, S.A. v. Cerveceria India, Inc., 892 F.2d 1021 (Fed.Cir.1989) (preponderance of the evidence test applicable in proceedings under the Lanham Act to cancel a registration for abandonment).

Illustration 3 is based on *Miller Brewing Co., supra*.

Comment c. Abandonment occurs under § 45 of the Lanham Act if any course of conduct by the trademark owner causes the mark to become generic "or otherwise to lose its significance as a mark." 15 U.S.C.A. § 1127. A number of cases indicate that an intent to resume use will not prevent abandonment if the designation has lost its significance as a trademark. See, e.g., American Photographic Pub. Co. v. Ziff-Davis Pub. Co., 135 F.2d 569 (7th Cir.1943); Royal Baking Powder Co. v. Raymond, 70 Fed. 376 (C.C.Ill.1895), affirmed 85 Fed. 231 (7th Cir.1898); Sherwood Co. v. Sherwood Distilling Co., 177 Md. 455, 9 A.2d 842 (1939); Golenpaul v. Rosett, 174 Misc. 114, 18 N.Y.S.2d 889 (1940). But see Beech-Nut Packing Co. v. P. Lorillard Co., 273 U.S. 629, 47 S.Ct. 481, 71 L.Ed. 810 (1927). See also McCarthy, *supra*, § 17.03[4]; Pattishall, The Impact of Intent in Trade Identity Cases, 60 Trademark Rep. 575, 584–86 (1970). The willingness of others to pay for the use of the mark is evidence of continuing good will in the designation. See Defiance Button Machine Co. v. C & C Metal Products Corp., 759 F.2d 1053 (2d Cir.), cert. denied 474 U.S. 844, 106 S.Ct. 131, 88 L.Ed.2d 108 (1985); Sterling Brewers, Inc. v. Schenley Industries, Inc., 441 F.2d 675 (C.C.P.A. 1971).

Failure to take action against third-party users will result in abandonment under the rule stated in Subsection (2)(b) of this Section only if such uses cause the designation to lose its significance as a trademark. See, e.g., Sweetheart Plastics, Inc. v. Detroit Forming, Inc., 743 F.2d 1039 (4th Cir.1984); Wallpaper Mfrs., Ltd. v. Crown Wallcovering Corp., 680 F.2d 755 (C.C.P.A.1982); United States Jaycees v. Philadelphia Jaycees, 639 F.2d 134 (3d Cir.1981); Bd. of Governors of U. of North Carolina v. Helpingstine, 714 F.Supp. 167 (M.D.N.C.1989). Third-party use is usually relevant only to the "strength" of the mark. See, e.g., Amstar Corp. v. Domino's Pizza, Inc., 615 F.2d 252 (5th Cir.), cert. denied 449 U.S. 899, 101 S.Ct. 268, 66 L.Ed.2d 129 (1980); Quality Inns International, Inc. v. McDonald's Corp., 695 F.Supp. 198 (D.Md.1988).

Illustration 4 is based on the facts in *Golenpaul, supra*. See also American Photographic Pub., *supra*.

§ 31. Unreasonable Delay (Laches)

If the owner of a trademark, trade name, collective mark, or certification mark unreasonably delays in commencing an action for infringement or otherwise asserting the owner's rights and thereby causes prejudice to another who may be subject to liability to the owner under the rules stated in this Chapter, the owner may be barred in whole or in part from the relief that would otherwise be available under §§ 35–37.

Comment:

a. Laches. An unreasonable delay in the assertion of trademark rights can affect the relief available to the owner of a trademark in an action for infringement. See §§ 35–37. Because of the public interest in protecting consumers from confusion as to the source or sponsorship of goods and services, unreasonable delay by the trademark owner does not necessarily constitute a complete defense to liability. However, in many circumstances such a delay will operate to limit the nature or scope of the remedy awarded against an infringer. See Comments *d* and *e*.

Remedies for trademark infringement, including damages, accounting of profits, and injunctive relief, are awarded subject to principles of equity, see §§ 35–37, and laches can be an important factor in assessing the appropriateness of particular relief. Delay by a trademark owner in asserting its rights after it knew or should have known of an infringement can prejudice the defendant by increasing the amount of the plaintiff's loss, by aggravating the burden that the requested remedy would impose on the defendant, or by undermining the ability of the court to ascertain the facts. In such instances, if the delay is unreasonable, the imposition of a particular remedy may be inequitable. Among the considerations that are relevant in evaluating a claim of laches are the length and justification for the delay, the certainty and extent of the harm to the trademark owner if the requested remedy is denied, the extent of the harm to the defendant that is attributable to the plaintiff's delay if the requested remedy is granted, and the public interest in avoiding confusion.

Laches may be raised in actions for the infringement of registered trademarks under § 32 of the Lanham Act as well as in actions involving unregistered trademarks at common law and under § 43(a) of the Lanham Act. Section 33(b)(8) of the Lanham Act permits laches to be raised even against an incontestable trademark registration, and §§ 34 and 35 of the Act provide that awards of both injunctive and monetary relief are subject "to the principles of equity." 15 U.S.C.A. §§ 1115–17.

Some decisions state that a delay in asserting trademark rights may show "acquiescence" on the part of the plaintiff. See § 29, Comment *c*. The doctrine of laches, however, rests on the consequences of the plaintiff's delay and not upon the communication of consent. If the trademark owner has in fact expressly or implicitly consented to the defendant's conduct, the owner may be barred from relief under the rule stated in § 29.

The role of statutes of limitations in trademark infringement actions remains uncertain. There is general agreement that it is the doctrine of laches rather than the statute of limitations that normally governs the availability of injunctive relief since infringement is typically a continuing wrong. A few cases indicate that the statute of limitations may bar claims for monetary relief with respect to damages incurred outside the statutory period. Other cases treat the action for trademark infringement as inherently equitable and rely solely on principles of laches to determine the availability of both monetary and injunctive relief. These latter cases, however, sometimes incorporate the analogous statutory limitations period into the analysis of laches through a presumption that laches will ordinarily bar the recovery of damages incurred outside the analogous limitations period. Some cases also adopt a presumption that delay for less than the limitations period does not constitute laches, but all courts recognize that in some circumstances even a short delay may so prejudice the defendant that the denial of monetary relief is appropriate.

b. Prejudice to defendant. A delay by the trademark owner in asserting its rights is not in itself sufficient to support a claim of laches. The delay must so prejudice the interests of the defendant that it would be inequitable to grant the requested relief. In cases that uphold a claim of laches, prejudice is typically found in the increased burden that the delayed relief would impose on the defendant. Allegations of prejudice in trademark infringement actions usually relate to the potential loss of the good will that has attached to the use of the designation by the defendant. For example, the value of the resources expended by the defendant in advertising and promoting the mark during the period of the plaintiff's delay will be lost in the event of a subsequent injunction barring the defendant's use. The same is true with respect to expenditures associated with territorial or product expansion under the mark by the defendant. Even the incremental accumulation of good will through sales made under the designation by the defendant can be sufficient to render subsequent relief inequitable in the face of an unreasonable delay by the plaintiff. Prejudice to the defendant may also arise from a delay that undermines the ability of the court to ascertain the facts relevant to the cause of action.

Cases sometimes recite that reliance by the defendant on the inaction of the trademark owner is a necessary element of laches. A number of cases, however, recognize laches even when the defendant was unaware of the existence of the prior user. Laches has also been founded on prejudice that is unrelated to any reliance by the defendant, such as a loss of evidence relevant to the infringement claim. As a general matter, only a causal connection between the delay by the plaintiff and the potential prejudice to the defendant is required.

Harm that is properly attributable to the defendant's own conduct rather than to the plaintiff's delay will not contribute to a finding of laches. For example, in some circumstances the defendant's continued investment in the designation after a notice of objection from the trademark owner may appropriately be deemed to be at the defendant's own risk. Thus, in some cases the relevant date for purposes of determining laches may be the date of the plaintiff's objection to the use rather than the date of the commencement of the action.

c. Unreasonable delay. The doctrine of laches is not applicable if the plaintiff's delay is reasonable under the particular circumstances of the case. The doctrine is not intended to encourage precipitous litigation, and a trademark owner is not required to take action at the first indication of possible infringement. The plaintiff is not ordinarily chargeable with any delay prior to an actual intrusion upon its rights. The plaintiff in some cases may also be justified in delaying a protest or the commencement of litigation until the viability of the defendant's infringing business is evident. Similarly, reasonable time consumed in objecting to the use and awaiting the defendant's response will not contribute to a finding of laches. The same is true with respect to delays attributable to on-going settlement negotiations. In some circumstances, the existence of other litigation involving the plaintiff's mark may justify a delay in commencing an action against the defendant, particularly when the issues in the litigation are relevant to the claim against the defendant and the plaintiff has notified the defendant of an intent to institute legal action at the conclusion of the other litigation.

An increase in the level of infringement attributable only to the normal growth of the defendant's business ordinarily is not sufficient to excuse a prior delay on the part of the trademark owner. However, changes in the nature of the threat posed by the defendant's conduct can sometimes overcome a claim of laches. Thus, a change by the defendant in the manner of use of the mark or an expansion into new products or new territories that increases the risk of confusion may be sufficient to excuse a prior delay by the plaintiff. In some cases it may be equitable to recognize laches only with respect to use of the mark by the defendant on certain products or in certain territories.

Delay caused by the plaintiff's justifiable ignorance of the defendant's infringing conduct will not support a claim of laches. Proof of actual knowledge of the defendant's use, however, is not necessary in order to establish laches. Proof that the trademark owner should have known of the infringing conduct can be sufficient, particularly when the potential prejudice to the defendant is substantial. Section 22 of the Lanham Act provides that registration of a mark under the Act is "constructive notice of the registrant's claim of ownership." A federal registration issued to a subsequent user may thus be sufficient to establish that the prior user knew or should have known of the facts revealed in the registration, and in some cases may justify the imposition of a duty on the prior user to undertake a reasonable inquiry to ascertain other relevant facts about the registrant's use. However, laches remains an equitable doctrine, and the fact of a defendant's federal registration is not necessarily conclusive on the issue of the plaintiff's notice of the infringing use.

d. Effect on monetary relief. A finding of laches reflects a judgment that it would be inequitable in light of the plaintiff's delay to grant the requested relief. The relative equities must thus be evaluated in light of the nature of the particular relief sought by the trademark owner. In some circumstances laches may preclude an award of monetary relief for past harm while not disabling the plaintiff from obtaining damages or profits accruing after the plaintiff's objection to the use or after the commencement of the litigation. In other cases, justice may require that the plaintiff be barred from all monetary relief.

A strong case for the recognition of laches can arise in connection with a demand for an accounting of the profits earned by the defendant during the period of the plaintiff's delay. Courts have frequently denied an accounting of profits to a trademark owner who has knowingly permitted the defendant to conduct business for an extended time before raising a claim to the profits generated by the defendant's efforts. The distinction between the "equitable" remedy of an accounting and the "legal" remedy of damages has not generally been maintained in actions for unfair competition, see § 36, Comment *b*, and the "equitable" doctrine of laches has frequently been invoked to preclude the recovery of damages by the trademark owner. The certainty of the fact and amount of damage to the trademark owner, the length and reasons for the delay, and the degree to which the delay has increased the defendant's potential monetary liability are all important factors in assessing the merits of a laches claim. Although not necessarily determinative, the defendant's good faith is also important, and evidence indicating an intent to trade on the good will of the trademark owner through confusion can shift the balance of equities in favor of the plaintiff.

e. Effect on injunctive relief. In applying the doctrine of laches in trademark infringement actions, the court should consider the public interest in protecting consumers from the continued use of confusing designations. Thus, while a denial of monetary relief for past infringements may rest solely on the relative equities as between the parties, the public interest is an explicit factor in decisions relating to injunctions.

There is no rule that precludes the recognition of laches in connection with a request for injunctive relief. However, because of the public interest in preventing the deception of consumers, delay by the trademark owner will not ordinarily disable it from obtaining an injunction if there is strong evidence of likely or actual confusion. The underlying equities may nevertheless affect the scope of injunctive relief, with absolute prohibitions against use sometimes displaced by mandatory precautionary measures such as disclaimers or labelling requirements in an attempt to ameliorate the prejudice to the defendant. In some circumstances it may be appropriate to recognize laches as a bar to an injunction only with respect to use in certain territories or on certain products. Unreasonable delay may also disable the trademark owner from obtaining preliminary relief prior to a complete evaluation of the risk of confusion.

Evidence establishing that the defendant intended to capitalize on the good will of the trademark owner through confusion is generally sufficient to overcome a laches claim raised against a request for injunctive relief. The intent to deceive not only undermines the defendant's claim to equity but also is evidence that an injunction is necessary to prevent the confusion of prospective purchasers.

When the likelihood of public confusion is uncertain, the relative harm to the parties in granting or denying an injunction can be determinative in resolving a claim of laches. In the case of a noncompeting use that creates only a marginal risk of confusion, for example, the prejudice to a defendant compelled to abandon the good will created through its use of the mark during the plaintiff's delay may in some cases outweigh any threatened harm to the trademark owner or the public.

REPORTERS' NOTE

The general doctrine of laches is described in Restatement, Second, Torts § 939 (1979). Application of the principle in actions for trademark infringement is discussed in Gilson, Trademark Protection and Practice § 8.12[12]; McCarthy, Trademarks and Unfair Competition §§ 31.01–14.

Comment a. "It is hornbook law that laches consists of two essential elements: (1) inexcusable delay in instituting suit, and (2) prejudice resulting to the defendant from such delay." University of Pittsburgh v. Champion Products Inc., 686 F.2d 1040 (3d Cir.), cert. denied 459 U.S. 1087, 103 S.Ct. 571, 74 L.Ed.2d 933 (1982). On the factors relevant to a finding of laches, see, e.g., Clamp Manufacturing Co. v. Enco Manufacturing Co., 870 F.2d 512, 515 (9th Cir.), cert. denied 493 U.S. 872, 110 S.Ct. 202, 107 L.Ed.2d 155 (1989) (strength and value of the trademark rights, the trademark owner's diligence in enforcing its rights, the harm to the trademark owner if relief is denied, the defendant's good faith, the existence of competition between the plaintiff and defendant, and the harm suffered by the defendant because of the delay). The trial court's determination of laches is generally reviewed under an abuse of discretion standard. See, e.g., Clamp Manufacturing, *supra*; Piper Aircraft Corp. v. Wag–Aero, Inc., 741 F.2d 925 (7th Cir.1984). Cf. Gump's, Inc. v. Byers' Choice, Ltd., 22 U.S.P.Q.2d 1797 (N.D.Cal.1992) (laches is determined by the court).

Under the 1988 amendments to the Lanham Act, equitable principles including laches are expressly applicable in actions for the infringement of federally-registered marks even if the registration has become incontestable. 15 U.S.C.A. § 1115(b)(8). Laches is also applicable to claims at common law and under state trademark registration statutes. See, e.g., Saratoga Vichy Spring Co. v. Lehman, 625 F.2d 1037 (2d Cir.1980). On the application of laches in inter partes proceedings in the Patent and Trademark Office, see Gilson, *supra*, § 8.12[12][d]; McCarthy, *supra*, §§ 20.11, 20.20.

That the statute of limitations does not bar injunctive relief against unfair competition, see, e.g., University of Pittsburgh, *supra*; Independent Nail & Packing Co. v. Stronghold Screw Products, Inc., 205 F.2d 921 (7th Cir.), cert. denied 346 U.S. 886, 74 S.Ct. 138, 98 L.Ed. 391 (1953); Dwinell–Wright Co. v. White House Milk Co., 132 F.2d 822 (2d Cir.1943) (L. Hand, J.); Construction Technology, Inc. v. Lockformer Co., 704 F.Supp. 1212 (S.D.N.Y.1989). For cases indicating that the statute of limitations can bar the recovery of damages incurred outside the limitations period, see Dwinell–Wright, *supra* (dictum); Construction Technology, *supra*; Cellasto Corp. v. Int'l Tel. & Tel. Corp., 215 U.S.P.Q. 998 (E.D.Mich.1982). Cf. Hoste v. Radio Corp. of America, 654 F.2d 11 (6th Cir.1981) and Mount v. Book–of–the–Month Club, Inc., 555 F.2d 1108 (2d Cir.1977), interpreting the statute of limitations provision in the Copyright Act, 17 U.S.C.A. § 507(b), to bar only damages incurred prior to the limitations period. The Lanham Act does not contain a limitations provision. The courts have been more consistent in invoking analogous state statutes of limitations in actions for deceptive marketing under § 43(a) than in actions for the infringement of registered trademarks. See Construction Technology, *supra*; PepsiCo, Inc. v. Dunlop Tire & Rubber Corp., 578 F.Supp. 196 (S.D.N.Y.1984); Fox Chemical Co. v. Amsoil, Inc., 445 F.Supp. 1355 (D.Minn.1978). In infringement actions, the doctrine of laches rather then a statute of limitations is typically invoked to determine the availability of both injunctive and monetary relief. See, e.g., Clamp Mfg. Co., *supra*; Tandy Corp. v. Malone & Hyde, Inc., 769 F.2d 362 (6th Cir.1985), cert. denied 476 U.S. 1158, 106 S.Ct. 2277, 90 L.Ed.2d 719 (1986). See also Callmann, Unfair Competition, Trademarks and Monopolies (4th ed.) § 22.30 (statute of limitations is generally inapplicable because trademark infringement is usually a continuing tort); Stimson, Statute of Limitations in Trademark Actions, 71 Trademark Rep. 605 (1981) (statute of limitations is inapplicable because trademark actions are predominately equitable). Cases holding that a delay beyond the analogous limitations period creates a presumption of laches include *University of Pittsburgh*, *supra*; *Construction Technology*, *supra*. See also Layton Pure Food Co. v. Church

& Dwight Co., 182 Fed. 35 (8th Cir. 1910). But see, e.g., Clamp Manufacturing, *supra*. Cases invoking a presumption against a finding of laches if the delay is less than the analogous limitations period include Elvis Presley Enterprises, Inc. v. Elvisly Yours, Inc., 936 F.2d 889 (6th Cir.1991); Ameritech, Inc. v. American Information Technologies Corp., 811 F.2d 960 (6th Cir.1987); Tandy Corp., *supra*; see AmBrit, Inc. v. Kraft, Inc., 812 F.2d 1531 (11th Cir.1986), cert. denied 481 U.S. 1041, 107 S.Ct. 1983, 95 L.Ed.2d 822 (1987); Frito–Lay, Inc. v. Bachman Co., 3 U.S.P.Q.2d 1472 (S.D.N.Y.1987). However, these cases also typically rely on findings that the plaintiff's delay was excusable or resulted in little prejudice to the defendant and recognize that the presumption against laches can be overcome in appropriate circumstances. See also Pomeroy, Equity Jurisprudence (5th ed.) § 419b ("the defense of laches may still be sustained where the lapse of time is less than the statutory period, if grounded upon additional circumstances").

Comment b. Some cases include reliance by the defendant as a necessary element of laches. See, e.g., NAACP v. NAACP Legal Defense & Educational Fund, Inc., 753 F.2d 131 (D.C.Cir.), cert. denied 472 U.S. 1021, 105 S.Ct. 3489, 87 L.Ed.2d 623 (1985). However, laches has been recognized in favor of defendants who had no knowledge of the plaintiff's use. See, e.g., Safeway Stores, Inc. v. Safeway Quality Foods, Inc., 433 F.2d 99 (7th Cir.1970); Chandon Champagne Corp. v. San Marino Wine Corp., 335 F.2d 531 (2d Cir.1964). The cases generally require only that the delay cause undue prejudice to the defendant. See, e.g., Conagra, Inc. v. Singleton, 743 F.2d 1508 (11th Cir.1984); Loma Linda Food Co. v. Thomson & Taylor Spice Co., 279 F.2d 522 (C.C.P.A.1960) ("[p]rejudice may result without any reliance").

The prejudice alleged by defendants in trademark infringement actions typically relates to the threatened loss of good will created through use and investment in the designation during the plaintiff's delay. Advertising and other promotional expenditures incurred during the delay are often cited. See, e.g., E–Systems, Inc. v. Monitek, Inc., 720 F.2d 604 (9th Cir.1983); Anheuser–Busch, Inc. v. Du Bois Brewing Co., 175 F.2d 370 (3d Cir.1949), cert. denied 339 U.S. 934, 70 S.Ct. 664, 94 L.Ed. 1353 (1950). Defendant's investment in expansion under the mark in new territories, see, e.g., beef & brew, inc. v. Beef & Brew, Inc., 389 F.Supp. 179 (D.Or.1974), or new products, see, e.g., E–Systems, *supra*, can constitute prejudice sufficient to establish laches. Expenditures in acquiring a business and its associated marks can also suffice. See, e.g., Saratoga Vichy Spring Co. v. Lehman, 625 F.2d 1037 (2d Cir.1980); Charvet S.A. v. Dominique France, Inc., 568 F.Supp. 470 (S.D.N.Y.1983), affirmed 736 F.2d 846 (2d Cir.1984). Incremental growth in the defendant's business during the delay or even the threatened loss of good will accumulated through a constant level of sustained usage of the mark can also sometimes justify a finding of laches. See, e.g., Armco, Inc. v. Armco Burglar Alarm Co., 693 F.2d 1155 (5th Cir.1982); Georgia–Pacific Corp. v. Great Plains Bag Co., 614 F.2d 757 (C.C.P.A.1980). Cf. Ralston Purina Co. v. Midwest Cordage Co., 373 F.2d 1015 (C.C.P.A. 1967) (prejudice through continuing usage may require substantial delay);

Cuban Cigar Brands N.V. v. Upmann International, Inc., 457 F.Supp. 1090 (S.D.N.Y.1978), affirmed 607 F.2d 995 (2d Cir.1979) (mere continuation of business insufficient to support laches). The required prejudice, however, can take other forms such as the loss or deterioration of evidence. See Charvet S.A., *supra* ; NAACP, *supra* (dictum); Tustin Community Hospital, Inc. v. Santa Ana Community Hospital Ass'n, 89 Cal.App.3d 889, 153 Cal.Rptr. 76 (1979) (increased difficulty in proving damages) (dictum).

Expenditures or other conduct undertaken by a defendant after a protest from the trademark owner may be entitled to little or no weight in evaluating a claim of laches, particularly if the possibility of subsequent legal action was apparent. See, e.g., Conan Properties, Inc. v. Conans Pizza, Inc., 752 F.2d 145 (5th Cir.1985); Piper Aircraft Corp. v. Wag–Aero, Inc., 741 F.2d 925 (7th Cir.1984); Citibank, N.A. v. Citibanc Group, Inc., 724 F.2d 1540 (11th Cir.1984); Armco, Inc. v. Armco Burglar Alarm Co., 693 F.2d 1155 (5th Cir.1982); Tisch Hotels, Inc. v. Americana Inn, Inc., 350 F.2d 609 (7th Cir.1965); Finance Co. of America v. BankAmerica Corp., 502 F.Supp. 593 (D.Md.1980); California Western School of Law v. California Western University, 125 Cal.App.3d 1002, 178 Cal.Rptr. 685 (1981).

Comment c. The trademark owner is not chargeable with delay until it knows or should know of the infringing conduct. E.g., Piper Aircraft Corp. v. Wag–Aero, Inc., 741 F.2d 925 (7th Cir.1984) ("first became, or reasonably should have become, aware of defendant's infringement"); Armco, Inc. v. Armco Burglar Alarm Co., 693 F.2d 1155 (5th Cir.1982) ("knew or should have known"); Safeway Stores, Inc. v. Safeway Quality Foods, Inc., 433 F.2d 99 (7th Cir.1970) ("chargeable with information it might have received had due inquiry been made"). See also Restatement, Second, Torts § 939, Comment *a.* The cases do not generally recognize as conclusive the constructive notice arising from a subsequent user's federal registration. See, e.g., Valmor Products Co. v. Standard Products Corp., 464 F.2d 200 (1st Cir.1972) (emphasizing the equitable nature of the doctrine); Chandon Champagne Corp. v. San Marino Wine Corp., 335 F.2d 531 (2d Cir.1964) (questioning the contrary position in Patent and Trademark Office proceedings). Cf. E–Systems, Inc. v. Monitek, Inc., 720 F.2d 604 (9th Cir.1983) (noting the fact of constructive notice in addition to other sources of information); Carter–Wallace, Inc. v. Procter & Gamble Co., 434 F.2d 794 (9th Cir.1970) (defendant's registration had probably come to the attention of the plaintiff).

A justifiable delay in commencing legal action will not contribute to a finding of laches. "A reasonable businessman should be afforded some latitude to assess both the impact of another's use of an allegedly infringing trademark as well as the wisdom of pursuing litigation on the issue." Tandy Corp. v. Malone & Hyde, Inc., 769 F.2d 362, 366 (6th Cir.1985), cert. denied 476 U.S. 1158, 106 S.Ct. 2277, 90 L.Ed.2d 719 (1986). Time consumed in settlement negotiations will ordinarily be excused. Compare Piper Aircraft Corp. v. Wag–Aero, Inc., 741 F.2d 925 (7th Cir.1984) (three-and-one-half-year delay during negotiations does not count toward laches) with Charvet S.A. v. Dominique France, Inc., 568 F.Supp. 470 (S.D.N.Y.1983), affirmed 736 F.2d 846

(2d Cir.1984) (desultory and sporadic negotiations did not excuse lengthy delay). The parties involvement in administrative proceedings concerning the mark will ordinarily excuse a delay in filing a civil action for infringement. E.g., Citibank, N.A. v. Citytrust, 644 F.Supp. 1011 (E.D.N.Y.1986); Finance Co. of America v. BankAmerica Corp., 502 F.Supp. 593 (D.Md.1980); Alfred Dunhill, Inc. v. Kasser Distillers Products Corp., 350 F.Supp. 1341 (E.D.Pa.1972), affirmed 480 F.2d 917 (3d Cir.1973). Contra, James Burrough Ltd. v. Sign of Beefeater, Inc., 572 F.2d 574 (7th Cir.1978). Litigation commenced by the trademark owner against other infringers may also excuse a delay in bringing suit against the defendant, at least when the defendant is aware of the plaintiff's objection to the use. See, e.g., Electronic Communications, Inc. v. Electronic Components for Industry Co., 443 F.2d 487 (8th Cir.), cert. denied 404 U.S. 833, 92 S.Ct. 80, 30 L.Ed.2d 63 (1971); Armstrong Cork Co. v. Armstrong Plastic Covers Co., 434 F.Supp. 860 (E.D.Mo.1977).

Changes by the defendant in the appearance or manner of use of the mark that increase the threat to the plaintiff's trademark rights may excuse an earlier delay in commencing an infringement action. See, e.g., Independent Nail & Packing Co. v. Stronghold Screw Products, Inc., 205 F.2d 921 (7th Cir.), cert. denied 346 U.S. 886, 74 S.Ct. 138, 98 L.Ed. 391 (1953) (laches rejected when the defendant changed the manner in which the mark was used); Standard Oil Co. v. Standard Oil Co., 252 F.2d 65 (10th Cir.1958) (same); SCI Systems Inc. v. Solidstate Controls Inc., 748 F.Supp. 1257 (S.D.Ohio 1990) ("progressive encroachment" through changes in the appearance of the defendant's mark and expansion into new product markets can excuse a prior delay); American Rice, Inc. v. Arkansas Rice Growers Cooperative Association, 532 F.Supp. 1376 (S.D.Tex.1982), affirmed 701 F.2d 408 (5th Cir.1983) (alterations in the defendant's mark increased the risk of confusion). Cf. Scott Paper Co. v. Scott's Liquid Gold, Inc., 439 F.Supp. 1022 (D.Del.1977), reversed on other grounds 589 F.2d 1225 (3d Cir.1978) (no laches recognized when the possibility of confusion only became apparent after the defendant's increased advertising and expansion into the plaintiff's channels of trade). If the defendant expands into new geographic markets, the plaintiff may not be barred by a prior delay from relief in the new territories. See, e.g., Conan Properties, Inc. v. Conans Pizza, Inc., 752 F.2d 145 (5th Cir.1985); Parrot Jungle, Inc. v. Parrot Jungle, Inc., 512 F.Supp. 266 (S.D.N.Y.1981). Although the trademark owner is not chargeable with any delay prior to the time that the defendant's conduct first intrudes upon its rights, Johanna Farms, Inc. v. Citrus Bowl, Inc., 468 F.Supp. 866 (E.D.N.Y.1978), an increase in the extent of an existing infringement attributable only to the natural growth of the defendant's business may not be sufficient to overcome the prejudice to the defendant resulting from the delay in instituting the action. See, e.g., Prudential Insurance Co. v. Gibraltar Financial Corp., 694 F.2d 1150 (9th Cir. 1982), cert. denied 463 U.S. 1208, 103 S.Ct. 3538, 77 L.Ed.2d 1389 (1983); Polaroid Corp. v. Polarad Electronics Corp., 287 F.2d 492 (2d Cir.), cert. denied 368 U.S. 820, 82 S.Ct. 36, 7 L.Ed.2d 25 (1961).

For examples of the length of delay in laches decisions, see McCarthy, *supra*, § 31.09.

Comment d. Many decisions recognizing laches as a bar to monetary liability find that the prejudice to the defendant is insufficient to bar injunctive relief. See, e.g., McLean v. Fleming, 96 U.S. 245, 24 L.Ed. 828 (1878); University of Pittsburgh v. Champion Products Inc., 686 F.2d 1040 (3d Cir.), cert. denied 459 U.S. 1087, 103 S.Ct. 571, 74 L.Ed.2d 933 (1982); Grotrian, Helfferich, Schulz, Th. Steinweg Nachf. v. Steinway & Sons, 523 F.2d 1331 (2d Cir.1975); Rolls–Royce Motors, Ltd. v. A & A Fiberglass, Inc., 428 F.Supp. 689 (N.D.Ga.1976) (laches is relevant to the recovery of damages under both federal and state law, but not to injunctive relief); Tustin Community Hospital, Inc. v. Santa Ana Community Hospital Ass'n, 89 Cal.App.3d 889, 153 Cal.Rptr. 76 (1979) (dictum distinguishing laches as a bar to damages and as a bar to an injunction). Similarly, monetary relief is sometimes barred only with respect to acts committed prior to notice of objection or the commencement of litigation. See, e.g., James Burrough Ltd. v. Sign of Beefeater, Inc., 572 F.2d 574 (7th Cir.1978); Whittaker Corp. v. Execuair Corp., 736 F.2d 1341 (9th Cir.1984); Houston Sports Association v. Astro–Card Co., 520 F.Supp. 1178 (S.D.Tex.1981).

On laches as a bar to an accounting of defendant's profits, see, e.g., McLean, *supra*; Brittingham v. Jenkins, 914 F.2d 447 (4th Cir.1990); University of Pittsburgh, *supra*. Under § 35 of the Lanham Act, 15 U.S.C.A. § 1117, awards of both damages and profits are "subject to the principles of equity." See also Restatement, Second, Torts § 939, Comment *c* (laches can be applicable to damages and accountings of profits); Restatement of Torts § 751, Comment *d* (laches is applicable to claims for damages and accountings in trademark infringement actions). "Where once [laches in the law of intellectual property] barred just equitable relief, today it is a substantive defense and bars legal relief as well * * *." Piper Aircraft Corp. v. Wag–Aero, Inc., 741 F.2d 925 (7th Cir.1984) (Posner, J., concurring). Cases recognizing laches as a bar to the recovery of plaintiff's damages include, e.g., Skippy, Inc. v. CPC Int'l, Inc., 674 F.2d 209 (4th Cir.), cert. denied 459 U.S. 969, 103 S.Ct. 298, 74 L.Ed.2d 280 (1982); James Burrough Ltd., *supra*; Grotrian, Helfferich, *supra*; Tustin Community Hospital, *supra* (dictum). Although the defendant's bad faith is relevant to the determination of laches, it will not necessarily preclude a finding of laches barring monetary relief. See, e.g., Skippy, Inc., *supra*; Grotrian, Helfferich, *supra*.

Comment e. Cases recognizing laches as a bar to injunctive relief include, e.g., Ancient Egyptian Arabic Order of Nobles of the Mystic Shrine v. Michaux, 279 U.S. 737, 49 S.Ct. 485, 73 L.Ed. 931 (1929); NAACP v. NAACP Legal Defense & Educational Fund, Inc., 753 F.2d 131 (D.C.Cir.), cert. denied 472 U.S. 1021, 105 S.Ct. 3489, 87 L.Ed.2d 623 (1985); E–Systems, Inc. v. Monitek, Inc., 720 F.2d 604 (9th Cir.1983); Procter & Gamble Co. v. J.L. Prescott Co., 102 F.2d 773 (3d Cir.), cert. denied 308 U.S. 557, 60 S.Ct. 80, 84 L.Ed. 461 (1939). In some circumstances, laches may preclude relief only with respect to certain territories or products. See, e.g., Conan Properties, Inc. v. Conans Pizza, Inc., 752 F.2d 145 (5th Cir.

1985) (laches did not bar injunction against subsequent expansion under the mark); Parrot Jungle, Inc. v. Parrot Jungle, Inc., 512 F.Supp. 266 (S.D.N.Y.1981) (same).

Delay in seeking preliminary relief may indicate an absence of the irreparable harm *pendente lite* relevant to the issuance of a preliminary injunction. See, e.g., Citibank, N.A. v. Citytrust, 756 F.2d 273 (2d Cir.1985) (delay of 10 weeks justified the withholding of a preliminary injunction); GTE Corp. v. Williams, 731 F.2d 676 (10th Cir.1984); Warner Lambert Co. v. McCrory's Corp., 718 F.Supp. 389 (D.N.J.1989), all distinguishing such delay from the doctrine of laches as a bar to permanent relief. See also Gilson, *supra*, § 8.12[12][l][iv]; McCarthy, *supra*, § 31.10; Raskopf & Edelman, Delay in Filing Preliminary Injunction Motions: How Long is Too Long?, 80 Trademark Rep. 36 (1990).

In assessing the merits of a laches claim raised against a request for injunctive relief, the public interest in avoiding confusion may sometimes outweigh any potential prejudice to the defendant. See, e.g., Conagra, Inc. v. Singleton, 743 F.2d 1508 (11th Cir.1984); Underwriters Laboratories, Inc. v. United Laboratories, Inc., 203 U.S.P.Q. 180 (N.D.Ill.1978); Tustin Community Hospital, Inc. v. Santa Ana Community Hospital Ass'n, 89 Cal.App.3d 889, 153 Cal.Rptr. 76 (1979). Thus, when the likelihood of confusion is clear, laches will not ordinarily bar an injunction. See, e.g., McLean v. Fleming, 96 U.S. 245, 24 L.Ed. 828 (1878); cf. Ultra-White Co. v. Johnson Chemical Industries, Inc., 465 F.2d 891 (C.C.P.A.1972) (cancellation of registration granted). On the other hand, when the risk of confusion is less serious, the prejudice to the defendant may be sufficient to preclude injunctive relief. See, e.g., E–Systems, *supra*; Prudential Insurance Co. v. Gibraltar Financial Corp., 694 F.2d 1150 (9th Cir.1982), cert. denied 463 U.S. 1208, 103 S.Ct. 3538, 77 L.Ed.2d 1389 (1983); American Dietaids Co. v. Plus Products, 412 F.Supp. 691 (S.D.N.Y.), affirmed 551 F.2d 299 (2d Cir.1976). On similar reasoning, laches is more likely to preclude an injunction when the use by the defendant involves noncompeting goods. See, e.g., Chandon Champagne Corp. v. San Marino Wine Corp., 335 F.2d 531 (2d Cir.1964); Polaroid Corp. v. Polarad Electronics Corp., 287 F.2d 492 (2d Cir.), cert. denied 368 U.S. 820, 82 S.Ct. 36, 7 L.Ed.2d 25 (1961); Dwinell–Wright Co. v. White House Milk Co., 132 F.2d 822 (2d Cir.1943) (L. Hand, J.).

Laches will not ordinarily bar an injunction against an intentional infringer. See, e.g., Saxlehner v. Eisner & Mendelson Co., 179 U.S. 19, 21 S.Ct. 7, 45 L.Ed. 60 (1900); Ameritech, Inc. v. American Information Technologies Corp., 811 F.2d 960 (6th Cir.1987); Harlequin Enterprises Ltd. v. Gulf & Western Corp., 644 F.2d 946 (2d Cir.1981); Grotrian, Helfferich, Schulz, Th. Steinweg Nachf. v. Steinway & Sons, 523 F.2d 1331 (2d Cir.1975); My–T Fine Corp. v. Samuels, 69 F.2d 76 (2d Cir.1934) (L. Hand, J.). The relevant intent, however, is that of capitalizing on the plaintiff's good will through confusion; mere knowledge of the prior use will not necessarily preclude a finding of laches.

§ 32. Plaintiff's Misconduct (Unclean Hands)

If a designation used as a trademark, trade name, collective mark, or certification mark is deceptive, or if its

use is otherwise in violation of public policy, or if the owner of the designation has engaged in other substantial misconduct directly related to the owner's assertion of rights in the trademark, trade name, collective mark, or certification mark, the owner may be barred in whole or in part from the relief that would otherwise be available under §§ 35–37.

Comment:

a. Unclean hands. Misconduct on the part of a trademark owner may in some circumstances limit or preclude an award of damages, profits, or injunctive relief in an action for trademark infringement. See §§ 35–37. As in the case of laches, see § 31, unclean hands does not necessarily constitute a defense to liability, frequently operating instead merely to limit the nature or scope of the available relief. The Comments treat the forms of unclean hands typically encountered in trademark infringement actions, but do not exhaust the potential scope of the doctrine. Other misconduct by the trademark owner toward the public, the defendant, or the court may also justify a partial or total denial of relief. The doctrine of unclean hands is applicable in actions for the infringement of registered trademarks under § 32 of the Lanham Act and in actions involving unregistered marks under § 43(a) of the Act and at common law.

Misconduct need not be criminal or tortious to constitute unclean hands, but it must be sufficiently serious in comparison with the defendant's conduct or in its threat to the public to justify a limitation on the relief available to the plaintiff. Although unclean hands is not limited to willful misconduct, the plaintiff's intent is an important factor in the application of the doctrine.

The unclean hands doctrine is intended to deny relief that would otherwise reward or assist in a course of misconduct. Thus, the doctrine is applicable only when the misconduct is sufficiently related to the trademark rights asserted by the plaintiff that judicial protection in the context of the particular case would be inequitable. Misconduct by the plaintiff that is unrelated to the trademark rights for which protection is sought does not constitute unclean hands. When the designation in which trademark rights are claimed is deceptive, see Comment *b*, or when the use of the designation as a trademark by the plaintiff violates a recognized public policy, see Comment *c*, the misconduct relates directly to the rights asserted and the doctrine of unclean hands may therefore limit the available relief. When the misconduct is less directly related to the plaintiff's assertion of trademark rights, the court must determine whether the requested relief would nevertheless be inequitable as assisting the plaintiff to achieve an improper objective. See Comment *d.* In applying the doctrine of unclean hands, the court must also weigh the public interest in preventing continuation of the defendant's infringing conduct. See Comment *e.*

b. Deceptive designations. The doctrine of unclean hands limits the relief available for the infringement of a deceptive designation. If a designation used as a trademark, trade name, collective mark, or certification mark misdescribes the goods, services, or business with which it is used in a manner likely to influence the purchasing decisions of a significant number of prospective purchasers, the designation is deceptive. See § 14, Comment *c.* Thus, the doctrine of unclean hands is applicable against a plaintiff's assertion of rights in designations that materially misrepresent the ingredients or other characteristics of the plaintiff's goods or services, the nature of the plaintiff's business, or the geographic origin of its products. See § 14, Illustration 3. The doctrine is also applicable if a substantial change in the ingredients or formulation of the plaintiff's product renders continued use of the trademark associated with the former version deceptive in the absence of adequate disclosure. The use of a deceptive designation may also subject the plaintiff to liability for deceptive marketing under the rule stated in § 2.

The doctrine of unclean hands is applicable if the plaintiff has used the designation to misrepresent the source of its goods or services. Under the rules relating to priority as stated in § 19, it is sufficient for the imposition of liability that the trademark rights asserted by the plaintiff have priority over those of the defendant, regardless of whether the plaintiff's rights are also superior to those of third persons. *Id.*, Comment *a.* However, if the evidence establishes that the plaintiff has used the designation in an attempt to trade on the good will of a third person, relief against a subsequent user may be limited under the rule stated here.

c. Designations violating public policy. The use of certain designations as trademarks, trade names, collective marks, or certification marks may violate public policy. For example, in addition to deceptive marks, both the Lanham Act and the Model State Trademark Bill prohibit the registration of immoral or scandalous marks; marks that disparage or falsely suggest a connection with persons, institutions, beliefs, or national symbols; marks consisting of insignia of the United States or of any state, municipality, or foreign nation; and marks consisting of a name, signature, or portrait identifying a particular living individual without written consent. 15 U.S.C.A.

§ 1052(a)-(c); Model State Trademark Bill § 2(a)-(d) (1992). Although these statutory provisions merely prohibit the registration of such marks, a court may conclude in a particular case that the adoption and use of such a mark also subjects the user to a claim of unclean hands. A similar conclusion may be justified in connection with the use of designations that violate an expressed public policy protecting privacy or publicity rights. See § 47, Comment *a*.

d. Other related misconduct. Unclean hands may limit the relief available in an action for trademark infringement even when the plaintiff's mark is not itself deceptive or otherwise in violation of public policy. In order to affect the availability or extent of relief, however, the plaintiff's misconduct must be sufficiently related to the assertion of trademark rights to justify a limitation on the scope of trademark protection.

Allegations of unclean hands are sometimes raised against trademark owners who have misrepresented the goods or services marketed under the designation. Unless the trademark itself is deceptive, however, such misconduct may not be sufficiently related to the plaintiff's assertion of trademark rights to justify a limitation on the remedies available against an infringer. The fact of a misrepresentation will not then deprive the plaintiff or the public of protection against the likelihood of confusion arising from a defendant's infringing use. The plaintiff, however, may be subject to liability to the defendant or others under the rules relating to deceptive marketing stated in Chapter Two.

A similar analysis is applicable to misconduct in violation of the antitrust laws. Although trademark misuse may give rise to unclean hands, the fact that the trademark owner has violated the antitrust laws in marketing its goods or services is not necessarily sufficient to invoke the unclean hands doctrine. Limitations on the relief available against infringement may be justified only when the antitrust violation is directly related to the trademark rights asserted against the defendant.

A misrepresentation of federal trademark registration through improper use of the federal registration symbol directly relates to the owner's assertion of trademark rights, but the doctrine of unclean hands will ordinarily apply only if the misrepresentation has misled or was intended to mislead other potential users of the designation.

Illustrations:

1. *A* markets a laxative under the trademark FIG TREE. Although *A* 's laxative contains no ingredients derived from figs, a significant number of consumers have been induced to purchase

the product in the mistaken belief that it is made from figs. In a trademark infringement action brought by *A* against a subsequent user of the designation, *A* 's use of a deceptive designation constitutes unclean hands. *A* may thus be barred in whole or in part from the relief that would otherwise be available under §§ 35–37.

2. *A* markets a plastic vegetable bin under the trademark POLY–FLEX. In an attempt to accentuate the innovative design of its product, *A* stamps on its bins the notation "Patent Pending," although no application for a patent has been filed. *B* subsequently begins marketing a similar product under the same designation. In an action for trademark infringement brought by *A*, the court may conclude that *A* 's misrepresentation is not sufficiently related to the trademark rights asserted against *B* to constitute unclean hands. However, *A* may be subject to liability to *B* or to other competitors under the rule stated in § 2. See § 3, Illustration 3.

e. Extent of disability. The law of unfair competition has not maintained a sharp distinction between "equitable" and "legal" remedies. See § 36, Comment *b*. Thus, the "equitable" doctrine of unclean hands can be a factor limiting the "legal" remedy of damages as well as the "equitable" remedies of an accounting and injunction. See §§ 35–37.

When a claim of unclean hands is raised against a request for injunctive relief, the court must take account of the public interest in preventing confusion. If a failure to enjoin the defendant's infringement would subject the public to a significant risk of harm, even substantial misconduct by the plaintiff will not preclude an injunction, particularly when the plaintiff's misconduct can be challenged directly through a counterclaim or an independent action. In other cases it may be appropriate to award an injunction conditioned on the cessation of the plaintiff's misconduct. If the plaintiff has already ceased the misconduct in circumstances indicating little likelihood of resumption, the doctrine of unclean hands will not ordinarily limit injunctive relief, although it may remain relevant to an award of damages or profits accruing during the period of the misconduct.

REPORTERS' NOTE

This Section combines and expands the former treatment of unclean hands in trademark litigation in Restatement of Torts §§ 726, 749 (1938). On the general concept of unclean hands, see Restatement, Second, Torts § 940 (1979). On the application of the concept in actions for trademark infringement, see Gilson, Trademark Protection and Practice

§ 8.12[13]; McCarthy, Trademarks and Unfair Competition §§ 31.15–20.

Comment a. Sections 34 and 35 of the Lanham Act authorize awards of both monetary and injunctive relief subject "to the principles of equity." 15 U.S.C.A. §§ 1116–17. Section 33(b) of the Act, 15 U.S.C.A. § 1115(b), also recognizes "equitable principles" as a defense against the conclusive evidentiary effect of an incontestable trademark registration, § 33(b)(8), in addition to misconduct consisting of fraud in obtaining the registration, § 33(b)(1), misrepresentations of source, § 33(b)(3), and use of the mark to violate the antitrust laws, § 33(b)(7).

Although the plaintiff's misconduct need not be criminal or tortious to constitute unclean hands, Precision Instrument Mfg. Co. v. Automotive Maintenance Machinery Co., 324 U.S. 806, 65 S.Ct. 993, 89 L.Ed. 1381 (1945), it must be directly related to the rights asserted against the defendant. "What is material is not that the plaintiff's hands are dirty, but that he dirtied them in acquiring the right he now asserts, or that the manner of the dirtying renders inequitable the assertion of such rights against the defendant." Republic Molding Corp. v. B.W. Photo Utilities, 319 F.2d 347, 349 (9th Cir.1963) (misrepresentation of patent pending was not sufficiently related to plaintiff's passing off claim to constitute unclean hands).

If the plaintiff has not acted in bad faith, a claim of unclean hands is usually rejected. See, e.g., Wilson Jones Co. v. Gilbert & Bennett Mfg. Co., 332 F.2d 216 (2d Cir.1964); Blaw–Knox Co. v. Siegerist, 300 F.Supp. 507 (E.D.Mo.1968), affirmed 414 F.2d 375 (8th Cir.1969); Q–Tips, Inc. v. Johnson & Johnson, 108 F.Supp. 845 (D.N.J.1952), affirmed 206 F.2d 144 (3d Cir.), cert. denied 346 U.S. 867, 74 S.Ct. 106, 98 L.Ed. 377 (1953).

Comment b. The Supreme Court in Clinton E. Worden & Co. v. California Fig Syrup Co., 187 U.S. 516, 23 S.Ct. 161, 47 L.Ed. 282 (1903), refused to protect the designation SYRUP OF FIGS because fig syrup was not a substantial ingredient of the plaintiff's product. See also Coca–Cola Co. v. Koke Co., 254 U.S. 143, 41 S.Ct. 113, 65 L.Ed. 189 (1920) (continued use of the mark COCA–COLA after the elimination of cocaine from the plaintiff's product was not sufficiently misleading to preclude relief against infringement). On unclean hands arising from misrepresentations of geographic origin, see Allan B. Wrisley Co. v. Iowa Soap Co., 104 Fed. 548 (C.C.S.D.Iowa 1900), appeal dismissed 105 Fed. 999 (8th Cir.1900) (OLD COUNTRY SOAP used on a domestic product). Relief has also been denied when a mark associated by consumers with goods manufactured in one location is used to misrepresent the geographic origin of goods made in another location. See American Thermos Bottle Co. v. W.T. Grant Co., 282 Fed. 426 (1st Cir.1922). On deception attributable to a substantial change in the ingredients or other characteristics of the product sold under a trademark, compare Renaud Sales Co. v. Davis, 104 F.2d 683 (1st Cir.1939) (relief precluded by assignee's unclean hands arising from use of the mark on inferior perfume) and Mulhens & Kropff, Inc. v. Ferd Muelhens, Inc., 43 F.2d 937 (2d Cir.), cert. denied 282 U.S. 881, 51 S.Ct. 84, 75 L.Ed. 777 (1930) (refusing an injunction to an assignee with respect to products not based on the original secret formula) and Independent Baking Powder Co. v. Boorman, 175 Fed. 448 (C.C.N.J. 1910) (dictum suggesting forfeiture of rights resulting from assignee's substitution of ingredients) with Rick v. Buchansky, 609 F.Supp. 1522 (S.D.N.Y.), dismissed 770 F.2d 157 (2d Cir.1985) (changes in composition of musical group did not cause abandonment of the service mark) and E.I. du Pont de Nemours and Co. v. G.C. Murphy Co., 199 U.S.P.Q. 807 (Tm.Tr.App.Bd.1978) (change in paint formula did not result in abandonment of trademark rights). See also Clinton E. Worden & Co., *supra* (dictum).

Although only relative and not absolute priority is required in order to subject a subsequent user to liability for infringement, see § 19, Comment *a*, adoption of a designation by the plaintiff with an intent to trade on the reputation of a prior user may constitute unclean hands limiting relief against subsequent users. See Ubeda v. Zialcita, 226 U.S. 452, 33 S.Ct. 165, 57 L.Ed. 296 (1913); Kay Dunhill, Inc. v. Dunhill, Fabrics, Inc., 44 F.Supp. 922 (S.D.N.Y.1942) (no unclean hands when the evidence did not establish a fraudulent intent). Cf. Borg–Warner Corp. v. York–Shipley, Inc., 293 F.2d 88 (7th Cir.), cert. denied 368 U.S. 939, 82 S.Ct. 381, 7 L.Ed.2d 338 (1961) (denying an accounting of profits to a trademark owner who used the mark in a manner intended to cause confusion with the defendant).

Comment c. The former treatment of this topic similarly recognized a limitation on the protection of designations used in violation of public policy. See Restatement of Torts § 726. On the interpretation of the statutory prohibitions against the registration of such marks, see McCarthy, *supra*, §§ 13.12, 19.25–28. The Lanham Act exclusions have been interpreted as embracing the protection of privacy and publicity interests. See University of Notre Dame Du Lac v. J.C. Gourmet Food Imports Co., 703 F.2d 1372 (Fed.Cir. 1983).

Comment d. A few cases have recognized unclean hands with respect to misrepresentations not directly involving the plaintiff's trademark. See, e.g., Strey v. Devine's, Inc., 217 F.2d 187 (7th Cir.1954); Moxie Nerve Food Co. v. Modox Co., 152 Fed. 493 (C.C.R.I.1907); Magic Foam Sales Corp. v. Mystic Foam Corp., 44 Ohio Op. 185, 98 N.E.2d 439 (C.P.1950). Cf. Q–Tips, Inc. v. Johnson & Johnson, 108 F.Supp. 845 (D.N.J.1952), affirmed 206 F.2d 144 (3d Cir.), cert. denied 346 U.S. 867, 74 S.Ct. 106, 98 L.Ed. 377 (1953) (unintentional misrepresentation of patent protection was insufficient to bar relief against trademark infringement). Most cases, however, refuse to invoke the defense when the trademark is not directly connected with the alleged misrepresentation. See, e.g., Fuddruckers, Inc. v. Doc's B.R. Others, Inc., 826 F.2d 837 (9th Cir.1987); Tveter v. AB Turn–O–Matic, 633 F.2d 831 (9th Cir.1980), cert. denied 451 U.S. 911, 101 S.Ct. 1983, 68 L.Ed.2d 300 (1981); Republic Molding Corp. v. B.W. Photo Utilities, 319 F.2d 347 (9th Cir.1963); W.E. Bassett Co. v. Revlon, Inc., 305 F.Supp. 581 (S.D.N.Y.1969), affirmed 435 F.2d 656 (2d Cir.1970). If the trademark is used to facilitate the misrepresentation, the unclean hands doctrine may be applicable. See Borg–Warner Corp. v. York–Shipley, Inc., 293 F.2d 88 (7th Cir.), cert. denied 368 U.S. 939, 82 S.Ct. 381, 7 L.Ed.2d 338

(1961) (trademark used in an attempt to create confusion of source).

Misuse of a trademark in violation of the antitrust laws is recognized as a defense to the evidentiary effect of an incontestable registration in § 33(b)(7) of the Lanham Act. 15 U.S.C.A. § 1115(b)(7). The misuse doctrine was analyzed in Carl Zeiss Stiftung v. V.E.B. Carl Zeiss, Jena, 298 F.Supp. 1309 (S.D.N.Y.1969), affirmed 433 F.2d 686 (2d Cir.1970), cert. denied 403 U.S. 905, 91 S.Ct. 2205, 29 L.Ed.2d 680 (1971). The court, holding that "[a]n essential element of the antitrust misuse defense in a trademark case is proof that the mark itself has been the basic and fundamental vehicle required and used to accomplish the violation," found the allegations of territorial restrictions, tying, and price discrimination were only collaterally related to the plaintiff's trademark rights and dismissed the misuse defense. A similar result was reached in Coca–Cola Co. v. Howard Johnson Co., 386 F.Supp. 330 (N.D.Ga.1974). The validity of an antitrust misuse defense was upheld in Phi Delta Theta Fraternity v. J.A. Buchroeder & Co., 251 F.Supp. 968 (W.D.Mo.1966), in connection with an alleged attempt to use trademark rights to monopolize the market for goods bearing fraternity insignia. See also Electrical Information Publications, Inc. v. C–M Periodicals, Inc., 163 U.S.P.Q. 624 (N.D.Ill.1969).

A sufficient nexus between the plaintiff's misconduct and the assertion of trademark rights has been found in a variety of contexts. In Bambu Sales, Inc. v. Testini, 12 U.S.P.Q.2d 1479 (E.D.N.Y.1988), the court refused to strike an unclean hands defense to monetary relief premised on an allegation that the business plaintiff sought to protect was illegal. See also Knights of the Ku Klux Klan v. Strayer, 34 F.2d 432 (3d Cir.1929). Cf. Erva Pharmaceuticals, Inc. v. American Cyanamid Co., 755 F.Supp. 36 (D.P.R.1991) (dismissing plaintiff's action for infringement of a trademark used on a misbranded drug). In United States Jaycees v. Cedar Rapids Jaycees, 794 F.2d 379 (8th Cir.1986), the court affirmed the denial of an injunction that it believed was sought by the licensor merely to punish a licensee who had disputed the trademark owner's policy of sex discrimination. But see United States Jaycees v. Philadelphia Jaycees, 639 F.2d 134 (3d Cir.1981), ordering an injunction on similar facts.

Although several cases have held that misuse of the federal trademark registration symbol can constitute unclean hands, see, e.g., Urecal Corp. v. Masters, 413 F.Supp. 873 (N.D.Ill. 1976); Fox–Stanley Photo Products, Inc. v. Otaguro, 339 F.Supp. 1293 (D.Mass.1972), the claim is generally rejected in the absence of an intent to deceive. See, e.g., Copeland's Enterprises, Inc. v. CNV, Inc., 945 F.2d 1563 (Fed.Cir.1991) (misuse of registration symbol can prevent registration of the mark if done with an intent to deceive); Shatel Corp. v. Mao Ta Lumber and Yacht Corp., 697 F.2d 1352 (11th Cir.1983); Nupro Co. v. Nypro Inc., 221 U.S.P.Q. 693 (D.Mass.1983); Waples–Platter Cos. v. General Foods Corp., 439 F.Supp. 551 (N.D.Tex.1977).

Illustration 1 is suggested by Clinton E. Worden & Co. v. California Fig Syrup Co., 187 U.S. 516, 23 S.Ct. 161, 47 L.Ed. 282 (1903). Illustration 2 is suggested by *Republic Molding Corp.*, *supra*. See, e.g., Tveter, *supra*.

Comment e. Unclean hands may bar a trademark owner from both monetary and injunctive relief. See, e.g., Manhattan Medicine Co. v. Wood, 108 U.S. 218, 2 S.Ct. 436, 27 L.Ed. 706 (1883) (common law); Bambu Sales, Inc. v. Testini, 12 U.S.P.Q.2d 1479 (E.D.N.Y.1988) (Lanham Act); Urecal Corp. v. Masters, 413 F.Supp. 873 (N.D.Ill.1976) (common law); Magic Foam Sales Corp. v. Mystic Foam Corp., 44 Ohio Op. 185, 98 N.E.2d 439 (C.P.1950) (common law). See also the former statement of the rule in Restatement of Torts § 749, Comment *h*.

The public interest is often an explicit factor in the application of the unclean hands doctrine in trademark infringement actions. "In the interests of right and justice the court should not automatically condone the defendant's infractions because the plaintiff is also blameworthy, thereby leaving two wrongs unremedied and increasing the injury to the public." Republic Molding Corp. v. B.W. Photo Utilities, 319 F.2d 347, 349 (9th Cir.1963). See, e.g., Ames Pub. Co. v. Walker–Davis Publications, Inc., 372 F.Supp. 1 (E.D.Pa.1974), noting that when the plaintiff has been guilty of misconduct the scope of the injunction may be directed more toward the vindication of public rather than private interests. See also Restatement, Second, Torts § 940, Comment *a*. On the award of relief conditioned upon a cessation of the plaintiff's misconduct, see Ames Pub. Co., *supra*. If the plaintiff has ceased the alleged misconduct with no likelihood of resumption, it will not ordinarily be barred from injunctive relief. See, e.g., Coca–Cola Co. v. Koke Co., 254 U.S. 143, 41 S.Ct. 113, 65 L.Ed. 189 (1920); Fund of Funds, Ltd. v. First American Fund of Funds, 274 F.Supp. 517 (S.D.N.Y.1967); Q–Tips, Inc. v. Johnson & Johnson, 108 F.Supp. 845 (D.N.J.1952), affirmed 206 F.2d 144 (3d Cir.), cert. denied 346 U.S. 867, 74 S.Ct. 106, 98 L.Ed. 377 (1953); Moxie Nerve Food Co. v. Modox Co., 152 Fed. 493 (C.C.R.I. 1907).

TOPIC 5. LICENSING AND ASSIGNMENT OF RIGHTS

Section

---

§ 33. Licensing of Trademarks

The owner of a trademark, trade name, collective mark, or certification mark may license another to use the designation. If the licensor exercises reasonable control over the nature and quality of the goods, services, or business on which the designation is used by the licensee, any rights in the designation arising from the licensee's use accrue to the benefit of the licensor. Failure of the licensor to exercise reasonable control over the use of the

designation by the licensee can result in abandonment of the designation under the rule stated in § 30(2)(b).

Comment:

a. Historical development. A license is an agreement under which the owner of a trademark, trade name, collective mark, or certification mark authorizes use of the designation by another. Unlike an assignment (see § 34), a license does not transfer ownership of the designation. Unlike a consent agreement (see § 29, Comment *b*), a license authorizes another to exploit the good will attached to the designation through a use that is likely to be associated by the public with the trademark owner. The use of the designation by the licensee thus accrues to the benefit of the trademark owner. See Comment *b*.

Collective and certification marks are adopted for use by third persons and do not identify goods or services controlled by the owner of the mark. See §§ 10 and 11. Use of the designation by a member of the collective group or by a seller of the certified goods or services is not a use by a licensee under the rule stated in this Section.

Trademarks were initially used to identify goods that had been manufactured by a particular person or business. See § 9, Comment *b*. The historical conception of trademarks as symbols indicating the physical source of the goods led a number of early courts to conclude that the owner of a trademark could not license others to use the mark without destroying the significance of the designation as an indication of source. Licenses were sometimes declared invalid as a fraud on the public, and licensors risked forfeiture of their rights in the mark through a finding of abandonment.

The narrow conception of trademarks as indications of physical source was eventually replaced by a recognition that trademarks may signify other connections between goods bearing the mark and the trademark owner, including the trademark owner's approval or sponsorship of the goods. The "source" identified by a trademark may now be a distributor, retailer, or other entity that selects the goods on which the mark appears. Trademarks thus came to be understood as indications of consistent and predictable quality assured through the trademark owner's control over the use of the designation. Emphasis on the quality assurance function of trademarks led modern courts to uphold the validity of trademark licenses when the control retained by the licensor was sufficient under the circumstances to insure that the licensee's goods or services would meet the expectations created by the presence of the trademark. Early cases found sufficient control when the licensor provided the principal ingredient for the product, enforced the use of a specific product formula, or controlled the licensee through stock ownership or other business relationship.

The right of a trademark owner to license the use of its mark by others was confirmed in 1946 by the enactment of the Lanham Act. Section 5 of the Act provides that the use of a mark by "related companies" inures to the benefit of the registrant or applicant for registration. 15 U.S.C.A. § 1055. A "related company" is one "whose use of a mark is controlled by the owner of the mark with respect to the nature and quality of the goods or services on or in connection with which the mark is used." *Id.* § 1127. The common law now recognizes the licensing of trademarks under similar principles.

b. Effect of a trademark license. A licensee is not subject to liability to the licensor for any use of the mark that is within the scope of the license, even if the licensor fails to exercise control over the licensee's use. See § 29. If the trademark owner exercises reasonable control over the nature and quality of the licensee's goods or services, the benefits of the licensee's use accrue to the trademark owner. The owner may thus rely on use by controlled licensees to prove secondary meaning, see § 13, the extent of the owner's geographic priority, see § 19, or the fact of continuing use of the mark, see § 30. If the license authorizes use on goods or services other than those previously marketed by the trademark owner, the licensee's use can also extend the trademark owner's rights into additional product markets.

An uncontrolled or "naked" license allows use of the trademark on goods or services for which the trademark owner cannot offer a meaningful assurance of quality. When a trademark owner fails to exercise reasonable control over the use of the mark by a licensee, the presence of the mark on the licensee's goods or services misrepresents their connection with the trademark owner since the mark no longer identifies goods or services that are under the control of the owner of the mark. Although prospective purchasers may continue to perceive the designation as a trademark, the courts have traditionally treated an erosion of the designation's capacity for accurate identification resulting from uncontrolled licensing as a loss of trademark significance, thus subjecting the owner of the mark to a claim of abandonment under the rule stated in § 30(2)(b).

The significance of a trademark as an accurate indication of source or sponsorship is not threatened unless there is substantial uncontrolled use by licensees. Thus, if the uncontrolled use continues for only a short time, or represents only an insignificant proportion of the total use of the mark, a court will not ordinarily find abandonment. If substantial uncontrolled use is confined to a particular geographic or product market, a court may conclude that the mark has been abandoned only in that geographic area or in connection with use on that product. The trademark owner then retains its priority in the use of the mark in other areas or on other products. The burden of proving the fact and extent of uncontrolled use by licensees is on the person alleging abandonment.

c. Requirement of reasonable control. The presence of a trademark on goods or services does not guarantee any specific level of quality. Just as the trademark owner is free to choose the quality of its own goods or services, it is free to choose the quality of the goods or services marketed under the designation by its licensees. However, the presence of a trademark ordinarily indicates to prospective purchasers that the trademark owner has concluded that the goods or services are of sufficient quality to be marketed under its designation. The requirement of reasonable control is intended to maintain consistency in the quality of the goods or services marketed under the trademark by the licensor and its licensees by insuring that decision-making authority over quality remains with the owner of the mark.

The Lanham Act does not define the extent or manner of supervision necessary to satisfy the requirement of reasonable control. Cases both under the Act and at common law apply a flexible standard responsive to the particular facts of each case. The ultimate issue is whether the control exercised by the licensor is sufficient under the circumstances to satisfy the public's expectation of quality assurance arising from the presence of the trademark on the licensee's goods or services. Any evidence relating to the likelihood that the quality of the licensee's goods or services will depart from the standards imposed or anticipated by the owner of the trademark is relevant in determining the adequacy of the licensor's control.

The nature and extent of the control required under this Section is determined by the expectations that the licensee's use of the mark creates in consumers and the supervision that is reasonably necessary to insure that those expectations are not endangered. The expectations of consumers depend in part on the character of the licensee's use. If a licensee uses the trademark of a beer or soft drink manufacturer on clothing or glassware, for example, prospective purchasers may be unlikely to assume that the owner of the trademark has more than perfunctory involvement in the production or quality of the licensee's goods even if the manner of use clearly indicates sponsorship by the trademark owner. On the other hand, if the licensee's use is on goods similar or identical to those produced by the trademark owner, purchasers may be likely to assume that the goods are actually manufactured by the owner of the mark. Greater control by the licensor may then be necessary to safeguard the interests of consumers who may purchase the goods on the basis of the licensor's reputation for quality. If the use authorized by the trademark owner is not perceived by prospective purchasers as an indication of source or sponsorship, but rather as a purely ornamental use, the designation as used by the licensee does not function as a trademark. The requirement of reasonable control over the nature and quality of the licensee's product is then inapplicable, and no rights accrue to the owner of the designation as a result of the licensee's use. See also § 20, Comment *e*.

Although the absence of contractual obligations relating to the quality of the licensee's goods or services can be evidence of a lack of reasonable control, actual control exercised by the licensor can satisfy the requirement imposed by this Section despite the lack of express contractual obligations. Trademark licenses, however, frequently contain express terms specifying standards of quality, ingredients, manufacturing methods, or other conditions or obligations intended to insure a level of quality satisfactory to the licensor. If the trademark owner is justified in relying on the reputation and expertise of the licensee, the existence of contractual obligations undertaken by the licensee may be sufficient in itself to constitute reasonable quality control under the rule stated in this Section, at least in the absence of evidence indicating significant deviations from the agreed standards or procedures. In other cases, the risk of deviations in quality may be too great to permit reliance solely on the presence of contractual obligations. Thus, if the licensee is inexperienced, or if the goods or services are particularly complex or otherwise require careful supervision, or if the risk to the public from inadequate supervision is substantial, greater control such as periodic inspections of facilities or products may be necessary.

Contractual provisions requiring the use of ingredients or parts supplied by the licensor or other approved source may in some cases constitute sufficient quality control. Under some circumstances the licensor may reasonably adopt and rely on the standards, inspections, or enforcement procedures of third persons such as independent testing organizations or government agencies. Similarly, supervision exercised by a controlled licensee over the use of the designation by sublicensees can be sufficient to protect the continued validity of the mark. Legal or practical control by the licensor over the operations of a licensee arising from stock ownership, common management, or family relationships can also contribute to a finding of reasonable quality control.

The law of trademarks relies primarily on the self-interest of the trademark owner to insure adequate control over the use of the mark by licensees. Because a finding of inadequate control can result in a forfeiture of trademark rights, courts impose a heavy burden on the person asserting a lack of reasonable control by a licensor. As a general matter, courts are reluctant to interfere with the marketing arrangements adopted by trademark owners, and minimal control over the quality of a licensee's goods or services is often sufficient to satisfy the requirement imposed under this Section.

d. Licensee standing and estoppel. Since a license does not transfer ownership of the mark, licensees ordinarily have no standing to bring an action for trademark infringement against another user of the mark. However, if the license is exclusive even as against use by the licensor, the licensee's interest may be sufficiently analogous to ownership to support the licensee's standing to bring an infringement action. In addition, if unauthorized use of the trademark by another is likely to deceive or mislead prospective purchasers to the likely commercial detriment of a licensee, the other user may be subject to liability to the licensee for deceptive marketing under the rule stated in § 2.

A licensee who has used a designation under a license from another is ordinarily estopped from asserting ownership of the designation as against the licensor. In several cases, licensees have also been estopped from challenging the validity of the licensed mark on the basis of abandonment or lack of distinctiveness. However, licensee estoppel is an equitable doctrine, and a court remains free to consider the particular circumstances of the case, including the nature of the licensee's claim and the terms of the license. The case for estoppel is strongest when the licensee's challenge rests on its own conduct under the license, such as an assertion of ownership based on the licensee's use of the mark during the term of the license or a claim of abandonment based on inadequate supervision of the licensee by the licensor. The public interest in permitting the licensee's challenge is also relevant to the application of the estoppel doctrine. Thus, in an appropriate case a court may conclude that the public interest in avoiding exclusive rights in generic or functional designations is sufficient to preclude estoppel of a challenge on such grounds brought by a licensee. In addition, former licensees should not ordinarily be estopped from challenging the ownership or validity of the licensor's mark on the basis of facts arising after the termination of the license.

REPORTERS' NOTE

The prior Restatement of this topic did not contain a separate section on trademark licensing, although some applications of the rule stated here were included in a section on the transfer of trademark rights. See Restatement of Torts § 756 (1938). See generally Gilson, Trademark Protection and Practice §§ 6.01–03; McCarthy, Trademarks and Unfair Competition §§ 18.13–24.

Comment a. The initial reluctance to permit the licensing of trademarks is apparent in, e.g, American Broadcasting Co. v. Wahl Co., 121 F.2d 412 (2d Cir.1941); Everett O. Fisk & Co. v. Fisk Teachers' Agency, Inc., 3 F.2d 7 (8th Cir.1924); Macmahan Pharmacal Co. v. Denver Chemical Mfg. Co., 113 Fed. 468 (8th Cir. 1901). Cases upholding trademark licenses prior to the enactment of the Lanham Act include, e.g., E.I. du Pont De Nemours & Co. v. Celanese Corp., 167 F.2d 484 (C.C.P.A.1948); Coca–Cola Co. v. Bennett, 238 Fed. 513 (8th Cir.1916); Keebler Weyl Baking Co. v. J.S. Ivins' Son, 7 F.Supp. 211 (E.D.Pa.1934). On the development of the rules governing trademark licensing, see Shniderman, Trade–Mark Licensing—A Saga of Fantasy and Fact, 14 Law & Contemp.Probs. 248 (1949). See also K Mart Corp. v. Cartier, Inc., 486 U.S. 281, 108 S.Ct. 1811, 100 L.Ed.2d 313 (1988) (Brennan, J., concurring). On the rationale for the requirement of quality control, see, e.g., Dawn Donut Co. v. Hart's Food Stores, Inc., 267 F.2d 358, 367 (2d Cir.1959) ("If the licensor is not compelled to take some reasonable steps to prevent misuses of his trademark in the hands of others the public will be deprived of its most effective protection against misleading uses of a trademark."); Syntex Laboratories, Inc. v. Norwich Pharmacal Co., 315 F.Supp. 45, 56 (S.D.N.Y.1970), affirmed 437 F.2d 566 (2d Cir.1971) ("[T]he purpose of the control requirement is to avoid the danger that the public may be deceived as to the quality of a product sold under a recognized name.").

On the distinction between the use of a collective or certification mark by persons other than the owner of the designation and the licensed use of a trademark, see § 11, Comment *a*, and the accompanying Reporters' Note, and also the Reporters' Note accompanying § 10, Comment *b*.

For an introduction to state and federal disclosure and registration rules applicable to franchising licensing, see McCarthy, *supra*, §§ 18.22–23. On the potential liability of a licensor for the torts of its licensees, see *id.* § 18.24.

Comment b. Controlled use by a licensee accrues to the benefit of the trademark owner. See, e.g., 15 U.S.C.A. § 1055; Church of Scientology Int'l v. Elmira Mission of the Church of Scientology, 794 F.2d 38 (2d Cir.1986); Printers Services Co. v. Bondurant, 20 U.S.P.Q.2d 1626 (C.D.Cal.1991); Distillerie Flli Ramazzotti v. Banfi Products Corp., 52 Misc.2d 593, 276 N.Y.S.2d 413 (Sup. Ct.1966), affirmed 27 A.D.2d 905, 280 N.Y.S.2d 892 (1967); Ideal Toy Corp. v. Cameo Exclusive Products Inc., 170 U.S.P.Q. 596 (Tm.Tr.App.Bd. 1971); General Mills, Inc. v. DCA Food Industries Inc., 149 U.S.P.Q. 225 (Tm.Tr.App.Bd.1966). Section 5 of the Lanham Act as amended in 1988, 15 U.S.C.A. § 1055, explicitly recognizes the acquisition of trademark rights by a licensor through a first use of the mark by a controlled licensee.

"The Lanham Act clearly carries forward the view * * * that controlled licensing does not work an abandonment of the licensor's registration, while a system of naked licensing does." Dawn Donut Co. v. Hart's Food Stores, Inc., 267 F.2d 358, 367 (2d Cir.1959). See, e.g., Haymaker Sports, Inc. v. Turian, 581 F.2d 257 (C.C.P.A.1978); Universal City Studios, Inc. v. Nintendo Co., 578 F.Supp. 911 (S.D.N.Y.1983), affirmed on other grounds 746 F.2d 112 (2d Cir.1984); First National Bank v. Autoteller Systems Service Corp., 9 U.S.P.Q.2d 1740 (Tm.Tr.App.Bd. 1988). See also Express, Inc. v. Sears, Roebuck & Co., 840 F.Supp. 502 (S.D.Ohio 1993) (quoting Restatement Third, Unfair Competition § 33, Comment *b* (Tent. Draft No.3 (1991))). Abandonment will not be found if the quantum of uncontrolled use is too insubstantial to undermine the source significance of the mark. See United States Jaycees v. Philadelphia Jaycees, 639 F.2d 134 (3d Cir. 1981) (source significance of the mark was maintained by substantial controlled use). See also Bureau National Interprofessionnel Du Cognac v. Int'l Better Drinks Corp., 6 U.S.P.Q.2d 1610 (Tm.Tr.App.Bd.1988) (no actual use by the uncontrolled licensee). On abandonment in a limited area through uncontrolled licensing, see Sheila's Shine Products, Inc. v. Sheila Shine, Inc., 486 F.2d 114 (5th Cir.1973). On abandonment limited to particular products, see Dawn Donut, *supra* (dictum); Winnebago Industries, Inc. v. Oliver & Winston, Inc., 207 U.S.P.Q. 335 (Tm.Tr.App. Bd.1980) (dictum). See also McCarthy, *supra*, § 18.15. On the burden of proof imposed on a party asserting abandonment through uncontrolled licensing, see, e.g., Moore Business Forms, Inc. v. Ryu, 960 F.2d 486 (5th Cir.1992) ("stringent standard"); Kentucky Fried Chicken Corp. v. Diversified Packaging Corp., 549 F.2d 368 (5th Cir.1977) ("heavy burden"); Edwin K. Williams & Co. v. Edwin K. Williams & Co.-East, 542 F.2d 1053 (9th Cir.1976), cert. denied 433 U.S. 908, 97 S.Ct. 2973, 53 L.Ed.2d 1092 (1977) ("high burden"); American Foods, Inc. v. Golden Flake, Inc., 312 F.2d 619 (5th Cir.1963) ("strict proof"). Even an uncontrolled license is effective between the parties to the agreement as a manifestation of consent to the licensee's use. Leon's Frozen Custard, Inc. v. Leon Corp., 182 Wis.2d 236, 513 N.W.2d 636 (App.1994) (Anderson, J., dissenting in part) (citing Restatement Third, Unfair Competition § 29, Comment *b* (Tent. Draft No.3 (1991))).

Comment c. On the general requirement of reasonable control, see, e.g., Dawn Donut Co. v. Hart's Food Stores, Inc., 267 F.2d 358, 367 (2d Cir.1959) ("affirmative duty of policing in a reasonable manner"); General Motors Corp. v. Gibson Chemical & Oil Corp., 786 F.2d 105, 110 (2d Cir.1986) ("The critical question in determining whether a licensing program is controlled sufficiently by the licensor to protect his mark is whether the licensees' operations are policed adequately to guarantee the quality of the products sold under the mark."); Syntex Laboratories, Inc. v. Norwich Pharmacal Co., 315 F.Supp. 45, 56 (S.D.N.Y.1970), affirmed 437 F.2d 566 (2d Cir.1971) (licensor had "adequate basis for the reasonable belief that the high quality of the * * * product would be maintained"). A number of courts and commentators explicitly recognize that the extent of the required control varies with the circumstances of the case. See, e.g., United States Jaycees v. Philadelphia Jaycees, 639 F.2d 134 (3d Cir.1981); Edwin K. Williams & Co. v. Edwin K. Williams & Co.-East, 542 F.2d 1053 (9th Cir.1976), cert.

denied 433 U.S. 908, 97 S.Ct. 2973, 53 L.Ed.2d 1092 (1977); Taffy Original Designs, Inc. v. Taffy's, Inc., 161 U.S.P.Q. 707, 713 (N.D.Ill.1966) ("The necessary degree of control must vary from situation to situation, from product to product."). See also Lahart, Control—The Sine Qua Non of a Valid Trademark License, 50 Trademark Rep. 103, 134 (1960) ("The protection of the public from deception and fraud, as well as the general welfare of the community, obviously requires that the control over the quality of drugs or food must be greater than the control over dyestuffs, dance instructions, etc."). Several commentators have argued that little control should be required in the context of licenses relating to collateral goods such as wearing apparel or other products that are substantially removed from the goods marketed by the trademark owner since the owner is unlikely to possess expertise in the production of the licensed product and consumers are less likely to rely on the mark as an indication of quality. See Marks, Trademark Licensing—Toward a More Flexible Standard, 78 Trademark Rep. 641 (1988); Keating, Promotional Trademark Licensing: A Concept Whose Time Has Come, 89 Dick.L.Rev. 363 (1985). The degree of control necessary to protect the validity of a mark is often described as "minimal." See, e.g, Kentucky Fried Chicken Corp. v. Diversified Packaging Corp., 549 F.2d 368 (5th Cir.1977); Engineered Mechanical Services, Inc. v. Applied Mechanical Technology, Inc., 584 F.Supp. 1149 (M.D.La.1984); Hurricane Fence Co. v. A–1 Hurricane Fence Co., 468 F.Supp. 975 (S.D.Ala.1979).

A trademark license need not be in writing. See, e.g., Transgo, Inc. v. Ajac Transmission Parts Corp., 768 F.2d 1001 (9th Cir.1985), cert. denied 474 U.S. 1059, 106 S.Ct. 802, 88 L.Ed.2d 778 (1986); Taffy Original Designs, *supra*; Nestle Co. v. Nash–Finch Co., 4 U.S.P.Q.2d 1085 (Tm.Tr. App.Bd.1987). The absence of contractual provisions relating to quality control is not determinative if the licensor exercises sufficient actual control. See, e.g., Dawn Donut, *supra*; Carl Zeiss Stiftung v. V.E.B. Carl Zeiss, Jena, 293 F.Supp. 892 (S.D.N.Y.1968), affirmed 433 F.2d 686 (2d Cir.1970), cert. denied 403 U.S. 905, 91 S.Ct. 2205, 29 L.Ed.2d 680 (1971). Contra, Robinson Co. v. Plastics Research and Dev. Corp., 264 F.Supp. 852 (W.D.Ark.1967).

The presence of quality control provisions in a licensing agreement is not necessarily sufficient in itself to satisfy the obligation of the licensor under this Section. See, e.g., Alligator Co. v. Robert Bruce, Inc., 176 F.Supp. 377 (E.D.Pa.1959). However, the licensor's reliance on the licensee's contractual obligations, alone or in combination with other measures, may be sufficient if the reliance is reasonable in light of the licensee's reputation and expertise. See, e.g., Stock Pot Restaurant, Inc. v. Stockpot, Inc., 737 F.2d 1576 (Fed.Cir. 1984); Edwin K. Williams & Co., *supra*; Morgan Creek Productions, Inc. v. Capital Cities/ABC, Inc., 22 U.S.P.Q.2d 1881 (C.D.Cal.1991); Land O'Lakes Creameries, Inc. v. Oconomowoc Canning Co., 221 F.Supp. 576 (E.D.Wis.1963), affirmed 330 F.2d 667 (7th Cir.1964). In some cases reasonable reliance on the licensee's own quality control measures may be sufficient even in the absence of express contractual requirements. See, e.g., Taco Cabana Int'l, Inc. v. Two Pesos, Inc., 932 F.2d

1113 (5th Cir.1991), affirmed ___ U.S. ___, 112 S.Ct. 2753, 120 L.Ed.2d 615 (1992); Transgo, *supra*; Printers Services Co. v. Bondurant, 20 U.S.P.Q.2d 1626 (C.D.Cal.1991); Embedded Moments, Inc. v. Int'l Silver Co., 648 F.Supp. 187 (E.D.N.Y.1986); Syntex Laboratories, *supra*. The absence of complaints by consumers or other indications of unsatisfactory quality is evidence of the reasonableness of the licensor's reliance. See, e.g., Transgo, *supra*; Printers Services, *supra*; Syntex Laboratories, *supra*; Land O'Lakes Creameries, *supra*.

In some cases the requirement of reasonable control can be satisfied if the licensor itself provides the major parts or ingredients for the licensee's product. See, e.g., Transgo, *supra*; Sterling Drug Inc. v. Lincoln Laboratories, Inc., 322 F.2d 968 (7th Cir. 1963); Coca–Cola Co. v. Bennett, 238 Fed. 513 (8th Cir.1916); Hurricane Fence Co., *supra*. Excessive restrictions on the licensee's ability to do business with others, however, may constitute an illegal tying arrangement under antitrust law. Compare, e.g., Northern v. McGraw–Edison Co., 542 F.2d 1336 (8th Cir.1976), cert. denied 429 U.S. 1097, 97 S.Ct. 1115, 51 L.Ed.2d 544 (1977), and Siegel v. Chicken Delight, Inc., 448 F.2d 43 (9th Cir.1971), cert. denied 405 U.S. 955, 92 S.Ct. 1172, 31 L.Ed.2d 232 (1972), with Jack Walters & Sons Corp. v. Morton Building, Inc., 737 F.2d 698 (7th Cir.), cert. denied 469 U.S. 1018, 105 S.Ct. 432, 83 L.Ed.2d 359 (1984); Hamro v. Shell Oil Co., 674 F.2d 784 (9th Cir.1982); Principe v. McDonald's Corp., 631 F.2d 303 (4th Cir.1980), cert. denied 451 U.S. 970, 101 S.Ct. 2047, 68 L.Ed.2d 349 (1981); and Kentucky Fried Chicken Corp. v. Diversified Packaging Corp., 549 F.2d 368 (5th Cir.1977). See generally Jefferson Parish Hospital Dist. No. 2 v. Hyde, 466 U.S. 2, 104 S.Ct. 1551, 80 L.Ed.2d 2 (1984); Gilson, *supra*, § 6.02; McCarthy, *supra*, § 18.19.

The licensor's obligation of reasonable control can be satisfied through supervision or testing conducted by third persons. See Turner v. HMH Pub. Co., 380 F.2d 224 (5th Cir.), cert. denied 389 U.S. 1006, 88 S.Ct. 566, 19 L.Ed.2d 601 (1967) (control by licensee over sublicensees); Crown Fabrics Corp. v. American Viscose Corp., 145 F.2d 246 (C.C.P.A.1944) (testing agency); Accurate Merchandising, Inc. v. American Pacific, 186 U.S.P.Q. 197 (S.D.N.Y.1975) (supervision by shareholder of licensor); Syntex Laboratories, *supra* (licensee was subject to governmental regulations). See also Borchard & Osman, Trademark Sublicensing and Quality Control, 70 Trademark Rep. 99 (1980).

Ownership of the licensee in whole or in part by the licensor is evidence of the control required under this Section. See, e.g., Sterling Drug, *supra*; Health Industries, Inc. v. European Health Spas, 489 F.Supp. 860 (D.S.D.1980). Similarly, common control of the licensor and licensee by members of the same family can be evidence of reasonable quality control. See Hurricane Fence Co., *supra*; Taffy Original Designs, *supra*. But see Heaton Enterprises, Inc. v. Lang, 7 U.S.P.Q.2d 1842 (Tm.Tr.App. Bd.1988).

Examples of limited supervision held sufficient to satisfy the requirement of reasonable control include *Dawn Donut Co., supra*; *Embedded Moments, Inc., supra*; *Nestle Co., supra*. Cases finding insufficient control by the licensor include Haymaker Sports, Inc. v. Turian, 581

F.2d 257 (C.C.P.A.1978) (dictum); Sheila's Shine Products, Inc. v. Sheila Shine, Inc., 486 F.2d 114 (5th Cir. 1973); First Interstate Bancorp v. Stenquist, 16 U.S.P.Q.2d 1704 (N.D.Cal.1990); Universal City Studios, Inc. v. Nintendo Co., 578 F.Supp. 911 (S.D.N.Y.1983), affirmed on other grounds 746 F.2d 112 (2d Cir.1984); First National Bank v. Autoteller Systems Service Corp., 9 U.S.P.Q.2d 1740 (Tm.Tr.App.Bd. 1988).

Comment d. A licensee ordinarily has no independent standing to bring an action for trademark infringement. See, e.g., Pure Food Products, Inc. v. American Bakeries Co., 176 U.S.P.Q. 233 (N.D.Ill.1972); Hertz Corp. v. Knickerbocker, 206 F.Supp. 305 (S.D.N.Y.1962); Cine–Pak Corp. v. Pathecolor, Inc., 187 F.Supp. 498 (D.N.J.1960). Several cases, however, recognize the standing of exclusive licensees to maintain an action for unauthorized use of the trademark under § 43(a) of the Lanham Act. See, e.g., Frisch's Restaurants, Inc. v. Elby's Big Boy, Inc., 670 F.2d 642 (6th Cir.), cert. denied 459 U.S. 916, 103 S.Ct. 231, 74 L.Ed.2d 182 (1982); Norman M. Morris Corp. v. Weinstein, 466 F.2d 137 (5th Cir.1972); Business Trends Analysts v. Freedonia Group, Inc., 650 F.Supp. 1452 (S.D.N.Y.1987); Della Palma Ice Cream, Inc. v. Caffe Delle Palme, 623 F.Supp. 138 (E.D.N.Y. 1985); Silverstar Enterprises, Inc. v. Aday, 537 F.Supp. 236 (S.D.N.Y. 1982); D.M. & Antique Import Corp. v. Royal Saxe Corp., 311 F.Supp. 1261 (S.D.N.Y.1969). In some circumstances even a nonexclusive licensee may have standing to bring an action under § 43(a) if it is likely to be damaged by the unauthorized use. See Quabaug Rubber Co. v. Fabiano Shoe Co., 567 F.2d 154 (1st Cir.1977); Traditional Living, Inc. v. Energy Log Homes, Inc., 464 F.Supp. 1024 (N.D.Ala.1978); National Lampoon, Inc. v. American Broadcasting Cos., 376 F.Supp. 733 (S.D.N.Y.), affirmed 497 F.2d 1343 (2d Cir.1974). If the use to which the licensee objects has been authorized by the owner of the trademark, however, there may be no likelihood of confusion. See Ballet Makers, Inc. v. United States Shoe Corp., 633 F.Supp. 1328 (S.D.N.Y. 1986); Silverstar Enterprises, *supra*.

Actions for the infringement of registered trademarks under § 32 of the Lanham Act must be brought "by the registrant," 15 U.S.C.A. § 1114, which includes the registrant's "legal representative, predecessors, successors and assigns." 15 U.S.C.A. § 1127. A licensee is thus precluded from maintaining an action under § 32 unless the transaction is characterized as an assignment. See, e.g., DEP Corp. v. Interstate Cigar Co., 622 F.2d 621 (2d Cir.1980), questioning contrary dictum in Quabaug Rubber Co., *supra*; Frisch's Restaurant, Inc. v. Elby's Big Boy, Inc., 849 F.2d 1012 (6th Cir.1988) (declining to resolve the standing of an exclusive licensee under § 32 in light of its right to proceed under § 43(a)); Silverstar Enterprises, *supra* (agreement was a license and not an assignment). See generally Gilson, *supra*, § 8.16[1].

Decisions estopping a licensee from asserting a claim of ownership adverse to the licensor include, e.g., Seven–Up Bottling Co. v. Seven–Up Co., 561 F.2d 1275 (8th Cir.1977); Pacific Supply Cooperative v. Farmers Union Central Exchange, Inc., 318 F.2d 894 (9th Cir.1963), cert. denied 375 U.S. 965, 84 S.Ct. 483, 11 L.Ed.2d 414 (1964); Smith v. Dental Products Co., 140 F.2d 140 (7th Cir.), cert.

denied 322 U.S. 743, 64 S.Ct. 1146, 88 L.Ed. 1576 (1944); Norden Restaurant Corp. v. Sons of the Revolution, 51 N.Y.2d 518, 434 N.Y.S.2d 967, 415 N.E.2d 956 (1980), cert. denied 454 U.S. 825, 102 S.Ct. 115, 70 L.Ed.2d 100 (1981). Cases precluding a licensee's challenge to the validity of a mark on the basis of a lack of distinctiveness include, e.g., Beer Nuts, Inc. v. King Nut Co., 477 F.2d 326 (6th Cir.), cert. denied 414 U.S. 858, 94 S.Ct. 66, 38 L.Ed.2d 326 (1973); Bandag Inc. v. Lewis General Tires, Inc., 207 U.S.P.Q. 745 (W.D.N.Y. 1980); Council of Better Business Bureaus, Inc. v. Better Business Bureau, Inc., 200 U.S.P.Q. 282 (S.D.Fla. 1978); Baker Boy Bakeries, Inc. v. Old World Baking Co., 116 U.S.P.Q. 567 (N.D.Ill.1958). Cf. Levine v. McDonald's Corp., 209 U.S.P.Q. 526 (D.Ariz.1979) (licensee estopped from challenging licensor's registration as fraudulent). But cf. Donald F. Duncan, Inc. v. Royal Tops Manufacturing Co., 343 F.2d 655 (7th Cir.1965) (interpreting the estoppel doctrine in a manner that allowed a former licensee to challenge the designation as generic); National Union Electric Corp. v. Emerson Electronics, S.p.A., 194 U.S.P.Q. 335 (S.D.N.Y.1975) (declining to enjoin a licensee's legal challenge to the validity of the mark). Some cases expressly distinguish the decision of the United States Supreme Court in Lear, Inc. v. Adkins, 395 U.S. 653, 89 S.Ct. 1902, 23 L.Ed.2d 610 (1969), which rejected the use of licensee estoppel to bar challenges to the validity of a licensed patent. See Danskin, Inc. v. Dan River, Inc., 498 F.2d 1386 (C.C.P.A. 1974); Beer Nuts, Inc., *supra*.

Several cases have invoked the estoppel doctrine to preclude a licensee from arguing that the mark has been abandoned as a result of the licensor's failure to control the licensee's use. See Professional Golfers Association v. Bankers Life & Casualty Co., 514 F.2d 665 (5th Cir.1975); Union Tank Car Co. v. Lindsay Soft Water Corp., 257 F.Supp. 510 (D.Neb.1966), affirmed sub nom. Heaton Distributing Co. v. Union Tank Car Co., 387 F.2d 477 (8th Cir.1967) (barring a claim of inadequate control even over other licensees); Distillerie Flli Ramazzotti v. Banfi Products Corp., 52 Misc.2d 593, 276 N.Y.S.2d 413 (Sup.Ct.1966), affirmed 27 A.D.2d 905, 280 N.Y.S.2d 892 (1967). But see Edwin K. Williams & Co. v. Edwin K. Williams & Co.-East, 542 F.2d 1053 (9th Cir.1976), cert. denied 433 U.S. 908, 97 S.Ct. 2973, 53 L.Ed.2d 1092 (1977) (deciding licensee's lack of control argument on the merits); Sheila's Shine Products, Inc. v. Sheila Shine, Inc., 486 F.2d 114 (5th Cir. 1973) (licensor is estopped from challenging uncontrolled licensee's use). The case for estoppel is weaker when the licensee asserts a lack of control by the licensor over other users. But see Union Tank Car, *supra*.

A licensee should not be precluded from challenging the licensor's interest in the trademark on the basis of facts arising after the termination of the license. See, e.g., Professional Golfers Association, *supra*; National Council of YMCA v. Columbia YMCA, 8 U.S.P.Q.2d 1682 (D.S.C. 1988); Council of Better Business Bureaus, *supra*; Urantia Foundation v. First Urantia Soc., Inc., 219 U.S.P.Q. 66 (S.D.Tex.1982).

On licensee estoppel, see generally Gilson, *supra*, § 6.03[7]; McCarthy, *supra*, § 18.20; Treece, Licensee Estoppel in Patent and Trademark Cases, 53 Iowa L.Rev. 525 (1967).

§ 34. Assignment of Trademarks

The owner of a trademark, trade name, collective mark, or certification mark may transfer ownership of the designation to another through an assignment. An assignment of ownership transfers the assignor's priority in the use of the designation to the assignee only if the assignee also acquires the line of business that is associated with the designation or otherwise maintains continuity in the use of the designation by continuing the line of business without substantial change. An assignment of ownership that does not maintain continuity in the use of the designation can result in abandonment of the designation under the rule stated in § 30.

Comment:

a. Scope. This Section states the rules governing the consequences of an assignment of rights in a trademark, trade name, collective mark, or certification mark. The Section governs only transfers of ownership and does not apply to agreements intended merely to license the use of a designation by another. Rules relating to the licensing of marks are stated in § 33. See also § 29 on the effect of an assignment as consent.

b. History and rationale. A trademark identifies the goods or services of the trademark owner and distinguishes them from the goods or services of others. See § 9. The mark thus symbolizes the reputation and good will of the line of business with which it is associated, and no protectable interest exists in a designation independent of the good will that the designation represents. If trademarks were freely transferable apart from the associated line of business, the ability of trademarks to communicate useful information to consumers would be undermined. The transfer of trademark rights to another is consistent with the identifying function of trademarks only if the mark is used by the assignee in connection with substantially the same business. This conception of the nature of trademark rights gave rise to the common law rule that a trademark cannot be transferred "in gross," with the result that an assignment of a trademark without a simultaneous transfer of the good will symbolized by the mark is not effective to transfer the assignor's rights in the mark to the assignee. The requirement that an assignment of a trademark must be accompanied by an assignment of the business good will associated with the mark is codified in § 10 of the Lanham Act. 15 U.S.C.A. § 1060.

Early applications of the rule against assignments in gross focused on whether the assignment included the tangible assets used in the assignor's business. The transfer of assets such as equipment, formulas, or other factors of production can be evidence that an assignment of the mark is not in gross, but rather encompasses the good will symbolized by the designation. The good will associated with many businesses, however, is not dependent on the possession of particular assets. In addition, the traditional focus on the transfer of tangible assets is not necessarily sufficient to protect against the possibility of consumer confusion since a transfer of tangible assets does not insure that the assignee of the mark will use the assets to produce goods or services comparable with those formerly marketed under the designation. Accordingly, courts now evaluate each assignment in light of the circumstances of the particular case, including both the terms of the transfer and the nature of the assignee's subsequent use. Recent decisions recognize that the central inquiry is whether the use of the mark by the assignee is likely to confuse prospective purchasers by departing from the expectations created by the presence of the trademark. The traditional requirement of an accompanying transfer of good will can thus be understood as requiring that the assignment not disrupt the existing significance of the mark to consumers.

An assignment of a trademark may be intended to accomplish several objectives. In the most common case, the assignee seeks to acquire the assignor's rights in the mark in order to carry on the assignor's business. The assignee thus expects to have the benefit of the assignor's priority in the use of the mark against claims by third persons. In such circumstances the rule against assignments in gross insures that the assignee has a legitimate right to assert the priority of the assignor. In other cases, however, the purpose of the assignment is merely to prevent the assignor from asserting a claim against the assignee's use of a similar mark, and the assignee has no intention of exploiting the assignor's good will or priority in the mark. Since the rule against assignments in gross does not invalidate the agreement as between the parties, an assignment can be effective to accomplish this latter purpose without regard to the transfer of good will. See § 29.

c. Transfer of priority of use. An assignee does not succeed to the assignor's priority in the use of the designation unless the transaction permits the assignee to continue the line of business with which the mark is associated. Although early cases required a transfer of tangible assets from the assignor's business, more recent cases recognize that a transfer of tangible assets is merely one factor that may indicate whether the assignment will permit the assignee to preserve continuity in the use of the designation. For example, the associational significance of a mark used in a business that does not depend on specialized assets can be maintained without a transfer of tangible property. In some circumstances, the management or personnel of a business may be the most important element in assuring the continuity of the business represented by the mark. On the other hand, a failure to transfer highly specialized assets such as patented machines or secret formulas can be evidence that the associational significance of the mark will not be maintained. In the final analysis, the question is whether the assignee has acquired enough of the assignor's business to maintain continuity in the use of the designation. Thus, some courts now recognize that an assignment of a mark followed by the assignee's use of the designation to identify goods, services, or a business substantially similar to the assignor's is itself sufficient to permit the assignee to assert the assignor's priority in the use of the designation. An assignee's use is substantially similar to the use by the assignor if the expectations of consumers who rely on the presence of the designation after the assignment will be substantially fulfilled. The changes that are permitted without disrupting the assignee's succession to the assignor's priority thus depend on the nature of the goods or services. Consumers expect that the quality and characteristics of some types of goods or services will change over time even when the business is continued by the same owner, and similar changes by an assignee are thus permissible. On the other hand, if the goods are unique, such as goods produced under a patent or secret formula, or have a reputation for a specific characteristic, deception is likely if the assignee does not maintain those qualities in the goods marketed under the designation.

Assignments typically occur as part of the sale of a business and a transfer of the trade name identifying the business and the trademarks identifying the goods or services of the business. However, an owner may instead transfer only a distinct line of business together with the associated trademark, while continuing the remainder of the business under other marks. An owner may also transfer the business and associated trademarks in only a particular geographic area. In each of these cases, the transaction will be effective to transfer the assignor's priority in the use of the assigned designation to the assignee.

An assignee may license the assignor to use the trademark after an assignment. If the assignment satisfies the requirements stated in this Section and the subsequent license back to the assignor satisfies the requirements stated in § 33, the priority arising from the assignor's original use of the trademark is maintained.

Illustrations:

1. *A* uses the mark FLUFF for its dry cleaning detergent beginning in November, 1966. In August, 1971, *B* begins to use the mark FLUFF BACK for dry cleaning detergent in the same market. In October, 1971, *A* assigns its rights in the FLUFF mark to *C*. In an infringement suit brought by *C* against *B*, *C* has priority in the use of the trademark unless the transfer from *A* to *C* was an assignment in gross.

2. *A* first uses the mark THE MONEY TREE for banking services in New Jersey in January, 1972. In August, 1972, *B* in good faith and without notice of *A* 's prior use begins to use the same mark for similar services in Chicago. *A* registers the mark under the Lanham Act in April, 1974. *C* subsequently obtains an assignment of *B* 's mark and begins to conduct business under the mark in Chicago. If the assignment from *B* to *C* was not an assignment in gross, *C* succeeds to *B* 's priority in the use of the mark and thus is not subject to liability to *A* for infringement in the area in which *B* used the mark in good faith prior to *A* 's registration. See § 19, Comment *e*.

d. Transfers to exclusive distributors. When a manufacturer markets trademarked goods through an exclusive distributor, the source identified by the trademark may be either the manufacturer or the distributor. In many instances the manufacturer controls the nature and quality of the goods and the distributor merely resells the finished product. In other instances, however, the distributor may determine specifications and otherwise control the quality of the goods sold under the trademark. The perception of consumers as to the source identified by the trademark may thus be uncertain or ambiguous. Courts in such cases will ordinarily recognize an agreement allocating or assigning ownership of the trademark between the manufacturer and distributor without regard to any accompanying transfer of tangible assets or other indicia of good will, unless the result is clearly inconsistent with the actual significance of the mark to consumers. Thus, an assignment of United States trademark rights by a foreign manufacturer to its United States distributor ordinarily will not be regarded as an assignment in gross, even if the transfer occurs after the designation has acquired trademark significance in this country.

e. Security interests in trademarks. A trademark may be used as collateral for a debt. The creation of a security interest in a trademark is not an assignment of the mark under the rule stated in this Section and thus does not affect the debtor's ownership or priority in the use of the mark. A transfer of ownership of the mark to a creditor upon a default by the debtor, however, is an assignment that is subject to the rules in this Section. Thus, a creditor who on default obtains a mark without the associated business does not succeed to the debtor's priority of use. Although such a transfer in gross is effective as between the parties themselves, the creditor's rights in the mark against third persons will be determined by its own use and not that of the debtor. See Comment *f.* A creditor who seeks to obtain the full value of a trademark as collateral must therefore obtain an interest not only in the trademark, but also in the associated line of business through a security interest in physical assets or other aspects of the debtor's business sufficient to permit continuity in the use of the designation. See Comment *c.*

f. Effect of assignment in gross. The assignee of an assignment in gross does not succeed to the assignor's priority in the use of the mark. A few courts have held that an assignment in gross also constitutes an abandonment of the mark. The issue of abandonment, however, is properly governed by the rules stated in § 30, and the effect of an assignment in gross thus depends on the application of those rules to the facts of the particular case. An assignment typically results in a cessation of use by the assignor. The assignment may also be evidence of the assignor's intent not to resume use. Thus, an assignment in gross followed by a period of nonuse by the assignor can result in abandonment of the assignor's priority in the use of the mark under the rule stated in § 30(2)(a). Substantial use by an assignee following an assignment in gross can also cause the mark to lose its significance as an accurate indication of source, thus resulting in abandonment under the rule stated in § 30(2)(b). However, an assignment in gross does not necessarily entail either of these consequences. For example, after an assignment in gross the mark may for a time retain its original trademark significance, and thus an assignment back to the original assignor, or a subsequent transfer of the associated business to the assignee, can avoid abandonment and preserve the original priority in the use of the mark.

If an assignment in gross results in the abandonment of the assignor's priority in the mark under the rules stated in § 30, new rights may be acquired in the designation through subsequent use. See § 30, Comment *a.* Thus, an assignee under an assignment in gross may acquire rights through its own use of the mark, but its priority is then determined by the assignee's use and not the prior use by the assignor. A third person may also acquire rights in the mark on the basis of use prior to that of the assignee. However, if the original source significance of the mark continues after the abandonment, use by the assignee or by third persons may result in consumer confusion. In such cases, the subsequent user may be subject to the defense of unclean hands when asserting rights in the mark. See § 32, Comment *b*.

g. Assignment of personal name designations. An individual's personal name may function as a trademark if the name has acquired distinctiveness as required under the rule stated in § 13. See § 14, Comment *e*. A personal name mark can ordinarily be assigned to another along with the business that the name has come to represent. The personal name, however, may also continue to symbolize the identity and personal reputation of the named individual. An assignment of a personal name mark will not ordinarily be interpreted to preclude the named individual from all subsequent use of the name in business unless the intention to do so is clearly expressed. Thus, courts frequently attempt to accommodate the assignor's continuing interest in legitimate use of the name with the interest of the assignee and the public in the prevention of confusion.

The rule relating to the fair use of trademarks stated in § 28 is applicable to the continued use of a personal name by an assignor. Thus, unless otherwise agreed, the assignor may use the name in good faith to indicate his or her connection with another business if the name is used in a reasonable manner calculated to avoid a likelihood of confusion with the assignee. For example, in some circumstances a court may permit the assignor to use the personal name in promotional material describing a new business, but not as a prominent feature of a trade name or trademark. See § 35, Comment *d*. The scope of permissible use by the assignor of a personal name mark will generally depend on the relative significance of the name in symbolizing the good will of the assigned business as distinguished from the personal skill, talent, and identity of the assignor.

In a few circumstances the commercial significance of a personal name mark may be so closely related to the personality or ability of the named individual that the mark is incapable of assignment because the associated good will cannot be transferred to another. This is generally the case, for example, with personal name marks symbolizing the business good will of professionals such as attorneys or physicians.

REPORTERS' NOTE

The rules governing assignments of trademarks appeared in Restatement of Torts §§ 755–756 (1938). See generally Gilson, Trademark Protection and Practice § 3.07; McCarthy, Trademarks and Unfair Competition §§ 18.01–12.

Comment a. Section 10 of the Lanham Act, 15 U.S.C.A. § 1060, states, "Assignments shall be by instruments in writing duly executed," and provides for the recording in the Patent and Trademark Office of assignments of registered marks and applications for registration. Applications based on intent to use, however, cannot be assigned prior to actual use of the mark except to "a successor to the business of the applicant, or portion thereof, to which the mark pertains, if that business is ongoing and existing." *Id.* A written assignment is unnecessary to transfer common law rights. See, e.g., Speed Products Co. v. Tinnerman Products, Inc., 179 F.2d 778 (2d Cir.1949); Airport Canteen Services, Inc. v. Farmer's Daughter, Inc., 184 U.S.P.Q. 622 (Tm.Tr.App.Bd.1974). Cf. Uniform Commercial Code § 1–206 (statute of frauds provision applicable to certain contracts for the sale of personal property). Trademark rights are ordinarily presumed to pass with a sale of the associated business absent evidence of a contrary intent. See, e.g., Speed Products, *supra* ; Loma Linda Food Co. v. Thomson & Taylor Spice Co., 279 F.2d 522 (C.C.P.A.1960); Discount Muffler Shop, Inc. v. Meineke Realty Corp., 535 F.Supp. 439 (N.D.Ohio 1982); Airport Canteen Services, *supra.*

Comment b. Courts consistently recognize that a trademark has no independent existence apart from the good will that the mark represents. See, e.g., United Drug Co. v. Theodore Rectanus Co., 248 U.S. 90, 97, 39 S.Ct. 48, 50, 63 L.Ed. 141, 145 (1918) ("There is no such thing as property in a trademark except as a right appurtenant to an established business or trade in connection with which the mark is employed."); Marshak v. Green, 746 F.2d 927, 929 (2d Cir. 1984) ("[A trademark] has no independent significance apart from the good will it symbolizes."). Section 10 of the Lanham Act permits assignments only "with the goodwill of the business in which the mark is used, or with that part of the goodwill of the business connected with the use of and symbolized by the mark." 15 U.S.C.A. § 1060.

The rule prohibiting assignments in gross is designed to prevent the confusion of consumers. See, e.g., Green River Bottling Co. v. Green River Corp., 997 F.2d 359 (7th Cir.1993); Visa, U.S.A., Inc. v. Birmingham Trust National Bank, 696 F.2d 1371 (Fed.Cir.1982), cert. denied 464 U.S. 826, 104 S.Ct. 98, 78 L.Ed.2d 104 (1983); Syntex Laboratories, Inc. v. Norwich Pharmacal Co., 315 F.Supp. 45 (S.D.N.Y.1970), affirmed 437 F.2d 566 (2d Cir.1971); J. Atkins Holdings Ltd. v. English Discounts, Inc., 729 F.Supp. 945 (S.D.N.Y.1990). In a few instances, however, courts have applied the assignment in gross rule to invalidate assignments in the absence of any likelihood of consumer confusion. In Haymaker Sports, Inc. v. Turian, 581 F.2d 257 (C.C.P.A.1978), a trademark was assigned to escrow agents as collateral for a debt, and the assignor continued to operate the business under a trademark license from the assignees. The majority found the assignment invalid and canceled the registration of the mark, although the dissenters forcefully argued that consumers were not confused because the mark was continuously used by the assignor to identify its goods.

Comment c. McCarthy, *supra,* § 18.07, notes that the "clear trend is that a transfer of tangible or physical assets is not crucial" to an effective assignment. Numerous cases have upheld trademark assignments without a transfer of tangible assets. See, e.g., Hy–Cross Hatchery, Inc. v. Osborne, 303 F.2d 947 (C.C.P.A. 1962); Glamorene Products Corp. v. Procter & Gamble Co., 538 F.2d 894 (C.C.P.A.1976); Visa, U.S.A., Inc. v. Birmingham Trust National Bank, 696 F.2d 1371 (Fed.Cir.1982), cert. denied 464 U.S. 826, 104 S.Ct. 98, 78 L.Ed.2d 104 (1983); Sterling Brewers, Inc. v. Schenley Industries, Inc., 441 F.2d 675, 680 (C.C.P.A.1971) ("[W]e see no reason why tangible assets must necessarily be included in the assignment of a trademark with the good will of the business associated with it.").

Continuity in the use of a trademark can be established in numerous ways. In Bambu Sales, Inc. v. Sultana Crackers, Inc., 683 F.Supp. 899 (E.D.N.Y.1988), the assignee had been the exclusive distributor of the trademarked goods in the United States prior to the assignment and was recognized as possessing the good will associated with the mark. A subsequent assignment without physical assets was upheld. See Comment *d*. When the goods are based on a secret formula or patent, transfer of the formula or patent may be necessary. See, e.g., Mulhens & Kropff, Inc. v. Ferd Muelhens, Inc., 43 F.2d 937 (2d Cir.), cert. denied 282 U.S. 881, 51 S.Ct. 84, 75 L.Ed. 777 (1930). If the value of the mark depends on the talents or skills of particular individuals, the relocation of those individuals to the assignee may be sufficient. See Marshak v. Green, 746 F.2d 927 (2d Cir.1984) (dictum). But cf. Liquid Glass Enterprises, Inc. v. Liquid Glass Industries, Ltd., 14 U.S.P.Q.2d 1976 (E.D.Mich.1989) (a statement in the assignment purporting to transfer "goodwill" is not dispositive).

An assignment can be supported either by a transfer of assets or by subsequent use of the mark by the assignee on substantially similar goods or services. See, e.g., Defiance Button Machine Co. v. C & C Metal Products, 759 F.2d 1053, 1059 (2d Cir.), cert. denied 474 U.S. 844, 106 S.Ct. 131, 88 L.Ed.2d 108 (1985) ("Nonetheless, assignments of marks separate from the underlying business have been upheld when the assignee 'is producing a product * * * substantially similar to that of the assignor [such that] consumers would not be deceived or harmed' or when there is 'continuity of management,'" quoting Marshak, *supra*); Main Street Outfitters, Inc. v. Federated Department Stores, Inc., 730 F.Supp. 289 (D.Minn.1989); Bambu Sales, Inc., *supra*.

An assignment is ineffective to transfer the assignor's priority if the assignee uses the mark on substantially different goods or services. PepsiCo, Inc. v. Grapette Co., 416 F.2d 285 (8th Cir.1969) (acquisition of a mark used on a cola drink did not confer priority when the assignee used the mark on a pepper drink); Independent Baking Powder Co. v. Boorman, 175 Fed. 448 (C.C.N.J. 1910) (priority of mark used on alum baking powder could not be transferred for use on phosphate powder). Cf. Clark & Freeman Corp. v. Heartland Co., 811 F.Supp. 137 (S.D.N.Y. 1993) (women's boots and men's shoes). Whether the goods or services of the assignee are substantially different from those originally identified by the mark depends on whether confusion is likely. Visa, U.S.A., Inc., *supra*. The change in the goods or services must be substantial in order to deprive the assignee of the assignor's priority, and normal or expected variations or alterations in the quality or characteristics of the product will not invalidate the assignment. The leading case is *Hy-Cross Hatchery, Inc., supra,* in which an assignee who acquired the trademark of a chicken hatchery without receiving any physical assets or instructions in the assignor's business methods succeeded to the priority of the assignor despite the assignee's use of the mark on different varieties of chicken. See also Glamorene Products Corp., *supra* (assignment was valid although the assignee changed the formulation of the dry cleaning detergent sold under the mark); Bambu Sales, Inc., *supra* (change by the assignee to a thinner cigarette paper found not substantial).

Early cases cast doubt on whether the assignor could assign a mark and the portion of the assignor's business represented by the mark and then continue in the same business under another designation. See Independent Baking Powder, *supra* ; Eiseman v. Schiffer, 157 Fed. 473 (C.C.N.Y.1907). Other cases, see, e.g., Abraham & Straus, Inc. v. Truval Mfrs., Inc., 138 F.2d 77 (C.C.P.A. 1943), and § 10 of the Lanham Act, 15 U.S.C.A. § 1060, permit such transfers if the portion of the business associated with the assigned mark is transferred to the assignee. Assignments limited to distinct geographic areas have also been upheld. See Int'l Armament Corp. v. Matra Manurhin Int'l, Inc., 630 F.Supp. 741 (E.D.Va.1986) (assignment of United States rights); Coca-Cola Bottling Co. v. Coca-Cola Co., 269 Fed. 796 (D.Del.1920) (assignment in specified states); California Wine & Liquor Corp. v. William Zakon & Sons, 297 Mass. 373, 8 N.E.2d 812 (1937) (assignment of New England rights).

Transactions involving the assignment of a mark with a license back to the assignor have also been upheld. See, e.g., E. & J. Gallo Winery v. Gallo Cattle Co., 967 F.2d 1280 (9th Cir.1992) (transaction in settlement of infringement claim); Visa, U.S.A., Inc., *supra* ; Geo. A. Hormel & Co. v. Hereford Heaven Brands, Inc., 341 F.2d 158 (C.C.P.A.1965). See also McCarthy, *supra,* § 18.01[9]. A one-year lease of a restaurant granting the lessee the exclusive right to use the accompanying trademark for the year and containing a covenant that the lessee would not compete for one year after the termination of the lease was held to be a valid assignment in Stock Pot Restaurant, Inc. v. Stockpot, Inc., 737 F.2d 1576 (Fed. Cir.1984). Intra-family transactions allocating the right to sell cosmetics bearing the trademark of the family-owned business were held not to constitute assignments in gross in Marcon, Ltd. v. Helena Rubenstein, Inc., 694 F.2d 953 (4th Cir.1982).

Illustration 1 is suggested by the facts in *Glamorene Products Corp., supra.*

Illustration 2 is based on Money Store v. Harriscorp Finance, Inc., 689 F.2d 666 (7th Cir.1982).

Comment d. The ownership of marks as between manufacturers and exclusive distributors is discussed in McCarthy, *supra,* § 16.16. Courts will ordinarily enforce agreements between manufacturers and distributors allocating ownership of a trademark. See, e.g., E.F. Prichard Co. v. Consumers Brewing Co., 136 F.2d 512 (6th Cir.1943), cert. denied 321 U.S. 763, 64 S.Ct. 486, 88 L.Ed. 1060 (1944); Columbia Nastri & Carta

Carbone, S/p/A v. Columbia Ribbon & Carbon Mfg. Co., 367 F.2d 308 (2d Cir.1966). Cf. Premier Dental Products Co. v. Darby Dental Supply Co., 794 F.2d 850, 854 (3d Cir.), cert. denied 479 U.S. 950, 107 S.Ct. 436, 93 L.Ed. 385 (1986) ("The ownership of a trademark as between a manufacturer and an exclusive distributor is largely determined by the parties' agreement," but "it is not dispositive.").

An assignment from a foreign manufacturer to a domestic distributor was upheld against an assignment in gross claim in Premier Dental Products, *supra.* See also Scandinavia Belting Co. v. Asbestos & Rubber Works, Inc., 257 Fed. 937 (2d Cir.), cert. denied 250 U.S. 644, 39 S.Ct. 494, 63 L.Ed. 1186 (1919) (assignment by English owner to American exclusive distributor was sufficient to transfer ownership for purposes of securing federal registration); J. Atkins Holdings, Ltd. v. English Discounts, Inc., 729 F.Supp. 945, 950 (S.D.N.Y.1990) (assignment by foreign manufacturer to domestic company did not violate the rule precluding "naked" assignments since the transaction "is designed to continue the employment of the trademarks in connection with the same goods on which their reputation is based"); Bambu Sales, Inc. v. Sultana Crackers, Inc., 683 F.Supp. 899 (E.D.N.Y. 1988).

In the absence of an agreement courts generally presume that the foreign manufacturer rather than the domestic distributor is the owner of the domestic trademark rights. See, e.g., Ilapak Research & Dev. S.A. v. Record SpA., 762 F.Supp. 1318 (N.D.Ill.1991); Energy Jet, Inc. v. Forex Corp., 589 F.Supp. 1110 (E.D.Mich.1984). On the factors relevant in rebutting that presumption, see, e.g., Ilapak, *supra*; Energy Jet, *supra*; Omega Nutrition U.S.A., Inc. v. Spectrum Marketing, Inc., 756 F.Supp. 435 (N.D.Cal.1991).

Comment e. The creation of a security interest in a trademark is not a present assignment subject to the assignment in gross rule. Li'l' Red Barn, Inc. v. Red Barn System, Inc., 322 F.Supp. 98 (N.D.Ind.1970), affirmed 174 U.S.P.Q. 193 (7th Cir. 1972); In re Roman Cleanser Co., 802 F.2d 207 (6th Cir.1986) (Thomas, J., concurring). However, an assignment of the trademark to a creditor upon default without an assignment of the associated business has been held to be an assignment in gross. Haymaker Sports, Inc. v. Turian, 581 F.2d 257 (C.C.P.A.1978).

It has been held that a filing pursuant to the rules in Article 9 of the Uniform Commercial Code is sufficient to perfect a security interest in even a federally registered mark notwithstanding the filing provisions relating to assignments in § 10 of the Lanham Act, 15 U.S.C.A. § 1060. See In re Roman Cleanser Co., *supra*; In re TR–3 Industries, 41 Bankr. 128 (Bankr.C.D.Cal.1984). Commentators, however, acknowledge uncertainty as to the proper method of perfecting security interests in registered trademarks. See Porto, The Scope of UCC Article 9: Is Filing Under Article 9 Sufficient to Perfect a Security Interest in a Patent or Trademark?, 93 Comm.L.J. 384 (1988); Comment, Perfection of Security Interests in Intellectual Property: Federal Statutes Preempt Article 9, 57 Geo.Wash.L.Rev. 135 (1988). See also McCarthy, *supra*, § 18.01[7].

The general rules that govern assignments of trademarks apply to sales in bankruptcy and other judicial transfers. The attachment and sale of the trademark of a musical group, for example, was held to be an assignment in gross in Marshak v. Green, 746 F.2d 927 (2d Cir.1984). However, a judicial sale is effective to transfer the debtor's rights in the mark to the purchaser if the assets constituting the underlying good will are also transferred. See, e.g., American Dirigold Corp. v. Dirigold Metals Corp., 125 F.2d 446 (6th Cir. 1942); Peeples v. Wolfe, 19 Utah 2d 258, 430 P.2d 574 (1967). See generally McCarthy, *supra*, § 18.09.

Comment f. Some cases suggest that an assignment in gross constitutes an abandonment of the mark. See, e.g., Johanna Farms, Inc. v. Citrus Bowl, Inc., 468 F.Supp. 866 (E.D.N.Y.1978). Such statements normally appear in cases determining whether the assignee has succeeded to the assignor's priority as against a third person. In such circumstances, "abandonment" may mean only that the assignee must rely for priority on its own use rather than the prior use by the assignor. In other circumstances it has been recognized that an assignment in gross does not automatically result in the abandonment of the mark, and that the normal rules relating to abandonment remain applicable. Hy–Cross Hatchery, Inc. v. Osborne, 303 F.2d 947 (C.C.P.A. 1962) (dictum); Li'l' Red Barn, Inc. v. Red Barn System, Inc., 322 F.Supp. 98 (N.D.Ind.1970), affirmed 174 U.S.P.Q. 193 (7th Cir.1972) (continued use by the assignor after the assignment prevents abandonment); Old Charter Distillery Co. v. Ooms, 73 F.Supp. 539 (D.D.C.1947), affirmed sub nom. Continental Distilling Corp. v. Old Charter Distillery Co., 188 F.2d 614 (D.C.Cir.1950) (assignment in gross does not preclude a subsequent valid assignment).

The assignee's priority in the use of a mark after an assignment in gross is determined by the assignee's own use and not that of the assignor. See Mister Donut of America, Inc. v. Mr. Donut, Inc., 418 F.2d 838 (9th Cir.1969); Morgan Creek Productions, Inc. v. Capital Cities/ABC, Inc., 22 U.S.P.Q.2d 1881 (C.D.Cal.1991) (dictum). If an assignee uses the mark on substantially different goods or services in a manner likely to deceive prospective purchasers, however, it may be precluded from asserting trademark rights under the rule relating to unclean hands as stated in § 32 without regard to whether the transfer was in gross. See Renaud Sales Co. v. Davis, 104 F.2d 683 (1st Cir.1939). See also In re Roman Cleanser Co., 802 F.2d 207 (6th Cir. 1986) (dictum).

Comment g. For a discussion of personal names as trademarks, see § 14, Comment *e*. On the assignment of personal name marks, see McCarthy, *supra*, § 18.10.

A personal name used as a trademark may be assigned with the business that it represents. Russia Cement Co. v. Le Page, 147 Mass. 206, 17 N.E. 304 (1888); Guth v. Guth Chocolate Co., 224 Fed. 932 (4th Cir.), cert. denied 239 U.S. 640, 36 S.Ct. 161, 60 L.Ed. 481 (1915); Goldwyn Pictures Corp. v. Goldwyn, 296 Fed. 391 (2d Cir.1924). See also, e.g., Levitt Corp. v. Levitt, 593 F.2d 463 (2d Cir.1979); Hanover Mfg. Co. v. Ed Hanover Trailers, Inc., 434 S.W.2d 109 (Tex.1968).

The assignor of a personal name trademark is not precluded from all subsequent use of the personal name in business unless the assignment clearly expresses such an intention. Poorman v. Julian, 22 Ill.App.2d 208, 160 N.E.2d 169 (1959); Madrigal Audio Laboratories, Inc. v. Cello, Ltd., 799 F.2d 814 (2d Cir.1986). For cases attempting to balance the right of the assignor to continue use of the personal name with the right of the assignee to be free from consumer confusion, see, e.g., Madrigal Audio Laboratories, *supra*; Levitt Corp., *supra*; Karsh v. Haiden, 120 Cal. App.2d 75, 260 P.2d 633 (1953).

In a few situations, the good will symbolized by a personal name trademark may be so intimately bound to the particular skills of the named individual that the trademark cannot be assigned. See Blakely v. Sousa, 197 Pa. 305, 47 A. 286 (1900); Messer v. The Fadettes, 168 Mass. 140, 46 N.E. 407 (1897). Cf. Rick v. Buchansky, 609 F.Supp. 1522 (S.D.N.Y.), dismissed 770 F.2d 157 (2d Cir.1985) (manager of a musical group is the owner of the group's trademark despite the turnover of members). See McCarthy, The Rights of Publicity and Privacy § 5.3[A].

An assignment of the right to use a personal name that consumers associate with a particular business by one who has no connection with that business is analogous to an assignment in gross and does not confer priority in the use of the name on the assignee. See Hat Corp. v. D.L. Davis Corp., 4 F.Supp. 613 (D.Conn.1933) (assignment of personal name by the son of the president of a famous hat manufacturer was an assignment in gross since the son had not been involved in the business); see also Nardini's Restaurant, Inc. v. Sterling Restaurant Co., 93 N.H. 364, 42 A.2d 325 (1945).

TOPIC 6. REMEDIES

Section

---

§ 35. Injunctions: Trademark Infringement and Deceptive Marketing

(1) Unless inappropriate under the rule stated in Subsection (2), injunctive relief will ordinarily be awarded against one who is liable to another for:

(a) deceptive marketing under the rules stated in §§ 2–8; or

(b) infringement of the other's trademark, trade name, collective mark, or certification mark under the rule stated in § 20; or

(c) dilution of the other's trademark, trade name, collective mark, or certification mark under the rule stated in § 25.

(2) The appropriateness and scope of injunctive relief depend upon a comparative appraisal of all the factors of the case, including the following primary factors:

(a) the nature of the interest to be protected;

(b) the nature and extent of the wrongful conduct;

(c) the relative adequacy to the plaintiff of an injunction and of other remedies;

(d) the relative harm likely to result to the legitimate interests of the defendant if an injunction is granted and to the legitimate interests of the plaintiff if an injunction is denied;

(e) the interests of third persons and of the public;

(f) any unreasonable delay by the plaintiff in bringing suit or otherwise asserting its rights;

(g) any related misconduct on the part of the plaintiff; and

(h) the practicality of framing and enforcing the injunction.

Comment:

a. Scope. This Section states the rules governing the award of injunctive relief in actions for deceptive marketing, trademark infringement, and trademark dilution. The usual remedy in tort actions is an award of damages, and the equitable remedy of an injunction was traditionally available only when the remedy of damages was inadequate. With the merger of law and equity, courts are now generally free to select the remedy or combination of remedies that most effectively protects the interests threatened by the defendant's misconduct. See Restatement, Second, Torts § 938, Comment *c*. In unfair competition cases, the wrong is ordinarily not a single act but a course of business conduct, and the plaintiff is thus subjected to continuing harm. Frequently, the harm is not reparable by an award of monetary relief because of the difficulty of proving the amount of loss and a causal connection with the defendant's wrongful conduct. See § 36. Thus, the judicial preference for injunctive relief in unfair competition cases is not an exception to ordinary remedial principles, but rather an application of those principles in a context in which injunctive relief is ordinarily the most appropriate remedy.

Section 34 of the Lanham Act, 15 U.S.C.A. § 1116, authorizes courts to grant injunctions "according to the principles of equity and upon such terms as the court may deem reasonable" to restrain the infringement of marks registered under the Act and the infringement of unregistered marks or other deceptive practices actionable under § 43(a) of the Lanham Act. State trademark registration and unfair trade practices statutes similarly authorize the issuance of injunctions. State antidilution statutes also provide for injunctive relief. See § 25. The principles stated in this Section govern the appropriateness and scope of injunctive relief under these various statutory provisions as well as injunctive relief in actions at common law.

The general rules relating to injunctive relief stated in Restatement, Second, Torts, Chapter 48 apply in actions for unfair competition. Only those rules that have particular significance to deceptive marketing, trademark infringement, or trademark dilution are considered here. This Section is derived from Restatement, Second, Torts § 936, which sets forth the general factors relating to the appropriateness of injunctions in tort actions. See also §§ 933–935, stating the standard of "appropriateness" for injunctive relief, and §§ 937–943, describing in detail the factors relevant in determining "appropriateness."

b. Appropriateness of injunctive relief. In cases of deceptive marketing, trademark infringement, or trademark dilution, a prevailing plaintiff is ordinarily awarded injunctive relief to protect both the plaintiff and the public from the likelihood of future harm. If repetition of the wrongful conduct is likely, an injunction will issue even if the defendant acted in good faith. Evidence that the defendant's conduct was willful or fraudulent can justify injunctive relief even in the absence of evidence that the misconduct is likely to recur. However, if the defendant acted in good faith and ceased the misconduct upon notification of the plaintiff's rights under circumstances making a resumption unlikely, an injunction may be denied as unnecessary for the protection of the plaintiff or the public.

Although injunctive relief is routinely granted in unfair competition cases, the remedy remains subject to equitable principles, and the court is free to balance the interests of the parties in light of the circumstances of the case. It is more likely, however, that the equities of the case will influence the scope and nature of the injunction; only in unusual circumstances is an injunction denied when the defendant is subject to liability. The plaintiff's interest in protecting the good will symbolized by its trademark or in preserving a truthful marketplace is unlikely to be adequately secured by monetary relief, and the equities thus normally favor the award of an injunction. The public interest in preventing confusion and deception also typically weighs in favor of an injunction. However, if the plaintiff's interest is not substantial in comparison with the legitimate interests of the defendant and the defendant's conduct was undertaken in good faith, the balance of equities may not justify injunctive relief. Similarly, denial of an injunction may sometimes be appropriate if the plaintiff has unreasonably delayed in asserting its rights, see § 31, or has engaged in misconduct related to the rights asserted in the action. See § 32.

c. Factors determining the scope of injunctive relief. In deceptive marketing cases, the scope of the injunction should be sufficient to prevent future deception without unreasonably interfering with the defendant's right to advertise its goods or services in a truthful manner. In trademark infringement cases, the likelihood of confusion standard determines the appropriate scope of injunctive relief, although adequate recognition should also be given to the defendant's right to use subject matter that is not eligible for protection as a trademark. See Comment *e*. Similarly, injunctive relief awarded pursuant to state antidilution statutes should be carefully tailored to the limited scope of the substantive rights recognized under such statutes.

In many cases it may be difficult as a practical matter to fashion an injunction that corresponds precisely to the wrongful conduct, and courts have considerable discretion to narrow or broaden the scope of relief according to the facts of the case. Among the factors that are important in formulating an injunction are the manner in which the plaintiff is harmed, the possible means by which the harm can be avoided, the justification advanced for the defendant's conduct, the potential burden that would be imposed on the legitimate interests of the defendant, and the potential effect upon lawful competition between the parties. If the defendant has acted in good faith and prospective purchasers can be adequately protected by disclaimers or other limited relief, or if a broad prohibition would seriously inhibit legitimate competition, the scope of the injunction may be appropriately narrow. If the defendant intended to deceive or confuse prospective purchasers, however, the injunction may extend beyond the precise scope of the original wrong in order to prevent future misconduct.

In determining the appropriate scope of injunctive relief, the court may also consider the extent to which the plaintiff has invested in planned expansion under the mark into other products or other geographic markets. Although such activities, if unknown to consumers, are not relevant to the likelihood of confusion, see § 21, Comment *j*, they may justify broader relief if a likelihood of confusion is otherwise established.

The constitutional right of free expression as applicable to commercial speech may also affect the scope of injunctive relief in unfair competition cases. Although market participants do not have a constitutional right to engage in deceptive or confusing commercial speech, restrictions on speech that extend beyond those reasonably necessary to prevent the wrongful conduct may infringe on protected rights. In addition, courts may tolerate a greater risk of deception or confusion when the defendant's conduct occurs in connection with the creation and marketing of expressive works such as parody or art, and the scope of injunctive relief in such cases may be accordingly narrow.

d. Absolute versus qualified injunctions. A trademark owner who proves infringement is ordinarily awarded an absolute injunction prohibiting further use of the designation as a trademark by the defendant. However, if the defendant demonstrates a legitimate interest in continued use of the designation, a limited injunction may achieve a more equitable balance between the interests of the plaintiff and the defendant. In determining whether an absolute or qualified injunction is appropriate, courts consider the nature of the defendant's interest in continued use, the extent to which consumer confusion can be avoided by a qualified injunction, and the defendant's good faith in initiating the use.

Mandatory disclaimers and other forms of qualified injunctions are often only partially effective in eliminating the likelihood of confusion, and thus such qualified relief is appropriate only when the defendant demonstrates a substantial interest in use of the designation. Inherently distinctive marks (see § 13) are usually accorded broad protection since a defendant generally has little justification for the subsequent use of such designations. On the other hand, qualified injunctions permitting continued use under specified conditions may sometimes be appropriate in connection with descriptive, geographic, or personal name designations. Subsequent users may have a legitimate interest in employing such terms in their original descriptive, geographic, or personal name sense. Thus, in the case of a descriptive mark, an injunction limiting the size and location of the defendant's use or requiring an accompanying disclaimer may significantly reduce the likelihood of confusion while permitting a truthful description of the defendant's product. Qualified injunctions are also sometimes appropriate to preserve a defendant's legitimate interest in the use of his or her own name or the name of the place in which the defendant's business is located.

In choosing between absolute and qualified relief, the court may properly consider whether the defendant has acted in good faith. If the defendant uses a descriptive term with an intent to create confusion or to trade on the good will of the plaintiff, an absolute injunction will ordinarily be awarded. Similarly, if the defendant has no connection with the personal name or geographic location identified by the plaintiff's mark, an absolute injunction is ordinarily appropriate. An absolute injunction is also ordinarily appropriate if the defendant acquired an interest in the personal name or established its business in the particular geographic location for the purpose of exploiting the good will attached to another's trademark. Courts are also unlikely to be solicitous toward a defendant who has assigned a personal name trademark and its associated business and who subsequently resumes use of the name in competition with the assignee.

When a qualified injunction is appropriate, the court has wide discretion to formulate the qualifications and conditions necessary to minimize the likelihood of confusion or deception without unduly restraining lawful conduct. Thus, the court may impose affirmative conditions on the defendant's continued use of the designation. In some cases the prominent appearance of the defendant's own name or mark may be required. In others, an explicit statement that the defendant is not connected with the plaintiff may be appropriate. Other disclosures may also be required in order to avoid misleading prospective purchasers. See, e.g., § 2, Comment *e*; § 24, Comment *d*. In some instances, however, confusion or deception can be effectively avoided only by an absolute injunction.

e. Generic and functional subject matter. Matter that is generic or functional is part of the public domain and its use may not be enjoined in an action for trademark infringement. See §§ 15–17. In some cases, however, a mark may be functional or generic in one market but not in another. In such instances an injunction may issue against another's use in the latter market. Similarly, although it is improper to enjoin the use of functional or generic subject matter, a subsequent user may be required to distinguish its goods or services from those of a prior user if a significant number of prospective purchasers view the presence of the material as an indication of source. See § 15, Comment *d*; § 16, Comment *d*. Thus, in such cases, a subsequent user may be enjoined from using the functional or generic subject matter unless accompanied by the prominent use of a distinguishing trademark, disclaimer, or other precautionary measure.

f. Geographic scope of injunctive relief. At common law, a trademark owner acquires rights only in the geographic area in which it is the prior good faith user of the mark. See § 19, Comment *b*.

Under the Lanham Act, a registrant may obtain priority in areas beyond those of its actual use or association with the mark. *Id.*, Comment *e.* Notwithstanding such statutory priority, however, a plaintiff is not entitled to an injunction prohibiting use by another in the absence of a likelihood of confusion. The appropriate geographic scope of injunctive relief in an action for trademark infringement can be difficult to determine, since the strength of the plaintiff's association with the trademark will often decrease incrementally with the distance from the area of the plaintiff's primary use. Because the protection of prospective purchasers from confusion remains paramount, the factors used to determine likelihood of confusion under § 21 are also important in fashioning the appropriate geographic scope of an injunction. Thus, courts may give relatively broader geographic protection when there is substantial similarity between the products and marketing methods of the plaintiff and the defendant. Similarly, although a court may carefully limit an injunction to the areas of the plaintiff's actual use when the evidence of likelihood of confusion is relatively weak and the defendant has acted in good faith, a finding of intentional infringement may justify more extensive relief. Thus, a court may enjoin a use intended by the defendant to preempt or undermine the trademark owner's ability to expand into a particular territory if the trademark owner establishes priority and a likelihood of future entry.

Both the common law and the Lanham Act contemplate concurrent use of the same mark in separate geographic markets by owners who have each adopted the mark in good faith and who thus have priority in their respective areas of use. If one or both of the users subsequently expands into areas contiguous to the other, it may be impossible to fashion relief that fully avoids a likelihood of confusion. The court may refuse relief in the contested area to either party, or if substantial confusion is likely, it may require both parties to adopt additional distinguishing matter for goods or services marketed in that area. In establishing the parameters of injunctive relief in cases of lawful concurrent users, a court should take account of the realities of the marketplace. In some instances it may be impossible for a trademark owner to restrict the advertising or resale of its goods or services to its area of priority. Similarly, a national user of a mark who is subject to the prior rights of another user in a local area may be unable to prevent entry of its national advertising into the local market. In each case the court must fashion a remedy that best limits the likely confusion of prospective purchasers while permitting both concurrent users to employ reasonable marketing methods.

The appropriate geographic scope of injunctive relief under state antidilution statutes has not yet been resolved. In actions for trademark infringement under the Lanham Act and at common law, courts typically issue injunctions that are unlimited in territorial effect when the activities of the parties are national in scope. The power of a federal court to issue a national injunction under federal law is uncontested, and the implicit assumption is that the similarity of unfair competition law throughout the states permits an analogous practice under state law. However, many states do not have antidilution statutes, and the interpretation of such statutes has not been consistent. The issuance of an injunction under state law that purports to regulate conduct in another state that is otherwise lawful may be inappropriate. Thus, although a court may have jurisdiction to grant broader relief, an injunction against dilution should ordinarily be limited to activity within the state under whose antidilution statute liability has been imposed or to activity in other states with statutory provisions that have been similarly interpreted.

g. Mandatory and prohibitory injunctions. The most common form of injunctive relief in trademark infringement and deceptive marketing actions is a prohibition against continued use of the infringing designation or deceptive representation. However, courts also have broad discretion to formulate injunctions requiring the defendant to take affirmative steps to insure against future wrongdoing or to cure past misconduct. The court may require, for example, the recall of infringing goods or the recall or destruction of deceptive promotional materials. Courts are reluctant, however, to mandate steps to correct past infringements or past deceptive marketing in the absence of a substantial risk of continuing harm to the plaintiff or the public. Thus, a defendant will not ordinarily be required to engage in corrective advertising unless the adverse effects of the misconduct are likely to persist in the absence of such measures. On the plaintiff's entitlement to compensation for the cost of its own corrective measures, see § 36, Comment *f.*

h. Preliminary relief. The rule stated in this Section deals primarily with injunctions granted as final relief, but the factors stated in Subsection (2) are also relevant to the imposition of provisional remedies. Although courts differ on the precise formulation, all courts recognize that the appropriateness of preliminary relief depends upon the likelihood that the plaintiff will suffer irreparable harm in the absence of such relief, the plaintiff's likelihood of success on the merits, the balance of equities between the parties, and the interest of the public. Absent special circumstances, courts will ordinarily grant a preliminary injunction in a trademark infringement action if there is strong evidence of a likelihood of confusion. In deceptive marketing cases, proof of direct competition between the parties and a material misrepresentation that is likely to deceive prospective purchasers is ordinarily sufficient for preliminary relief. When the plaintiff's likelihood of success on the merits is less clear, the relative hardship to each party resulting from a grant or denial of preliminary relief becomes more significant. For example, if the designation is the defendant's surname or if the defendant has made a substantial investment in the designation and has otherwise acted in good faith, the defendant's interest in continued use may weigh against the issuance of an absolute injunction prior to a final determination on the merits. The balance of equities prior to trial may indicate that qualified relief such as a mandatory disclaimer or the required use of other distinguishing elements is appropriate, or even that preliminary relief of any kind is unwarranted. Other equitable factors including the intent of the defendant and any delay or related misconduct on the part of the plaintiff are also relevant to the granting of preliminary relief.

A 1984 amendment to the Lanham Act, 15 U.S.C.A. § 1116(d), expressly authorizes the court to order pretrial ex parte seizures of goods bearing marks that are counterfeits of registered trademarks. Orders under this section are regarded as equitable in nature and depend upon a showing similar to that required for other preliminary relief. However, because of the ex parte nature of the seizure order, the statute requires clear proof that seizure is appropriate and that less drastic remedies would be inadequate. The statute also authorizes an action for damages in favor of any person injured as a result of a wrongful seizure.

REPORTERS' NOTE

This Section is based on Restatement, Second, Torts § 936 (1977), which describes the factors relevant in determining the appropriateness of injunctive relief in tort actions. See also Gilson, Trademark Protection and Practice § 8.07; McCarthy, Trademarks and Unfair Competition §§ 30.01–23; Dobbs, Law of Remedies § 6.4 (1993). The rules relating to injunctive relief in unfair competition actions were stated in Restatement of Torts § 744 (1938).

Comment a. It is widely recognized that injunctive relief is a customary remedy in actions for trademark infringement and unfair competition. See, e.g., Champion Spark Plug Co. v. Sanders, 331 U.S. 125, 67 S.Ct. 1136, 91 L.Ed. 1386 (1947); National Football League Properties, Inc. v. Wichita Falls Sportswear, Inc., 532 F.Supp. 651 (W.D.Wash.1982). See also McCarthy, *supra*, § 30.01; Restatement, Second, Torts, Scope Note to Ch. 48 at 557: "This list of torts that are frequently the subject of suit for an injunction should include * * * the various forms of unfair competition and wrongful trade practices * * *."

The history of the traditional principles governing injunctive relief in tort actions is traced in Restatement, Second, Torts § 938, Comment *c*. That section also recognizes that the use of injunctive relief as the customary remedy in unfair competition actions is not a departure from the traditional rule, but rather "represents crystallized applications of that rule to situations in which the narrow definition of tort set up by the substantive law administered by the damage remedy, or the impracticability of that remedy, or the unique suitability of injunction, has made the appropriateness of an injunction obvious." *Id.*, Comment *b*. There is evidence that the traditional requirement of irreparable injury or inadequacy of the remedy at law is no longer viable as a general principle. See Laycock, The Death of the Irreparable Injury Rule (1991).

Comment b. The factors listed in this Section are taken from Restatement, Second, Torts § 936. See also *id.* §§ 937, 941–943. On the effect of laches and unclean hands, see §§ 31 and 32 of this Restatement.

The Second Circuit requires an explicit balancing of the equities prior to an award of injunctive relief in trademark infringement actions. See, e.g., Avon Shoe Co. v. David Crystal, Inc., 279 F.2d 607 (2d Cir.), cert. denied 364 U.S. 909, 81 S.Ct. 271, 5 L.Ed.2d 224 (1960); Mushroom Makers, Inc. v. R.G. Barry Corp., 580 F.2d 44 (2d Cir.1978), cert. denied 439 U.S. 1116, 99 S.Ct. 1022, 59 L.Ed.2d 75 (1979); McGregor–Doniger Inc. v. Drizzle Inc., 599 F.2d 1126 (2d Cir.1979); Vitarroz Corp. v. Borden, Inc., 644 F.2d 960 (2d Cir.1981); Jim Beam Brands Co. v. Beamish & Crawford Ltd., 937 F.2d 729 (2d Cir. 1991), cert. denied ___ U.S. ___, 112 S.Ct. 1169, 117 L.Ed.2d 415 (1992). In noncompeting goods cases, injunctive relief is sometimes denied if the prior user is unlikely to expand into the subsequent user's product market, the quality of the subsequent user's goods will not damage the reputation of the prior user, and the subsequent use is in good faith. See Mushroom Makers, *supra*. See also Chandon Champagne Corp. v. San Marino Wine Corp., 335 F.2d 531 (2d Cir.1964) (denying an injunction to a small prior user who had delayed enforcing its rights, noting the "serious harm an injunction would cause the defendant as against the trifling benefit to the plaintiffs"); Stuart v. Collins, 489 F.Supp. 827 (S.D.N.Y.1980) (awarding monetary relief but denying an injunction because the plaintiff could no longer exploit the mark due to the defendant's extensive use).

Cessation of the wrongful conduct will not necessarily avoid the issuance of an injunction. See, e.g., Brunswick Corp. v. Spinit Reel Co., 832 F.2d 513 (10th Cir.1987); I. Appel Corp. v. Munsingwear, Inc., 646 F.Supp. 685 (S.D.N.Y.1986). Injunctions were denied when innocent infringements were discontinued in M–F–G Corp. v. EMRA Corp., 817 F.2d 410 (7th Cir.1987); Schutt Mfg. Co. v. Riddell, Inc., 673 F.2d 202 (7th Cir. 1982); Parkway Baking Co. v. Freihofer Baking Co., 255 F.2d 641 (3d Cir.1958). See generally McCarthy, *supra*, § 30.06. In Polo Fashions, Inc. v. Dick Bruhn, Inc., 793 F.2d 1132 (9th Cir.1986), the court held that a willful infringer must "irrefutably" demonstrate that an injunction is unnecessary. Injunctions in deceptive marketing cases may be withheld if there is no likelihood of future deception. See Menendez v. Saks and Co., 485 F.2d 1355 (2d Cir.1973), reversed on other grounds 425 U.S. 682, 96 S.Ct. 1854, 48 L.Ed.2d 301 (1976); Burndy Corp. v. Teledyne Industries, Inc., 748 F.2d 767 (2d Cir. 1984).

Comment c. The scope of injunctive relief is determined by the nature of the wrongful conduct. In deceptive marketing actions the prevention of consumer deception determines the appropriate scope of relief. See, e.g., U–Haul Int'l, Inc. v. Jartran, Inc., 793 F.2d 1034 (9th Cir. 1986); Better Business Bureau, Inc. v. Medical Directors, Inc., 681 F.2d 397 (5th Cir.1982); Geisel v. Poynter Products, Inc., 283 F.Supp. 261 (S.D.N.Y.1968). Prevention of a likelihood of confusion determines the appropriate scope of injunctive relief in trademark infringement actions. See, e.g., Aktiebolaget Electrolux v. Armatron Int'l, Inc., 999 F.2d 1 (1st Cir.1993); Charles Jacquin Et Cie, Inc. v. Destileria Serralles, Inc., 921 F.2d 467 (3d Cir.1990) (injunction limited to use on products likely to cause confusion); Plus Products v. Plus Discount Foods, Inc., 722 F.2d 999 (2d Cir.1983); Holiday Inns of America, Inc. v. B & B Corp., 409 F.2d 614 (3d Cir.1969); Miss Universe, Inc. v. Patricelli, 408 F.2d 506 (2d Cir.1969). Cf. Wynn Oil Co. v. American Way Service Corp., 943 F.2d 595 (6th Cir. 1991) (injunction against the use of "confusingly similar" marks is not impermissibly vague).

Uncertainties regarding the scope of injunctive relief are typically resolved against the wrongdoer. See, e.g., Champion Spark Plug Co. v. Sanders, 331 U.S. 125, 67 S.Ct. 1136, 91 L.Ed. 1386 (1947); National Football League Properties, Inc. v. Wichita Falls Sportswear, Inc., 532 F.Supp. 651 (W.D.Wash.1982). However, an injunction should not prohibit legitimate competitive activities. B.H. Bunn Co. v. AAA Replacement Parts Co., 451 F.2d 1254 (5th Cir. 1971) (relief should be "only that which is required to distinguish the two products, and no more"); Trail Chevrolet, Inc. v. General Motors Corp., 381 F.2d 353 (5th Cir.1967) (prohibition against all use of the CHEVROLET mark was too broad because the defendant has the right to inform customers that it sells used Chevrolet automobiles); Feathercombs, Inc. v. Solo Products Corp., 306 F.2d 251 (2d Cir.), cert. denied 371 U.S. 910, 83 S.Ct. 253, 9 L.Ed.2d 170 (1962). For cases supporting broader injunctions in instances of intentional or egregious misconduct, including prohibitions of conduct not itself unlawful, see, e.g., Chevron Chemical Co. v. Voluntary Purchasing Groups, Inc., 659 F.2d 695 (5th Cir.1981), cert. denied 457 U.S. 1126, 102 S.Ct. 2947, 73 L.Ed.2d 1342 (1982); Kentucky Fried Chicken Corp. v. Diversified Packaging Corp., 549 F.2d 368 (5th Cir.1977). See also National Football League Properties, *supra* (broader injunction justified by defendant's failure to comply with the intent of a prior injunction). More limited relief may be appropriate when the equities of the case are closely balanced. See, e.g., Manhattan Industries, Inc. v. Sweater Bee by Banff, Ltd., 627 F.2d 628 (2d Cir. 1980) (disclaimers may be sufficient when both parties have made substantial investments in their marks); AMF Inc. v. Sleekcraft Boats, 599 F.2d 341 (9th Cir.1979) (limited injunction granted when both parties had used the mark for 10 years in good faith and an absolute injunction was unnecessary to prevent confusion).

The constitutional right of free speech can limit the scope of injunctive relief in unfair competition cases. Commercial speech is protected under the first amendment, and restrictions that go beyond the prevention of false or misleading commercial speech must be narrowly drawn and advance a substantial governmental interest. See, e.g., Central Hudson Gas & Elec. Corp. v. Public Service Com., 447 U.S. 557, 100 S.Ct. 2343, 65 L.Ed.2d 341 (1980). Cf. Board of Trustees v. Fox, 492 U.S. 469, 109 S.Ct. 3028, 106 L.Ed.2d 388 (1989) (restrictions on commercial speech need not meet a "least restrictive means" test). Cases suggesting that injunctions broad enough to prohibit truthful advertising may be constitutionally defective include *U-Haul Int'l Inc., supra*; *Better Business Bureau, supra.* See also Rogers v. Grimaldi, 875 F.2d 994 (2d Cir.1989) (tolerating a risk of some confusion arising from the use of a movie title with artistic relevance to the film because of the public interest in free expression).

First amendment limitations on the scope of protection accorded to trademarks in the context of parody and other expressive activities are considered in § 20, Comment *b*; § 25, Comments *g, i.*

Comment d. Courts have broad authority to fashion qualified injunctions. See, e.g., Springs Mills, Inc. v. Ultracashmere House, Ltd., 724 F.2d 352 (2d Cir.1983) (disclaimer); AMF Inc. v. Sleekcraft Boats, 599 F.2d 341 (9th Cir.1979) (requiring use of a separate logo with the infringing mark); Moore Business Forms, Inc. v. Seidenburg, 619 F.Supp. 1173 (W.D.La. 1985) (defendant required to establish a telephone intercept to disclaim association with the plaintiff); American Ass'n for Advancement of Science v. Hearst Corp., 498 F.Supp. 244 (D.D.C.1980) (prohibiting use of the name SCIENCE for a magazine unless accompanied by the word "Digest"); Pizitz, Inc. v. Pizitz Mercantile Co., 467 F.Supp. 1089 (N.D.Ala. 1979) (detailed advertising campaign containing disclaimers required prior to expansion into the trademark owner's territory).

Whether a qualified injunction permitting use of a mark with a disclaimer is appropriate depends on the strength of the defendant's legitimate interest in continued use of the mark and the probable effectiveness of the disclaimer in preventing confusion. In some cases disclaimers may be ineffective. See, e.g., Home Box Office, Inc. v. Showtime/Movie Channel, Inc., 832 F.2d 1311 (2d Cir.1987); United States Jaycees v. Philadelphia Jaycees, 639 F.2d 134 (3d Cir.1981), both rejecting the lower court's reliance on qualified relief. See also Jacoby & Raskoff, Disclaimers as a Remedy for Trademark Infringement Litigation: More Trouble Than They Are Worth?, 76 Trademark Rep. 35 (1986); Radin, Disclaimers as a Remedy for Trademark Infringement: Inadequacies and Alternatives, 76 Trademark Rep. 59 (1986). However, in appropriate circumstances courts continue to rely on qualified injunctions to protect the interests of both plaintiff and defendant. See, e.g., Soltex Polymer Corp. v. Fortex Industries, Inc., 832 F.2d 1325 (2d Cir.1987); Spring Mills, Inc., *supra.*

When the infringing mark consists of defendant's personal name, courts frequently attempt to balance the right to use one's own name in business against the need to protect the plaintiff and the public from confusion. See, e.g., E. & J. Gallo Winery

v. Gallo Cattle Co., 967 F.2d 1280 (9th Cir.1992) (enjoining the use of a personal name as a trademark with retail but not wholesale sales); Basile, S.p.A. v. Basile, 899 F.2d 35 (D.C.Cir. 1990). A variety of qualified injunctions have been employed for this purpose. Several decisions attempt to prohibit use of the name as or as part of the defendant's trademark or trade name while permitting use in a subsidiary capacity. See Joseph Scott Co. v. Scott Swimming Pools, Inc., 764 F.2d 62 (2d Cir.1985) (preliminary injunction enjoining use of personal name in a trade name, but allowing use to describe past accomplishments and expertise); Taylor Wine Co. v. Bully Hill Vineyards, Inc., 569 F.2d 731 (2d Cir.1978), appeal after remand 590 F.2d 701 (2d Cir.1978) (preliminary injunction allowing defendant to use full name on wine bottles in signature form only); Gucci v. Gucci Shops, Inc., 688 F.Supp. 916 (S.D.N.Y.1988) (trademark may not include the name "Gucci," but the words "by Paolo Gucci" may appear beside the trademark if they are not more prominent than the mark). Courts sometimes require the inclusion of a first name or initials if such use will avoid confusion. See, e.g., L.E. Waterman Co. v. Modern Pen Co., 235 U.S. 88, 35 S.Ct. 91, 59 L.Ed. 142 (1914); Emilio Pucci Societa a Responsibilita Limitata v. Pucci Corp., 10 U.S.P.Q.2d 1541 (N.D.Ill. 1988); Dolby v. Robertson, 654 F.Supp. 815 (N.D.Cal.1986). Cf. Scarves by Vera, Inc. v. Todo Imports Ltd., 544 F.2d 1167 (2d Cir. 1976) ("Vera y Cosmetica, S.A." suggested to avoid confusion with plaintiff's VERA trademark). Disclaimers are also sometimes employed. See, e.g., R.J. Toomey Co. v. Toomey, 683 F.Supp. 873 (D.Mass.1988); Dolby, *supra.*

If a personal name is used with an intent to deceive, an absolute injunction is generally granted. See, e.g., De Nobili Cigar Co. v. Nobile Cigar Co., 56 F.2d 324 (1st Cir.1932); John Walker & Sons, Ltd. v. Bethea, 305 F.Supp. 1302 (D.S.C.1969). Similarly, if the defendant's name has no market reputation, courts are more likely to award the plaintiff broad relief. See Basile, *supra*; Bertolli USA, Inc. v. Filippo Bertolli Fine Foods, Ltd., 662 F.Supp. 203 (S.D.N.Y.1987). A broad injunction ordinarily will also be granted to protect an assignee of a personal name mark from competitive use of the name by the assignor. See Levitt Corp. v. Levitt, 593 F.2d 463 (2d Cir. 1979). On the general principles applicable to injunctions in personal name cases, see McCarthy, *supra,* §§ 13.03–.08.

The leading case utilizing a qualified injunction to reconcile the defendant's interest in describing its geographic location with the plaintiff's trademark rights in a geographic term is American Waltham Watch Co. v. United States Watch Co., 173 Mass. 85, 53 N.E. 141 (1899). See also, e.g., Midwest Research Institute v. S & B Promotions, Inc., 677 F.Supp. 1007 (W.D.Mo.1988) (audio and print disclaimers required on self-help tapes); Puget Sound Rendering, Inc. v. Puget Sound By–Products, 26 Wash.App. 724, 615 P.2d 504 (1980) (PUGET SOUND enjoined unless qualified by additional geographic or descriptive language). However, in some instances a complete prohibition against the use of a geographic term may be the only practical means of avoiding a likelihood of confusion. See, e.g., Eastern Columbia, Inc. v. Waldman, 30 Cal.2d 268, 181 P.2d 865 (1947).

Comment e. A term may be generic in one market but not in another. See Bayer Co. v. United Drug Co., 272 Fed. 505 (S.D.N.Y.1921) (defendant enjoined from using the term "Aspirin" in the wholesale but not retail market). For cases noting that a subsequent user may be required to take steps to reduce the potential confusion caused by its use of a generic term, see, e.g., Kellogg Co. v. National Biscuit Co., 305 U.S. 111, 59 S.Ct. 109, 83 L.Ed. 73 (1938); Blinded Veterans Ass'n v. Blinded American Veterans Foundation, 872 F.2d 1035 (D.C.Cir.1989); DuPont Cellophane Co. v. Waxed Products Co., 85 F.2d 75 (2d Cir.), cert. denied 299 U.S. 601, 57 S.Ct. 194, 81 L.Ed. 443 (1936).

A subsequent user of a generic term that has acquired secondary meaning may avoid confusion by clearly identifying the source of its product. See Miller Brewing Co. v. Jos. Schlitz Brewing Co., 605 F.2d 990 (7th Cir.1979), cert. denied 444 U.S. 1102, 100 S.Ct. 1067, 62 L.Ed.2d 787 (1980) (passing off claim rejected because defendant adequately identified itself as the source of the product); King–Seeley Thermos Co. v. Aladdin Industries, Inc., 321 F.2d 577 (2d Cir.1963) (in addition to limiting use of the generic term "thermos" to lower case letters and enjoining defendant's use of the words "genuine" or "original," the court required that the use be preceded by the name of the defendant company in its possessive form). Some cases require an accompanying disclaimer with the use of a generic term that has secondary meaning. See, e.g., Blinded Veterans Ass'n, *supra* (recommending use of a prominent disclaimer of association with the prior user). See also the cases cited in the Reporters' Note accompanying § 15, Comment *d.* Explanatory disclosures may sometimes be necessary to prevent a misdescription of the goods otherwise implied by the use of a generic term. See Eastern Air Lines, Inc. v. New York Air Lines, Inc., 559 F.Supp. 1270 (S.D.N.Y.1983).

For examples of qualified injunctions intended to prevent confusion arising from the use of functional elements that have acquired secondary meaning, see the cases cited in the Reporters' Note accompanying § 16, Comment *d.*

Comment f. Even in cases of nationwide priority under the Lanham Act, injunctive relief is not available in remote areas where the mark is not associated with the registrant. See, e.g., American Foods, Inc. v. Golden Flake, Inc., 312 F.2d 619 (5th Cir.1963); Dawn Donut Co. v. Hart's Food Stores, Inc., 267 F.2d 358 (2d Cir.1959). Cf. Charles Jacquin Et Cie, Inc. v. Destileria Serralles, Inc., 921 F.2d 467 (3d Cir.1990) (geographic scope of injunctions under § 43(a) of the Lanham Act and common law are determined by the trademark owner's market penetration).

On the problem of national advertising by a concurrent trademark user, see Flavor Corp. v. Kemin Industries, Inc., 503 F.2d 729 (8th Cir. 1974) (national advertisements must include notation that "This product is not available in Georgia and Florida"). See also Sterling Drug, Inc. v. Bayer AG, 14 F.3d 733 (2d Cir.1994) (court must take account of the "realities of the marketplace" in determining the scope of an injunction against advertising activities by a foreign infringer, citing Restatement Third, Unfair Competition § 35, Comment *f* (Tent. Draft No.3 (1991))); Frisch's Restaurants, Inc. v. Elby's Big Boy,

Inc., 670 F.2d 642 (6th Cir.), cert. denied 459 U.S. 916, 103 S.Ct. 231, 74 L.Ed.2d 182 (1982).

The cases are inconsistent on the appropriate scope of injunctive relief under state antidilution statutes. Compare American Dairy Queen Corp. v. RTO, Inc., 16 U.S.P.Q.2d 1077 (N.D.Ill.1990) (dictum recognizing only statewide protection under an antidilution statute) and Hyatt Corp. v. Hyatt Legal Services, 610 F.Supp. 381 (N.D.Ill.1985) (injunction against dilution stayed as to "all advertisements not expected, in the normal course, to be received within the State of Illinois") with Instrumentalist Co. v. Marine Corps League, 509 F.Supp. 323 (N.D.Ill.1981), affirmed 694 F.2d 145 (7th Cir.1982) (nationwide injunction issued). Cf. Carson v. Here's Johnny Portable Toilets, Inc., 810 F.2d 104 (6th Cir.1987) (approving nationwide injunction under Michigan common law right of publicity but permitting the defendant to seek a modification for any state where the substantive law allowed the prohibited activity). The Model State Trademark Bill § 13 (1992) provides that, unless the violation is willful, the trademark owner in a dilution action is "entitled only to injunctive relief in this state." See generally Amend, The Geographic Scope of Injunctions in Intellectual Property Cases, 77 Trademark Rep. 49 (1987).

Comment g. A mandatory recall of infringing promotional materials or products is an unusual but recognized remedy. See Perfect Fit Industries, Inc. v. Acme Quilting Co., 646 F.2d 800 (2d Cir.1981) (recall of infringing trade dress proper when the defendant was a willful infringer, litigation had delayed relief to the plaintiff, and the trial court's evaluation of the burdens and benefits of the recall was not clearly erroneous). See also, e.g., Nikon Inc. v. Ikon Corp., 987 F.2d 91 (2d Cir.1993); Feathercombs, Inc. v. Solo Products Corp., 306 F.2d 251 (2d Cir.), cert. denied 371 U.S. 910, 83 S.Ct. 253, 9 L.Ed.2d 170 (1962) (destruction of infringing sales literature); Kiki Undies Corp. v. Promenade Hosiery Mills, Inc., 308 F.Supp. 489 (S.D.N.Y.1969); Gaylord Products, Inc. v. Golding Wave Clip Co., 161 F.Supp. 746 (W.D.N.Y.1958) (recall of infringing merchandise). Cf. Playskool, Inc. v. Product Dev. Group, Inc., 699 F.Supp. 1056 (E.D.N.Y.1988) (recall of products ordered because misleading statements on packaging created a safety hazard). But see Kraft General Foods, Inc. v. Friendship Dairies, Inc., 19 U.S.P.Q.2d 1691 (S.D.N.Y.1991) (denying recall of perishable product); Supelco, Inc. v. Alltech Associates, 1 U.S.P.Q.2d 1149 (E.D.Pa.1986) (cost of recalling brochures with limited useful life found excessive); Thomas Nelson, Inc. v. Cherish Books Ltd., 595 F.Supp. 989 (S.D.N.Y.1984) (recall and destruction denied as too costly, but defendant ordered to pay the cost of corrective advertising). For a case requiring notification to the trade of the substance of the court's judgment, see Midwest Fur Producers Ass'n v. Mutation Mink Breeders Ass'n, 127 F.Supp. 217 (D.Wis.1954).

Comment h. Provisional relief in trademark infringement actions is discussed in Gilson, *supra*, § 8.07[1]; McCarthy, *supra*, §§ 30.15–23.

The various circuits use different formulations to describe the standard for preliminary relief, but there are few substantive differences. See, e.g., Int'l Kennel Club of Chicago, Inc. v. Mighty Star, Inc., 846 F.2d 1079 (7th Cir.1988) (plaintiff must prove the inadequacy of the remedy at law, irreparable harm, a balance of hardships in its favor, a reasonable likelihood of prevailing on the merits, and an absence of harm to the public interest if relief is granted); Calvin Klein Cosmetics Corp. v. Lenox Laboratories, Inc., 815 F.2d 500 (8th Cir. 1987) (irreparable harm to the plaintiff, the balance between that harm and the injury to other parties if relief is granted, probability of success on the merits, and the public interest); Church of Scientology Int'l v. Elmira Mission of Church of Scientology, 794 F.2d 38 (2d Cir.1986) (irreparable harm and either a probability of success or serious questions going to the merits and a balance of hardships favoring the plaintiff); Sardi's Restaurant Corp. v. Sardie, 755 F.2d 719, 723 (9th Cir.1985) (plaintiff must show "(1) a combination of probable success on the merits *and* the possibility of irreparable injury *or* (2) the existence of serious questions going to the merits *and* that the balance of hardships tips sharply in his favor"). In trademark infringement cases, irreparable harm is often presumed when there is a likelihood of confusion. See, e.g., Vision Sports, Inc. v. Melville Corp., 888 F.2d 609 (9th Cir. 1989); Church of Scientology, *supra* ; Processed Plastic Co. v. Warner Communications, Inc., 675 F.2d 852 (7th Cir.1982). A similar presumption of irreparable harm is often invoked in connection with false comparative advertising claims. See, e.g., Abbott Laboratories v. Mead Johnson & Co., 971 F.2d 6 (7th Cir. 1992); McNeilab, Inc. v. American Home Products Corp., 848 F.2d 34 (2d Cir.1988).

On the importance of the balance of equities, see, e.g., Calvin Klein Cosmetics Corp., *supra* ; American Hospital Supply Corp. v. Hospital Products Ltd., 780 F.2d 589, 593 (7th Cir. 1986) (preliminary injunction granted only if "the harm to the plaintiff if the injunction is denied, multiplied by the probability that the denial would be an error (that the plaintiff, in other words, will win at trial), exceeds the harm to the defendant if the injunction is granted, multiplied by the probability that granting the injunction would be an error"). Other equitable factors are also relevant to an award of preliminary relief. See, e.g., National Board of Y.M.C.A. v. Flint Y.M.C.A., 764 F.2d 199 (6th Cir. 1985) (acquiescence by the plaintiff is a sufficient basis for a denial of preliminary relief). On the effect of delay in seeking a preliminary injunction, see the cases cited in the Reporters' Note accompanying § 31, Comment *e*.

Preliminary injunctions have also been granted in deceptive marketing cases. See, e.g., McNeilab, Inc., *supra* ; Camel Hair and Cashmere Institute of America, Inc. v. Associated Dry Goods Corp., 799 F.2d 6 (1st Cir.1986); Coca–Cola Co. v. Tropicana Products, Inc., 690 F.2d 312 (2d Cir.1982). See also Abbott Laboratories, *supra* (remanding the denial of a preliminary injunction); Vidal Sassoon, Inc. v. Bristol–Myers Co., 661 F.2d 272 (2d Cir.1981) (first amendment interests do not require alteration of the traditional standards for preliminary injunctive relief in cases involving misleading commercial speech).

Ex parte pretrial orders for seizure of counterfeit goods are authorized under 15 U.S.C.A. § 1116(d). See, e.g., Vuitton v. White, 945 F.2d 569 (3d Cir.1991) (denial of an ex parte seizure order in a counterfeit goods case held to be an abuse of discretion); General Motors Corp. v. Gibson Chemical & Oil Corp., 786 F.2d 105 (2d Cir.1986). See also Pepe (U.K.) Ltd. v. Ocean View Factory Outlet Corp., 770 F.Supp. 754 (D.P.R. 1991) (ex parte seizure order awarded for violations of § 43(a) and state law). For a case declining to dismiss a claim of wrongful seizure against attorneys who made misleading statements in support of a seizure order, see Skierkewiecz v. Gonzalez, 711 F.Supp. 931 (N.D.Ill.1989). See generally McCoy and Myers, Ex Parte Seizure Order Practice After the Trademark Counterfeiting Act of 1984, 14 Am.Intell.Prop.L.A.Q.J. 237 (1986).

§ 36. Damages: Trademark Infringement and Deceptive Marketing

(1) One who is liable to another for deceptive marketing under the rules stated in §§ 2–8 or for infringement of the other's trademark, trade name, collective mark, or certification mark under the rule stated in § 20 is liable for the pecuniary loss to the other caused by the deceptive marketing or infringement, unless an award of damages for such pecuniary loss is prohibited by statute or is otherwise inappropriate under the rule stated in Subsection (3).

(2) The pecuniary loss for which damages may be recovered under this Section includes:

(a) loss resulting to the plaintiff from sales or other revenues lost because of the actor's conduct;

(b) loss resulting from sales made by the plaintiff at prices that have been reasonably reduced because of the actor's conduct;

(c) harm to the market reputation of the plaintiff's goods, services, business, or trademark; and

(d) reasonable expenditures made by the plaintiff in order to prevent, correct, or mitigate the confusion or deception of prospective purchasers resulting from the actor's conduct.

(3) Whether an award of damages for pecuniary loss is appropriate depends upon a comparative appraisal of all the factors of the case, including the following primary factors:

(a) the degree of certainty with which the plaintiff has established the fact and extent of the pecuniary loss caused by the actor's conduct;

(b) the relative adequacy to the plaintiff of other remedies, including an accounting of the actor's profits;

(c) the intent of the actor and the extent to which the actor knew or should have known that the conduct was unlawful;

(d) the role of the actor in bringing about the infringement or deceptive marketing;

(e) any unreasonable delay by the plaintiff in bringing suit or otherwise asserting its rights; and

(f) any related misconduct on the part of the plaintiff.

Comment:

a. Scope. This Section states the rules governing the recovery of damages for deceptive marketing and trademark infringement. Damages measure the loss suffered by the plaintiff. An accounting of profits, which measures the defendant's gain rather than the plaintiff's loss, is governed by the rules stated in § 37.

The general rules relating to the recovery of compensatory damages in tort actions apply in actions for unfair competition. This Section addresses only issues that have particular significance to an award of damages for trademark infringement or deceptive marketing. The following Sections of the Restatement, Second, of Torts are also relevant: §§ 902 and 903 defining "damages" and "compensatory damages"; § 907 stating the rule for recovery of nominal damages; §§ 908 and 909 stating the rule for recovery of punitive damages (see Comment *n, infra*); § 912 stating the requirement of "certainty" (see Comments *h* and *i, infra*); and §§ 435A and 435B stating rules relating to intended and unintended consequences of tortious conduct.

This Section is applicable to the award of damages under § 35(a) of the Lanham Act, 15 U.S.C.A. § 1117(a), which authorizes the recovery of damages both in actions for the infringement of registered trademarks under § 32 of the Act and in actions for deceptive marketing and infringement of unregistered marks under § 43(a) of the Act. The rules stated in this Section are also applicable in actions at common law and under state trademark registration statutes. Other state statutes such as the Unfair Trade Practices and Consumer Protection Acts (see the Statutory Note accompanying § 1) are sometimes interpreted to authorize a private cause of action for trademark infringement and deceptive marketing. The rules stated in this Section apply in such actions unless inconsistent with the applicable statutory language. This Section is not applicable to claims for trademark dilution as described in § 25, since the antidilution statutes on which such claims are founded generally provide only for injunctive relief.

b. History of the damage remedy; law and equity. Prior to the merger of law and equity, a plaintiff alleging trademark infringement or unfair competition could bring an action at law for damages or an action in equity for injunctive relief. Because of the difficulty of establishing the fact and extent of loss attributable to a competitor's unfair competition and the threat of continuing harm, the equitable action for injunctive relief became the preferred remedy. Courts of equity, in order to avoid the need for a separate action at law, sometimes awarded damages or an accounting of the defendant's profits in addition to injunctive relief. These monetary awards were subject to traditional equitable principles such as laches and unclean hands. The modern rules governing the recovery of monetary relief in actions for trademark infringement and unfair competition reflect this history. Section 35(a) of the Lanham Act makes the award of damages and profits "subject to the principles of equity." This Section adopts the view that these equitable factors also remain applicable to claims for monetary relief at common law.

The early preference for the action in equity blurred the distinction between a recovery of the plaintiff's damages and an award of the defendant's profits. In a competitive market, proof of loss resulting from the wrongful conduct of a particular competitor is often difficult. The plaintiff's sales are subject to a variety of forces, including business cycles, shifts in consumer demand, and the legitimate marketing strategies of competitors. An accounting of the defendant's profits was thus often advantageous to the trademark owner, since upon proof of the defendant's gross sales the burden shifts to the defendant to prove the proportion of sales not attributable to the infringement and the costs properly deductible from gross revenue in calculating the net profit for which the defendant is accountable. See § 37. However, the defendant's profits may bear only a slight relationship to the loss sustained by the plaintiff, and an accounting of profits can therefore produce a potential windfall to the plaintiff. The remedy of an accounting was thus generally reserved for cases of willful infringement. Many courts, however, did not recognize a sharp distinction between cases in which the plaintiff offered direct proof of actual loss such as diverted sales or harm to reputation and cases in which the plaintiff instead sought a recovery measured by the amount of the defendant's gain. Some courts assumed that the sales made by the defendant had been diverted from the plaintiff and thus regarded the defendant's profits as a measure of the plaintiff's damages. Courts thus sometimes construed the plaintiff's claim as one for "damages" even when the proof consisted solely of evidence relating to the defendant's profits. Other courts referred to the same claim as one for an "accounting of damages." The term "profits" was sometimes used to describe recoveries measured by either the plaintiff's profits lost through diverted sales or the defendant's profits earned through the tortious conduct. In some cases courts discussed monetary relief without specifying which measure was at issue. Fraud was thus often said to be a prerequisite to an award of both damages and profits even after fraud was no longer an element of the substantive cause of action.

A claim for deceptive marketing, like that for trademark infringement, initially required proof of fraud as an element of substantive liability. The common law gradually retreated from this requirement, and the enactment of § 43(a) of the Lanham Act in 1946 created a federal cause of action for deceptive marketing with no requirement of an intent to deceive. See § 2, Comment *f*. In some courts fraudulent intent nevertheless remained a prerequisite to monetary relief.

The rules stated in this Section and in § 37 reflect the more recent cases that recognize a distinction between claims for damages and claims for an accounting of the defendant's profits. Both claims remain subject to equitable principles, and the court should consider whether an award of damages or profits is appropriate in light of the facts of the particular case. The equities supporting a claim to monetary relief by a plaintiff who has proven actual pecuniary loss, however, are normally stronger than those of a plaintiff who seeks to recover the defendant's profits in the absence of proven loss. Although proof of an intent to deceive is a prerequisite to an award of the defendant's profits under the rule stated in § 37, it is not a prerequisite to the recovery of damages under this Section.

c. Relationship to other remedies. An injunction is the most common remedy in unfair competition cases. See § 35. Liability for trademark infringement and deceptive marketing requires proof only of a likelihood of harm, and an injunction restraining the unlawful conduct is normally an adequate and appropriate remedy absent proof of actual harm. An injunction is often insufficient, however, if the plaintiff has suffered a pecuniary loss or if the defendant has been unjustly enriched by the wrongful conduct.

An award of damages is designed to compensate the plaintiff for proven pecuniary loss, and the burden is on the plaintiff to establish the fact and amount of such loss. The relative equities between an injured plaintiff and even an unintentional wrongdoer suggest that an award of proven damages is appropriate in most cases. On the other hand, an accounting of the defendant's profits serves more complex objectives. Although the defendant's profits may sometimes represent an alternative measure of the plaintiff's damages, an award of profits often is intended, not as compensation, but to prevent unjust enrichment or to insure an adequate deterrent against further wrongdoing. The defendant also bears a substantial burden of proof in apportioning sales and costs. Courts have generally required proof of bad faith as a prerequisite to an accounting of profits. See § 37.

In some cases courts have permitted the recovery of both damages under the rule stated in this Section and an accounting of the defendant's profits under the rule stated in § 37, with the caveat that the plaintiff may not recover twice for the same loss. The prohibition against double recovery most clearly applies when the goods of the parties directly compete and the plaintiff seeks to recover both damages for losses attributable to diverted sales and the profits earned on sales made by the defendant. Although the two sums are not necessarily identical since the parties may have different profit margins and not all of the defendant's sales may represent sales diverted from the plaintiff, in the absence of contrary evidence the court may conclude that the defendant's profits adequately reflect the sales lost by the plaintiff. In such cases an award of both profits and damages is therefore prohibited under the rule precluding double recovery for the same loss. Recovery of both profits and damages is most clearly appropriate when the profits of the defendant are used as a measure of the loss attributable to sales diverted from the plaintiff, and the plaintiff in addition proves other losses such as harm to reputation.

Although some courts have suggested that a plaintiff may recover both damages and profits when the goods or services of the parties do not compete, in many cases such a result may be inappropriate. An award of the defendant's profits in a case involving noncompeting products cannot reflect diverted sales; the purpose of the award ordinarily is to deprive the defendant of unjust enrichment and to deter future misconduct. In such circumstances the defendant's profits are awarded to the plaintiff notwithstanding the fact that they do not directly reflect any harm caused by the infringement or deceptive marketing. If the plaintiff in fact suffers harm such as injury to its reputation, that harm may be regarded as compensated by the award of the defendant's profits to the extent that the profits exceed the plaintiff's proven losses. Similarly, if the plaintiff's proven losses exceed the defendant's profits, an award of damages will not only compensate the plaintiff, but will also eliminate the defendant's unjust enrichment and serve to deter future misconduct. Thus, when the parties do not directly compete, an award of profits or damages, whichever is greater, may best serve the objectives of monetary relief.

Illustrations:

1. *A* and *B* sell competing safes. *B* tells prospective purchasers that its safe has an explosion chamber identical to that found in *A* 's safe. In fact, *A* is the only producer of safes with explosion chambers and *B* 's safe is merely constructed to appear as if the safe has an explosion chamber. *A* 's profit on each safe is $1,000. *B*, because it does not have the expense of installing an explosion chamber, makes a profit of $1,500 on each safe. If the remedies are otherwise appropriate, *A* may recover either $1,000 in damages for each sale proven to have been lost as a result of *B* 's deceptive marketing, or *B* 's profit of $1,500 on each of *B* 's sales attributable to the misrepresentation. *A* may not recover both damages for lost sales under the rule stated in this Section and *B* 's profits under the rule stated in § 37.

2. The facts being otherwise as stated in Illustration 1, *A* also spends $1,500 for advertisements intended to overcome the injury to the reputation of its product caused by the sale of *B* 's safes. *A* may recover both the cost of the advertisements under this Section and *B* 's profits under the rules stated in § 37.

3. *A* sells expensive men's suits under the trademark JACKSON. *B* begins selling inexpensive men's shirts using the JACKSON mark, causing purchasers to believe that the shirts are manufactured by *A*. *B* makes a profit of $20,000 on sales of the shirts. Some purchasers who are dissatisfied with the quality of *B* 's shirts decide not to purchase *A* 's suits, causing a loss to *A* in the amount of $5,000. A court may properly conclude that an award to *A* of *B* 's profits, in addition to depriving *B* of its unjust gains from the infringement, is also adequate to compensate *A* for its lost sales.

d. Lost revenues. If a damage remedy is appropriate under the rules stated in this Section, the plaintiff may recover lost profits or other lost revenues such as royalties or donations that would have been received by the plaintiff but for the defendant's wrongful conduct. The plaintiff may recover such losses regardless of whether the lost revenues were diverted to the defendant.

The defendant's wrongful conduct may sometimes compel the plaintiff to sell its goods at a lower price. To recover for the resulting pecuniary loss, the plaintiff must establish that the reduction in price was reasonable under the circumstances and caused by the defendant's misconduct.

In some cases the plaintiff may attempt to establish the amount of its loss by proving the royalty rate normally charged for licensing the trademark use made by the defendant. This measure is typically invoked in cases involving licensees who continue to use the mark after termination of the license. The former royalty rate may then be one of several reasonable measures of the plaintiff's loss. However, damages measured by a reasonable royalty rate provide little disincentive against infringement since they leave the infringer no worse off than one who properly obtains a license, and in some cases the royalty measure may also fail to account for the absence of other benefits and burdens present in an actual licensing relationship.

e. Loss of market reputation. The defendant's infringement or deceptive marketing may diminish the market reputation of the plaintiff's trademark, goods, services, or business. The threat to reputation may be direct, as when the defendant misrepresents the quality of the plaintiff's goods in comparative advertising, or indirect, as when the defendant sells inferior goods under the plaintiff's trademark. In both instances the plaintiff may lose future sales because of the misrepresentation even after the defendant's misconduct has ceased. Such reputational injury, if proved with sufficient certainty, is a recoverable loss under this Section.

f. Corrective advertising. Correction of the defendant's misrepresentation or warnings to prospective purchasers not to be misled may avoid a loss of sales or injury to reputation and may thus mitigate the plaintiff's damages for which the defendant would otherwise be liable. Expenditures reasonably incurred by the plaintiff in connection with such corrections or warnings can be recovered as damages under this Section.

It is often difficult to determine the reasonableness of expenditures allegedly undertaken to correct the defendant's misrepresentation or to warn prospective purchasers. The fact that the plaintiff has engaged in the curative activities, however, is evidence that the expenditures were reasonable. On the other hand, a claim for expenditures to be undertaken in the future should be subject to greater scrutiny, and recovery for future expenses may be inappropriate unless the plaintiff can demonstrate a lack of resources or other reasonable justification for the failure to take the corrective measures prior to the litigation. The appropriate amount of an award for corrective advertising depends on the facts of the particular case. Although the amount of the defendant's expenditures in promoting the infringing mark or deceptive claim is relevant, there is no necessary relationship between the defendant's expenditures and the level of corrective expenditures by the plaintiff that may be reasonable.

g. Appropriateness of damage award. The recovery of damages for unfair competition is subject to equitable principles both at common law and under the Lanham Act. If the plaintiff proves pecuniary harm resulting from the defendant's infringement or misrepresentation, damages should be recoverable even if the defendant acted in good faith, since the claim of an innocent plaintiff for compensation ordinarily outweighs any equities favoring the innocent wrongdoer. There are circumstances, however, in which an award of damages may be inappropriate. When the plaintiff's proof of the fact of loss is weak, imposing the risk of that uncertainty on an innocent defendant may be inequitable. When the fact of loss is proven with reasonable certainty, however, an award of damages may be appropriate despite the plaintiff's inability to prove the precise amount of loss. Even when both the fact and amount of loss are proven with certainty, other factors such as the plaintiff's delay or unclean hands may make an award of damages inappropriate.

Monetary relief is not available in an action for the infringement of a mark registered under the Lanham Act if the registrant fails to display a notice of trademark registration, unless the infringer had actual notice of the registration. 15 U.S.C.A. § 1111. Monetary relief may be available, however, through an action under § 43(a) of the Lanham Act or at common law. The Lanham Act also prohibits monetary relief against certain parties who innocently contribute to an infringement or misrepresentation. See Comment *k*.

h. Causation and proof of loss. The plaintiff may recover for all losses caused by the defendant's wrongful conduct, whether or not the losses were anticipated by the defendant. The plaintiff, however, bears the burden of proving causation. Proof of a general decline in sales or a disruption of anticipated business growth following the defendant's misconduct can be sufficient in some cases to justify an inference of causation. However, many potential intervening factors can affect the plaintiff's sales, and the presence of such factors bears on the sufficiency of the plaintiff's proof. Proof of a decline in sales combined with evidence tending to discount the importance of other market factors, such as evidence of positive business conditions and the success of similar businesses not subject to the defendant's tortious conduct, can be sufficient to establish a causal connection between the plaintiff's decline in sales and the misconduct of the defendant.

i. Certainty of loss. Although the plaintiff bears the burden of proving both the fact and extent of its pecuniary loss, the difficulty of quantifying loss in a market context frequently justifies a less exacting standard of proof for the amount than for the fact of loss. Once the fact of loss caused by the defendant's misconduct has been established, the plaintiff's burden may be satisfied by evidence that furnishes a reasonable basis for computing damages. The plaintiff is not obliged to provide individualized proof of lost sales. As the fact and extent of the loss become more uncertain, however, the risk increases that an award of damages will represent a windfall to the plaintiff and a penalty to the defendant. In such cases, the appropriateness of a damage award depends on whether the other circumstances of the case justify imposing that risk on the defendant.

An actor can be subject to liability for trademark infringement or deceptive marketing upon proof of a likelihood of confusion or deception, but the recovery of damages ordinarily requires proof that some consumers have actually been confused or deceived. However, direct proof of actual confusion or deception is often unavailable, and the proof may consist instead of circumstantial evidence such as consumer surveys, market analysis, or the nature of the defendant's misconduct. See also § 23. In trademark infringement cases involving directly competing goods, proof of actual confusion may permit the further inference that sales have been diverted from the plaintiff to the defendant. In other cases, the link between the infringement or deception and the plaintiff's sales may be less clear. In deceptive marketing cases, for example, consumers deceived into believing that the defendant's product contains a particular ingredient may be diverted from any of a number of sellers whose products in fact contain that ingredient. Damages for lost sales are thus more likely to be appropriate when the misrepresentation relates directly to the plaintiff, as when the defendant specifically compares its goods to those of the plaintiff, or claims for its goods an ingredient or characteristic otherwise available only from the plaintiff, or misrepresents its goods as those of the plaintiff.

j. Defendant's intent. The defendant's intent is an important factor in determining the relief that is appropriate in both trademark infringement and deceptive marketing cases. Although this Section permits an award of damages against a defendant who acted without an intent to confuse or deceive, the decision to award damages is properly influenced by the nature of the defendant's conduct. When the defendant intentionally seeks to confuse or deceive, the court may accept less certain proof of loss in order to discourage similar behavior in the future. The court also may infer that a defendant who intends to divert sales from the plaintiff through an infringement or misrepresentation is likely to have succeeded. See § 22, Comment *c*. When the defendant's unlawful conduct is unintentional, the balance of equities may suggest that an injunction is sufficient unless the plaintiff presents convincing evidence of pecuniary loss. Although some courts have expressed the view that good faith is a defense to any claim for monetary relief in trademark infringement or deceptive marketing actions, that rule has been invoked almost exclusively in response to requests for an accounting of the defendant's profits, which present issues distinct from those associated with awards of damages. See § 37, Comment *e*.

k. Role of the defendant. A defendant who adopts an infringing trademark or who initiates a misrepresentation is ordinarily subject to liability under this Section for any harm sustained by the plaintiff, even if the defendant acted in good faith. See Comment *j*. Liability for trademark infringement or deceptive marketing, however, can also extend to others who play a less central role in the infringement or deception. The good faith of such defendants is an important factor in determining whether an award of damages is appropriate. Retailers who sell goods bearing an infringing mark or who republish a misrepresentation originating with the manufacturer of the goods are subject to liability, but the extent to which the resale or republication was innocent and the extent to which monetary relief is available from the initial source of the goods are relevant in determining whether an award of damages against the retailer is appropriate. Printers, publishers, and suppliers who contribute to an infringement or deception, although subject to liability, are not liable for monetary remedies unless they had knowledge of the intent to infringe or deceive. See §§ 7 and 26. Manufacturers and distributors who market goods or services to others who in turn market the goods or services in a manner that constitutes infringement or deceptive marketing are subject to contributory liability only if they acted intentionally or negligently. See §§ 8, 27. Thus, in some circumstances such a manufacturer or distributor may appropriately be subject to an award of monetary relief.

l. Plaintiff's delay or misconduct. Although the rule stated in this Section recognizes a general entitlement to damages for pecuniary loss caused by trademark infringement or deceptive marketing, the award of damages remains subject to the equities of the case. A plaintiff who delays in asserting its rights may be barred from recovering damages even when the proof of loss is clear. See § 31. Misconduct on the part of the plaintiff may also be sufficient to preclude the recovery of damages. See § 32.

m. Enhanced damages under the Lanham Act. Section 35(a) of the Lanham Act, 15 U.S.C.A. § 1117(a), applicable to infringements of registered trademarks and violations of § 43(a), recognizes broad discretion in the court to determine an appropriate monetary award. The court may award an amount up to three times the amount found as actual damages, provided that the award shall "constitute compensation and not a penalty." This discretion in assessing damages is a recognition of the difficulties inherent in proving the amount of loss in a market context. If the plaintiff proves that certain consumers were diverted to the defendant, for example, the court may infer that other consumers were similarly diverted. However, the power to enhance damages is not ordinarily exercised if the defendant has acted in good faith.

The use of a counterfeit mark can result in an automatic trebling of damages under § 35(b) of the Lanham Act. 15 U.S.C.A. § 1117(b). A counterfeit mark is a spurious mark that is indistinguishable from the registered mark and used on the goods or services for which the genuine mark is registered. A person who intentionally uses a mark knowing that it is a counterfeit is liable for treble damages absent extenuating circumstances.

n. Punitive damages. A successful plaintiff in an action for unfair competition may recover punitive damages under the rules generally applicable to awards of punitive damages in tort actions. See Restatement, Second, Torts § 908. The purpose of punitive damages is to punish the wrongdoer for egregious conduct, and normally proof of malice or willful misconduct is required. Punitive damages are not available in actions under the Lanham Act.

o. Attorney's fees. In an action under the Lanham Act, the court may award reasonable attorney's fees in "exceptional cases." 15 U.S.C.A. § 1117(b). Fees are typically awarded only in cases of deliberate infringement or when the prosecution of the claim is in bad faith. Most states do not provide for the recovery of attorney's fees in actions at common law. However, many state deceptive trade practices statutes, including the Unfair Trade Practices and Consumer Protection Act (see the Statutory Note accompanying § 1) and the Uniform Deceptive Trade Practices Act (see the Statutory Note accompanying § 2), authorize awards of attorney's fees.

REPORTERS' NOTE

This Section states the rules governing the recovery of damages in actions for trademark infringement and deceptive marketing. These rules were stated in Restatement of Torts §§ 745–746 (1938). See generally, Gilson, Trademark Protection and Practice § 8.08; McCarthy, Trademarks and Unfair Competition §§ 30.27–31; Nims, Unfair Competition and Trade–Marks §§ 419–23 (4th ed.1947); Koelemay, Monetary Relief for Trademark Infringement Under the Lanham Act, 72 Trademark Rep. 458 (1982).

Comment a. Courts often assume that the rules governing the recovery of monetary relief in unfair competition actions are similar at common law and under the Lanham Act. See, e.g., Champion Spark Plug Co. v. Sanders, 331 U.S. 125, 131, 67 S.Ct. 1136, 1139, 91 L.Ed. 1386, 1391 (1947) (accounting denied under both the Trade Mark Act of 1905 and the law of unfair competition since "an injunction will satisfy the equities of the case"); DC Comics, Inc. v. Filmation Associates, 486 F.Supp. 1273 (S.D.N.Y.1980); Rolls–Royce Motors Ltd. v. A. & A. Fiberglass, Inc., 428 F.Supp. 689 (N.D.Ga.1976) (laches relevant to a claim for damages under both federal and state law); Electronics Corp. v. Honeywell, Inc., 358 F.Supp. 1230 (D.Mass.), affirmed 487 F.2d 513 (1st Cir.1973), cert. denied 415 U.S. 960, 94 S.Ct. 1491, 39 L.Ed.2d 575 (1974); Gillette Co. v. Ed Pinaud, Inc., 178 F.Supp. 618 (S.D.N.Y.1959).

Many states have adopted unfair trade practice acts that provide monetary remedies for deceptive or unfair practices. Some of these statutes have been interpreted to include claims by competitors for trademark infringement and deceptive marketing. See the Statutory Note accompanying § 1 and the Reporters' Note to § 1, Comment *g*. In some circumstances the monetary remedies available under these statutes may be more liberal than those available under the Lanham Act. See, e.g., Polo Fashions, Inc. v. Craftex, Inc., 816 F.2d 145 (4th Cir.1987). Section 13(G) of the Model State Trademark Bill (1992) authorizes the recovery of monetary relief in dilution actions if the defendant "willfully intended" to cause the dilution.

Comment b. The interaction of law and equity in the development of the rules governing the recovery of damages in actions for trademark infringement and unfair competition is described in Nims, Unfair Competition and Trade–Marks §§ 419–23 (4th ed.1947). "The case law on monetary recovery in trademark infringement cases is a confusing melange of common law and equity principles * * *." McCarthy, *supra*, § 30.24. In many cases courts of equity awarded damages for trademark infringement and unfair competition. See, e.g., P.E. Sharpless Co. v. Lawrence, 213 Fed. 423 (3d Cir.1914); Hennessy v. Wilmerding–Loewe Co., 103 Fed. 90 (C.C.Cal.1900); Foster Mfg. Co. v. Cutter–Tower Co., 215 Mass. 136, 101 N.E. 1083 (1913). Cases recognizing laches as a limitation on the recovery of damages in an equitable action include, e.g., Bissell Chilled Plow Works v. T.M. Bissell Plow Co., 121 Fed. 357 (C.C.Mich.1902); Low v. Fels, 35 Fed. 361 (C.C.Pa.1888). Laches remains relevant to an award of damages even after the merger of law and equity. See, e.g., Rolls–Royce Motors Ltd. v. A. & A. Fiberglass, Inc., 428 F.Supp. 689 (N.D.Ga. 1976) (laches applicable to the recovery of damages under both state and federal law); Tustin Community Hospital, Inc. v. Santa Ana Community Hospital Association, 89 Cal.App.3d 889, 153 Cal.Rptr. 76 (1979) (dictum). Cases recognizing unclean hands as a limitation on the recovery of damages in equity include, e.g., Manhattan Medicine Co. v. Wood, 108 U.S. 218, 2 S.Ct. 436, 27 L.Ed. 706 (1883).

Although equitable principles remain relevant in determining the appropriateness of monetary relief in actions for trademark infringement, the Supreme Court has held that a party seeking damages for infringement under the Lanham Act is entitled to a jury trial. Dairy Queen, Inc. v. Wood, 369 U.S. 469, 82 S.Ct. 894, 8 L.Ed.2d 44 (1962). See also, e.g., L.L. Bean, Inc. v. Drake Publishers, Inc., 629 F.Supp. 644 (D.Me. 1986); Stuart v. Collins, 489 F.Supp. 827 (S.D.N.Y.1980); Holiday Inns, Inc. v. Lussi, 42 F.R.D. 27 (N.D.N.Y. 1967). A jury trial is similarly available for damage claims in common law trademark infringement and unfair competition actions tried in federal court. See Lee Pharmaceuticals v. Mishler, 526 F.2d 1115 (2d Cir. 1975); L.L. Bean, Inc., *supra.* See generally Gilson, *supra,* § 8.06; McCarthy, *supra,* §§ 32.38–42. The right to a jury trial in state court actions involving claims for both legal and equitable relief, however, may be subject to different rules. See McCarthy, *supra,* § 32.41; James, Hazard and Leubsdorf, Civil Procedure (4th ed.) § 8.8. The precise allocation of responsibility between judge and jury with respect to the factors relevant to an award of monetary relief in trademark infringement and deceptive marketing cases remains unsettled. See, e.g., Stuart, *supra*; Five Platters, Inc. v. Purdie, 419 F.Supp. 372 (D.Md.1976); Conifer Laboratories, Inc. v. Unitech Chemical Mfg. Co., 167 U.S.P.Q. 398 (D.Minn.1970); Gilson, *supra,* § 8.06[4][a].

The confusion regarding the various measures of monetary relief for unfair competition that is reflected in the early case law is elaborately described in Koelemay, Monetary Relief for Trademark Infringement Under the Lanham Act, 72 Trademark Rep. 458 (1982). See also McCarthy, *supra,* § 30.24. The inconsistent use of the terms "damages" and "profits" is noted in Nims, Unfair Competition and Trade–Marks § 419: "As a result of this confusing use of these terms, decisions are often difficult to understand and apply." See, e.g., Flexitized, Inc. v. National Flexitized Corp., 335 F.2d 774 (2d Cir.1964), cert. denied 380 U.S. 913, 85 S.Ct. 899, 13 L.Ed.2d 799 (1965) (using the term "accounting of profits" to refer to the plaintiff's profits); Regis v. Jaynes, 191 Mass. 245, 77 N.E. 774 (1906) ("accounting of the plaintiff's damages").

Comment c. Courts have consistently stated that in a proper case a plaintiff may recover both damages and defendant's profits. See, e.g., Mishawaka Rubber & Woolen Mfg. Co. v. S.S. Kresge Co., 316 U.S. 203, 62 S.Ct. 1022, 86 L.Ed. 1381 (1942); Hamilton–Brown Shoe Co. v. Wolf Brothers & Co., 240 U.S. 251, 36 S.Ct. 269, 60 L.Ed. 629 (1916); Aladdin Mfg. Co. v. Mantle Lamp Co., 116 F.2d 708 (7th Cir.1941). The plaintiff may not recover both profits and damages, however, if the profits made by the defendant are derived from the same lost sales claimed as damages. Friend v. H.A. Friend & Co., 416 F.2d 526 (9th Cir.1969), cert. denied 379 U.S. 914, 90 S.Ct. 916, 25 L.Ed.2d 94 (1970); Century Distilling Co. v. Continental Distilling Corp., 205 F.2d 140 (3d Cir.), cert. denied 346 U.S. 900, 74 S.Ct. 226, 98 L.Ed. 400 (1953). Both profits and damages have been awarded when the infringement occurred on competing goods and elements of damage in addition to diverted sales were proven. See, e.g., Stuart v. Collins, 489 F.Supp. 827 (S.D.N.Y.1980) (profits plus damages for loss of good will).

Subsection (2) lists the traditional elements of recoverable damages. See, e.g., Obear–Nester Glass Co. v. United Drug Co., 149 F.2d 671 (8th Cir.), cert. denied 326 U.S. 761, 66 S.Ct. 141, 90 L.Ed. 458 (1945). The elements reflect losses to the plaintiff as distinguished from gains to the defendant. These elements of damage have also been held applicable in deceptive marketing cases under § 43(a) of the Lanham Act. See ALPO Petfoods, Inc. v. Ralston Purina Co., 913 F.2d 958 (D.C.Cir.1990). In some circumstances the defendant's gains may be used as a means of calculating the plaintiff's losses. See, e.g., Brunswick Corp. v. Spinit Reel Co., 832 F.2d 513 (10th Cir.1987) (sales made by the defendant may place an upper limit on the damages suffered by the plaintiff).

Comment d. Profits lost on diverted sales are recoverable as damages in both trademark infringement and deceptive marketing actions. See, e.g., Brunswick Corp. v. Spinit Reel Co., 832 F.2d 513 (10th Cir. 1987); Flexitized, Inc. v. National Flexitized Corp., 335 F.2d 774 (2d Cir.1964), cert. denied 380 U.S. 913, 85 S.Ct. 899, 13 L.Ed.2d 799 (1965); Grant Airmass Corp. v. Gaymar Industries, Inc., 645 F.Supp. 1507 (S.D.N.Y.1986); Ronson Art Metal Works, Inc. v. Gibson Lighter Mfg. Co., 3 A.D.2d 227, 159 N.Y.S.2d 606 (1957). Cf. PPX Enterprises, Inc. v. Audiofidelity Enterprises, Inc., 818 F.2d 266 (2d Cir.1987) (remanding for calculation of damages in false advertising case). See also Restatement of Torts § 746; McCarthy, *supra*, § 30.-27. On recovery for a prospective loss of sales, see Broan Mfg. Co. v. Associated Distributors, Inc., 923 F.2d 1232 (6th Cir.1991).

Some courts have awarded damages for trademark infringement based on the royalty rate normally charged for licensing the unauthorized use. See Boston Professional Hockey Ass'n, Inc. v. Dallas Cap & Emblem Mfg., Inc., 597 F.2d 71 (5th Cir.1979); Holiday Inns, Inc. v. Airport Holiday Corporation, 493 F.Supp. 1025 (N.D.Tex.1980), affirmed 683 F.2d 931 (5th Cir.1982) (holdover licensee). Cf. Sands, Taylor & Wood Co. v. Quaker Oats Co., 978 F.2d 947 (7th Cir.1992), cert. denied ___ U.S. ___, 113 S.Ct. 1879, 123 L.Ed.2d 497 (1993) (a reasonable royalty can be an appropriate measure of recovery when the defendant has not acted in bad faith) (dictum). See also Ramada Inns, Inc. v. Gadsden Motel Co., 804 F.2d 1562 (11th Cir.1986) (holdover franchisee); Columbia Nastri & Carta Carbone, S/p/A v. Columbia Ribbon & Carbon Mfg. Co., 367 F.2d 308 (2d Cir.1966) (royalty agreement, although expired, may be evidence of the value attached to the trademark by the parties). A royalty measure was rejected in Bandag, Inc. v. Al Bolser's Tire Stores, Inc., 750 F.2d 903 (Fed.Cir.1984), as not bearing a "rational relationship to the rights appropriated." The defendant had falsely represented that it was a franchisee of the trademark owner, but the court rejected a reasonable royalty measure of damages as excessive because the defendant did not receive the full range of services accorded to actual franchisees.

Comment e. Plaintiffs may recover damages for harm to reputation resulting from the defendant's conduct. Restatement of Torts § 746; see, e.g., Heaton Distributing Co. v. Union Tank Car Co., 387 F.2d 477 (8th Cir.1967); Aladdin Mfg. Co. v. Mantle Lamp Co., 116 F.2d 708 (7th Cir.1941); Singer Mfg. Co. v. Redlich, 109 F.Supp. 623 (S.D.Cal.1952).

Comment f. The plaintiff is generally permitted to recover the costs of reasonable corrective advertising expended prior to the litigation. See ALPO Petfoods, Inc. v. Ralston Purina Co., 997 F.2d 949 (D.C.Cir.1993) (the plaintiff's corrective advertising need not specifically address the defendant's deceptive claim); U-Haul Int'l, Inc. v. Jartran, Inc., 793 F.2d 1034 (9th Cir.1986); Otis Clapp & Son, Inc. v. Filmore Vitamin Co., 754 F.2d 738 (7th Cir.1985); Cuisinarts, Inc. v. Robot-Coupe Int'l Corp., 580 F.Supp. 634 (S.D.N.Y.1984). See also Fancee Free Mfg. Co. v. Fancy Free Fashions, Inc., 148 F.Supp. 825 (S.D.N.Y.1957) (awarding the cost of advising the trade of two similar marks). Some courts have rejected claims seeking recovery for prospective corrective advertising costs. See Zazu Designs v. L'Oreal, S.A., 979 F.2d 499 (7th Cir.1992) (insufficient proof of injury to the plaintiff's trademark); Mastercard Int'l, Inc. v. Arbel Corp., 13 U.S.P.Q.2d 1958 (S.D.N.Y. 1989). See also West & Co. v. Arica Institute, Inc., 194 U.S.P.Q. 32 (S.D.N.Y.1976), affirmed 557 F.2d 338 (2d Cir.1977) (rejecting prospective corrective advertising claim for lack of proof of actual harm to reputation). A recovery for prospective corrective advertising was awarded upon proof that the plaintiff had been financially unable to undertake the corrective advertising in Big O Tire Dealers, Inc. v. Goodyear Tire and Rubber Co., 561 F.2d 1365 (10th Cir.1977), cert. dismissed 434 U.S. 1052, 98 S.Ct. 905, 54 L.Ed.2d 805 (1978).

Some courts in awarding damages for prospective corrective advertising measure the plaintiff's recovery as a percentage of the defendant's expenditures on the infringing or deceptive promotion. See West Des Moines State Bank v. Hawkeye Bancorporation, 722 F.2d 411 (8th Cir.1983); Big O Tire Dealers, *supra.* But see Zazu Designs, *supra* (recovery for prospective corrective advertising in a trademark infringement action should not exceed the value of the plaintiff's mark). For a criticism of prospective corrective advertising awards, see Comment, Money Damages and Corrective Advertising: An Economic Analysis, 55 U.Chi.L.Rev. 629 (1988).

Comment g. There is no consensus on the elements of proof required for the recovery of damages in trademark infringement and deceptive marketing cases. When proof of loss is clear, plaintiffs have recovered damages without proof of the defendant's bad faith or other aggravating factors. See Fuller Products Co. v. Fuller Brush Co., 299 F.2d 772 (7th Cir.), cert. denied 370 U.S. 923, 82 S.Ct. 1565, 8 L.Ed.2d 503 (1962) (damages awarded without proof of fraud); Borg-Warner Corp. v. York-Shipley, Inc., 293 F.2d 88 (7th Cir.), cert. denied 368 U.S. 939, 82 S.Ct. 381, 7 L.Ed.2d 338 (1961) (actual damages can be awarded without evidence of bad faith, although an accounting of profits was denied because of the plaintiff's misconduct); Gehl v. Hebe Co., 276 Fed. 271 (7th Cir.1921) (trademark infringer's good faith may bear on punitive but not actual damages); Fancee Free Mfg. Co. v. Fancy Free Fashions, Inc., 148 F.Supp. 825 (S.D.N.Y.1957) (awarding damages including the cost of a circular intended to dispel confusion but not the defendant's profits in the absence of an intent to trade on the plaintiff's good will). See also El Greco Leather Products Co. v. Shoe World, Inc., 806 F.2d 392 (2d Cir. 1986), cert. denied 484 U.S. 817, 108 S.Ct. 71, 98 L.Ed.2d 34 (1987), remanding for a determination of damages against an innocent infringer; on remand the court concluded that damages would be inequitable in view of the absence of an intent to deceive. El Greco Leather Products Co. v. Shoe World, Inc., 726 F.Supp. 25 (E.D.N.Y.1989).

Although recovery of the defendant's profits may be limited to cases of intentional misconduct, see § 37, it has been held that courts should not routinely use equitable considerations to prevent the recovery of the plaintiff's proven damages. General Electric Co. v. Speicher, 877 F.2d 531 (7th Cir.1988); Louis Vuitton S.A. v. Lee, 875 F.2d 584 (7th Cir.1989) (damages recoverable against an innocent infringer). See ALPO Petfoods, Inc. v. Ralston Purina Co., 913 F.2d 958 (D.C.Cir.1990) (damages recoverable in a deceptive marketing case upon proof of actual loss despite a lack of bad faith). Contra, Hammons Mobile Homes, Inc. v. Laser Mobile Home Transport, Inc., 501 N.E.2d 458 (Ind. App.1986). A number of the cases that appear to require intentional misconduct as a prerequisite to the recovery of monetary relief do not carefully distinguish between an award of the plaintiff's damages and an accounting of the defendant's profits. See, e.g., Carl Zeiss Stiftung v. VEB Carl Zeiss Jena, 433 F.2d 686 (2d Cir.1970), cert. denied 403 U.S. 905, 91 S.Ct. 2205, 29 L.Ed.2d 680 (1971); El Greco Leather Products, *supra.*

Although § 29 of the Lanham Act, 15 U.S.C.A. § 1111, requires the display of a notice of federal registration as a prerequisite to the recovery of monetary relief in infringement actions under § 32, the absence of notice does not preclude monetary relief in actions under § 43(a) or state law. See Polo Fashions, Inc. v. J & W Enterprises, 786 F.2d 1156 (4th Cir. 1986); Bambu Sales, Inc. v. Sultana Crackers, Inc., 683 F.Supp. 899 (E.D.N.Y.1988).

Comment h. The defendant may be liable even for unanticipated consequences of its wrongful conduct. See, e.g., Ramada Inns, Inc. v. Gadsden Motel Co., 804 F.2d 1562 (11th Cir.1986) (damages for injuries "proximately resulting" from the infringement); Aladdin Mfg. Co. v. Mantle Lamp Co., 116 F.2d 708 (7th Cir. 1941). See also Restatement, Second, Torts §§ 435A, 435B.

The plaintiff has the burden of proving both the cause and extent of lost sales. Otis Clapp & Son, Inc. v. Filmore Vitamin Co., 754 F.2d 738 (7th Cir.1985); Maltina Corp. v. Cawy Bottling Co., 613 F.2d 582 (5th Cir.1980) (damages not proved in light of plaintiff's limited manufacturing capacity); Break–Away Tours, Inc. v. British Caledonian Airways, 704 F.Supp. 178 (S.D.Cal.1988) (proof of several misdirected telephone calls and letters was insufficient to establish lost sales.) Courts will not necessarily presume that the plaintiff would have made the sales actually made by the defendant. See Obear–Nester Glass Co. v. United Drug Co., 149 F.2d 671 (8th Cir.), cert. denied 326 U.S. 761, 66 S.Ct. 141, 90 L.Ed. 458 (1945). The plaintiff's lost sales must be attributable to the defendant's infringement or misrepresentation and not to general competition.

Burndy Corp. v. Teledyne Industries, Inc., 748 F.2d 767 (2d Cir.1984) (no proof that the plaintiff's loss resulted from the defendant's misrepresentation as opposed to lower prices); Toro Co. v. Textron, Inc., 499 F.Supp. 241 (D.Del.1980). Although a material misrepresentation may be presumed to cause damage for purposes of subjecting a defendant to liability for deceptive marketing, see §§ 2 and 3, the presumption is not necessarily sufficient for the recovery of damages. See Electronics Corp. v. Honeywell, Inc., 487 F.2d 513 (1st Cir.1973), cert. denied 415 U.S. 960, 94 S.Ct. 1491, 39 L.Ed.2d 575 (1974).

When the plaintiff relies on circumstantial evidence to prove lost sales, other possible causes may preclude an inference of causation. Compare Otis Clapp & Son, *supra* (comparison of the plaintiff's historical growth rate with the growth rate during the period of the infringement held insufficient to prove causation) with Brunswick Corp. v. Spinit Reel Co., 832 F.2d 513 (10th Cir.1987) (proof that the plaintiff's sales declined substantially more than the market as a whole, combined with proof of actual confusion and direct competition, was sufficient to prove damages). See Can–Am Engineering Co. v. Henderson Glass, Inc., 814 F.2d 253 (6th Cir.1987); Borg–Warner Corp. v. York–Shipley, Inc., 293 F.2d 88 (7th Cir.), cert. denied 368 U.S. 939, 82 S.Ct. 381, 7 L.Ed.2d 338 (1961) (other intervening market factors that may account for the loss must be considered). See also Restatement, Second, Torts § 912, Comment *d*.

It is particularly difficult to prove damages in the form of a prospective loss of sales. See, e.g., Truck Equipment Service Co. v. Fruehauf Corp., 536 F.2d 1210 (8th Cir.), cert. denied 429 U.S. 861, 97 S.Ct. 164, 50 L.Ed.2d 139 (1976) (failure to expand production facilities resulting in loss of future sales was not attributable to the infringement); D.C. Comics, Inc. v. Filmation Associates, 486 F.Supp. 1273 (S.D.N.Y.1980) (denying damages for loss of future sales). But see Broan Mfg. Co. v. Associated Distributors, Inc., 923 F.2d 1232 (6th Cir.1991) (remanding for admission of evidence on future lost sales).

Comment i. Restatement, Second, Contracts § 352, Comment *a* (1979), requires that the amount of loss be proven only with reasonable and not mathematical certainty and recognizes that courts may reduce the degree of certainty required in light of the circumstances of the case, including the willfulness of the breach. Restatement, Second, Torts § 912 (1977), provides that the plaintiff is entitled to compensatory damages if "he establishes by proof the extent of the harm and the amount of money representing adequate compensation with as much certainty as the nature of the tort and the circumstances permit." See Broan Mfg. Co. v. Associated Distributors, Inc., 923 F.2d 1232 (6th Cir.1991) (relying on a "sharp distinction" between the required proof of the fact and amount of damages); Otis Clapp & Son, Inc. v. Filmore Vitamin Co., 754 F.2d 738 (7th Cir.1985) (lower burden to prove the amount rather than the fact of loss); Fuller Products Co. v. Fuller Brush Co., 299 F.2d 772 (7th Cir.), cert. denied 370 U.S. 923, 82 S.Ct. 1565, 8 L.Ed.2d 503 (1962) (plaintiff must prove a reasonable basis for computing damages); Borg–Warner Corp. v. York–Shipley, Inc., 293 F.2d 88 (7th Cir.), cert. denied 368 U.S. 939, 82 S.Ct. 381, 7 L.Ed.2d 338 (1961) (damages are not speculative although not calculated with exactness if there is a reasonable basis for the computation); D.C. Comics, Inc. v. Filmation Associates, 486 F.Supp. 1273 (S.D.N.Y.1980); Hammons Mobile Homes, Inc. v. Laser Mobile Home Transport, Inc., 501 N.E.2d 458 (Ind.App.1986) ("mathematical certainty as to the amount is not necessary"). But see Lindy Pen Co. v. Bic Pen Corp., 982 F.2d 1400 (9th Cir.), cert. denied ___ U.S. ___, 114 S.Ct. 64, 116 L.Ed.2d 34 (1993) (lost profits denied as too speculative). Cases under the Lanham Act have suggested that in the absence of clear proof of loss, the recovery of monetary relief may depend on the nature of the violation and the intent of the defendant. See, e.g., Harper House, Inc. v. Thomas Nelson, Inc., 889 F.2d 197, 209 n.8 (9th Cir.1989); Bandag, Inc. v. Al Bolser's Tire Stores, Inc., 750 F.2d 903 (Fed.Cir.1984).

Proof of actual confusion or deception is normally a prerequisite to the recovery of compensatory damages. See, e.g., Getty Petroleum Corp. v. Island Transportation Corp., 878 F.2d 650 (2d Cir.1989); PPX Enterprises, Inc. v. Audiofidelity Enterprises, Inc., 818 F.2d 266 (2d Cir.1987); PAF S.r.l. v. Lisa Lighting Co., 712 F.Supp. 394 (S.D.N.Y.1989); Cesare v. Work, 36 Ohio App.3d 26, 520 N.E.2d 586 (1987). Evidence of actual confusion sufficient to support an award of damages can consist of consumer surveys or the testimony of dealers or customers. See Schutt Mfg. Co. v. Riddell, Inc., 673 F.2d 202 (7th Cir.1982). In deceptive marketing cases the plaintiff must show actual consumer reliance on the misrepresentation, although not individualized loss of sales. Toro Co. v. Textron, Inc., 499 F.Supp. 241 (D.Del. 1980) (proof can consist of direct evidence or surveys). See also PPX Enterprises, *supra* (false statement was so clearly material that actual deception can be assumed); Parkway Baking Co. v. Freihofer Baking Co., 255 F.2d 641 (3d Cir.1958).

Comment j. On the presumption of injury arising from proof of the defendant's deceptive intent, see, e.g., Resource Developers, Inc. v. Statue of Liberty–Ellis Island Foundation, Inc., 926 F.2d 134 (2d Cir.1991) (although proof of actual confusion is required for an award of damages, proof of the defendant's intent to deceive shifts the burden to the defendant to show the absence of confusion). The intent relevant to an award of monetary relief is an intention to cause confusion or to deceive prospective purchasers; use of a mark under a good faith claim of ownership will not generally weigh against the defendant. See Carl Zeiss Stiftung v. VEB Carl Zeiss Jena, 433 F.2d 686 (2d Cir.1970), cert. denied 403 U.S. 905, 91 S.Ct. 2205, 29 L.Ed.2d 680 (1971). See also § 22, Comment *c*.

Comment k. Monetary remedies were denied against innocent resellers or republishers in El Greco Leather Products Co. v. Shoe World,Inc., 726 F.Supp. 25 (E.D.N.Y. 1989), and Finity Sportswear, Ltd. v. Airnit, Inc., 631 F.Supp. 769 (S.D.N.Y.1985). Cases limiting monetary and other relief in instances of contributory liability are collected in the Reporters' Notes accompanying §§ 7, 8, 26, and 27.

Comment l. A delay by the plaintiff in asserting its rights may prevent an award of monetary remedies even when the delay is insufficient to bar all relief. See, e.g., Grotrian, Helfferich, Schulz, Th. Steinweg

Nachf. v. Steinway & Sons, 523 F.2d 1331 (2d Cir.1975). See generally § 31.

Unclean hands can bar the recovery of both damages and profits. See Bambu Sales, Inc. v. Testini, 12 U.S.P.Q.2d 1479 (E.D.N.Y.1988). Some misconduct may prevent the recovery of profits but not actual damages. See Borg-Warner Corp. v. York-Shipley, Inc., 293 F.2d 88 (7th Cir.), cert. denied 368 U.S. 939, 82 S.Ct. 381, 7 L.Ed.2d 338 (1961), denying an accounting of profits but not an injunction and damages. See generally § 32.

Comment m. Courts have not ordinarily awarded enhanced damages under § 35(a) of the Lanham Act unless actual damages are shown. See Caesar's World, Inc. v. Venus Lounge, Inc., 520 F.2d 269 (3d Cir. 1975). Courts typically require proof of willful or intentional misconduct before damages are increased. See, e.g., Boston Professional Hockey Ass'n v. Dallas Cap & Emblem Mfg., Inc., 597 F.2d 71 (5th Cir.1979); Deering, Milliken & Co. v. Gilbert, 269 F.2d 191 (2d Cir.1959); American Express Co. v. Lipscomb, 210 U.S.P.Q. 827 (E.D.Mich.1981). But cf. ALPO Petfoods, Inc. v. Ralston Purina Co., 997 F.2d 949 (D.C.Cir. 1993) (enhanced damages can be appropriate as rough compensation for lost profits that cannot be calculated with sufficient certainty to support a direct award). Since the passage of the Trademark Counterfeiting Act of 1984, 98 Stat. 1837, § 35(b) of the Lanham Act has required the trebling of damages in most cases of intentional counterfeiting. See Louis Vuitton S.A. v. Lee, 875 F.2d 584 (7th Cir.1989); Louis Vuitton, S.A. v. After Dark Boutique, 680 F.Supp. 1507 (N.D.Fla.1988); Fendi S.A.S. Di Paola Fendi E Sorelle v. Cosmetic World, Ltd., 642 F.Supp. 1143 (S.D.N.Y. 1986). The difference between counterfeiting and traditional trademark infringement, however, is one of degree, depending chiefly on intent and the similarity of the infringing mark to the genuine mark. See Louis Vuitton S.A. v. Lee, *supra*; Louis Vuitton, S.A. v. After Dark Boutique, *supra*; Sun Products Group, Inc. v. B & E Sales Co., 700 F.Supp. 366 (E.D.Mich.1988).

The exercise of the trial court's discretion under the Lanham Act to determine an equitable level of monetary relief will not be overturned absent clear error. See, e.g., Ramada Inns, Inc. v. Gadsden Motel Co., 804 F.2d 1562 (11th Cir.1986); Holiday Inns, Inc. v. Alberding, 683 F.2d 931 (5th Cir.1982). The determination of enhanced damages rests with the judge rather than the jury. Stuart v. Collins, 489 F.Supp. 827 (S.D.N.Y. 1980).

Comment n. Restatement, Second, Torts § 908 sets out the rules relating to the recovery of punitive damages in tort actions. These rules are applicable to unfair competition cases in those states in which punitive damages are available. See, e.g., Getty Petroleum Corp. v. Island Transportation Corp., 878 F.2d 650 (2d Cir.1989) (New York law authorizes punitive damages in unfair competition actions for "gross, wanton, or willful fraud or other morally culpable conduct to an extreme degree"); Murphy Door Bed Co. v. Interior Sleep Systems, Inc., 874 F.2d 95 (2d Cir.1989) (New York law); Transgo, Inc. v. Ajac Transmission Parts Corp., 768 F.2d 1001 (9th Cir.1985), cert. denied 474 U.S. 1059, 106 S.Ct. 802, 88 L.Ed.2d 778 (1986) (California law); Big O Tire Dealers, Inc. v.

Goodyear Tire and Rubber Co., 561 F.2d 1365 (10th Cir.1977), cert. dismissed 434 U.S. 1052, 98 S.Ct. 905, 54 L.Ed.2d 805 (1978) (Colorado law). The Lanham Act does not authorize the recovery of punitive damages. Getty Petroleum Corp. v. Bartco Petroleum Corp., 858 F.2d 103 (2d Cir. 1988), cert. denied 490 U.S. 1006, 109 S.Ct. 1642, 104 L.Ed.2d 158 (1989).

Comment o. In response to the Supreme Court's decision in Fleischmann Distilling Corp. v. Maier Brewing Co., 386 U.S. 714, 87 S.Ct. 1404, 18 L.Ed.2d 475 (1967), holding that attorney's fees were not recoverable under the Lanham Act, Congress amended § 35 of the Act to authorize the recovery of attorney's fees by the prevailing party in "exceptional cases." Fees are generally awarded only when the infringement or deception is willful, see, e.g., Ferrero U.S.A., Inc. v. Ozak Trading, Inc., 952 F.2d 44 (3d Cir.1991) ("malicious, fraudulent, deliberate, or willful"); ALPO Petfoods, Inc. v. Ralston Purina Co., 913 F.2d 958 (D.C.Cir.1990); Roulo v. Russ Berrie & Co., 886 F.2d 931 (7th Cir.1989), cert. denied 493 U.S. 1075, 110 S.Ct. 1124, 107 L.Ed.2d 1030 (1990); Sealy, Inc. v. Easy Living, Inc., 743 F.2d 1378 (9th Cir.1984); Jellibeans, Inc. v. Skating Clubs, Inc., 716 F.2d 833 (11th Cir. 1983), or when a claim is prosecuted in bad faith. Universal City Studios, Inc. v. Nintendo Co., 797 F.2d 70 (2d Cir.), cert. denied 479 U.S. 987, 107 S.Ct. 578, 93 L.Ed.2d 581 (1986). Cf. Scotch Whisky Ass'n v. Majestic Distilling Co., 958 F.2d 594 (4th Cir.), cert. denied ___ U.S. ___, 113 S.Ct. 181, 121 L.Ed.2d 126 (1992) (bad faith is not required for an award of fees to a prevailing defendant).

On the recovery of attorney's fees in unfair competition actions at state law, see, e.g., Thompson v. Spring–Green Lawn Care Corp., 126 Ill. App.3d 99, 81 Ill.Dec. 202, 466 N.E.2d 1004 (1984) (attorney's fees were not recoverable at common law but could be awarded under the state deceptive trade practices act in cases of willful violations); Bell v. Davidson, 597 P.2d 753 (Okl.1979) (attorney's fees recoverable for willful violations of the deceptive trade practices act); Tradewell Stores, Inc. v. T.B. & M., Inc., 7 Wash.App. 424, 500 P.2d 1290 (1972) (attorney's fees recoverable in trade name infringement case under state consumer protection act despite the defendant's good faith). See generally Gilson, *supra*, § 8.08[4]; McCarthy, *supra*, § 30.30.

§ 37. Accounting of Defendant's Profits: Trademark Infringement and Deceptive Marketing

(1) One who is liable to another for deceptive marketing under the rules stated in §§ 2–8 or for infringement of the other's trademark, trade name, collective mark, or certification mark under the rule stated in § 20 is liable for the net profits earned on profitable transactions resulting from the unlawful conduct, but only if:

(a) the actor engaged in the conduct with the intention of causing confusion or deception; and

(b) the award of profits is not prohibited by statute and is otherwise appropriate under the rule stated in Subsection (2).

(2) Whether an award of profits is appropriate depends upon a comparative appraisal of all the factors of the case, including the following primary factors:

(a) the degree of certainty that the actor benefitted from the unlawful conduct;

(b) the relative adequacy to the plaintiff of other remedies, including an award of damages;

(c) the interests of the public in depriving the actor of unjust gains and discouraging unlawful conduct;

(d) the role of the actor in bringing about the infringement or deceptive marketing;

(e) any unreasonable delay by the plaintiff in bringing suit or otherwise asserting its rights; and

(f) any related misconduct on the part of the plaintiff.

Comment:

a. Scope. This Section states rules governing the award of an accounting of the defendant's profits in actions for deceptive marketing and trademark infringement. An accounting of profits measures and transfers to the plaintiff the gains resulting to the defendant from the wrongful conduct. Although the defendant's profits may sometimes be an approximate measure of the plaintiff's damages, an accounting of profits is subject to the rules stated in this Section rather than the rules governing an award of damages stated in § 36.

Section 35 of the Lanham Act permits, "subject to the principles of equity," the recovery of "defendant's profits." 15 U.S.C.A. § 1117. Section 35 is applicable to actions under § 43(a) of the Lanham Act for deceptive marketing and the infringement of unregistered trademarks as well as to actions under § 32 for the infringement of registered marks. The common law rules governing the remedy of an accounting are analogous to those applicable under the Lanham Act. The rules stated in this Section are also applicable to accountings of defendants' profits awarded under state legislation imposing liability for trademark infringement or deceptive marketing unless inconsistent with the statutory language.

b. History of the accounting remedy. The rules relating to an award of the defendant's profits, like those governing the award of damages, have been influenced by the historical distinction between law and equity and the doctrinal development of the law of unfair competition. See § 36, Comment *b*. Accountings of profits in unfair competition cases were initially granted as ancillary relief in actions in equity, thus permitting an award of monetary and injunctive relief in the same action. In England after the enactment of Lord Cairns' Act (21 & 22 Vict. C. 27), a plaintiff in equity could recover either profits or damages, but was required to make an election. In the United States an election was not required, and the plaintiff could recover both profits and damages, subject to a prohibition against double recovery. See § 36, Comment *c*.

An award of the defendant's profits was traditionally justified as compensation to the plaintiff for harm caused by the defendant's misconduct. Recognizing the difficulty of proving lost sales, courts frequently adopted the inference that the profits earned by the defendant represented profits diverted from the plaintiff. The correspondence is clearly imperfect, however, since in most cases there is no reason to expect that every sale made by the defendant has been diverted from the plaintiff or that the profit margins of the parties are necessarily the same. Nonetheless, the accounting remedy is an attractive alternative to plaintiffs who otherwise must bear the burden of proving the fact and amount of loss, but who in an accounting are required to prove only the defendant's sales, leaving the defendant to prove deductible costs and any profits not attributable to the misconduct.

The view of an accounting as a surrogate for plaintiff's lost profits resulted in a rule that an accounting was appropriate only in cases involving directly competing goods, since noncompeting goods could not divert sales from the plaintiff. However, deliberate infringement on noncompeting goods may not be sufficiently deterred if the plaintiff's inability to prove damages leaves an injunction as the only available remedy. Thus, courts gradually adopted the view that in an appropriate case an accounting of the defendant's profits could be awarded to prevent unjust enrichment and to deter future infringement. This perspective emphasizes the gains earned by the defendant rather than the losses incurred by the plaintiff. The deterrence justification also suggests that an award of profits is inappropriate in cases of innocent infringement.

The multiple rationales for an award of the defendant's profits complicate analysis of the applicable rules. This Section recognizes that courts award an accounting of profits under numerous theories. In many cases it is unnecessary to adopt a specific theory since the consequences of the various rationales frequently overlap. In some cases, however, it may be necessary to adjust the terms of the accounting to reflect the specific objective sought by the award and the equities of the particular case.

c. Relation to other remedies. Injunctive relief is the most common remedy in actions for unfair competition. See § 35. The rule governing damages stated in § 36 generally authorizes an award of damages whenever the plaintiff's loss is proved with reasonable certainty. An award of defendant's profits, however, is ordinarily reserved for cases of intentional misconduct. See Comment *e*. If the defendant's profits are awarded under this Section, the plaintiff may recover damages under the rule stated in § 36 only if double recovery for the same loss is avoided. See § 36, Comment *c*.

d. Recoverable profits. An accounting awards only profits on sales that are attributable to the defendant's wrongful conduct. However, the wrongful conduct need not be the sole cause of the sales on which profits are awarded. Some sales may be caused in part by the defendant's misconduct and in part by other factors such as the intrinsic merit of the defendant's goods or the convenience of purchasers. If the wrongful conduct is a substantial factor in producing a sale, the defendant is liable for the resulting profit without diminution for other contributing factors.

The plaintiff has the burden of proving the defendant's gross profits with reasonable certainty; mathematical precision is not required. The defendant bears the burden of establishing which, if any, of the total sales are not attributable to the misconduct. Although a court will ordinarily infer that all sales of goods bearing an infringing designation are attributable to the infringement, the inference may be rebutted by evidence establishing that the purchasers were aware of the true source of the goods, for example, or that the sales resulted solely from the inherent merits of the defendant's product without regard to its source or sponsorship.

If the defendant's misconduct results in numerous individual sales, each sale is an independent wrong to the plaintiff. The plaintiff may thus recover the defendant's profits on profitable transactions without a deduction for losses suffered on unprofitable transactions. However, if the transactions are related, as when an unprofitable sale is a preliminary step to a later transaction, the defendant is liable only for any resulting net profit.

e. Bad faith. An award of the defendant's profits creates a potential windfall to the plaintiff and a potential penalty to the defendant. Although the victim of an innocent infringement may ordinarily enjoin future infringements and recover proven losses, see §§ 35 and 36, courts generally require proof of intentional misconduct as a prerequisite to an accounting of the defendant's profits.

Some early cases suggested three classes of infringement: innocent, deliberate or willful, and fraudulent. Deliberate or willful infringement consisted of the use of another's mark with knowledge of the other's claim of ownership but with a reasonable belief that the use was not an infringement. Fraudulent infringement was one in which the actor intended to confuse or deceive prospective purchasers. Although several cases have awarded an accounting of profits when the defendant deliberately but in good faith used a mark with knowledge of the plaintiff's prior use, application of the accounting remedy to uses undertaken in good faith can chill lawful behavior. A defendant who reasonably believes, for example, that its goods are sufficiently unrelated to those of the plaintiff to avoid confusion, or that the plaintiff's mark is functional or generic, may be deterred from using the designation by the risk of substantial monetary liability unrelated to any injury to the plaintiff, thus effectively expanding the scope of the plaintiff's trademark rights. The better view limits an accounting of profits to acts intended to create confusion or to deceive prospective purchasers.

f. Appropriateness of an award of profits. Although bad faith is a prerequisite to the recovery of the defendant's profits, an accounting is not necessarily appropriate in every case in which bad faith is established. An accounting of profits remains an equitable remedy, subject to a balancing of the relative equities of the plaintiff, the defendant, and the public. Even in the presence of bad faith, a variety of factors may counsel against an accounting, including the adequacy of other remedies considered in light of the rationale for the accounting. For example, when actual loss has been proven, an award of damages may sometimes be a sufficient remedy. The extent to which the defendant would otherwise be unjustly enriched by the tortious conduct and the need for an effective deterrent also remain important in determining whether an accounting is appropriate. Misconduct by the plaintiff or delay in asserting its rights are also relevant to the award of an accounting. See §§ 31 and 32.

An accounting of the defendant's profits may be awarded in actions for deceptive marketing as well as in actions for trademark infringement, but the remedy is less likely to be appropriate in the former case. A defendant who falsely describes the qualities of its own product may be unjustly enriched by the deception, but often no specific competitor will have a compelling claim to the defendant's profits. There is also a risk of multiple recoveries of the same profits. On the other hand, a false comparison made by the defendant with the product of a specific competitor, or a misrepresentation of source, may result in substantial harm to a specific plaintiff, thus sometimes justifying an accounting of profits.

g. Computation of net profits. When an accounting of the defendant's profits is appropriate, the plaintiff is entitled to recover the net profits on sales attributable to the wrongful conduct. The defendant bears the burden of proving any costs or expenses to be deducted from gross income in calculating net profit. The defendant may deduct the cost of labor and materials expended in producing the infringing goods and the direct costs associated with the performance of infringing services. Deductions are measured by the defendant's actual costs rather than the market value of the labor and materials unless the price paid by the defendant is clearly artificial, as may be the case in purchases from wholly-owned subsidiaries. Discounts, rebates, bonuses, and similar savings to the defendant are ordinarily taken into account in determining deductible costs. Selling costs as well as manufacturing costs are deductible, including the expenses of promotion and advertising, sales commissions, trade discounts, salaries of sales personnel, and transportation costs. Other expenses directly associated with producing the relevant gross income are also deductible. The value of a defendant's own labor, however, and salaries or wages paid to persons responsible for the tortious conduct, are not ordinarily deductible. Distributions of profits to partners or stockholders are also not ordinarily deductible.

Income tax paid by the defendant on the profits for which it is accountable should not generally be deducted in computing the defendant's liability. Since the defendant can ordinarily claim the amount paid under an accounting as a deductible business expense, it can recoup some or all of the income tax previously paid on the profits included in the award. Similarly, the plaintiff is ordinarily obligated to pay income tax on the recovery from the defendant. Thus, the denial of a deduction for income taxes paid by the defendant on the profits awarded to the plaintiff best implements the goals of compensating the plaintiff and preventing the unjust enrichment of the defendant. Taxes other than income tax that are attributable to the infringement are ordinarily included as deductible expenses.

h. Apportionment of costs. If the defendant manufactures several products and is subject to liability for conduct relating to only one, the defendant's costs must be apportioned among the various products. Internal apportionments made by the defendant are not necessarily determinative. Only costs directly attributable to the production of the infringing goods are deductible. Variable costs and any portion of general expenses that would not have been incurred if the infringing goods had not been produced are properly deductible. If the manufacture and marketing of the infringing goods caused no increase in general expenses, no portion should be deducted in calculating profits. Thus, although normal accounting practice may allocate overhead and general expenses over all products, such an allocation is not necessarily appropriate for purposes of determining the net profits for which the defendant must account. However, increases in overhead and general expenses caused by the production and marketing of the infringing goods may not be capable of precise calculation. In some cases a percentage allocation based on total production or total sales may be an acceptable approximation of the defendant's deductible costs.

REPORTERS' NOTE

This Section states the rules governing an accounting of the defendant's profits. These rules were originally stated in §§ 747 and 748 of the Restatement of Torts (1938). See generally Gilson, Trademark Protection and Practice § 8.08[3]; McCarthy, Trademarks and Unfair Competition §§ 30.25–26; Nims, Unfair Competition and Trademarks §§ 424–27 (4th ed.1947); Koelemay, Monetary Relief for Trademark Infringement Under the Lanham Act, 72 Trademark Rep. 458 (1982).

Comment a. Most courts do not draw a distinction between the rules governing monetary relief at common law and under the Lanham Act. See § 36, Reporters' Note to Comment *a.* State legislation also provides for an accounting of the profits derived from an infringement. See, e.g., Model State Trademark Bill § 14 (1992).

Comment b. The description of the history of the accounting remedy is taken from Restatement of Torts § 747, Comment *b.* Commentators have deplored the confused and inconsistent case law on the accounting remedy in trademark and unfair competition cases. See, e.g., Nims, *supra,* § 419; Price, Financial Recovery in an Action for Trademark Infringement, 47 Trademark Rep. 1297 (1957). Compare, e.g., Hamilton–Brown Shoe Co. v. Wolf Bros. & Co., 240 U.S. 251, 36 S.Ct. 269, 60 L.Ed. 629 (1916) (suggesting that an accounting is appropriate for all infringements) with Champion Spark Plug Co. v. Sanders, 331 U.S. 125, 67 S.Ct. 1136, 91 L.Ed. 1386 (1947) (denying an accounting because injunctive relief satisfied the "equities of the case"). The nature of the defendant's knowledge or intent that is sufficient to support an accounting has also been unclear. In P.E. Sharpless Co. v. Lawrence, 213 Fed. 423 (3d Cir.1914), for example, the court stated that profits could be awarded in the absence of fraud in actions for trademark infringement but not for unfair competition. See also, e.g., Aladdin Mfg. Co. v. Mantle Lamp Co., 116 F.2d 708 (7th Cir. 1941), suggesting that fraud is required for an award of damages but not profits.

Recovery of defendant's profits is sometimes viewed as a means of overcoming the difficulty of proving actual damages. See, e.g., Mishawaka Rubber & Woolen Mfg. Co. v. S.S. Kresge Co., 316 U.S. 203, 62 S.Ct. 1022, 86 L.Ed. 1381 (1942); Culligan, Inc. v. Rheaume, 268 Wis. 298, 67 N.W.2d 279 (1954). Restatement of Torts § 747, Comment *g*, stated that an accounting was not available when the infringing goods did not directly compete with those of the trademark owner because "the accounting for defendant's profits is, historically, a substitute for damages for the plaintiff's loss of sales." See, e.g., Blue Ribbon Feed Co. v. Farmers Union Cent. Exchange, Inc., 731 F.2d 415 (7th Cir.1984); Pure Foods, Inc. v. Minute Maid Corp., 214 F.2d 792 (5th Cir.), cert. denied 348 U.S. 888, 75 S.Ct. 208, 99 L.Ed. 697 (1954). See also Polo Fashions, Inc. v. Craftex, Inc., 816 F.2d 145 (4th Cir.1987) (defendant's profits viewed as a measure of the plaintiff's loss under the North Carolina Deceptive Trade Practice Act).

The leading case to announce the rule that an accounting of the defendant's profits can be justified on theories of unjust enrichment and deterrence is Monsanto Chemical Co. v. Perfect Fit Products Mfg. Co., 349 F.2d 389 (2d Cir.1965), cert. denied 383 U.S. 942, 86 S.Ct. 1195, 16 L.Ed.2d 206 (1966). See also Playboy Enterprises, Inc. v. Baccarat Clothing Co., 692 F.2d 1272 (9th Cir. 1982); Maltina Corp. v. Cawy Bottling Co., 613 F.2d 582 (5th Cir.1980); Maier Brewing Co. v. Fleischmann Distilling Corp., 390 F.2d 117 (9th Cir.), cert. denied 391 U.S. 966, 88 S.Ct. 2037, 20 L.Ed.2d 879 (1968). Plaintiffs have been awarded an accounting of the defendant's profits in noncompeting goods cases notwithstanding a lack of actual damage in order to insure a deterrent against willful infringement. See Springs Mills, Inc. v. Ultracashmere House, Ltd., 724 F.2d 352 (2d Cir.1983); W.E. Bassett Co. v. Revlon, Inc., 435 F.2d 656 (2d Cir.1970).

Comment c. See the Reporters' Note to § 36, Comment *c*, for authority supporting the rule that the plaintiff may recover both damages and defendant's profits provided that double recovery for the same loss is avoided.

Comment d. See generally Restatement of Torts § 747, Comment *c*. The rule that the plaintiff may recover only profits attributable to the infringement is illustrated by Truck Equipment Service Co. v. Fruehauf Corp., 536 F.2d 1210 (8th Cir.), cert. denied 429 U.S. 861, 97 S.Ct. 164, 50 L.Ed.2d 139 (1976) (recovery of profits limited to defendant's sales in geographic areas in which the mark was identified with the plaintiff).

The plaintiff has the burden of proving the defendant's gross sales, but need not do so with mathematical precision. See, e.g., Wesco Mfg. Inc. v. Tropical Attractions of Palm Beach, Inc., 833 F.2d 1484 (11th Cir. 1987) (proof based on the defendant's tax returns and other evidence of infringing sales found sufficient since the defendant is in the best position to prove exact sales and profits).

The defendant bears the burden of apportioning gross sales to causes other than the infringement. See Hamilton–Brown Shoe Co. v. Wolf Bros. & Co., 240 U.S. 251, 36 S.Ct. 269, 60 L.Ed. 629 (1916) (suggesting that attribution of a portion of the sales to the inherent merits of the product is often impossible); Wynn Oil Co. v. American Way Service Corp., 943 F.2d 595 (6th Cir.1991); Century Distilling Co. v. Continental Distilling Corp., 205 F.2d 140, 144 (3d Cir.), cert. denied 346 U.S. 900, 74 S.Ct. 226, 98 L.Ed. 400 (1953) ("if a windfall is to result from the failure to achieve mathematical precision in gauging the percentage of the infringer's sales not attributable to confusion it belongs to the wronged, not the wrongdoer"); Obear–Nester Glass Co. v. United Drug Co., 149 F.2d 671 (8th Cir.), cert. denied 326 U.S. 761, 66 S.Ct. 141, 90 L.Ed. 458 (1945) (presumption that the defendant's gross sales resulted from the infringement was successfully rebutted); Holiday Inns, Inc. v. Airport Holiday Corp., 493 F.Supp. 1025 (N.D.Tex.1980), affirmed 683 F.2d 931 (5th Cir.1982) (30% of the defendant's hotel profits found attributable to the infringement of the plaintiff's trademark). "The plaintiff of course is not entitled to profits demonstrably not attributable to the unlawful use of his mark." Mishawaka Rubber & Woolen Mfg. Co. v. S.S. Kresge Co., 316 U.S. 203, 206, 62 S.Ct. 1022, 1024, 86 L.Ed. 1381, 1385 (1942); Maier Brewing Co. v. Fleischmann Distilling Corp., 390 F.2d 117 (9th Cir.), cert. denied 391 U.S. 966, 88 S.Ct. 2037, 20 L.Ed.2d 879 (1968).

The leading case holding that the defendant is not entitled to offset losses from independent transactions in determining profits is Wolfe v. National Lead Co., 272 F.2d 867 (9th Cir.1959), cert. denied 362 U.S. 950, 80 S.Ct. 860, 4 L.Ed.2d 868 (1960) (citing Duplate Corp. v. Triplex Safety Glass Co., 298 U.S. 448, 56 S.Ct. 792, 80 L.Ed. 1274 (1936) (a patent case), and Restatement of Torts § 747, Comment *d*). See also Burger King Corp. v. Mason, 855 F.2d 779 (11th Cir.1988) (holdover franchisee could not set off losses from some restaurants against profits from others, but was permitted to offset one year's losses against another year's gains from the same restaurant).

Comment e. The decision of the Supreme Court in Hamilton-Brown Shoe Co. v. Wolf Bros. & Co., 240 U.S. 251, 36 S.Ct. 269, 60 L.Ed. 629 (1916), is sometimes read to authorize an accounting of defendant's profits in all cases of infringement regardless of the defendant's intent, although the Court in that case found that the defendant had intentionally infringed the plaintiff's mark. However, the Supreme Court denied an accounting for trademark infringement in Champion Spark Plug Co. v. Sanders, 331 U.S. 125, 67 S.Ct. 1136, 91 L.Ed. 1386 (1947). Some cases authorize an award of profits for a deliberate but good faith use of another's mark. See Burger King Corp. v. Mason, 855 F.2d 779 (11th Cir.1988); Wolfe v. National Lead Co., 272 F.2d 867 (9th Cir.1959), cert. denied 362 U.S. 950, 80 S.Ct. 860, 4 L.Ed.2d 868 (1960). A leading decision limiting an accounting of the defendant's profits to cases of willful infringement is George Basch Co. v. Blue Coral, Inc., 968 F.2d 1532, 1537 (2d Cir.), cert. denied ___ U.S. ___, 113 S.Ct. 510, 121 L.Ed.2d 445 (1992) ("under any theory, a finding of defendant's willful deceptiveness is a prerequisite for awarding profits," citing Restatement Third, Unfair Competition § 37 (Tent. Draft No.3 (1991))). Other recent decisions also limit an award of profits to cases of bad faith. See, e.g., Aktiebolaget Electrolux v. Armatron Int'l, Inc., 999

F.2d 1 (1st Cir.1993) (if the defendant's profits do not represent sales diverted from the plaintiff, fraud or other inequitable conduct is required to support an accounting); Lindy Pen Co. v. Bic Pen Corp., 982 F.2d 1400 (9th Cir.), cert. denied ___ U.S. ___, 114 S.Ct. 64, 126 L.Ed.2d 34 (1993) (denying an accounting in the absence of "willful" infringement); Frisch's Restaurants, Inc. v. Elby's Big Boy, 849 F.2d 1012 (6th Cir. 1988); Schroeder v. Lotito, 747 F.2d 801 (1st Cir.1984) (Rhode Island law requires fraudulent intent for an award of profits); Maier Brewing Co. v. Fleischmann Distilling Corp., 390 F.2d 117 (9th Cir.), cert. denied 391 U.S. 966, 88 S.Ct. 2037, 20 L.Ed.2d 879 (1968) (when the infringement is "entirely innocent" an injunction satisfies the equities of the case); El Greco Leather Products Co. v. Shoe World, Inc., 726 F.Supp. 25 (E.D.N.Y. 1989) ("unjust enrichment" rationale does not authorize profits against a good faith infringer). Cf. Sands, Taylor & Wood Co. v. Quaker Oats Co., 978 F.2d 947 (7th Cir.1992), cert. denied ___ U.S. ___, 113 S.Ct. 1879, 123 L.Ed.2d 497 (1993) (an award of profits against a defendant who had no knowledge of the plaintiff's mark would not be "equitable"). See also Nalpac, Ltd. v. Corning Glass Works, 784 F.2d 752, 755 (6th Cir.1986), holding that bad faith is required for an accounting:

> The fact that one believes he has a right to adopt a mark already in use because in his view no conflict exists since the products are separate and distinct cannot, by itself, stamp his conduct as bad faith, even after the Patent Office has refused the mark registration. Any such doctrine would preempt a mark exclusively in favor of a senior user for all related products.

(quoting Mushroom Makers, Inc. v. R.G. Barry Corp., 441 F.Supp. 1220, 1230 (S.D.N.Y.1977), affirmed 580 F.2d 44 (2d Cir.1978), cert. denied 439 U.S. 1116, 99 S.Ct. 1022, 59 L.Ed.2d 75 (1979)). In Reader's Digest Ass'n v. Conservative Digest, Inc., 821 F.2d 800 (D.C.Cir.1987), the Court of Appeals for the District of Columbia noted that it had "left open" the possibility of an award of profits under § 43(a) based solely on unjust enrichment in the absence of bad faith, but subsequently held that bad faith is required. See ALPO Petfoods, Inc. v. Ralston Purina Co., 913 F.2d 958 (D.C.Cir.1990). But see Roulo v. Russ Berrie & Co., 886 F.2d 931 (7th Cir.1989), cert. denied 493 U.S. 1075, 110 S.Ct. 1124, 107 L.Ed.2d 1030 (1990) (willful infringement is not required for an award of profits) (dictum). Reliance on the advice of counsel can be evidence of good faith. See Cuisinarts, Inc. v. Robot–Coupe Int'l Corp., 580 F.Supp. 634 (S.D.N.Y.1984). See also El Greco Leather Products Co., *supra* (trial court's finding of no infringement, although reversed on appeal, is evidence that the defendant did not act in bad faith).

Comment f. Even in cases of bad faith, the award of an accounting remains subject to principles of equity. See George Basch Co. v. Blue Coral, Inc., 968 F.2d 1532 (2d Cir.), cert. denied ___ U.S. ___, 113 S.Ct. 510, 121 L.Ed.2d 445 (1992) (citing Restatement Third, Unfair Competition § 37 (Tent. Draft No.3 (1991))); Faberge, Inc. v. Saxony Products, Inc., 605 F.2d 426 (9th Cir.1979) (upholding the denial of an accounting because the costs of litigation and a requirement of relabeling were sufficient to deter further infringement); Red Devil Tools v. Tip Top Brush Co., 50 N.J. 563, 236 A.2d 861 (1967). For a case explicitly recognizing that a variety of factors including the intent of the defendant and the certainty of harm to the plaintiff should be considered in determining whether an accounting is appropriate, see Robert Bruce, Inc. v. Sears, Roebuck & Co., 343 F.Supp. 1333 (E.D.Pa.1972). In Mister Twister, Inc. v. JenEm Corp., 710 F.Supp. 202 (S.D.Ohio 1989), an injunction was held sufficient and an accounting of profits denied when the charter of the corporate defendant had been canceled and the individual defendant was in bankruptcy. See also El Greco Leather Products Co. v. Shoe World, Inc., 726 F.Supp. 25 (E.D.N.Y.1989) (the availability of a remedy against a third person may be considered).

In fashioning appropriate relief the courts also consider the public interest in deterring future misconduct. See, e.g., Playboy Enterprises, Inc. v. Baccarat Clothing Co., 692 F.2d 1272 (9th Cir.1982); Maier Brewing Co. v. Fleischmann Distilling Corp., 390 F.2d 117 (9th Cir.), cert. denied 391 U.S. 966, 88 S.Ct. 2037, 20 L.Ed.2d 879 (1968).

In a deceptive marketing case an award of profits can raise the prospect of multiple recoveries and may therefore be inappropriate unless the defendant's profits derive from a diversion of sales from a particular plaintiff. See ALPO Petfoods, Inc. v. Ralston Purina Co., 913 F.2d 958 (D.C.Cir.1990) (the willfulness required for an accounting of profits entails the "targeting" of a specific competitor); Burndy Corp. v. Teledyne Industries, Inc., 748 F.2d 767 (2d Cir.1984).

In Borg–Warner Corp. v. York–Shipley, Inc., 293 F.2d 88 (7th Cir.), cert. denied 368 U.S. 939, 82 S.Ct. 381, 7 L.Ed.2d 338 (1961), misconduct by the trademark owner was found sufficient to deny an accounting of the infringer's profits, although not an injunction and an award of actual damages. However, a plaintiff's misconduct should bar an accounting only if the misconduct is related to the rights asserted in the action and is of such severity or culpability as to justify the withholding of such relief. Durbin Brass Works, Inc. v. Schuler, 532 F.Supp. 41 (E.D.Mo.1982). See generally § 32.

Comment g. See generally Restatement of Torts § 748, from which much of Comment *g* is derived. On apportionment and the computation of net profits, see Bussert and Davis, Calculating Profits Under Section 35 of the Lanham Act: A Practitioner's Guide, 82 Trademark Rep. 182 (1992). The accepted rule is that the plaintiff bears the burden of proving the defendant's gross sales and the defendant has the burden of proving deductible costs. E.g., 15 U.S.C.A. § 1117; Maltina Corp. v. Cawy Bottling Co., 613 F.2d 582 (5th Cir.1980); Obear–Nester Glass Co. v. United Drug Co., 149 F.2d 671 (8th Cir.), cert. denied 326 U.S. 761, 66 S.Ct. 141, 90 L.Ed. 458 (1945); S.C. Johnson & Son, Inc. v. Drop Dead Co., 144 U.S.P.Q. 257 (S.D.Cal.1965). Labor, raw materials, and other costs associated with the production of infringing goods are generally deductible. E.g., W.E. Bassett Co. v. Revlon, Inc., 435 F.2d 656 (2d Cir.1970); Century Distilling Co. v. Continental Distilling Corp., 205 F.2d 140 (3d Cir.), cert. denied 346 U.S. 900, 74 S.Ct. 226, 98 L.Ed. 400 (1953).

Attorney's fees expended by the defendant in defending the infringement action are not deductible, at least when the infringement is willful. Wolfe v. National Lead Co., 272 F.2d 867 (9th Cir.1959), cert. denied 362 U.S. 950, 80 S.Ct. 860, 4 L.Ed.2d 868 (1960). Compensation paid to persons directly responsible for the infringement is not ordinarily deductible. See *id.*; Durbin Brass Works, Inc. v. Schuler, 532 F.Supp. 41 (E.D.Mo.1982); Champion Spark Plug Co. v. Sanders, 108 F.Supp. 674 (E.D.N.Y.1952), affirmed 204 F.2d 125 (2d Cir.1953). But cf. American Express Co. v. American Express Limousine Service Ltd., 785 F.Supp. 334 (E.D.N.Y.1992) (commissions paid by corporate defendant to individual defendants held deductible under the equities of the case). Distributions of profits to partners or stockholders are also not ordinarily deductible. Aladdin Mfg. Co. v. Mantle Lamp Co., 116 F.2d 708 (7th Cir. 1941).

The leading case holding that income tax paid by the defendant is not deductible is *Wolfe, supra.* See also, e.g., Century Distilling Co., *supra*; Stuart v. Collins, 489 F.Supp. 827 (S.D.N.Y.1980) (noting that the defendant's payment of the accounting award is deductible for tax purposes). But see W.E. Bassett Co., *supra*; USM Corp. v. Marson Fastener Corp., 392 Mass. 334, 467 N.E.2d 1271 (1984). In L.P. Larson Jr., Co. v. William Wrigley, Jr., Co., 277 U.S. 97, 48 S.Ct. 449, 72 L.Ed. 800 (1928), Justice Holmes held that the deductibility of income tax depends on the facts of the particular case.

Comment h. The burden of apportioning deductible expenses between infringing and noninfringing goods is on the defendant. Beyond the variable costs directly associated with the manufacture and sale of the infringing goods, some courts allocate a proportion of overhead and other fixed costs. See, e.g., Warner Bros., Inc. v. Gay Toys, Inc., 598 F.Supp. 424 (S.D.N.Y.1984). See also W.E. Bassett Co. v. Revlon, Inc., 435 F.2d 656 (2d Cir.1970) (permitting an allocation of overhead). Restatement of Torts § 748, Comment *j*, permitted a deduction only for the marginal increase in costs resulting from the production of the infringing goods. See Century Distilling Co. v. Continental Distilling Corp., 205 F.2d 140 (3d Cir.), cert. denied 346 U.S. 900, 74 S.Ct. 226, 98 L.Ed. 400 (1953); USM Corp. v. Marson Fastener Corp., 392 Mass. 334, 467 N.E.2d 1271 (1984). See also Polo Fashions, Inc. v. Craftex, Inc., 816 F.2d 145 (4th Cir.1987) (deduction of only marginal costs with no allocation of overhead may be appropriate in some contexts) (dictum). Some courts have applied a "sales-ratio" method, apportioning costs by the ratio of sales of the infringing product to total sales, but the determination can also take into account other circumstances of the case. See Wolfe v. National Lead Co., 272 F.2d 867 (9th Cir.1959), cert. denied 362 U.S. 950, 80 S.Ct. 860, 4 L.Ed.2d 868 (1960). A few cases have denied a proportional deduction for overhead when sales of the infringing product constitute only a small percentage of total sales. Maltina Corp. v. Cawy Bottling Co., 613 F.2d 582 (5th Cir. 1980) (just over 6%); S.C. Johnson & Son, Inc. v. Drop Dead Co., 144 U.S.P.Q. 257 (S.D.Cal.1965) (6%).

CHAPTER FOUR

APPROPRIATION OF TRADE VALUES

Introductory Note: This Chapter states the principles governing liability for the appropriation of intangible trade values. Topic 1 states a general rule rejecting the recognition of exclusive rights in intangible trade values, subject to a series of specified exceptions. Topic 2 states the rules comprising the law of trade secrets. A majority of the states have adopted the Uniform Trade Secrets Act, which codifies the common law doctrines relating to the protection of trade secrets. The rules stated in Topic 2 are applicable to both statutory and common law trade secret cases. Rules governing the right of publicity, which protects against certain appropriations of the commercial value of a person's identity, are treated in Topic 3.

TOPIC 1. MISAPPROPRIATION

---

§ 38. Appropriation of Trade Values

One who causes harm to the commercial relations of another by appropriating the other's intangible trade values is subject to liability to the other for such harm only if:

(a) the actor is subject to liability for an appropriation of the other's trade secret under the rules stated in §§ 39–45; or

(b) the actor is subject to liability for an appropriation of the commercial value of the other's identity under the rules stated in §§ 46–49; or

(c) the appropriation is actionable by the other under federal or state statutes or international agreements, or is actionable as a breach of contract, or as an infringement of common law copyright as preserved under federal copyright law.

Comment:

a. Scope and relationship to other rules. Chapter One of this Restatement recognizes the freedom to engage in business and to compete with others for the patronage of prospective customers. The law of unfair competition imposes liability only in connection with particular methods of competition that undermine rather than advance the competitive process. See § 1. Chapter Two of this Restatement states rules governing liability for deceptive practices that deprive consumers of the accurate information necessary for the efficient operation of a competitive market. Chapter Three states rules prohibiting the infringement of trademarks and other trade designations in order to prevent consumer confusion and encourage investment in good will. This Chapter states the rules relating to liability for the appropriation of information and other intangible trade values. This Section states the general rule governing the protection of such trade values. Sections 39–45 state the rules applicable to the protection of trade secrets. Sections 46–49 state the rules protecting the commercial value of a person's identity.

The primary sources of protection for intangible trade values are the federal patent and copyright laws. These statutory systems offer extensive protection to eligible subject matter and also significantly limit the protection of intangible trade values under state statutory and common law. See Comment *e*.

The rules stated in this Chapter deal with rights in intangible trade values. Conduct that interferes with other protected interests may subject the actor to liability under other rules of tort law. An appropriation of tangible assets, for example, may be actionable under the law of conversion, and an appropriation of a person's identity may infringe upon noncommercial interests protected under the law of privacy. See § 46, Comment *b*. Similarly, conduct that induces a breach of contract may be actionable under the general principles of tort law prohibiting interference with contractual relationships. Interference with mere prospective economic relationships, however, does not ordinarily subject a competitor to liability unless the interference is accomplished through "wrongful means." See Restatement, Second, Torts § 768. The rules stated in this Chapter determine whether the appropriation of an intangible trade value is a "wrongful means" of competition for purposes of that rule. Intangible trade values may also be the subject of contractual obligations, and the traditional remedies for breach of contract supplement the protection afforded under this Chapter. However, agreements that unreasonably restrain trade are not enforceable, and the rules stated in this Chapter can be helpful in determining whether a particular restraint is reasonable. See § 41, Comment *d*.

b. Misappropriation. Protection against the misappropriation of intangible trade values insures an incentive to invest in the creation of intangible assets and prevents the potential unjust enrichment that may result from the appropriation of an investment made by another. However, the recognition of exclusive rights in intangible trade values can impede access to valuable information and restrain competition. Unlike appropriations of physical assets, the appropriation of information or other intangible asset does not ordinarily deprive the originator of simultaneous use. The recognition of exclusive rights may thus deny to the public the full benefits of valuable ideas and innovations by limiting their distribution and exploitation. In addition, the principle of unjust enrichment does not demand restitution of every gain derived from the efforts of others. A small shop, for example, may freely benefit from the customers attracted by a nearby department store, a local manufacturer may benefit from increased demand attributable to the promotional efforts of a national manufacturer of similar goods, and a newspaper may benefit from reporting on the activities of local athletic teams. Similarly, the law has long recognized the right of a competitor to copy the successful products and business methods of others absent protection under patent, copyright, or trademark law.

Achieving a proper balance between protection and access is often a complicated and difficult undertaking. Because of the complexity and indeterminacy of the competing interests, rights in intangible trade values such as ideas, innovations, and information have been created primarily through legislation. The patent and copyright statutes illustrate the intricacy required to harmonize the competing public and private interests implicated in the recognition of rights in intangible trade values. Both statutes contain elaborate mechanisms intended to balance the interests in protection and access. Protection under the patent act, for example, is limited to innovations that are new, useful, and non-obvious to persons having ordinary skill in the art. The copyright act grants rights in works of authorship subject to a complex system of exemptions and limitations. Both statutes grant rights only for a limited term, after which the discovery or writing enters the public domain and may be freely appropriated by others.

The common law of unfair competition has generally recognized rights against the appropriation of intangible trade values only when the recognition of such rights is supported by other interests that justify protection, and then only when the scope of the resulting rights can be clearly defined. The protection of trade secrets, for example, reflects the established interests in preserving confidential relationships and promoting physical security. See §§ 39–45. Protection against an appropriation of the commercial value of a person's identity implicates interests in privacy, reputation, and personal autonomy. See §§ 46–49. In the absence of such additional interests, the common law has resisted the recognition of general rights against the appropriation of information and other intangible trade values.

In 1918, the United States Supreme Court in International News Service v. Associated Press, 248 U.S. 215, 39 S.Ct. 68, 63 L.Ed. 211 (1918), recognized a common law tort of "misappropriation" that afforded protection against the appropriation by a competitor of commercially valuable information otherwise in the public domain. Although the decision has been frequently cited, it has been sparingly applied. Notwithstanding its longevity, the decision has had little enduring effect. See Comment *c*. In many cases it has been invoked when narrower rules of unfair competition would have achieved the same result. In most of the areas in which it has been expansively applied, its application has now been supplanted by legislation.

The rule stated in this Section limits common law tort liability for appropriations of intangible trade values to cases involving an appropriation of trade secrets, an appropriation of the commercial value of another's identity, or an appropriation of a work of authorship that is not fixed in a tangible medium of expression and thus protectable under common law copyright. See Comment *d.* Although courts have occasionally invoked the *INS* decision on an ad hoc basis to grant relief against other commercial appropriations, they have not articulated coherent principles for its application. It is clear that no general rule of law prohibits the appropriation of a competitor's ideas, innovations, or other intangible assets once they become publicly known. In addition, the federal patent and copyright statutes now preempt a considerable portion of the domain in which the common law tort might otherwise apply. See Comment *e.* The better approach, and the one most likely to achieve an appropriate balance between the competing interests, does not recognize a residual common law tort of misappropriation.

c. International News Service v. Associated Press. In International News Service v. Associated Press, 248 U.S. 215, 39 S.Ct. 68, 63 L.Ed. 211 (1918), the United States Supreme Court recognized a cause of action under federal common law for the misappropriation of a competitor's intangible trade values. The International News Service had copied information from Associated Press news dispatches published in eastern newspapers and transmitted news stories based on the information to INS-affiliated newspapers on the west coast for publication in competition with western members of the Associated Press. Although acknowledging the public's right to copy the uncopyrighted news reports, the Supreme Court held that the appropriation of news by a competitor for use in direct competition with the originator was actionable as unfair competition:

> In doing this defendant, by its very act, admits that it is taking material that has been acquired by complainant as the result of organization and the expenditure of labor, skill, and money, and which is salable by complainant for money, and that defendant in appropriating it and selling it as its own is endeavoring to reap where it has not sown, and by disposing of it to newspapers that are competitors of complainant's members is appropriating to itself the harvest of those who have sown. Stripped of all disguises, the process amounts to an unauthorized interference with the normal operation of complainant's legitimate business precisely at the point where the profit is to be reaped, in order to divert a material portion of the profit from those who have earned it to those who have not; with special advantage to defendant in the competition because of the fact that it is not burdened with any part of the expense of gathering the news. The transaction

> speaks for itself, and a court of equity ought not to hesitate long in characterizing it as unfair competition in business.

248 U.S. at 239–40, 39 S.Ct. at 72–73, 63 L.Ed. at 221.

Although the decision appears to rest on a rationale of unjust enrichment potentially applicable to a wide range of competitive conduct, subsequent decisions have recognized that broad application of the unjust enrichment rationale in a competitive marketplace would unreasonably restrain competition and undermine the public interest in access to valuable information. The facts of the *INS* decision are unusual and may serve, in part, to limit its rationale. The originator of valuable information or other intangible assets normally has an opportunity to exploit the advantage of a lead time in the market. This can provide the originator with an opportunity to recover the costs of development and in many cases is sufficient to encourage continued investment. However, the appropriation in *INS* deprived Associated Press of any lead-time advantage, at least on the West Coast. Associated Press thus faced a direct threat to its primary market by a competitor who had incurred none of the development costs associated with collecting the news. Such circumstances present the most compelling case for protection against appropriation, although even on these facts Justice Brandeis argued persuasively in dissent that the proper balance between protection and access could be drawn only through legislation.

The limited extent to which the *INS* rationale has been incorporated into the common law of the states indicates that the decision is properly viewed as a response to unusual circumstances rather than as a statement of generally applicable principles of common law. Many subsequent decisions have expressly limited the *INS* case to its facts. In addition, in many of the decisions that invoke the misappropriation doctrine, other principles of unfair competition law are more directly applicable. For example, some courts have invoked the misappropriation doctrine to impose liability in trademark and trade dress cases notwithstanding proof of a likelihood of confusion sufficient to establish liability under traditional principles of trademark law. Similarly, some cases have invoked the doctrine against appropriations involving breaches of confidence or other improper conduct actionable under the rules protecting trade secrets.

In most of the small number of cases in which the misappropriation doctrine has been determinative, the defendant's appropriation, like that in *INS*, resulted in direct competition in the plaintiff's primary market. Several cases, for example, invoke the doctrine to impose liability for an appropriation of news on facts more or less analogous to those in the *INS* case. Similarly, the misappropriation doctrine for a time played a significant role in restraining the unauthorized reproduction and sale of musical performances and sound recordings. Injunctions based on the misappropriation doctrine were granted against the sale of unauthorized recordings of radio broadcasts in competition with authorized recordings and against record and tape pirates selling unauthorized copies of popular sound recordings in competition with the originals. These decisions are now effectively superseded by the protection available under the 1976 Copyright Act to sound recordings and to broadcasts that are simultaneously recorded upon transmission. Even with respect to directly competitive appropriations, however, the implementation of enduring and appropriately circumscribed protection is generally best achieved through legislation rather than common law adjudication.

Appeals to the misappropriation doctrine are almost always rejected when the appropriation does not intrude upon the plaintiff's primary market. Only rarely have courts applied the doctrine to appropriations of intangible trade values for use in secondary or derivative markets. Absent proof of consumer confusion or a violation of other recognized principles of unfair competition law, such results go beyond even the broad rationale of the *INS* case.

d. Common law copyright. Prior to January 1, 1978, the effective date of the 1976 Copyright Act, the doctrine of common law copyright played an important role in preventing the appropriation of works of authorship. Common law copyright protected an author's proprietary and privacy interests in unpublished works by affording a right of first publication, thus precluding exploitation of the work by others prior to its publication by the author. After publication, protection against appropriation was governed by federal statutory copyright. However, under the 1976 Copyright Act, federal copyright protection subsists from the creation of a work, 17 U.S.C.A. § 302, defined as the first fixation of the work in any tangible medium of expression. *Id.* § 101. Both published and unpublished works are thus within the scope of the 1976 Copyright Act, which expressly preempts much of the former common law protection for unpublished works. See Comment *e.* State law remains free to protect from appropriation only those works that are not within the subject matter of federal copyright law, including works of authorship that have not been fixed in a tangible medium of expression.

It was well established at common law that the public performance of a work did not constitute "publication" and therefore did not divest common law copyright. Thus, while there is little case law, common law copyright might be invoked to prevent the appropriation of unfixed works such as extemporaneous speeches or live musical performances. However, although state common law copyright protection for unfixed works is not preempted by the 1976 Copyright Act, the significance of such protection is diminished by modern recording technologies that facilitate the fixation of works and the consequent acquisition of federal copyright protection. In addition, the appropriation of an unfixed work will often invade interests protected under other principles of law. The appropriation of an idea offered to another through an oral presentation, for example, can be actionable under the law of trade secrets. See § 39, Comment *h*. Similarly, unfixed performances may occur in circumstances that justify the implication of an obligation of confidentiality or in controlled settings that afford the opportunity to impose physical or contractual restrictions on recording or other reproduction. The unauthorized exploitation of an unfixed performance can also be actionable as an infringement of the right of publicity if it appropriates the commercial value of the performer's identity. See § 47, Comment *d*. Nevertheless, protection for works of authorship at common law has historically been pursued through the doctrine of common law copyright. Since the federal copyright statute expressly preserves common law protection for unfixed works of authorship, see 17 U.S.C.A. § 301, the continued recognition of rights in this narrowly-defined subject matter through the doctrine of common law copyright does not present the problems associated with judicial recognition of a more general misappropriation tort. However, comprehensive protection for unfixed works of authorship, which can encompass works extending from formal performances to casual conversations, may require limitations best implemented through legislation. Statutes in many states, for example, prohibit the unauthorized commercial recording of live performances.

e. Preemption by federal patent and copyright law. Many potential applications of the misappropriation doctrine are preempted by federal patent and copyright law. Beginning with the companion decisions in Sears, Roebuck & Co. v. Stiffel Co., 376 U.S. 225, 84 S.Ct. 784, 11 L.Ed.2d 661 (1964), and Compco Corp. v. Day–Brite Lighting, Inc., 376 U.S. 234, 84 S.Ct. 779, 11 L.Ed.2d 669 (1964), the United States Supreme Court has endeavored to define the permissible scope of state statutory and common law restrictions on copying. See § 16, Comment *c*. Emphasizing that the system of federal patent protection depends "almost entirely on a backdrop of free competition in the exploitation of unpatented designs and innovations," the Supreme Court in Bonito Boats, Inc. v. Thunder Craft Boats, Inc., 489 U.S. 141, 151, 156–57, 109 S.Ct. 971, 977, 980–81, 103 L.Ed.2d 118, 138 (1989), declared that "[a] state law that substantially interferes with the enjoyment of an unpatented utilitarian or design conception which has been freely disclosed by its author to the public at large impermissibly contravenes" federal patent policy. Thus, states may not apply the misappropriation doctrine to prevent the copying of products or ideas for mechanical or other utilitarian innovations that have been disclosed to the public.

Section 301 of the 1976 Copyright Act, 17 U.S.C.A. § 301, precludes the recognition under state law of rights "equivalent" to any of the exclusive rights of copyright in works that are "within the subject matter" of the Copyright Act. State rules protecting interests outside the scope of copyright, such as those affording relief against deception, consumer confusion, or breaches of confidence, are not preempted as "equivalent" to copyright. See § 16, Comment *c*; § 39, Comment *c*. However, primary among the rights of copyright in § 106, 17 U.S.C.A. § 106, is the exclusive right of reproduction. Courts have consistently concluded that in most if not all of its applications, the misappropriation doctrine affords a right "equivalent" to copyright. Preemption of state misappropriation law under § 301 thus turns on whether the object of state protection is within the subject matter preempted by the 1976 Copyright Act. Section 301 expressly authorizes state protection for unfixed works, which are ineligible for federal copyright under § 102(a), 17 U.S.C.A. § 102(b). See Comment *d*. State restrictions on appropriating the copyrightable aspects of works fixed in a tangible medium of expression, however, are clearly preempted. A more difficult issue arises in connection with the application of the misappropriation doctrine to protect the non-copyrightable aspects or elements of such works, including ideas or facts taken apart from the form in which they are expressed. Some courts and commentators have argued that the exclusion of ideas and facts from copyright protection in § 102(b) of the Copyright Act demonstrates that such material is not "within the subject matter of copyright," thus permitting protection under state law. However, § 102(b) can be seen, not as an exclusion of subject matter, but as a limitation on the scope of protection available to copyrighted works. Many cases therefore conclude that protection under state law for ideas, facts, or other non-copyrightable aspects of compilations and other works within the subject matter of copyright is preempted under § 301. Even if not preempted under a literal interpretation of § 301, state protection of facts and ideas may interfere with the balance between protection and access struck by Congress in the 1976 Copyright Act and may thus be preempted under the supremacy clause. State protection of facts and ideas can also interfere with rights under the first amendment.

Although the preemptive scope of federal patent and copyright law remains uncertain, the potential for interference with the policies underlying the federal intellectual property regime counsels against the recognition of broad and indeterminate rights against misappropriation.

REPORTERS' NOTE

Comment a. Notwithstanding the Supreme Court's 1918 decision in International News Service v. Associated Press, the Restatement of Torts published in 1939 contained no acknowledgement of the misappropriation doctrine.

Comment b. Many early commentators warned against broad recognition of the misappropriation doctrine. See, e.g., Kocourek, Comment, 13 Ill.L.Rev. 708 (1919); Handler, Unfair Competition, 21 Iowa L.Rev. 175, 189 (1936) ("For one to reap with impunity the fruits of another's labor may be reprehensible, but the creation of new species of property interests and new series of monopolies by the courts may be disastrous to free enterprise."); Chafee, Unfair Competition, 53 Harv.L.Rev. 1289 (1940); Brown, Advertising and the Public Interest: Legal Protection of Trade Symbols, 57 Yale L.J. 1165 (1948). On the other hand, some commentators applauded the decision. See Rogers, Unfair Competition, 17 Mich.L.Rev. 490 (1919); Callmann, He Who Reaps Where He Has Not Sown: Unjust Enrichment in the Law of Unfair Competition, 55 Harv. L.Rev. 595 (1942); Green, Protection of Trade Relations Under Tort Law, 47 Va.L.Rev. 559 (1961). More recent commentary on the misappropriation doctrine includes Baird, Common Law Intellectual Property and the Legacy of *International News Service v. Associated Press*, 50 U.Chi. L.Rev. 411 (1983); Gordon, On Owning Information: Intellectual Property and the Restitutionary Impulse, 78 Va.L.Rev. 149 (1992); Rahl, The Right to "Appropriate" Trade Values, 23 Ohio St.L.J. 56 (1962); Raskind, The Misappropriation Doctrine as a Competitive Norm of Intellectual Property Law, 75 Minn.L.Rev. 875 (1991).

There is no general common law prohibition against benefiting from the efforts of others. See, e.g., Emerson v. Davies, 8 F.Cas. 615, 619 (C.C.D.Mass.1845) ("Every book in literature, science and art, borrows, and must necessarily borrow, and use much which was well known and used before."); WCVB–TV v. Boston Athletic Ass'n, 926 F.2d 42, 45 (1st Cir. 1991) ("But the man who clears a swamp, the developer of a neighborhood, the academic scientist, the school teacher, and millions of others, each day create 'value' (over and above what they are paid) that the law permits others to receive without charge."); National Football League v. Governor of Delaware, 435 F.Supp. 1372, 1378 (D.Del.1977) ("It is true that Delaware is thus making profits [from the use of the plaintiffs' football scores in a state lottery] it would not make but for the existence of the NFL, but I find this difficult to distinguish from the multitude of charter bus companies who generate profit from servicing those of plaintiffs' fans who want to go to the stadium or, indeed, the sidewalk popcorn salesman who services the crowd as it surges towards the gate.").

A number of recent cases expressly acknowledge the balancing of interests inherent in the recognition of exclusive rights in intangible property. See, e.g., United States Golf

Ass'n v. St. Andrews Systems, Data–Max, Inc., 749 F.2d 1028, 1035 (3d Cir.1984) ("[T]he dilemma posed by the doctrine can best be viewed as an attempt to provide the necessary incentives to the creators of intellectual property without unnecessarily restricting the public's free access to information."); Board of Trade v. Dow Jones & Co., 98 Ill.2d 109, 119, 74 Ill.Dec. 582, 587, 456 N.E.2d 84, 89 (1983) ("Competing with the policy that protection should be afforded one who expends labor and money to develop products is the concept that freedom to imitate and duplicate is vital to our free market economy."). See also, e.g., Roho, Inc. v. Marquis, 902 F.2d 356, 360 (5th Cir.1990) ("Although copyists undoubtedly incur the enmity of the product's creator, they serve the public interest by promoting competition and price reductions."). For arguments that the balancing is best accomplished through legislation, see, e.g., International News Service v. Associated Press, 248 U.S. 215, 39 S.Ct. 68, 63 L.Ed. 211 (1918) (Brandeis, J., dissenting); Cheney Bros. v. Doris Silk Corp., 35 F.2d 279 (2d Cir.1929), cert. denied 281 U.S. 728, 50 S.Ct. 245, 74 L.Ed. 1145 (1930) (L. Hand, J.); Board of Trade, *supra* (Simon, J., dissenting). See also Handler, *supra*, 21 Iowa L.Rev. at 189–90 ("Judge-made monopolies find their origin and their regulation in the law of torts and the protection of the public interest is at best unsystematic and fortuitous."); Gordon, *supra*, 78 Va.L.Rev. at 281 ("Legislatures likely will continue to be the best institutions for implementing protection for intellectual products * * *.").

Comment c. A number of decisions limit the *INS* case to its facts. See, e.g., Cheney Bros. v. Doris Silk Corp., 35 F.2d 279, 280 (2d Cir.1929), cert. denied 281 U.S. 728, 50 S.Ct. 245, 74 L.Ed. 1145 (1930) (L. Hand, J.) ("[W]e think that no more was covered than situations substantially similar to those then at bar."); National Comics Pub., Inc. v. Fawcett Pub., Inc., 191 F.2d 594 (2d Cir.1951) (L. Hand, J.); Speedry Products, Inc. v. Dri Mark Products, Inc., 271 F.2d 646 (2d Cir.1959) (the *INS* case "is sui generis"); Famolare, Inc. v. Melville Corp., 472 F.Supp. 738 (D.Hawaii 1979), affirmed 652 F.2d 62 (9th Cir.1981). Early cases declining to apply the misappropriation rationale include, e.g., Triangle Pub., Inc. v. New England Newspaper Pub. Co., 46 F.Supp. 198, 203 (D.Mass.1942) ("[I]t is not unfair competition in Massachusetts to use information assembled by a competitor"); Clipper Belt Lacer Co. v. Detroit Belt Lacer Co., 223 Mich. 399, 194 N.W. 125 (1923) (declining to apply *INS* to the defendant's sale of hooks designed to fit the plaintiff's machines); Germanow v. Standard Unbreakable Watch Crystals, Inc., 283 N.Y. 1, 27 N.E.2d 212 (1940) (declining to apply *INS* to a competitor's appropriation of the plaintiff's measuring system for watch crystals); New England Tel. & Tel. Co. v. National Merchandising Corp., 335 Mass. 658, 141 N.E.2d 702 (1957) (refusing to apply the misappropriation doctrine to prevent the defendant's sale of covers for the plaintiff's telephone directories bearing advertising sold by the defendant). But see National Tel. Directory Co. v. Dawson Mfg. Co., 214 Mo. App. 683, 263 S.W. 483 (1924) (applying *INS* on similar facts).

The misappropriation doctrine prevailed in several cases on facts similar to *INS*. See Associated Press v. KVOS, Inc., 80 F.2d 575 (9th Cir.

1935), reversed for lack of jurisdiction, 299 U.S. 269, 57 S.Ct. 197, 81 L.Ed. 183 (1936) (appropriation of news by a radio station); Pottstown Daily News Pub. Co. v. Pottstown Broadcasting Co., 411 Pa. 383, 192 A.2d 657 (1963) (same); McCord Co. v. Plotnick, 108 Cal.App.2d 392, 239 P.2d 32 (1951) (appropriation of news by a competing publication). See also National Exhibition Co. v. Fass, 143 N.Y.S.2d 767 (Sup.Ct.1955) and Twentieth Century Sporting Club, Inc. v. Transradio Press Service, Inc., 165 Misc. 71, 300 N.Y.S. 159 (Sup.Ct. 1937), both enjoining the appropriation of information from radio broadcasts of sporting events for the purpose of recreating the event on other radio stations. But see Loeb v. Turner, 257 S.W.2d 800 (Tex.Civ.App. 1953), permitting the defendant's recreated broadcast of a stock car race based on the plaintiff's radio broadcast when the plaintiff and defendant served different cities. Compare WCVB–TV v. Boston Athletic Ass'n, 926 F.2d 42 (1st Cir.1991), refusing to enjoin the defendant's unauthorized broadcast of the Boston Marathon, with Pittsburgh Athletic Co. v. KQV Broadcasting Co., 24 F.Supp. 490 (W.D.Pa.1938), enjoining the defendant from broadcasting the plaintiff's baseball games from vantage points outside the stadium.

The misappropriation doctrine played a significant role in the early protection of sound recordings. In Waring v. WDAS Broadcasting Station, Inc., 327 Pa. 433, 194 A. 631 (1937), the doctrine was applied under Pennsylvania law to prevent unauthorized radio broadcasts of the plaintiff's recordings. Judge Learned Hand's opinion in RCA Mfg. Co. v. Whiteman, 114 F.2d 86 (2d Cir.), cert. denied 311 U.S. 712, 61 S.Ct. 393, 85 L.Ed. 463 (1940), denied an injunction on similar facts, holding that the public sale of the recordings divested the plaintiff of common law rights. The 1976 Copyright Act denies an exclusive right of public performance in sound recordings. 17 U.S.C.A. § 114. See also Metropolitan Opera Ass'n v. Wagner–Nichols Recorder Corp., 199 Misc. 786, 101 N.Y.S.2d 483 (1950), affirmed 279 A.D. 632, 107 N.Y.S.2d 795 (1951), which applied the misappropriation doctrine under New York law to enjoin the defendant's sale of unauthorized recordings made from radio broadcasts of the Metropolitan Opera. Under the 1976 Copyright Act, recording of the radio broadcasts by the plaintiff at the time of transmission would invest federal copyright protection. 17 U.S.C.A. § 101 (definition of "fixed"). The misappropriation doctrine was also invoked in a number of cases to prevent the unauthorized duplication and sale of sound recordings by record pirates. See, e.g., A & M Records, Inc. v. M.V.C. Distributing Corp., 574 F.2d 312 (6th Cir.1978); Capitol Records, Inc. v. Mercury Records Corp., 221 F.2d 657 (2d Cir.1955) (with a dissent by L. Hand); United States Sporting Products, Inc. v. Johnny Stewart Game Calls, Inc., 865 S.W.2d 214 (Tex.App. 1993); Capitol Records, Inc. v. Spies, 130 Ill.App.2d 429, 264 N.E.2d 874 (1970); Mercury Record Productions, Inc. v. Economic Consultants, Inc., 64 Wis.2d 163, 218 N.W.2d 705 (1974), cert. denied 420 U.S. 914, 95 S.Ct. 1107, 43 L.Ed.2d 386 (1975); Gai Audio, Inc. v. Columbia Broadcasting System, Inc., 27 Md.App. 172, 340 A.2d 736 (1975) (awarding compensatory and punitive damages); Columbia Broadcasting System, Inc. v. Melody Recordings, Inc., 134 N.J.Super. 368, 341 A.2d 348 (1975). On February 15, 1972, sound recordings became eligible for protection under federal copyright law, thus preempting state protection. See 17 U.S.C.A. §§ 114, 301. Protection under state law for pre–1972 recordings is expressly preserved in § 301(c) of the 1976 Copyright Act until the year 2047.

Unauthorized retransmissions of radio and television broadcasts also prompted claims founded on *INS*. Compare Mutual Broadcasting System, Inc. v. Muzak Corp., 177 Misc. 489, 30 N.Y.S.2d 419 (1941) (issuing an injunction against the retransmission of plaintiff's radio broadcast of the 1941 World Series) with Intermountain Broadcasting & Television Corp. v. Idaho Microwave, Inc., 196 F.Supp. 315 (D.Idaho 1961) (declining to apply the *INS* case to cable television retransmission, emphasizing the lack of direct competition). Retransmission by cable and satellite carriers is now subject to a complex system of regulation under the 1976 Copyright Act, 17 U.S.C.A. §§ 111, 119. Cf. Orth–O–Vision, Inc. v. Home Box Office, 474 F.Supp. 672 (S.D.N.Y.1979) (state misappropriation claim directed at the unauthorized retransmission of a copyrighted broadcast is preempted). Unauthorized reception of transmissions is also regulated by the Federal Communications Act, 47 U.S.C.A. § 151 et seq., but misappropriation claims have continued. See KMLA Broadcasting Corp. v. Twentieth Century Cigarette Vendors Corp., 264 F.Supp. 35 (C.D.Cal.1967) (injunction issued against a defendant who provided equipment capable of receiving plaintiff's subscription radio broadcasts); American Television and Communications Corp. v. Manning, 651 P.2d 440 (Colo.App.1982) (sale of unauthorized receiving equipment enjoined).

Although the United States Supreme Court has occasionally cited the *INS* decision, it has never reaffirmed the misappropriation doctrine. See, e.g., Feist Publications, Inc. v. Rural Telephone Service Co., 499 U.S. 340, 111 S.Ct. 1282, 113 L.Ed.2d 358 (1991) and Harper & Row, Publishers, Inc. v. Nation Enterprises, 471 U.S. 539, 105 S.Ct. 2218, 85 L.Ed.2d 588 (1985), both citing *INS* for the proposition that ideas and facts are not copyrightable. In San Francisco Arts & Athletics, Inc. v. United States Olympic Committee, 483 U.S. 522, 107 S.Ct. 2971, 97 L.Ed.2d 427 (1987), the Court cited *INS* in upholding the constitutionality of a federal statute granting the United States Olympic Committee exclusive rights in the commercial use of the word "Olympic." In Carpenter v. United States, 484 U.S. 19, 108 S.Ct. 316, 98 L.Ed.2d 275 (1987), *INS* was invoked to support the conclusion that confidential and unpublished business information was "property" for purposes of the federal wire and mail fraud statutes. Cf. KVOS, Inc. v. Associated Press, 299 U.S. 269, 57 S.Ct. 197, 81 L.Ed. 183 (1936) (declining to consider the merits of the *INS* decision due to the absence of subject matter jurisdiction); Fashion Originators' Guild, Inc. v. FTC, 312 U.S. 457, 61 S.Ct. 703, 85 L.Ed. 949 (1941) (noting that after Erie Railroad Co. v. Tompkins, 304 U.S. 64, 58 S.Ct. 817, 82 L.Ed. 1188 (1938), the substantive issue in *INS* is a matter of state law). The dissenting opinion of Justice Brandeis in the *INS* case is cited in Kewanee Oil Co. v. Bicron Corp., 416 U.S. 470, 94 S.Ct. 1879, 40 L.Ed.2d 315 (1974) and Goldstein v. California, 412 U.S. 546, 93 S.Ct. 2303, 37

L.Ed.2d 163 (1973), for the proposition that ideas in general circulation are part of the public domain.

In many of the decisions that invoke the misappropriation doctrine, relief can be justified on more traditional grounds. See, e.g., Lexton–Ancira Real Estate Fund, 1972 v. Heller, 826 P.2d 819 (Colo.1992) (although affirming relief on a misappropriation claim, the court noted that a variety of deceptive practices including trade name infringement contributed to the plaintiff's injury); Roy Export Co. Establishment v. Columbia Broadcasting System, Inc., 672 F.2d 1095 (2d Cir.), cert. denied 459 U.S. 826, 103 S.Ct. 60, 74 L.Ed.2d 63 (1982) (misappropriation doctrine applied while noting that "such an amorphous cause of action is capable of mischievous application," but also finding infringement of common law copyright); Dior v. Milton, 9 Misc.2d 425, 155 N.Y.S.2d 443 (Sup.Ct.), affirmed 2 A.D.2d 878, 156 N.Y.S.2d 996 (1956) (misappropriation applied to protect dress designs, but access had been gained through fraud and misrepresentation); Standard & Poor's Corp. v. Commodity Exchange, Inc., 683 F.2d 704 (2d Cir. 1982) (preliminary injunction issued against the use of plaintiff's stock index in defendant's stock futures contracts, but also finding a likelihood of confusion). Cf. Wilson v. Electro Marine Systems, Inc., 915 F.2d 1110 (7th Cir.1990) (declining to apply the misappropriation doctrine in the absence of fraud or breach of confidence).

A number of cases invoke the misappropriation doctrine to protect trademarks and other trade designations. In some decisions the *INS* case is cited despite proof of a likelihood of confusion that would permit relief under traditional rules of trademark infringement. See, e.g., Fisher v. Star Co., 231 N.Y. 414, 132 N.E. 133, cert. denied 257 U.S. 654, 42 S.Ct. 94, 66 L.Ed. 419 (1921) (plaintiff's cartoon characters were found to have acquired secondary meaning). In other decisions, however, the misappropriation doctrine has been applied to justify protection for the ornamental or merchandising value of a trademark or trade name when there was little apparent likelihood of consumer confusion. See, e.g., Boston Athletic Association v. Sullivan, 867 F.2d 22 (1st Cir.1989); Warner Bros., Inc. v. Gay Toys, Inc., 658 F.2d 76 (2d Cir.1981); Flexitized, Inc. v. National Flexitized Corp., 335 F.2d 774 (2d Cir.1964), cert. denied 380 U.S. 913, 85 S.Ct. 899, 13 L.Ed.2d 799 (1965); Universal City Studios, Inc. v. Kamar Industries, Inc., 217 U.S.P.Q. 1162 (S.D.Tex.1982); Universal City Studios, Inc. v. Montgomery Ward & Co., 207 U.S.P.Q. 852 (N.D.Ill.1980). Cf. Board of Trade v. Dow Jones & Co., 98 Ill.2d 109, 456 N.E.2d 84 (1983) (an injunction against the unauthorized use of a well-known stock index in stock market futures contracts was issued to prevent an appropriation of the originator's good will). The scope of protection afforded to trade symbols under traditional principles of trademark law, including the requirement of a likelihood of confusion (see, e.g., § 20, Comment *e*), the right of fair use (§ 28), and the limitations on protection against dilution (see § 25), reflects a sensitive balancing of competing interests that should not be undermined by appeals to a general misappropriation rationale. Many cases refuse to allow the misappropriation doctrine to circumvent traditional limitations on the protection of trade symbols. See, e.g., WCVB–TV v. Boston Athletic

Ass'n, 926 F.2d 42 (1st Cir.1991); Toho Co. v. Sears, Roebuck & Co., 645 F.2d 788 (9th Cir.1981); Diversified Marketing, Inc. v. Estee Lauder, Inc., 705 F.Supp. 128 (S.D.N.Y.1988); Sykes Laboratory, Inc. v. Kalvin, 610 F.Supp. 849 (C.D.Cal.1985); Eastern Air Lines, Inc. v. New York Air Lines, Inc., 559 F.Supp. 1270 (S.D.N.Y.1983).

When the appropriation by the defendant does not interfere with the plaintiff's exploitation of the asset in its primary market, appeals to the *INS* case are regularly rejected absent a violation of other protected interests. In United States Golf Ass'n v. St. Andrews Systems, Data–Max, Inc., 749 F.2d 1028, 1029–30 (3d Cir.1984), the court refused to enjoin defendant's use of the plaintiff's golf handicapping formula in the defendant's handicapping service. The court, distinguishing the directly-competitive appropriation in *INS*, noted that "in using the formula [defendant] will not compete directly with the U.S.G.A., and thus will not interfere with the economic incentive of the U.S.G.A. to maintain and update its handicapping formula." Similarly, in National Football League v. Governor of Delaware, 435 F.Supp. 1372, 1378 (D.Del.1977), the court rejected a claim of misappropriation raised by the NFL against the use of football scores in a state lottery, emphasizing that the state was not appropriating the performances from which the NFL derives its profits. Other cases rejecting misappropriation claims when the defendant's use was not in direct competition with the plaintiff include, e.g., Universal City Studios, Inc. v. Ideal Pub. Corp., 195 U.S.P.Q. 761 (S.D.N.Y.1977) (denying an injunction against publication of a magazine devoted to the plaintiff's television series); Intermountain Broadcasting & Television Corp. v. Idaho Microwave, Inc., 196 F.Supp. 315 (D.Idaho 1961) (retransmission of the plaintiff's television signal to a different market); Gary Van Zeeland Talent, Inc. v. Sandas, 84 Wis.2d 202, 267 N.W.2d 242 (1978) (distinguishing collateral assets like customer lists from trade values marketed to customers); Loeb v. Turner, 257 S.W.2d 800 (Tex.Civ.App.1953) (recreation of a radio broadcast in a different city). In a few cases revenues from licenses have been treated as part of the plaintiff's primary market. See Pittsburgh Athletic Co. v. KQV Broadcasting Co., 24 F.Supp. 490 (W.D.Pa.1938) (unauthorized broadcast of baseball games in competition with the licensed broadcast); Metropolitan Opera Ass'n v. Wagner–Nichols Recorder Corp., 199 Misc. 786, 101 N.Y.S.2d 483 (1950), affirmed 279 App.Div. 632, 107 N.Y.S.2d 795 (1951) (sale of unauthorized recordings of radio transmissions in competition with licensed recordings). But in *Board of Trade, supra*, an injunction was issued against the use of a stock index in futures contracts despite the court's conclusion that the use did not threaten the originator's incentives or revenues—a result specifically rejected in *United States Golf Ass'n, supra*. See also Standard & Poor's Corp. v. Commodity Exchange, Inc., 683 F.2d 704 (2d Cir.1982) (holding on facts similar to *Board of Trade* that the issue presented "sufficiently serious questions" to permit a preliminary injunction). Cf. Golden Nugget, Inc. v. American Stock Exchange, Inc., 828 F.2d 586 (9th Cir.1987) (distinguishing *INS* and *Board of Trade* and declining to enjoin the trading of options on plaintiff's corporate stock without the plaintiff's consent).

Comment d. The history and current scope of common law copyright are described in Goldstein, Copyright §§ 15.4–15.6; Nimmer on Copyright § 8.23. Common law copyright is preempted under § 301 of the 1976 Copyright Act, 17 U.S.C.A. § 301, except as applied to works not fixed in any tangible medium of expression or to other works outside the scope of federal copyright. Although common law copyright was limited to unpublished works, the public performance of a work did not constitute "publication" and therefore did not divest common law copyright. Ferris v. Frohman, 223 U.S. 424, 32 S.Ct. 263, 56 L.Ed. 492 (1912) (public performance of a play); Heim v. Universal Pictures Co., 154 F.2d 480 (2d Cir.1946) (public performance of a song); Nutt v. National Institute Inc. for Improvement of Memory, 31 F.2d 236 (2d Cir.1929) (delivery of lectures); King v. Mister Maestro, Inc., 224 F.Supp. 101 (S.D.N.Y.1963) (delivery of a speech). Thus, claims for infringement of unfixed works appropriated from a public or private performance may be cognizable at common law. Several cases, however, indicate that common law copyright might not extend to unfixed works. See Roy Export Co. Establishment Etc. v. Columbia Broadcasting System, Inc., 503 F.Supp. 1137 (S.D.N.Y.1980), affirmed 672 F.2d 1095 (2d Cir.), cert. denied 459 U.S. 826, 103 S.Ct. 60, 74 L.Ed.2d 63 (1982); Rowe v. Golden West Television Productions, 184 N.J.Super. 264, 445 A.2d 1165 (1982). Courts have been reluctant to recognize common law rights in conversations. See Falwell v. Penthouse Int'l, Ltd., 521 F.Supp. 1204, 1207 (W.D.Va.1981) ("The existence of common law copyright protection for the spoken word has not been established by any court.") and Estate of Hemingway v. Random House, Inc., 23 N.Y.2d 341, 296 N.Y.S.2d 771, 244 N.E.2d 250 (1968), both noting that the facts did not support liability for breach of confidence. Cf. Sinatra v. Wilson, 2 Media L.Rptr. 2008, 2010 n.2 (S.D.N.Y.1977) (denying defendant's motion to dismiss, but noting plaintiff's "heavy burden of showing that [plaintiff] clearly indicated to defendants his wish to exercise control over the publication of these statements"); Marvin Worth Productions v. Superior Films Corp., 319 F.Supp. 1269 (S.D.N.Y.1970) (dictum suggesting that conversations can be protectable).

In some cases the doctrine of common law copyright has been applied to idea submissions that are better analyzed under the rules governing trade secrets, confidential relationships, or contracts. See Silver v. Television City, Inc., 207 Pa.Super. 150, 215 A.2d 335 (1965); Jenkins v. News Syndicate Co., 128 Misc. 284, 219 N.Y.S. 196 (Sup.Ct.1926). In other cases, common law copyright in unfixed works may overlap with the protection available to a performer under the right of publicity. See Zacchini v. Scripps–Howard Broadcasting Co., 47 Ohio St.2d 224, 351 N.E.2d 454 (1976), reversed 433 U.S. 562, 97 S.Ct. 2849, 53 L.Ed.2d 965 (1977) (relief against the appropriation of plaintiff's live performance was granted by the Ohio Court of Appeals on grounds of common law copyright; the Ohio Supreme Court and the United States Supreme Court treated plaintiff's claim as one for infringement of the right of publicity); Columbia Broadcasting System, Inc. v. Documentaries Unlimited, Inc., 42 Misc.2d 723 and 726, 248 N.Y.S.2d 809 (Sup.Ct.1964) (common law copyright recognized in a broadcaster's news announcement of the assassination of President Kennedy, acknowledging the appropriated "voice and style" as aspects of the broadcaster's personality). See § 47, Comment *d*.

California has a statute of general application that recognizes rights in the "representation or expression" of original works of authorship not fixed in any tangible medium of expression. Cal.Civ.Code § 980. Many states have enacted more limited statutes prohibiting the unauthorized commercial recording of live performances or transmissions. See Copyright Law Reporter (CCH) ¶ 10,901.

Comment e. The Supreme Court's opinion in *Bonito Boats* distinguished the Court's earlier decision in Kewanee Oil Co. v. Bicron Corp., 416 U.S. 470, 94 S.Ct. 1879, 40 L.Ed.2d 315 (1974), which held that state trade secret law is not preempted. The Court noted that unlike the protection of trade secrets, the prohibition against duplication by molding in *Bonito Boats* effectively withdrew subject matter from the public domain. See § 39, Comment *c*. That the misappropriation doctrine cannot be used to prevent product copying, see, e.g., Famolare, Inc. v. Melville Corp., 472 F.Supp. 738 (D.Hawaii 1979), affirmed 652 F.2d 62 (9th Cir. 1981) (shoe design).

Cases holding that misappropriation claims directed at works protectable under federal copyright law are preempted include, e.g., Warner Bros., Inc. v. American Broadcasting Cos., 720 F.2d 231 (2d Cir.1983) (cartoon character); Universal City Studios, Inc. v. T–Shirt Gallery, Ltd., 634 F.Supp. 1468 (S.D.N.Y.1986) (elements of a television series); Mayer v. Josiah Wedgwood & Sons, Ltd., 601 F.Supp. 1523 (S.D.N.Y.1985) (graphic design); Schuchart & Associates, Professional Engineers, Inc. v. Solo Serve Corp., 540 F.Supp. 928 (W.D.Tex.1982) (architectural drawings); Giangrasso v. CBS, Inc., 534 F.Supp. 472 (E.D.N.Y.1982) (radio script). Section 301(c) of the Copyright Act specifically exempts from preemption state protection of sound recordings fixed prior to February 15, 1972, the date on which sound recordings were added to the subject matter of federal copyright law. See Goldstein v. California, 412 U.S. 546, 93 S.Ct. 2303, 37 L.Ed.2d 163 (1973), holding that the preemptive effect of the 1909 Copyright Act did not extend to subject matter left "unattended" by federal law. Statutes in many states remain in effect to protect pre–1972 sound recordings. See Copyright Law Reporter (CCH) ¶ 10,901.

The House Judiciary Committee Report accompanying the 1976 Copyright Act, in a discussion of the *International News Service* case, expressed the view that a cause of action for misappropriation may not be equivalent to copyright, emphasizing the "consistent pattern" of appropriation against which relief was granted in *INS*. H.R.Rep.No. 94–1476, 94th Cong., 2d Sess. 132 (1976). However, at the time the House Report was prepared, § 301 of the copyright revision bill specifically preserved "rights against misappropriation not equivalent to" copyright. The reference to misappropriation was deleted prior to enactment. In a few of the cases holding misappropriation claims preempted, the courts have distinguished the discussion in the House Report on the basis of the quantity and systematic nature of the appropriation involved in *INS*. See Financial Information, Inc. v. Moody's Investors Service, Inc., 808 F.2d 204 (2d Cir.1986), cert. denied 484 U.S. 820, 108 S.Ct. 79, 98 L.Ed.2d 42 (1987); Nash v. CBS, Inc., 704 F.Supp. 823 (N.D.Ill.1989), affirmed 899 F.2d 1537 (7th Cir.1990).

Language in a few cases suggests that since facts and ideas cannot be protected under copyright, they remain eligible for protection under state law. See Mayer, *supra* (dictum); Rand McNally & Co. v. Fleet Management Systems, Inc., 591 F.Supp. 726 (N.D.Ill.1983) (dictum); Bromhall v. Rorvik, 478 F.Supp. 361 (E.D.Pa.1979). See also Goldstein, Copyright § 15.2.3; Nimmer on Copyright § 101[B][2]. Most cases, however, hold that recognition under state law of a right to prevent the appropriation of facts, research, or ideas from a work fixed in a tangible medium of expression is preempted under § 301. See, e.g., Financial Information, *supra*; Ehat v. Tanner, 780 F.2d 876 (10th Cir.1985), cert. denied 479 U.S. 820, 107 S.Ct. 86, 93 L.Ed.2d 39 (1986); Harper & Row Pub., Inc. v. Nation Enterprises, 723 F.2d 195 (2d Cir.1983), reversed on other grounds 471 U.S. 539, 105 S.Ct. 2218, 85 L.Ed.2d 588 (1985); Nash, *supra*, 704 F.Supp. at 832 ("If the rule were otherwise, states would be free to regulate materials Congress has assigned to the public domain."); Gem Products, Inc. v. Robertshaw Controls Co., 229 U.S.P.Q. 740 (C.D.Cal.1986); Mitchell v. Penton/Industrial Pub. Co., 486 F.Supp. 22 (N.D.Ohio 1979); Garrido v. Burger King Corp., 558 So.2d 79 (Fla.App. 1990). See also Abrams, Copyright, Misappropriation, and Preemption: Constitutional and Statutory Limits of State Law Protection, 1983 Sup.Ct. Rev. 509 (1983).

State protection that interferes with the balance struck by federal copyright law is presumably subject to preemption even if not specifically prohibited under § 301. In a number of cases decided under the prior copyright act, the courts concluded that state protection for facts or ideas was void under the supremacy clause. See, e.g., Hoehling v. Universal City Studios, Inc., 618 F.2d 972, 980 (2d Cir.), cert. denied 449 U.S. 841, 101 S.Ct. 121, 66 L.Ed.2d 49 (1980) ("Where, as here, historical facts, themes, and research have been deliberately exempted from the scope of copyright protection to vindicate the overriding goal of encouraging contributions to recorded knowledge, the states are pre-empted from removing such material from the public domain."); Synercom Technology, Inc. v. University Computing Co., 474 F.Supp. 37 (N.D.Tex.1979); H.W. Wilson Co. v. National Library Service Co., 402 F.Supp. 456 (S.D.N.Y. 1975). That the preemptive effect of federal copyright law extends beyond the literal scope of § 301, see, e.g., Goldstein, Copyright § 15.3; Abrams, *supra*; Ginsburg, No "Sweat"? Copyright and Other Protection of Works of Information after *Feist v. Rural Telephone*, 92 Colum.L.Rev. 338 (1992).

TOPIC 2. TRADE SECRETS

Section

---

§ 39. Definition of Trade Secret

A trade secret is any information that can be used in the operation of a business or other enterprise and that is sufficiently valuable and secret to afford an actual or potential economic advantage over others.

Comment:

a. Rationale for protection. The protection of confidential business information dates at least to Roman law, which afforded relief against a person who induced another's employee to divulge secrets relating to the master's commercial affairs. The modern law of trade secrets evolved in England in the early 19th century, apparently in response to the growing accumulation of technical know-how and the increased mobility of employees during the industrial revolution. In the United States the protection of trade secrets was recognized at common law by the middle of the 19th century, and by the end of the century the principal features of contemporary trade secret law were well established.

The protection of trade secrets advances several interests. Early cases emphasized the unfairness inherent in obtaining a competitive advantage through a breach of confidence. The imposition of liability for the appropriation of a trade secret protects the plaintiff from unfair competition and deprives the defendant of unjust enrichment attributable to bad faith. The development of rules protecting trade secrets formed part of a more general attempt to articulate standards of fair competition. More recently, the protection of trade secrets has been justified as a means to encourage investment in research by providing an opportunity to capture the returns from successful innovations. The rules protecting trade secrets also promote the efficient exploitation of knowledge by discouraging the unproductive hoarding of useful information and facilitating disclosure to employees, agents, licensees, and others who can assist in its productive use. Finally, the protection afforded under the law of trade secrets against breaches of confidence and improper physical intrusions furthers the interest in personal privacy.

The subject matter and scope of trade secret protection is necessarily limited by the public and private interest in access to valuable information. The freedom to compete in the marketplace includes, in the absence of patent, copyright, or trademark protection (see §§ 16 and 17), the freedom to copy the goods, methods, processes, and ideas of others. The freedom to copy, however, does not extend to information that is inaccessible by proper means. Liability for the appropriation of a trade secret thus rests on a breach of confidence or other wrongful conduct in acquiring, using, or disclosing secret information.

b. Doctrinal development. Early trade secret cases, responding to requests for injunctive relief against breaches of confidence, frequently supported the exercise of equity jurisdiction by describing the plaintiff's interest in the trade secret as a property right, often said to derive from the discovery of valuable information. Similar characterizations sometimes appear in the modern case law. The property rationale emphasizes the nature of the appropriated information, especially its value and secrecy. Even the earliest cases, however, also include an examination of the propriety of the defendant's conduct. The plaintiff's property right was effective only against defendants who used or acquired the information improperly. No exclusive rights were recognized against those who acquired the information by proper means. Other cases, choosing to begin their analysis with an examination of the defendant's behavior, concluded that the essence of a trade secret action is a breach of confidence or other improper conduct, sometimes explicitly disavowing any property dimension to a trade secret. The influential formulation in § 757 of the Restatement of Torts (1939), reporting that the property conception "has been frequently advanced and rejected," concluded that the prevailing theory of liability rests on "a general duty of good faith." *Id.*, Comment *a.* Both the former Restatement and the supporting case law, however, also require that the information qualify for protection as a trade secret, thus incorporating the elements of secrecy and value that underlie the property rationale.

The dispute over the nature of trade secret rights has had little practical effect on the rules governing civil liability for the appropriation of a trade secret. The cases generally require that the plaintiff establish both the existence of a trade secret under the principles described in this Section and the fact of misconduct by the defendant under the rules stated in § 40. Many cases acknowledge that the primary issue is the propriety of the defendant's conduct as a means of competition. The substantive scope of the rights recognized under the law of trade secrets thus reflects the accommodation of numerous interests, including the trade secret owner's claim to protection against the defendant's bad faith or improper conduct, the right of competitors and others to exploit information and skills in the public domain, and the interest of the public in encouraging innovation and in securing the benefits of vigorous competition.

In 1979, the National Conference of Commissioners on Uniform State Laws promulgated the Uniform Trade Secrets Act. The Prefatory Note states that the "Uniform Act codifies the basic principles of common law trade secret protection." The original Act or its 1985 revision has been adopted in a majority of the states. (See the Statutory Note following this Section.) Except as otherwise noted, the principles of trade secret law described in this Restatement are applicable to actions under the Uniform Trade Secrets Act as well as to actions at common law. The concept of a trade secret as defined in this Section is intended to be consistent with the definition of "trade secret" in § 1(4) of the Act.

Some states have adopted criminal statutes specifically addressed to the appropriation of trade secrets. In other states, more general criminal statutes have been interpreted to reach such appropriations. In some circumstances the appropriation of a trade secret may also violate the federal wire and mail fraud statutes (18 U.S.C.A. §§ 1341, 1343) and the National Stolen Property Act (18 U.S.C.A. § 2314). The definition of a trade secret contained in this Section, however, is directly applicable only to the imposition of civil liability under the rules stated in § 40. It does not apply, other than by analogy, in actions under criminal statutes or in other circumstances not involving civil liability for the appropriation of a trade secret, such as the protection of trade secrets from disclosure under the Freedom of Information Act (5 U.S.C. § 552).

c. Relation to patent and copyright law. Federal patent law offers protection to "any new and useful process, machine, manufacture, or composition of matter," 35 U.S.C.A. § 101, unless the invention "would have been obvious at the time the invention was made to a person having ordinary skill in the art to which said subject matter pertains." 35 U.S.C.A. § 103. Federal design patents protect "any new, original and ornamental design for an article of manufacture," again subject to the requirement of non-obviousness. 35 U.S.C.A. § 135. Unlike the limited protection against improper acquisition, disclosure, and use accorded to the owner of a trade secret under the rules stated in § 40, the holder of a patent enjoys a general right to exclude others from making, using, or selling the patented invention, 35 U.S.C.A. § 271, enforceable even against persons relying on independent discovery or reverse engineering. An application for a patent must include a specification containing "a written description of the invention, and of the manner and process of making and using it," and "the best mode contemplated by the inventor of carrying out" the invention. 35 U.S.C.A. §§ 111 and 112. Upon issuance of a patent, the specification and other materials comprising the patent file become available for public inspection. 37 C.F.R. § 1.11. Thus, for matter disclosed in the patent, issuance terminates the secrecy required for continued protection as a trade secret, even if the patent is subsequently declared invalid. See Comment *f.* Pending, denied, and abandoned patent applications, however, are not generally open to public inspection. 35 U.S.C.A. § 122; 37 C.F.R. § 1.14. Thus, the filing of a patent application does not in itself preclude continued protection of the invention as a trade secret.

The United States Supreme Court in Kewanee Oil Co. v. Bicron Corp., 416 U.S. 470, 94 S.Ct. 1879, 40 L.Ed.2d 315 (1974), held that federal patent law does not preempt the protection of inventions and other information under state trade secret law. The Court concluded that the requirement of secrecy fundamental to the protection of trade secrets (see Comment *f*) avoids interference with the federal patent policy of access to information in the public domain. It also concluded that the limitations on the scope of state trade secret protection (see § 40) make it unlikely that the federal policy of inducing public disclosure in exchange for the protection of a patent will be significantly undermined by reliance on trade secret protection for patentable inventions. In a subsequent decision, however, the Supreme Court emphasized that any rule of state law that substantially interferes with the use of information that has already been disclosed to the public or that is readily ascertainable from public sources is preempted. Bonito Boats, Inc. v. Thunder Craft Boats, Inc., 489 U.S. 141, 109 S.Ct. 971, 103 L.Ed.2d 118 (1989).

Federal copyright law protects "original works of authorship fixed in any tangible medium of expression," 17 U.S.C.A. § 102(a), against unauthorized reproduction, use in the preparation of derivative works, distribution, public performance, or public display. 17 U.S.C.A. § 106. Protection is limited, however, to the manner in which the authorship is expressed and does not extend to "any idea, procedure, process, system, method of operation, concept, principle, or discovery" embodied in the work. 17 U.S.C.A. § 102(b). Copyright protection subsists from the creation of a work and is not contingent upon public dissemination. See 17 U.S.C.A. § 302. A claim of federal copyright is thus not in itself inconsistent with a claim to trade secret protection for information contained in the work. Although § 301 of the Copyright Act preempts the recognition under state law of "rights that are equivalent to any of the exclusive rights" of copyright in works "within the subject matter" of the statute, the protection afforded to trade secrets under the rules stated in § 40 has been held to lie outside the preemptive scope of the Copyright Act.

Registration of a copyright is not a condition of copyright protection. 17 U.S.C.A. § 408. The registration of a copyright claim in an unpublished work ordinarily requires the deposit of a complete copy of the work, 17 U.S.C.A. § 408(b)(1), which is then open to public inspection. 17 U.S.C.A. § 705. However, the regulations of the Copyright Office permit the deletion of material constituting trade secrets from deposits made in connection with computer programs and also authorize the granting of special relief from the normal deposit requirements in other cases. The status as a trade secret of information contained in a work that is the subject of a copyright registration is determined under the general principles governing secrecy and accessibility described in Comment *f*.

d. Subject matter. A trade secret can consist of a formula, pattern, compilation of data, computer program, device, method, technique, process, or other form or embodiment of economically valuable information. A trade secret can relate to technical matters such as the composition or design of a product, a method of manufacture, or the know-how necessary to perform a particular operation or service. A trade secret can also relate to other aspects of business operations such as pricing and marketing techniques or the identity and requirements of customers (see § 42, Comment *f*). Although rights in trade secrets are normally asserted by businesses and other commercial enterprises, nonprofit entities such as charitable, educational, governmental, fraternal, and religious organizations can also claim trade secret protection for economically valuable information such as lists of prospective members or donors.

The prior Restatement of this topic limited the subject matter of trade secret law to information capable of "continuous use in the operation of a business," thus excluding information relating to single events such as secret bids and impending business announcements or information whose secrecy is quickly destroyed by commercial exploitation. See Restatement of Torts § 757, Comment *b* (1939). Both the case law and the prior Restatement, however, offered protection against the "improper" acquisition of such short-term information under rules virtually identical to those applicable to trade secrets. See *id.* § 759, Comment *c*. The Restatement, Second, of Agency in § 396 similarly protects both trade secrets and "other similar confidential matters" from unauthorized use or disclosure following the termination of an agency relationship. The definition of "trade secret" adopted in the Uniform Trade Secrets Act does not include any requirement relating to the duration of the information's economic value. See Uniform Trade Secrets Act § 1(4) and the accompanying Comment. The definition adopted in this Section similarly contains no requirement that the information afford a continuous or long-term advantage.

A person claiming rights in a trade secret bears the burden of defining the information for which protection is sought with sufficient definiteness to permit a court to apply the criteria for protection described in this Section and to determine the fact of an appropriation. In the case of technical information, a physical embodiment of the information in the form of a specific product, process, or working model often provides the requisite definition. However, there is no requirement that the information be incorporated or embodied in a tangible form if it is otherwise sufficiently delineated. The degree of definiteness required in a particular case is also properly influenced by the legitimate interests of the defendant. Thus, a court may require greater specificity when the plaintiff's claim involves information that is closely integrated with the general skill and knowledge that is properly retained by former employees. See § 42, Comment *d.*

An agreement between the parties that characterizes specific information as a "trade secret" can be an important although not necessarily conclusive factor in determining whether the information qualifies for protection as a trade secret under this Section. As a precaution against disclosure, such an agreement is evidence of the value and secrecy of the information, see Comments *e* and *f*, and can also supply or contribute to the definiteness required in delineating the trade secret. The agreement can also be important in establishing a duty of confidence. See § 41. However, because of the public interest in preserving access to information that is in the public domain, such an agreement will not ordinarily estop a defendant from contesting the existence of a trade secret. (On the protection of information by contract, see § 41, Comment *d.*)

It is not possible to state precise criteria for determining the existence of a trade secret. The status of information claimed as a trade secret must be ascertained through a comparative evaluation of all the relevant factors, including the value, secrecy, and definiteness of the information as well as the nature of the defendant's misconduct.

e. Requirement of value. A trade secret must be of sufficient value in the operation of a business or other enterprise to provide an actual or potential economic advantage over others who do not possess the information. The advantage, however, need not be great. It is sufficient if the secret provides an advantage that is more than trivial. Although a trade secret can consist of a patentable invention, there is no requirement that the trade secret meet the standard of inventiveness applicable under federal patent law.

The value of information claimed as a trade secret may be established by direct or circumstantial evidence. Direct evidence relating to the content of the secret and its impact on business operations is clearly relevant. Circumstantial evidence of value is also relevant, including the amount of resources invested by the plaintiff in the production of the information, the precautions taken by the plaintiff to protect the secrecy of the information (see Comment *g*), and the willingness of others to pay for access to the information.

The plaintiff's use of the trade secret in the operation of its business is itself some evidence of the information's value. Identifiable benefits realized by the trade secret owner through use of the information are also evidence of value. Some early cases elevated use by the trade secret owner to independent significance by establishing such use as an element of the cause of action for the appropriation of a trade secret. Such a "use" requirement, however, imposes unjustified limitations on the scope of trade secret protection. The requirement can deny protection during periods of research and development and is particularly burdensome for innovators who do not possess the capability to exploit their innovations. See Comment *h*. The requirement also places in doubt protection for so-called "negative" information that teaches conduct to be avoided, such as knowledge that a particular process or technique is unsuitable for commercial use. Cases in many jurisdictions expressly renounce any requirement of use by the trade secret owner. It is also rejected under the Uniform Trade Secrets Act. See the Comment to § 1 of the Act. Use by the person asserting rights in the information is not a prerequisite to protection under the rule stated in this Section.

f. Requirement of secrecy. To qualify as a trade secret, the information must be secret. The secrecy, however, need not be absolute. The rule stated in this Section requires only secrecy sufficient to confer an actual or potential economic advantage on one who possesses the information. Thus, the requirement of secrecy is satisfied if it would be difficult or costly for others who could exploit the information to acquire it without resort to the wrongful conduct proscribed under § 40. Novelty in the patent law sense is not required. Although trade secret cases sometimes announce a "novelty" requirement, the requirement is synonymous with the concepts of secrecy and value as described in this Section and the correlative exclusion of self-evident variants of the known art.

Information known by persons in addition to the trade secret owner can retain its status as a trade secret if it remains secret from others to whom it has potential economic value. Independent discovery by another who maintains the secrecy of the information, for example, will not preclude relief against an appropriation by a third person. Similarly, confidential disclosures to employees, licensees, or others will not destroy the information's status as a trade secret. Even limited non-confidential disclosure will not necessarily terminate protection if the recipients of the disclosure maintain the secrecy of the information.

Information that is generally known or readily ascertainable through proper means (see § 43) by others to whom it has potential economic value is not protectable as a trade secret. Thus, information that is disclosed in a patent or contained in published materials reasonably accessible to competitors does not qualify for protection under this Section. Similarly, information readily ascertainable from an examination of a product on public sale or display is not a trade secret. Self-evident variations or modifications of known processes, procedures, or methods also lack the secrecy necessary for protection as a trade secret. However, it is the secrecy of the claimed trade secret as a whole that is determinative. The fact that some or all of the components of the trade secret are well-known does not preclude protection for a secret combination, compilation, or integration of the individual elements.

The theoretical ability of others to ascertain the information through proper means does not necessarily preclude protection as a trade secret. Trade secret protection remains available unless the information is readily ascertainable by such means. Thus, if acquisition of the information through an examination of a competitor's product would be difficult, costly, or time-consuming, the trade secret owner retains protection against an improper acquisition, disclosure, or use prohibited under the rules stated in § 40. However, any person who actually acquires the information through an examination of a publicly available product has obtained the information by proper means and is thus not subject to liability. See § 43. Similarly, the theoretical possibility of reconstructing the secret from published materials containing scattered references to portions of the information or of extracting it from public materials unlikely to come to the attention of the appropriator will not preclude relief against the wrongful conduct proscribed under § 40, although one who actually acquires the secret from such sources is not subject to liability.

Circumstantial evidence is admissible to establish that information is not readily ascertainable through proper means and hence is eligible for protection as a trade secret. Precautions taken by the claimant to preserve the secrecy of the information (see Comment *g*), the willingness of licensees to pay for disclosure of the secret, unsuccessful attempts by the defendant or others to duplicate the information by proper means, and resort by a defendant to improper means of acquisition are all probative of the relative accessibility of the information. When a defendant has engaged in egregious misconduct in order to acquire the information, the inference that the information is sufficiently inaccessible to qualify for protection as a trade secret is particularly strong. See § 43, Comment *d*.

Although courts have recognized that trade secret rights may not be asserted in information that is in the public domain, the cases disagree on the consequences of a loss of secrecy that occurs between the time of a defendant's confidential receipt of the trade secret and the defendant's subsequent unauthorized use or disclosure. Some decisions refuse to consider the availability of the information from public domain sources at the time of the alleged appropriation, at least when the defendant's knowledge derives from the confidential disclosure rather than from the public sources. Other decisions, more narrowly construing the obligations attendant upon a confidential disclosure, hold that protection against unauthorized use or disclosure is not available after the information has ceased to be a secret. (On the remedial consequences of a loss of secrecy occurring *after* a defendant's appropriation, see § 44, Comment *f*; § 45, Comment *h*.) However, in many of the cases that refuse as a matter of law to take into account a loss of secrecy, the information was in fact only theoretically rather than readily ascertainable from the public domain at the time of the defendant's use or disclosure, thus justifying relief under either rule.

When information is no longer sufficiently secret to qualify for protection as a trade secret, its use should not serve as a basis for the imposition of liability under the rules stated in § 40. If the information has become readily ascertainable from public sources so that no significant benefit accrues to a person who relies instead on other means of acquisition, the information is in the public domain and no longer protectable under the law of trade secrets. Even those courts that decline to take into account a loss of secrecy following a confidential disclosure to the defendant often assert in dicta that no liability attaches if the defendant actually extracts the information from public sources. When the information is readily ascertainable from such sources, however, actual resort to the public domain is a formality that should not determine liability. The public interest in avoiding unnecessary restraints on the exploitation of valuable information supports the conclusion that protection as a trade secret terminates when the information is no longer secret. The defendant remains liable, however, for any unauthorized use or disclosure that occurred prior to the loss of secrecy. This position is consistent with the language and policy of the Uniform Trade Secrets Act. Section 1(2) of the Act defines "misappropriation" as the improper acquisition, disclosure, or use of a "trade secret," and § 1(4) excludes from the definition of "trade secret" information "generally known * * * or readily ascertainable by proper means." Termination of trade secret rights upon a loss of secrecy is also consistent with the limitations on injunctive and monetary relief in §§ 2 and 3 of the Act (and in §§ 44 and 45 of this Restatement) applicable to appropriations occurring prior to the loss of secrecy.

Illustrations:

1. *A*, a pharmaceutical company, develops a more efficient process for the production of a particular drug. *A* discloses the process in confidence to an engineering firm in order to facilitate the construction of a new manufacturing plant and later discloses the process to specific employees involved in the production of the drug. *A* also discloses the process in confidence to *B*, another pharmaceutical company, under a licensing agreement. *C*, a third pharmaceutical company, independently discovers and secretly implements the process. *D*, a fourth pharmaceutical company, bribes an employee of *A* to disclose the process. If the process otherwise remains unknown and not readily ascertainable through proper means, it is sufficiently secret to be protected as a trade secret. *D* is thus subject to liability to *A* for the appropriation of *A* 's trade secret under the rules stated in § 40. *C* is not subject to liability to *A* because *C* 's acquisition of the trade secret was not improper. See § 43.

2. *A*, a company in the business of selling building maintenance supplies to large commercial users, employs *B* as a general manager. After termination of the employment, *B* starts a competing business and solicits some of *A* 's customers whose identities *B* learned while employed by *A*. If the identities of the customers solicited by *B* are readily ascertainable in the trade as prospective purchasers of the types of products sold by *A* and *B*, the customer identities are not protectable as a trade secret. See § 42, Comment *f*.

3. The facts being otherwise as stated in Illustration 2, *B* also copies files prepared by *A* containing detailed data on the requirements, past purchases, and key personnel of individual customers. *B* uses information from the files in soliciting the customers. If a court concludes that the compiled data is valuable and not readily ascertainable from other sources, the information is protectable as a trade secret. *B* is then subject to liability to *A*

for the appropriation of *A* 's trade secrets under the rules stated in § 40.

4. *A* confidentially discloses a trade secret to *B* during negotiations concerning a possible licensing agreement. *A* and *B* eventually terminate the negotiations without reaching agreement, and *B* refrains from all use of the information. Later, the secret is revealed in an article published by *A*, and *B* subsequently begins to use the information. The information is no longer protectable as a trade secret, and *B* is not subject to liability to *A* regardless of whether *B* actually extracted the information from the published article or relied on the prior confidential disclosure.

5. *A* manufactures heavy-duty centrifugal blowers. Drawings containing dimensions and specifications for components of the blowers are taken without authorization by *B*, a former employee of *A*, and used to manufacture a competing product. Although the approximate dimensions and specifications of *A* 's products can be determined by measuring blowers sold by *A* on the open market, the evidence establishes that the information resulting from such measurements would be less accurate than the drawings taken by *B* and less valuable in manufacturing competing products. The acquisition of information as accurate as that contained in the drawings taken by *B* would require a statistical analysis of measurements taken from a large number of *A* 's blowers. The court may properly conclude that the information contained in the drawings is not readily ascertainable by proper means and is thus sufficiently secret to be protected as a trade secret. *B* is thus subject to liability to *A* for the appropriation of *A* 's trade secrets under the rules stated in § 40.

g. Precautions to maintain secrecy. Precautions taken to maintain the secrecy of information are relevant in determining whether the information qualifies for protection as a trade secret. Precautions to maintain secrecy may take many forms, including physical security designed to prevent unauthorized access, procedures intended to limit disclosure based upon the "need to know," and measures that emphasize to recipients the confidential nature of the information such as nondisclosure agreements, signs, and restrictive legends. Such precautions can be evidence of the information's value (see Comment *e*) and secrecy (see Comment *f*). The prior Restatement of this topic included the precautions taken to maintain the secrecy of the information as one of a number of factors relevant in determining the existence of a trade secret. See Restatement of Torts § 757, Comment *b* (1939). The Uniform Trade Secrets Act requires a trade secret to be "the subject of efforts that are reasonable under the circumstances to maintain its secrecy." Section 1(4)(ii). Whether viewed as an independent requirement or as an element to be considered with other factors relevant to the existence of a trade secret, the owner's precautions should be evaluated in light of the other available evidence relating to the value and secrecy of the information. Thus, if the value and secrecy of the information are clear, evidence of specific precautions taken by the trade secret owner may be unnecessary.

The precautions taken by the trade secret owner are also relevant to other potential issues in an action for the appropriation of a trade secret. They can signal to employees and other recipients that a disclosure of the information by the trade secret owner is intended to be in confidence. See § 41. They can also be relevant in determining whether a defendant possessed the knowledge necessary for the imposition of liability under the rules stated in § 40 (see § 40, Comment *d*), whether particular means of acquisition are improper under the rule stated in § 43 (see § 43, Comment *c*), and whether an accidental disclosure results in the loss of trade secret rights (see § 40, Comment *e*).

h. "Law of ideas." Cases involving the submission of ideas by employees, customers, inventors, and others to businesses capable of reducing the idea to practice are sometimes analyzed under separate rules referred to as the "law of ideas." Idea submission cases often arise in the context of suggestions for new or improved products submitted to manufacturers, or in connection with programming and other ideas submitted to the entertainment industries. Plaintiffs seeking compensation for their ideas typically rely on contract claims alleging an express or implied-in-fact promise by the recipient to pay for the submitted idea. In some cases, however, compensation is sought through tort or restitutionary claims. These non-contractual claims are generally resolved through an analysis of the nature of the information and the circumstances of the submission that is fundamentally indistinguishable from the rules governing trade secrets. Some decisions explicitly incorporate such claims within the scope of trade secret law.

To sustain a claim in tort for the appropriation of an idea, most courts require the submitted idea to be "novel" in the sense of not being generally known (cf. Comment *f*) and sufficiently "concrete" to permit an assessment of its value and the fact of its use by the recipient (cf. Comment *d*). The courts also examine the circumstances of the disclosure to determine whether the recipient is bound by an obligation of confidentiality. Factors such as the relationship between the submitter and recipient, prior dealings between the parties, the customs of the industry, and the recipient's solicitation or opportunity to refuse the disclosure are relevant in determining the recipient's obligations. Cf. § 41.

With the rejection under the Uniform Trade Secrets Act and under this Section of any requirement of use by the owner of a trade secret, see Comment *e*, there is no longer a formal distinction between trade secrets and the ideas that form the subject matter of the idea submission cases. The developing rules governing the rights of submitters and recipients of ideas in the absence of an express or implied-in-fact contract can thus be understood as specific applications of the general rules stated here. The rules in this Restatement relating to the protection of trade secrets are therefore applicable, either directly or by analogy, to claims in tort alleging the appropriation of ideas.

Since the public and private interests favoring access to information that is in the public domain are also relevant in analyzing contractual claims, many jurisdictions require proof of novelty and concreteness for the enforcement of express or implied-in-fact contracts to pay for submitted ideas. Thus, the rules stated here may also be helpful in analyzing contractual liability in idea submission cases.

STATUTORY NOTE

The Uniform Trade Secrets Act or other civil trade secret statute of general applicability is in effect as follows:

Alabama .... ALA. C. § 8–27–1 et seq.
Alaska .... ALASKA S. § 45.50.910 et seq.
Arizona .... ARIZ. R.S. § 44–401 et seq.
Arkansas .... ARK. C.A. § 4–75–601 et seq.
California .... CAL. Civ.C. § 3426 et seq.
Colorado .... COLO. R.S. § 7–74–101 et seq.
Connecticut .... CONN. G.S. § 35–50 et seq.
Delaware .... DEL. C., tit. 6, § 2001 et seq.
Dist. of Columbia ...... D.C. C. § 48–501 et seq.
Florida .... FLA. S. § 688.001 et seq.
Georgia .... GA. C.A. § 10–1–760 et seq.
Hawaii .... HAW. R.S. § 482B–1 et seq.
Idaho .... IDAHO C. § 48–801 et seq.
Illinois .... ILL. C.S., ch. 765, § 1065/1 et seq.
Indiana .... IND. C. § 24–2–3–1 et seq.
Iowa .... IOWA C. § 550.1 et seq.
Kansas .... KAN. S.A. § 60–3320 et seq.
Kentucky .... KY. R.S. § 365.880 et seq.
Louisiana .... LA. R.S.A. § 51:1431 et seq.
Maine .... ME. R.S.A., tit. 10, § 1541 et seq.
Maryland .... MD. Comm.L., § 11–1201 et seq.

Massachusetts	MASS. G.L.A., ch. 93, § 42 et seq.
Minnesota	MINN. S.A. § 325C.01 et seq.
Mississippi	MISS. C.A. § 75–26–1 et seq.
Montana	MONT. C.A. § 30–14–401 et seq.
Nebraska	NEB. R.S. § 87–501 et seq.
Nevada	NEV. R.S.A. § 600A.010 et seq.
New Hampshire	N.H. R.S.A. § 350–B:1 et seq.
New Mexico	N.M. S.A. § 57–3A–1 et seq.
North Carolina	N.C. G.S. § 66–152 et seq.
North Dakota	N.D. Cent. C. § 47–25.1–01 et seq.
Oklahoma	OKLA. S.A., tit. 78, § 85 et seq.
Ohio	OHIO R.C. § 1333.51
Oregon	OR. R.S. § 646.461 et seq.
Rhode Island	R.I. G.L.A. § 6–41–1 et seq.
South Carolina	S.C. C.A. § 39–8–1 et seq.
South Dakota	S.D. Comp. L.A. § 37–29–1 et seq.
Utah	UTAH C.A. § 13–24–1 et seq.
Virginia	VA. C.A. § 59.1–336 et seq.
Washington	WASH. R.C.A. § 19.108.010 et seq.
West Virginia	W.VA. C.A. § 47–22–1 et seq.
Wisconsin	WIS. S. § 134.90

REPORTERS' NOTE

The principal treatises on the law of trade secrets are M. Jager, Trade Secrets Law and R. Milgrim, Milgrim on Trade Secrets. This topic was treated in Restatement of Torts §§ 757–759 (1939). A definition of "trade secret" appeared in § 757, Comment *b*. Courts have continued to rely on the Restatement of Torts in cases governed by the Uniform Trade Secrets Act. See, e.g., Religious Technology Center v. Wollersheim, 796 F.2d 1076 (9th Cir.1986), cert. denied 479 U.S. 1103, 107 S.Ct. 1336, 94 L.Ed.2d 187 (1987); Optic Graphics, Inc. v. Agee, 87 Md.App. 770, 591 A.2d 578 (1991); Minuteman, Inc. v. Alexander, 147 Wis.2d 842, 434 N.W.2d 773 (1989). The rules in this Restatement are applicable both to common law actions and actions under the Uniform Trade Secrets Act or analogous civil legislation.

Comment a. The protection of confidential business information under Roman law is analyzed in Schiller, Trade Secrets and Roman Law: The Actio Servi Corrupti, 30 Colum.L.Rev. 837 (1930). The first reported trade secret case in England is said to be Newbery v. James, 35 Eng.Rep. 1011 (Ch.1817), in which the court denied an injunction citing its inability to enforce an order protecting a secret not disclosed to the court. Three years later in Yovatt v. Winyard, 37 Eng.Rep. 425 (Ch.1820), the court enjoined a former employee from further use or disclosure of surreptitiously copied medicinal formulas. A third party who had acquired a trade secret through another's breach of confidence was enjoined in Morison v. Moat, 68 Eng.Rep. 492 (Ch.1851). The first American case involving trade secrets may be Vickery v. Welch, 36 Mass. 523 (1837), holding that a contract for the sale of rights in a secret process was not void as a restraint of trade. Most well-known of the early American decisions on trade secrets is Peabody v. Norfolk, 98 Mass. 452 (1868), which enforced a former employee's promise not to disclose the employer's trade secrets and emphasized that confidential disclosures do not destroy the secrecy necessary for trade secret protection. Another early case, Tabor v. Hoffman, 118 N.Y. 30, 23 N.E. 12 (1889), recognized the right of others to acquire information through reverse engineering, although it found on the facts that the plaintiff's trade secrets were not disclosed by the marketed product. Other early cases recognized that an obligation of confidentiality could be found even in the absence of an express promise and that liability could extend to third persons who acquired the trade secret through another's breach of confidence. See Pressed Steel Car Co. v. Standard Steel Car Co., 210 Pa. 464, 60 A. 4 (1904); Stone v. Goss, 65 N.J.Eq. 756, 55 A. 736 (1903). See generally Jager, Trade Secrets Law §§ 2.01–02.

The United States Supreme Court in Kewanee Oil Co. v. Bicron Corp., 416 U.S. 470, 481, 94 S.Ct. 1879, 1886, 40 L.Ed.2d 315, 325 (1974), summarized the traditional rationales for the protection of trade secrets: "The maintenance of standards of commercial ethics and the encouragement of invention are the broadly stated policies behind trade secret law." On trade secret law as protection against unfair or unethical competition, see also, e.g., CVD, Inc. v. Raytheon Co., 769 F.2d 842 (1st Cir.1985), cert. denied 475 U.S. 1016, 106 S.Ct. 1198, 89 L.Ed.2d 312 (1986); ILG Industries, Inc. v. Scott, 49 Ill.2d 88, 273 N.E.2d 393 (1971). On the incentive rationale, see also, e.g., Rockwell Graphic Systems, Inc. v. DEV Industries, Inc., 925 F.2d 174 (7th Cir.1991); CVD, Inc., *supra* ; American Can Co. v. Mansukhani, 742 F.2d 314 (7th Cir. 1984). Trade secret law also promotes the efficient exploitation of information by encouraging the dissemination of ideas through confidential disclosures. Kewanee Oil Co., *supra,* 416 U.S. at 485–86, 94 S.Ct. at 1888, 40 L.Ed.2d at 327–28; Burten v. Milton Bradley Co., 763 F.2d 461 (1st Cir.1985); Painton & Co. v. Bourns, Inc., 442 F.2d 216 (2d Cir.1971). The Supreme Court in *Kewanee Oil Co.* also emphasized another rationale for the protection of trade secrets: "A most fundamental human right, that of privacy, is threatened when industrial espionage is condoned or is made profitable." 416 U.S. at 487, 94 S.Ct. at 1889, 40 L.Ed.2d at 329. See also Bonito Boats, Inc. v. Thunder Craft Boats, Inc., 489 U.S. 141, 155, 109 S.Ct. 971, 980, 103 L.Ed.2d 118, 137 (1989). The Court has also recognized, however, that the scope of trade secret protection is limited by the public interest in promoting competition and maintaining access to valuable information. Kewanee Oil Co., *supra* ; Bonito Boats, Inc., *supra.* See also, e.g., American Can Co., *supra* ; Brunswick Corp. v. Outboard Marine Corp., 79 Ill.2d 475, 38 Ill.Dec. 781, 404 N.E.2d 205 (1980).

Comment b. Early cases invoking a property rationale to justify an award of equitable relief include, e.g., Peabody v. Norfolk, 98 Mass. 452 (1868); Cincinnati Bell Foundry Co. v. Dodds, 10 Ohio Dec. Reprint 154 (Super.Ct.1887); Elaterite Paint & Mfg. Co. v. S.E. Frost Co., 105 Minn. 239, 117 N.W. 388 (1908). Modern cases also sometimes adopt a property perspective. See, e.g., Chicago Lock Co. v. Fanberg, 676 F.2d 400 (9th Cir.1982); Scharmer v. Carrollton Mfg. Co., 525 F.2d 95 (6th Cir. 1975); Anaconda Co. v. Metric Tool & Die Co., 485 F.Supp. 410 (E.D.Pa. 1980); Microbiological Research Corp. v. Muna, 625 P.2d 690 (Utah 1981); Mann v. Tatge Chemical Co., 201 Kan. 326, 440 P.2d 640 (1968). See also Carpenter v. United States, 484 U.S. 19, 108 S.Ct. 316, 98 L.Ed.2d 275 (1987) (confidential information is property for purposes of the federal mail fraud statute); Ruckelshaus v. Monsanto Co., 467 U.S. 986, 104 S.Ct. 2862, 81 L.Ed.2d 815 (1984) (trade secrets are property protected under the fifth amendment); E.I. Du Pont De Nemours and Co. v. United States, 288 F.2d 904 (Ct.Cl.1961) (trade secrets are property under the Internal Revenue Code). Many cases emphasize that property rights in trade secrets terminate upon public disclosure. E.g., Ruckelshaus, *supra*; Chicago Lock Co., *supra*; Scharmer, *supra*; Tabor v. Hoffman, 118 N.Y. 30, 23 N.E. 12 (1889). Even the early cases recognize that the plaintiff's property rights are not infringed by an acquisition of the secret through proper means. E.g., Peabody, *supra*; Eastman Co. v. Reichenbach, 20 N.Y.S. 110 (Sup.Ct. 1892), affirmed 29 N.Y.S. 1143 (1894); Tabor, *supra*.

Cases concluding that the basis of a trade secret action is a breach of good faith rather than an invasion of property rights include, e.g., Smith v. Snap–On Tools Corp., 833 F.2d 578, 579 (5th Cir.1987) ("The essence of the tort of trade secret misappropriation is the inequitable use of the secret."); Northern Petrochemical Co. v. Tomlinson, 484 F.2d 1057 (7th Cir. 1973); Servo Corp. v. General Electric Co., 393 F.2d 551 (4th Cir.1968); Valco Cincinnati, Inc. v. N & D Machining Service, Inc., 24 Ohio St.3d 41, 492 N.E.2d 814 (1986). In E.I. Du Pont De Nemours Powder Co. v. Masland, 244 U.S. 100, 102, 37 S.Ct. 575, 576, 61 L.Ed. 1016, 1019 (1917), Justice Holmes said, "The word property as applied to trade-marks and trade secrets is an unanalyzed expression of certain secondary consequences of the primary fact that the law makes some rudimentary requirements of good faith." The choice of rationale is rarely determinative of the defendant's liability. But see, e.g., Intermedics, Inc. v. Ventritex, Inc., 822 F.Supp. 634 (N.D.Cal.1993) (finding the choice of rationale relevant to the application of the "continuing tort" doctrine); Anaconda Co., *supra* (finding the property rationale conclusive on a statute of limitations issue). Compare also Kamin v. Kuhnau, 232 Or. 139, 374 P.2d 912 (1962) (emphasizing breach of confidence rather than the existence of a trade secret in declining to recognize accessibility of the information as a defense) with Den–Tal–Ez, Inc. v. Siemens Capital Corp., 389 Pa.Super. 219, 566 A.2d 1214 (1989) (emphasizing the property conception in concluding that readily-ascertainable information is not protectable as a trade secret).

Cases viewing trade secret law as an aspect of the general prohibition against unfair methods of competition include, e.g., Computer Assoc. Int'l, Inc. v. Altai, Inc., 982 F.2d 693 (2d Cir.1992); American Can Co. v. Mansukhani, 742 F.2d 314 (7th Cir.1984); Chicago Lock Co., *supra*; Sarkes Tarzian, Inc. v. Audio Devices, Inc., 166 F.Supp. 250 (S.D.Cal.1958), affirmed 283 F.2d 695 (9th Cir.1960), cert. denied 365 U.S. 869, 81 S.Ct.

903, 5 L.Ed.2d 859 (1961); Newell v. O.A. Newton & Son Co., 104 F.Supp. 162 (D.Del.1952); Eastman Co., *supra*. Liability for trade secret appropriation has also been imposed under state Unfair Trade Practices and Consumer Protection Acts. (See the Statutory Note following § 1.) See, e.g., Peggy Lawton Kitchens, Inc. v. Hogan, 18 Mass.App.Ct. 937, 466 N.E.2d 138 (1984); Lamb v. Quality Inspection Services, Inc., 398 So.2d 643 (La.App.1981). The Uniform Trade Secrets Act has itself been described as an unfair competition statute. See Stork–Werkspoor Diesel V.V. v. Koek, 534 So.2d 983 (La.App. 1988).

On criminal liability for an appropriation of information under the federal mail and wire fraud statutes, 18 U.S.C.A. §§ 1341, 1343, see Carpenter v. United States, 484 U.S. 19, 108 S.Ct. 316, 98 L.Ed.2d 275 (1987); United States v. Riggs, 739 F.Supp. 414 (N.D.Ill.1990). On liability under the National Stolen Property Act, 18 U.S.C.A. §§ 2314–15, see, e.g., United States v. Brown, 925 F.2d 1301 (10th Cir.1991) (requiring theft of a tangible embodiment of the intellectual property); United States v. Greenwald, 479 F.2d 320 (6th Cir.), cert. denied 414 U.S. 854, 94 S.Ct. 154, 38 L.Ed.2d 104 (1973); United States v. Bottone, 365 F.2d 389 (2d Cir.), cert. denied 385 U.S. 974, 87 S.Ct. 514, 17 L.Ed.2d 437 (1966); United States v. Riggs, *supra*. See also 18 U.S.C.A. § 1905, imposing criminal liability for the unauthorized disclosure of trade secrets by officers and employees of the federal government. On criminal liability for trade secret appropriation, see generally Jager, Trade Secrets Law § 4.01[4]; Milgrim on Trade Secrets § 1.10. On the protection of trade secrets from disclosure under the Freedom of Information Act, see Jager, *supra*, §§ 12.01–06.

Comment c. Trade secret protection terminates upon disclosure of the information in a patent. E.g., Scharmer v. Carrollton Mfg. Co., 525 F.2d 95 (6th Cir.1975); Felmlee v. Lockett, 466 Pa. 1, 351 A.2d 273 (1976). See Comment *f*. Related information not disclosed in the patent, however, remains eligible for protection as a trade secret. Henry Hope X–Ray Products, Inc. v. Marron Carrel, Inc., 674 F.2d 1336 (9th Cir.1982); Christianson v. Colt Industries Operating Corp., 870 F.2d 1292 (7th Cir.), cert. denied 493 U.S. 822, 110 S.Ct. 81, 107 L.Ed.2d 47 (1989). The filing of a patent application is not a public disclosure and thus does not preclude continued protection as a trade secret. Scharmer, *supra*; A.O. Smith Corp. v. Petroleum Iron Works Co., 73 F.2d 531 (6th Cir.1934), modified on other grounds 74 F.2d 934 (6th Cir.1935).

On the preemptive effect of federal patent law, see, in addition to the *Kewanee Oil* and *Bonito Boats* cases discussed in the Comment, Aronson v. Quick Point Pencil Co., 440 U.S. 257, 99 S.Ct. 1096, 59 L.Ed.2d 296 (1979) (upholding state enforcement of a contract to pay royalties for the manufacture of a product disclosed in confidence to the promisor but that later entered the public domain). See also § 16, Comment *c*. However, an attempt to extend protection under state trade secret law to information that is in the public domain is preempted. See Roboserve, Ltd. v. Tom's Foods, Inc., 940 F.2d 1441 (11th Cir.1991); Avco Corp. v. Precision Air Parts, Inc., 210 U.S.P.Q. 894 (M.D.Ala.1980), affirmed on other grounds 676 F.2d 494 (11th Cir.), cert. denied 459 U.S. 1037, 103 S.Ct.

450, 74 L.Ed.2d 604 (1982). Cf. Vault Corp. v. Quaid Software Ltd., 655 F.Supp. 750 (E.D.La.1987), affirmed 847 F.2d 255 (5th Cir.1988) (state statutory restriction on reverse engineering of software is preempted).

The preemptive effect of federal copyright law as delineated in § 301 of the Copyright Act does not extend to state trade secret protection, even when the trade secrets are embodied in works of authorship, provided that the state cause of action is premised upon improper acquisition or breach of confidence. See Trandes Corp. v. Guy F. Atkinson Co., 996 F.2d 655 (4th Cir.), cert. denied ___ U.S. ___, 114 S.Ct. 443, 126 L.Ed.2d 377 (1993); Computer Assoc. Int'l, Inc. v. Altai, Inc., 982 F.2d 693 (2d Cir.1992); Warrington Associates, Inc. v. Real–Time Engineering Systems, Inc., 522 F.Supp. 367 (N.D.Ill.1981); Balboa Insurance Co. v. Trans Global Equities, 218 Cal.App.3d 1327, 267 Cal. Rptr. 787, cert. denied 498 U.S. 940, 111 S.Ct. 347, 112 L.Ed.2d 311 (1990); Boeing Co. v. Sierracin Corp., 108 Wash.2d 38, 738 P.2d 665 (1987). Cf. M. Bryce & Assoc., Inc. v. Gladstone, 107 Wis.2d 241, 319 N.W.2d 907 (App.), cert. denied 459 U.S. 944, 103 S.Ct. 258, 74 L.Ed.2d 201 (1982) (1909 Copyright Act).

A claim of copyright in a work of authorship does not preclude a simultaneous claim of trade secret protection for information embodied in the work if sufficient secrecy has been maintained. See Technicon Medical Information Systems Corp. v. Green Bay Packaging Inc., 687 F.2d 1032 (7th Cir.1982), cert. denied 459 U.S. 1106, 103 S.Ct. 732, 74 L.Ed.2d 955 (1983); Bishop v. Wick, 11 U.S.P.Q.2d 1360 (N.D.Ill.1988); Warrington Associates, *supra*.

Comment d. "[T]he value of a trade secret lies in the competitive advantage it gives its owner over competitors." Ruckelshaus v. Monsanto Co., 467 U.S. 986, 1012 n.15, 104 S.Ct. 2862, 2877 n.15, 81 L.Ed.2d 815, 838 n.15 (1984). See also, e.g., Sikes v. McGraw–Edison Co., 665 F.2d 731 (5th Cir.), cert. denied 458 U.S. 1108, 102 S.Ct. 3488, 73 L.Ed.2d 1369 (1982). The requirement in § 1(4)(i) of the Uniform Trade Secrets Act that a trade secret possess "independent economic value" has been interpreted as a codification of the common law requirement of competitive advantage. See Electro–Craft Corp. v. Controlled Motion, Inc., 332 N.W.2d 890, 900 (Minn. 1983).

The Uniform Trade Secrets Act protects eligible "information," including "a formula, pattern, compilation, program, device, method, technique, or process." Although information relating to products or processes is a common subject of trade secret law, the cases provide numerous examples of other protectable information. See, e.g., Sigma Chemical Co. v. Harris, 794 F.2d 371 (8th Cir. 1986) (capabilities of suppliers); SI Handling Systems, Inc. v. Heisley, 753 F.2d 1244, 1260 (3d Cir.1985) (pricing methods); Clark v. Bunker, 453 F.2d 1006 (9th Cir.1972) (marketing plans); Tan–Line Studios, Inc. v. Bradley, 1 U.S.P.Q.2d 2032 (E.D.Pa. 1986) (business methods). Computer programs have become an important subject of trade secret law. See, e.g., Rivendell Forest Prod., Ltd. v. Georgia–Pacific Corp., 28 F.3d 1042 (10th Cir.1994) (Uniform Trade Secrets Act); Trandes Corp. v. Guy F. Atkinson Co., 996 F.2d 655 (4th Cir.), cert. denied ___ U.S. ___, 114 S.Ct. 443, 126 L.Ed.2d 377 (1993) (Uniform

Trade Secrets Act); Integrated Cash Management Services, Inc. v. Digital Transactions, Inc., 920 F.2d 171 (2d Cir.1990) (common law). On trade secret protection for customer identities and related information, see § 42, Comment *f*. Nonprofit organizations can assert trade secret rights in information that has potential economic value. Religious Technology Center v. Scott, 869 F.2d 1306 (9th Cir.1989) (scriptural materials alleged to be of importance in retaining members may be protectable, distinguishing the court's earlier decision in Religious Technology Center v. Wollersheim, 796 F.2d 1076 (9th Cir.1986)). See also, e.g., Plains Cotton Cooperative Ass'n v. Goodpasture Computer Service, Inc., 807 F.2d 1256 (5th Cir.), cert. denied 484 U.S. 821, 108 S.Ct. 80, 98 L.Ed.2d 42 (1987) (rejecting on the merits a trade secret claim by a nonprofit agricultural cooperative).

Few cases have focused on the former requirement in Restatement of Torts § 757, Comment *b*, that a trade secret must be of "continuous use in the operation of the business." But see Lehman v. Dow Jones & Co., 783 F.2d 285 (2d Cir.1986) (using the requirement to deny trade secret protection in an idea submission case) (dictum); Wisconsin Electric Power Co. v. Public Service Com., 110 Wis.2d 530, 329 N.W.2d 178 (1983) (emphasizing the "continuous use" requirement in strictly construing the term "trade secret" in a criminal statute). Cf. Kendall/Hunt Pub. Co. v. Rowe, 424 N.W.2d 235 (Iowa 1988) (a constantly changing list of names is too "ephemeral" for protection as a trade secret). But see Sikes v. McGraw–Edison Co., 665 F.2d 731 (5th Cir.), cert. denied 458 U.S. 1108, 102 S.Ct. 3488, 73 L.Ed.2d 1369 (1982) (a temporary advantage can be sufficient for protection as a trade secret).

If the trade secret claim relates to abstract ideas rather than concrete applications, it may be difficult for the plaintiff to demonstrate economic value. See Richter v. Westab, Inc., 529 F.2d 896 (6th Cir.1976); Wilson v. Barton & Ludwig, Inc., 163 Ga. App. 721, 296 S.E.2d 74 (1982). A lack of definiteness may also preclude proof of secrecy. See Trandes Corp., *supra*; Jostens, Inc. v. National Computer Systems, Inc., 318 N.W.2d 691 (Minn.1982). A physical embodiment of the information such as a working model can provide the requisite definition, see, e.g., Sikes, *supra*; Mann v. Tatge Chemical Co., 201 Kan. 326, 440 P.2d 640 (1968), but it is not required if the information is otherwise sufficiently concrete. See, e.g., Jones v. Ulrich, 342 Ill.App. 16, 95 N.E.2d 113 (1950). Failure to particularize the claimed trade secret with sufficient precision may also make it impossible for the court to determine whether the secret has been appropriated or to formulate appropriate relief. See MAI Systems Corp. v. Peak Computer, Inc., 991 F.2d 511 (9th Cir.1993), cert. dismissed ___ U.S. ___, 114 S.Ct. 671, 126 L.Ed.2d 640 (1994); AMP Inc. v. Fleischhacker, 823 F.2d 1199 (7th Cir.1987). The degree of definiteness required of the plaintiff may also reflect the equities of the case, including the legitimate interests of the defendant. For example, to protect the ability of former employees to utilize their general knowledge and skill (see § 42, Comment *d*), a court may impose a rigorous burden on the former employer to define the precise contours of the claimed trade secret. See, e.g., AMP Inc., *supra*; Dynamics Research Corp. v. Analytic Sciences Corp., 9 Mass.App.Ct. 254, 400 N.E.2d 1274 (1980). See generally Jager, Trade Secrets Law § 5.05[4].

An agreement that defines particular information as a "trade secret" does not conclusively establish that the information qualifies for protection under this Section. See Gary Van Zeeland Talent, Inc. v. Sandas, 84 Wis.2d 202, 267 N.W.2d 242 (1978) (declaration of trade secret status in an employment contract does not estop a subsequent challenge by the employee). See also, e.g., Cambridge Filter Corp. v. Int'l Filter Co., 548 F.Supp. 1301 (D.Nev.1982); Sarkes Tarzian, Inc. v. Audio Devices, Inc., 166 F.Supp. 250 (S.D.Cal.1958), affirmed 283 F.2d 695 (9th Cir.1960), cert. denied 365 U.S. 869, 81 S.Ct. 903, 5 L.Ed.2d 859 (1961); American Paper & Packaging Products, Inc. v. Kirgan, 183 Cal.App.3d 1318, 228 Cal. Rptr. 713 (1986); Dynamics Research Corp., *supra*. In some instances the terms of the agreement may justify an inference that the parties did not intend to treat particular information as confidential. See Ferroline Corp. v. General Aniline & Film Corp., 207 F.2d 912 (7th Cir.1953), cert. denied 347 U.S. 953, 74 S.Ct. 678, 98 L.Ed. 1098 (1954); Michels v. Dyna–Kote Industries, Inc., 497 N.E.2d 586 (Ind. App.1986).

In determining the existence of a trade secret, many cases rely on the factors identified in Restatement of Torts § 757, Comment *b* (1939):

> Some factors to be considered in determining whether given information is one's trade secret are: (1) the extent to which the information is known outside of his business; (2) the extent to which it is known by employees and others involved in his business; (3) the extent of measures taken by him to guard the secrecy of the information; (4) the value of the information to him and to his competitors; (5) the amount of effort or money expended by him in developing the information; (6) the ease or difficulty with which the information could be properly acquired or duplicated by others.

See, e.g., SI Handling Systems, Inc. v. Heisley, 753 F.2d 1244 (3d Cir. 1985); B.C. Ziegler and Co. v. Ehren, 141 Wis.2d 19, 414 N.W.2d 48 (App. 1987); ILG Industries, Inc. v. Scott, 49 Ill.2d 88, 273 N.E.2d 393 (1971). The Restatement factors have also been invoked in decisions under the Uniform Trade Secrets Act. See, e.g., Trandes Corp., *supra*; Amoco Production Co. v. Laird, 622 N.E.2d 912 (Ind.1993); Network Telecommunications, Inc. v. Boor–Crepeau, 790 P.2d 901 (Colo.App.1990); Optic Graphics, Inc. v. Agee, 87 Md.App. 770, 591 A.2d 578 (1991); Minuteman, Inc. v. Alexander, 147 Wis.2d 842, 434 N.W.2d 773 (1989). Other factors such as the nature of the defendant's misconduct and the public interest in permitting access to the particular information are also relevant. See, e.g., In re Innovative Construction Systems, Inc., 793 F.2d 875 (7th Cir. 1986) (trade secret rights asserted against former employees are narrowly construed in order to preserve competition and employee mobility); Metallurgical Industries Inc. v. Fourtek, Inc., 790 F.2d 1195 (5th Cir.1986) (the degree of defendant's misconduct may influence the determination of trade secret status).

The existence of a trade secret is properly considered a question of fact to be decided by the judge or jury as fact-finder. Rockwell Graphic Systems, Inc. v. DEV Industries, Inc., 925 F.2d 174 (7th Cir.1991) (Illinois law); Chevron U.S.A., Inc. v. Roxen Service, Inc., 813 F.2d 26 (2d Cir. 1987) (New York law); Lear Siegler, Inc. v. Ark-Ell Springs, Inc., 569 F.2d 286 (5th Cir.1978) (Mississippi law); Valco Cincinnati, Inc. v. N & D Machining Service, Inc., 24 Ohio St.3d 41, 492 N.E.2d 814 (1986); West Mountain Poultry Co. v. Gress, 309 Pa.Super. 361, 455 A.2d 651 (1982). Contra, Secure Services Technology, Inc. v. Time & Space Processing, Inc., 722 F.Supp. 1354 (E.D.Va.1989) (existence of a trade secret is a question of law under California law); Corroon & Black-Rutters & Roberts, Inc. v. Hosch, 109 Wis.2d 290, 325 N.W.2d 883 (1982) (question of law under Wisconsin law). The conclusion of the fact-finder as to the existence of a trade secret is entitled on appeal to the usual deference accorded findings of fact. See, e.g., Defiance Button Machine Co. v. C & C Metal Products Corp., 759 F.2d 1053 (2d Cir.), cert. denied 474 U.S. 844, 106 S.Ct. 131, 88 L.Ed.2d 108 (1985); Syntex Ophthalmics, Inc. v. Novicky, 745 F.2d 1423 (Fed.Cir.1984), vacated on other grounds 470 U.S. 1047, 105 S.Ct. 1740, 84 L.Ed.2d 807 (1985), reinstated 767 F.2d 901 (Fed.Cir.1985), cert. denied 475 U.S. 1083, 106 S.Ct. 1463, 89 L.Ed.2d 719 (1986); Zoecon Industries v. American Stockman Tag Co., 713 F.2d 1174 (5th Cir.1983); Saunders v. Florence Enameling Co., 540 So.2d 651 (Ala.1988). (In jurisdictions that view the existence of a trade secret as a question of law, the conclusion of the trial court is not entitled to special deference on appeal. See B.C. Ziegler and Co. v. Ehren, 141 Wis.2d 19, 414 N.W.2d 48 (App.1987) (Wisconsin law).) The burden is on the plaintiff to establish that the information qualifies for protection as a trade secret. E.g., Amoco Production, *supra*; Engineered Mechanical Services, Inc. v. Langlois, 464 So.2d 329 (La.App.1984); Microbiological Research Corp. v. Muna, 625 P.2d 690 (Utah 1981); Basic Chemicals, Inc. v. Benson, 251 N.W.2d 220 (Iowa 1977). See generally Jager, *supra*, § 5.01.

Comment e. On the requirement of value, see, e.g., Ruckelshaus v. Monsanto Co., 467 U.S. 986, 104 S.Ct. 2862, 81 L.Ed.2d 815 (1984); Phillips v. Frey, 20 F.3d 623 (5th Cir.1994) (a trade secret "must give the owner a competitive advantage"); Metallurgical Industries, Inc. v. Fourtek, Inc., 790 F.2d 1195 (5th Cir. 1986); Sikes v. McGraw-Edison Co., 665 F.2d 731 (5th Cir.), cert. denied 458 U.S. 1108, 102 S.Ct. 3488, 73 L.Ed.2d 1369 (1982) (jury instruction); FMC Corp. v. Spurlin, 596 F.Supp. 609 (W.D.Pa.1984) (a trade secret must afford a "competitive advantage"); SmokEnders, Inc. v. Smoke No More, Inc., 184 U.S.P.Q. 309 (S.D.Fla.1974); Organic Chemicals, Inc. v. Carroll Products, Inc., 211 U.S.P.Q. 628 (W.D.Mich.1981). The criterion is carried forward in § 1(4)(i) of the Uniform Trade Secrets Act through the requirement of "independent economic value." See, e.g., Electro-Craft Corp. v. Controlled Motion, Inc., 332 N.W.2d 890 (Minn.1983).

A trade secret need not be patentable. Kewanee Oil Co. v. Bicron Corp., 416 U.S. 470, 94 S.Ct. 1879, 40 L.Ed.2d 315 (1974); Atlantic Wool Combing Co. v. Norfolk Mills, Inc., 357 F.2d 866 (1st Cir.1966); A.O. Smith Corp. v. Petroleum Iron Works Co., 73 F.2d 531 (6th Cir.1934), modified on other grounds 74 F.2d 934 (6th Cir.1935); Peabody v. Norfolk, 98 Mass. 452 (1868). Even a modest advance may be eligible for protection as a trade secret. See, e.g., Sheridan v. Mallinckrodt, Inc., 568 F.Supp. 1347 (N.D.N.Y.1983) ("slight" advance sufficient); Organic Chemicals, *supra* (a trade secret can be anticipated in the prior art); Sinclair v. Aquarius Electronics, Inc., 42 Cal. App.3d 216, 116 Cal.Rptr. 654 (1974) (mere mechanical improvement can be a trade secret). Cf. Nickelson v. General Motors Corp., 361 F.2d 196 (7th Cir.1966) ("trivial" advance not protectable).

Value can be established by direct evidence of the usefulness of the information in conducting business. See, e.g., Metallurgical Industries, *supra*. Although a trade secret may consist of information discovered fortuitously, a significant expenditure of time, money, or effort in the production of the information is evidence of value. See, e.g., Surgidev Corp. v. Eye Technology, Inc., 648 F.Supp. 661 (D.Minn.1986), affirmed 828 F.2d 452 (8th Cir.1987); Koch Engineering Co. v. Faulconer, 227 Kan. 813, 610 P.2d 1094 (1980). A substantial investment by the person asserting trade secret rights, however, does not insure that the resulting information will qualify as a trade secret. See National Rejectors, Inc. v. Trieman, 409 S.W.2d 1 (Mo.1966). Precautions undertaken to protect the secrecy of the information can also indicate value. Rockwell Graphic Systems, Inc. v. DEV Industries, Inc., 925 F.2d 174 (7th Cir.1991). See Comment *g*. The willingness of licensees to pay for access to the secret and a defendant's decision to resort to improper means to acquire the secret are also evidence that the information is valuable. See Tan–Line Studios Inc. v. Bradley, 1 U.S.P.Q.2d 2032 (E.D.Pa. 1986).

The former treatment of this topic described a trade secret as information "used in one's business." Restatement of Torts § 757, Comment *b* (1939). Use by the claimant is recited as a requirement in a number of early decisions. E.g., Victor Chemical Works v. Iliff, 299 Ill. 532, 132 N.E. 806 (1921). See Milgrim on Trade Secrets § 2.02[1]. Other cases reject any requirement of use by the trade secret owner. E.g., Syntex Ophthalmics, Inc. v. Tsuetaki, 701 F.2d 677 (7th Cir.1983) (Illinois law); Ferroline Corp. v. General Aniline & Film Corp., 207 F.2d 912 (7th Cir. 1953) (New Jersey law); Sinclair v. Aquarius Electronics, Inc., 42 Cal. App.3d 216, 116 Cal.Rptr. 654 (1974). See, e.g., Sikes v. McGraw–Edison Co., 665 F.2d 731 (5th Cir.), cert. denied 458 U.S. 1108, 102 S.Ct. 3488, 73 L.Ed.2d 1369 (1982) (commercial marketing not required); Prince Mfg., Inc. v. Automatic Partner, Inc., 191 U.S.P.Q. 450 (N.J.Super.1976) (same). See also Jager, Trade Secrets Law § 5.02[2]. Dicta in several cases suggest that "negative" information concerning "what not to do" may be ineligible for protection as a trade secret. See Hurst v. Hughes Tool Co., 634 F.2d 895 (5th Cir.), cert. denied 454 U.S. 829, 102 S.Ct. 123, 70 L.Ed.2d 105 (1981); Standard Brands, Inc. v. Zumpe, 264 F.Supp. 254 (E.D.La.1967). But cf. Metallurgical Industries, Inc. v. Fourtek, Inc., 790 F.2d 1195 (5th Cir.1986) (questioning the validity of a distinction between positive and negative information). The Comment to § 1 of the Uniform Trade Secrets Act states that the Act's definition of "trade secret" is intended to encompass such negative information.

Comment f. Novelty in the patent law sense is not required for trade secret protection. Kewanee Oil Co. v. Bicron Corp., 416 U.S. 470, 94 S.Ct. 1879, 40 L.Ed.2d 315 (1974). Most definitions of "trade secret" at common law do not contain a requirement of "novelty". It is also absent from the definition of "trade secret" in the Uniform Trade Secrets Act. See § 1(4). Some cases explicitly reject a "novelty" requirement. See, e.g., Cataphote Corp. v. Hudson, 422 F.2d 1290 (5th Cir.1970) (Mississippi law); Water Services, Inc. v. Tesco Chemicals, Inc., 410 F.2d 163 (5th Cir.1969) (Georgia law); SmokEnders, Inc. v. Smoke No More, Inc., 184 U.S.P.Q. 309 (S.D.Fla.1974) (Florida law). Other cases, equating "novelty" with secrecy, invoke the concept to preclude protection for matters commonly known or readily ascertainable. "However, some novelty will be required if merely because that which does not possess novelty is usually known; secrecy, in the context of trade secrets, thus implies at least minimum novelty." Kewanee, *supra*, 416 U.S. at 476, 94 S.Ct. at 1879, 40 L.Ed.2d at 322–23. See, e.g., SI Handling Systems, Inc. v. Heisley, 753 F.2d 1244 (3d Cir. 1985) (novelty demonstrates secrecy); Henry Hope X–Ray Products, Inc. v. Marron Carrel, Inc., 674 F.2d 1336 (9th Cir.1982) (novelty means that the matter is not public knowledge); Fishing Concepts, Inc. v. Ross, 226 U.S.P.Q. 692 (D.Minn.1985) (aggregation of common practices is not novel); CPG Products Corp. v. Mego Corp., 214 U.S.P.Q. 206 (S.D.Ohio 1981) (novelty means that the process is not common knowledge); Anaconda Co. v. Metric Tool & Die Co., 485 F.Supp. 410 (E.D.Pa.1980) (novelty demonstrates secrecy).

Early cases emphasizing that absolute secrecy is not a prerequisite for trade secret protection include, e.g., Vulcan Detinning Co. v. American Can Co., 72 N.J.Eq. 387, 67 A. 339 (1907); Peabody v. Norfolk, 98 Mass. 452 (1868). Confidential disclosures to employees, licensees, and others will not destroy the secrecy necessary for protection as a trade secret. See § 41. Trade secret rights can survive even relatively broad dissemination if the disclosures are made in confidence, see, e.g., Aries Information Systems, Inc. v. Pacific Management Systems Corp., 366 N.W.2d 366 (Minn.App.1985); Data General Corp. v. Digital Computer Controls, Inc., 297 A.2d 433 (Del.Ch.1971), affirmed 297 A.2d 437 (Del.1972), although the precautions required of the trade secret owner may increase with increasing dissemination. See Comment *g*; § 43, Comment *c*. Trade secret protection can also survive limited nonconfidential disclosure if the information does not become generally known or readily ascertainable by competitors. Metallurgical Industries, Inc. v. Fourtek, Inc., 790 F.2d 1195 (5th Cir.1986). A trade secret can also consist of a secret compilation or combination of known elements. Syntex Ophthalmics, Inc. v. Novicky, 745 F.2d 1423 (Fed.Cir. 1984), vacated on other grounds 470 U.S. 1047, 105 S.Ct. 1740, 84 L.Ed.2d 807 (1985), reinstated 767 F.2d 901 (Fed.Cir.1985), cert. denied 475 U.S. 1083, 106 S.Ct. 1463, 89 L.Ed.2d 719 (1986); Water Services, Inc. v. Tesco Chemicals, Inc., 410 F.2d 163 (5th Cir.1969); Imperial Chemical Industries, Ltd. v. National Distillers and Chemical Corp., 342 F.2d 737 (2d Cir. 1965); Mann v. Tatge Chemical Co., 201 Kan. 326, 440 P.2d 640 (1968).

The relative secrecy of information claimed as a trade secret is measured by the difficulty in acquiring the information by proper means. E.g., Clark v. Bunker, 453 F.2d 1006 (9th Cir.1972); Anaconda Co. v. Metric Tool & Die Co., 485 F.Supp. 410 (E.D.Pa.1980); Amoco Production Co. v. Laird, 622 N.E.2d 912 (Ind.1993) (acquisition by proper means need not be "economically infeasible"; it can be sufficient if acquisition requires "a substantial investment of time, expense, or effort"); Robert S. Weiss and Assoc., Inc. v. Wiederlight, 208 Conn. 525, 546 A.2d 216 (1988); Technicon Data Systems Corp. v. Curtis 1000, Inc., 224 U.S.P.Q. 286 (Del.Ch.1984); Space Aero Products Co. v. R.E. Darling Co., 238 Md. 93, 208 A.2d 74, cert. denied, 382 U.S. 843, 86 S.Ct. 77, 15 L.Ed.2d 83 (1965). Thus, public sale of a product does not preclude continued protection against the improper acquisition or use of information that is difficult, costly, or time-consuming to extract through reverse engineering. E.g., American Can Co. v. Mansukhani, 728 F.2d 818 (7th Cir.1982); ILG Industries, Inc. v. Scott, 49 Ill.2d 88, 273 N.E.2d 393 (1971); Tabor v. Hoffman, 118 N.Y. 30, 23 N.E. 12 (1889). See also Uniform Trade Secrets Act, Comment to § 1. If the information is in fact obtained through reverse engineering, however, the actor is not subject to liability because the information has not been acquired improperly. See § 43. Public distribution of a computer program in object code, for example, does not necessarily forfeit trade secret rights in the underlying source code against one who obtains the source code through a breach of confidence or other improper conduct rather than through an analysis of the marketed program. See Integrated Cash Management Services, Inc. v. Digital Transactions, Inc., 920 F.2d 171 (2d Cir.1990); ISC–Bunker Ramo Corp. v. Altech, Inc., 765 F.Supp. 1310 (N.D.Ill.1990); Q–Co Industries, Inc. v. Hoffman, 625 F.Supp. 608 (S.D.N.Y.1985); Telex Corp. v. Int'l Business Machines Corp., 367 F.Supp. 258, 325 (N.D.Okla.1973), affirmed 510 F.2d 894 (10th Cir.), cert. dismissed 423 U.S. 802, 96 S.Ct. 8, 46 L.Ed.2d 244 (1975); Barr–Mullin, Inc. v. Browning, 108 N.C.App. 590, 424 S.E.2d 226 (1993). Trade secret protection can also survive a limited public sale or display that does not provide competitors with a reasonable opportunity for inspection and analysis. See, e.g., Motorola, Inc. v. Computer Displays Int'l, Inc., 739 F.2d 1149 (7th Cir. 1984) (brief display did not divulge trade secrets); K–2 Ski Co. v. Head Ski Co., 506 F.2d 471 (9th Cir.1974) (secrecy was not destroyed by a public display that was not observed by other manufacturers); Kubik, Inc. v. Hull, 56 Mich.App. 335, 224 N.W.2d 80 (1974) (competitors would have difficulty obtaining the product for inspection due to limited sales).

"Information is readily ascertainable if it is available in trade journals, reference books, or published materials." Uniform Trade Secrets Act, Comment to § 1. See, e.g., T. P. Laboratories, Inc. v. Huge, 261 F.Supp. 349 (E.D.Wis.1965), affirmed 371 F.2d 231 (7th Cir.1966); Public Systems, Inc. v. Towry, 587 So.2d 969 (Ala.1991); Dynamics Research Corp. v. Analytic Sciences Corp., 9 Mass. App.Ct. 254, 400 N.E.2d 1274 (1980); Van Products Co. v. General Welding and Fabricating Co., 419 Pa. 248, 213 A.2d 769 (1965); Microbiological Research Corp. v. Muna, 625 P.2d 690 (Utah 1981). However, if the publications containing the information are unavailable or unlikely to come to the attention of others to whom the information has value, it can be argued that the information remains sufficiently secret for protection. "'[R]eadily ascertainable' should not apply to obscure publications * * *." Jager, Trade Secrets Law § 5.04[3][a][ii]. The federal policy requiring public disclosure in return for the limited monopoly of a patent, however, may justify automatic termination of trade secret rights upon the issuance of a patent without regard to the likelihood that the disclosed information will come to the attention of other potential users. See Rototron Corp. v. Lake Shore Burial Vault Co., 712 F.2d 1214 (7th Cir.1983); Scharmer v. Carrollton Manufacturing Co., 525 F.2d 95 (6th Cir.1975). The rationale may be less forceful with respect to information disclosed in foreign patents. See Milgrim on Trade Secrets § 2.06[5].

Among the facts relevant in determining relative secrecy are the plaintiff's precautions against disclosure, see, e.g., Rockwell Graphic Systems, Inc. v. DEV Industries, Inc., 925 F.2d 174 (7th Cir.1991); Surgidev Corp. v. Eye Technology, Inc., 648 F.Supp. 661 (D.Minn.1986), affirmed 828 F.2d 452 (8th Cir.1987); Space Aero Products Co. v. R.E. Darling Co., 238 Md. 93, 208 A.2d 74, cert. denied 382 U.S. 843, 86 S.Ct. 77, 15 L.Ed.2d 83 (1965), the willingness of others to pay for access to the information, Clark v. Bunker, 453 F.2d 1006 (9th Cir.1972), the inability of others to duplicate the information, e.g., Water Services, Inc. v. Tesco Chemicals, Inc., 410 F.2d 163 (5th Cir.1969); L.M. Rabinowitz & Co. v. Dasher, 82 N.Y.S.2d 431 (Sup. Ct.1948), and the defendant's resort to improper means of acquisition, Clark, *supra* ; Tan–Line Studios Inc. v. Bradley, 1 U.S.P.Q.2d 2032 (E.D.Pa.1986).

The following cases adopt the position that the right to enforce an obligation of confidentiality arising from the confidential disclosure of information then qualifying as a trade secret continues even after a subsequent loss of secrecy through public sales or other disclosure by the plaintiff. E.g., Goldberg v. Medtronic, Inc., 686 F.2d 1219 (7th Cir.1982) (disagreed with as to Minnesota law in Electro–Craft Corp. v. Controlled Motion, Inc., 332 N.W.2d 890 (Minn.1983)); Franke v. Wiltschek, 209 F.2d 493 (2d Cir.1953); Smith v. Dravo Corp., 203 F.2d 369 (7th Cir.1953) (disagreed with as to Pennsylvania law in Van Products Co. v. General Welding and Fabricating Co., 419 Pa. 248, 213 A.2d 769 (1965)); Kamin v. Kuhnau, 232 Or. 139, 374 P.2d 912 (1962); Classic Instruments, Inc. v. VDO–Argo Instruments, Inc., 73 Or.App. 732, 700 P.2d 677 (1985); Reading & Bates Construction Co. v. O'Donnell, 627 S.W.2d 239 (Tex.App.1982); Atlas Bradford Co. v. Tuboscope Co., 378 S.W.2d 147 (Tex.Civ.App.1964). Many of these cases note, however, that actual reliance by the defendant on the public domain sources is permissible. See, e.g., Goldberg, *supra* ; Franke, *supra* ; Smith, *supra* ; Kamin, *supra.*

The position adopted in this Restatement that protection under the law of trade secrets terminates when the information becomes generally known or readily ascertainable by proper means is supported by, e.g., Rockwell Graphic Systems, Inc. v. DEV Industries, Inc., 925 F.2d 174 (7th Cir.1991); SI Handling Systems, Inc. v. Heisley, 753 F.2d 1244 (3d Cir.1985); Henry Hope X–Ray Products, Inc. v. Marron Carrel, Inc., 674 F.2d 1336 (9th Cir.1982); Scharmer v. Carrollton Mfg. Co., 525 F.2d 95

(6th Cir.1975); Northup v. Reish, 200 F.2d 924 (7th Cir.1953); Electro–Craft Corp. v. Controlled Motion, Inc., 332 N.W.2d 890 (Minn.1983); Laurie Visual Etudes, Inc. v. Chesebrough–Pond's Inc., 83 A.D.2d 505, 441 N.Y.S.2d 88 (1981); Kubik, Inc. v. Hull, 56 Mich.App. 335, 224 N.W.2d 80 (1974); Van Products Co. v. General Welding and Fabricating Co., 419 Pa. 248, 213 A.2d 769 (1965); Den–Tal–Ez Inc. v. Siemens Capital Corp., 389 Pa.Super. 219, 566 A.2d 1214 (1989); Gallowhur Chemical Corp. v. Schwerdle, 37 N.J.Super. 385, 117 A.2d 416 (1955). This position is also consistent with the policy of the Uniform Trade Secrets Act, which limits injunctive relief to that necessary "to eliminate the commercial advantage or 'lead time' with respect to good faith competitors that a person has obtained through misappropriation." Uniform Trade Secrets Act, Comment to § 2.

Illustration 1 is based on the principles governing confidential disclosures discussed in § 41. Independent discovery by another does not preclude protection as a trade secret if the information remains sufficiently inaccessible to others. See Electro–Craft Corp. v. Controlled Motion, Inc., 332 N.W.2d 890 (Minn.1983) (dictum).

Illustrations 2 and 3 are based on Leo Silfen, Inc. v. Cream, 29 N.Y.2d 387, 328 N.Y.S.2d 423, 278 N.E.2d 636 (1972). See also § 42, Comment *f*.

Illustration 4 is supported by, e.g., Scharmer v. Carrollton Mfg. Co., 525 F.2d 95 (6th Cir.1975) (patent disclosure).

Illustration 5 is based on ILG Industries, Inc. v. Scott, 49 Ill.2d 88, 273 N.E.2d 393 (1971).

Comment g. Illustrations of physical security measures intended to prevent unauthorized access and other precautions intended to insure the confidentiality of disclosures made to employees and others are collected in Jager, Trade Secrets Law § 5.05[2]; Milgrim on Trade Secrets § 2.04. Precautions taken to maintain secrecy can be evidence of the information's value, Rockwell Graphic Systems, Inc. v. DEV Industries, Inc., 925 F.2d 174 (7th Cir.1991), and relative secrecy, Metallurgical Industries Inc. v. Fourtek, Inc., 790 F.2d 1195 (5th Cir.1986); Arco Industries Corp. v. Chemcast Corp., 633 F.2d 435 (6th Cir.1980); Kubik, Inc. v. Hull, 56 Mich.App. 335, 224 N.W.2d 80 (1974). Cf. Victor Chemical Works v. Iliff, 299 Ill. 532, 132 N.E. 806 (1921) (precautions are not sufficient for protection if other evidence establishes that the information is generally known). Precautions can also signal to employees and other recipients of the secret that the information is confidential. See, e.g, Surgidev Corp. v. Eye Technology, Inc., 828 F.2d 452 (8th Cir.1987); Electro–Craft Corp. v. Controlled Motion, Inc., 332 N.W.2d 890 (Minn.1983); O. & W. Thum Co. v. Tloczynski, 114 Mich. 149, 72 N.W. 140 (1897). Precautions taken by the trade secret owner are also relevant in determining whether a defendant knew or had reason to know that use or disclosure of the information was wrongful, see § 40, whether a defendant used improper means to acquire the secret, see E.I. duPont deNemours & Co. v. Christopher, 431 F.2d 1012 (5th Cir. 1970), cert. denied 400 U.S. 1024, 91 S.Ct. 581, 27 L.Ed.2d 637 (1971); § 43, Comment *c*, and whether an accidental disclosure to the defendant results in a loss of trade secret rights, see Defiance Button Machine Co. v. C

& C Metal Products Corp., 759 F.2d 1053 (2d Cir.), cert. denied 474 U.S. 844, 106 S.Ct. 131, 88 L.Ed.2d 108 (1985); B.C. Ziegler and Co. v. Ehren, 141 Wis.2d 19, 414 N.W.2d 48 (App.1987); § 40, Comment *e*.

When other evidence establishes secrecy and the existence of a confidential relationship, courts are properly reluctant to deny protection on the basis of alleged inadequacies in the plaintiff's security precautions. After noting that "[t]he significance of the security precautions taken by the possessor of a trade secret must be viewed in the context of the law of trade secrets, taken as a whole," the court in USM Corp. v. Marson Fastener Corp., 379 Mass. 90, 98 n.9, 393 N.E.2d 895, 900 n.9 (1979), stated, "We think it appropriate to balance a plaintiff's conduct in maintaining its security measures against the conduct of a defendant in acquiring the information." *Id.* at 98, 393 N.E.2d at 900. See, e.g., Syntex Ophthalmics, Inc. v. Novicky, 214 U.S.P.Q. 272, 277 (N.D.Ill.1982), affirmed 701 F.2d 677 (7th Cir.1983) ("[W]here the security lapses were not the cause of the misappropriation, those lapses should not be the basis for denying protection."); Pioneer Hi-Bred Int'l v. Holden Foundation Seeds, Inc., 35 F.3d 1226 (8th Cir.1994) (quoting Syntex, *supra*); Tan-Line Studios, Inc. v. Bradley, 1 U.S.P.Q.2d 2032, 2039 (E.D.Pa.1986) ("The issue, however, is not whether plaintiff utilized adequate precautions. Rather, the issue is whether a confidential relationship existed * * *."). See also, e.g, In re Innovative Constr. Sys., Inc., 793 F.2d 875 (7th Cir.1986); K-2 Ski Co. v. Head Ski Co., 506 F.2d 471 (9th Cir.1974); Computer Print Sys., Inc. v. Lewis, 281 Pa.Super. 240, 422 A.2d 148 (1980).

Comment h. For an introduction to the "law of ideas," see Goldstein, Copyright §§ 15.7–15.9; Nimmer on Copyright §§ 16.01–08. The distinction between trade secret cases and idea submission cases engendered by the narrow definition of trade secret in Restatement of Torts § 757, Comment *b* (1939), is illustrated in, e.g., Lehman v. Dow Jones & Co., 783 F.2d 285 (2d Cir.1986) and Richter v. Westab, Inc., 529 F.2d 896 (6th Cir.1976), both emphasizing the lack of a continuing advantage. See Comment *d*. See also Hudson Hotels Corp. v. Choice Hotels Int'l, Inc., 995 F.2d 1173 (2d Cir.1993). Cases explicitly applying trade secret law to idea submissions include, e.g., Smith v. Snap-On Tools Corp., 833 F.2d 578 (5th Cir.1987); Burten v. Milton Bradley Co., 763 F.2d 461 (1st Cir. 1985); Sikes v. McGraw-Edison Co., 665 F.2d 731 (5th Cir.), cert. denied 458 U.S. 1108, 102 S.Ct. 3488, 73 L.Ed.2d 1369 (1982); Sinclair v. Aquarius Electronics, Inc., 42 Cal. App.3d 216, 116 Cal.Rptr. 654 (1974); Mann v. Tatge Chemical Co., 201 Kan. 326, 440 P.2d 640 (1968). See also, e.g., Wilson v. Barton & Ludwig, Inc., 163 Ga.App. 721, 296 S.E.2d 74 (1982) (using trade secret cases to evaluate the novelty of the submitted idea).

Most cases require "novelty" as a prerequisite to the protection of submitted ideas under both tort and implied-in-fact contract theories. E.g., Murray v. National Broadcasting Co., 844 F.2d 988 (2d Cir.), cert. denied 488 U.S. 955, 109 S.Ct. 391, 102 L.Ed.2d 380 (1988); Lehman, *supra*; Hamilton National Bank v. Belt, 210 F.2d 706 (D.C.Cir.1953); Werlin v. Reader's Digest Ass'n, 528 F.Supp. 451 (S.D.N.Y.1981); Downey v. General Foods Corp., 31 N.Y.2d 56, 334 N.Y.S.2d 874, 286 N.E.2d 257 (1972). Although the necessity of protecting the recipient through a novelty requirement may be less compelling when the parties have expressly agreed on the terms of the disclosure, most decisions indicate that proof of novelty is also required for the enforcement of an express contract. See, e.g., Masline v. New York, N.H. & H.R. Co., 95 Conn. 702, 112 A. 639 (1921); Garrido v. Burger King Corp., 558 So.2d 79 (Fla.App.1990), appeal after remand 605 So.2d 1026 (1992); Kienzle v. Capital Cities/American Broadcasting Co., 774 F.Supp. 432 (E.D.Mich.1991) (Michigan law) (dictum); Tate v. Scanlan Int'l, Inc., 403 N.W.2d 666 (Minn. App.1987); Bergman v. Electrolux Corp., 558 F.Supp. 1351 (D.Nev.1983) (Nevada law); Granoff v. Merrill Lynch & Co., 775 F.Supp. 621 (S.D.N.Y.1991), affirmed 962 F.2d 2 (2d Cir.1992) (New York law); Downey, *supra*. The requirement of "concreteness" is evident in, e.g., Sikes, *supra*; Richter, *supra*; Hamilton National Bank, *supra*; Bergman, *supra*; Werlin, *supra*; Mann, *supra*; Tate, *supra*. California law, however, permits the enforcement of express and implied-in-fact contracts for the use of ideas without proof of novelty, see Desny v. Wilder, 46 Cal.2d 715, 299 P.2d 257 (1956) (novelty unnecessary), or concreteness, see Minniear v. Tors, 266 Cal.App.2d 495, 72 Cal.Rptr. 287 (1968) (novelty and concreteness unnecessary), perhaps in recognition of the kinds of ideas that can be of significant value in the entertainment industries. The requirements under California law are apparently more severe with respect to breach of confidence actions. See Faris v. Enberg, 97 Cal.App.3d 309, 158 Cal.Rptr. 704 (1979) ("novelty and elaboration" are relevant in supporting an inference of confidentiality); Tele–Count Engineers, Inc. v. Pacific Tel. and Tel. Co., 168 Cal. App.3d 455, 214 Cal.Rptr. 276 (1985) (idea must be novel to warrant protection under a breach of confidence theory). See Goldstein, *supra*, § 15.7 ("Courts apply the requirements [of novelty and concreteness] least rigorously when the cause of action is for breach of an express contract, somewhat more rigorously in implied in fact contract actions, and more rigorously still in quasi-contract actions.").

For examples of the various legal theories raised in idea submission cases, see, e.g., Sinclair, *supra* (trade secret and express contract); Landsberg v. Scrabble Crossword Game Players, Inc., 802 F.2d 1193 (9th Cir. 1986) (implied-in-fact contract); Whitfield v. Lear, 751 F.2d 90 (2d Cir.1984) (same); Minniear, *supra* (same); Matarese v. Moore–McCormack Lines, Inc., 158 F.2d 631 (2d Cir.1946) (unjust enrichment); Werlin, *supra* (same); Smith, *supra* (trade secret and breach of confidence); Lehman, *supra* (breach of confidence); Burten, *supra* (trade secret and breach of confidence); Faris, *supra* (breach of confidence). On the ownership of ideas developed by employees, see § 42, Comment *e*.

§ 40. Appropriation of Trade Secrets

One is subject to liability for the appropriation of another's trade secret if:

(a) the actor acquires by means that are improper under the rule stated in § 43 information that the

actor knows or has reason to know is the other's trade secret; or

(b) the actor uses or discloses the other's trade secret without the other's consent and, at the time of the use or disclosure,

(1) the actor knows or has reason to know that the information is a trade secret that the actor acquired under circumstances creating a duty of confidence owed by the actor to the other under the rule stated in § 41; or

(2) the actor knows or has reason to know that the information is a trade secret that the actor acquired by means that are improper under the rule stated in § 43; or

(3) the actor knows or has reason to know that the information is a trade secret that the actor acquired from or through a person who acquired it by means that are improper under the rule stated in § 43 or whose disclosure of the trade secret constituted a breach of a duty of confidence owed to the other under the rule stated in § 41; or

(4) the actor knows or has reason to know that the information is a trade secret that the actor acquired through an accident or mistake, unless the acquisition was the result of the other's failure to take reasonable precautions to maintain the secrecy of the information.

Comment:

a. Scope. The rules stated in this Section are applicable to common law actions in tort or restitution for the appropriation of another's trade secret, however denominated, including actions for "misappropriation," "infringement," or "conversion" of a trade secret, actions for "unjust enrichment" based on the unauthorized use of a trade secret, and actions for "breach of confidence" in which the subject matter of the confidence is a trade secret. Except as otherwise noted, the rules governing trade secrets as stated in this Restatement are also intended to be consistent with and applicable to actions under the Uniform Trade Secrets Act. This Section does not govern the imposition of liability for conduct that infringes other protected interests such as interference with contractual relations (see Restatement, Second, Torts §§ 766–774A (1979)), breach of the duty of loyalty owed by an employee or other agent (see Restatement, Second, Agency §§ 387–398 (1958)), or a breach of confidence not involving a trade secret (see § 41, Comment *c*).

The rules stated in this Section are not applicable to actions for breach of contract, including breach of a promise not to use or disclose a trade secret or a promise not to compete with the owner of a trade secret. Such agreements are governed by the rules generally applicable to the formation and enforcement of contracts, including the limitations on the enforcement of contracts in restraint of trade stated in Restatement, Second, Contracts §§ 186–188 (1981). The rules stated in this Chapter, however, can be useful in interpreting and implementing the principles embodied in those limitations. See § 41, Comment *d*. The existence of an express or implied-in-fact contract protecting trade secrets does not preclude a separate cause of action in tort under the rules in this Section. The terms of the contract may be relevant to a number of issues in such an action, including the existence of a protectable trade secret (see § 39, Comment *d*) and the creation of a duty of confidence (see § 41, Comment *b*).

In an action for the appropriation of a trade secret, the plaintiff bears the burden of proving both a proprietary interest in information that qualifies for protection as a trade secret under the rule stated in § 39 and an acquisition, use, or disclosure of the information by the defendant in violation of the rules stated here. A proprietary interest sufficient for relief under this Section can arise through the discovery of a trade secret or through the acquisition of rights in a trade secret discovered by another. On the rights of an employer in trade secrets discovered by an employee, see § 42, Comment *e*. Since neither novelty nor absolute secrecy is a prerequisite for protection as a trade secret, see § 39, Comment *f*, each of several independent discoverers can have a proprietary interest in the same information.

b. Improper acquisition. The prior Restatement of this topic imposed liability only for the wrongful use or disclosure of another's trade secret. Improper acquisition of a trade secret was not independently actionable. See Restatement of Torts § 757 (1939). Wrongful use or disclosure is also frequently recited in the case law as an element of the cause of action for trade secret appropriation. The cases requiring proof of wrongful use or disclosure, however, typically involve information that has been acquired by the defendant through a confidential disclosure from the trade secret owner. In such cases the acquisition of the secret is not improper; only a subsequent use or disclosure in breach of the defendant's duty of confidence is wrongful. Even in these circumstances the courts have recognized a plaintiff's right to obtain relief prior to any wrongful use or disclosure if such misconduct by the defendant is sufficiently likely. See § 44, Comment *c*. A defendant's willingness to resort to improper means in order to acquire a trade secret is itself evidence of a substantial risk of subsequent use or disclosure. Subsection (a) of this Section follows the rule adopted in § 1(2)(i) of the Uniform Trade Secrets Act, which imposes liability for the acquisition of a trade secret by improper means. Thus, a person who obtains a trade secret through a wiretap or who induces or knowingly accepts a disclosure of the secret in breach of confidence is subject to liability. See § 43, Comment *c*. Subsequent use or disclosure of a trade secret that has been improperly acquired constitutes a further appropriation under the rule stated in Subsection (b)(2) of this Section. The relief available to the trade secret owner in such circumstances, however, may be more extensive than that available prior to any use or disclosure of the secret by the defendant.

Illustration:

1. *A* and *B* are competitors. *B* knows that *A* has a secret process that substantially reduces manufacturing costs. *C*, an employee of *A* who learned the secret through a confidential disclosure by *A*, offers to sell *A* 's secret to *B*. *B* knows that *C* is employed by *A* and that a disclosure by *C* would be a breach of *C* 's duty of confidence. If *B* purchases the trade secret from *C*, *B* is subject to liability to *A* under the rule stated in Subsection (a) of this Section. If *B* subsequently uses or discloses the secret, *B* is also subject to liability to *A* under the rule stated in Subsection (b)(2) of this Section.

c. Improper use or disclosure. There are no technical limitations on the nature of the conduct that constitutes "use" of a trade secret for purposes of the rules stated in Subsection (b). As a general matter, any exploitation of the trade secret that is likely to result in injury to the trade secret owner or enrichment to the defendant is a "use" under this Section. Thus, marketing goods that embody the trade secret, employing the trade secret in manufacturing or production, relying on the trade secret to assist or accelerate research or development, or soliciting customers through the use of information that is a trade secret (see § 42, Comment *f*) all constitute "use." The nature of the unauthorized use, however, is relevant in determining appropriate relief. See §§ 44 and 45.

The unauthorized use need not extend to every aspect or feature of the trade secret; use of any substantial portion of the secret is sufficient to subject the actor to liability. Similarly, the actor need not use the trade secret in its original form. Thus, an actor is liable for using the trade secret with independently created improvements or modifications if the result is substantially derived from the trade secret. The extent to which the actor's sales or other benefits are attributable to such independent improvements or modifications, however, can affect the computation of monetary relief. See § 45, Comment *f.* However, if the contribution made by the trade secret is so slight that the actor's product or process can be said to derive from other sources of information or from independent creation, the trade secret has not been "used" for purposes of imposing liability under the rules stated in Subsection (b). Although the trade secret owner bears the burden of proving unauthorized use, proof of the defendant's knowledge of the trade secret together with substantial similarities between the parties' products or processes may justify an inference of use by the defendant.

The owner of a trade secret may be injured by unauthorized disclosure of a trade secret as well as by unauthorized use. A public disclosure injures the trade secret owner by destroying the secrecy necessary for continued protection of the information as a trade secret. See § 39, Comment *f.* A private disclosure can increase the likelihood of both unauthorized use and further disclosure. An actor may thus be subject to liability under the circumstances described in Subsection (b) in connection with either a public or private disclosure of a trade secret. To subject the actor to liability, the unauthorized disclosure need not be express. Any conduct by the actor that enables another to learn the trade secret, including the sale or transfer of goods or other tangible objects from which the trade secret can be obtained, is a "disclosure" of the secret under the rules stated in this Section.

The unauthorized disclosure of a trade secret ordinarily occurs as part of an attempt to exploit the commercial value of the secret through use in competition with the trade secret owner or through a sale of the information to other potential users. The scope of liability at common law and under the Uniform Trade Secrets Act for disclosures that do not involve commercial exploitation of the secret information is unclear. If the trade secret is disclosed primarily for the purpose of causing harm to the trade secret owner, a court may properly conclude that the actor is subject to liability despite an absence of commercial exploitation. Thus, a former employee who publicly discloses trade secrets of the former employer in retaliation for a termination of the employment is subject to liability under this Section. In other circumstances, however, the disclosure of another's trade secret for purposes other than commercial exploitation may implicate the interest in freedom of expression or advance another significant public interest. A witness who is compelled by law to disclose another's trade secret during the course of a judicial proceeding, for example, is not subject to liability. The existence of a privilege to disclose another's trade secret depends upon the circumstances of the particular case, including the nature of the information, the purpose of the disclosure, and the means by which the actor acquired the information. A privilege is likely to be recognized, for example, in connection with the disclosure of information that is relevant to public health or safety, or to the commission of a crime or tort, or to other matters of substantial public concern.

d. Knowledge of wrongful possession. The owner of a trade secret is protected under Subsection (b) of this Section only against a use or disclosure of the trade secret that the actor knows or has reason to know is wrongful. If the actor has not acquired the information through a confidential disclosure from the trade secret owner, see Subsection (b)(1), use or disclosure of the information will not subject the actor to liability unless the actor knew or had reason to know that the use or disclosure was wrongful due to the manner in which the actor acquired the trade secret. See Subsection (b)(2)-(4). Thus, if an actor acquires a trade secret by improper means, such as by inducing or knowingly accepting a disclosure of the information from a third person that is in breach of a duty of confidence, the actor is subject to liability for any subsequent use or disclosure of the secret. See Subsection (b)(2). However, an actor who acquires a trade secret from a third person without notice of that person's breach of confidence has not acquired the information by improper means and is not subject to liability for use or disclosure unless the actor subsequently receives notice that its possession of the information is wrongful. See Subsection (b)(3).

To subject an actor to liability under the rules stated in Subsection (b)(2)-(4), the owner need not prove that the actor knew that its possession of the trade secret was wrongful; it is sufficient if the actor had reason to know. Thus, if a reasonable person in the position of the actor would have inferred that he or she was in wrongful possession of another's trade secret, the actor is subject to liability for any subsequent use or disclosure. A number of cases also subject an actor to liability if, based on the known facts, a reasonable person would have inquired further and learned that possession of the information was wrongful. Studious ignorance of the circumstances surrounding the acquisition of the information thus will not necessarily avoid liability under this Section. Among the facts relevant in establishing the actor's actual or constructive knowledge are the actor's knowledge of any precautions against disclosure taken by the trade secret owner, the actor's familiarity with industry customs or practices that would justify an assumption that a disclosure to the actor by a third person was unauthorized, information known to the actor regarding the nature of the relationship between the trade secret owner and the person from whom the actor acquired the secret, and any direct communications to the actor from the trade secret owner. The actor's reliance on claims of ownership or other assurances given by the person from whom the actor acquired the information is sufficient to avoid liability only if the actor's reliance is reasonable under the circumstances.

If an actor possesses the actual or constructive knowledge required under Subsection (b)(2)-(4) of this Section at the time of the initial acquisition of the secret, the actor is subject to liability for all use or disclosure of the trade secret. If the actor obtains such knowledge after acquisition of the trade secret, the actor is subject to liability for any use or disclosure occurring subsequent to receipt of the requisite knowledge, but is not liable for prior use or disclosure. However, although receipt of the requisite knowledge is sufficient to subject the actor to liability for subsequent conduct, the relief available to the trade secret owner may be limited by the equities of the case. Thus, if before receiving the required knowledge the actor has in good faith paid value for the trade secret, undertaken significant investment in equipment or research relating to the secret, or otherwise substantially changed its position in reliance on the information, the imposition of particular remedies for subsequent use or disclosure may be inappropriate. See § 44, Comment *b*; § 45, Comment *b*.

Illustrations:

2. *A*, a manufacturer of paints, developed a secret process for the production of exterior house paint. The process was revealed to *B*, a laboratory assistant in *A* 's research department, after *B* agreed not to disclose the information to unauthorized persons. Upon leaving the employment with *A*, *B* accepted a position in the research department of *C*, a competing paint manufacturer. *C* had tried unsuccessfully for several years to duplicate *A* 's process and was aware of *B* 's prior employment in *A* 's laboratory. Three weeks after joining *C* 's research staff, *B* submitted a report to *C* describing a process that produced paints identical to *A* 's. The process was immediately implemented by *C*. A court may properly conclude that *C* knew or had reason to know that *B* had made an unauthorized disclosure of *A* 's trade secret and that *C* is therefore subject to liability to *A* under the rule stated in Subsection (b)(3) of this Section.

3. *A*, the owner of computer software containing trade secrets relating to the efficient operation of assembly lines, dis-

closes the software in confidence to *B*, a computer consultant. *B* subsequently offers to sell the software to *C*, a manufacturer. *C* neither knows nor has reason to know that the software contains trade secrets belonging to *A*. *C* purchases the software from *B* for $100,000 and substantially modifies its computer system and assembly line to accommodate the new software. After *C* has used the software for one year, *A* learns of the improper disclosure by *B* and notifies *C* of the circumstances surrounding *B* 's acquisition of the software. *C* is not subject to liability to *A* for use of the software prior to the receipt of *A* 's notice. *C* is subject to liability to *A* for any use of the software subsequent to the notice, but the relief available to *A* may be limited because of *C* 's good faith purchase and subsequent expenditures in implementing the system. See § 44, Comment *b* ; § 45, Comment *b*.

e. Accidental disclosure. An accidental or mistaken disclosure of the trade secret to the actor under the rule stated in Subsection (b)(4) of this Section may result from a mistake by the owner of the trade secret, the actor, or a third person. If the disclosure to the actor is not the result of the owner's failure to take reasonable precautions to protect the trade secret, an actor who knows or has reason to know that the information is a trade secret that has been disclosed to the actor through an accident or mistake is subject to liability for subsequent use or disclosure. If the actor in good faith has substantially changed its position in reliance on the information prior to acquiring the requisite knowledge, however, the relief available to the trade secret owner may be appropriately limited. See § 44, Comment *b* ; § 45, Comment *b*.

Illustration:

4. The identities of the customers doing business with *A*, a brokerage firm, are found to qualify for protection as a trade secret under the rule stated in § 39. All of *A* 's customer lists are kept in locked rooms and employees are instructed that all information regarding customer identities is confidential. *A* 's employees have been directed to shred all waste paper containing customer names before releasing the paper to *B*, a waste paper dealer. An employee of *A* who was instructed to dispose of excess envelopes did not realize that the envelopes had already been addressed to *A* 's customers and did not shred the envelopes before delivering them to *B*. *C*, a competing brokerage firm, purchased the envelopes from *B* at waste paper prices with knowledge that the delivery of the envelopes to *B* was a mistake. *C* uses the information to solicit *A* 's customers. If the court finds that *C* 's acquisition of the customer identities was not the result

of a failure by *A* to take reasonable precautions to protect the confidentiality of the information, *C* is subject to liability to *A* under the rule stated in Subsection (b)(4) of this Section.

REPORTERS' NOTE

The prior Restatement of this topic limited liability for the appropriation of trade secrets to instances of wrongful use or disclosure. See Restatement of Torts § 757 (1939). This Section follows § 1(2)(i) of the Uniform Trade Secrets Act in also recognizing liability for the acquisition of a trade secret by improper means.

Comment a. The scope of the rule stated in this Section is intended to be identical with the coverage of the Uniform Trade Secrets Act, described in its Prefatory Note as encompassing "the various property, quasi-contractual, and violation of fiduciary relationship theories of noncontractual liability utilized at common law." See also § 7 of the Act, which expressly preserves common law actions for contractual remedies relating to trade secrets and "other civil remedies that are not based upon misappropriation of a trade secret." See, e.g., Micro Display Systems, Inc. v. Axtel, Inc., 699 F.Supp. 202 (D.Minn.1988) (causes of action not dependent on the misuse of trade secrets are not displaced by the Uniform Trade Secrets Act); Rehabilitation Specialists, Inc. v. Koering, 404 N.W.2d 301 (Minn.App.1987) (action for breach of an employee's duty of loyalty through solicitation of the employer's customers during the term of employment is not displaced by the Act). Similarly, neither the Uniform Trade Secrets Act nor this Section is applicable to actions for breaches of confidence involving subject matter outside the scope of trade secret law. See, e.g., Boeing Co. v. Sierracin Corp., 108 Wash.2d 38, 738 P.2d 665 (1987) (dictum describing the preemptive scope of the Act); Saliterman v. Finney, 361 N.W.2d 175 (Minn.App.1985).

Actions for breach of contract are not within the scope of this Section and are similarly excluded from the scope of the Uniform Trade Secrets Act. See the Comment accompanying § 7 of the Act. The existence of a contract, however, does not preclude a separate cause of action for trade secret appropriation under the rules stated here. See, e.g., Zoecon Industries v. American Stockman Tag Co., 713 F.2d 1174 (5th Cir.1983); Klockner–Humboldt–Deutz Aktiengellschaft, Koln v. Hewitt–Robins, Inc., 205 U.S.P.Q. 257 (D.S.C.1978); Den–Tal–Ez, Inc. v. Siemens Capital Corp., 9 U.S.P.Q.2d 1932 (Pa.Super.1988); Boeing Co., *supra* (affirming liability for both trade secret appropriation under the Uniform Trade Secrets Act and breach of contract). The distinction between contract and tort theories may have implications for issues such as choice of law, see Jager, Trade Secrets Law § 4.02, jurisdiction, see *id.* § 4.01[1], and the applicable statute of limitations, see *id.* § 4.03.

The relevant limitations period in trade secret actions at common law is determined by the statute of limitations applicable to tort actions, frequently that for injury to personal property, see, e.g, Construction Technology, Inc. v. Lockformer Co., 704

F.Supp. 1212 (S.D.N.Y.1989) (New York law); USM Corp. v. Tremco Inc., 710 F.Supp. 1140 (N.D.Ohio 1988) (Ohio law), or for miscellaneous torts, see, e.g., Whittaker Corp. v. Execuair Corp., 736 F.2d 1341 (9th Cir.1984) (California law); AVCO Corp. v. Precision Air Parts, Inc., 676 F.2d 494 (11th Cir.), cert. denied 459 U.S. 1037, 103 S.Ct. 450, 74 L.Ed.2d 604 (1982) (Alabama law). Some common law decisions treat the appropriation of a trade secret as a continuing tort, thus permitting the trade secret owner to seek relief for any misuse occurring during the statutory period, even if the defendant first commenced use outside the limitations period. See Underwater Storage, Inc. v. United States Rubber Co., 371 F.2d 950 (D.C.Cir.1966), cert. denied 386 U.S. 911, 87 S.Ct. 859, 17 L.Ed.2d 784 (1967); Anaconda Co. v. Metric Tool & Die Co., 485 F.Supp. 410 (E.D.Pa.1980). Other decisions hold that there is no continuing tort with respect to use occurring after a public disclosure of the secret. See Prescott v. Morton Int'l, Inc., 769 F.Supp. 404 (D.Mass.1990); Construction Technology, *supra*; Kistler Instrumente A.G. v. PCB Piezotronics, Inc., 419 F.Supp. 120 (W.D.N.Y. 1976). Still others reject any attempt to avoid the limitations period through a continuing tort theory. See, e.g., Avco Corp., *supra*; Monolith Portland Midwest Co. v. Kaiser Aluminum & Chemical Corp., 407 F.2d 288 (9th Cir.1969). Results also differ as to the effect of a plaintiff's ignorance of the appropriation. Compare Monolith Portland Midwest, *supra*, with Whittaker Corp., *supra*. Actions under the Uniform Trade Secrets Act are subject to the three-year limitations period provided in § 6 of the Act, measured from the time the appropriation was or should have been discovered. The Act rejects the continuing tort theory, see, e.g., Intermedics, Inc. v. Ventritex, Inc., 822 F.Supp. 634 (N.D.Cal.1993), although it is unclear whether violations of the separate substantive standards prohibiting improper acquisition and unauthorized use or disclosure, or disclosures by a defendant to several persons, constitute independent appropriations under the Act. Compare Ashton–Tate Corp. v. Ross, 916 F.2d 516 (9th Cir.1990) (later unauthorized use following initial improper acquisition does not extend the limitations period) with McCormack & Dodge Corp. v. ABC Management Systems, Inc., 222 U.S.P.Q. 432 (Wash.Super.1983) (each unauthorized sale of a software system incorporating the trade secret is an independent appropriation under the Act). See also Intermedics, *supra* (no separate appropriation with respect to other trade secrets acquired from the plaintiff in the same transaction). Even if the limitations period has run with respect to an action against the initial appropriator, actions against third persons who acquire the trade secret with knowledge of the appropriation are not necessarily barred. See USM Corp., *supra* (common law). See generally Jager, *supra*, § 4.03; Milgrim on Trade Secrets § 7.04.

Cases reciting the elements of a cause of action for trade secret appropriation are collected in Jager, *supra*, § 5.04[1]; Milgrim, *supra*, § 7.07[1]. The plaintiff bears the burden of proving the existence of a trade secret and appropriation by the defendant. E.g., Air Products and Chemicals, Inc. v. Chas. S. Tanner Co., 219 U.S.P.Q. 223 (D.S.C.1983); Engineered Mechanical Services, Inc. v. Langlois, 464 So.2d 329 (La.App.

1984). "Trade secret processes are not passed upon officially, as are patented processes. Therefore, they are attended by no presumptions and the burden of proof is on the plaintiff * * *." Cataphote Corp. v. Hudson, 444 F.2d 1313, 1316–17 (5th Cir.1971). The burden is similar under the Uniform Trade Secrets Act. See, e.g., Boeing Co. v. Sierracin Corp., 108 Wash.2d 38, 738 P.2d 665 (1987).

A proprietary interest in a trade secret can be established through evidence of either discovery or acquisition of ownership. See, e.g., Rohm and Haas Co. v. Adco Chemical Co., 689 F.2d 424 (3d Cir.1982) (discovery and retention of rights); Van Products Co. v. General Welding and Fabricating Co., 419 Pa. 248, 213 A.2d 769 (1965) (plaintiff must establish rights through discovery or ownership). Mere possession is insufficient to establish a proprietary interest. See Water Management, Inc. v. Stayanchi, 15 Ohio St.3d 83, 472 N.E.2d 715 (1984) (a former employee was not liable for appropriation because the alleged trade secrets belonged to the plaintiff's customers); Ancraft Products Co. v. Universal Oil Products Co., 84 Ill.App.3d 836, 40 Ill.Dec. 70, 405 N.E.2d 1162 (1980) (denying relief since the plaintiff had possession but not ownership of the plans embodying the secrets). Cf. Sims v. Mack Truck Corp., 608 F.2d 87 (3d Cir.1979), cert. denied 445 U.S. 930, 100 S.Ct. 1319, 63 L.Ed.2d 764 (1980) (summary judgment denied because of a dispute as to the plaintiff's ownership). Some courts have found a sufficient proprietary interest in an exclusive licensee of the trade secret. See Frank M. Denison, D.D.S., Inc. v. Westmore Dental Arts, P.C., 212 U.S.P.Q. 601 (W.D.Pa.1981); Koch Engineering Co. v. Faulconer, 227 Kan. 813, 610 P.2d 1094 (1980). On the possibility of multiple ownership through independent discovery, see Uniform Trade Secrets Act, Comment to § 1; Surgidev Corp. v. Eye Technology, Inc., 648 F.Supp. 661 (D.Minn.1986), affirmed 828 F.2d 452 (8th Cir.1987) (dictum); Electro–Craft Corp. v. Controlled Motion, Inc., 332 N.W.2d 890 (Minn.1983) (dictum). Although an occasional case lists detriment to the trade secret owner as an element of the cause of action for appropriation, see, e.g., Continental Data Systems, Inc. v. Exxon Corp., 638 F.Supp. 432 (E.D.Pa.1986), neither the Uniform Trade Secrets Act nor the former statement of the rule in Restatement of Torts § 757 (1939) requires such proof. Although use within the scope of consent given by the trade secret owner does not subject the user to liability, use that exceeds the consent can be actionable. See, e.g., McCormack & Dodge Corp. v. ABC Management Systems, Inc., 222 U.S.P.Q. 432 (Wash.Super.1983) (licensee liable for use outside the geographic scope of the license).

Comment b. Cases that list use or disclosure by the defendant as an element of the cause of action for trade secret appropriation typically involve employees or other defendants whose initial acquisition of the secret was not improper. See, e.g., Texas Urethane, Inc. v. Seacrest Marine Corp., 608 F.2d 136 (5th Cir. 1979); E.W. Bliss Co. v. Struthers–Dunn, Inc., 408 F.2d 1108 (8th Cir. 1969); Heyman v. AR. Winarick, Inc., 325 F.2d 584 (2d Cir.1963); SCM Corp. v. Union Camp Corp., 169 U.S.P.Q. 140 (M.D.Fla.1970). But cf. Metallurgical Industries Inc. v. Fourtek, Inc., 790 F.2d 1195 (5th Cir.1986) (no liability absent use even when the defendant learned the trade secret with notice that the disclosure was improper).

Section 1(2)(i) of the Uniform Trade Secrets Act recognizes liability for the improper acquisition of a trade secret as distinguished from any subsequent use or disclosure. See, e.g., Minuteman, Inc. v. Alexander, 147 Wis.2d 842, 434 N.W.2d 773 (1989); Rehabilitation Specialists, Inc. v. Koering, 404 N.W.2d 301 (Minn.App.1987). Cf. Sybron Corp. v. Wetzel, 46 N.Y.2d 197, 413 N.Y.S.2d 127, 385 N.E.2d 1055 (1978) (hiring of a competitor's former employee with an intent to appropriate the competitor's trade secrets is itself a tortious act at common law for purposes of jurisdiction under the state long-arm statute).

Comment c. "Use" is not limited to the sale of goods embodying or produced by means of the trade secret. See, e.g., Telex Corp. v. Int'l Business Machines Corp., 510 F.2d 894 (10th Cir.), cert. dismissed 423 U.S. 802, 96 S.Ct. 8, 46 L.Ed.2d 244 (1975) (use found through a reduction in defendant's research costs on a product abandoned prior to marketing); Engelhard Industries, Inc. v. Research Instrumental Corp., 324 F.2d 347 (9th Cir.1963), cert. denied 377 U.S. 923, 84 S.Ct. 1220, 12 L.Ed.2d 215 (1964) (defendant held liable although its product incorporating the trade secret was not actually sold until after a public disclosure of the secret by the plaintiff); United Parcel Service v. Chandler, 1993 WL 21070 (D.N.J.1993) (use by the defendant in filing a patent application); Continental Data Systems, Inc. v. Exxon Corp., 638 F.Supp. 432 (E.D.Pa.1986) (defendant's lack of sales is not a defense) (dictum). But cf. Hurst v. Hughes Tool Co., 634 F.2d 895 (5th Cir.), cert. denied 454 U.S. 829, 102 S.Ct. 123, 70 L.Ed.2d 105 (1981) (dictum that learning "what not to do" is insufficient to constitute "use" of a trade secret, at least when the secret is not a major part of the defendant's data). See also Metallurgical Industries Inc. v. Fourtek, Inc., 790 F.2d 1195 (5th Cir. 1986) (no use found by a purchaser of equipment incorporating the plaintiff's trade secrets since the equipment had not been placed into operation). On solicitation as a "use" of customer identities, see, e.g., MAI Systems Corp. v. Peak Computer, Inc., 991 F.2d 511 (9th Cir.1993), cert. dismissed ___ U.S. ___, 114 S.Ct. 671, 126 L.Ed.2d 640 (1994) and American Credit Indemnity Co. v. Sacks, 213 Cal.App.3d 622, 262 Cal.Rptr. 92 (1989), both distinguishing an announcement of new employment from a solicitation of customers.

Use of a modified or improved version of the trade secret will not avoid liability if the version is substantially derived from the protected information. See, e.g., In re Innovative Construction Systems, Inc., 793 F.2d 875 (7th Cir.1986); Sikes v. McGraw–Edison Co., 665 F.2d 731 (5th Cir.), cert. denied 458 U.S. 1108, 102 S.Ct. 3488, 73 L.Ed.2d 1369 (1982); Tri–Tron Int'l v. Velto, 525 F.2d 432 (9th Cir. 1975); Cataphote Corp. v. Hudson, 422 F.2d 1290 (5th Cir.1970) (drawing an analogy to the doctrine of equivalents in patent law); Affiliated Hospital Products, Inc. v. Baldwin, 57 Ill. App.3d 800, 15 Ill.Dec. 528, 373 N.E.2d 1000 (1978); Sinclair v. Aquarius Electronics, Inc., 42 Cal. App.3d 216, 116 Cal.Rptr. 654 (1974). Even if the defendant's final product or process differs significantly from that of the plaintiff, substantial use of the trade secret in the course of the defendant's research can be sufficient to constitute an appropriation. See, e.g., Superior Flux & Mfg. Co. v. H & S Industries, Inc., 210 U.S.P.Q. 669 (N.D.Ohio 1980). If, despite the defendant's knowledge of the plaintiff's trade secret, the defendant's product or process results from independent creation or information in the public domain, the defendant is not subject to liability. See, e.g, American Can Co. v. Mansukhani, 742 F.2d 314 (7th Cir.1984); Reinforced Earth Co. v. Neumann, 201 U.S.P.Q. 205 (D.Md. 1978); Selection Research Inc. v. Murman, 230 Neb. 786, 433 N.W.2d 526 (1989).

Proof of a disclosure to the defendant and similarities between the products or processes of the parties can create an inference of use by the defendant. E.g., Phillips v. Frey, 20 F.3d 623 (5th Cir.1994); Smith v. Dravo Corp., 203 F.2d 369 (7th Cir. 1953); Sims v. Mack Truck Corp., 488 F.Supp. 592 (E.D.Pa.1980); Mann v. Tatge Chemical Co., 201 Kan. 326, 440 P.2d 640 (1968). Cf. Garter–Bare Co. v. Munsingwear Inc., 723 F.2d 707 (9th Cir.), cert. denied 469 U.S. 980, 105 S.Ct. 381, 83 L.Ed.2d 316 (1984) (shifting "burden" to the defendant); Integrated Cash Management Services, Inc. v. Digital Transactions, Inc., 732 F.Supp. 370 (S.D.N.Y.1989), affirmed 920 F.2d 171 (2d Cir.1990) (same); Kamin v. Kuhnau, 232 Or. 139, 374 P.2d 912 (1962) (same). The similarities, however, must be evaluated in light of the scope of the trade secret and the content of the public domain. See, e.g., American Can Co., *supra* (similarities are less probative of use when there is an extensive public domain); Berry v. Glidden Co., 92 F.Supp. 909 (S.D.N.Y.1950).

On liability for unauthorized disclosure of trade secrets, see, e.g., Precision Plating & Metal Finishing Inc. v. Martin–Marietta Corp., 435 F.2d 1262 (5th Cir.1970), cert. denied 404 U.S. 1002, 92 S.Ct. 571, 30 L.Ed.2d 556 (1971) (monetary relief for public disclosure of a trade secret); CPG Products Corp. v. Mego Corp., 214 U.S.P.Q. 206 (S.D.Ohio 1981) (threat of destruction of the trade secret through disclosure justified a preliminary injunction). Cf. 18 U.S.C.A. § 1905, imposing criminal liability for unauthorized disclosure of trade secrets by federal employees. Injunctions in trade secret cases frequently prohibit both unauthorized use and disclosure. See, e.g., Drill Parts & Service Co. v. Joy Mfg. Co., 439 So.2d 43 (Ala.1983) (injunction against use or sale of drawings containing trade secrets).

The existence in some circumstances of a privilege to disclose another's trade secret was briefly noted in Restatement of Torts § 757, Comment *d* (1939). See System Operations, Inc. v. Scientific Games Dev. Corp., 425 F.Supp. 130 (D.N.J.1977) (dictum indicating that a state lottery director could disclose to the lottery ticket manufacturer trade secrets of another company relating to the testing and security of tickets, citing the former Restatement); Re v. Horstmann, 1987 WL 16710 (Del.Super.1987) (recognizing a privilege to disclose to law enforcement officials trade secrets relevant to criminal fraud that had been disclosed to the defendants in confidence, citing the former Restatement). Cf. United States v. Wallington, 889 F.2d 573 (5th Cir.1989) (upholding a federal statute prohibiting the disclosure of trade secrets by federal employees, but noting in dictum that in an "extraordinary" case an employee's constitutional interest in free expression might outweigh the interest in confidentiality); Lachman v. Sperry–Sun Well Surveying Co., 457 F.2d 850 (10th Cir.1972) (refusing to impose liability for breach of a nondisclosure provision in a contract to survey an oil well when the survey company disclosed to the adjoining landowner that the well encroached on the landowner's property). The policies underlying the privilege are similar to those supporting the numerous state and federal "whistleblower" statutes that prohibit retaliatory personnel actions by employers against employees who disclose violations to public officials. See, e.g., 5 U.S.C.A. § 2320(b)(8); Mich.Comp.Laws §§ 15.361–369; N.Y.Lab.Law § 740. But cf. Cal.Lab.Code § 1102.5(c) (expressly excluding from the protection of the statute actions of employees that violate the confidentiality of trade secrets). That there is no absolute right under the first amendment to disclose truthful confidential information, even by the media, see, e.g., Cohen v. Cowles Media Co., 501 U.S. 663, 111 S.Ct. 2513, 115 L.Ed.2d 586 (1991) (first amendment does not prevent an award of damages for breach of a promise of confidentiality made by a newspaper); Seattle Times Co. v. Rhinehart, 467 U.S. 20, 104 S.Ct. 2199, 81 L.Ed.2d 17 (1984) (a newspaper defendant in a defamation action had no constitutional right to disseminate information acquired through discovery in violation of a protective order). Cf., e.g., Standard & Poor's Corp. v. Commodity Exchange, Inc., 541 F.Supp. 1273 (S.D.N.Y.1982) (denying a motion by a newspaper to vacate an order sealing a hearing transcript that contained trade secrets).

Comment d. A defendant is not liable for the use or disclosure of another's trade secret absent actual or constructive knowledge that the use or disclosure is wrongful. See, e.g., Amberley Co. v. Brown Co., 408 F.2d 1358 (6th Cir.1969); Ferroline Corp. v. General Aniline & Film Corp., 207 F.2d 912 (7th Cir.1953), cert. denied 347 U.S. 953, 74 S.Ct. 678, 98 L.Ed. 1098 (1954) (burden of proving the requisite knowledge is on the plaintiff); Conmar Products Corp. v. Universal Slide Fastener Co., 172 F.2d 150 (2d Cir.1949); Construction Technology, Inc. v. Lockformer Co., 704 F.Supp. 1212 (S.D.N.Y.1989); Computer Print Systems, Inc. v. Lewis, 281 Pa.Super. 240, 422 A.2d 148 (1980). But cf. Koehring Co. v. National Automatic Tool Co., 257 F.Supp. 282 (S.D.Ind. 1966), affirmed 385 F.2d 414 (7th Cir. 1967) (defendant is liable for unjust enrichment resulting from innocent use). When the defendant knows that its possession of the secret is improper, it is subject to liability for any subsequent use or disclosure. E.g., Servo Corp. v. General Electric Co., 337 F.2d 716 (4th Cir.1964), cert. denied 383 U.S. 934, 86 S.Ct. 1061, 15 L.Ed.2d 851 (1966); FMC Corp. v. Spurlin, 596 F.Supp. 609 (W.D.Pa. 1984) (denying summary judgment because of a dispute as to the defendant's knowledge); Anaconda Co. v. Metric Tool & Die Co., 485 F.Supp. 410 (E.D.Pa.1980); Tabor v. Hoffman, 118 N.Y. 30, 23 N.E. 12 (1889).

Actual knowledge is not required in order to subject a defendant to liability for the use or disclosure of another's trade secret. Uniform Trade Secrets Act § 1(2) ("reason to know"); Computer Assoc. Int'l, Inc. v. Altai, Inc., 982 F.2d 693 (2d Cir.1992) ("constructive notice is sufficient"); Anaconda Co., *supra* ("knew or should have known"); Ralph Andrews Productions, Inc. v. Paramount Pictures Corp., 222 Cal.App.3d 676, 271 Cal. Rptr. 797 (1990) ("constructive notice"); Curtiss–Wright Corp. v. Edel–Brown Tool & Die Co., 381 Mass. 1, 407 N.E.2d 319 (1980) (knows or "should know"). A defendant may be subject to liability if under the facts a reasonable person would have inquired further and gained the required knowledge. See, e.g., Computer Associates, *supra*; Metallurgical Industries Inc. v. Fourtek, Inc., 790 F.2d 1195 (5th Cir.1986); Rohm and Haas Co. v. Adco Chemical Co., 689 F.2d 424 (3d Cir.1982); Colgate–Palmolive Co. v. Carter Products, Inc., 230 F.2d 855 (4th Cir.), cert. denied 352 U.S. 843, 77 S.Ct. 43, 1 L.Ed.2d 59 (1956); Ralph Andrews Productions, *supra*; Curtiss–Wright Corp., *supra*. Cf. Hard Rock Cafe Licensing Corp. v. Concession Services, Inc., 955 F.2d 1143 (7th Cir.1992) (stating in a trademark case that "willful blindness is equivalent to actual knowledge").

Cases indicating that a defendant is not liable for use or disclosure unless it knows or has reason to know that the information in its possession is a secret include Data General Corp. v. Grumman Systems Support Corp., 825 F.Supp. 340 (D.Mass.1993); *Anaconda Co., supra*; *Curtiss–Wright Corp., supra*. Facts establishing the defendant's actual or constructive knowledge of the impropriety of the acquisition are also ordinarily sufficient to establish knowledge of the secrecy of the information. See Restatement of Torts § 757, Comment *m* (1939).

Letters and other communications sent to the defendant by the trade secret owner can establish that the defendant knew its use or disclosure was wrongful. See, e.g., Cybertek Computer Products, Inc. v. Whitfield, 203 U.S.P.Q. 1020 (Cal.Super.1977); Components for Research, Inc. v. Isolation Products, Inc., 241 Cal.App.2d 726, 50 Cal.Rptr. 829 (1966). The defendant's familiarity with practices or customs in the industry that would suggest that a third person's disclosure to the defendant was unauthorized is also relevant. See, e.g., Warrington Associates, Inc. v. Real–Time Engineering Systems, Inc., 522 F.Supp. 367 (N.D.Ill.1981); Ralph Andrews Productions, *supra*; Curtiss–Wright Corp., *supra*. Cf. Conmar Products Corp., *supra* (lack of industry custom of confidentiality is evidence of the defendant's good faith). The extent of the defendant's knowledge of the disclosing party's employment or other relationship with the trade secret owner is similarly relevant. See, e.g., Colgate–Palmolive Co., *supra*. See also Data General, *supra* (the defendant's knowledge must often be proven by circumstantial evidence). Reliance on assurances given by the disclosing party will not necessarily avoid liability. See, e.g., Lamb–Weston, Inc. v. McCain Foods, Ltd., 941 F.2d 970 (9th Cir.1991); Metallurgical Industries, *supra*; Ralph Andrews Productions, *supra*.

If the defendant learns that it has unauthorized possession of another's trade secret only after a period of innocent exploitation, it is subject to liability only for any subsequent use. See Forest Laboratories, Inc. v. Pillsbury Co., 452 F.2d 621 (7th Cir.1971); Conmar Products Corp., *supra*; Computer Print Systems, *supra*. The statement of the rule in Restatement of Torts § 758 (1939) could preclude the imposition of liability against a person who had in good faith paid value for the information or otherwise substantially changed position in reliance on the information prior to the receipt of notice. This Section adopts the rule in § 2 and § 3 of the Uniform Trade Secrets Act, which treat a material and prejudicial change of position prior to notice as relevant only to the appropriateness of particular remedies for subsequent use. See the Comment to § 2 of the Act.

Illustration 2 is suggested by the facts in Rohm and Haas Co. v. Adco Chemical Co., 689 F.2d 424 (3d Cir. 1982). In connection with Illustration 3, compare *Conmar Products Corp., supra* (defendant's good faith investment in equipment outweighed plaintiff's interest in protection against use subsequent to notice) with *Forest Laboratories, supra*, and *Computer Print Systems, supra*, both rejecting defendants' claims of good faith purchase on the facts.

Comment e. The rule in Subsection (b)(4) relating to accidental disclosure is carried forward from Restatement of Torts § 757(d) (1939). See also Uniform Trade Secrets Act § 1(2)(ii)(C). The Comment accompanying the Act emphasizes that a defendant is not liable if the accidental or mistaken disclosure results from a failure by the trade secret owner to take reasonable precautions to maintain the secrecy of the information.

Illustration 4 is based on B.C. Ziegler and Co. v. Ehren, 141 Wis.2d 19, 414 N.W.2d 48 (App.1987). See Williams v. Curtiss–Wright Corp., 681 F.2d 161 (3d Cir.1982) (preliminary injunction issued against the use of a trade secret that may have been erroneously disclosed to the defendant by a customer of the plaintiff); Myers v. Williams, 819 F.Supp. 919 (D.Or.1993) (preliminary injunction granted against threatened disclosure of a drug formula mistakenly released by the FDA in response to a Freedom of Information Act request); Drill Parts & Service Co. v. Joy Mfg. Co., 439 So.2d 43 (Ala.1983) (injunction issued against use or disclosure by a defendant who obtained secret plans bearing a restrictive legend from the trash of a subcontractor of the plaintiff). But cf. Kewanee Oil Co. v. Bicron Corp., 416 U.S. 470, 94 S.Ct. 1879, 40 L.Ed.2d 315 (1974) (dictum listing "accidental disclosure" as a fair means of acquisition). If the accidental disclosure results from the trade secret owner's failure to take reasonable precautions to protect the secrecy of the information, the defendant is not subject to liability. See Defiance Button Machine Co. v. C & C Metal Products Corp., 759 F.2d 1053 (2d Cir.), cert. denied 474 U.S. 844, 106 S.Ct. 131, 88 L.Ed.2d 108 (1985) (plaintiff held not entitled to protection for a customer list accidentally left in the memory of a computer sold to the defendant); Fisher Stoves, Inc. v. All Nighter Stove Works, Inc., 626 F.2d 193 (1st Cir. 1980) (dictum indicating that the plaintiff could not prevent defendant's use of a list of plaintiff's dealers accidentally left by the plaintiff at the defendant's store).

§ 41. Duty of Confidence

A person to whom a trade secret has been disclosed owes a duty of confidence to the owner of the trade secret for purposes of the rule stated in § 40 if:

(a) the person made an express promise of confidentiality prior to the disclosure of the trade secret; or

(b) the trade secret was disclosed to the person under circumstances in which the relationship between the parties to the disclosure or the other facts surrounding the disclosure justify the conclusions that, at the time of the disclosure,

(1) the person knew or had reason to know that the disclosure was intended to be in confidence, and

(2) the other party to the disclosure was reasonable in inferring that the person consented to an obligation of confidentiality.

Comment:

a. Scope. This Section describes when the recipient of a trade secret disclosure is bound by a duty of confidence. Section 42 treats the special considerations that influence the application of the principles discussed in this Section when the disclosure occurs within an employment relationship.

b. Confidential disclosures. A duty of confidence enforceable under the rules stated in § 40 can be created by an express promise of confidentiality made by the recipient of the disclosure. A duty of confidence may also be inferred from the relationship between the parties and the circumstances surrounding the disclosure. However, no duty of confidence will be inferred unless the recipient has notice of the confidential nature of the disclosure. Although no specific form of notice is required, the circumstances must indicate that the recipient knew or had reason to know that the disclosure was intended as confidential. In addition, the circumstances must justify the other party's belief that the recipient has consented to the duty of confidence. Thus, a disclosure to one who has indicated an unwillingness to accept the confidence or who has no opportunity prior to the disclosure to object to the imposition of the confidence will not create an obligation of confidentiality in the recipient.

In some cases the customs of the particular business or industry may be sufficient to indicate to the recipient that a particular disclosure is intended as confidential. The customary expectations surrounding the disclosure of information in noncommercial settings may differ from those arising in connection with disclosures in commercial contexts. The customary expectations regarding the confidentiality of information disclosed within the research facilities of an industrial firm, for example, may differ from those regarding disclosures in a nonprofit research laboratory. Precautions undertaken by the trade secret owner to maintain the secrecy of the information, if known to the recipient, can be evidence that the recipient knew or had reason to know of the owner's expectation of confidentiality. Solicitation of the disclosure by the recipient can also contribute to an inference of confidentiality, particularly if the disclosure is prompted by a misrepresentation or other improper conduct on the part of the recipient. In some cases an express agreement regarding the confidentiality of particular information may be evidence of the parties' expectations regarding the confidentiality of other information not within the scope of the agreement.

If the owner of a trade secret discloses information for a limited purpose that is known to the recipient at the time of the disclosure, the recipient is ordinarily bound by the limitation unless the recipient has indicated an unwillingness to accept the disclosure on such terms. During negotiations with prospective buyers, customers, or licensees, for example, it is sometimes necessary to disclose trade secrets in order to permit the other party to evaluate the merits of the proposed transaction. The law of trade secrets provides the necessary assurance that the limited purpose of such disclosures will be respected.

In the absence of an agreement to the contrary, the sale of a product embodying a trade secret is not ordinarily regarded as a confidential disclosure. The purchaser is thus free to exploit any information acquired through an examination or analysis of the product. However, a transaction such as a lease or a bailment may be more likely to support an inference of confidentiality if the parties understand the transfer to be for a limited purpose. The transfer of a machine embodying trade secrets for the purpose of repair, for example, does not ordinarily authorize the transferee to use or disclose trade secrets learned as a result of the transaction.

Courts frequently recognize an obligation to refrain from the unauthorized use or disclosure of information that is communicated between parties in a so-called "confidential relationship." Certain business relationships such as employer-employee and licensor-licensee are sometimes characterized as "confidential." The fact that the parties are engaged in such an on-going relationship is relevant in determining whether a specific disclosure creates a duty of confidence, but not every disclosure made in the context of a particular relationship is properly treated as confidential. Even within a relationship generally characterized as "confidential," the purpose of the disclosure, the past practice of the parties, the customs of the industry, and the other circumstances of the disclosure remain relevant in determining the recipient's obligations. Thus, although the disclosure to a licensee of a secret formula that is the subject of a license is normally regarded as confidential, a disclosure of other information to a licensee with no indication that the information is confidential may not give rise to a duty of confidence. The special considerations applicable to disclosures within an employment relationship are considered in § 42.

Illustrations:

1. *A*, a manufacturer, develops a new food-processing machine that incorporates innovations eligible for protection as trade secrets. *B*, an engineering professor at a local university, asks permission from *A* to inspect the machine. *A* grants permission without expressing any need or desire for confidentiality. *B* subsequently uses information acquired during the inspection to design a competing machine. In the absence of evidence establishing that *B* knew or had reason to know that the inspection was intended by *A* to be for a limited purpose or was otherwise intended as confidential, *B* is not subject to liability under the rules stated in § 40.

2. *A* and *B* are negotiating for the sale of *A*'s soft drink business to *B*. *A* discloses the secret formula used to produce the soft drink in order to permit *B* to assess the value of *A*'s business. *B* subsequently terminates the negotiations and begins to use the formula. *B* is subject to liability to *A* under the rules stated in § 40 since *B* knew or had reason to know that the disclosure was for the limited purpose of enabling *B* to evaluate the merits of the proposed transaction.

3. The facts being otherwise as stated in Illustration 2, during the negotiations for *A*'s business *A* also discloses to *B* plans for a chain of fast-food restaurants that *A* intends to open after the soft drink business is sold. *B* subsequently opens several restaurants modeled after those described by *A*. Since the disclosure was not made for a limited purpose apparent from the nature of the parties' business relationship, *B* is not subject to liability to *A* under the rules stated in § 40 unless other evidence establishes that *B* knew or had reason to know that *A* intended the disclosure to be confidential and that *A* was reasonable in believing that *B* consented to the duty of confidence.

c. Breach of confidence as a separate tort. Some courts have recognized liability in tort for the unauthorized disclosure of confidential business information found to be ineligible for protection as a trade secret. In some cases the claim is designated as one for "breach of confidence," while in others it is described as one for "unfair competition." Many of these cases rest on a narrow definition of "trade secret" that excludes non-technical information such as customer identities or information that is not subject to continuous, long-term use. Such information is now subsumed under the broader definition of "trade secret" adopted in § 39. In other cases the imposition of liability for breach of confidence may be justified by interests other than the protection of valuable commercial information, such as the interests that prompt recognition of the general duty of loyalty owed by an employee to an employer, see § 42, Comment *b*, or the special duties of confidence owed in particular relationships such as attorney and client or doctor and patient. However, in the absence of interests justifying broader duties, the plaintiff should be required to demonstrate that the information qualifies for protection as a trade secret under the rule stated in § 39. The recognition of more extensive rights against the use or disclosure of commercial information can restrict access to knowledge that is properly regarded as part of the public domain. Cf. § 39, Comment *f*.

d. Contractual protection of trade secrets. The owner of a trade secret may seek protection against unauthorized use or disclosure through a contract with the recipient of a disclosure. Such contracts may take several forms, including a promise by the recipient not to compete with the trade secret owner, a general promise to refrain from disclosing or using any confidential information acquired within the context of a particular relationship or transaction, or a promise to refrain from using or disclosing particular information specified in the agreement. Use or disclosure in violation of such agreements can result in liability for breach of contract under the rules stated in the Restatement, Second, of Contracts. However, since such agreements can reduce or eliminate potential competition, they are subject to the traditional rules governing contracts in restraint of trade and are accordingly enforceable only when ancillary to a valid transaction and otherwise reasonable. See Restatement, Second, Contracts §§ 186–188. As a general matter, a restraint is unreasonable if it is greater than necessary to protect the legitimate interests of the promisee or if the promisee's interest in protection is outweighed by the likely harm to the promisor or to the public. *Id.* § 188, Comment *a*.

In many jurisdictions a reasonable covenant not to compete is enforceable against the promisor. The rules governing the protection of trade secrets as stated in this Restatement can sometimes be helpful in evaluating the reasonableness of such a covenant. A promise by an employee not to compete with the employer after the termination of the employment or by a seller of a business not to compete with the buyer after the sale may be justified as a reasonable attempt to protect confidential information, provided that the duration and geographic scope of the covenant are appropriately related to the promisee's legitimate interests. When this justification is offered to support the enforcement of a covenant not to compete, the rules governing trade secrets, although not determinative, can be useful in identifying both the legitimate interests served by the covenant and the appropriate limitations on the scope of protection.

The reasonableness of an agreement that merely prohibits the use or disclosure of particular information depends primarily upon whether the information protected by the agreement qualifies as a trade secret. If the information qualifies for protection under the rule stated in § 39, a contract prohibiting its use or disclosure is generally enforceable according to its terms. Although in some cases courts have enforced nondisclosure agreements directed at information found ineligible for protection as a trade secret, many of these decisions merely reflect a more narrow definition of trade secret than that adopted in § 39. However, a nondisclosure agreement that encompasses information that is generally known or in which the promisee has no protectable interest, such as a former employee's promise not to use information that is part of the employee's general skill and training (see § 42, Comment *d*), may be unenforceable as an unreasonable restraint of trade. Agreements that deny the promisor the right to use information that is in the public domain are ordinarily enforceable only if justified on the basis of interests other than the protection of confidential information.

Some courts have indicated that nondisclosure agreements are subject to the same durational and geographic limitations traditionally applied to covenants not to compete. However, a nondisclosure agreement can be reasonable even if the agreement is not limited to a specific geographic area. Once a secret is disclosed, knowledge of the information cannot normally be confined to a particular area. Unauthorized disclosure in any geographic area can therefore result in harm to the trade secret owner. Similarly, unauthorized use in any area may deprive the trade secret owner of potential licensing opportunities. Thus, although the more onerous burden of a covenant not to compete is normally enforceable only if confined within appropriate geographic limits, an absolute prohibition against the use or disclosure of a trade secret is ordinarily justified by the legitimate interests of the trade secret owner. The absence of an express duration on a promise not to use or disclose a trade secret should also not in itself render the agreement unenforceable since in the absence of a clear intention to the contrary a nondisclosure agreement is ordinarily interpreted as imposing an obligation of confidentiality only until the information becomes generally known or readily ascertainable by proper means. However, enforcement of an agreement that is interpreted to prohibit the promisor from using information even after it has entered the public domain cannot be justified by the interest in protecting confidential information, although it may be justified on some other basis. For example, licensing agreements that require the continuation of royalty payments for the use of a trade secret even after the secret becomes generally known are ordinarily enforceable. Such agreements may be justified as a reasonable attempt by the parties to measure the value of the head start obtained by the licensee through the initial disclosure of the trade secret. Similarly, in some circumstances an agreement not to use information that is in the public domain may be justified by a legitimate interest in protecting the reputation or good will of the promisee. The rules stated here do not purport to encompass the full range of justifications that may support the enforcement of an agreement not to use or disclose particular information. These rules may be helpful, however, in determining the appropriate limits on the enforceability of an agreement that the promisee seeks to justify on the basis of interests analogous to those protected under the law of trade secrets.

Illustrations:

4. *A* engages in a dry-cleaning business in a market with a radius of two miles. *A* sells the business and a secret process used in the business to *B*. In the absence of an applicable statute restricting or prohibiting enforcement of covenants not to compete, a promise by *A* not to engage in the dry-cleaning business is enforceable if the promise is limited to a reasonable time and to a radius of two miles.

5. The facts being otherwise as stated in Illustration 4, *A* also promises not to use or disclose the process, with no stated durational or geographic limitations. The promise is enforceable if interpreted to apply only until the process is no longer secret.

6. The facts being otherwise as stated in Illustration 5, *B* grants to *A* a license to use the secret process in other markets in return for royalty payments. Subsequently, the process falls into the public domain and others begin to use the process in competition with both *A* and *B*. *A*, although continuing to use the process, refuses to continue the royalty payments. If the agreement is interpreted to require *A* to continue the royalty payments even after the process is no longer secret, *B* may continue to enforce the royalty agreement against *A*.

REPORTERS' NOTE

Comment a. Disclosure or use of another's trade secret in breach of a duty of confidence was recognized as a basis of liability in Restatement of Torts § 757(b) (1939). Similar principles are applicable under § 1(2) of the Uniform Trade Secrets Act. See generally Jager, Trade Secrets Law § 5.04[3][b]; Milgrim on Trade Secrets § 4.03.

Comment b. A duty of confidence can be created by an express or implied-in-fact promise or by operation of law. Kamin v. Kuhnau, 232 Or. 139, 374 P.2d 912 (1962); Aerospace America, Inc. v. Abatement Technologies, Inc., 738 F.Supp. 1061 (E.D.Mich.1990). Even when the parties have entered into an express confidentiality agreement, a tort action under the rules stated in § 40 can be maintained for disclosure or use of the trade secret in violation of the confidence. See § 40, Comment *a* and the accompanying Reporters' Note.

A disclosure that occurs in a transaction carried on at arm's length is not ordinarily regarded as confidential absent evidence of a contrary understanding by the parties. Smith v. Snap–On Tools Corp., 833 F.2d 578 (5th Cir.1987); RTE Corp. v. Coatings, Inc., 84 Wis.2d 105, 267 N.W.2d 226 (1978). However, confidentiality may be inferred from the nature of the relationship between the parties, see Roberts v. Sears, Roebuck and Co., 573 F.2d 976 (7th Cir.), cert. denied 439 U.S. 860, 99 S.Ct. 179, 58 L.Ed.2d 168 (1978) (submission of an idea by an employee held to be in confidence), or from the customary practices of the industry, see Vantage Point, Inc. v. Parker Brothers, Inc., 529 F.Supp. 1204 (E.D.N.Y.1981), affirmed 697 F.2d 301 (2d Cir.1982).

If the circumstances of the disclosure do not otherwise indicate to the recipient that there is an expectation of confidentiality, the trade secret owner must give notice that the information is to be kept in confidence. See, e.g., Pacific Title, Inc. v. Pioneer National Title Ins. Co., 33 Wash.App. 874, 658 P.2d 684 (1983). The notification must precede the disclosure. See Smith, *supra* ; RTE Corp., *supra* (manufacturer sought to create a confidential relationship only after the disclosure); Hurst v. Hughes Tool Co., 634 F.2d 895 (5th Cir.), cert. denied 454 U.S. 829, 102 S.Ct. 123, 70 L.Ed.2d 105 (1981) (inventor mentioned the expectation of compensation only after the disclosure). Cf. Bush v. Goldman Sachs & Co., 544 So.2d 873 (Ala.1989) (notification of confidentiality given to one person may not bind others who acquire the information from that person). An obligation of confidentiality will not ordinarily be imposed on a person who had no opportunity to decline the disclosure. See Tele–Count Engineers, Inc. v. Pacific Tel. and Tel. Co., 168 Cal.App.3d 455, 214 Cal.Rptr. 276 (1985); Faris v. Enberg, 97 Cal. App.3d 309, 158 Cal.Rptr. 704 (1979).

For cases discussing solicited disclosures, see Smith, *supra* (confidentiality may be implied when the recipient actively solicits the disclosure) (dictum); Pachmayr Gun Works, Inc. v. Olin Mathieson Chemical Corp., 502 F.2d 802 (9th Cir.1974) (disclosure held confidential when the defendant induced the disclosure under false pretenses); Crocan Corp. v. Sheller–Globe Corp., 385 F.Supp. 251 (N.D.Ill.1974). On disclosure for a limited purpose, see, e.g., Metallurgical Industries, Inc. v. Fourtek, Inc., 790 F.2d 1195 (5th Cir.1986) (disclosure of an invention to a supplier of machines that would incorporate the innovation held confidential); Nucor Corp. v. Tennessee Forging Steel Service, Inc., 476 F.2d 386 (8th Cir. 1973) (submission of building plans to subcontractors for the purpose of preparing bids was a confidential disclosure); Kamin, *supra* (manufacturer employed to develop inventor's ideas was not entitled to appropriate the ideas for its own use); Tabor v. Hoffman, 118 N.Y. 30, 23 N.E. 12 (1889) (transfer of equipment for purposes of repair).

Disclosures made to enable prospective purchasers or licensees to appraise the value of the business or trade secret are ordinarily held to be confidential. See, e.g., Phillips v. Frey, 20 F.3d 623 (5th Cir.1994) (disclosure during negotiations with a prospective purchaser); Schreyer v. Casco Products Corp., 190 F.2d 921 (2d Cir.1951), cert. denied 342 U.S. 913, 72 S.Ct. 360, 96 L.Ed. 683 (1952) (disclosure during negotiations with a prospective licensee); Heyman v. AR. Winarick, Inc., 325 F.2d 584 (2d Cir. 1963) (information disclosed to permit a purchaser to assess the merits of the bargain); Speedry Chemical Products, Inc. v. Carter's Ink Co., 306 F.2d 328 (2d Cir.1962) (valuable information disclosed during licensing negotiations would be confidential) (dictum). Cf. Cloud v. Standard Packaging Corp., 376 F.2d 384 (7th Cir.1967) (disclosure to a prospective supplier held on the facts to be at arm's length and not confidential).

The relationship of licensor-licensee is often characterized as "confidential." See Hyde Corp. v. Huffines, 158 Tex. 566, 314 S.W.2d 763, cert. denied 358 U.S. 898, 79 S.Ct. 223, 3 L.Ed.2d 148 (1958); Default Proof Credit Card System, Inc. v. State Street Bank & Trust Co., 753 F.Supp. 1566 (S.D.Fla.1990). Cf. Aerospace America, *supra* (no confidential relationship existed between a manufacturer and a distributor in the absence of an express agreement or notice that the disclosure was intended as confidential).

For a case recognizing reverse engineering as a proper means to acquire a trade secret that was embodied in a product purchased from the trade secret owner, see Roboserve, Ltd. v. Tom's Foods, Inc., 940 F.2d 1441 (11th Cir.1991). For a case holding reverse engineering improper when the product was loaned to the recipient in confidence, see Mineral Deposits Ltd. v. Zigan, 773 P.2d 606 (Colo.App.1988). But see Elle v. Babbitt, 259 Or. 590, 488 P.2d 440 (1971) (lease of a machine held not to create a confidential relationship) (dictum).

On Illustration 1, see, e.g., Cloud v. Standard Packaging Corp., 376 F.2d 384 (7th Cir.1967). Illustration 2 is suggested by Heyman v. AR. Winarick, Inc., 325 F.2d 584 (2d Cir.1963).

Comment c. Some of the decisions that grant relief against a breach of confidence in spite of the absence of a trade secret seek support in Justice Holmes's famous statement in E.I. Du Pont De Nemours Powder Co. v. Masland, 244 U.S. 100, 102, 37 S.Ct. 575, 575, 61 L.Ed. 1016, 1019 (1917): "Whether the plaintiffs have any valuable secret or not the defendant knows the facts, whatever they are, through a special confidence that he accepted. The property may be denied, but the confidence cannot be." The issue in *Masland*, however, was whether the defendant could be prohibited from disclosing the alleged trade secret to expert witnesses in preparation for trial. The case does not support the imposition of liability in the absence of evidence that the plaintiff has a protectable interest in the information. See Kubik, Inc. v. Hull, 56 Mich.App. 335, 224 N.W.2d 80 (1974); National Starch Products, Inc. v. Polymer Industries, Inc., 273 App. Div. 732, 79 N.Y.S.2d 357 (1948); Milgrim on Trade Secrets § 1.01[1].

Cases in which a broader definition of "trade secret" might have made consideration of a separate breach of confidence claim unnecessary include, e.g., Lehman v. Dow Jones & Co., 783 F.2d 285 (2d Cir.1986); Saliterman v. Finney, 361 N.W.2d 175 (Minn.App. 1985). For cases in which a breach of confidence claim was invoked to enforce a current employee's duty of loyalty to the employer, see Nucor Corp. v. Tennessee Forging Steel Service, Inc., 476 F.2d 386 (8th Cir. 1973); Tan–Line Studios, Inc. v. Bradley, 1 U.S.P.Q.2d 2032 (E.D.Pa. 1986). Cases suggesting that a generalized breach of confidence claim can be invoked to protect valuable commercial information without regard to its status as a trade secret include Roboserve, Ltd. v. Tom's Foods, Inc., 940 F.2d 1441 (11th Cir. 1991); Self Directed Placement Corp. v. Control Data Corp., 908 F.2d 462 (9th Cir.1990); Tele–Count Engineers, Inc. v. Pacific Tel. and Tel. Co., 168 Cal.App.3d 455, 214 Cal.Rptr. 276 (1985); Boeing Co. v. Sierracin Corp., 108 Wash.2d 38, 738 P.2d 665 (1987) (breach of confidence claim not displaced by the Uniform Trade Secrets Act). The *Roboserve* case illustrates the danger inherent in imposing liability for breach of confidence without regard to the nature of the protected information. After determining that the defendant was not liable under trade secret law for using information available through an inspection of a machine in the public domain, the court nevertheless suggested the possibility of liability under a breach of confidence theory. Other cases recognize that the policies limiting the scope of trade secret protection are also applicable when the claim is described instead as one for breach of confidence. See Johns–Manville Corp. v. Guardian Industries Corp., 586 F.Supp. 1034 (E.D.Mich.1983), affirmed 770 F.2d 178 (Fed.Cir.1985).

Comment d. Agreements that create an unreasonable restraint on trade are unenforceable. Restatement, Second, Contracts § 186 (1979). A covenant not to compete given by an employee to the employer or by the seller of a business to the buyer is an unreasonable restraint of trade if: "(a) the restraint is greater than is needed to protect the promisee's legitimate interest, or (b) the promisee's need is outweighed by the hardship to the promisor and the likely injury to the public." *Id.* § 188(1). Covenants not to compete must be limited in duration and geographic area to a scope that is justified by the legitimate interests of the promisee. *Id.*, Comment *e*. See, e.g., Central Water Works Supply, Inc. v. Fisher, 240 Ill.App.3d 952, 181 Ill.Dec. 545, 608 N.E.2d 618 (1993) (covenants not to compete given by former employees are evaluated more strictly than covenants ancillary to the sale of a business). Statutes in some jurisdictions further restrict or prohibit the enforcement of covenants not to compete. See Aspelund and Eriksen, Employee Noncompetition Law §§ 9.01–05.

A promise to refrain from the use or disclosure of commercial information is ordinarily unenforceable unless the information is sufficiently secret to justify the restraint. See Rototron Corp. v. Lake Shore Burial Vault Co., 712 F.2d 1214 (7th Cir. 1983); Rigging Int'l Maintenance Co. v. Gwin, 128 Cal.App.3d 594, 180 Cal. Rptr. 451 (1982); Thomas v. Best Mfg. Corp., 234 Ga. 787, 218 S.E.2d 68 (1975); American Family Life Assurance Co. v. Tazelaar, 135 Ill. App.3d 1069, 90 Ill.Dec. 789, 482 N.E.2d 1072 (1985); Dynamics Research Corp. v. Analytic Sciences Corp., 9 Mass.App.Ct. 254, 400 N.E.2d 1274 (1980); Kaumagraph Co. v. Stampagraph Co., 235 N.Y. 1, 138 N.E. 485 (1923); Gary Van Zeeland Talent, Inc. v. Sandas, 84 Wis.2d 202, 267 N.W.2d 242 (1978).

Cases expressing the view that contractual restrictions can protect confidential information that does not technically qualify as a trade secret often rest on a narrower definition of "trade secret" than that adopted in § 39. See, e.g., Modern Controls, Inc. v. Andreadakis, 578 F.2d 1264 (8th Cir.1978); Johns–Manville Corp. v. Guardian Industries Corp., 586 F.Supp. 1034 (E.D.Mich.1983), affirmed 770 F.2d 178 (Fed.Cir.1985); Organic Chemicals, Inc. v. Carroll Products, Inc., 211 U.S.P.Q. 628 (W.D.Mich.1981) (dictum); Continental Group, Inc. v. Kinsley, 422 F.Supp. 838 (D.Conn.1976); Structural Dynamics Research Corp. v. Engineering Mechanics Research Corp., 401 F.Supp. 1102 (E.D.Mich.1975). However, since enforcement turns on the reasonableness of the restraint, the precise definition of a "trade secret" is not necessarily determinative in such cases. Although the existence of an express contract to refrain from the disclosure or use of particular information may justify somewhat broader protection than that available under tort law, see, e.g., Richardson v. Suzuki Motor Co., 868 F.2d 1226 (Fed.Cir.), cert. denied 493 U.S. 853, 110 S.Ct. 154, 107 L.Ed.2d 112 (1989); Lear Siegler, Inc. v. Ark–Ell Springs, Inc., 569 F.2d 286 (5th Cir.1978), the public policies that operate to restrict the scope of trade secret protection are also relevant to the enforcement of confidentiality agreements. See, e.g., AMP Inc. v. Fleischhacker, 823 F.2d 1199 (7th Cir.1987); Victor Chemical Works v. Iliff, 299 Ill. 532, 132 N.E. 806 (1921).

Some courts, reviewing nondisclosure agreements under the standards traditionally applied to covenants not to compete, require not only a protectable interest in the information but also both durational and geographic limitations. See Gary Van Zeeland Talent, *supra*; Disher v. Fulgoni, 124 Ill.App.3d 257, 79 Ill. Dec. 735, 464 N.E.2d 639 (1984) (overruled on this issue by statute in Ill.C.S., ch.765, § 1065/8); State Medical Oxygen & Supply, Inc. v. American Medical Oxygen Co., 240 Mont. 70, 782 P.2d 1272 (1989). Cf. Wesley–Jessen, Inc. v. Armento, 519 F.Supp. 1352 (N.D.Ga.1981) and Durham v. Stand-by Labor, Inc., 230 Ga. 558, 198 S.E.2d 145 (1973), requiring durational but not geographic limitations. But see Nalco Chemical Co. v. Hydro Technologies, Inc., 984 F.2d 801 (7th Cir.1993) and Woven Electronics Corp. v. Advance Group, Inc., 930 F.2d 913 (4th Cir.1991) (durational and geographic limitations are unnecessary in non-disclosure agreements involving trade secrets). Other cases interpret nondisclosure agreements as imposing an obligation of confidentiality only as long as the underlying information remains secret. See Conmar Products Corp. v. Universal Slide Fastener Co., 172 F.2d 150 (2d Cir.1949); Henry Hope X-Ray Products, Inc. v. Marron Carrel, Inc., 674 F.2d 1336 (9th Cir.1982); Dollac Corp. v. Margon Corp., 164 F.Supp. 41 (D.N.J.1958), affirmed 275 F.2d 202 (3d Cir.1960). The cases that require durational and geographic limitations often reflect the concern that broad restrictions on use or disclosure will unfairly inhibit employee mobility. The appropriate inquiry to balance the legitimate interests of the employer and the employee, however, is whether the information is protectable as a trade secret. See, e.g., Amex Distributing Co. v. Mascari, 150 Ariz. 510, 724 P.2d 596 (App. 1986); Aspelund and Eriksen, Employee Noncompetition Law § 3.12; Jager, Trade Secret Law § 13.03.

Interests other than confidentiality may also justify the enforcement of contractual restrictions on the use of information. Thus, courts have enforced royalty agreements that extend beyond the public disclosure of the trade secret. See Aronson v. Quick Point Pencil Co., 440 U.S. 257, 99 S.Ct. 1096, 59 L.Ed.2d 296 (1979); Warner–Lambert Pharmaceutical Co. v. John J. Reynolds, Inc., 178 F.Supp. 655 (S.D.N.Y.1959), affirmed 280 F.2d 197 (2d Cir.1960); Laff v. John O. Butler Co., 64 Ill.App.3d 603, 21 Ill. Dec. 314, 381 N.E.2d 423 (1978), cert. denied 444 U.S. 844, 100 S.Ct. 88, 62 L.Ed.2d 57 (1979). See also, e.g., Universal Gym Equipment Inc. v. ERWA Exercise Equipment Ltd., 827 F.2d 1542 (Fed.Cir.1987) (agreement prohibiting a licensee from using design features of a publicly marketed product after the termination of the license was perhaps justified to protect the good will of the licensor). A number of cases hold that the interest in protecting established customer relationships can be sufficient to support enforcement of a covenant not to compete. E.g., McRand, Inc. v. Van Beelen, 138 Ill.App.3d 1045, 93 Ill.Dec. 471, 486 N.E.2d 1306 (1985); 4408, Inc. v. Losure, 175 Ind.App. 658, 373 N.E.2d 899 (1978); Eastern Distributing Co. v. Flynn, 222 Kan. 666, 567 P.2d 1371 (1977); North Pacific Lumber Co. v. Moore, 275 Or. 359, 551 P.2d 431 (1976); John G. Bryant Co. v. Sling Testing and Repair, Inc., 471 Pa. 1, 369 A.2d 1164 (1977). See Jager, Trade Secrets Law § 13.05.

Illustration 4 is suggested by Illustrations 1 and 2 to Restatement, Second, Contracts § 188, Comment *f*.

§ 42. Breach of Confidence by Employees

An employee or former employee who uses or discloses a trade secret owned by the employer or former employer in breach of a duty of confidence is subject to liability for appropriation of the trade secret under the rule stated in § 40.

Comment:

a. Scope. This Section is a specific application of the general rules stated in §§ 40 and 41 prohibiting the use or disclosure of a trade secret in violation of a duty of confidence. The issues discussed in this Section are primarily applicable to persons who are regarded under the law of agency as employees or "servants" of the trade secret owner as distinguished from "independent contractors." See Restatement, Second, Agency §§ 2, 220. The Section applies to the use or disclosure of trade secrets by both current and former employees. Current employees, however, are also subject to a general duty of loyalty that is broader than the specific obligations arising under the law of trade secrets. See Comment *b*. The obligations imposed by trade secret law on persons who provide services to the trade secret owner as independent contractors such as attorneys, financial advisors, or consultants are determined according to the general principles governing duties of confidence as stated in § 41. In some circumstances, however, the rules relating to employees as stated in this Section may be useful by analogy in cases involving independent contractors. To advance interests other than the maintenance of fair competition, some professionals such as attorneys and physicians are also subject to obligations of confidentiality apart from those arising under the law of trade secrets.

b. Duties of employees and former employees. During the duration of an employment relationship, an employee is subject to a duty of loyalty applicable to all conduct within the scope of the employment. See Restatement, Second, Agency § 387. The duty of loyalty encompasses a general duty not to compete with the employer in the subject matter of the employment, *id.* § 393, including a duty to refrain from using confidential information acquired through the employment in competition with the employer. *Id.* § 395. Thus, if a current employee enters into competition with the employer, liability may be imposed without regard to the existence or appropriation of trade secrets. The duty of loyalty also includes a duty not to disclose the employer's confidential information to others. *Id.* When it is alleged that a current employee has disclosed to third persons valuable information acquired in the course of the employment, the emphasis is properly on whether there has been a breach of loyalty by the employee and not on the character of the particular information. However, it is not ordinarily regarded as a breach of loyalty to "disclose" information that is common knowledge or that the employee has no reason to believe is confidential. *Id.*, Comment *b*. Although a current employee can be subject to liability for the appropriation of a trade secret under the rules stated in this Chapter, the liability of current employees for the unauthorized use or disclosure of valuable information is more typically determined under the rules governing the general duty of loyalty owed by an employee to the employer.

The rules governing liability for the appropriation of trade secrets play a more central role in regulating the behavior of employees after the termination of the employment relationship. Once the employment has ended, the former employee has the right to compete with the former employer absent an enforceable agreement to the contrary. Restrictive covenants limiting competition by former employees are enforceable only if the restriction is reasonable. See § 41, Comment *d.* However, even in the absence of an enforceable covenant a former employee remains subject to the general rules prohibiting use or disclosure of another's trade secrets in breach of a duty of confidence.

Application of the rules protecting trade secrets in cases involving competition by former employees requires a careful balancing of interests. There is a strong public interest in preserving the freedom of employees to market their talents and experience in order to earn a livelihood. The mobility of employees also promotes competition through the dissemination of useful skills and information. In many instances, however, employers cannot conduct business efficiently without disclosing valuable trade secrets to their employees. Absent reasonable protection against the unauthorized use or disclosure of such information by former employees, employers would be forced to adopt expensive and inefficient restrictions on access to information. Businesses would also be less likely to invest in research and development if competitors could easily appropriate the gains from such investments through disclosures by former employees. Thus, the interests of both the former employer and the former employee must be weighed in light of the circumstances of the particular case in order to insure sufficient protection for trade secrets without unduly restraining the mobility of employees.

c. Employment as a confidential relationship. The employment relationship by its nature ordinarily justifies an inference that the employee consents to a duty of confidence with respect to any information acquired through the employment that the employee knows or has reason to know is confidential. See § 41, Comment *b.* The duty to refrain from unauthorized use or disclosure of confidential information continues after termination of the employment relationship. However, some information developed during the employment relationship may belong to the employee rather than the employer. See Comment *e.* Former employees are also entitled to exploit their general skill, knowledge, training, and experience, even when acquired or enhanced through the resources of the former employer. See Comment *d.* Although some courts have justified particular decisions in favor of employees on the absence of a confidential relationship, these cases are often better understood as resting on the absence of a protectable trade secret owned by the employer or on a lack of adequate notice to the employee of the confidential nature of the information. If an employer establishes ownership of a trade secret and circumstances sufficient to put the employee on notice that the information is confidential, the employment relationship will ordinarily justify the recognition of a duty of confidence.

d. General skill, knowledge, training, and experience. Information that forms the general skill, knowledge, training, and experience of an employee cannot be claimed as a trade secret by a former employer even when the information is directly attributable to an investment of resources by the employer in the employee. The Statute of Apprentices enacted in England in 1562, 5 Eliz. I, ch. 4, which mandated a seven-year period of apprenticeship to a master, was in part an early attempt to reconcile the interest of employers in capturing the benefits of their investment in the training of employees and the interest of employees in a competitive market for their services. The modern balance relies primarily on the recognition of a duty of loyalty during the period of employment, see Comment *b*, the ability of employers and employees in most states to contract for reasonable restrictions on the employee's freedom to compete with the employer after termination of the employment, see § 41, Comment *d*, and the recognition of rights in specific information that is eligible for protection as a trade secret. Thus, absent an enforceable covenant not to compete, a former employee may utilize in competition with the former employer the general skills, knowledge, training, and experience acquired during the employment, but the employee remains obligated to refrain from using or disclosing the employer's trade secrets.

Whether particular information is properly regarded as a trade secret of the former employer or as part of the general skill, knowledge, training, and experience of the former employee depends on the facts and circumstances of the particular case. An employer who is asserting rights in information against a former employee bears the burden of proving the existence and ownership of a trade secret. Trade secret rights are more likely to be recognized in specialized information unique to the employer's business than in information more widely known in the industry or derived from skills generally possessed by persons employed in the industry. The relative contribution of the employer and employee to the development of the information can also be relevant. The fact that other competitors have been unsuccessful in independent attempts to develop the information may suggest that the information qualifies for protection as a trade secret. Courts are also more likely to conclude that particular information is a trade secret if the employee on termination of the employment appropriates some physical embodiment of the information such as written formulas, blueprints, plans, or lists of customers. However, although information that is retained in the employee's memory may be less likely to be regarded as a trade secret absent evidence of intentional memorization, the inference is not conclusive.

The distinction between trade secrets and general skill, knowledge, training, and experience is intended to achieve a reasonable balance between the protection of confidential information and the mobility of employees. If the information is so closely integrated with the employee's overall employment experience that protection would deprive the employee of the ability to obtain employment commensurate with the employee's general qualifications, it will not ordinarily be protected as a trade secret of the former employer.

e. Allocation of ownership between employers and employees. The law of agency has established rules governing the ownership of valuable information created by employees during the course of an employment relationship. See Restatement, Second, Agency § 397. In the absence of a contrary agreement, the law ordinarily assigns ownership of an invention or idea to the person who conceives it. However, valuable information that is the product of an employee's assigned duties is owned by the employer, even when the information results from the application of the employee's personal knowledge or skill:

> If, however, one is employed to do experimental work for inventive purposes, it is inferred ordinarily, although not so specifically agreed, that patentable ideas arrived at through the experimentation are to be owned by the employer. This is even more clear where one is employed to achieve a particular result which the invention accomplishes. On the other hand, if one is employed merely to do work in a particular line in which he is an expert, there is no inference that inventions which he makes while so working belong to the employer.

Restatement, Second, Agency § 397, Comment *a*.

An employee is ordinarily entitled to claim ownership of patents and trade secrets developed outside the scope of the employee's assigned duties, even if the invention or idea relates to the employer's business and was developed using the employer's time, personnel, facilities, or equipment. In the latter circumstances, however, the employer is entitled to a "shop right"—an irrevocable, nonexclusive, royalty-free license to use the innovation. Similarly, employees retain ownership of information comprising their general skill, knowledge, training, and experience. See Comment *d*. The allocation of ownership between employers and employees is also subject to alteration by contract. See Comment *g*.

If a trade secret developed by an employee is owned by the employer, the employee is subject to liability under the rule stated in § 40 for any unauthorized use or disclosure. If the trade secret is owned by the employee, the employee is free, when no longer subject to the duty of loyalty owed by current employees, to use the information or to disclose it to others even if the former employer retains a "shop right" in the trade secret.

Although the rules governing ownership of valuable information created during an employment relationship are most frequently applied to inventions, the rules are also applicable to information such as customer lists, marketing ideas, and other valuable business information. If an employee collects or develops such information as part of the assigned duties of the employment, the information is owned by the employer. Thus, if the information qualifies for protection as a trade secret, unauthorized use or disclosure will subject the employee to liability under the rule stated in § 40.

Illustrations:

1. *A*, a manufacturer of household chemicals, employs *B*, a chemist, to develop new products. In the course of the employment, *B* develops a formula for a new floor cleaner that is a significant improvement over existing products. After leaving the employment with *A*, *B* is induced by *C*, a competitor of *A*, to disclose the secret formula. Because *B* was hired by *A* specifically to develop new products, the formula is owned by *A*; *B* and *C* are subject to liability to *A*.

2. The facts being otherwise as stated in Illustration 1, *B* is hired by *A* to analyze the formulas of products sold by *A*'s competitors. After leaving the employment with *A*, *B* is hired to perform a similar task for *C*, a competitor of *A*. In analyzing the formulas for *C*, *B* relies on the general skill and training acquired during the former employment. *B* and *C* are not subject to liability to *A*.

3. *A* is a toy maker. *B*, who is hired by *A* as a toy designer, invents a new manufacturing process valuable in *A*'s business. *B* terminates the employment with *A* and begins work for *C*, a competing toy maker, and assists in implementing the new manufacturing process at *C*'s factory. Because the new process was not the product of *B*'s assigned duties while employed by *A*, in the absence of an agreement to the contrary the rights in the process are owned by *B*; *B* and *C* are not subject to liability to *A*.

However, *A* may have a "shop right" in the manufacturing process if *B* developed the process using *A* 's time, personnel, facilities, or equipment.

f. Customer lists. The general rules that govern trade secrets are applicable to the protection of information relating to the identity and requirements of customers. Customer identities and related customer information can be a company's most valuable asset and may represent a considerable investment of resources. Although issues relating to the protection of customer lists may arise in a variety of contexts, most cases involve the solicitation of a company's customers by a former employee who acquired information about the customers in the course of the former employment. The public and private interests that are implicated in the protection of customer information are best accommodated through application of the traditional rules governing trade secrets, covenants not to compete, and the duty of loyalty owed to an employer by a current employee.

A customer list is not protectable as a trade secret under the rule stated in § 39 unless it is sufficiently valuable and secret to afford an economic advantage to a person who has access to the list. Thus, if the potential customers for a particular product or service are readily identifiable, their identities do not constitute a trade secret. On the other hand, specialized customer information that cannot easily be duplicated, such as a list of homeowners who employ commercial cleaning services or a compilation of specific information about individual customers, may be sufficiently valuable and secret to qualify as a trade secret. The fact that an employee has appropriated a written list or has made an attempt to memorize customer information prior to terminating the employment may justify an inference that the information is valuable and not readily ascertainable by proper means. However, solicitation of the same customers by a number of competitors is evidence that the customer identities are generally known or readily ascertainable in the trade. Some of the customer list cases involve the identities of customers on delivery routes. In most cases the identities of such customers are readily ascertainable by observing the delivery vehicle. Information concerning the particular requirements of individual customers may be eligible for protection as a trade secret if such knowledge is difficult to obtain and valuable in gaining or retaining patronage.

When information relating to the identities or requirements of customers qualifies for protection as a trade secret, the rules described in Comment *e* are applicable in determining ownership. If the employer discloses the list of customers to the employee, or if the employee is specifically assigned to identify potential customers, the employer is ordinarily the owner of the information. On the other hand, in the absence of an enforceable covenant not to compete, an employee who possessed the relevant customer information prior to the former employment is free to use the information in competition with the former employer after termination of the employment relationship.

If the identities of the former employer's customers are not protectable as a trade secret, a former employee is entitled, absent an enforceable agreement to the contrary, to solicit the customers in competition with the former employer once the employment has ended. A few courts, particularly in delivery route cases, have nevertheless enjoined such solicitation when the former employee had developed substantial personal relationships with the customers. However, such a prohibition can unfairly limit employee mobility. If the customer list or related information does not qualify for protection as a trade secret, the former employer should ordinarily be limited to the protection available through a reasonable covenant not to compete. See § 41, Comment *d.*

g. Contractual protection. The rules governing the protection and ownership of trade secrets are generally subject to reasonable modification by the parties. By means of a reasonable covenant not to compete, an employer may achieve protection against the competitive use by a former employee of information not technically protectable as a trade secret. See § 41, Comment *d.* Similarly, a nondisclosure agreement prohibiting the use or disclosure of particular information can clarify and extend the scope of an employer's rights. *Id.* However, the rules governing trade secrets remain relevant in assessing the reasonableness and hence the enforceability of such contractual restrictions. *Id.*

The common law accords to an employer ownership of inventions and discoveries made by an employee only when the information is the product of the employee's assigned duties. See Comment *e.* However, absent an applicable statutory prohibition, agreements relating to the ownership of inventions and discoveries made by employees during the term of the employment are generally enforceable according to their terms. Employment agreements sometimes include provisions granting the employer ownership of all inventions and discoveries conceived by the employee during the term of the employment. In some situations, however, it may be difficult to prove when a particular invention was conceived. The employee may have an incentive to delay disclosure of the invention until after the employment is terminated in order to avoid the contractual or common law claims of the employer. It may also be difficult to establish whether a post-employment invention was improperly derived from the trade secrets of the former employer. Some employment agreements respond to this uncertainty through provisions granting the former employer ownership of inventions and discoveries relating to the subject matter of the former employment that are developed by the employee even after the termination of the employment. Such agreements can restrict the former employee's ability to exploit the skills and training desired by other employers and may thus restrain competition and limit employee mobility. The courts have therefore subjected such "holdover" agreements to scrutiny analogous to that applied to covenants not to compete. Thus, the agreement may be unenforceable if it extends beyond a reasonable period of time or to inventions or discoveries resulting solely from the general skill and experience of the former employee.

REPORTERS' NOTE

Comment a. The rules governing the protection of trade secrets in employment relationships are discussed in Jager, Trade Secrets Law § 8.01; Milgrim on Trade Secrets § 5.02.

Comment b. The Restatement, Second, of Agency distinguishes the duties owed by agents and former agents. An agent has a duty not to compete with the principal and not to use or disclose confidential information to the detriment of the principal. *Id.* § 395. A former agent has no duty not to compete but remains subject to the duty not to disclose trade secrets or other confidential information. *Id.* § 396. The scope of information subject to a duty of confidence is also broader for current agents than for former agents. Compare *id.* § 395, Comment *b* with § 396, Comment *b*. See, e.g., Nucor Corp. v. Tennessee Forging Steel Service, Inc., 476 F.2d 386 (8th Cir.1973) (proof of a trade secret is unnecessary to impose liability on a current employee for breach of confidence); Lear Siegler, Inc. v. Ark–Ell Springs, Inc., 569 F.2d 286 (5th Cir.1978) (breach of confidence by a former employee requires proof of a trade secret, distinguishing a breach of loyalty by a current employee) (dictum); Vigitron, Inc. v. Ferguson, 120 N.H. 626, 419 A.2d 1115 (1980) (injunction issued against a breach of confidence by a current employee without proof of a trade secret). Cf. Augat, Inc. v. Aegis, Inc., 409 Mass. 165, 565 N.E.2d 415 (1991) (current employee was not liable for disclosing sales figures already known in the industry).

Cases discussing the competing interests implicated by the law of trade secrets as applied to the employment relationship include, e.g., Valco Cincinnati, Inc. v. N & D Machining Service, Inc., 24 Ohio St.3d 41, 46, 492 N.E.2d 814, 818 (1986) ("Underlying almost every case in which a former employee is accused of the unauthorized disclosure or use of trade secrets is the matter of balancing or reconciling '* * * the conflicting rights of an employer to enjoy the use of secret processes and devices which were developed through his own initiative and investment and the right of employees to earn a livelihood by utilizing their personal skill, knowledge and experience.' " (quoting GTI Corp. v. Calhoon, 309 F.Supp. 762, 768 (S.D.Ohio 1969))); Wexler v. Greenberg, 399 Pa. 569, 160 A.2d 430 (1960) (courts weigh heavily the right of employees to pursue their livelihood free of restrictions arising from prior employment); SI Handling Systems, Inc. v. Heisley, 753 F.2d 1244, 1264 (3d Cir.1985) (although protection of trade secrets is necessary to ensure that an "optimum amount of 'entrusting' " will occur in the employment relationship, restrictions on former employees diminishes the dissemination of ideas and reduces competition (quoting Wexler, *supra*, 160 A.2d at 435)).

Comment c. Sections 395 and 396 of the Restatement, Second, of Agency recognize a general duty of confidence arising from an employment relationship. See also, e.g., NCH Corp. v. Broyles, 749 F.2d 247 (5th Cir.1985); American Stay Co. v. Delaney, 211 Mass. 229, 97 N.E. 911 (1912) (the "bare relation" of master and servant imposes an obligation of confidentiality); Rice Researchers, Inc. v. Hiter, 512 So.2d 1259 (Miss. 1987) (officers and directors); Thermotics, Inc. v. Bat–Jac Tool Co., 541 S.W.2d 255 (Tex.Civ.App.1976); Julius Hyman & Co. v. Velsicol Corp., 123 Colo. 563, 233 P.2d 977, cert. denied 342 U.S. 870, 72 S.Ct. 113, 96 L.Ed. 654 (1951). The duty of confidence is sometimes described as an implied term in the employment agreement. See, e.g., O. & W. Thum Co. v. Tloczynski, 114 Mich. 149, 72 N.W. 140 (1897). However, no duty of confidence arises with respect to information that the employee neither knows nor has reason to know is confidential. Mercer v. C.A. Roberts Co., 570 F.2d 1232 (5th Cir.1978) (employees could have reasonably assumed that the information was not confidential); Electro–Craft Corp. v. Controlled Motion, Inc., 332 N.W.2d 890 (Minn.1983) (employees were not put on notice that the employer considered the information to be confidential). See, e.g., Surgidev Corp. v. Eye Technology, Inc., 828 F.2d 452 (8th Cir.1987) (employer's actions found sufficient to indicate that the information should not be disclosed).

Some of the cases questioning the existence of a confidential relationship in particular employment situations are better understood as resting on an absence of protectable information. See Shatterproof Glass Corp. v. Guardian Glass Co., 322 F.Supp. 854 (E.D.Mich.1970), affirmed 462 F.2d 1115 (6th Cir.), cert. denied 409 U.S. 1039, 93 S.Ct. 518, 34 L.Ed.2d 487 (1972) (holding that certain hourly employees were not in a confidential relationship with the employer, but also finding no appropriation of protectable information); Mercer, *supra* (suggesting that not every employment relationship is confidential, but finding that the contested information was not a trade secret); Wexler v. Greenberg, 399 Pa. 569, 160 A.2d 430 (1960) (no confidential relationship existed with respect to information resulting from the employee's general skill and training).

Comment d. The rule denying employers an interest in the general skill, knowledge, training, and experience of former employees reflects the public interest in protecting employee mobility. See, e.g., AMP Inc. v. Fleischhacker, 823 F.2d 1199, 1202 (7th Cir.1987) ("Our society is extremely mobile and our free economy is based upon competition. One who has worked in a particular field cannot be compelled to erase from his mind all of the general skills, knowledge and expertise acquired through his experience. These skills are valuable to such employee in the market place for his services." (quoting ILG Industries v. Scott, 49 Ill.2d 88, 93–94, 273 N.E.2d 393, 396 (1971))); Wexler v. Greenberg, 399 Pa. 569, 160 A.2d 430 (1960). The fact that the employee's general skill and knowledge has been enhanced by the former employment does not entitle the former employer to prohibit subsequent exploitation on behalf of another. E.g., Vigitron, Inc. v. Ferguson, 120 N.H. 626, 419 A.2d 1115 (1980); National Dev. Co. v. Gray, 316 Mass. 240, 55 N.E.2d 783 (1944). See generally von Kalinowski, Key Employees and Trade Secrets, 47 Va.L.Rev. 583 (1961).

Courts are properly reluctant to recognize claims by employers in information that cannot be easily segregated from the general skill and knowledge of former employees. See, e.g., AMP Inc., *supra*; Dynamics Research Corp. v. Analytic Sciences Corp., 9 Mass.App.Ct. 254, 400 N.E.2d 1274 (1980). When a former employee uses information from memory rather than from physical records taken from the former employer, courts may be more likely to regard the information as part of the employee's general knowledge and experience. See, e.g., AMP Inc., *supra*; NCH Corp. v. Broyles, 749 F.2d 247 (5th Cir.1985) (distinguishing a former employee's use of a route book from reliance on casual memory). Cf. Schulenburg v. Signatrol, Inc., 33 Ill.2d 379, 212 N.E.2d 865 (1965), cert. denied 383 U.S. 959, 86 S.Ct. 1225, 16 L.Ed.2d 302 (1966) (systematic attempts to memorize information will not immunize former employees from liability). Although the distinction between information retained in memory and information embodied in appropriated records can be relevant in determining whether the information qualifies for protection, the defendant's reliance on memory is not a defense if the information is in fact a trade secret. MAI Systems Corp. v. Peak Computer, Inc., 991 F.2d 511 (9th Cir.1993), cert. dismissed ___ U.S. ___, 114 S.Ct. 671, 126 L.Ed.2d 640 (1994); American Republic Ins. Co. v. Union Fidelity Life Ins. Co., 295 F.Supp. 553 (D.Or. 1968), reversed on other grounds 470 F.2d 820 (9th Cir.1972); Sperry Rand Corp. v. Rothlein, 241 F.Supp. 549 (D.Conn.1964) (it is irrelevant whether the trade secret "came out in a defendant's hand or in his head"); Allen v. Johar, Inc., 308 Ark. 45, 823 S.W.2d 824 (1992); Morgan's Home Equipment Corp. v. Martucci, 390 Pa. 618, 136 A.2d 838 (1957).

Cases illustrating the difficulties inherent in distinguishing the general skill and knowledge of a former employee from the trade secrets of a former employer include, e.g., Ingersoll–Rand Co. v. Ciavatta, 110 N.J. 609, 542 A.2d 879 (1988); Amoco Production Co. v. Lindley, 609 P.2d 733 (Okla.1980); Schulenburg, *supra*. See GTI Corp. v. Calhoon, 309 F.Supp. 762, 769 (S.D.Ohio 1969) (asking, "First, did the employees derive the necessary knowledge to make their products from their employment with plaintiff or from their general knowledge of the arts of manufacture? Second, could the defendants proceed as they did independently of the knowledge gained as plaintiff's employee?"). Whether particular information is a protectable trade secret of the former employer depends on the facts of the particular case. An important factor is whether the information is general to the trade or peculiar to the former employer. See, e.g., GTI Corp., *supra*. If other competitors have tried unsuccessfully to solve a particular problem, a solution retained from a prior employment is unlikely to be considered part of the employee's general skill and knowledge. See Head Ski Co. v. Kam Ski Co., 158 F.Supp. 919 (D.Md.1958). Although information disclosed to the employee by the former employer may be more likely to be regarded as a trade secret than information produced through the employee's own efforts, see, e.g., Wexler v. Greenberg, 399 Pa. 569, 160 A.2d 430 (1960) (dictum); Structural Dynamics Research Corp. v. Engineering Mechanics Research Corp., 401 F.Supp. 1102 (E.D.Mich. 1975), the latter can also be a trade secret owned by the employer. See Comment *e*.

Comment e. The common law rules governing ownership of inventions created during an employment relationship are stated in Restatement, Second, Agency § 397. See generally Jager, Trade Secrets Law § 8.01; Milgrim on Trade Secrets § 5.02; Baker & Brunel, Restructuring the Judicial Evaluation of Employed Inventors' Rights, 35 St. Louis L.J. 399 (1991). See, e.g., National Dev. Co. v. Gray, 316 Mass. 240, 55 N.E.2d 783 (1944); Kinkade v. New York Shipbuilding Corp., 21 N.J. 362, 122 A.2d 360 (1956). See also Ingersoll–Rand Co. v. Ciavatta, 110 N.J. 609, 542 A.2d 879 (1988) (noting the freedom to allocate ownership by contract).

The development of the rules allocating ownership of information between employers and employees is evident in a series of opinions in the United States Supreme Court. See Solomons v. United States, 137 U.S. 342, 11 S.Ct. 88, 34 L.Ed. 667 (1890) (invention conceived by employees hired to design a particular device or achieve a prescribed result is the property of the employer); Standard Parts Co. v. Peck, 264 U.S. 52, 44 S.Ct. 239, 68 L.Ed. 560 (1924) (employer is entitled to the inventions of an employee hired to work on a particular problem); United States v. Dubilier Condenser Corp., 289 U.S. 178, 53 S.Ct. 554, 77 L.Ed. 1114, amended 289 U.S. 706, 53 S.Ct. 687, 77 L.Ed. 1462 (1933) (inventions of a general employee belong to the employee, but if the employee uses the employer's time, materials, and facilities in developing the invention, the employer is entitled to a nonexclusive, irrevocable license). Other cases make clear that the employer's claim to ownership does not depend on whether the employee was hired to create the specific invention, but rather on whether the invention arose out of the duties to which the employee was assigned. See National Dev. Co., *supra* ; Vigitron, Inc. v. Ferguson, 120 N.H. 626, 629–30, 419 A.2d 1115, 1117 (1980) ("The product of one who is hired to invent, accomplish a prescribed result, or aid in the development of products belongs to the employer in the absence of a written contract to assign."). See also Pursche v. Atlas Scraper and Engineering Co., 300 F.2d 467 (9th Cir. 1961), cert. denied 371 U.S. 911, 83 S.Ct. 251, 9 L.Ed.2d 170 (1962) (employer is entitled to inventions of an employee who, although not initially hired to invent, was later assigned to use his inventive talents on behalf of the employer); Houghton v. United States, 23 F.2d 386, 390 (4th Cir.), cert. denied 277 U.S. 592, 48 S.Ct. 528, 72 L.Ed. 1004 (1928) ("It matters not in what capacity the employee may originally have been hired, if he be set to experimenting with the view of making an invention * * * what he accomplishes by the experiments belongs to the employer."); Aero Bolt & Screw Co. v. Iaia, 180 Cal.App.2d 728, 5 Cal.Rptr. 53 (1960) (an employee is "hired to invent" when he or she has a duty to invent). Cf. Cahill v. Regan, 5 N.Y.2d 292, 184 N.Y.S.2d 348, 157 N.E.2d 505 (1959) (employer is not entitled to the invention of an employee directed to work on an idea conceived by the employee prior to the employment).

A few states have enacted employee patent right statutes that invalidate provisions in employment contracts requiring employees to assign rights in inventions that do not relate to the employer's business and that do not result from work performed for the employer if the invention was made on the employee's own time and without the use of the employer's equipment, supplies, facilities, or trade secrets. See, e.g., Cal.Labor C. § 2870; Ill.C.S., ch. 765, § 1060/1; Minn.S.A. § 181.78; N.C.G.S. § 66–57.1; Wash.R.C.A. § 49.44.140. See generally Gullette, State Legislation Governing Ownership Rights in Inventions Under Employee Invention Agreements, 62 J.Pat.Off.Soc. 732 (1980).

On the ownership of copyrightable subject matter created during an employment relationship, see 17 U.S.C.A. § 201(b) (employer is the owner of a "work made for hire") and 17 U.S.C.A. § 101 (definition of "work made for hire" includes "a work prepared by an employee within the scope of his or her employment"). See Community for Creative Non–Violence v. Reid, 490 U.S. 730, 109 S.Ct. 2166, 104 L.Ed.2d 811 (1989).

Illustrations 1 and 2 are suggested by the facts in Wexler v. Greenberg, 399 Pa. 569, 160 A.2d 430 (1960). In *Wexler*, a chemist was specifically assigned to duplicate the formulas of competing products. The chemist later reproduced the formulas for a subsequent employer. The court held that the information formed part of the chemist's general knowledge and skill and was thus not protectable by the former employer.

Illustration 3 is suggested by the facts in New Method Die & Cut–Out Co. v. Milton Bradley Co., 289 Mass. 277, 194 N.E. 80 (1935). See also Structural Dynamics Research Corp. v. Engineering Mechanics Research Corp., 401 F.Supp. 1102 (E.D.Mich. 1975) (software developed by general employees held not a trade secret of the employer because it represented the general skill and training of the employees); Amoco Production Co. v. Lindley, 609 P.2d 733 (Okla.1980) (software developed by an employee was not shown to be a trade secret that could be claimed by the employer).

Comment f. Restatement of Torts § 757, Comment *b*, recognized customer lists as part of the subject matter of trade secret law. See generally Jager, Trade Secrets Law § 3.01; Milgrim on Trade Secrets § 2.09. Customer lists have also been held to be protectable as trade secrets under the Uniform Trade Secrets Act. See, e.g., MAI Systems Corp. v. Peak Computer, Inc., 991 F.2d 511 (9th Cir.1993), cert. dismissed ___ U.S. ___, 114 S.Ct. 671, 126 L.Ed.2d 640 (1994); Allen v. Johar, Inc., 308 Ark. 45, 823 S.W.2d 824 (1992); American Credit Indemnity Co. v. Sacks, 213 Cal.App.3d 622, 262 Cal.Rptr. 92 (1989); Courtesy Temporary Service, Inc. v. Camacho, 222

Cal.App.3d 1278, 272 Cal.Rptr. 352 (1990). See also the Illinois version of the Uniform Trade Secrets Act, specifically including a "list of actual or potential customers or suppliers." Ill.C.S., ch. 765, § 1065/2(d).

Numerous cases recognize customer lists as a potential subject of trade secret protection. See, e.g., Defiance Button Machine Co. v. C & C Metal Products Corp., 759 F.2d 1053 (2d Cir.), cert. denied 474 U.S. 844, 106 S.Ct. 131, 88 L.Ed.2d 108 (1985) (customer list developed through substantial effort and kept in confidence is protectable) (dictum); Leo Silfen, Inc. v. Cream, 29 N.Y.2d 387, 328 N.Y.S.2d 423, 278 N.E.2d 636 (1972) (customer list not protected because the customer identities were readily ascertainable); Follmer, Rudzewicz & Co. v. Kosco, 420 Mich. 394, 362 N.W.2d 676 (1984) (confidential information concerning individual customers is protectable); Town & Country House & Home Service, Inc. v. Newbery, 3 N.Y.2d 554, 170 N.Y.S.2d 328, 147 N.E.2d 724 (1958) (list of residential customers using cleaning services held protectable); Morgan's Home Equip. Corp. v. Martucci, 390 Pa. 618, 136 A.2d 838 (1957) (customer list and customer information protectable as a trade secret; whether the information is embodied in a written list or committed to memory is irrelevant); Van Products Co. v. General Welding & Fabricating Co., 419 Pa. 248, 213 A.2d 769 (1965) (distillation of readily available commercial lists is not protectable); NCH Corp. v. Broyles, 749 F.2d 247 (5th Cir.1985) (prohibiting the use of a written route book to solicit customers of the former employer). For a review of the multi-factor test used under California law to decide customer list cases prior to the adoption of the Uniform Trade Secrets Act, see Hollingsworth Solderless Terminal Co. v. Turley, 622 F.2d 1324 (9th Cir.1980).

The interest of a former employee in the opportunity to solicit the customers of a former employer was recognized in Continental Car–Na–Var Corp. v. Moseley, 24 Cal.2d 104, 148 P.2d 9 (1944) (distinguishing the "route cases" in which the former employee has a special relationship with the customers); Woolley's Laundry Inc. v. Silva, 304 Mass. 383, 23 N.E.2d 899 (1939) (acquaintance with former customers is part of the employee's general skill and knowledge); Hollingsworth Solderless Terminal Co., *supra* ("a person has a substantial interest in the unrestrained pursuit of his livelihood"). Restatement, Second, Agency § 396 states that after termination of an agency relationship the agent has no duty to refrain from competing with the principal. Under the Restatement formulation, a former agent remains under a duty not to use or disclose "written lists of names" received in confidence, but is entitled to use "names of customers retained in his memory, if not acquired in violation of his duty as agent." But see the cases cited in the Reporters' Note to Comment *d* that refuse to recognize reliance on memory as a defense.

On the ownership of customer lists, see, e.g., United Centrifugal Pumps v. Cusimano, 9 U.S.P.Q.2d 1171 (W.D.Ark.1988) (rejecting a claim of ownership by an employee hired to develop the customer information); Reid v. Mass Co., 155 Cal.App.2d 293, 318 P.2d 54 (1957) (employer owns customer information developed at its direction); Empire Steam Laundry v. Lozier, 165 Cal. 95, 130 P. 1180 (1913) (same).

Interests beyond the protection of trade secrets may sometimes justify an injunction against soliciting the customers of a former employer. See Adler, Barish, Daniels, Levin and Creskoff v. Epstein, 482 Pa. 416, 393 A.2d 1175 (1978), cert. denied 442 U.S. 907, 99 S.Ct. 2817, 61 L.Ed.2d 272 (1979) (solicitation began during the former employment, thus implicating the employees' duty of loyalty, and the solicitation interfered with existing contractual relationships).

Cases indicating that post-employment solicitation of customers on delivery routes can be prohibited include George v. Burdusis, 21 Cal.2d 153, 130 P.2d 399 (1942) (the friendly relationship between a delivery employee and the employer's customers can justify an injunction against solicitation on behalf of a new employer); Dairy Dale Co. v. Azevedo, 211 Cal. 344, 295 P. 10 (1931) (names, addresses, and requirements of customers held protectable as part of the good will of the business); Pasadena Ice Co. v. Reeder, 206 Cal. 697, 704, 275 P. 944, 947 (1929) (solicitation of delivery route customers prohibited because the former employees knew the customers' "peculiar likes and fancies and other characteristics, a knowledge of which would greatly aid them in securing and retaining the business" of former customers). However, traditional trade secret principles were applied to deny protection in delivery route cases in, e.g., Woolley's Laundry Inc., *supra* (laundry route customers not protected from post-employment solicitation by a former employee who reconstructed the list from memory); Carl A. Colteryahn Dairy, Inc. v. Schneider Dairy, 415 Pa. 276, 203 A.2d 469 (1964) (former employee was entitled to exploit the personal relationships with former dairy route customers). On the use of restrictive covenants to protect customer relationships, see SI Handling Systems, Inc. v. Heisley, 753 F.2d 1244, 1259 (3d Cir.1985) (solicitation of customers by former employees is so "natural, logical and part of human fellowship, that an employer who fears this kind of future competition must protect himself by a preventive contract with his employee" (quoting Spring Steels, Inc. v. Molloy, 400 Pa. 354, 363, 162 A.2d 370, 375 (1960))). Cases upholding restrictive covenants intended to protect customer relationships or confidential customer information include, e.g., McRand, Inc. v. Van Beelen, 138 Ill.App.3d 1045, 93 Ill.Dec. 471, 486 N.E.2d 1306 (1985); Wolf and Co. v. Waldron, 51 Ill.App.3d 239, 9 Ill.Dec. 346, 366 N.E.2d 603 (1977); Eastern Distributing Co. v. Flynn, 222 Kan. 666, 567 P.2d 1371 (1977); North Pacific Lumber Co. v. Moore, 275 Or. 359, 551 P.2d 431 (1976); Walker Employment Serv., Inc. v. Parkhurst, 300 Minn. 264, 219 N.W.2d 437 (1974); Chambers–Dobson, Inc. v. Squier, 238 Neb. 748, 472 N.W.2d 391 (1991).

Comment g. Authority relating to the use and enforcement of nondisclosure agreements and covenants not to compete is collected in the Reporters' Note to § 41, Comment *d.*

For cases examining the reasonableness of "holdover" agreements assigning to the former employer inventions discovered by former employees after termination of the employment, see, e.g., Ingersoll–Rand Co. v. Ciavatta, 110 N.J. 609, 542 A.2d 879 (1988) ("holdover" agreement held unenforceable as applied to inventions conceived after the employment and not derived from proprietary information of the former employer); GTI Corp. v. Calhoon, 309 F.Supp. 762 (S.D.Ohio 1969) (five-year "hold-over" agreement unenforceable as an unreasonable restraint on the employee's use of general skill and training). See also, e.g., Dorr–Oliver, Inc. v. United States, 432 F.2d 447 (Ct.Cl.1970).

§ 43. Improper Acquisition of Trade Secrets

"Improper" means of acquiring another's trade secret under the rule stated in § 40 include theft, fraud, unauthorized interception of communications, inducement of or knowing participation in a breach of confidence, and other means either wrongful in themselves or wrongful under the circumstances of the case. Independent discovery and analysis of publicly available products or information are not improper means of acquisition.

Comment:

a. Scope of protection. The owner of a trade secret does not have an exclusive right to possession or use of the secret information. Protection is available only against a wrongful acquisition, use, or disclosure of the trade secret. See § 40. Use or disclosure of a trade secret in breach of a duty of confidence is treated in §§ 41 and 42. This Section considers the acquisition, use, and disclosure of trade secrets by persons who have not obtained the secret through a confidential disclosure.

b. Proper means of acquisition. Unless a trade secret has been acquired under circumstances giving rise to a duty of confidence, a person who obtains the trade secret by proper means is free to use or disclose the information without liability. Unlike the holder of a patent, the owner of a trade secret has no claim against another who independently discovers the secret. Similarly, others remain free to analyze products publicly marketed by the trade secret owner and, absent protection under a patent or copyright, to exploit any information acquired through such "reverse engineering." A person may also acquire a trade secret through an analysis of published materials or through observation of objects or events that are in public view or otherwise accessible by proper means.

Illustrations:

1. *A* sells a drug compounded from a secret formula. *B*, a competing drug manufacturer, purchases a quantity of *A* 's drug on the open market and learns the formula through scientific analysis. *B* then begins to market a similar product. *B* has not acquired *A* 's trade secret by improper means.

2. *A*, a chemical company, discovers a new process for producing methanol and begins construction of a manufacturing plant incorporating the process. Although the construction site is clearly visible from a major highway that adjoins the site, *A* takes no precautions to prevent passersby from observing construction of the plant. *B*, a competing chemical company, sends several of its engineers to observe *A* 's construction site. The engineers take photographs of the partially-completed plant from the adjoining highway. Subsequent analysis of the photographs reveals *A* 's new process. *B* has not acquired *A* 's trade secret by improper means.

c. Improper means of acquisition. It is not possible to formulate a comprehensive list of the conduct that constitutes "improper" means of acquiring a trade secret. If a trade secret is acquired through conduct that is itself a tortious or criminal invasion of the trade secret owner's rights, the acquisition ordinarily will be regarded as improper. Thus, a person who obtains a trade secret by burglarizing the offices of a competitor acquires the secret by improper means. So also does one who obtains a trade secret by wiretapping the owner's telephone or by employing fraudulent representations to induce the owner to disclose the trade secret. A person who obtains a trade secret by inducing or knowingly accepting a disclosure from a third person who has acquired the secret by improper means, or who induces or knowingly accepts a disclosure from a third person that is in breach of a duty of confidence owed by the third person to the trade secret owner, also acquires the secret by improper means.

The acquisition of a trade secret can be improper even if the means of acquisition are not independently wrongful. The propriety of the acquisition must be evaluated in light of all the circumstances of the case, including whether the means of acquisition are inconsistent with accepted principles of public policy and the extent to which the acquisition was facilitated by the trade secret owner's failure to take reasonable precautions against discovery of the secret by the means in question. Among the factors relevant to the reasonableness of the trade secret owner's precautions are the foreseeability of the conduct through which the secret was acquired and the availability and cost of effective precautions against such an acquisition, evaluated in light of the economic value of the trade secret.

Illustrations:

3. The facts being otherwise as stated in Illustration 2, *B* 's engineers are unable to photograph *A* 's plant from the adjoining highway because of a large fence erected by *A* to prevent observa-

tion of the construction site from the surrounding area. However, because of the size of the site and the nature of the plant, it would be difficult and expensive for *A* to maintain a temporary roof over the site during construction. *B* hires a pilot who flies over the site in a small airplane while *B*'s engineers photograph portions of the partially-completed facility. Subsequent analysis of the photographs reveals *A*'s new process. A court may conclude that *A* has taken reasonable precautions against the discovery of the process and that *B* has acquired *A*'s trade secret by improper means.

4. *A*, a large manufacturing company, employs *B* as an engineer. Angered by a termination of the employment, *B* makes unauthorized photocopies of engineering drawings depicting trade secrets used in the machines that manufacture *A*'s most successful product. *B* offers to provide the photocopies to *C*, a competing manufacturer. *C* accepts the photocopies from *B* with knowledge that *B* is a former employee of *A*. *C* has acquired *A*'s trade secrets by improper means.

5. *A* manufactures a computer system for the transmission, display, and storage of medical data. The system has been licensed for use in several large hospitals under agreements that require the licensees to maintain the confidentiality of trade secrets embodied in *A*'s system. *B* is hired as a consultant by one of *A*'s licensees and is informed of the confidential nature of *A*'s system. *B* decides to design and market a competing system. After normal working hours and without the permission of the licensee, *B* spends a substantial number of hours subjecting *A*'s system to a series of electronic tests in order to learn the trade secrets. *B* has acquired *A*'s trade secrets by improper means.

d. Existence of a trade secret. A person is not subject to liability for an appropriation of information under the rules stated in § 40 unless the information qualifies for protection as a trade secret under the rule stated in § 39. Thus, although an actor may be subject to liability under other rules for conduct that is actionable as an invasion of other protected interests, the acquisition of information that is not a trade secret will not subject the actor to liability under § 40 regardless of the means of acquisition. Information that is readily ascertainable by proper means is not protectable as a trade secret, see § 39, Comment *f*, and the acquisition of such information even by improper means is therefore not actionable under § 40. However, the accessibility of information, and hence its status as a trade secret, is evaluated in light of the difficulty and cost of acquiring the information by proper means. See § 39, Comment *f*. In some circumstances the actor's decision to employ improper means of acquisition is itself evidence that the information is not readily ascertainable through proper means and is thus protectable as a trade secret. Because of the public interest in deterring the acquisition of information by improper means, doubts regarding the status of information as a trade secret are likely to be resolved in favor of protection when the means of acquisition are clearly improper.

REPORTERS' NOTE

This Section carries forward the rules relating to improper means of acquiring trade secrets that originally appeared in Restatement of Torts § 757(a) (1939). See *id.*, Comment *f.* The prohibition against acquisition by improper means is codified in §§ 1 and 2 of the Uniform Trade Secrets Act, which defines "improper means" as "including theft, bribery, misrepresentation, breach or inducement of a breach of a duty to maintain secrecy, or espionage through electronic or other means." *Id.* § 1(1).

Comment b. The United States Supreme Court has emphasized that trade secret law does not restrict the use of information acquired through independent discovery or reverse engineering of publicly distributed products. See Bonito Boats, Inc. v. Thunder Craft Boats, Inc., 489 U.S. 141, 109 S.Ct. 971, 103 L.Ed.2d 118 (1989); Kewanee Oil Co. v. Bicron Corp., 416 U.S. 470, 94 S.Ct. 1879, 40 L.Ed.2d 315 (1974). The Comment to § 1 of the Uniform Trade Secrets Act includes as "proper means" of acquiring a trade secret independent invention, reverse engineering, license from the trade secret owner, observation of items in public use or display, and acquisition from published literature. On the freedom to obtain a trade secret through reverse engineering, see, e.g., SI Handling Systems, Inc. v. Heisley, 753 F.2d 1244 (3d Cir.1985); Chicago Lock Co. v. Fanberg, 676 F.2d 400 (9th Cir. 1982); Angell Elevator Lock Co. v. Manning, 348 Mass. 623, 205 N.E.2d 245 (1965). On the freedom to acquire a trade secret through independent discovery or from public domain materials, see, e.g., American Can Co. v. Mansukhani, 742 F.2d 314 (7th Cir. 1984); Texas Urethane, Inc. v. Seacrest Marine Corp., 608 F.2d 136 (5th Cir.1979); Microbiological Research Corp. v. Muna, 625 P.2d 690 (Utah 1981).

Illustration 1 is based on Restatement of Torts § 757, Illustration 2. Compare Technicon Data Systems Corp. v. Curtis 1000, Inc., 224 U.S.P.Q. 286 (Del.Ch.1984), from which Illustration 5 is taken.

Illustration 2 is based on the result in Interox America v. PPG Industries, Inc., 736 F.2d 194 (5th Cir. 1984). Compare E.I. duPont deNemours & Co. v. Christopher, 431 F.2d 1012 (5th Cir.1970), cert. denied 400 U.S. 1024, 91 S.Ct. 581, 27 L.Ed.2d 637 (1971), from which Illustration 3 is taken.

Comment c. For cases involving means of acquisition that are wrongful in themselves, see, e.g., Phillips v. Frey, 20 F.3d 623 (5th Cir.1994) (misrepresentation); University Computing Co. v. Lykes—Youngstown Corp., 504 F.2d 518 (5th Cir.1974) (theft); Solo Cup Co. v. Paper Machinery

Corp., 240 F.Supp. 126 (E.D.Wis. 1965), affirmed in part 359 F.2d 754 (7th Cir.1966) (same); Sandler v. Gordon, 94 Cal.App.2d 254, 210 P.2d 314 (1949) (same); Continental Data Systems, Inc. v. Exxon Corp., 638 F.Supp. 432 (E.D.Pa.1986) (misrepresentation); Den–Tal–Ez, Inc. v. Siemens Capital Corp., 389 Pa.Super. 219, 566 A.2d 1214 (1989) (same). See also, e.g., Kewanee Oil Co. v. Bicron Corp., 416 U.S. 470, 94 S.Ct. 1879, 40 L.Ed.2d 315 (1974) (listing theft and wiretapping as examples of improper means of acquisition).

Intentionally inducing a breach of confidence is an improper means of acquiring a trade secret. Uniform Trade Secrets Act § 1(1); Restatement of Torts § 757, Comment *h.* See, e.g., Telex Corp. v. Int'l Business Machines Corp., 510 F.2d 894 (10th Cir.), cert. dismissed 423 U.S. 802, 96 S.Ct. 8, 46 L.Ed. 244 (1975); Atlantic Wool Combing Co. v. Norfolk Mills, Inc., 357 F.2d 866 (1st Cir.1966); Anaconda Co. v. Metric Tool & Die Co., 485 F.Supp. 410 (E.D.Pa.1980). Cf. Telerate Systems, Inc. v. Caro, 689 F.Supp. 221 (S.D.N.Y.1988) (inducing breach of a contractual restriction on use is an improper means of acquisition). See generally Milgrim on Trade Secrets § 5.04[4]. A person who accepts a disclosure knowing that it is in breach of a duty of confidence also acquires the trade secret improperly, see, e.g., Bryan v. Kershaw, 366 F.2d 497 (5th Cir.1966), cert. denied 386 U.S. 959, 87 S.Ct. 1030, 18 L.Ed.2d 108 (1967); Colgate–Palmolive Co. v. Carter Products, Inc., 230 F.2d 855 (4th Cir.), cert. denied 352 U.S. 843, 77 S.Ct. 43, 1 L.Ed.2d 59 (1956); Colony Corp. v. Crown Glass Corp., 102 Ill.App.3d 647, 58 Ill.Dec. 283, 430 N.E.2d 225 (1981), but the remedies appropriate against such a person may differ from those appropriate against an actor who actively induces the disclosure. See Milgrim, *supra*, § 5.04[4][c].

Otherwise lawful conduct that is wrongful under the circumstances of the case also constitutes improper means of acquiring a trade secret. Uniform Trade Secrets Act, Comment to § 1; Restatement of Torts § 757, Comment *f.* An often-cited example is E.I. duPont deNemours & Co. v. Christopher, 431 F.2d 1012 (5th Cir.1970), cert. denied 400 U.S. 1024, 91 S.Ct. 581, 27 L.Ed.2d 637 (1971), which is the basis for Illustration 3. The *Christopher* case was cited with apparent approval in Kewanee Oil Co. v. Bicron Corp., 416 U.S. 470, 476, 94 S.Ct. 1879, 1883, 40 L.Ed.2d 315, 322 (1974). The Supreme Court noted that "[t]he maintenance of commercial ethics" is one of the policies animating the protection of trade secrets, and also that "[a] most fundamental human right, that of privacy, is threatened when industrial espionage is condoned or is made profitable." *Id.* at 487, 94 S.Ct. at 1889, 40 L.Ed.2d at 329.

Illustration 3 is based on the *Christopher* case, *supra.* In concluding that the defendant's acquisition was improper, the court stated that although reasonable security precautions such as ordinary fences or roofs may be required, "[c]ommercial privacy must be protected from espionage which could not have been reasonably anticipated or prevented." 431 F.2d at 1016. Compare Drill Parts & Service Co v. Joy Mfg. Co., 439 So.2d 43 (Ala.1983) (defendant held liable for the use of drawings bearing a restrictive notice that it had removed from the trash after disposal by one of the plaintiff's subcontractors) with Defiance Button Machine Co. v. C & C Metal Products Corp., 759 F.2d 1053 (2d Cir.), cert. denied 474 U.S. 844, 106 S.Ct. 131, 88 L.Ed.2d 108 (1985) (plaintiff's failure to erase customer files prior to the sale of a computer constituted inadequate precautions).

Illustration 4 is suggested by, e.g., Solo Cup Co. v. Paper Machinery Corp., 240 F.Supp. 126 (E.D.Wis. 1965), affirmed 359 F.2d 754 (7th Cir. 1966). Illustration 5 is based on Technicon Data Systems Corp. v. Curtis 1000, Inc., 224 U.S.P.Q. 286 (Del.Ch.1984). See also, e.g., Telerate Systems, Inc. v. Caro, 689 F.Supp. 221 (S.D.N.Y.1988) (improper means used to access the plaintiff's computer program).

Comment d. In Defiance Button Machine Co. v. C & C Metal Products Corp., 759 F.2d 1053 (2d Cir.), cert. denied 474 U.S. 844, 106 S.Ct. 131, 88 L.Ed.2d 108 (1985), a defendant who purchased a computer from a competitor subsequently induced a former employee of the competitor to access a customer list left in the computer memory. The Second Circuit held that the propriety of the defendant's means of acquisition was irrelevant in light of the conclusion that the information was no longer protectable as a trade secret. See also, e.g., Wilkin v. Sunbeam Corp., 377 F.2d 344 (10th Cir.), cert. denied 389 U.S. 973, 88 S.Ct. 472, 19 L.Ed.2d 464 (1967) (alleged fraud in acquisition does not eliminate the need to establish the existence of a trade secret); Eaton Corp. v. Appliance Valves Co., 634 F.Supp. 974, 984 (N.D.Ind.1984), affirmed 790 F.2d 874 (Fed.Cir.1986) (removal of patent documents from a former employer's files did not constitute an appropriation of trade secrets since the information was publicly available); Abraham Zion Corp. v. Lebow, 593 F.Supp. 551 (S.D.N.Y. 1984), affirmed 761 F.2d 93 (2d Cir. 1985) (employee's unauthorized use of a garment pattern was not actionable because the information was ascertainable by examining the finished product). In some circumstances, however, the use of improper means of acquisition can itself indicate that the information is sufficiently inaccessible to qualify for protection as a trade secret. See, e.g., Clark v. Bunker, 453 F.2d 1006 (9th Cir.1972); Tan–Line Sun Studios, Inc. v. Bradley, 1 U.S.P.Q.2d 2032, 2039 (E.D.Pa. 1986).

§ 44. Injunctions: Appropriation of Trade Secrets

(1) If appropriate under the rule stated in Subsection (2), injunctive relief may be awarded to prevent a continuing or threatened appropriation of another's trade secret by one who is subject to liability under the rule stated in § 40.

(2) The appropriateness and scope of injunctive relief depend upon a comparative appraisal of all the factors of the case, including the following primary factors:

(a) the nature of the interest to be protected;

(b) the nature and extent of the appropriation;

(c) the relative adequacy to the plaintiff of an injunction and of other remedies;

(d) the relative harm likely to result to the legitimate interests of the defendant if an injunction is granted and to the legitimate interests of the plaintiff if an injunction is denied;

(e) the interests of third persons and of the public;

(f) any unreasonable delay by the plaintiff in bringing suit or otherwise asserting its rights;

(g) any related misconduct on the part of the plaintiff; and

(h) the practicality of framing and enforcing the injunction.

(3) The duration of injunctive relief in trade secret actions should be limited to the time necessary to protect the plaintiff from any harm attributable to the appropriation and to deprive the defendant of any economic advantage attributable to the appropriation.

Comment:

a. Scope. This Section states the principles governing injunctive relief in actions for the appropriation of a trade secret. The general rules relating to injunctive relief in tort actions stated in Chapter 48 of the Restatement, Second, of Torts apply in actions for the appropriation of trade secrets. Only those rules that have particular significance to injunctions in trade secret cases are considered here. This Section is derived from Restatement, Second, Torts § 936, which sets forth the general factors relating to the appropriateness of injunctions in tort actions. See also §§ 933–935, stating the standard of "appropriateness" for injunctive relief, and §§ 937–943, describing in detail the factors relevant in determining appropriateness. Additional considerations may influence the award of preliminary injunctive relief. See Comment *g*.

The appropriation of a trade secret is more closely analogous to tortious interference with rights in tangible property than is trademark infringement or deceptive marketing, which depend on the perceptions of prospective purchasers. The general rules on injunctions in tort actions stated in Restatement, Second, Torts §§ 933–943 are thus more likely to be directly applicable in trade secret cases than in other unfair competition actions.

This Restatement does not treat the rules governing the various techniques available to preserve the secrecy of trade secrets during litigation, such as protective orders, in camera proceedings, and the sealing of records. See Uniform Trade Secrets Act § 5.

b. Relation to other remedies. The usual remedy in tort actions is an award of damages, and the equitable remedy of an injunction was traditionally available only when the remedy of damages was inadequate. With the merger of law and equity, courts are generally free to select the remedy or combination of remedies that most effectively protects the interests threatened by the defendant's misconduct. See Restatement, Second, Torts § 938, Comment *c*. In trade secret cases, the primary interest of the plaintiff is in the secrecy and exclusive use of the appropriated information. As in the case of other forms of unfair competition, the harm caused by the appropriation of a trade secret may not be fully reparable through an award of monetary relief due to the difficulty of proving the amount of loss and the causal connection with the defendant's misconduct. Thus, a defendant's continuing or threatened use or disclosure of a trade secret normally justifies an award of injunctive relief.

In many trade secret cases, both injunctive and monetary relief are appropriate: monetary relief to compensate the plaintiff for existing losses and injunctive relief to prevent future loss through further use or disclosure of the trade secret. In some cases, however, an injunction may be the only appropriate remedy, as when the defendant has not yet disclosed or used a trade secret acquired by improper means or when a defendant threatens to breach a duty of confidence arising from a confidential disclosure of the trade secret. In other cases, unqualified injunctive relief may be inappropriate, as when the defendant in good faith makes a substantial investment in reliance on the trade secret prior to receiving knowledge sufficient to subject the defendant to liability for further use. See § 45, Comment *b*.

c. Appropriateness of injunctive relief. Injunctive relief is often appropriate in trade secret cases to insure against additional harm from further unauthorized use of the trade secret and to deprive the defendant of additional benefits from the appropriation. If the information has not become generally known, an injunction may also be appropriate to preserve the plaintiff's rights in the trade secret by preventing a public disclosure. If the trade secret has already entered the public domain, an injunction may be appropriate to remedy any head start or other unfair advantage acquired by the defendant as a result of the appropriation. However, if the defendant retains no unfair advantage from the appropriation, an injunction against the use of information that is no longer secret can be justified only on a rationale of punishment and deterrence. Because of the public interest in promoting competition, such punitive injunctions are ordinarily inappropriate in trade secret actions.

An injunction may sometimes be appropriate to prevent a threatened use or disclosure of a trade secret. The scope of such an injunction should be carefully framed to avoid undue restraint on legitimate competition. For example, a court will not ordinarily enjoin an employee who has knowledge of a former employer's trade secret from engaging in a particular occupation or working for a particular competitor in the absence of an enforceable covenant not to compete or clear evidence that the contemplated employment will result in disclosure of the secret. However, if there is a substantial risk of disclosure, an injunction prohibiting the disclosure or prohibiting participation in a particular project that presents a special risk of disclosure may be appropriate.

Although injunctive relief is routinely granted in trade secret cases, the remedy remains subject to equitable principles, including the factors stated in Subsection (2) of this Section. The appropriateness of injunctive relief must be determined in light of the interests of both the parties and the public, including the interest of the plaintiff in preserving the commercial advantage inherent in the trade secret, the interest of the defendant in avoiding interference with legitimate business transactions, and the interest of the public in fostering innovation and promoting vigorous competition. For example, although employers are entitled to protection against appropriations of trade secrets by employees, employees are entitled, absent an enforceable contractual restraint, to market their skills and training to others. These competing interests are properly considered not only in defining the subject matter eligible for protection as a trade secret, see § 42, Comment *d*, but also in fashioning appropriate relief. The traditional equitable principles of laches, estoppel, and unclean hands are also applicable in trade secret cases.

Under the rules stated in § 40, innocent use of another's trade secret is not actionable. A defendant is subject to liability only for use occurring after the defendant acquires actual or constructive knowledge that the information is the trade secret of another. See § 40, Comment *d*. There is some authority for the rule that a good faith user who pays value for the secret or otherwise invests in its use before receiving notice of the appropriation is not subject to liability for continued use after notice. A more appropriate balance of interests can be achieved in such cases, however, by limiting the remedy rather than precluding liability for subsequent use. Although it may sometimes be inequitable to prohibit the defendant from continued use of the secret after notice, it may be appropriate to impose other remedies such as an injunction conditioning further use on the payment of a reasonable royalty. See Uniform Trade Secrets Act § 2(b).

A court contemplating injunctive relief in a trade secret case must also consider its ability to fashion and enforce the injunction so as to protect the legitimate interests of the trade secret owner without unduly interfering with legitimate competition by the defendant. For example, an injunction should be sufficiently precise to give the defendant fair notice of the information that is encompassed within the terms of the injunction.

d. Factors determining the scope of injunctive relief. The factors listed in Subsection (2) of this Section are relevant in determining the scope as well as the appropriateness of injunctive relief. An injunction ordinarily prohibits only use or disclosure of the trade secret and information substantially derived from the trade secret. Practical considerations, however, may sometimes justify broader relief. In some cases, for example, an injunction limited to the trade secret and its derivatives may be impossible to enforce due to the difficulty of distinguishing further improper use or disclosure of the trade secret from independent discovery. An injunction against participation in a particular project or business may then be appropriate. Similarly, in some cases, although liability may be clear, the exact boundaries of the trade secret may be difficult to define. The proper balance between the plaintiff's right to protection and the defendant's right to fair notice of prohibited conduct may then require the court to include a somewhat broader or somewhat narrower field of information within the scope of the injunction.

When the trade secret is narrow in scope and closely related to publicly available information, the injunction should be carefully restricted to the contours of the trade secret in order to avoid encroachment on the public domain. Nevertheless, if the trade secret is an essential component of a larger process or product, other aspects of which are in the public domain, in some cases the only effective means of protecting the trade secret may be an injunction against use of the process or manufacture of the product.

Geographic limitations on the scope of injunctive relief in trade secret cases are ordinarily inappropriate. A defendant will normally be enjoined from disclosing or using the trade secret even outside the geographic market of the trade secret owner. The defendant's use of the secret in any market may increase the risk of disclosure to the public and may deprive the plaintiff of potential licensing revenues. Even when direct injury to the plaintiff is unlikely, an injunction unlimited in geographic scope is ordinarily appropriate to deprive the defendant of further unjust enrichment from the appropriation of the trade secret.

In some circumstances the unauthorized disclosure of another's trade secret for a purpose other than commercial exploitation may be privileged. See § 40, Comment *c*. Although there is little case law, any injunctive relief issued in such situations must accommodate protection of the plaintiff's trade secret with the free speech or other interests underlying the privilege.

e. Surrender of objects and assignment of patents. In order to insure full compensation to the trade secret owner and to deprive the defendant of all unjust gains, a court may properly require a defendant to return to the trade secret owner documents, blueprints, customer lists, or other tangible embodiments of the trade secret. See Uniform Trade Secrets Act § 2(c). If the defendant has obtained a patent covering either the trade secret or an invention derived from the trade secret, a court may also require the defendant to assign the patent to the owner of the trade secret.

f. Duration of injunctive relief. Injunctions are appropriate in trade secret cases to protect the plaintiff from further harm caused by the use or disclosure of the trade secret and to deprive the defendant of further unjust gain. However, the law of trade secrets does not afford protection against losses or gains that are not attributable to the defendant's appropriation. This principle establishes the appropriate duration of injunctive relief in trade secret cases. Thus, injunctive relief should ordinarily continue only until the defendant could have acquired the information by proper means. Injunctions extending beyond this period are justified only when necessary to deprive the defendant of a head start or other unjust advantage that is attributable to the appropriation. See Uniform Trade Secrets Act § 2(a). More extensive injunctive relief undermines the public interest by restraining legitimate competition.

The issuance of a patent or other public disclosure renders the disclosed information ineligible for continued protection as a trade secret. See § 39, Comment *f*. Some courts, however, have issued or continued injunctions after public disclosure of the trade secret against defendants who appropriated the information while it was still secret. Other courts hold that public disclosure precludes the subsequent issuance of an injunction and justifies termination of an injunction previously granted. When the trade secret is publicly disclosed by the plaintiff or a third person after the defendant's appropriation, the proper inquiry is whether injunctive relief remains necessary to protect against future injury to the plaintiff or future unjust enrichment to the defendant that is attributable to the defendant's wrongful actions prior to the public disclosure. Whether an injunction remains appropriate thus depends on the facts of the particular case. For example, early access to information subsequently disclosed in a patent may allow the defendant to bring to market or reduce to practice the teachings of the patent more quickly than otherwise possible. Similarly, the public disclosure may not encompass all aspects of the information appropriated by the defendant. Limited injunctive relief may thus remain appropriate to eliminate an improper economic advantage that would otherwise be retained by the defendant after the public disclosure of the trade secret. If the public disclosure results from the defendant's own unauthorized conduct, injunctive relief may remain appropriate until the information would have become readily ascertainable to the defendant through proper means. However, if the defendant's public disclosure results in extensive use of the information by others, a continuing injunction against the defendant may yield little benefit to the plaintiff. It may also be difficult to determine the appropriate duration of such an injunction. Since the defendant is subject to liability for the pecuniary loss to the plaintiff resulting from the destruction of the trade secret and for its own pecuniary gain derived from the unauthorized disclosure, see § 45, in some cases a court may properly conclude that monetary relief is a sufficient remedy.

An injunction also should not ordinarily extend beyond the time when the defendant could have properly acquired and implemented the information through reverse engineering or independent discovery. Subsequent use by the defendant does not subject the plaintiff to harm that is attributable to the appropriation of the trade secret. In some cases this duration may be measured by the time it would take a person of ordinary skill in the industry to discover the trade secret by independent means or to obtain the trade secret through the reverse engineering of publicly marketed products. The opinions of experts familiar with the particular industry are thus relevant in determining an appropriate duration. The experience of other competitors in attempting to acquire the information by proper means is also relevant in determining the time it would have taken the defendant to acquire the information in the absence of the appropriation. The defendant may also show that because of a comparative advantage unrelated to the appropriation, the period of lawful development would have been shorter than that for others in the industry. The duration of the injunction, however, should be sufficient to deprive the defendant of any head start or other economic advantage attributable to the appropriation. In some cases courts have issued injunctions for a specific period reflecting the time when the defendant could have acquired the information by proper means. In other cases courts have awarded unlimited injunctions, with the burden on the defendant to seek a modification of the injunction when the commercial advantage from the appropriation has ended. The most efficient procedure depends on the ease and certainty with which the appropriate duration of relief can be determined in advance. In either case the defendant remains liable for any expenses of reverse engineering or independent development that the defendant has saved as a result of the appropriation. See § 45, Comment *f*.

Illustrations:

1. *A* produces a chemical through a process eligible for protection as a trade secret. *B*, a former employee of *A* who learned the process in confidence, establishes a competing business to produce the chemical using the secret process. *C*, a research chemist at a major university, later independently discovers the process and describes it in an article published in a prominent chemistry journal. An injunction against *B*'s use or disclosure of the process should not extend beyond the time of the public disclosure by *C* and any additional period necessary to eliminate any economic advantage to *B* resulting from *B*'s head start in exploiting the information prior to the public disclosure.

2. *A*, a manufacturer, initiates a research project intended to produce a precision tape recorder. *B* works as an engineer on the project through its successful completion and subsequently leaves the employment with *A* to establish a competing business using trade secrets learned during the former employment. Before *B* begins marketing the product, *A* brings an action in which *B* is found liable for appropriating *A*'s trade secrets. The evidence indicates that it would take six months to acquire the trade secrets through reverse engineering of the tape recorders that *A* has begun to market and to embody the secrets in a finished product. If an injunction is otherwise appropriate, the court may properly conclude that *B* should be enjoined from use or disclosure of the trade secrets for six months following the commencement of sales by *A*. Alternatively, the court may properly conclude that *B* should be enjoined from use or disclosure of the trade secrets for an unlimited time, subject to *B*'s right to apply for a termination of the injunction upon proof that the period required for successful reverse engineering and implementation has passed. *B* is also subject to liability to *A* for any costs associated with reverse engineering that have been saved by *B* as result of the appropriation. See § 45, Comment *f*.

g. Preliminary relief. The rule stated in this Section deals primarily with injunctions granted as final relief, but the factors stated in Subsection (2) are also relevant to the imposition of provisional remedies. Although courts differ on the precise formulation, all courts recognize that the appropriateness of preliminary relief depends upon the likelihood that the plaintiff will suffer irreparable harm in the absence of preliminary relief, the plaintiff's likelihood of success on the merits, the balance of equities between the parties, and the interest of the public. In evaluating the possibility of irreparable harm in trade secret cases, the courts have recognized that the loss to a trade secret owner from the unauthorized use or disclosure of a trade secret is often difficult to remedy through a subsequent award of monetary relief.

REPORTERS' NOTE

Comment a. Remedies in trade secret cases were considered in Restatement of Torts § 757, Comment *e* (1939), which recognized that an injunction against "future harm by disclosure or adverse use" is an appropriate remedy. Section 2 of the Uniform Trade Secrets Act provides for injunctive relief against an "actual or threatened" appropriation of a trade secret. See generally Jager, Trade Secrets Law § 7.02; Milgrim on Trade Secrets § 7.08; Johnson, Remedies in Trade Secret Litigation, 72 Nw.U.L.Rev. 1004 (1978).

On the protection of trade secrets during litigation, see Jager, *supra*, § 5.06; Milgrim, *supra*, § 7.06. Section 5 of the Uniform Trade Secrets Act requires the court in actions under the Act to "preserve the secrecy of an alleged trade secret by reasonable means." See generally Miller, Confidentiality, Protective Orders, and Public Access to the Courts, 105 Harv.L.Rev. 428 (1991).

Comment b. Injunctive relief is a common remedy in trade secret cases. See generally Jager, Trade Secrets Law § 7.02; Milgrim on Trade Secrets § 7.08[1]. There is evidence that the rule requiring irreparable harm or inadequacy of the remedy at law as a prerequisite for injunctive relief may no longer be viable even as a general principle. See Laycock, The Death of the Irreparable Injury Rule (1991).

The prior Restatement emphasized that the owner of a trade secret could be granted "two or more remedies in the same action if the court is competent to administer them." Restatement of Torts § 757, Comment *e*. Many trade secret cases award both monetary and injunctive relief. See, e.g., USM Corp. v. Marson Fastener Corp., 392 Mass. 334, 467 N.E.2d 1271 (1984) (accounting and injunction); Cherne Industrial, Inc. v. Grounds & Associates, Inc., 278 N.W.2d 81 (Minn.1979) (accounting and injunction); Tri–Tron Int'l v. Velto, 525 F.2d 432 (9th Cir.1975) (damages and injunction).

Comment c. For cases discussing the functions of injunctive relief in trade secret actions, see, e.g., Winston Research Corp. v. Minnesota Mining and Mfg. Co., 350 F.2d 134 (9th Cir.1965) (an injunction denies the defendant unjust enrichment and protects the plaintiff from further injury); Surgidev Corp. v. Eye Technology, Inc., 828 F.2d 452 (8th Cir. 1987); Kubik, Inc. v. Hull, 56 Mich. App. 335, 224 N.W.2d 80 (1974) (equitable relief should bear a reasonable relationship to the injuries suffered by the plaintiff; punitive relief is not appropriate). Some cases have granted punitive injunctions that go beyond protecting the injured party or preventing unjust enrichment. See, e.g., Franke v. Wiltschek, 209 F.2d 493 (2d Cir.1953) (injunction granted although the trade secret was largely disclosed in an expired patent; Judge Frank in dissent argued that damages were adequate compensation and that a punitive injunction was inappropriate); Valco Cincinnati, Inc. v. N & D Machining Service, Inc., 24 Ohio St.3d 41, 492 N.E.2d 814 (1986) (upholding a permanent injunction in order to punish the defendant for unethical conduct).

Courts have issued injunctions against a threatened use or disclosure of trade secrets. See, e.g., Baxter Int'l, Inc. v. Morris, 976 F.2d 1189 (8th Cir.1992) (enjoining disclosure by a former employee but permitting acceptance of the new employment); Allis–Chalmers Mfg. Co. v. Continental Aviation & Engineering Corp., 255 F.Supp. 645 (E.D.Mich.1966) (enjoining former employee's participation in a specific research project); Den–Tal–Ez Inc. v. Siemens Capital Corp., 9 U.S.P.Q.2d 1932 (Pa.Super.1988); Air Products and Chemicals, Inc. v. Johnson, 296 Pa.Super. 405, 442 A.2d 1114 (1982); B.F. Goodrich Co. v. Wohlgemuth, 117 Ohio App. 493, 192 N.E.2d 99 (1963) (injunction based on evidence of former employee's intent to disclose). Cf. E.I. duPont de Nemours & Co. v. American Potash & Chemical Corp., 41 Del.Ch. 533, 200 A.2d 428 (1964) (summary judgment denied to the defendant because the evidence might establish a sufficient threat of wrongful use or disclosure). Cases finding the risk of use or disclosure insufficient to justify injunctive relief include AMP, Inc. v. Fleischhacker, 823 F.2d 1199 (7th Cir.1987) (dictum); Continental Group, Inc. v. Amoco Chemicals Corp., 614 F.2d 351 (3d Cir.1980) (distinguishing the standard for enforcement of a covenant not to compete); Teradyne, Inc. v. Clear Communications Corp., 707 F.Supp. 353 (N.D.Ill. 1989); Tubular Threading, Inc. v. Scandaliato, 443 So.2d 712 (La.App. 1983). See also § 2 of the Uniform Trade Secrets Act, which authorizes an injunction against a "threatened" appropriation.

Restatement of Torts § 757, Comment *e*, concluded that equitable defenses generally applicable to injunctive relief are available in trade secret cases. For cases involving laches, see, e.g., Tracerlab, Inc. v. Industrial Nucleonics Corp., 313 F.2d 97 (1st Cir.1963) (material issue of fact as to whether the plaintiff was guilty of laches); Anaconda Co. v. Metric Tool & Die Co., 485 F.Supp. 410 (E.D.Pa.1980) (laches is directed to the court's equitable discretion; applied to bar damages but not injunctive relief); FMC Corp. v. Spurlin, 596 F.Supp. 609 (W.D.Pa.1984) (laches precluded summary judgment); Shatterproof Glass Corp. v. Guardian Glass Co., 322 F.Supp. 854 (E.D.Mich.1970), affirmed 462 F.2d 1115 (6th Cir.), cert. denied 409 U.S. 1039, 93 S.Ct. 518, 34 L.Ed.2d 487 (1972) (claim barred by laches) (dictum). For cases recognizing the applicability of the doctrine of unclean hands in trade secret actions, see, e.g., Winston Research Corp. v.

Minnesota Mining and Mfg. Co., 350 F.2d 134 (9th Cir.1965) (unclean hands not established); A.H. Emery Co. v. Marcan Products Corp., 389 F.2d 11 (2d Cir.), cert. denied 393 U.S. 835, 89 S.Ct. 109, 21 L.Ed.2d 106 (1968) (same); Cataphote Corp. v. Hudson, 422 F.2d 1290 (5th Cir.1970) (unclean hands doctrine would preclude protection for secrets improperly obtained by the plaintiff) (dictum); American Cyanamid Co. v. Power Conversion, Inc., 71 Misc.2d 213, 336 N.Y.S.2d 6 (Sup.Ct.1972) (unclean hands doctrine recognized). See generally Milgrim on Trade Secrets § 7.08[1][e].

An injunction protecting trade secrets should be sufficiently precise to give the defendant fair notice of the prohibited conduct. See, e.g., American Can Co. v. Mansukhani, 742 F.2d 314 (7th Cir.1984); E.W. Bliss Co. v. Struthers–Dunn, Inc., 408 F.2d 1108 (8th Cir.1969) (preliminary injunction found overly broad and vague); Syntex Ophthalmics, Inc. v. Tsuetaki, 701 F.2d 677 (7th Cir.1983) (permitting the defendants to seek judicial interpretation of the injunction); Televation Telecommunication Systems, Inc. v. Saindon, 169 Ill.App.3d 8, 119 Ill. Dec. 500, 522 N.E.2d 1359 (1988) (injunction prohibiting the manufacture of products "based on or incorporating plaintiff's trade secrets" was sufficiently precise under the circumstances of the case).

Comment d. A defendant may be enjoined from using the trade secret and anything substantially derived from the trade secret. A few cases invoke the patent law doctrine of equivalents to determine the appropriate limits of the plaintiff's protection. See Cataphote Corp. v. Hudson, 422 F.2d 1290 (5th Cir.1970) (doctrine of equivalents "useful as an analogy, though no more than that"); Bolt Associates, Inc. v. Alpine Geophysical Associates, 365 F.2d 742 (3d Cir.1966) (doctrine invoked in interpreting a contract); Minnesota Mining & Mfg. Co. v. Technical Tape Corp., 221 N.Y.S.2d 58 (Sup.Ct.1961), affirmed 18 A.D.2d 679, 235 N.Y.S.2d 830 (1962) (doctrine invoked in interpreting an injunction). See also Motorola, Inc. v. Computer Displays Int'l, Inc., 739 F.2d 1149 (7th Cir. 1984) (applying the doctrine of equivalents to a consent decree).

An injunction should not unnecessarily restrict the use of information that is outside the scope of the trade secret. See, e.g., Sigma Chemical Co. v. Harris, 794 F.2d 371 (8th Cir. 1986); Smith v. Dravo Corp., 203 F.2d 369 (7th Cir.1953); American Can Co. v. Mansukhani, 742 F.2d 314 (7th Cir.1984) (when the trade secret is closely related to information in the public domain, relief should be carefully framed to avoid restraint on legitimate competition; see also the appeal of the permanent injunction, 814 F.2d 421 (7th Cir.1987)); Winston Research Corp. v. Minnesota Mining and Mfg. Co., 350 F.2d 134 (9th Cir. 1965). See also, e.g., Jillian's Billiard Club, Inc. v. Beloff Billiards, Inc., 35 Mass.App.Ct. 372, 619 N.E.2d 635 (1993) (injunction issued against use of appropriated data but not all competition with the plaintiff, citing Restatement Third, Unfair Competition § 44, Comment *c* (Tent. Draft No.4 (1993))); Hayes–Albion v. Kuberski, 421 Mich. 170, 364 N.W.2d 609 (1984) (an injunction against former employees should ordinarily extend only to the use of the trade secret rather than to all competition with the former employer). In some cases, however, broader prohibitions may be necessary to provide effective relief.

See, e.g., General Electric Co. v. Sung, 843 F.Supp. 776 (D.Mass.1994) (injunction prohibiting manufacture of a product "inextricably connected" to the trade secret); Head Ski Co. v. Kam Ski Co., 158 F.Supp. 919 (D.Md. 1958); ILG Industries, Inc. v. Scott, 49 Ill.2d 88, 273 N.E.2d 393 (1971) (prohibiting manufacture of a product in which the trade secret was an essential component); Allis–Chalmers Mfg. Co. v. Continental Aviation & Engineering Corp., 255 F.Supp. 645 (E.D.Mich.1966) (new employment was sufficiently likely to result in disclosure of confidential information that a preliminary injunction against work on products related to the trade secrets was justified).

Geographic limitations are not ordinarily appropriate in trade secret injunctions. See Lamb–Weston, Inc. v. McCain Foods, Ltd., 941 F.2d 970 (9th Cir.1991) (world-wide injunction issued despite plaintiff's sales in only a few countries).

For cases illustrating the importance of shaping injunctive relief to balance the legitimate interests of the user and the public as well as the interests of the trade secret owner, see Detroit Edison Co. v. National Labor Relations Board, 440 U.S. 301, 99 S.Ct. 1123, 59 L.Ed.2d 333 (1979) (overturning an NLRB order requiring disclosure of confidential information by an employer to a labor union because the order did not contain adequate safeguards to protect the confidentiality of the information); Hercules, Inc. v. National Labor Relations Board, 833 F.2d 426 (2d Cir. 1987) (upholding an NLRB order requiring an employer to disclose trade secrets to a labor union in connection with the investigation of an accident site, subject to the union's execution of a confidentiality agreement).

Comment e. The prior Restatement provided for the surrender of physical embodiments of the trade secret. Restatement of Torts § 757, Comment *e.* Section 2(c) of the Uniform Trade Secrets Act authorizes a court to compel affirmative acts to protect the trade secret. For cases requiring surrender of documents or other materials embodying the trade secret, see Curtiss–Wright Corp. v. Edel–Brown Tool & Die Co., 381 Mass. 1, 407 N.E.2d 319 (1980); Sperry Rand Corp. v. A–T–O, Inc., 447 F.2d 1387 (4th Cir.1971), cert. denied 405 U.S. 1017, 92 S.Ct. 1292, 31 L.Ed.2d 479 (1972). Assignment of a patent to the trade secret owner was ordered in, e.g., Julius Hyman & Co. v. Velsicol Corp., 123 Colo. 563, 233 P.2d 977, cert. denied 342 U.S. 870, 72 S.Ct. 113, 96 L.Ed. 654 (1951); Colgate–Palmolive Co. v. Carter Products, Inc., 230 F.2d 855 (4th Cir.), cert. denied 352 U.S. 843, 77 S.Ct. 43, 1 L.Ed.2d 59 (1956).

Comment f. Cases limiting the duration of injunctive relief to the period it would take a legitimate competitor to acquire the information by proper means include, e.g., Lamb–Weston, Inc. v. McCain Foods, Ltd., 941 F.2d 970 (9th Cir.1991); Sigma Chemical Co. v. Harris, 794 F.2d 371 (8th Cir.1986); Schulenburg v. Signatrol, Inc., 33 Ill.2d 379, 212 N.E.2d 865 (1965), cert. denied 383 U.S. 959, 86 S.Ct. 1225, 16 L.Ed.2d 302 (1966) (injunction should terminate when the defendant could have legally produced the product); ILG Industries, Inc. v. Scott, 49 Ill.2d 88, 273 N.E.2d 393 (1971) (injunction should last no longer than the time required to discover the trade secret by lawful means); Televation Telecommunication Systems, Inc. v. Saindon, 169 Ill.App.3d 8, 119 Ill.Dec. 500, 522

N.E.2d 1359 (1988); Winston Research Corp. v. Minnesota Mining and Mfg. Co., 350 F.2d 134 (9th Cir. 1965); Surgidev Corp. v. Eye Technology, Inc., 828 F.2d 452 (8th Cir. 1987) (injunction against solicitation of customers granted only for the time required to develop the customer list independently); SI Handling Systems, Inc. v. Heisley, 753 F.2d 1244 (3d Cir.1985) (injunction for a period sufficient to negate the advantage from the appropriation). See also General Electric Co. v. Sung, 843 F.Supp. 776 (D.Mass.1994) (appropriate measure is the time it would take "independently to develop or reverse engineer" the technology, but also permitting the defendant to license the technology from other manufacturers). In Brunswick Corp. v. Outboard Marine Corp., 79 Ill.2d 475, 38 Ill.Dec. 781, 404 N.E.2d 205 (1980), the court emphasized that the time period for reverse engineering is measured from the first lawful access to the product, not from the time the defendant improperly acquired the trade secret. In Northern Petrochemical Co. v. Tomlinson, 484 F.2d 1057 (7th Cir.1973), the court held that if the period of time necessary for lawful discovery of the trade secret has passed before the defendant begins use of the information, no injunction should issue. See generally Jamieson, Just Deserts: A Model to Harmonize Trade Secret Injunctions, 72 Neb.L.Rev. 515 (1993); Johnson, Remedies in Trade Secret Litigation, 72 Nw.U.L.Rev. 1004 (1978); Comment, Trade Secrets: How Long Should an Injunction Last?, 26 U.C.L.A. L.Rev. 203 (1978). "[T]he period of time that would be required for independent development appears to be the prevailing standard." Milgrim on Trade Secrets § 7.08[1]. The Comment to § 2 of the Uniform Trade Secrets Act states the rule on duration as follows: "Subject to any additional period of restraint necessary to negate lead time, an injunction accordingly should terminate when a former trade secret becomes either generally known to good faith competitors or generally knowable to them because of the lawful availability of products that can be reverse engineered to reveal a trade secret."

In determining the period necessary for reverse engineering, expert testimony and evidence relating to the experience of other competitors is admissible. Schulenburg, *supra*; Salsbury Laboratories, Inc. v. Merieux Laboratories, Inc., 735 F.Supp. 1555 (M.D.Ga.1989), affirmed 908 F.2d 706 (11th Cir.1990) (the fact that other competitors were able to produce the product without the plaintiff's trade secret weighs against an injunction prohibiting production of the product by the defendant).

The leading case holding that an injunction is not available once the trade secret has been disclosed in a patent is Conmar Products Corp. v. Universal Slide Fastener Co., 172 F.2d 150 (2d Cir.1949). See also, e.g., Schreyer v. Casco Products Corp., 190 F.2d 921 (2d Cir.1951), cert. denied 342 U.S. 913, 72 S.Ct. 360, 96 L.Ed. 683 (1952) (damages are an adequate remedy to compensate for the head start resulting from access to the information prior to the patent disclosure); Picard v. United Aircraft Corp., 128 F.2d 632 (2d Cir.), cert. denied 317 U.S. 651, 63 S.Ct. 46, 87 L.Ed. 524 (1942). Contra, e.g., Shellmar Products Co. v. Allen–Qualley Co., 87 F.2d 104 (7th Cir.1936), cert. denied 301 U.S. 695, 57 S.Ct. 923, 81 L.Ed. 1350 (1937); A.O. Smith Corp. v. Petroleum Iron Works Co., 74 F.2d 934 (6th Cir.1935). When the public disclosure of a trade secret is due to the actions of the defendant rather than the plaintiff or a third person, several cases indicate that the defendant should not be permitted to rely on the loss of secrecy to avoid an injunction for the time necessary to acquire the information by proper means. See Syntex Ophthalmics, Inc. v. Tsuetaki, 701 F.2d 677 (7th Cir.1983); Underwater Storage, Inc. v. United States Rubber Co., 371 F.2d 950 (D.C.Cir.1966), cert. denied 386 U.S. 911, 87 S.Ct. 859, 17 L.Ed.2d 784 (1967); Space Aero Products Co. v. R.E. Darling Co., 238 Md. 93, 208 A.2d 74, cert. denied 382 U.S. 843, 86 S.Ct. 77, 15 L.Ed.2d 83 (1965).

Cases recognizing that an injunction is sometimes necessary to prevent the defendant from unjustly benefiting from a head start that is attributable to the appropriation include, e.g., Lamb–Weston, *supra*; K–2 Ski Co. v. Head Ski Co., 506 F.2d 471 (9th Cir.1974); Hyde Corp. v. Huffines, 158 Tex. 566, 314 S.W.2d 763, cert. denied 358 U.S. 898, 79 S.Ct. 223, 3 L.Ed.2d 148 (1958) (injunction continuing beyond the disclosure of the trade secret in a patent was justified to deprive the defendant of a head start gained from the breach of an earlier confidential disclosure).

Section 2(a) of the Uniform Trade Secrets Act authorizing injunctive relief requires termination of the injunction when the information is no longer secret, except to the extent necessary to "eliminate commercial advantage that otherwise would be derived from the misappropriation." See Lamb–Weston, *supra* (recognizing that under the Act a defendant may ask the court to vacate an injunction if the trade secret becomes publicly known). See also American Can Co. v. Mansukhani, 814 F.2d 421 (7th Cir.1987) (permitting the defendant to request a modification of the injunction if the trade secret enters the public domain); Curtiss–Wright Corp. v. Edel–Brown Tool & Die Co., 381 Mass. 1, 407 N.E.2d 319 (1980) (perpetual injunction affirmed on conflicting evidence of ability to reverse engineer, but recognizing the right of the defendant to seek a dissolution of the injunction based on changed circumstances). Cf. Hyde Corp., *supra* (defendant has the burden of persuading the court that the injunction should be less than perpetual; the dissent argued that the plaintiff has the burden of establishing the appropriateness of equitable relief). Cases that grant perpetual injunctions are not inconsistent with the principles stated in this Section if the courts are receptive to requests for subsequent modification. A few cases, however, appear to uphold perpetual injunctions on punitive grounds. See Franke v. Wiltschek, 209 F.2d 493 (2d Cir.1953) (injunction granted although the trade secret was largely disclosed in an expired patent; Judge Frank in dissent argued that a punitive injunction was inappropriate); Valco Cincinnati, Inc. v. N & D Machining Service, Inc., 24 Ohio St.3d 41, 492 N.E.2d 814 (1986) (upholding a perpetual injunction in order to punish the defendant in light of egregious circumstances; the dissent notes that a perpetual injunction undermines competition). See also Analogic Corp. v. Data Translation, Inc., 371 Mass. 643, 358 N.E.2d 804 (1976).

Comment g. Preliminary relief in trade secret cases is discussed in Jager, Trade Secrets Law §§ 7.02[1]-[2]; Milgrim on Trade Secrets § 7.05 (describing the varying formulations of the standard for preliminary relief in the federal circuits).

Application of the criteria for preliminary relief in trade secret cases is illustrated in, e.g., FMC Corp. v. Varco Int'l, Inc., 677 F.2d 500 (5th Cir. 1982); Litton Systems, Inc. v. Sundstrand Corp., 750 F.2d 952 (Fed. Cir.1984). The inadequacy of monetary relief and the risk of a destruction of trade secret rights through public disclosure frequently justify the conclusion that the plaintiff will suffer irreparable harm in the absence of preliminary relief. See, e.g., FMC Corp. v. Taiwan Tainan Giant Industrial Co., 730 F.2d 61, 63 (2d Cir.1984) ("A trade secret once lost is, of course, lost forever."); Chem–Trend Inc. v. McCarthy, 780 F.Supp. 458 (E.D.Mich.1991) (noting the difficulty of measuring the loss caused by an appropriation of plaintiff's customer list); CPG Products Corp. v. Mego Corp., 502 F.Supp. 42 (S.D.Ohio 1980) (noting the risk that the trade secret will enter the public domain); Barr–Mullin, Inc. v. Browning, 108 N.C.App. 590, 424 S.E.2d 226 (1993) (the nature of a trade secret makes irreparable harm likely). But cf. Campbell Soup Co. v. ConAgra, Inc., 977 F.2d 86 (3d Cir.1992) (no irreparable harm likely under the facts).

§ 45. Monetary Relief: Appropriation of Trade Secrets

(1) One who is liable to another for an appropriation of the other's trade secret under the rule stated in § 40 is liable for the pecuniary loss to the other caused by the appropriation or for the actor's own pecuniary gain resulting from the appropriation, whichever is greater, unless such relief is inappropriate under the rule stated in Subsection (2).

(2) Whether an award of monetary relief is appropriate and the appropriate method of measuring such relief depend upon a comparative appraisal of all the factors of the case, including the following primary factors:

(a) the degree of certainty with which the plaintiff has established the fact and extent of the pecuniary loss or the actor's pecuniary gain resulting from the appropriation;

(b) the nature and extent of the appropriation;

(c) the relative adequacy to the plaintiff of other remedies;

(d) the intent and knowledge of the actor and the nature and extent of any good faith reliance by the actor;

(e) any unreasonable delay by the plaintiff in bringing suit or otherwise asserting its rights; and

(f) any related misconduct on the part of the plaintiff.

Comment:

a. Scope. This Section states the rules governing the recovery of monetary relief in actions for the appropriation of a trade secret. Monetary relief may consist of compensatory damages measured by the loss to the plaintiff or restitutionary relief measured by the unjust gain to the defendant. This Section states the rules applicable to both measures of monetary relief.

The general rules relating to the recovery of compensatory damages in tort actions apply in actions for the appropriation of trade secrets. This Section addresses only issues that have particular significance to the recovery of damages in trade secret actions. The following sections of the Restatement, Second, of Torts are also relevant: §§ 902 and 903 defining "damages" and "compensatory damages"; § 907 stating the rule for recovery of nominal damages; §§ 908 and 909 stating the rules for recovery of punitive damages; § 912 stating the requirement of "certainty"; and §§ 435A and 435B stating rules relating to intended and unintended consequences of tortious conduct.

The general rules relating to the restitution of benefits tortiously acquired are also applicable in actions for the appropriation of trade secrets. See Restatement of Restitution § 136 (1937).

b. Appropriateness of monetary relief. Loss to the plaintiff or gain to the defendant can result from either unauthorized use or unauthorized disclosure of a trade secret. The courts have recognized the need for flexibility in formulating monetary remedies in order to achieve both compensatory and restitutionary objectives.

The plaintiff is generally entitled to recover any proven pecuniary loss attributable to the appropriation of the trade secret. The plaintiff bears the burden of proving the fact and cause of any loss for which recovery is sought. However, the plaintiff is required to prove the amount of such loss with only as much certainty as is reasonable under the circumstances. See Restatement, Second, Torts § 912. If otherwise appropriate, the plaintiff may also recover any gain acquired by the defendant as a result of the appropriation, subject to the limitation on double recovery. See Comment *c*.

The knowledge and intent of the defendant are relevant in determining appropriate relief. A defendant is not subject to liability under the rules stated in § 40 until the defendant has actual or constructive knowledge that the use or disclosure of the trade secret is wrongful. See § 40, Comment *d*. If the defendant has invested in the trade secret prior to acquiring such knowledge, it may be inequitable to deprive the defendant of all gains attributable to subsequent use of the trade secret. The award of a reasonable royalty for use made after notice and an injunction conditioning further use upon payment of a reasonable royalty may be an appropriate remedy. See Comment *g*.

The conduct of the plaintiff may also affect the appropriateness of monetary relief. The traditional equitable doctrines of laches, estoppel, and unclean hands are applicable to the award of monetary as well as injunctive relief in trade secret actions. Cf. §§ 31 and 32.

c. Relationship of legal and equitable remedies. The rules governing the award of monetary relief for the appropriation of a trade secret derive from both legal and equitable principles. Cf. § 36, Comment *b*. The traditional measure of damages awards relief measured by the loss to the plaintiff resulting from the appropriation. The nature of a competitive marketplace, however, often makes it difficult for a plaintiff to prove lost sales or other losses attributable to the appropriation of a trade secret. Similarly, the value of a trade secret that has been destroyed through public disclosure is often speculative. The remedy of restitution is thus an important form of monetary relief in trade secret cases. The restitution remedy awards to the plaintiff the enrichment unjustly acquired by the defendant as a result of the appropriation of the plaintiff's trade secret. In some situations the defendant's enrichment is represented by profits from sales made possible by the appropriation; in others, by savings achieved through the use of the trade secret in the defendant's business. In some cases the measure of the plaintiff's compensatory damages and the measure of the defendant's unjust enrichment may converge. For example, relief based on the defendant's profits on sales can measure either the gain derived by the defendant or the loss to the plaintiff from diverted business. Similarly, relief based on a reasonable royalty for the defendant's use may measure either the defendant's savings or the plaintiff's lost revenue. Thus, many cases do not maintain a sharp distinction between compensatory and restitutionary remedies.

Although a few cases have required the plaintiff to elect between compensatory damages and restitution, others permit the plaintiff to pursue both measures provided that there is no double recovery. The better rule permits the plaintiff to prove either or both measures since in many circumstances the loss to the plaintiff and the gain to the defendant do not fully overlap. Both compensatory and restitutionary objectives are ordinarily satisfied, however, if the plaintiff is permitted to recover only the greater of the two measures. The restitutionary remedy serves to deprive the defendant of unjust gains, but it also has the effect of compensating the plaintiff to the extent of the award for any losses resulting from the appropriation. Similarly, an award of the plaintiff's proven losses also has the effect of reducing the defendant's unjust enrichment by the amount of the award. An award of the greater of the two remedies thus ordinarily serves the objectives of both forms of relief and best prevents double recovery. See also § 36, Comment *c*.

Illustration:

1. *A* and *B* are competing manufacturers of radar antennas. *C*, a former employee of *A*, discloses *A* 's trade secrets to *B* in breach of a duty of confidence owed to *A*. *B*, with notice of *C* 's breach of confidence, relies on the trade secrets to underbid *A* on a government contract. The use of *A* 's trade secrets saves *B* $175,000 in manufacturing costs and causes *A* $231,000 in lost profits on the government contract. In an action against *B* for the appropriation of *A* 's trade secrets, an award of both *B* 's savings and *A* 's lost profits would result in double recovery. In addition to appropriate injunctive relief, *A* may recover $231,000, which is the greater of the loss to *A* and the gain to *B* that is attributable to the appropriation.

d. Measures of monetary relief. Courts have recognized at least four methods of measuring monetary relief in trade secret cases. The first method measures the loss to the plaintiff caused by the appropriation. The plaintiff's loss usually consists of profits lost on sales diverted from the plaintiff by the appropriation, loss of royalties or other income that would have been earned by the plaintiff but for the appropriation, or the value of the trade secret if it has been destroyed through a public disclosure by the defendant. The second measure awards to the plaintiff the defendant's profits earned on sales that are attributable to the trade secret. A third method, the "standard of comparison" measure, is derived from patent infringement cases and measures the savings to the defendant that are attributable to the use of the trade secret. This method compares the costs to the defendant of achieving the same result with and without the improper use of the trade secret and awards the difference to the plaintiff. The fourth method awards to the plaintiff a reasonable royalty for the defendant's use of the trade secret. A reasonable royalty is the price that would be agreed upon by a willing buyer and a willing seller for the use made of the trade secret by the defendant. The method is not limited to a percentage of the defendant's sales or profits and may instead rely on any appropriate measure of the fair market value of the defendant's use. Selection of the appropriate method of measuring monetary relief depends on the facts and circumstances of the particular case. See Comments *e-g*.

e. Relief measured by plaintiff's loss. A frequent element of loss resulting from the appropriation of a trade secret is the lost profit that the plaintiff would have earned in the absence of the use by the defendant. The plaintiff may prove lost profits by identifying specific customers diverted to the defendant. The plaintiff may also prove lost profits through proof of a general decline in sales or a disruption of business growth following the commencement of use by the defendant, although the presence of other market factors that may affect the plaintiff's sales bears on the sufficiency of the plaintiff's proof. If the evidence justifies the conclusion that the sales made by the defendant would have instead been made by the plaintiff in the absence of the appropriation, the plaintiff may establish its lost profits by applying its own profit margin to the defendant's sales. Upon sufficient proof, the plaintiff may also recover lost profits on sales of spare parts, service, supplies, or other items normally purchased from the original seller. In some cases it may be appropriate to measure the plaintiff's loss by a reasonable royalty on the sales made by the defendant. See Comment *g*.

A plaintiff may also recover any other proven pecuniary loss attributable to the appropriation. Courts have permitted recovery of the costs of remedial efforts such as promotional expenses undertaken to recapture customers lost as a result of the defendant's appropriation. The plaintiff is also entitled to recover losses associated with sales of its own goods at reduced prices resulting from the wrongful competition of the defendant.

Damages resulting from the unauthorized disclosure of a trade secret are frequently more difficult to measure than damages caused by unauthorized use. For example, in some cases a defendant's unauthorized disclosure to one competitor of the plaintiff may cause the trade secret to become known to other competitors or to enter the public domain, thus destroying the value of the secret. The appropriate measure of relief may then be the fair market value of the trade secret at the time of the appropriation. This measure can depend upon a variety of factors, including the likelihood that the trade secret would have become known in the absence of the defendant's appropriation. See Comment *h*. If the destroyed trade secret is a central asset of the plaintiff's business, the plaintiff can in some cases measure damages by the reduction in the capital value of the business caused by the appropriation.

f. Relief measured by defendant's gain. The traditional form of restitutionary relief in an action for the appropriation of a trade secret is an accounting of the defendant's profits on sales attributable to the use of the trade secret. The general rules governing accountings of profits are applicable in trade secret actions. The plaintiff is entitled to recover the defendant's net profits. The plaintiff has the burden of establishing the defendant's sales; the defendant has the burden of establishing any portion of the sales not attributable to the trade secret and any expenses to be deducted in determining net profits. The rules governing the deductibility of expenses and the allocation of overhead are analogous to those stated in § 37, Comments *g* and *h*, on accountings in actions for trademark infringement. The defendant must account not only for profits earned on sales of products incorporating the trade secret, but also on other sales dependent on the appropriation. For example, profits on the sale of consumable supplies used in a machine embodying the trade secret or profits on spare parts and service may be included in the accounting to the extent that such profits were made possible by the defendant's sale of the original product.

If the trade secret accounts for only a portion of the profits earned on the defendant's sales, such as when the trade secret relates to a single component of a product marketable without the secret, an award to the plaintiff of defendant's entire profit may be unjust. The royalty that the plaintiff and defendant would have agreed to for the use of the trade secret made by the defendant may be one measure of the approximate portion of the defendant's profits attributable to the use. See Comment *g*.

If the benefit derived by the defendant consists primarily of cost savings, such as when the trade secret is a more efficient method of production, the "standard of comparison" measure that determines relief based on the savings achieved through the use of the trade secret may be the most appropriate measure of relief. The standard of comparison measure determines the defendant's gain by comparing the defendant's actual costs with the costs that the defendant would have incurred to achieve the same result without the use of the appropriated trade secret. When it would have been possible for the defendant to acquire the trade secret by proper means such as reverse engineering or independent development, the appropriate comparison may be between the costs of such acquisition and the cost of using the appropriated information. In determining the costs of proper acquisition, the court may consider the actual development costs of the plaintiff and, if available, the development or reverse engineering costs of third persons. When acquisition of the trade secret by proper means is unlikely, the appropriate comparison may be between the costs of using the trade secret and the costs of alternative methods available to the defendant to achieve the same result.

Under the principles discussed in § 44, Comment *f*, it is often appropriate to enjoin the defendant's use of a trade secret only for the period of time that would have been required for the defendant to acquire the information by proper means. In such cases, however, the defendant remains liable for any development or reverse engineering costs saved as a result of the appropriation that are not otherwise accounted for through an award of the defendant's profits or other monetary relief.

Illustrations:

2. *A* and *B* are competing manufacturers of poultry vaccines. *A* spends $400,000 to develop a secret process for the production of a new vaccine. *B* appropriates the trade secret and begins to produce the vaccine in competition with *A*. *B* earns $50,000 in net profits on sales of the vaccine. In the absence of evidence indicating loss to *A* in excess of $50,000, *A* may recover *B* 's $50,000 profit in addition to the award of an injunction prohibiting further use of the process by *B*.

3. The facts being otherwise as stated in Illustration 2, *B* establishes that other competitors have already succeeded in duplicating *A* 's secret process by analyzing samples of *A* 's vaccine and that *B* would have been similarly successful. The cost of such an analysis is $150,000. The court may properly conclude that an injunction against *B* 's use of the process would be inappropriate and that an award to *A* of $150,000 representing *B* 's savings in analysis costs and $50,000 representing the net profits earned by *B* prior to the time it would have been able to market the vaccine in the absence of the appropriation is an appropriate remedy.

4. *A*, a shipper, invents several techniques and devices to improve efficiency in the unloading of ships. *B*, a former employee of *A*, discloses the trade secrets to *C*, a competing shipper, in breach of a duty of confidence. *C*, with notice of *B* 's breach of confidence, adopts the techniques and devices in its business. In addition to appropriate injunctive relief, *A* may recover from *C* any savings that have resulted from *C* 's use of *A* 's trade secrets.

g. Reasonable royalty. A reasonable royalty measure of relief awards to the plaintiff the price that would be set by a willing buyer and a willing seller for the use of the trade secret made by the defendant. However, the royalty agreed to in an actual market transaction reflects a price at which both parties gain from the transaction. To the extent that a court-awarded reasonable royalty accurately reflects the marketplace, the royalty may compensate the plaintiff for loss but it does not necessarily deprive the defendant of the full gain attributable to the appropriation. Since the imposition of a reasonable royalty requires the defendant to pay only the amount it would have paid had it fairly bargained for use of the plaintiff's secret, it may not adequately discourage the appropriation of trade secrets.

There are at least three situations in which the reasonable royalty measure of relief has been applied. First, when the defendant has made a substantial good faith investment in the trade secret prior to receiving notice of the plaintiff's claim, it may be inequitable to require the relinquishment of all profits earned by the defendant after notice. An award of damages measured by a reasonable royalty for use subsequent to the notice and an injunction conditioning future use on the payment of a reasonable royalty gives the plaintiff the market value of the trade secret but protects the defendant's good faith reliance. Second, when the plaintiff's loss, although difficult to measure, is apparently greater than any gain acquired by the defendant, a reasonable royalty may be the most appropriate measure of relief. For example, if the defendant's inefficiency results in little or no profit from the exploitation of the trade secret and the loss to the plaintiff cannot otherwise be established, a reasonable royalty may be the best available approximation of the plaintiff's loss. Third, in cases in which the defendant's gain from the trade secret is difficult to measure but apparently exceeds the plaintiff's loss, a reasonable royalty may be the best means of approximating the defendant's unjust enrichment.

The purpose for which the reasonable royalty measure is invoked and the equities of the particular case may properly influence the calculation of the appropriate royalty. To insure adequate deterrence and to prevent unjust enrichment, a court may resolve issues relating to the amount of the royalty against a defendant who has willfully appropriated the trade secret.

Illustration:

5. The facts being otherwise as stated in Illustration 4, *C* has no notice of *B* 's breach of confidence until after *C* has invested in equipment designed to implement the trade secrets in its business. A court may properly conclude that the appropriate remedy is a monetary award measured by a reasonable royalty for use of the trade secret by *C* subsequent to the notice of *B* 's breach of confidence and an injunction conditioning future use by *C* on the payment of a reasonable royalty.

h. Limitation on monetary relief. Monetary remedies, whether measured by the loss to the plaintiff or the gain to the defendant, are appropriate only for the period of time that the information would have remained unavailable to the defendant in the absence of the appropriation. This period may be measured by the time it would have taken the defendant to obtain the information by proper means such as reverse engineering or independent development. Similarly, the issuance of a patent or other public disclosure of the information by the plaintiff or a third person terminates the secrecy necessary to the protection of the trade secret. Monetary relief based on the defendant's use of the information after the loss of secrecy is therefore appropriate only to the extent necessary to remedy a head start or other unfair advantage attributable to the defendant's prior access to the information. The limitations on the appropriate duration of injunctive relief as stated in § 44, Comment *f*, are thus also generally applicable to the calculation of monetary relief.

The rules governing the appropriate period of liability for monetary relief in actions in tort for the appropriation of a trade secret are not necessarily applicable in actions in contract for breach of agreements relating to the use or disclosure of trade secrets. Remedies for breach of contracts relating to trade secrets are ordinarily measured by the terms of the obligations imposed under the agreement. Licensing agreements, for example, can ordinarily provide for royalty payments covering a period that ends before or after any public disclosure of the trade secret. See § 41, Comment *d*. Similarly, although a nondisclosure agreement that is interpreted to extend beyond a public disclosure of the trade secret may be unenforceable as an unreasonable restraint of trade, *id.*, obligations under a nondisclosure agreement may terminate according to its terms prior to any public disclosure. The use of a trade secret in breach of an enforceable agreement, however, can give rise to both a claim for breach of contract and a claim for appropriation in tort under the rules stated in § 40. Durational limits contained in the agreement may influence but do not necessarily determine the appropriate duration of monetary relief awarded in a tort action pursuant to the rules stated here.

i. Punitive damages. A successful plaintiff in an action at common law for the appropriation of a trade secret may recover punitive damages under the rules generally applicable in the jurisdiction to the award of punitive damages in tort actions. See Restatement, Second, Torts § 908. The purpose of punitive damages is to deter and punish egregious conduct, and normally proof of malice or willful misconduct is required. Section 3(b) of the Uniform Trade Secrets Act provides for an award of punitive damages not exceeding twice the amount of compensatory and restitutionary damages in cases of "willful and malicious misappropriation."

j. Attorney's fees. Most states do not provide for an award of attorney's fees in actions at common law. In actions under the Uniform Trade Secrets Act, reasonable attorney's fees may be awarded if the appropriation is "willful and malicious," if the claim of appropriation is made in bad faith, or if a motion to terminate an injunction is made or resisted in bad faith. *Id.* § 4.

REPORTERS' NOTE

Comment a. Monetary relief for the appropriation of a trade secret was discussed only briefly in the former Restatement of this topic. See Restatement of Torts § 757, Comment *e* (1938). See generally Jager, Trade Secrets Law § 7.03; Milgrim on Trade Secrets § 7.08[3]; Johnson, Remedies in Trade Secret Litigation, 72 Nw.U.L.Rev. 1004 (1978); Prandl, Damages for Misappropriation of Trade Secret, 22 Tort Ins.L.J. 447 (1987). See also § 3 of the Uniform Trade Secrets Act.

Comment b. The cases reflect considerable flexibility in the calculation of appropriate monetary relief in trade secret actions. See, e.g., University Computing Co. v. Lykes—Youngstown Corp., 504 F.2d 518, 538 (5th Cir.1974) ("[E]very case requires a flexible and imaginative approach to the problem of damages. * * * [C]ases reveal that most courts adjust the measure of damages to accord with the commercial setting of the injury, the likely future consequences of the misappropriation, and the nature and extent of the use the defendant put the trade secret to after misappropriation.").

For cases recognizing both compensation and unjust enrichment as objectives of monetary relief, see, e.g., Telex Corp. v. Int'l Business Machines Corp., 510 F.2d 894 (10th Cir.), cert. dismissed 423 U.S. 802, 96 S.Ct. 8, 46 L.Ed.2d 244 (1975) (recovery of elements representing plaintiff's loss and defendant's gain); Carter Products, Inc. v. Colgate–Palmolive Co., 214 F.Supp. 383 (D.Md.1963); Jet Spray Cooler, Inc. v. Crampton, 377 Mass. 159, 385 N.E.2d 1349 (1979). A few cases suggest that remedies in trade secret cases should foster commercial morality. See, e.g., Adolph Gottscho, Inc. v. American Marking Corp., 18 N.J. 467, 114 A.2d 438, cert. denied 350 U.S. 834, 76 S.Ct. 69, 100 L.Ed. 744 (1955) (injunction granted despite public disclosure); Kilbarr Corp. v. Business Systems Inc., 679 F.Supp. 422 (D.N.J.1988), affirmed 869 F.2d 589 (3d Cir.1989) (refusing to limit an accounting of profits to the period of the defendant's head start). However, full compensatory and restitutionary relief is ordinarily sufficient to accomplish such an objective.

The plaintiff bears the burden of proving any loss for which relief is sought, but the amount of loss must be proved only with such certainty as is reasonable under the circumstances. See Electro–Miniatures Corp. v. Wendon Co., 771 F.2d 23 (2d Cir.1985); Tri–Tron Int'l v. Velto, 525 F.2d 432 (9th Cir.1975) (the rule precluding an award of speculative profits goes to the fact and cause of the lost profits rather than to the amount); DeVries v. Starr, 393 F.2d 9 (10th Cir.1968); Julius Hyman & Co. v. Velsicol Corp., 123 Colo. 563, 233 P.2d 977, cert. denied 342 U.S. 870, 72 S.Ct. 113, 96 L.Ed. 654 (1951). But cf. Elcor Chemical Corp. v. Agri–Sul, Inc., 494 S.W.2d 204 (Tex.Civ. App.1973) (insufficient evidence to support an award of damages).

Comment c. Monetary remedies may be awarded in conjunction with injunctive relief. See, e.g., Tri–Tron Int'l v. Velto, 525 F.2d 432 (9th Cir. 1975) (damages and injunction); USM Corp. v. Marson Fastener Corp., 392 Mass. 334, 467 N.E.2d 1271 (1984) (accounting and injunction); Cherne Industrial, Inc. v. Grounds & Associates, Inc., 278 N.W.2d 81 (Minn.1979) (same). In some cases an injunction may eliminate the need for monetary relief. See, e.g., Winston Research Corp. v. Minnesota Mining and Mfg. Co., 350 F.2d 134 (9th Cir.1965) (defendant was enjoined before any sales of the appropriated product). In other cases, monetary relief may be the more appropriate remedy. See, e.g., Schreyer v. Casco Products Corp., 190 F.2d 921 (2d Cir.1951), cert. denied 342 U.S. 913, 72 S.Ct. 360, 96 L.Ed. 683 (1952) (accounting of profits from defendant's head start in using information later disclosed in a patent was an adequate remedy); Tolchester Lines, Inc. v. Dowd, 253 F.Supp. 643 (S.D.N.Y.1966) (monetary relief may be sufficient when an injunction would have the effect of denying the defendant a livelihood).

Section 136 of the Restatement of Restitution (1937) recognizes the importance of a remedy based on unjust enrichment in light of the difficulty of proving damages in trade secret actions. The merger of law and equity allows plaintiffs in most circumstances to pursue both legal and equitable remedies. Section 3(a) of the Uniform Trade Secrets Act authorizes the recovery of both "actual loss" and any "unjust enrichment" not taken into account in calculating actual loss.

Numerous cases hold that monetary relief in trade secret actions is limited to the greater of the plaintiff's loss or the defendant's gain. Clark v. Bunker, 453 F.2d 1006 (9th Cir.1972) (plaintiff is entitled to lost profits but not less than the defendant's gain from the appropriation); Sperry Rand Corp. v. A–T–O, Inc., 447 F.2d 1387 (4th Cir.1971), cert. denied 405 U.S. 1017, 92 S.Ct. 1292, 31 L.Ed.2d 479 (1972) (awarding plaintiff's lost profits in an amount larger than the defendant's savings); Tolchester Lines, *supra* (plaintiff is entitled to defendant's profits and any damages exceeding that amount); Curtiss–Wright Corp. v. Edel–Brown Tool & Die Co., 381 Mass. 1, 407 N.E.2d 319 (1980) (the appropriate measure is the greater of the plaintiff's lost profits or the defendant's gain); Jet Spray Cooler, Inc. v. Crampton, 377 Mass. 159, 385 N.E.2d 1349 (1979) (plaintiff is entitled to lost profits, but not less than the monetary gain to the defendant).

Illustration 1 is derived from *Sperry Rand Corp., supra.*

Comment d. For discussions of the various measures of monetary relief in trade secret cases, see, e.g., Telex Corp. v. Int'l Business Machines Corp., 510 F.2d 894 (10th Cir.), cert. dismissed 423 U.S. 802, 96 S.Ct. 8, 46 L.Ed.2d 244 (1975); University Computing Co. v. Lykes—Youngstown Corp., 504 F.2d 518 (5th Cir. 1974); Jet Spray Cooler, Inc. v. Crampton, 377 Mass. 159, 385 N.E.2d 1349 (1979). See generally Prandl, Damages for Misappropriation of Trade Secret, 22 Tort Ins.L.J. 447 (1987); Annot., Proper Measure and Elements of Damages for Misappropriation of Trade Secret, 11 A.L.R.4th 12 (1982).

Comment e. The actual loss to the plaintiff caused by the defendant's appropriation is an appropriate measure of monetary relief. See, e.g., Tri–Tron Int'l v. Velto, 525 F.2d 432 (9th Cir.1975); Sperry Rand Corp. v. A–T–O, Inc., 447 F.2d 1387 (4th Cir.1971), cert. denied 405 U.S. 1017, 92 S.Ct. 1292, 31 L.Ed.2d 479 (1972); Kamin v. Kuhnau, 232 Or. 139, 374 P.2d 912 (1962). See also § 3 of the Uniform Trade Secrets Act.

Lost profits on sales that would have been made by the plaintiff but for the appropriation were awarded in, e.g., *Sperry Rand Corp., supra* (loss of specific contract); Clark v. Bunker, 453 F.2d 1006 (9th Cir.1972) (adopting the presumption that the plaintiff would have made all the sales in the area absent the defendant's appropriation); Telex Corp. v. Int'l Business Machines Corp., 510 F.2d 894 (10th Cir.), cert. dismissed 423 U.S. 802, 96 S.Ct. 8, 46 L.Ed.2d 244 (1975) (lost rental income). Evidence of a decline in plaintiff's sales subsequent to the appropriation is relevant in establishing lost profits. DeVries v. Starr, 393 F.2d 9 (10th Cir.1968). Plaintiff's lost profits are sometimes measured by applying the plaintiff's profit margin to the sales made by the defendant. See Jet Spray Cooler, Inc. v. Crampton, 377 Mass. 159, 385 N.E.2d 1349 (1979) (approving the principle although the evidence did not support its application); DeVries, *supra*; Tri–Tron Int'l, *supra*. The loss of future profits likely to result from the appropriation may also be compensable. See Sperry Rand Corp., *supra* (future sale of spare parts); Financial Programs, Inc. v. Falcon Financial Services, Inc., 371 F.Supp. 770 (D.Or. 1974) (future profits on diverted accounts calculated on the basis of past experience); Dozor Agency, Inc. v. Rosenberg, 218 A.2d 583 (Pa.1966) (loss of future premiums calculated on the basis of past experience). The plaintiff was awarded damages reflecting the reduced price received for its own goods as a result of competition attributable to the defendant's appropriation in Julius Hyman & Co. v. Velsicol Corp., 123 Colo. 563, 233 P.2d 977, cert. denied 342 U.S. 870, 72 S.Ct. 113, 96 L.Ed. 654 (1951).

A royalty adopted by the parties in an "agreement in principle" was applied as the appropriate measure of damages in Vitro Corp. v. Hall Chemical Co., 292 F.2d 678 (6th Cir.1961). See also Kamin, *supra*. A reasonable royalty reflecting the likely loss to the plaintiff was awarded in Carter Products, Inc. v. Colgate–Palmolive Co., 214 F.Supp. 383 (D.Md.1963). See also Goldberg v. Medtronic, Inc., 686 F.2d 1219 (7th Cir.1982) (10% royalty on defendant's sales awarded when it was unlikely that the plaintiff could have marketed the trade secret on its own).

In Precision Plating & Metal Finishing Inc. v. Martin–Marietta Corp., 435 F.2d 1262 (5th Cir.1970), cert. denied 404 U.S. 1002, 92 S.Ct. 571, 30 L.Ed.2d 556 (1971), the value of the trade secret was destroyed by the defendant's disclosure. The court affirmed an award of damages based on the "fair market value" of the trade secret. See also Smith v. Dravo Corp., 208 F.2d 388 (7th Cir.1953) (plaintiffs recovered capital investment losses caused by the appropriation of their trade secret); Registered Physical Therapists, Inc. v. Jepson, 584 P.2d 857 (Utah 1978) (awarding damages measured by the value of the plaintiff's business when the appropriation required the plaintiff to terminate operation).

Comment f. An accounting of the defendant's profits from unauthorized use of the plaintiff's trade secret is a common remedy. See, e.g., Clark v. Bunker, 453 F.2d 1006 (9th Cir.1972); Schreyer v. Casco Products Corp., 190 F.2d 921 (2d Cir. 1951), cert. denied 342 U.S. 913, 72 S.Ct. 360, 96 L.Ed. 683 (1952); Carter Products, Inc. v. Colgate–Palmolive Co., 214 F.Supp. 383 (D.Md. 1963); Julius Hyman & Co. v. Velsicol Corp., 123 Colo. 563, 233 P.2d 977, cert. denied 342 U.S. 870, 72 S.Ct. 113, 96 L.Ed. 654 (1951). Section 3 of the Uniform Trade Secrets Act provides that the plaintiff may recover "the unjust enrichment caused by misappropriation that is not taken into account in computing actual loss." See also Restatement of Restitution § 136 (an accounting of profits in trade secret cases is the "usual method of seeking restitution"); Restatement, Second, Agency § 404, Comment *b* (an agent who uses assets, including trade secrets, belonging to the principal is subject to liability for "the value of the use," including profits). See also *id.* § 407, Comment *a* (agent is liable for the amount received from a sale of the principal's trade secret).

The plaintiff is entitled to the defendant's net profits from sales of goods incorporating the trade secret. E.g., Jet Spray Cooler, Inc. v. Crampton, 377 Mass. 159, 385 N.E.2d 1349 (1979). The defendant may also be held accountable for sales of other products that are dependent upon sales of the appropriated product. Adolph Gottscho, Inc. v. American Marking Corp., 26 N.J. 229, 139 A.2d 281 (1958) (defendant's profits on ink and solvents were included in an accounting of profits from the appropriation of a trade secret for the design of a marking machine). The plaintiff bears the burden of establishing sales; the defendant has the burden of establishing deductible expenses and any sales not attributable to the use of the trade secret. E.g., USM Corp. v. Marson Fastener Corp., 392 Mass. 334, 467 N.E.2d 1271 (1984); Julius Hyman & Co, *supra.*

Courts are divided on the deductibility by the defendant of bad debts arising from sales of products incorporating the trade secret. Compare Jet Spray Cooler, *supra* (treated as a deductible manufacturing expense) with Julius Hyman & Co., *supra* (the defendant should assume the risk of credit extensions). On the deductibility of income taxes paid by the defendant on the profits for which it is accountable, see § 37, Comment *g.* Cf. USM Corp., *supra* (dictum suggesting that a deduction for income taxes is generally proper, but permitting a claim by the plaintiff to any tax benefits accruing to the defendant as a result of the defendant's payment of the awarded profits); Julius Hyman & Co., *supra* (deductibility of income taxes conditioned on payment to the plaintiff of any tax benefits to the defendant arising from payment of the judgment). On the deductibility of salaries and consulting fees paid to the individual defendants, compare Jet Spray Cooler, *supra* (salaries deductible if reasonable) with Julius Hyman & Co., *supra* (denying the deduction).

In allocating overhead among products derived from the appropriation and other products marketed by the defendant, the courts generally apply an incremental cost allocation that allows deductions only for additional expenses made necessary by the manufacture or sale of the products subject to the accounting. USM

Corp., *supra*; Carboline Co. v. Jarboe, 454 S.W.2d 540 (Mo.1970). The defendant may set off losses from prior accounting periods against subsequent profits only if the profits are dependent on expenses incurred in the prior period, such as advertising costs that result in profits in a succeeding year. See Carter Products, *supra*; Adolph Gottscho, Inc., *supra*.

The leading case applying the "standard of comparison" measure is Int'l Industries, Inc. v. Warren Petroleum Corp., 248 F.2d 696 (3d Cir. 1957), cert. dismissed 355 U.S. 943, 78 S.Ct. 529, 2 L.Ed.2d 523 (1958) (plaintiff was awarded the defendant's savings measured by the difference in cost between rail transportation and transportation by boat that was made possible by the use of the trade secret). See, e.g., Matarese v. Moore–McCormack Lines, Inc., 158 F.2d 631 (2d Cir.1946) (awarding the defendant's savings from implementing the plaintiff's ideas relating to loading operations less the cost of implementation). The standard of comparison method has also been invoked to support recovery of development and reverse engineering costs saved by the defendant as a result of the appropriation. See, e.g., Salsbury Laboratories, Inc. v. Merieux Laboratories, Inc., 908 F.2d 706 (11th Cir.1990); Telex Corp. v. Int'l Business Machines, Corp., 510 F.2d 894 (10th Cir.), cert. dismissed 423 U.S. 802, 96 S.Ct. 8, 46 L.Ed.2d 244 (1975) (awarding savings in development costs although the defendant did not produce a marketable product); Servo Corp. v. General Electric Co., 393 F.2d 551 (4th Cir.1968); Analogic Corp. v. Data Translation, Inc., 371 Mass. 643, 358 N.E.2d 804 (1976) (suggesting that the dissolution of an injunction after the period necessary for reverse engineering may be conditioned on payment to the plaintiff of costs saved by the defendant).

Illustrations 2 and 3 are suggested by the facts in *Salsbury Laboratories, supra*. Illustration 4 is suggested by the facts in *Matarese, supra*.

Comment g. A reasonable royalty measure of damages is expressly authorized in § 3(a) of the Uniform Trade Secrets Act. A reasonable royalty has been described as the royalty that would have been agreed to by a willing buyer and a willing seller. See, e.g., University Computing Co. v. Lykes—Youngstown Corp., 504 F.2d 518 (5th Cir.1974); Forest Laboratories, Inc. v. Pillsbury Co., 452 F.2d 621 (7th Cir.1971). The fact that payment of a reasonable royalty does not deprive the defendant of the entire unjust gain was recognized in Carter Products, Inc. v. Colgate–Palmolive Co., 214 F.Supp. 383 (D.Md. 1963), in which the court awarded a reasonable royalty plus additional profits on sales. See also Molinaro v. Burnbaum, 201 U.S.P.Q. 150 (D.Mass. 1978). Cf. Pioneer Hi–Bred Int'l v. Holden Foundation Seeds, Inc., 35 F.3d 1226 (8th Cir.1994) (reasonable royalty measure "is most appropriate when the other theories would result in no recovery or when the parties actually had or contemplated a royalty arrangement").

A reasonable royalty is most often awarded as compensation for the plaintiff's loss when actual damages cannot be determined more directly. See University Computing Co., *supra*; Vitro Corp. v. Hall Chemical Co., 292 F.2d 678 (6th Cir.1961); Carter Products, *supra*. The reasonable royalty measure has also been invoked when the defendant began its use of the trade secret in good faith. See Forest Laboratories, *supra* (reasonable royalty awarded for use by the defendant after notice of the plaintiff's claim). Cf. San Manuel

Copper Corp. v. Redmond, 8 Ariz. App. 214, 445 P.2d 162 (1968), applying the reasonable royalty measure in connection with an appropriation that was not "willful." In some circumstances the defendant's good faith reliance may make any monetary relief inappropriate. See § 3(a) of the Uniform Trade Secrets Act.

A reasonable royalty has been used to apportion the defendant's profits when it would be inequitable to award the plaintiff the entire profit on defendant's sales. See Laurie Visual Etudes, Inc. v. Chesebrough–Pond's, Inc., 105 Misc.2d 413, 432 N.Y.S.2d 457 (Sup.Ct.1980), reversed on other grounds 83 A.D.2d 505, 441 N.Y.S.2d 88 (1981) (defendant contributed substantially to the product's success); Goldberg v. Medtronic, Inc., 686 F.2d 1219 (7th Cir.1982) (awarding a 10% royalty on the defendant's sales because it was unlikely that the plaintiff could have marketed the trade secret without entering into a licensing agreement). See also Egry Register Co. v. Standard Register Co., 23 F.2d 438 (6th Cir.1928) (a patent infringement case apportioning profits by a reasonable royalty when the patented device was only one component of the defendant's product).

In determining the amount of a reasonable royalty, the courts have considered a variety of factors including the nature and importance of the trade secret, the nature and extent of the defendant's use, royalties discussed by the parties or common in the industry, resulting or foreseeable changes in the competitive position of the parties, the development costs of the plaintiff, the availability of alternatives to the trade secret, and other factors that might affect an agreement between willing buyers and sellers. See University Computing Co., *supra*; Forest Laboratories, *supra*; Carter Products, *supra* (royalty rate charged by the plaintiff to other manufacturers is relevant); Vitro Corp., *supra* (royalties established in an "agreement in principle" used to determine a reasonable royalty); Laurie Visual Etudes, *supra* (royalties based on prior negotiations between the parties). The royalty is not limited to a percentage of the defendant's sales. University Computing Co., *supra*.

Illustration 5 reflects the rule in § 2 of the Uniform Trade Secrets Act. See also Forest Laboratories, *supra*. In an extreme case the defendant's good faith reliance may justify the denial of all injunctive and monetary relief. See § 3(a) and the Comment to § 2 of the Uniform Trade Secrets Act.

Comment h. The Comment to § 3 of the Uniform Trade Secrets Act states the rule on the duration of monetary relief as follows: "Like injunctive relief, a monetary recovery for trade secret misappropriation is appropriate only for the period in which information is entitled to protection as a trade secret, plus the additional period, if any, in which a misappropriator retains an advantage over good faith competitors because of misappropriation." Cases limiting monetary relief under principles analogous to those applicable to the duration of injunctive relief include, e.g., Schreyer v. Casco Products Corp., 190 F.2d 921 (2d Cir.1951), cert. denied 342 U.S. 913, 72 S.Ct. 360, 96 L.Ed. 683 (1952) (affirming an accounting of profits attributable to an acceleration of the date when production by the defendant would otherwise have been possible); Engelhard Industries, Inc. v. Research Instrumental Corp., 324 F.2d 347 (9th Cir.

1963), cert. denied 377 U.S. 923, 84 S.Ct. 1220, 12 L.Ed.2d 215 (1964) (accounting of defendant's profits during the head start period is appropriate); Reinforced Molding Corp. v. General Electric Co., 592 F.Supp. 1083 (W.D.Pa.1984) (accounting of profits limited to the period required for independent development); Structural Dynamics Research Corp. v. Engineering Mechanics Research Corp., 401 F.Supp. 1102 (E.D.Mich.1975) (imposing a reasonable royalty during the period required for independent development); Carboline Co. v. Jarboe, 454 S.W.2d 540 (Mo.1970) (accounting of profits limited to the time required for reverse engineering). Cf. Kilbarr Corp. v. Business Systems Inc., 679 F.Supp. 422 (D.N.J. 1988), affirmed 869 F.2d 589 (3d Cir. 1989) (limitation of damages to the head start period was not appropriate when the defendant's appropriation effectively preempted the market).

Contractual royalties for the use of a trade secret may extend beyond public disclosure of the information. Warner–Lambert Pharmaceutical Co. v. John J. Reynolds, Inc., 178 F.Supp. 655 (S.D.N.Y.1959), affirmed 280 F.2d 197 (2d Cir.1960). See also Aronson v. Quick Point Pencil Co., 440 U.S. 257, 99 S.Ct. 1096, 59 L.Ed.2d 296 (1979) (federal patent law does not preempt state enforcement of a contractual obligation to pay royalties after a public disclosure of the trade secret). In awarding monetary relief in an action in tort for the appropriation of a trade secret, the court may consider but is not bound by the duration of any contractual obligation. See Sikes v. McGraw–Edison Co., 665 F.2d 731 (5th Cir.), cert. denied 458 U.S. 1108, 102 S.Ct. 3488, 73 L.Ed.2d 1369 (1982) (although confidentiality agreement terminated after two years, an award of defendant's profits from an appropriation of the trade secrets was not limited to the two-year period); compare Premix, Inc. v. Zappitelli, 561 F.Supp. 269 (N.D.Ohio 1983) (awarding lost profits for the agreed period of confidentiality in a breach of contract action).

Comment i. Courts approving punitive damage awards in trade secret cases include, e.g., Clark v. Bunker, 453 F.2d 1006 (9th Cir.1972); Sperry Rand Corp. v. A–T–O, Inc., 447 F.2d 1387 (4th Cir.1971), cert. denied 405 U.S. 1017, 92 S.Ct. 1292, 31 L.Ed.2d 479 (1972); Telex Corp. v. Int'l Business Machines Corp., 510 F.2d 894 (10th Cir.), cert. dismissed 423 U.S. 802, 96 S.Ct. 8, 46 L.Ed.2d 244 (1975); Boeing Co. v. Sierracin Corp., 108 Wash.2d 38, 738 P.2d 665 (1987) (Uniform Trade Secrets Act). See generally Jager, Trade Secrets Law § 7.03[3].

Comment j. For cases awarding attorney's fees under § 4 of the Uniform Trade Secrets Act, see, e.g., Boeing Co. v. Sierracin Corp., 108 Wash.2d 38, 738 P.2d 665 (1987); Aries Information Systems, Inc. v. Pacific Management Systems Corp., 366 N.W.2d 366 (Minn.App.1985). See generally Jager, Trade Secrets Law § 7.04; Milgrim on Trade Secrets § 7.08[3][e].

TOPIC 3. RIGHT OF PUBLICITY

Section

---

§ 46. Appropriation of the Commercial Value of a Person's Identity: The Right of Publicity

One who appropriates the commercial value of a person's identity by using without consent the person's name, likeness, or other indicia of identity for purposes of trade is subject to liability for the relief appropriate under the rules stated in §§ 48 and 49.

Comment:

a. Scope. This Topic addresses the common law and statutory rules that protect the commercial value of a person's identity. The appropriation of another's identity for purposes of trade can result in injury to both commercial and personal interests. This Restatement deals with rules affording relief against unfair methods of competition, and the rules stated in this Topic are therefore limited to the redress of commercial injuries. The interest protected by these rules is often described as the "right of publicity." Relief is also generally available under the law of torts for injuries to personal interests caused by the unauthorized commercial use of another's identity. The protection of these personal interests is often described as an aspect of the "right of privacy." See Comment *b*. Although not directly applicable, the rules stated here may be useful by analogy in evaluating claims under the right of privacy arising from an unauthorized commercial exploitation of a person's identity.

b. Relation to other rules. The principal historical antecedent of the right of publicity is the right of privacy. In 1902, the New York Court of Appeals in Roberson v. Rochester Folding Box Co., 171 N.Y. 538, 64 N.E. 442 (1902), rejected a claim for emotional distress resulting from the unauthorized use of the plaintiff's photograph in an advertisement. The following year the New York legislature enacted a statute imposing criminal and civil liability for unauthorized use of a person's name, portrait, or picture for "advertising purposes or for the purposes of trade." In 1905, the Supreme Court of Georgia in Pavesich v. New England Life Insurance Co., 122 Ga. 190, 50 S.E. 68 (1905), upheld a complaint against similar conduct at common law, relying on a noted article by Samuel Warren and Louis Brandeis entitled *The Right of Privacy,* 4 Harv.L.Rev. 193 (1890).

As described in an influential article by William Prosser, *Privacy,* 48 Calif.L.Rev. 383 (1960), the right of privacy came to be viewed as a complex of four torts, embracing unreasonable intrusions upon another's seclusion, public disclosure of private facts, publicity placing another in a false light, and the appropriation for the defendant's advantage of the plaintiff's name or likeness. Prosser's analysis was subsequently incorporated into the Restatement, Second, of Torts §§ 652A–652I (1977), which includes a rule imposing liability for an invasion of privacy against "[o]ne who appropriates to his own use or benefit the name or likeness of another." *Id.* § 652C.

The "appropriation" tort as described by Prosser and the Restatement, Second, of Torts subsumes harm to both personal and commercial interests caused by an unauthorized exploitation of the plaintiff's identity. Classification of the tort as an aspect of the right of privacy, however, led some courts to deny relief to well-known personalities whose celebrity precluded the allegations of injury to solitude or personal feelings normally associated with an invasion of privacy. The historical connection with personal privacy also impeded the transfer of rights in the commercial value of a person's identity. See Comment *g.* Courts in a number of jurisdictions eventually came to distinguish claims for injury to personal feelings caused by an unauthorized use of the plaintiff's identity from claims seeking redress for an appropriation of the commercial value of the identity. The latter claim was sometimes denominated a "right of publicity" to distinguish it from the protection available to personal interests under the "right of privacy." Thus, in some jurisdictions separate causes of action now redress the commercial and personal injuries resulting from an unauthorized commercial exploitation of a person's identity. The distinction between the publicity and privacy actions, however, relates primarily to the nature of the harm suffered by the plaintiff; similar substantive rules govern the determination of liability. In other jurisdictions, relief for both personal and commercial harm is available through a single common law or statutory cause of action. In many states, however, the parameters or even the existence of the right of publicity remains undetermined.

Some decisions suggest that an unauthorized use of a person's identity for purposes of trade injures only commercial interests if plaintiff is a celebrity and only personal interests if the plaintiff is not well known. However, celebrities are not precluded from establishing cognizable injury to personal interests in addition to commercial loss, nor are less well-known plaintiffs precluded from establishing commercial loss in addition to injury to personal interests, whether recoverable through a single or companion causes of action. See § 49.

Proof of deception or consumer confusion is not required for the imposition of liability under this Section. However, a person's name or likeness may be protectable as a trademark if it has become distinctive of the goods or services emanating from a particular commercial source. See § 14, Comments *e* and *f*. Unauthorized use of such a trademark in a manner likely to cause confusion regarding the source or sponsorship of goods or services will subject the user to liability for trademark infringement under the rule stated in § 20. Similarly, the unauthorized use of another's name or likeness in marketing goods or services can subject the user to liability for deceptive marketing under the rule stated in § 4 if the use is likely to cause prospective purchasers to believe that the identified person endorses or is otherwise connected with the goods or services. If the plaintiff's identity is used in a manner that is defamatory or places the plaintiff before the public in a false light, the user may be subject to liability for defamation or invasion of privacy. See Restatement, Second, Torts § 565, Illustration 1; § 652E, Illustration 1. Liability under any of these rules, however, is independent of liability for an infringement of the right of publicity under the rule stated in this Section.

c. Rationale for protection. Recognition of a right of publicity has been justified on numerous grounds. Like the right of privacy, the right of publicity protects an individual's interest in personal dignity and autonomy. With its emphasis on commercial interests, the right of publicity also secures for plaintiffs the commercial value of their fame and prevents the unjust enrichment of others seeking to appropriate that value for themselves. The right to prohibit unauthorized commercial exploitation of one's identity allows a person to prevent harmful or excessive commercial use that may dilute the value of the identity. Although proof of deception or confusion is not an element of liability under this Section, the right of publicity indirectly affords protection against false suggestions of endorsement or sponsorship. Some decisions also invoke an incentive rationale analogous to that supporting the recognition of exclusive rights under copyright and patent law.

The rationales underlying recognition of a right of publicity are generally less compelling than those that justify rights in trademarks or trade secrets. The commercial value of a person's identity often results from success in endeavors such as entertainment or sports that offer their own substantial rewards. Any additional incentive attributable to the right of publicity may have only marginal significance. In other cases the commercial value acquired by a person's identity is largely fortuitous or otherwise unrelated to any investment made by the individual, thus diminishing the weight of the property and unjust enrichment rationales for protection. In addition, the public interest in avoiding false suggestions of endorsement or sponsorship can be pursued through the cause of action for deceptive marketing. Thus, courts may be properly reluctant to adopt a broad construction of the publicity right. See § 47.

d. Appropriation of identity. The right of publicity protects the commercial value of a person's identity. The right is most often invoked to protect the value associated with the identity of a celebrity, and a few cases appear to require some minimum degree of fame or notoriety as a prerequisite for relief. However, the identity of even an unknown person may possess commercial value. See § 49, Comment *d.* Thus, an evaluation of the relative fame of the plaintiff is more properly relevant to the determination of appropriate relief.

The right of publicity is infringed by an appropriation of another's identity for purposes of trade. The use must therefore be sufficient to identify the person whose identity the defendant is alleged to have appropriated. If the appropriation consists of the use of a name, for example, the name as used by the defendant must be understood by the audience as referring to the plaintiff. Similarly, in the case of an alleged visual likeness, the plaintiff must be reasonably identifiable from the photograph or other depiction. Whether the plaintiff is identified by the defendant's use is a question of fact. Relevant evidence includes the nature and extent of the identifying characteristics used by the defendant, the defendant's intent, the fame of the plaintiff, evidence of actual identification made by third persons, and surveys or other evidence indicating the perceptions of the audience.

In most cases an appropriation of identity is accomplished through the use of a person's name or likeness. The person can be identified by a real name, nickname, or professional name, or by a likeness embodied in a photograph, drawing, film, or physical look-alike. In the absence of a narrower statutory definition, a number of cases have held that the unauthorized use of other indicia of a person's identity can infringe the right of publicity. Thus, the use or imitation of a person's voice or an imitation of a person's performing persona such as Charlie Chaplin's "Little Tramp" or Julius Marx's "Groucho" may violate the right of publicity if used for purposes of trade under the rule stated in § 47. The use of other identifying characteristics or attributes may also infringe the right of publicity, but only if they are so closely and uniquely associated with the identity of a particular individual that their use enables the defendant to appropriate the commercial value of the person's identity.

The interest in personal dignity and autonomy that underlies both publicity and privacy rights limits application of the right of publicity to natural persons. The protection available against the unauthorized use of corporate or institutional identities is determined by the rules governing trademarks and trade names. See Chapter 3.

e. Intent. Unless required by an applicable statutory provision, an intent to infringe another's right of publicity is not an element of liability. (See the similar rule for trademark infringement in § 20, Comment *c*.) Thus, the plaintiff is not required to prove that the defendant intended to identify the plaintiff. Similarly, a mistake regarding the plaintiff's consent is not a defense. Since liability for infringement of the right of publicity does not depend upon proof of falsity, see Comment *b*, the constitutional requirement of fault imposed in defamation and false light privacy actions is not applicable to the imposition of liability under this Section. However, the intent and knowledge of the defendant remains relevant to the resolution of other issues, including the requirement of identification, see Comment *d*, and the determination of appropriate relief, see § 49, Comment *c*. On the liability of innocent retailers and publishers of infringing material, see § 47, Comment *e*.

f. Consent. Conduct that would otherwise infringe the personal or commercial interests protected by the rights of privacy and publicity is not actionable if the conduct is within the scope of consent given by the holder of the right. See Restatement, Second, Torts § 652F, Comment *b*. Consent can be communicated through a formal agreement such as a license or assignment. See Comment *g*. In the absence of an applicable statute requiring consent in writing, consent can also be implied from conduct or inaction reasonably interpreted as manifesting consent. The general rules of tort law relating to the manifestation and effect of consent as stated in Restatement, Second, Torts §§ 892–892B are applicable in actions under this Section. On the effect of a mistake as to consent, see Comment *e*. The defense of consent extends only to conduct that is within the scope of the consent. Consent to use a person's identity may be restricted, for example, to certain products, or to certain media, or to a certain duration. Whether particular conduct is within the scope of consent given to the user is determined according to the general principles applicable to the interpretation of agreements. See Restatement, Second, Contracts, Chapter 10. If the use is outside the scope of consent, the defendant is subject to liability for any harm resulting from conduct that exceeds the consent. If it is impossible as a practical matter to separate the harm resulting from the excess use from harm caused by the consented use, the defendant is subject to liability for the entire harm.

Consent precludes the imposition of liability for the use of another's identity only if the use occurs prior to termination of the consent. Unless irrevocable, consent is terminated when the user knows or has reason to know that the other is no longer willing to permit the particular use. The unwillingness may be manifested by words or by conduct inconsistent with continued consent such as the commencement of legal action. However, if a person is estopped or otherwise precluded from terminating the consent, an attempted termination is not effective. A person may be precluded from terminating consent by the express or implied terms of an agreement with the user. A person may also be precluded from terminating consent if the termination would be inequitable because of the user's reasonable reliance on the consent, evaluated in light of the specific terms of any agreement between the parties.

g. Assignment and licensing of rights. The interest in the commercial value of a person's identity is in the nature of a property right and is freely assignable to others. Early cases questioned the transferability of commercial rights in a person's identity because of the historical connection with privacy rights, which are not generally transferable. The reluctance to recognize assignments was eventually overcome through the development of a distinct right of publicity. An assignment of the right of publicity transfers ownership to the assignee, who has standing to assert the right against others. However, an assignment of the right of publicity transfers only the right to exploit the commercial value of the assignor's identity; the personal interests protected under the right of privacy are not transferable, and thus invasions of those rights by third persons remain actionable by the assignor.

An assignment of the right of publicity is binding against the assignor, who may not thereafter exploit the commercial value of the identity in a manner that conflicts with the terms of the assignment. The assignment also operates as a consent to the assignee's use. Thus, conduct by the assignee that would otherwise violate the publicity or privacy rights of the assignor is privileged if the use is within the terms of the assignment. See Comment *f.*

An individual's name or likeness can become a trademark if it serves to identify the source or sponsorship of goods or services. See § 14, Comments *e* and *f.* An assignment of rights in such a mark is subject to the general rules governing the assignment of trademarks, including the requirement of a concurrent transfer of the line of business associated with the mark. See § 34, Comment *g.* The right of publicity, however, is not dependent upon a public association of the identity with a particular source of goods or services, and publicity rights may thus be assigned in gross without the transfer of any accompanying business or good will.

A license is a form of consent that establishes the terms under which the licensee may exploit the licensor's identity but which does not purport to transfer ownership of the commercial value of the identity. Unless an applicable statute requires a writing, a license may be oral or implied from conduct or inaction that manifests consent to a particular use of the identity. See Comment *f.* Since a licensee does not acquire ownership of the commercial value of the identity, the licensee does not ordinarily have standing to prevent use of the identity by others. However, when the license is exclusive, courts have held that the licensee has standing to object to commercial uses that infringe on the scope of the licensee's exclusive right.

If a personal name or likeness has become a trademark, a license to use the name or likeness to identify the source of goods or services is subject to the general requirement of trademark law that the licensor exercise reasonable control over the nature and quality of the licensee's goods or services. See § 33. The requirement of control is not otherwise applicable to the licensing of publicity rights.

Illustration:

1. *A*, a famous actress, assigns to *B* the right to exploit the commercial value of *A* 's identity. *C*, without the permission of either *A* or *B*, markets posters that feature *A* 's picture in a pose that places *A* before the public in a false light. *C* is subject to liability to *B*, but not to *A*, for an appropriation of the commercial value of *A* 's identity under the rule stated in this Section. *C* is subject to liability to *A*, but not to *B*, for placing *A* before the public in a false light under the rule stated in Restatement, Second, Torts § 652E.

h. Duration of rights. Many jurisdictions have not yet considered the descendibility of the right of publicity. Of those jurisdictions that have determined the issue through legislation or common law adjudication, the majority recognize the right as descendible, while in others the assertion of post-mortem rights is precluded by statute or case law.

Recognition of a descendible right of publicity may increase the value of the right during life by securing the expectations of potential licensees and assignees. As a general matter, however, the dignitary and proprietary interests that support the recognition of a right of publicity become substantially attenuated after death. Post mortem uses are also less likely to create a false suggestion of endorsement or sponsorship. Thus, in jurisdictions recognizing the right of publicity as descendible, the scope of permissible use by others may be greater in the case of post mortem publicity rights. See § 47, Comment *d.* The practical duration of post mortem rights is ordinarily limited by the diminishing commercial value of a person's identity in the period after death. In addition, the exercise of post mortem rights by heirs or legatees is subject to the traditional equitable principles of laches and estoppel. Statutes recognizing descendibility typically limit the duration of post mortem rights to a fixed term of years.

In several of the decisions that recognize the descendibility of the right of publicity at common law, post mortem rights are conditioned on commercial exploitation of the identity prior to death. Some of these decisions suggest that commercial exploitation in the person's primary profession is sufficient, while others appear to demand supplementary use of the identity in merchandising or licensing. The case law offers little justification for such a requirement. The rule creates needless uncertainty and has been rejected in a number of decisions. State statutes recognizing descendibility do not demand exploitation before death, and several statutes expressly repudiate such a requirement. Although commercial exploitation prior to death can be relevant in establishing the value of the appropriated identity, it should not be required as a condition of descent.

i. Relation to copyright. The 1976 Copyright Act protects "original works of authorship fixed in any tangible medium of expression." 17 U.S.C.A. § 102(a). States are preempted from recognizing rights "equivalent" to copyright in works "within the subject matter" of the Copyright Act. *Id.* § 301. Personal identities and the indicia by which they are recognized, however, are not generally within the subject matter of copyright. No copyright can be obtained, for example, on a person's name, voice, or physical likeness. Fixation of particular indicia of identity within a work of authorship does not bring the indicia within the subject matter of copyright. Copyright in a photograph or portrait of an individual, for example, extends only to the particular depiction, not to the underlying likeness of the person depicted. Similarly, copyright in a film or videotape of a person's performance does not extend to the personal likeness or other identifying characteristics of the performer, and copyright in a sound recording does not create exclusive rights in the identifying characteristics of the performer's voice. Thus, the subject matter of the right of publicity generally lies outside the scope of copyright. Moreover, the protection afforded by the right of publicity against the exploitation of a person's identity for purposes of trade is not ordinarily "equivalent" to the rights against reproduction, distribution, performance, and display recognized under copyright. Claims for infringement of the right of publicity are thus not generally preempted by federal law. In addition, ownership of copyright in a work that embodies the likeness or other indicia of a person's identity will not prevent the imposition of liability under the rule stated in this Section if the copyrighted work is used in a manner that infringes the person's right of publicity.

STATUTORY NOTE

State statutes recognizing a right of publicity or analogous right include the following:

California . . . . CAL. Civ.C. §§ 990; 3344
Florida . . . . FLA. S.A. § 540.08
Kentucky . . . . KY. R.S. § 391.170
Massachusetts . . . . MASS. G.L.A., ch. 214, § 3A
Nebraska . . . . NEB. R.S.A. § 20–202
Nevada . . . . NEV. R.S.A. §§ 598.980–88
New York . . . . N.Y. Civ.Rights L. §§ 50–51
Oklahoma . . . . OKLA S.A., tit. 12, §§ 1448–49; tit. 21, §§ 839.1–839.3
Rhode Island . . . . R.I. G.L.A. §§ 9–1–28; 9–1–28.1
Tennessee . . . . TENN. C.A. § 47–25–1101 et seq.
Texas . . . . TEX. Prop.C. § 26.001 et seq.
Virginia . . . . VA. C.A. § 8.01–40
Wisconsin . . . . WIS. S. § 895.50

REPORTERS' NOTE

The leading treatise on the right of publicity is J. McCarthy, The Rights of Publicity and Privacy. Liability for harm to both commercial and personal interests resulting from an unauthorized appropriation of a person's name or likeness is recognized in Restatement, Second, Torts §§ 652C, 652H (1976).

Comment b. The right of privacy in American law is traditionally traced to Warren and Brandeis, The Right to Privacy, 4 Harv.L.Rev. 193 (1890). The current version of the New York privacy statute enacted in response to the *Roberson* decision is codified at N.Y. Civil Rights Law §§ 50–51.

Illustrative of the early cases precluding celebrities from invoking a right of privacy to prevent unauthorized commercial use of their names or likenesses are O'Brien v. Pabst Sales Co., 124 F.2d 167 (5th Cir. 1941), cert. denied 315 U.S. 823, 62 S.Ct. 917, 86 L.Ed. 1220 (1942), and Pallas v. Crowley–Milner & Co., 334 Mich. 282, 54 N.W.2d 595 (1952). In some cases reliance on the privacy rationale has also influenced the rules governing transfer and descent of rights in the commercial value of a person's identity. See, e.g., Reeves v. United Artists Corp., 765 F.2d 79 (6th Cir.1985) (holding that the right of publicity is not descendible due to its foundation in privacy); Stephano v. News Group Publications, Inc., 64 N.Y.2d 174, 485 N.Y.S.2d 220, 474 N.E.2d 580 (1984) (declining to decide whether the New York privacy statute also controls the transfer and descent of publicity rights).

The first case to formally distinguish the rights of publicity and privacy is Haelan Laboratories, Inc. v. Topps Chewing Gum, Inc., 202 F.2d 866 (2d Cir.), cert. denied 346 U.S. 816, 74 S.Ct. 26, 98 L.Ed. 343 (1953). The distinction was quickly pursued in an influential article by Nimmer, The Right of Publicity, 19 Law & Contemp.Probs. 203 (1954). Many decisions now view the right of publicity as an independent doctrine distinct from the right of privacy. See, e.g., Carson v. Here's Johnny Portable Toilets, Inc., 698 F.2d 831 (6th Cir.1983); Martin Luther King, Jr., Center for Social Change, Inc. v. American Heritage Products, Inc., 250 Ga. 135, 296 S.E.2d 697 (1982); State ex rel. Elvis Presley Int'l Memorial Foundation v. Crowell, 733 S.W.2d 89 (Tenn.App.1987). Other cases continue to protect the commercial value of a person's identity through the privacy tort. See, e.g., Palmer v. Schonhorn Enterprises, Inc., 96 N.J.Super. 72, 232 A.2d 458 (1967). Statutory formulations prohibiting unauthorized commercial exploitation of another's identity are usually sufficiently broad to redress injuries to both commercial and personal interests. See, e.g., Stephano, *supra* (N.Y. statute encompasses both privacy and publicity rights).

In an appropriate case even celebrities accustomed to publicity may recover damages under the right of privacy for mental distress caused by an unauthorized commercial appropriation of their identity. Motschenbacher v. R.J. Reynolds Tobacco Co., 498 F.2d 821 (9th Cir.1974) (dictum); Clark v. Celeb Pub., Inc., 530 F.Supp. 979 (S.D.N.Y.1981); National Bank of Commerce v. Shaklee Corp., 503 F.Supp. 533 (W.D.Tex.1980); Grant v. Esquire, Inc., 367 F.Supp. 876 (S.D.N.Y.1973); Anderson v. Fisher Broadcasting Cos., 300 Or. 452, 712 P.2d 803 (1986) (dictum).

Proof of deception or confusion is not required in order to establish an infringement of the right of publicity. See, e.g., Rogers v. Grimaldi, 875 F.2d 994 (2d Cir.1989); Carson, *supra*; Maheu v. CBS, Inc., 201 Cal. App.3d 662, 247 Cal.Rptr. 304 (1988); Flores v. Mosler Safe Co., 7 N.Y.2d 276, 196 N.Y.S.2d 975, 164 N.E.2d 853 (1959); Aguilar v. Ragusa, 174 A.D.2d 1002, 572 N.Y.S.2d 164 (1991). However, if the defendant's unauthorized use creates a false suggestion of endorsement or a likelihood of confusion as to source or sponsorship, liability may also be imposed for deceptive marketing or trademark or trade name infringement. See, e.g., Waits v. Frito–Lay, Inc., 978 F.2d 1093 (9th Cir.1992), cert. denied ___ U.S. ___, 113 S.Ct. 1047, 122 L.Ed.2d 355 (1993) (liability under § 43(a) of the Lanham Act); Allen v. Men's World Outlet, Inc., 679 F.Supp. 360 (S.D.N.Y.1988) (same); Allen v. National Video, Inc., 610 F.Supp. 612 (S.D.N.Y.1985) (same); National Bank of Commerce, *supra* (unfair competition); Hirsch v. S.C. Johnson & Son, Inc., 90 Wis.2d 379, 280 N.W.2d 129 (1979) (trade name infringement). See also Newton v. Thomason, 22 F.3d 1455 (9th Cir. 1994) (upholding defendants' summary judgment under § 43(a) absent proof of confusion of endorsement).

Comment c. The desire to secure for plaintiffs the commercial value of their identity and to prevent the perceived unjust enrichment of an appropriator is evident throughout the case law on the right of publicity. The right "prevents unjust enrichment by providing a remedy against exploitation of the goodwill and reputation that a person develops in his name or likeness through the investment of time, effort, and money." Bi–Rite Enterprises, Inc. v. Button Master, 555 F.Supp. 1188, 1198 (S.D.N.Y.1983). See also, e.g., Uhlaender v. Henricksen, 316 F.Supp. 1277 (D.Minn.1970); Hirsch v. S.C. Johnson & Son, Inc., 90 Wis.2d 379, 280 N.W.2d 129 (1979). The right also protects against dilution of the commercial value of the identity caused by excessive or harmful uses. See Hirsch, *supra*; Lugosi v. Universal Pictures, 25 Cal.3d 813, 160 Cal.Rptr. 323, 603 P.2d 425 (1979) (Bird, J., dissenting). The incentive rationale is most persuasive when the defendant has appropriated a work product of the plaintiff in addition to the plaintiff's identity. Compare Zacchini v. Scripps–Howard Broadcasting Co., 433 U.S. 562, 97 S.Ct. 2849, 53 L.Ed.2d 965 (1977) (incentive rationale used to justify protection against an appropriation of the plaintiff's performance) with Memphis Dev. Foundation v. Factors Etc., Inc., 616 F.2d 956 (6th Cir.), cert. denied 449 U.S. 953, 101 S.Ct. 358, 66 L.Ed.2d 217 (1980) (noting that fame is often merely a by-product of other achievements). Several cases suggest that the right of publicity can be understood as an aspect of the broader prohibition against unfair competition. See Factors Etc., Inc. v. Creative Card Co., 444 F.Supp. 279, 283 (S.D.N.Y.1977), affirmed 579 F.2d 215 (2d Cir.1978), cert. denied 440 U.S. 908, 99 S.Ct. 1215, 59 L.Ed.2d 455 (1979); Lugosi, *supra* (Bird, J., dissenting); Hogan v. A.S. Barnes & Co., 114 U.S.P.Q. 314, 320 (Pa.Com. Pl.1957).

Comment d. Several cases indicate that the right of publicity is available only to plaintiffs who have achieved some degree of celebrity. See, e.g., Brewer v. Hustler Magazine, Inc., 749 F.2d 527 (9th Cir.1984); Ali v. Playgirl, Inc., 447 F.Supp. 723 (S.D.N.Y.1978); Martin Luther King, Jr., Center for Social Change, Inc. v. American Heritage Products, Inc., 250 Ga. 135, 296 S.E.2d 697 (1982). However, non-celebrities should also be permitted to recover upon proof that the appropriated identity possessed commercial value. See, e.g., Motschenbacher v. R.J. Reynolds Tobacco Co., 498 F.2d 821 (9th Cir.1974) (dictum); Tellado v. Time–Life Books, Inc., 643 F.Supp. 904 (D.N.J. 1986); Vinci v. American Can Co., 9 Ohio St.3d 98, 459 N.E.2d 507 (1984) (the "degree of notoriety" is relevant to damages rather than to liability); Canessa v. J.I. Kislak, Inc., 97 N.J.Super. 327, 350, 235 A.2d 62, 75 (1967) (the distinction between celebrities and others "is relevant only to the question of damages"); McCarthy, The Rights of Publicity and Privacy § 4.3.

The right of publicity is not infringed unless the plaintiff is identified by the defendant's use. "The [New York] statute is designed to protect a person's identity, not merely a property interest in his or her 'name', 'portrait' or 'picture', and thus it implicitly requires that plaintiff be capable of identification from the objectionable material itself * * *." Cohen v. Herbal Concepts, Inc., 63 N.Y.2d 379, 384, 482 N.Y.S.2d 457, 459, 472 N.E.2d 307, 309 (1984). Compare Hirsch v. S.C. Johnson & Son, Inc., 90 Wis.2d 379, 280 N.W.2d 129 (1979) (allegation that the nickname "Crazylegs" identified the plaintiff was sufficient to state a cause of action) with Hooker v. Columbia Pictures Industries, Inc., 551 F.Supp. 1060 (N.D.Ill.1982) (use of the plaintiff's name does not subject the defendant to liability if the name is not understood as identifying the plaintiff). See, e.g., Ali, *supra* (finding the defendant's drawing to be a "recognizable likeness" of the plaintiff); Cal.Civ.Code § 3344 (requiring in the case of a photograph that the plaintiff be "readily identifiable," determined by whether "one who views the photograph with the naked eye can reasonably determine that the person depicted" is the plaintiff). See also Okla.Stat. tit. 12, § 1448(I); Tex.Prop.Code Ann. § 26.001. "On [the issue of liability] the question is whether the figure is recogniz*able*, not the number of people who recognize it." Negri v. Schering Corp., 333 F.Supp. 101, 104 (S.D.N.Y.1971). See also Cohen, *supra*. The number of people who recognize or identify the plaintiff, however, is relevant on the issue of damages. See Negri, *supra* (dictum); Hirsch, *supra* (dictum).

Whether the plaintiff is identified by the defendant's use is a question of fact. Motschenbacher, *supra*; Hirsch, *supra*; Cohen, *supra*. Relevant evidence includes the number and nature of the identifying characteristics used by the defendant, see, e.g., Ali, *supra*; Lombardo v. Doyle, Dane & Bernbach, Inc., 58 A.D.2d 620, 396 N.Y.S.2d 661 (1977), and actual identification made by third persons. See Negri, *supra*; Cohen, *supra*. The defendant's intent to identify the plaintiff is also evidence that the plaintiff is in fact identified by the use. See Carson v. Here's Johnny Portable Toilets, Inc., 698 F.2d 831 (6th Cir.1983). Cf. White v. Samsung Electronics America, Inc., 971 F.2d 1395 (9th Cir.1992), cert. denied ___ U.S. ___, 113 S.Ct. 2443, 124 L.Ed.2d 660 (1993) (defendants informally named the disputed advertisement after the plaintiff).

A number of state statutes, adopting the formulation used by New York in the first privacy statute, N.Y. Civil Rights Law §§ 50–51, limit the subject matter of protection to a "name, portrait or picture." See Mass.Gen.L. ch. 214, § 3A; R.I.Gen. Laws § 9–1–28; Va.Code Ann. § 8.01–40; Wis.Stat. § 895.50. See also Fla.Stat. § 540.08 ("name, portrait, photograph or other likeness"); Ky.Rev.Stat.Ann. § 391.170 ("name and likeness"); Tenn.Code Ann. § 47–25–1103 ("name, photograph or likeness"). Cf. Restatement, Second, Torts § 652C ("name or likeness"). Other statutes are broader. See Cal. Civ.Code § 3344 ("name, voice, signature, photograph, or likeness"); Neb. Rev.Stat. § 20–202 ("name, picture, portrait, or personality"); Nev.Rev. Stat. § 598.980(1) ("name, voice, signature, photograph or likeness"); Okla.Stat. tit. 12, § 1449 (same); Tex. Prop.Code Ann. § 26.002 (same). However, the statutory formulations do not necessarily displace common law rights. See, e.g., Cal.Civ.Code § 3344(g); Fla.Stat. § 540.08(6); Okla.Stat. tit. 12, § 1449(G); Tenn. Code Ann. § 47–25–1106(e); Tex. Prop.Code Ann. § 26.014. But see Stephano v. News Group Publications, Inc., 64 N.Y.2d 174, 485 N.Y.S.2d 220, 474 N.E.2d 580 (1984)

(New York privacy and publicity rights are exclusively statutory).

On the unauthorized use of names, see, e.g., McFarland v. Miller, 14 F.3d 912 (3d Cir.1994) (stage name); Uhlaender v. Henricksen, 316 F.Supp. 1277 (D.Minn.1970); Hirsch, *supra* (nickname). On the unauthorized use of photographs, see, e.g., Factors Etc., Inc. v. Pro Arts, Inc., 579 F.2d 215 (2d Cir.1978), cert. denied 440 U.S. 908, 99 S.Ct. 1215, 59 L.Ed.2d 455 (1979); Haelan Laboratories, Inc. v. Topps Chewing Gum, Inc., 202 F.2d 866 (2d Cir.), cert. denied 346 U.S. 816, 74 S.Ct. 26, 98 L.Ed. 343 (1953); Tellado v. Time–Life Books, Inc., 643 F.Supp. 904 (D.N.J.1986); Negri, *supra*; Brinkley v. Casablancas, 80 A.D.2d 428, 438 N.Y.S.2d 1004 (1981). Some state statutes limit the imposition of liability in connection with group photographs or photographs depicting persons solely as unidentified members of the public. See Cal.Civ.Code § 3344(b); Fla.Stat. § 540.08(3)(c); Neb.Rev.Stat. § 20–202(3). Liability can extend to the use of a drawing that is a recognizable likeness of the plaintiff. See Ali, *supra* (a drawing can qualify as a "portrait or picture" under the New York privacy statute). Use of a photograph of a look-alike can also be actionable as a "portrait or picture" of the plaintiff. Allen v. National Video, Inc., 610 F.Supp. 612 (S.D.N.Y.1985) (dictum); Onassis v. Christian Dior–New York, Inc., 122 Misc.2d 603, 472 N.Y.S.2d 254 (Sup. Ct.1984), affirmed 110 A.D.2d 1095, 488 N.Y.S.2d 943 (1985). Cf. Nurmi v. Peterson, 10 U.S.P.Q.2d 1775 (C.D.Cal.1989) (a character who merely resembled the plaintiff was not a "likeness" under the California statute).

The leading case recognizing a claim for the appropriation of a voice for purposes of trade is Midler v. Ford Motor Co., 849 F.2d 460 (9th Cir.1988), which imposed liability for an imitation of the plaintiff's voice in a song used during a television commercial. The court distinguished a contrary holding in Sinatra v. Goodyear Tire & Rubber Co., 435 F.2d 711 (9th Cir.1970), cert. denied 402 U.S. 906, 91 S.Ct. 1376, 28 L.Ed.2d 646 (1971), arguing that the plaintiff in the latter case had asserted rights in the performance of the song itself rather than in a distinctive voice as an attribute of identity. See also Waits v. Frito–Lay, Inc., 978 F.2d 1093 (9th Cir.1992), cert. denied ___ U.S. ___, 113 S.Ct. 1047, 122 L.Ed.2d 355 (1993). But cf. Tin Pan Apple, Inc. v. Miller Brewing Co., 737 F.Supp. 826 (S.D.N.Y.1990) (New York privacy statute does not reach sound-alikes).

Some cases have found infringement in the imitation of a distinctive performing persona. See, e.g., Groucho Marx Productions, Inc. v. Day and Night Co., 523 F.Supp. 485 (S.D.N.Y.1981), reversed on other grounds 689 F.2d 317 (2d Cir.1982); Estate of Presley v. Russen, 513 F.Supp. 1339 (D.N.J.1981); Price v. Worldvision Enterprises, Inc., 455 F.Supp. 252 (S.D.N.Y.1978), affirmed 603 F.2d 214 (2d Cir.1979); Lombardo v. Doyle, Dane & Bernbach, Inc., 58 A.D.2d 620, 396 N.Y.S.2d 661 (1977) (upholding a claim at common law but not under the more restrictive language of N.Y.Civ.Rights Law §§ 50–51, which was later held by the New York Court of Appeals in Stephano v. News Group Publications, Inc., 64 N.Y.2d 174, 485 N.Y.S.2d 220, 474 N.E.2d 580 (1984), to be the exclusive source of publicity rights in

New York). Cf. McFarland, *supra*, 14 F.3d at 920 (recognizing rights "[w]here an actor's screen persona becomes so associated with him that it becomes inseparable from the actor's own public image") (dictum); Nurmi, *supra* (finding insufficient resemblance to the plaintiff). On the potential constitutional limitations on the scope of liability, see § 47, Comment *d*. Portrayal of a character in a theatrical work will not ordinarily endow the actor with publicity rights in the character itself, but use of a likeness of the particular actor in the role of the character can infringe the actor's right of publicity. See White v. Samsung Electronics America, Inc., 971 F.2d 1395 (9th Cir.1992), cert. denied ___ U.S. ___, 113 S.Ct. 2443, 124 L.Ed.2d 660 (1993) (the majority and dissenting opinions disagree as to whether the appropriated attributes identify the plaintiff actress or merely a particular role) (see also 989 F.2d 1512 (9th Cir.1993), denying a petition for rehearing en banc (Kozinski, J., dissenting"; Lugosi v. Universal Pictures, 25 Cal.3d 813, 160 Cal.Rptr. 323, 603 P.2d 425 (1979) (Bird, J., dissenting).

A few cases indicate that the right of publicity can be infringed through the use of other subject matter that serves to identify the plaintiff. See Carson v. Here's Johnny Portable Toilets, Inc., 698 F.2d 831 (6th Cir. 1983) (stage phrase "Here's Johnny" found sufficiently identified with the plaintiff); Motschenbacher v. R.J. Reynolds Tobacco Co., 498 F.2d 821 (9th Cir.1974) (plaintiff identified by his distinctive racing car); Lombardo, *supra* (refusing to dismiss a common law claim alleging the use of distinctive props and gestures). Cf. Rosemont Enterprises, Inc. v. Urban Systems, Inc., 72 Misc.2d 788, 340 N.Y.S.2d 144 (Sup.Ct.), modified 42 A.D.2d 544, 345 N.Y.S.2d 17 (1973) (name and biographical data); Palmer v. Schonhorn Enterprises, Inc., 96 N.J.Super. 72, 232 A.2d 458 (1967) (same).

Protection under the right of publicity is limited to natural persons. See, e.g., Fla.Stat. § 540.08 ("natural person"); Nev.Rev.Stat. § 598.980(2) ("natural person"); N.Y.Civ.Rights Law § 50 ("living person"); Tenn. Code Ann. § 47–25–1102 ("human being"); Pump, Inc. v. Collins Management, Inc., 746 F.Supp. 1159 (D.Mass. 1990) (expressing doubt that the Massachusetts statute covers commercial names or trademarks); Eagle's Eye, Inc. v. Ambler Fashion Shop, Inc., 627 F.Supp. 856 (E.D.Pa.1985) (the right of publicity does not protect trademarks). However, the right may be applicable to some collective names such as those adopted by musical groups if an appropriation of the name effectively appropriates the identities of the individual group members. See, e.g., Bi–Rite Enterprises, Inc. v. Button Master, 555 F.Supp. 1188 (S.D.N.Y.1983); Winterland Concessions Co. v. Sileo, 528 F.Supp. 1201 (N.D.Ill.1981), affirmed 735 F.2d 257 (7th Cir.1984). Cf. Philadelphia Orchestra Ass'n v. Walt Disney Co., 821 F.Supp. 341 (E.D.Pa. 1993) (dictum that the right of publicity extends to the name "The Philadelphia Orchestra"). See also N.Y. Gen.Bus. Law § 397 (prohibiting unauthorized use of the name or trademark of a non-profit organization "for advertising purposes or for purposes of trade").

Comment e. Statutes in several states require proof that the defendant "knowingly" appropriated the plaintiff's identity. Cal.Civ.Code § 3344(a); Okla.Stat. tit. 12,

§ 1449(A); Tenn.Code Ann. § 47–25–1105(a). But cf. Eastwood v. Superior Court, 149 Cal.App.3d 409, 198 Cal.Rptr. 342 (1983) (mistaken or inadvertent use remains actionable under California common law). State statutes more commonly limit the relevance of knowing use to the recovery of punitive damages. See Mass. Gen.L. ch. 214, § 3A (treble damages); Nev.Rev.Stat. § 598.-988(1)(b)(2); N.Y.Civ.Rights Law § 51; R.I.Gen.Laws § 9–1–28; Va. Code Ann. § 8.01–40. On the availability of punitive damages, see § 49, Comment *e*. An intent to identify the plaintiff is not an element of liability for infringement of the right of publicity at common law. Fairfield v. American Photocopy Equipment Co., 138 Cal.App.2d 82, 291 P.2d 194 (1955) (dictum); Kerby v. Hal Roach Studios, Inc., 53 Cal.App.2d 207, 127 P.2d 577 (1942); McCarthy, The Rights of Publicity and Privacy § 3.6. Similarly, mistake as to the plaintiff's consent is not a defense. Douglass v. Hustler Magazine, Inc., 769 F.2d 1128 (7th Cir.1985), cert. denied 475 U.S. 1094, 106 S.Ct. 1489, 89 L.Ed.2d 892 (1986) (dictum); Genesis Pub., Inc. v. Goss, 437 So.2d 169 (Fla.App.1983); Welch v. Mr. Christmas Inc., 57 N.Y.2d 143, 454 N.Y.S.2d 971, 440 N.E.2d 1317 (1982) (dictum that mistake as to consent is not a defense under the New York privacy statute); Myers v. U.S. Camera Pub. Corp., 9 Misc.2d 765, 167 N.Y.S.2d 771 (N.Y.C.Ct.1957) (mistake is relevant only to mitigation of damages under the New York privacy statute). McCarthy, *supra* § 3.6[E].

The constitutional requirement of fault applicable in certain defamation actions has not been applied to the right of publicity. See Hustler Magazine, Inc. v. Falwell, 485 U.S. 46, 52, 108 S.Ct. 876, 880, 99 L.Ed.2d 41, 49 (1988), which interpreted Zacchini v. Scripps–Howard Broadcasting Co., 433 U.S. 562, 97 S.Ct. 2849, 53 L.Ed.2d 965 (1977), as "ruling that the 'actual malice' standard does not apply to the tort of appropriation of a right of publicity." See, e.g., National Bank of Commerce v. Shaklee Corp., 503 F.Supp. 533 (W.D.Tex. 1980). However, the constitutional standards are applicable when a state appropriation of identity statute is used as a vehicle for the redress of false light privacy claims. Time, Inc. v. Hill, 385 U.S. 374, 87 S.Ct. 534, 17 L.Ed.2d 456 (1967) (New York privacy statute); Lerman v. Flynt Distributing Co., 745 F.2d 123 (2d Cir.1984), cert. denied 471 U.S. 1054, 105 S.Ct. 2114, 85 L.Ed.2d 479 (1985) (same); Davis v. High Society Magazine, Inc., 90 A.D.2d 374, 457 N.Y.S.2d 308 (1982) (same). See § 47, Comment *c*.

Comment f. Statutes in several states require that the consent be in writing. See Ky.Rev.Stat.Ann. § 391.170(2) (written consent for post mortem use); Mass.Gen.L. ch. 214, § 3A; Nev.Rev.Stat. § 598.988(1); N.Y.Civ.Rights Law § 51; R.I.Gen. Laws § 9–1–28; Tex.Prop.Code Ann. § 26.011 (post mortem use); Va.Code Ann. § 8.01–40; Wis.Stat. § 895.-50(2)(b). The requirement of written consent in the New York statute has been interpreted to preclude defenses based on oral or implied consent, Caesar v. Chemical Bank, 66 N.Y.2d 698, 496 N.Y.S.2d 418, 487 N.E.2d 275 (1985); Brinkley v. Casablancas, 80 A.D.2d 428, 438 N.Y.S.2d 1004 (1981), estoppel, Lomax v. New Broadcasting Co., 18 A.D.2d 229, 238 N.Y.S.2d 781 (1963), and industry custom, Sidney v. A.S. Beck Shoe Corp., 153 Misc. 166, 274 N.Y.S. 559 (Sup.Ct.1934), although the cases recognize such facts in mitigation of damages.

The scope of consent is determined according to the general principles of contract interpretation. See, e.g., Cepeda v. Swift and Co., 415 F.2d 1205 (8th Cir.1969); Sharman v. C. Schmidt & Sons, Inc., 216 F.Supp. 401 (E.D.Pa.1963); Andretti v. Rolex Watch U.S.A., Inc., 56 N.Y.2d 284, 452 N.Y.S.2d 5, 437 N.E.2d 264 (1982). Cf. Newton v. Thomason, 22 F.3d 1455 (9th Cir.1994) (upholding summary judgment on a defense of consent). Consent to the taking of a photograph does not in itself imply consent to commercial use. See, e.g, Bi–Rite Enterprises, Inc. v. Bruce Miner Co., 757 F.2d 440 (1st Cir. 1985); Smith v. WGN, Inc., 47 Ill. App.2d 183, 197 N.E.2d 482 (1964); Canessa v. J.I. Kislak, Inc., 97 N.J.Super. 327, 235 A.2d 62 (1967); Brinkley v. Casablancas, 80 A.D.2d 428, 438 N.Y.S.2d 1004 (1981). On liability for use outside the scope of consent, see, e.g., Ettore v. Philco Television Broadcasting Corp., 229 F.2d 481 (3d Cir.), cert. denied 351 U.S. 926, 76 S.Ct. 783, 100 L.Ed. 1456 (1956); Price v. Hal Roach Studios, Inc., 400 F.Supp. 836 (S.D.N.Y.1975); Dzurenko v. Jordache, Inc., 59 N.Y.2d 788, 464 N.Y.S.2d 730, 451 N.E.2d 477 (1983). On use after the expiration of consent, see, e.g., Welch v. Mr. Christmas Inc., 57 N.Y.2d 143, 454 N.Y.S.2d 971, 440 N.E.2d 1317 (1982). On the recognition of a "first sale" doctrine to protect subsequent resales of licensed merchandise, see Major League Baseball Players Ass'n v. Dad's Kid Corp., 806 F.Supp. 458 (S.D.N.Y.1992).

Comment g. For a general discussion of the rules relating to the assignment and licensing of publicity rights, see McCarthy, The Rights of Privacy and Publicity, ch. 10. For an early case holding that a person's right of privacy, construed as including the commercial value of the person's identity, is not assignable, see Hanna Mfg. Co. v. Hillerich & Bradsby Co., 78 F.2d 763 (5th Cir.), cert. denied 296 U.S. 645, 56 S.Ct. 248, 80 L.Ed. 458 (1935). The right of publicity was recognized as a right distinct from privacy in part to overcome the rule prohibiting assignment. See Haelan Laboratories, Inc. v. Topps Chewing Gum, Inc., 202 F.2d 866, 868 (2d Cir.), cert. denied 346 U.S. 816, 74 S.Ct. 26, 98 L.Ed. 343 (1953) ("We think that, in addition to and independent of that right of privacy (which in New York derives from statute), a man has a right in the publicity value of his photograph, *i.e.*, the right to grant the exclusive privilege of publishing his picture, and that such a grant may validly be made 'in gross,' *i.e.*, without an accompanying transfer of a business or of anything else." But see Stephano v. News Group Pub., Inc., 64 N.Y.2d 174, 485 N.Y.S.2d 220, 474 N.E.2d 580 (1984), holding that New York Civil Rights Law §§ 50–51 is the exclusive source of publicity rights in New York.) For other cases indicating that the right of publicity is assignable, see, e.g., Nature's Way Products, Inc. v. Nature–Pharma, Inc., 736 F.Supp. 245 (D.Utah 1990); Bi–Rite Enterprises, Inc. v. Button Master, 555 F.Supp. 1188 (S.D.N.Y. 1983); Price v. Hal Roach Studios, Inc., 400 F.Supp. 836 (S.D.N.Y.1975); Martin Luther King, Jr., Center for Social Change, Inc. v. American Heritage Products, Inc., 250 Ga. 135, 296 S.E.2d 697 (1982). Statutes in several states expressly declare that the right of publicity is transferable. See Cal.Civ.Code § 990(b) (post mortem rights); Nev.Rev.Stat. § 598.986(1);

Okla.Stat. tit. 12, § 1448(B) (post mortem rights); Tenn.Code Ann. § 47–25–1103(b); Tex.Prop.Code Ann. § 26.004 (post mortem rights). But see Neb.Rev.Stat. § 20–207 (actions for invasion of privacy, including the appropriation tort, are not assignable). Although publicity rights can be assigned, courts continue to hold that privacy rights are personal and nonassignable. See, e.g., Bi–Rite Enterprises, *supra* (distinguishing publicity and privacy rights).

The legal consequences of assignments and licenses of publicity rights were distinguished in Estate of Presley v. Russen, 513 F.Supp. 1339 (D.N.J.1981). Although non-exclusive licensees have no standing to prevent exploitation of the identity by others, see, e.g., Bi–Rite Enterprises, *supra*, exclusive licensees have standing to prevent a use that infringes on their exclusive rights. See, e.g., Bi–Rite Enterprises, Inc. v. Bruce Miner Co., 757 F.2d 440 (1st Cir.1985); Factors Etc., Inc. v. Pro Arts, Inc., 579 F.2d 215 (2d Cir.1978), cert. denied 440 U.S. 908, 99 S.Ct. 1215, 59 L.Ed.2d 455 (1979); Bi–Rite Enterprises, Inc. v. Button Master, 555 F.Supp. 1188 (S.D.N.Y.1983).

Comment h. Descendibility of the right of publicity at common law is recognized in Nature's Way Products, Inc. v. Nature–Pharma, Inc., 736 F.Supp. 245 (D.Utah 1990) (Utah law); Estate of Presley v. Russen, 513 F.Supp. 1339 (D.N.J.1981) (New Jersey law); Martin Luther King, Jr., Center for Social Change, Inc. v. American Heritage Products, Inc., 250 Ga. 135, 296 S.E.2d 697 (1982). See also State ex rel. Elvis Presley Int'l Memorial Foundation v. Crowell, 733 S.W.2d 89 (Tenn.App.1987) (upholding the descent of rights vested prior to subsequent state legislation recognizing descendibility). The latter two cases argue that descendibility increases the value of the right during life. Descendibility under California common law is unclear. See Guglielmi v. Spelling–Goldberg Productions, 25 Cal.3d 860, 160 Cal. Rptr. 352, 603 P.2d 454 (1979); Lugosi v. Universal Pictures, 25 Cal.3d 813, 160 Cal.Rptr. 323, 603 P.2d 425 (1979). The California cases are interpreted in Acme Circus Operating Co. v. Kuperstock, 711 F.2d 1538 (11th Cir.1983); Groucho Marx Productions, Inc. v. Day and Night Co., 689 F.2d 317 (2d Cir.1982). Descendibility is now recognized in Cal.Civ. Code § 990. Although the right of publicity was initially held to be descendible in several federal cases applying New York common law, see, e.g., Factors Etc., Inc. v. Pro Arts, Inc., 579 F.2d 215 (2d Cir.1978), cert. denied 440 U.S. 908, 99 S.Ct. 1215, 59 L.Ed.2d 455 (1979); Hicks v. Casablanca Records, 464 F.Supp. 426 (S.D.N.Y.1978), the New York Court of Appeals ultimately held that privacy and publicity rights in New York are governed exclusively by N.Y. Civ. Rights Law § 50, which is limited to "any living person." Stephano v. News Group Pub., Inc., 64 N.Y.2d 174, 485 N.Y.S.2d 220, 474 N.E.2d 580 (1984). Subsequent cases have held that the right of publicity is not descendible under New York law. See, e.g., Pirone v. MacMillan, Inc., 894 F.2d 579 (2d Cir.1990) (no post mortem rights under the New York statute); James v. Delilah Films, Inc., 144 Misc.2d 374, 544 N.Y.S.2d 447 (Sup.Ct.1989). The leading case rejecting descendibility at common law is Memphis Dev. Foundation v. Factors Etc., Inc., 616 F.2d 956 (6th Cir.), cert. denied 449 U.S. 953, 101 S.Ct. 358, 66 L.Ed.2d 217 (1980) (Tennessee law). But see State ex rel. Elvis Presley Int'l Memorial Foundation, *supra*. See also Reeves v. United Artists Corp., 765 F.2d 79 (6th Cir.1985) (right of publicity not descendible under Ohio common law, emphasizing the historical connection with privacy rights); Joplin Enterprises v. Allen, 795 F.Supp. 349 (W.D.Wash.1992) (refusing to extrapolate a descendible right of publicity from a state right to privacy tort) (dictum). Trademark rights established in a personal name or likeness continue after death without regard to the persistence of publicity rights. Cf. Groucho Marx Productions, *supra* (distinguishing trademark and publicity rights).

A number of states recognize post mortem publicity rights by statute, usually subject to a fixed duration. See Cal.Civ.Code § 990 (50 years); Fla.Stat. § 540.08(4) (40 years); Ky. Rev.Stat.Ann. § 391.170(2) (50 years); Neb.Rev.Stat. § 20–208 (right of action deemed to "survive the death of the subject," with no stated duration); Nev.Rev.Stat. § 598.984(1) (50 years); Okla.Stat. tit. 12, § 1448(G) (100 years); Tenn.Code Ann. § 47–25–1104 (10 years and thereafter until terminated by non-use for two years); Tex.Prop.Code Ann. § 26.012(d) (50 years); Va.Code Ann. § 8.01–40 (20 years). Statutes in other states do not provide for post mortem rights. See Mass.Gen.L. ch. 214, § 3A; N.Y.Civ.Rights Law § 50 ("living person"); R.I.Gen.Laws § 9–1–28; Wis.Stat. § 895.50 ("living person").

The majority in *Lugosi, supra*, argued that it was improper for a court to impose at common law the durational limits appropriate to the recognition of post mortem rights. Justice Bird in dissent argued for an analogy to the duration of copyright. See also Factors Etc., Inc. v. Pro Arts, Inc., 652 F.2d 278 (2d Cir.1981), cert. denied 456 U.S. 927, 102 S.Ct. 1973, 72 L.Ed.2d 442 (1982) (Mansfield, J., dissenting). The court in *Estate of Presley, supra*, recognizing post mortem rights at common law, commented that any durational limit was a matter for legislation. 513 F.Supp. at 1355 n.10.

Cases requiring lifetime exploitation as a condition of post mortem rights include Lugosi, *supra*; Acme Circus, *supra* (California common law); Nature's Way Products, *supra*; Sinkler v. Goldsmith, 623 F.Supp. 727 (D.Ariz.1985); Hicks, *supra*. In some cases the requirement is interpreted to entail exploitation beyond the person's primary profession, see Acme Circus, *supra*; Groucho Marx Productions, *supra* (both interpreting California common law), while other cases accept any effort to exploit the commercial value of the identity during life. See Groucho Marx Productions, Inc. v. Day and Night Co., 523 F.Supp. 485 (S.D.N.Y.1981), reversed on other grounds Groucho Marx Productions, Inc. v. Day and Night Co., 689 F.2d 317 (2d Cir.1982); Hicks, *supra* (both interpreting New York common law). Cases rejecting the exploitation requirement at common law include Price v. Hal Roach Studios, Inc., 400 F.Supp. 836 (S.D.N.Y. 1975); Martin Luther King, *supra*. See also Lugosi, *supra* (Bird, J., dissenting). The requirement of lifetime exploitation is specifically rejected in Cal.Civ.Code § 990(h); Nev. Rev.Stat. § 598.984(1); Okla.Stat. tit. 12, § 1448(H); Tenn.Code Ann. § 47–25–1103.

Comment i. Cases indicating that claims under state law for infringement of the right of publicity are not preempted by federal copyright law include Zacchini v. Scripps–

Howard Broadcasting Co., 433 U.S. 562, 97 S.Ct. 2849, 53 L.Ed.2d 965 (1977); Waits v. Frito–Lay, Inc., 978 F.2d 1093 (9th Cir.1992), cert. denied ___ U.S. ___, 113 S.Ct. 1047, 122 L.Ed.2d 355 (1993); Factors Etc., Inc. v. Pro Arts, Inc., 652 F.2d 278 (2d Cir.1981), cert. denied 456 U.S. 927, 102 S.Ct. 1973, 72 L.Ed.2d 442 (1982) (Mansfield, J., dissenting); Bi–Rite Enterprises, Inc. v. Button Master, 555 F.Supp. 1188 (S.D.N.Y.1983); Price v. Hal Roach Studios, Inc., 400 F.Supp. 836 (S.D.N.Y.1975); Lugosi v. Universal Pictures, 25 Cal.3d 813, 160 Cal.Rptr. 323, 603 P.2d 425 (1979) (Bird, J., dissenting). See also James v. Delilah Films, Inc., 144 Misc.2d 374, 544 N.Y.S.2d 447 (Sup.Ct.1989), and Ippolito v. Ono–Lennon, 139 Misc.2d 230, 526 N.Y.S.2d 877 (Sup. Ct.1988), affirmed 150 A.D.2d 300, 542 N.Y.S.2d 3 (1989), both indicating that claims under the New York privacy statute are not equivalent to copyright. The legislative history of § 301 of the Copyright Act, 17 U.S.C.A. § 301, supports the conclusion that publicity rights are not preempted. "The evolving common law rights of 'privacy,' 'publicity,' and trade secrets, and the general laws of defamation and fraud, would remain unaffected as long as the causes of action contain elements, such as an invasion of personal rights or a breach of trust or confidentiality, that are different in kind from copyright infringement." H.R.Rep.No. 94–1476, 94th Cong., 2d Sess. 132 (1976), reprinted in 1976 U.S. Code Cong. & Ad. News 5659, 5748.

The leading case holding a right of publicity claim preempted under § 301 of the Copyright Act is Baltimore Orioles, Inc. v. Major League Baseball Players Ass'n, 805 F.2d 663 (7th Cir.1986), cert. denied 480 U.S. 941, 107 S.Ct. 1593, 94 L.Ed.2d 782 (1987). See also Motown Record Corp. v. George A. Hormel & Co., 657 F.Supp. 1236 (C.D.Cal.1987). Cf. Sinatra v. Goodyear Tire & Rubber Co., 435 F.2d 711 (9th Cir.1970), cert. denied 402 U.S. 906, 91 S.Ct. 1376, 28 L.Ed.2d 646 (1971) (dictum finding preemption prior to the enactment of the 1976 Copyright Act). The *Baltimore Orioles* decision has been criticized for failing to distinguish copyright in a particular broadcast of a baseball game from rights in the underlying performance and identities of the players. See, e.g., Goldstein, Copyright § 15.22.1.1; McCarthy, The Rights of Publicity and Privacy § 11.13[C][4] (citing other secondary sources critical of the decision); Nimmer on Copyright § 1.01[B][2].

Although two early cases expressed the concern that the recognition of publicity rights could improperly restrict the market in copyrighted works, see Sinatra, *supra* ; Booth v. Colgate—Palmolive Co., 362 F.Supp. 343 (S.D.N.Y.1973), later cases hold that ownership of copyright in a work embodying the likeness or other indicia of another's identity is not a defense if the work is used in a manner that infringes the other's right of publicity. See, e.g., Factors, Etc., Inc. v. Pro Arts, Inc., 496 F.Supp. 1090 (S.D.N.Y.1980), reversed on other grounds 652 F.2d 278 (2d Cir. 1981), cert. denied 456 U.S. 927, 102 S.Ct. 1973, 72 L.Ed.2d 442 (1982); Price, *supra* ; Lugosi, *supra* (Bird, J., dissenting); McCarthy, *supra*, § 11.14[A][1].

§ 47. Use for Purposes of Trade

The name, likeness, and other indicia of a person's identity are used "for purposes of trade" under the rule

stated in § 46 if they are used in advertising the user's goods or services, or are placed on merchandise marketed by the user, or are used in connection with services rendered by the user. However, use "for purposes of trade" does not ordinarily include the use of a person's identity in news reporting, commentary, entertainment, works of fiction or nonfiction, or in advertising that is incidental to such uses.

Comment:

a. Use in advertising. The use of a person's identity for the purpose of advertising goods or services marketed by the user is a use "for purposes of trade" under the rule stated in § 46. The interest of a seller in attracting attention to a commercial solicitation is not sufficient to overcome the personal and economic interests protected by the right of publicity. Proof that prospective purchasers are likely to believe that the identified person endorses or sponsors the user's goods or services is not required for the imposition of liability. Thus, the unauthorized use of another's name or likeness in newspaper or magazine advertisements, in television or radio commercials, or in other solicitations of prospective purchasers will ordinarily subject the user to liability for infringement of the other's right of publicity. Appropriation of another's identity for use as a trademark or trade name is similarly actionable. Unauthorized use of a person's identity in solicitations for contributions or memberships by nonprofit entities such as charitable, educational, governmental, fraternal, and religious organizations also constitutes a use for purposes of trade.

In some circumstances the use of another's identity in advertising may not be actionable because of consent or other privilege. See § 46, Comment *f*. For example, use of a person's name or likeness for the purpose of identifying that person as the author or creator of the advertised goods is ordinarily permissible. Thus, a bookstore may include in its advertising the name and photograph of the author of an advertised book, and a movie theater may display the names and photographs of the actors appearing in the advertised motion picture. Use of another's name for the purpose of responding to statements made by that person about the user or the user's goods or services is also permissible.

The use of a person's identity in news reporting, commentary, entertainment, or works of fiction or nonfiction is not ordinarily an infringement of the right of publicity. See Comment *c*. Use of the person's identity in advertising or promoting such uses is also not actionable. Thus, the use of a celebrity's name or photograph in an advertisement for a biography of the celebrity or for a magazine containing an article about the celebrity will not subject the advertiser to liability for infringement of the celebrity's right of publicity. The rule allowing use of a person's identity to advertise a permissible use of the identity has been extended beyond advertisements for the particular work or issue in which the identity is used to general advertising for the medium in which the use appears. A magazine soliciting subscriptions, for example, may refer to a past article about a particular celebrity as an illustration of the magazine's customary content. Use of another's identity in a manner that falsely suggests an endorsement by the identified person, however, will subject the user to liability for deceptive marketing under the rule stated in § 4.

Illustrations:

1. *A* is an actress. *B*, a pharmaceutical company, publishes without consent an advertisement containing a photograph showing *A* as she appeared in one of her motion pictures, with simulated dialogue discussing one of *B* 's products. *B* is subject to liability to *A* for infringement of *A* 's right of publicity under the rule stated in § 46.

2. *A* is a former child actor. *B* operates a tavern under a trade name identical to the nickname of *A*, without *A* 's consent. A recognizable likeness of *A* appears on a sign outside the tavern and on merchandise and accessories used on the premises. *B* is subject to liability to *A* for infringement of *A* 's right of publicity under the rule stated in § 46.

3. *A*, the conductor of a renowned symphony orchestra, is the subject of a biography published by *B*, a publishing company. *B* announces publication of the book with an advertisement that contains *A* 's name and photograph. *B* has not infringed *A* 's right of publicity.

b. Use on merchandise. The sale of merchandise bearing a person's name or likeness ordinarily constitutes a use of the identity for purposes of trade under the rule stated in § 46. An unauthorized appropriation of another's name or likeness for use on posters, buttons, or other memorabilia is thus ordinarily actionable as an infringement of the right of publicity. Attempts to defend the sale of such merchandise on first amendment grounds through analogies to the marketing of books, magazines, and other traditional media of communication (see Comment *c*) have typically been rejected. In some circumstances, however, the informational content of the particular merchandise or its utility to purchasers as a means of expression may justify the conclusion that the use is protected under the first amendment. A candidate for public office, for example, cannot invoke the right of publicity to prohibit the distribution of posters or buttons bearing the candidate's name or likeness, whether used to signify support or opposition.

Illustration:

4. *A* is a well-known musician. *B*, a marketer of novelty items, sells posters depicting *A* performing at a recent concert. The posters were created from a photograph obtained by *B* from a news magazine. *B* does not have *A*'s consent to market the posters. *B* is subject to liability to *A* for infringement of *A*'s right of publicity under the rule stated in § 46.

c. Use in news, entertainment, and creative works. The right of publicity as recognized by statute and common law is fundamentally constrained by the public and constitutional interest in freedom of expression. The use of a person's identity primarily for the purpose of communicating information or expressing ideas is not generally actionable as a violation of the person's right of publicity. The scope of the activities embraced within this limitation on the right of publicity has been broadly construed. Thus, the use of a person's name or likeness in news reporting, whether in newspapers, magazines, or broadcast news, does not infringe the right of publicity. The interest in freedom of expression also extends to use in entertainment and other creative works, including both fiction and nonfiction. The use of a celebrity's name or photograph as part of an article published in a fan magazine or in a feature story broadcast on an entertainment program, for example, will not infringe the celebrity's right of publicity. Similarly, the right of publicity is not infringed by the dissemination of an unauthorized print or broadcast biography. Use of another's identity in a novel, play, or motion picture is also not ordinarily an infringement. The fact that the publisher or other user seeks or is successful in obtaining a commercial advantage from an otherwise permitted use of another's identity does not render the appropriation actionable. However, if the name or likeness is used solely to attract attention to a work that is not related to the identified person, the user may be subject to liability for a use of the other's identity in advertising. See Comment *a*. Similarly, if a photograph of the plaintiff is included in the defendant's publication merely for the purpose of appropriating the plaintiff's commercial value as a model rather than as part of a news or other communicative use, the defendant may be subject to liability for a merchandising use of the plaintiff's identity. See Comment *b*.

Some cases indicate that the right to use another's identity in news reports and similar works may be forfeited if the work contains substantial falsifications. Such cases, however, are more appropriately regarded as actions for defamation or for invasion of privacy by placing the plaintiff in a false light rather than for infringement of the right of publicity. When the imposition of liability turns on the truth or falsity of the defendant's statements, the defendant is also entitled to the constitutional safeguards that have been incorporated into the law of defamation and false light privacy.

Illustrations:

5. *A* is a well-known actress. *B*, a magazine publisher, places a photograph of *A* on the cover of an issue of the magazine. An article about *A*, consisting of several photographs and brief commentary, is included in the magazine. One of the photographs is taken from a scene in a recent movie in which *A* appeared partially unclothed. *B* has not infringed *A*'s right of publicity.

6. *A* is the subject of an unauthorized biography published by *B*. The biography is entitled "A" and contains a photograph of *A* on the dust jacket. The biography contains numerous false statements concerning facts and incidents in *A*'s life. *B* has not infringed *A*'s right of publicity. Whether *B* is subject to liability to *A* for the false statements contained in the biography is determined under the rules governing liability for defamation or invasion of privacy by placing another in a false light.

d. Limits of liability. The right of publicity has been extended in a few cases beyond advertising and merchandising uses to other substantial appropriations of a person's identity. Liability has been imposed, for example, in connection with an unauthorized broadcast of the plaintiff's performance or a sustained imitation of the plaintiff's performing style or performing persona that is marketed by the defendant as a simulation of the plaintiff's performance. If the defendant's appropriation falsely suggests the participation or endorsement of the plaintiff, liability may be imposed under the rules prohibiting deceptive marketing. See § 4. If the defendant has appropriated a work of authorship owned by the plaintiff, liability may be imposed for an infringement of federal statutory or state common law copyright. See § 38, Comment *d.* Broader restrictions on the use of another's identity in entertainment, news, or other creative works threaten significant public and constitutional interests. In an effort to balance the personal and proprietary interests recognized by the right of publicity with the public interests in free expression and in the creation of original works, some courts have engaged in an analysis analogous to the determination of fair use in copyright law. The substantiality and market effect of the appropriation have been analyzed in light of the informational or creative content of the defendant's use. In cases of imitation, the public interest in competition and in avoiding the monopolization of successful styles, together with the interest in the production of new works including parody and satire, will ordinarily outweigh any adverse effect on the plaintiff's market. When the defendant's appropriation consists, not of an imitation, but of an unauthorized broadcast or other reproduction of an actual performance by the plaintiff, the greater likelihood of commercial injury to the plaintiff and the reduced public interest in permitting the use may justify relief in exceptional circumstances. Since the personal and proprietary interests underlying the right of publicity (see § 46, Comment *c*) diminish after death, more substantial appropriations may be permissible after the death of the identified person even in jurisdictions in which the right is descendible. Statutes in some states can be interpreted to permit the use of another's identity in news reporting or other specified works without regard to the substantiality of the use or its effect on the plaintiff.

Illustrations:

7. *B*, the operator of a television station, broadcasts on its local news program a videotape of a "human cannonball" act performed by *A*, with favorable commentary. The videotape was made despite *A* 's objection at one of a series of performances by *A* scheduled throughout the duration of the local county fair. The broadcast by *B* includes *A* 's entire performance. A court may properly conclude in light of the substantiality and likely market effect of the appropriation that *B* is subject to liability to *A* for infringement of *A* 's right of publicity under the rule stated in § 46.

8. The facts being otherwise as stated in Illustration 7, the broadcast by *B* occurs two years after *A* 's death as part of a feature story on the history of the county fair. *A* 's right of publicity is owned by *A* 's son, *C*. A court may properly conclude in light of the absence of any injury to the personal interests of *A* and the minimal market effect of the appropriation on *C* that *B* is not subject to liability to *C*.

e. Liability of retailers and publishers. A retailer or distributor of merchandise that infringes a person's right of publicity has used the appropriated identity "for purposes of trade" under the rule stated in § 46. As in the case of retailers and distributors of goods that infringe another's trademark (see § 36, Comment *k*), such persons are subject to liability for infringement of the right of publicity without regard to their knowledge or intent. See § 46, Comment *e*. However, the absence of an intent to infringe on the plaintiff's publicity rights remains relevant in determining appropriate relief. See § 49, Comment *c*.

Publishers and broadcasters who disseminate infringing advertisements on behalf of others should be subject to liability for infringement of the right of publicity only under conditions analogous to those governing the liability of such persons for trademark infringement. See § 26. Thus, absent knowledge that the advertisement is infringing, the liability of a publisher or broadcaster should not extend beyond an injunction against further publication. Cf. § 32(2) of the Lanham Act, 15 U.S.C.A. § 1114(2).

REPORTERS' NOTE

Comment a. Statutes in several states adopt the substantive standard in New York Civil Rights Law § 51, which prohibits use "for advertising purposes or for the purposes of trade." See Mass.Gen.L. ch. 214, § 3A; R.I.Gen.Laws § 9–1–28; Va. Code Ann. § 8.01–40; Wis.Stat. § 895.50. See also Cal.Civ.Code § 3344 (use "on or in products, merchandise, or goods, or for purposes of advertising or selling, or soliciting purchases of, products, merchandise, goods, or services"), and the similar standards in Okla.Stat. tit. 12, § 1449; Nev.Rev.Stat. § 598.980(1); Tex. Prop.Code Ann. § 26.011. See also Fla.Stat. § 540.08 (use "for purposes of trade or for any commercial or advertising purpose"); Neb.Rev.Stat. § 20–202 ("advertising or commercial purposes"); Tenn.Code Ann. § 47–25–1105 (use "for purposes of advertising products, merchandise, or goods or services, or for purposes of fund raising, solicitation of donations, purchases of products, merchandise, goods or services").

For examples of the unauthorized use of another's identity in advertising, see, e.g., Midler v. Ford Motor Co., 849 F.2d 460 (9th Cir.1988); Motschenbacher v. R.J. Reynolds Tobacco Co., 498 F.2d 821 (9th Cir. 1974); Negri v. Schering Corp., 333 F.Supp. 101 (S.D.N.Y.1971); Beverley v. Choices Women's Medical Center, Inc., 78 N.Y.2d 745, 579 N.Y.S.2d 637, 587 N.E.2d 275 (1991); Lombardo v. Doyle, Dane & Bernbach, Inc., 58 A.D.2d 620, 396 N.Y.S.2d 661 (1977). See also the comprehensive list of cases cited in McCarthy, The Rights of Publicity and Privacy § 7.2. First amendment defenses to the use of another's identity in advertising were expressly rejected in, e.g., White v. Samsung Electronics America, Inc., 971 F.2d 1395 (9th Cir.1992), cert. denied ___ U.S. ___, 113 S.Ct. 2443, 124 L.Ed.2d 660 (1993) (distinguishing use in advertising from noncommercial uses); Tellado v. Time–Life Books, Inc., 643 F.Supp. 904 (D.N.J.1986); Fergerstrom v. Hawaiian Ocean View Estates, 50 Hawaii 374, 441 P.2d 141 (1968); Onassis v. Christian Dior–New York, Inc., 122 Misc.2d 603, 472 N.Y.S.2d 254 (Sup. Ct.1984), affirmed 110 A.D.2d 1095,

488 N.Y.S.2d 943 (1985). The fact that the appropriated material was originally published in a news report does not insulate its later republication in advertising. E.g., Continental Optical Co. v. Reed, 119 Ind.App. 643, 86 N.E.2d 306 (1949); Canessa v. J.I. Kislak, Inc., 97 N.J.Super. 327, 235 A.2d 62 (1967); Reilly v. Rapperswill Corp., 50 A.D.2d 342, 377 N.Y.S.2d 488 (1975); Flores v. Mosler Safe Co., 7 N.Y.2d 276, 196 N.Y.S.2d 975, 164 N.E.2d 853 (1959).

On the unauthorized use of a person's identity as a trademark or trade name, see, e.g., McFarland v. Miller, 14 F.3d 912 (3d Cir.1994); Carson v. Here's Johnny Portable Toilets, Inc., 698 F.2d 831 (6th Cir.1983); Hirsch v. S.C. Johnson & Son, Inc., 90 Wis.2d 379, 280 N.W.2d 129 (1979); Edison v. Edison Polyform Mfg. Co., 73 N.J.Eq. 136, 67 A. 392 (1907). Such unauthorized use can also preclude registration and protection of trademark rights in the designation. See § 32, Comment *c*.

Use of a person's name or likeness to identify the person as the author of an advertised work will not subject the user to liability. See, e.g., Kamakazi Music Corp. v. Robbins Music Corp., 534 F.Supp. 69 (S.D.N.Y.1982) (N.Y. Civil Rights Law); National Bank of Commerce v. Shaklee Corp., 503 F.Supp. 533 (W.D.Tex.1980) (dictum); Gee v. CBS, Inc., 471 F.Supp. 600, 662 (E.D.Pa.), affirmed 612 F.2d 572 (3d Cir.1979); Shaw v. Time–Life Records, 38 N.Y.2d 201, 379 N.Y.S.2d 390, 341 N.E.2d 817 (1975) (N.Y. Civil Rights Law). See also Fla.Stat. § 540.08(3)(b); Mass.Gen.L. ch. 214, § 3A; Neb.Rev.Stat. § 20–202(2); N.Y.Civ. Rights Law § 51; R.I.Gen. Laws § 9–1–28.

Use of a person's identity in advertising magazine or newspaper articles, biographies, films, or similar works relating to the identified individual is not an infringement of the right of publicity. See, e.g., Sidis v. F–R Pub. Corp., 113 F.2d 806, 810 (2d Cir.), cert. denied 311 U.S. 711, 61 S.Ct. 393, 85 L.Ed. 462 (1940) ("But since it was to advertise the article on [plaintiff], and the article itself was unobjectionable [under the N.Y. Civil Rights Law], the advertisement shares the privilege enjoyed by the article."); Friedan v. Friedan, 414 F.Supp. 77 (S.D.N.Y.1976) (N.Y. Civil Rights Law); Guglielmi v. Spelling–Goldberg Productions, 25 Cal.3d 860, 160 Cal.Rptr. 352, 603 P.2d 454 (1979) (Bird, J., concurring). Cf. Bolger v. Youngs Drug Products Corp., 463 U.S. 60, 68 n.14, 103 S.Ct. 2875, 2881 n.14, 77 L.Ed.2d 469, 478 n.14 (1983) (dictum indicating that advertisements for activities protected by the first amendment cannot be regulated as commercial speech). Statutes in some states expressly exempt use in advertisements that promote uses permitted under the statute. See Cal.Civ.Code § 990(n)(4); Nev.Rev. Stat. § 598.984(2)(f); Okla.Stat. tit. 12, § 1448(N)(4); Tex.Prop.Code Ann. § 26.012(a)(5). Reference to a previous article about an identified person in the course of soliciting subscriptions to the publication in which the article appeared has also been held to be a permissible advertising use. See, e.g., Lerman v. Flynt Distributing Co., 745 F.2d 123 (2d Cir. 1984), cert. denied 471 U.S. 1054, 105 S.Ct. 2114, 85 L.Ed.2d 479 (1985) (N.Y. Civil Rights Law); Cher v. Forum Int'l, Ltd., 692 F.2d 634 (9th Cir.1982), cert. denied 462 U.S. 1120, 103 S.Ct. 3089, 77 L.Ed.2d 1350 (1983) (dictum); Velez v. VV Pub. Corp., 135 A.D.2d 47, 524 N.Y.S.2d 186 (1988); Namath v. Sports Illustrated, 48 A.D.2d 487, 371 N.Y.S.2d

10 (1975), affirmed 39 N.Y.2d 897, 386 N.Y.S.2d 397, 352 N.E.2d 584 (1976); Booth v. Curtis Pub. Co., 15 A.D.2d 343, 223 N.Y.S.2d 737, affirmed 11 N.Y.2d 907, 228 N.Y.S.2d 468, 182 N.E.2d 812 (1962).

Illustration 1 is based on Negri v. Schering Corp., 333 F.Supp. 101 (S.D.N.Y.1971). Illustration 2 is based on McFarland v. E & K Corp., 18 U.S.P.Q.2d 1246 (D.Minn.1991). See also McFarland v. Miller, *supra*. Illustration 3 is based on Koussevitzky v. Allen, Towne & Heath, Inc., 188 Misc. 479, 68 N.Y.S.2d 779 (Sup.Ct.), affirmed 272 App.Div. 759, 69 N.Y.S.2d 432 (1947).

Comment b. Cases involving the unauthorized use of the plaintiff's likeness on posters include, e.g., Factors Etc., Inc. v. Pro Arts, Inc., 579 F.2d 215 (2d Cir.1978), cert. denied 440 U.S. 908, 99 S.Ct. 1215, 59 L.Ed.2d 455 (1979); Brinkley v. Casablancas, 80 A.D.2d 428, 438 N.Y.S.2d 1004 (1981). See also Titan Sports, Inc. v. Comics World Corp., 870 F.2d 85 (2d Cir.1989) (remanding for a determination of whether foldout photographs contained in defendant's magazine were a merchandising use). Other infringing merchandise has included buttons, see Bi-Rite Enterprises, Inc. v. Button Master, 555 F.Supp. 1188 (S.D.N.Y.1983), trading cards, see Haelan Laboratories, Inc. v. Topps Chewing Gum, Inc., 202 F.2d 866 (2d Cir.), cert. denied 346 U.S. 816, 74 S.Ct. 26, 98 L.Ed. 343 (1953), photographs, see Mendonsa v. Time Inc., 678 F.Supp. 967 (D.R.I.1988), T-shirts, see Winterland Concessions Co. v. Sileo, 528 F.Supp. 1201 (N.D.Ill.1981), affirmed 735 F.2d 257 (7th Cir.1984); Rosemont Enterprises, Inc. v. Choppy Productions, Inc., 74 Misc.2d 1003, 347 N.Y.S.2d 83 (Sup.Ct.1972), busts, see Martin Luther King, Jr., Center for Social Change, Inc. v. American Heritage Products, Inc., 250 Ga. 135, 296 S.E.2d 697 (1982), and games, see Uhlaender v. Henricksen, 316 F.Supp. 1277 (D.Minn.1970); Palmer v. Schonhorn Enterprises, Inc., 96 N.J.Super. 72, 232 A.2d 458 (1967); Rosemont Enterprises, Inc. v. Urban Systems, Inc., 72 Misc.2d 788, 340 N.Y.S.2d 144 (Sup.Ct.), modified 42 A.D.2d 544, 345 N.Y.S.2d 17 (1973).

Many of the merchandising cases expressly reject attempts to invoke a first amendment defense. See, e.g., Factors Etc., Inc. v. Pro Arts, Inc., *supra* (distinguishing an Elvis Presley "In Memory" poster from political campaign posters); Winterland Concessions, *supra* (distinguishing T-shirts from newspapers); Factors Etc., Inc. v. Creative Card Co., 444 F.Supp. 279, 285 (S.D.N.Y.1977), affirmed 579 F.2d 215 (2d Cir.1978), cert. denied 440 U.S. 908, 99 S.Ct. 1215, 59 L.Ed.2d 455 (1979) ("There is no constitutional protection for selling posters of Elvis Presley as Elvis Presley."); Lugosi v. Universal Pictures, 25 Cal.3d 813, 160 Cal.Rptr. 323, 603 P.2d 425 (1979) (Bird, J., dissenting, finding no first amendment implications in the sale of pencil sharpeners, soap, target games, candy dispensers, and stirring rods bearing the likeness of Bela Lugosi as Count Dracula); Palmer, *supra* (distinguishing games from magazines and biographies); Rosemont Enterprises, Inc. v. Urban Systems, Inc., *supra* (same). See also Hicks v. Casablanca Records, 464 F.Supp. 426 (S.D.N.Y.1978) (distinguishing use in a motion picture from the merchandising cases); Guglielmi v. Spelling-Goldberg Productions, 25 Cal.3d 860, 160 Cal.Rptr. 352, 603 P.2d 454 (1979) (Bird, J., concurring) (same). See

McCarthy, The Rights of Publicity and Privacy § 7.6.

In Paulsen v. Personality Posters, Inc., 59 Misc.2d 444, 299 N.Y.S.2d 501 (Sup.Ct.1968), the court refused to enjoin distribution of a "For President" poster depicting a comedian who had initiated a mock presidential campaign, emphasizing the traditional deference to political commentary. Other cases have noted in dicta that the sale of commercial merchandise bearing a person's name or likeness may in some circumstances be entitled to constitutional protection. See Guglielmi, *supra* (Bird, J., concurring); Martin Luther King, Jr., *supra* (Weltner, J., concurring); Rosemont Enterprises, Inc. v. Urban Systems, Inc., *supra* (weighing the media used, the subject matter, and the extent of the appropriation). In assessing first amendment interests, it is the nature and content of the use and not merely its physical form that is controlling. See Titan Sports, *supra*, 870 F.2d at 88 ("In applying [the New York Civil Rights Law], a court must be ever mindful of the inherent tension between the protection of an individual's right to control the use of his likeness and the constitutional guarantee of free dissemination of ideas, images, and newsworthy matter in whatever form it takes.").

Comment c. The right to use another's identity for purposes of news reporting is discussed in, e.g., Titan Sports, Inc. v. Comics World Corp., 870 F.2d 85 (2d Cir.1989); Jackson v. MPI Home Video, 694 F.Supp. 483 (N.D.Ill.1988); Mendonsa v. Time Inc., 678 F.Supp. 967 (D.R.I.1988); Ann-Margret v. High Society Magazine, Inc., 498 F.Supp. 401 (S.D.N.Y.1980). Cases involving interviews include, e.g., Cher v. Forum Int'l, Ltd., 692 F.2d 634 (9th Cir.1982), cert. denied 462 U.S. 1120, 103 S.Ct. 3089, 77 L.Ed.2d 1350 (1983); Falwell v. Penthouse Int'l, Ltd., 521 F.Supp. 1204 (W.D.Va. 1981); Current Audio, Inc. v. RCA Corp., 71 Misc.2d 831, 337 N.Y.S.2d 949 (Sup.Ct.1972). Biographies are also outside the scope of the publicity right. E.g., Frosch v. Grosset & Dunlap, Inc., 75 A.D.2d 768, 427 N.Y.S.2d 828 (1980); Rosemont Enterprises, Inc. v. Random House, Inc., 58 Misc.2d 1, 294 N.Y.S.2d 122 (Sup. Ct.1968), affirmed 32 A.D.2d 892, 301 N.Y.S.2d 948 (1969). But cf. Hogan v. A.S. Barnes & Co., 114 U.S.P.Q. 314 (Pa.C.P.1957) (liability imposed for the use of plaintiff's name and photographs in a golf instructional book, but also finding passing off). The breadth of the news right is evident in, e.g., New Kids On The Block v. News America Pub., Inc., 971 F.2d 302 (9th Cir.1992) (newspaper survey of readers); Dora v. Frontline Video, Inc., 15 Cal.App.4th 536, 18 Cal. Rptr.2d 790 (1993) (surfing documentary); Stephano v. News Group Pub., Inc., 64 N.Y.2d 174, 485 N.Y.S.2d 220, 474 N.E.2d 580 (1984) (fashion column); Welch v. Group W Productions, Inc., 138 Misc.2d 856, 525 N.Y.S.2d 466 (Sup.Ct.1987) (rebroadcast of a performance during an awards program); Paulsen v. Personality Posters, Inc., 59 Misc.2d 444, 299 N.Y.S.2d 501 (Sup.Ct.1968) (poster of a mock presidential candidate). The first amendment limitations on the right of publicity are discussed in McCarthy, The Rights of Publicity and Privacy ch. 8.

State right of publicity statutes frequently contain express exemptions for news reporting. See Cal.Civ. Code § 3344(d); Fla.Stat. § 540.08(3)(a); Neb.Rev.Stat. § 20–202(1); Nev.Rev.Stat. § 598.984(2)(c); Okla.

Stat. tit. 12, § 1449(D); Tenn.Code Ann. § 47–25–1107(a); Tex.Prop. Code Ann. § 26.012(b); Wis.Stat. § 895.50(3). The constitutional right of free speech extends to entertainment and other expressive works, including fiction. E.g., Schad v. Borough of Mt. Ephraim, 452 U.S. 61, 101 S.Ct. 2176, 68 L.Ed.2d 671 (1981); Zacchini v. Scripps–Howard Broadcasting Co., 433 U.S. 562, 97 S.Ct. 2849, 53 L.Ed.2d 965 (1977); Joseph Burstyn, Inc. v. Wilson, 343 U.S. 495, 72 S.Ct. 777, 96 L.Ed. 1098 (1952); Winters v. New York, 333 U.S. 507, 68 S.Ct. 665, 92 L.Ed. 840 (1948). Cases recognizing a right to use another's identity in entertainment and fiction include, e.g., Rogers v. Grimaldi, 875 F.2d 994 (2d Cir.1989); Hicks v. Casablanca Records, 464 F.Supp. 426 (S.D.N.Y.1978); Guglielmi v. Spelling–Goldberg Productions, 25 Cal.3d 860, 160 Cal.Rptr. 352, 603 P.2d 454 (1979) (Bird, J., concurring); Frosch, *supra.* See also Cal.Civ. Code § 990(n)(1) (exempting non-advertising use of a deceased person's identity in a "play, book, magazine, newspaper, musical composition, film, radio or television program"); Nev. Rev.Stat. § 598.984(2)(d); Okla.Stat. tit. 12, § 1448(N)(1); Tex.Prop.Code Ann. § 26.012(a). The fact that the user obtains a financial benefit from a news or entertainment use is not sufficient to render the appropriation actionable. E.g., Falwell, *supra*; Stephano, *supra*; Guglielmi, *supra* (Bird, J., concurring). See also Cal. Civ.Code § 3344(e); Okla.Stat. tit. 12, § 1449(E); Tenn.Code Ann. § 47–25–1107(b).

Use of a name or likeness in connection with news or entertainment may be actionable if the use is not sufficiently related to the underlying work. See, e.g., Lerman v. Flynt Distributing Co., 745 F.2d 123 (2d Cir.1984), cert. denied 471 U.S. 1054, 105 S.Ct. 2114, 85 L.Ed.2d 479 (1985) (dictum); Leverton v. Curtis Pub. Co., 192 F.2d 974 (3d Cir.1951); Grant v. Esquire, Inc., 367 F.Supp. 876 (S.D.N.Y.1973). However, because of the commitment to freedom of expression, the required relationship is liberally construed. See, e.g., New Kids on the Block, *supra*; Rogers, *supra*; Finger v. Omni Pub. Int'l, Ltd., 77 N.Y.2d 138, 564 N.Y.S.2d 1014, 566 N.E.2d 141 (1990); Murray v. New York Magazine Co., 27 N.Y.2d 406, 318 N.Y.S.2d 474, 267 N.E.2d 256 (1971). Photographs of a celebrity's public appearances or public performances are generally regarded as sufficiently newsworthy to permit publication in a newspaper or magazine without infringing the celebrity's right of publicity. See Douglass v. Hustler Magazine, Inc., 769 F.2d 1128 (7th Cir.1985), cert. denied 475 U.S. 1094, 106 S.Ct. 1489, 89 L.Ed.2d 892 (1986); Ann–Margret, *supra*; Davis v. High Society Magazine, Inc., 90 A.D.2d 374, 457 N.Y.S.2d 308 (1982) (dictum). However, publication of photographs of the plaintiff that are unrelated to news events merely for the purpose of appropriating the plaintiff's commercial value as a model may be an infringement, particularly when the use is one for which payment is customarily made. See Douglass, *supra*; Clark v. Celeb Pub., Inc., 530 F.Supp. 979 (S.D.N.Y.1981); Grant, *supra*; Myers v. U.S. Camera Pub. Corp., 9 Misc.2d 765, 167 N.Y.S.2d 771 (N.Y.C.Ct.1957). See also Titan Sports, *supra*, 870 F.2d at 88–89 (directing the trial court to consider whether the oversized photographs contained in defendant's magazine "are included primarily for their 'public interest aspect' or whether whatever public interest aspect might be involved 'is merely incidental to [the distributors'] commercial purpose,'" quoting Davis, *supra*, 457 N.Y.S.2d at 313).

Some of the cases interpreting New York law, which does not afford a common law cause of action for invasion of privacy, recognize an exception to the news and entertainment right under New York Civil Rights Law § 51 when the work contains substantial falsifications. See, e.g., Lerman, *supra* ; Spahn v. Julian Messner, Inc., 21 N.Y.2d 124, 286 N.Y.S.2d 832, 233 N.E.2d 840 (1967), appeal dismissed 393 U.S. 1046, 89 S.Ct. 676, 21 L.Ed.2d 600 (1969); Davis, *supra*. Cf. Eastwood v. Superior Court, 149 Cal.App.3d 409, 198 Cal.Rptr. 342 (1983) (California law). But see Zacchini, *supra* (distinguishing false light invasion of privacy from the right of publicity); Guglielmi, *supra* (Bird, J., concurring) (disagreeing with a falsification exception under California law). A similar exception is sometimes recognized in connection with otherwise permissible advertising for lawful uses of another's identity if the advertisement falsely suggests an endorsement or is otherwise deceptive. See Cher, *supra* ; Marcinkus v. NAL Pub. Inc., 138 Misc.2d 256, 522 N.Y.S.2d 1009 (Sup.Ct.1987). However, when a statute prohibiting the appropriation of a person's identity is used to afford a remedy for a false light privacy claim, the constitutional limitations on the false light tort are applicable. Time, Inc. v. Hill, 385 U.S. 374, 87 S.Ct. 534, 17 L.Ed.2d 456 (1967) (New York Civil Rights Law); Lerman, *supra* ; Davis, *supra*.

Illustration 5 is based on Ann–Margret v. High Society Magazine, Inc., 498 F.Supp. 401 (S.D.N.Y.1980). Illustration 6 is suggested by Frosch v. Grosset & Dunlap, Inc., 75 A.D.2d 768, 427 N.Y.S.2d 828 (1980).

Comment d. The leading case on infringement of the right of publicity through the appropriation of a performance is Zacchini v. Scripps–Howard Broadcasting Co., 433 U.S. 562, 97 S.Ct. 2849, 53 L.Ed.2d 965 (1977), which concerned the unauthorized broadcast of plaintiff's human cannonball act on a television news program. See Illustration 7. The Supreme Court noted that the appropriation of a performance "may be the strongest case for a 'right of publicity'—involving, not the appropriation of an entertainer's reputation to enhance the attractiveness of a commercial product, but the appropriation of the very activity by which the entertainer acquired his reputation in the first place." *Id.* at 576, 97 S.Ct. at 2858. The Court held that the broadcast of the plaintiff's entire act was too substantial to qualify as permissible news coverage. Compare Zacchini, *supra*, with Welch v. Group W Productions, Inc., 138 Misc.2d 856, 525 N.Y.S.2d 466 (Sup.Ct.1987) (broadcast of a television commercial as part of an advertising awards program did not infringe the publicity rights of the performer) and Current Audio, Inc. v. RCA Corp., 71 Misc.2d 831, 337 N.Y.S.2d 949 (Sup.Ct.1972) (sale of a recording of an Elvis Presley news conference did not infringe his right of publicity). See also Baltimore Orioles, Inc. v. Major League Baseball Players Ass'n, 805 F.2d 663 (7th Cir.1986), cert. denied 480 U.S. 941, 107 S.Ct. 1593, 94 L.Ed.2d 782 (1987) (holding a right of publicity claim involving a performance preempted by federal copyright law) (see § 46, Comment *i*); Ettore v. Philco Television Broadcasting Corp.,

229 F.2d 481 (3d Cir.), cert. denied 351 U.S. 926, 76 S.Ct. 783, 100 L.Ed. 1456 (1956) (imposing liability under unfair competition for the unauthorized television broadcast of a film of the plaintiff's boxing match). Analogous issues may arise in the future in connection with computer-generated works embodying performances of well-known entertainers created through the digital manipulation of images extracted from earlier works. See Beard, Casting Call at Forest Lawn: The Digital Resurrection of Deceased Entertainers—A 21st Century Challenge for Intellectual Property Law, 8 High Tech.L.J. 101 (1993). However, if the use is within the scope of the performer's express or implied consent, it is not an infringement. See, e.g., Leavy v. Cooney, 214 Cal.App.2d 496, 29 Cal.Rptr. 580 (1963) (enjoining theater performances of a film when consent was for television only).

For cases involving an imitation of the plaintiff's performance, see Estate of Presley v. Russen, 513 F.Supp. 1339 (D.N.J.1981) and Apple Corps Ltd. v. Leber, 229 U.S.P.Q. 1015 (Cal.Super.1986), both holding that the right of publicity was infringed by defendants' simulation of the plaintiffs' theatrical performances. Compare Price v. Worldvision Enterprises, Inc., 455 F.Supp. 252 (S.D.N.Y.1978), affirmed 603 F.2d 214 (2d Cir.1979) (refusing to permit an unauthorized imitation of the Laurel and Hardy performing personas in a television series) with Groucho Marx Productions, Inc. v. Day and Night Co., 689 F.2d 317 (2d Cir.1982) (dictum questioning the lower court's finding of infringement in connection with an imitation of the Marx Brothers' performing personas in a theatrical production). Cf. Hicks v. Casablanca Records, 464 F.Supp. 426 (S.D.N.Y.1978) (use of a name and selected biographical facts in a motion picture was not an actionable appropriation). An explicit analogy to the fair use doctrine in copyright law was drawn in, e.g., Groucho Marx Productions, Inc. v. Day and Night Co., 523 F.Supp. 485 (S.D.N.Y.1981), reversed on other grounds 689 F.2d 317 (2d Cir.1982); Apple Corps, *supra*. However, some state statutes permitting the use of another's identity in news or other specified works may be interpreted as authorizing such appropriations without regard to the substantiality or market effect of the use. See New Kids On The Block v. New America Pub., Inc., 971 F.2d 302 (9th Cir.1992) (California statutory exemption for news accounts is a "complete defense" designed to avoid first amendment issues); Joplin Enterprises v. Allen, 795 F.Supp. 349 (W.D.Wash.1992) (simulation of a performance as part of a dramatic work was not actionable because of the California statutory exemption for use in plays).

The scope of permissible use may be greater after the death of the identified individual. Cf. Estate of Presley, *supra* (no showing of irreparable harm from a simulated performance occurring after Elvis Presley's death). Compare Cal.Civ.Code § 3344 and Okla.Stat. tit. 12, § 1449 (both applicable to living persons) with Cal.Civ.Code § 990(n) and Okla. Stat. tit. 12, § 1448(N) (both including broader exemptions for use of a deceased person's identity). See McCarthy, The Rights of Publicity and Privacy § 8.16.

Illustration 7 is based on *Zacchini*, *supra*.

Comment e. On the liability of retailers of infringing goods, see, e.g.,

Factors Etc., Inc. v. Pro Arts, Inc., 444 F.Supp. 288 (S.D.N.Y.1977), affirmed 579 F.2d 215 (2d Cir.1978), cert. denied 440 U.S. 908, 99 S.Ct. 1215, 59 L.Ed.2d 455 (1979) (retailer included in a preliminary injunction); Brinkley v. Casablancas, 80 A.D.2d 428, 438 N.Y.S.2d 1004 (1981) (injunction but no damages awarded against an innocent retailer, with a concurring opinion stating in dictum that under some circumstances damages might also be appropriate). If a right of publicity statute is used as a vehicle to impose liability on a retailer or distributor for an appropriation that places the plaintiff before the public in a false light, the constitutional limitations on the false light privacy tort recognized in Time, Inc. v. Hill, 385 U.S. 374, 87 S.Ct. 534, 17 L.Ed.2d 456 (1967), are applicable. See Lerman v. Flynt Distributing Co., 745 F.2d 123 (2d Cir.1984), cert. denied 471 U.S. 1054, 105 S.Ct. 2114, 85 L.Ed.2d 479 (1985) (distributor did not act with "actual malice").

On the liability of publishers of infringing advertisements, compare Cabaniss v. Hipsley, 114 Ga.App. 367, 151 S.E.2d 496 (1966) (innocent publisher was not liable for the publication of another's infringing advertisement) with Rosenberg v. Lee's Carpet & Furniture Warehouse Outlet, Inc., 80 Misc.2d 479, 363 N.Y.S.2d 231 (Sup.Ct.1974) (damages awarded against an innocent newspaper). Right of publicity statutes in several states expressly preclude the imposition of liability on advertising media absent knowledge that the advertisement infringes the plaintiff's publicity rights. See Cal.Civ.Code §§ 3344(f), 990(n)(1); Nev.Rev.Stat. § 598.988(2); Okla.Stat. tit. 12, §§ 1448(L), 1449(F); Tenn.Code Ann. § 47–25–1107(c); Tex.Prop.Code Ann. § 26.012(c). See also McCarthy, The Rights of Publicity and Privacy § 3.7.

§ 48. Injunctions: Appropriation of the Commercial Value of a Person's Identity

(1) If appropriate under the rule stated in Subsection (2), injunctive relief may be awarded to prevent a continuing or threatened appropriation of the commercial value of another's identity by one who is subject to liability under the rule stated in § 46.

(2) The appropriateness and scope of injunctive relief depend upon a comparative appraisal of all the factors of the case, including the following primary factors:

(a) the nature of the interest to be protected;

(b) the nature and extent of the appropriation;

(c) the relative adequacy to the plaintiff of an injunction and of other remedies;

(d) the relative harm likely to result to the legitimate interests of the defendant if an injunction is granted and to the legitimate interests of the plaintiff if an injunction is denied;

(e) the interests of third persons and of the public;

(f) any unreasonable delay by the plaintiff in bringing suit or otherwise asserting his or her rights;

(g) any related misconduct on the part of the plaintiff; and

(h) the practicality of framing and enforcing the injunction.

Comment:

a. Scope. This Section states the principles governing injunctive relief in actions for infringement of the right of publicity. The usual remedy in tort actions is an award of damages, and the equitable remedy of an injunction was traditionally available only when the remedy of damages was found to be inadequate. With the merger of law and equity, courts are generally free to select the remedy or combination of remedies that most effectively protects the interests threatened by the defendant's misconduct. See Restatement, Second, Torts § 938, Comment *c*.

The general rules relating to injunctive relief in tort actions stated in Chapter 48 of the Restatement, Second, of Torts are applicable in actions for infringement of the right of publicity. This Section is derived from Restatement, Second, Torts § 936, which sets forth the general factors relating to the appropriateness of injunctive relief. See also §§ 933–935, stating the standard of "appropriateness" for injunctive relief, and §§ 937–943, describing in detail the factors relevant in determining appropriateness.

Injunctive relief is expressly authorized in many of the state statutes that protect the commercial value of a person's identity. Courts also ordinarily have inherent authority to issue injunctions to enforce statutes that do not make specific reference to injunctive relief. The principles stated in this Section govern the appropriateness and scope of injunctive relief in both statutory and common law right of publicity actions.

b. Appropriateness of injunctive relief. A continuing or threatened infringement of a person's right of publicity ordinarily justifies injunctive relief. As in the case of other forms of unfair competition, the pecuniary harm caused by an infringement of the right of publicity may not be easily reparable through an award of damages because of the difficulty of proving the amount of loss and a causal connection with the defendant's appropriation. Cf. § 35, Comment *a*; § 44,

Comment *b*. In addition, the commercial exploitation of a person's identity is often a continuing wrong for which injunctive relief is particularly appropriate. Thus, injunctive relief, alone or in combination with monetary relief, is the customary remedy in right of publicity cases. The availability of injunctive relief, however, may be limited by the equitable principles of estoppel, laches, and unclean hands. Cf. §§ 29, 31–32.

c. Scope of injunctions. Because of the limited scope of the right of publicity, an injunction will ordinarily prohibit only unauthorized use of the plaintiff's identity in advertising or merchandising activities. Conduct by the defendant that intrudes upon other protected interests such as the personal interests protected by the right of privacy can justify broader relief. If the plaintiff has consented to some commercial uses, the injunction may be tailored to prohibit only uses that exceed the scope of the consent. In some circumstances the constitutional right of free expression may also limit the scope of injunctive relief. If the infringing use occurs in the context of a work that communicates noncommercial speech, it may be appropriate to limit the scope of the injunction in order to minimize the intrusion on expression. In some cases the public and constitutional interest in freedom of speech may make any injunctive relief inappropriate.

The appropriate geographic scope of an injunction issued to protect the right of publicity is complicated by the variations among state statutes and common law rules. In other areas of unfair competition, courts typically issue injunctions that are unlimited in geographic scope. An implicit assumption in such cases is that the law of unfair competition is similar in the various states. See § 35, Comment *f*. The issuance of an injunction under state law prohibiting otherwise lawful conduct in another state raises serious concerns. Thus, although a court may have jurisdiction to grant broader relief, an injunction protecting the right of publicity should ordinarily be limited to conduct in jurisdictions that provide protection comparable to the forum state. A procedure permitting the defendant to request a modification of a geographically unlimited injunction upon a showing that the conduct is lawful under the law of another state can be an efficient method of addressing this issue.

Illustration:

1. Sitting at a sidewalk cafe in a public market, *A* puts his arm around his wife, *B*, and kisses her. A photographer for *C*, a local newspaper, takes a photograph of the event, which *C* publishes in a feature story about the market. *C* also permits *D*, the owner of the cafe, to use the photograph in an advertisement that

emphasizes the cafe's romantic ambience. *A* and *B* may obtain an injunction under the rule stated in § 46 restraining *D* from using the photograph in advertising. Since the use of the photograph in *C*'s newspaper story is not an invasion of *A*'s or *B*'s right of publicity or right of privacy, see Restatement, Second, Torts § 652D, Illustration 5, *A* and *B* may not obtain an injunction restraining *C* from using the photograph in newspaper stories about the market.

d. Preliminary relief. The principles stated in this Section deal primarily with injunctions granted as final relief, but the factors stated in Subsection (2) are also relevant to the imposition of provisional remedies. Although courts differ on the precise formulation, all courts recognize that the appropriateness of preliminary relief depends upon the likelihood that the plaintiff will suffer irreparable harm in the absence of preliminary relief, the plaintiff's likelihood of success on the merits, the balance of equities between the parties, and the interest of the public. In applying these criteria, courts have recognized that in many cases the unauthorized use of another's identity may produce harm to both commercial and personal interests that is not easily reparable by a subsequent monetary award.

REPORTERS' NOTE

On injunctive relief in right of publicity cases, see generally McCarthy, The Rights of Publicity and Privacy § 11.6.

Comment b. Some early cases held that the appropriation of another's name or likeness was an interference with a property right for which injunctive relief was appropriate even under the obsolete rule limiting injunctions to the protection of property rights. See, e.g., Munden v. Harris, 153 Mo.App. 652, 134 S.W. 1076 (1911); Edison v. Edison Polyform Mfg. Co., 73 N.J.Eq. 136, 67 A. 392 (1907). For cases recognizing that damages are often an inadequate remedy in publicity rights cases, see, e.g., Ali v. Playgirl, Inc., 447 F.Supp. 723 (S.D.N.Y.1978); Uhlaender v. Henricksen, 316 F.Supp. 1277 (D.Minn.1970).

Examples of permanent injunctions against infringement of the right of publicity include, e.g., Price v. Hal Roach Studios, Inc., 400 F.Supp. 836 (S.D.N.Y.1975); Uhlaender, *supra*; Brinkley v. Casablancas, 80 A.D.2d 428, 438 N.Y.S.2d 1004 (1981); Palmer v. Schonhorn Enterprises, Inc., 96 N.J.Super. 72, 232 A.2d 458 (1967). Impoundment of infringing merchandise may also be ordered. See Tenn. Code Ann. § 47–25–1106(b); Joel v. Various John Does, 499 F.Supp. 791 (E.D.Wis.1980) (statutory right of publicity and federal unfair competition claims). Cases considering equitable defenses in right of publicity actions include Elvis Presley Enterprises, Inc. v. Elvisly Yours, Inc., 936 F.2d 889 (6th Cir.1991) (acquiescence and estoppel defenses rejected on the facts); McFarland v. E & K Corp., 18 U.S.P.Q.2d 1246 (D.Minn.1991) (laches rejected on the facts); Estate of Presley v. Russen, 513 F.Supp. 1339 (D.N.J.1981) (laches and acquiescence rejected on the facts); Uhlaender, *supra* (unclean hands rejected on the facts). If the use by the defendant is de minimis, injunctive relief may be withheld. See Restatement, Second, Torts § 941, Comment *c*.

Comment c. Injunctions are ordinarily limited to those uses of the plaintiff's identity that infringe the right of publicity. See, e.g., Onassis v. Christian Dior–New York, Inc., 122 Misc.2d 603, 472 N.Y.S.2d 254 (Sup. Ct.1984), affirmed 110 A.D.2d 1095, 488 N.Y.S.2d 943 (1985) (injunction issued against appearances by a lookalike in commercial advertisements); Leavy v. Cooney, 214 Cal.App.2d 496, 29 Cal.Rptr. 580 (1963) (enjoining theater performances of a film when consent was for television only). On the first amendment implications of injunctive relief, cf. Zacchini v. Scripps–Howard Broadcasting Co., 433 U.S. 562, 97 S.Ct. 2849, 53 L.Ed.2d 965 (1977), noting that the plaintiff was seeking only monetary and not injunctive relief against a television station that broadcast the plaintiff's performance on a local news program. See McCarthy, The Rights of Publicity and Privacy § 8.4.

The appropriate geographic scope of injunctions in right of publicity actions is complicated by the variations in state law. Geographically unlimited injunctions were issued in Elvis Presley Enterprises, Inc. v. Elvisly Yours, Inc., 936 F.2d 889 (6th Cir. 1991); Carson v. Here's Johnny Portable Toilets, Inc., 810 F.2d 104 (6th Cir.1987) (inviting the defendant to seek a modification for conduct permissible in other states). See also Factors Etc., Inc. v. Pro Arts, Inc., 652 F.2d 278 (2d Cir.1981), cert. denied 456 U.S. 927, 102 S.Ct. 1973, 72 L.Ed.2d 442 (1982) (Mansfield, J., dissenting). But see Reilly v. Rapperswill Corp., 50 A.D.2d 342, 377 N.Y.S.2d 488 (1975), and Rosemont Enterprises, Inc. v. Urban Systems, Inc., 42 A.D.2d 544, 345 N.Y.S.2d 17 (1973), both limiting an injunction under New York Civil Rights Law § 51 to conduct within the state. However, an injunction under the same statute extended to conduct in England in Ali v. Playgirl, Inc., 447 F.Supp. 723 (S.D.N.Y.1978).

Illustration 1 is based on Restatement, Second, Torts § 652D, Illustration 5.

Comment d. For examples of preliminary injunctions in right of publicity cases, see, e.g., Factors Etc., Inc. v. Creative Card Co., 444 F.Supp. 279 (S.D.N.Y.1977), affirmed 579 F.2d 215 (2d Cir.1978), cert. denied 440 U.S. 908, 99 S.Ct. 1215, 59 L.Ed.2d 455 (1979); Ali v. Playgirl, Inc., 447 F.Supp. 723 (S.D.N.Y.1978); Onassis v. Christian Dior–New York, Inc., 122 Misc.2d 603, 472 N.Y.S.2d 254 (Sup.Ct.1984), affirmed 110 A.D.2d 1095, 488 N.Y.S.2d 943 (1985); Reilly v. Rapperswill Corp., 50 A.D.2d 342, 377 N.Y.S.2d 488 (1975).

Although a preliminary injunction will ordinarily be granted if the defendant's infringement is clear, see, e.g., Onassis, *supra*; Durgom v. Columbia Broadcasting System, Inc., 29 Misc.2d 394, 214 N.Y.S.2d 752 (Sup. Ct.1961), the balance of equities may sometimes justify the denial of preliminary relief, particularly when the fact of infringement is uncertain. See Marcinkus v. NAL Pub.,Inc., 138 Misc.2d 256, 522 N.Y.S.2d 1009 (Sup. Ct.1987) (refusing to order a recall of the defendant's book); Smith v. Goro, 66 Misc.2d 1011, 323 N.Y.S.2d 47 (Sup.Ct.1970) (preliminary injunction against publication denied); Albert v. New York Telephone Co., 28 Misc.2d 296, 204 N.Y.S.2d 36 (Sup.Ct.), affirmed 11 A.D.2d 656, 203 N.Y.S.2d 1019 (1960) (request for recall of telephone directories containing an unauthorized picture of the plaintiff denied).

§ 49. Monetary Relief: Appropriation of the Commercial Value of a Person's Identity

(1) One who is liable for an appropriation of the commercial value of another's identity under the rule stated in § 46 is liable for the pecuniary loss to the other caused by the appropriation or for the actor's own pecuniary gain resulting from the appropriation, whichever is greater, unless such relief is precluded by an applicable statute or is otherwise inappropriate under the rule stated in Subsection (2).

(2) Whether an award of monetary relief is appropriate and the appropriate method of measuring such relief depend upon a comparative appraisal of all the factors of the case, including the following primary factors:

(a) the degree of certainty with which the plaintiff has established the fact and extent of the pecuniary loss or the actor's pecuniary gain resulting from the appropriation;

(b) the nature and extent of the appropriation;

(c) the relative adequacy to the plaintiff of other remedies;

(d) the intent of the actor and whether the actor knew or should have known that the conduct was unlawful;

(e) any unreasonable delay by the plaintiff in bringing suit or otherwise asserting his or her rights; and

(f) any related misconduct on the part of the plaintiff.

Comment:

a. Scope. This Section states the rules governing the recovery of monetary relief in actions for infringement of the right of publicity. Monetary relief for an appropriation of the commercial value of a person's identity can consist of either compensatory damages measured by the loss to the plaintiff or restitutionary relief measured by the unjust gain to the defendant. This Section states the rules applicable to both measures of relief. The appropriation of another's identity may also cause emotional or reputational injuries. Compensation for such injuries is generally available under the rules governing liability for invasion of privacy. See Comment *b*.

The general rules relating to the recovery of compensatory damages in tort actions apply in actions for infringement of the right of publicity. This Section addresses only those issues that have particular significance to an award of damages in right of publicity cases. The following sections of the Restatement, Second, of Torts are also relevant: §§ 902 and 903 defining "damages" and "compensatory damages"; § 907 stating the rule for recovery of nominal damages; §§ 908 and 909 stating the rules for recovery of punitive damages; § 912 stating the requirement of "certainty"; and §§ 435A and 435B stating rules relating to intended and unintended consequences of tortious conduct. The general rules relating to the restitution of benefits tortiously acquired are also applicable in actions for infringement of the right of publicity. See Restatement of Restitution § 136 (1937).

State statutes that protect the right of publicity generally authorize the recovery of monetary relief. Some statutes provide for minimum statutory damages recoverable when loss in a greater amount is not proven. Several statutes expressly provide for an award of the defendant's profits. In the absence of a conflicting statutory provision, the general rules that govern the recovery of monetary relief at common law are also applicable in actions under state right of publicity statutes.

b. Relationship to other causes of action. The history of the publicity tort and its relationship to other causes of action have created confusion regarding the appropriate measure of damages. The right of publicity protects the commercial value of a person's identity, and the measure of damages properly focuses on the pecuniary loss to the plaintiff or the unjust pecuniary gain to the defendant. In some cases, however, the plaintiff may also be entitled to relief for injury to personal interests caused by the defendant's appropriation. Thus, if the defendant's use of the plaintiff's identity is defamatory, or places the plaintiff before the public in a false light, or involves the unreasonable disclosure of matters relating to the plaintiff's private life, or is an unreasonable intrusion upon the plaintiff's seclusion, the defendant is subject to liability for harm to the interests protected under the rules applicable to such conduct. However, an unauthorized use of a person's identity for purposes of trade can result in compensable injury to personal interests even in the absence of other independently tortious conduct. Thus, protection is available under the right of privacy for the personal interest in controlling the use and exploitation of one's own identity. Private individuals with little fame or prominence frequently suffer greater emotional than pecuniary harm from an unauthorized commercial appropriation of their identity. Celebrities, although often primarily concerned with protecting the commercial value of their identities, may also suffer emotional distress or humiliation from an unauthorized exploitation of their name or likeness. For example, both a private individual and a celebrity may suffer harm attributable to the indignity of a particular use or to an unwelcome association with particular goods or services. Compensation for such harm is available upon appropriate proof through an action for invasion of privacy. See § 46, Comment *b* ; Restatement, Second, Torts §§ 652C, 652H. However, unlike the interest in the commercial value of a person's identity protected by the right of publicity, privacy interests are personal. In most jurisdictions the interest in personal privacy cannot be assigned and does not survive death. Thus, if the right of publicity is owned by the plaintiff through descent or assignment, relief is ordinarily limited to the commercial harm caused by an unauthorized use. See § 46, Illustration 1.

The unauthorized use of a person's name or likeness in advertising may also create the false impression that the person endorses, sponsors, or is otherwise associated with the advertised product. See § 4, Illustration 5. In such cases, the defendant is also subject to liability for any monetary relief appropriate under the rules governing remedies for deceptive marketing as stated in § 36.

Illustrations:

1. *A*, a person who is not a celebrity, enrolled in *B* 's body-building course and consented to the taking of "before" and "after" photographs for the purpose of evaluating the results of the course. Ten years later, without *A* 's consent, *B* used the photographs in an advertising campaign. Friends and co-workers who saw the advertisements made fun of *A*, who no longer resembled the "after" picture, causing *A* embarrassment and humiliation. *B* is subject to liability to *A* under the rule stated in § 46 for any pecuniary loss suffered by *A* or any pecuniary gain acquired by *B* as a result of *B* 's appropriation of the commercial value of *A* 's identity. *B* is also subject to liability under the rules relating to invasion of privacy for the mental distress suffered by *A*. See Restatement, Second, Torts § 652C.

2. *A*, the author of a nationally-syndicated column of household hints, maintains a policy of never endorsing specific products. *B*, a manufacturer of household products, uses without consent *A* 's name and likeness in its advertising in a manner that

suggests an endorsement by *A*, causing *A* substantial emotional distress. *B* is subject to liability to *A* under the rules stated in both § 4 and § 46 for any pecuniary loss suffered by *A* or any pecuniary gain acquired by *B* as a result of *B* 's appropriation of the commercial value of *A* 's identity. *B* is also subject to liability to *A* under the rules relating to invasion of privacy for the mental distress suffered by *A*. See Restatement, Second, Torts § 652C.

c. Appropriateness of monetary relief. Monetary relief is a common remedy in actions for infringement of the right of publicity. The plaintiff bears the burden of proving the fact and cause of any pecuniary loss for which recovery is sought. However, the amount of loss must be shown only with such certainty as is reasonable under the circumstances. See Restatement, Second, Torts § 912. As with other forms of unfair competition, the finder of fact has considerable discretion in fixing appropriate compensation.

A defendant may be subject to liability under the rule stated in § 46 even if the violation of the plaintiff's rights is unintentional. See § 46, Comment *e* ; § 47, Comment *e*. However, the defendant's intent remains relevant in determining appropriate relief. In light of the meager case law, an analogy to the rules governing relief for other forms of unfair competition may be appropriate. Thus, although a defendant who unintentionally infringes another's right of publicity is subject to liability for compensatory damages, the court may properly require more certain proof of pecuniary loss to the plaintiff than in cases of intentional infringement. Cf. § 36, Comment *j*. Similarly, injunctive relief may be sufficient against a defendant who plays a subordinate role in the infringement, such as an innocent retailer. Cf. § 36, Comment *k*. Other factors such as a delay by the plaintiff in commencing the action or otherwise objecting to the use or misconduct by the plaintiff that is related to the rights asserted against the defendant are also properly considered in defense or mitigation of damages.

An accounting of the defendant's profits from an unauthorized use of the plaintiff's identity is most often justified as a means of deterring infringement and recapturing gains attributable to wrongful conduct. Since the defendant's gains do not necessarily correspond to the plaintiff's losses, an award of the defendant's profits can result in a windfall to the plaintiff. Cf. § 36, Comments *b* and *c*. Thus, the remedy of an accounting may be inappropriate in the case of an innocent infringer. Cf. § 37.

d. Measure of monetary relief. If otherwise appropriate, monetary relief may be awarded for the pecuniary loss to the plaintiff or the pecuniary gain to the defendant resulting from the unauthorized use of the plaintiff's identity. As in other areas of unfair competition, the plaintiff is permitted to establish either or both measures of relief, but may recover only the greater of the two amounts. This limitation satisfies both compensatory and restitutionary objectives without permitting double recovery for the same loss. See § 45, Comment *c*.

If the defendant's unauthorized use competes directly with a use made by the plaintiff, the appropriation may result in lost profits on sales or licenses. Celebrities who actively exploit their name or likeness may also recover for any reduction in the commercial value of their identity caused by the defendant's unauthorized use. Such a reduction in value may result, for example, from the manner or form of the unauthorized use, the quality or nature of the goods or services with which the plaintiff's identity is used, overexposure of the identity, or from other characteristics of the use that reduce the plaintiff's future economic opportunities. The costs of corrective measures undertaken by the plaintiff to restore injured reputation or good will may also be recoverable. A private figure may recover for a reduction in the commercial value of his or her identity upon proof that the unauthorized use has diminished the value of the identity for use in the plaintiff's own business.

Because of the difficulty in proving the loss to the plaintiff or the gain to the defendant that is attributable to an appropriation of identity, courts sometimes apply a measure of damages based on the fair market value of the unauthorized use. This measure, analogous to the reasonable royalty measure of damages in trade secret cases, see § 45, Comment *g*, can represent either the loss of compensation to the plaintiff for the value of the defendant's use or the unjust gain to the defendant in avoiding payment for the use. Among the evidence relevant in determining the value of the use are the manner in which the defendant has exploited the identity, the relative fame of the plaintiff, and the price that the plaintiff has received for similar uses in the past. Courts have also relied on expert testimony concerning the licensing fees paid to similarly-situated persons for comparable uses. Private persons may also recover damages measured by the value of the use by establishing the market price that the defendant would have been required to pay in order to secure similar services from other private persons or from professional models.

Damages measured by the fair market value of the appropriated use can compensate the plaintiff for loss but do not ordinarily deprive the defendant of the full gain attributable to the appropriation. The fair market value of the use reflects a price at which both parties benefit from the transaction. Thus, although in many cases damages measured by the market value of the use may be the only practical remedy, a court may properly give to the plaintiff the benefit of any doubt in determining fair market value in order to prevent unjust enrichment and to insure adequate deterrence.

Restitutionary relief in the form of an accounting of the defendant's profits is also available in actions for infringement of the right of publicity. When otherwise appropriate (see Comment *c*), the plaintiff may recover the proportion of the defendant's net profits that is attributable to the unauthorized use. The plaintiff bears the burden of establishing the defendant's sales; the defendant has the burden of establishing any portion of the sales that is attributable to factors other than the appropriation of the plaintiff's identity and any expenses properly deducted in determining net profits. See the analogous rules governing accountings in trademark infringement actions in § 37, Comments *g* and *h*. See also § 45, Comment *f*.

e. Punitive damages. Punitive damages are ordinarily available to successful plaintiffs in right of publicity actions under the general rules applicable to the award of punitive damages in tort actions. See Restatement, Second, Torts § 908. Normally, proof of malice or willful disregard of the plaintiff's rights is required. Statutes in several states permit the award of enhanced or punitive damages if the defendant "knowingly" infringes the plaintiff's right of publicity.

f. Attorney's fees. Most states do not provide for the award of attorney's fees in actions at common law. Statutes in some states specifically authorize an award of attorney's fees to a prevailing plaintiff or prevailing party in an action for infringement of the right of publicity.

REPORTERS' NOTE

Comment a. On the recovery of monetary relief in right of publicity actions, see generally McCarthy, The Rights of Publicity and Privacy §§ 11.7–10. The general rules governing the recovery of compensatory damages in tort actions are stated in Restatement, Second, Torts, ch. 47. Minimum statutory damages are authorized in Cal.Civ.Code §§ 990, 3344; Nev.Rev.Stat. § 598.988(1)(b); Tex.Prop.Code Ann. § 26.013.

Comment b. On the relationship between the right of publicity and the right of privacy, see § 46, Comment *b*. The plaintiff may ordinarily recover for injury to both personal and commercial interests caused by the appropriation. See, e.g., Clark v. Celeb Pub., Inc., 530 F.Supp. 979 (S.D.N.Y.1981); National Bank of Commerce v. Shaklee Corp., 503 F.Supp. 533 (W.D.Tex.1980); Grant v. Esquire, Inc., 367 F.Supp. 876 (S.D.N.Y.1973); Candebat v. Flanagan, 487 So.2d 207 (Miss.1986); Canessa v. J.I. Kislak, Inc., 97 N.J.Super. 327, 235 A.2d 62 (1967). See also Restatement, Second, Torts

§ 652H. Damages for emotional distress have been awarded as general damages without proof of specific loss. See, e.g., National Bank of Commerce, *supra* ; Faber v. Condecor, Inc., 195 N.J.Super. 81, 477 A.2d 1289 (1984); Olan Mills, Inc. v. Dodd, 234 Ark. 495, 353 S.W.2d 22 (1962); Fairfield v. American Photocopy Equipment Co., 158 Cal.App.2d 53, 322 P.2d 93 (1958). Cf. Manville v. Borg–Warner Corp., 418 F.2d 434 (10th Cir.1969) (although general damages are recoverable without proof of specific loss, some evidence of general damage is required). Even celebrities may recover damages for emotional distress in addition to pecuniary loss. See, e.g, Waits v. Frito–Lay, Inc., 978 F.2d 1093 (9th Cir.1992), cert. denied ___ U.S. ___, 113 S.Ct. 1047, 122 L.Ed.2d 355 (1993); Clark, *supra* ; National Bank of Commerce, *supra* ; Grant, *supra*. On monetary liability for a false suggestion of endorsement or sponsorship, see Waits, *supra* ; National Bank of Commerce, *supra*.

Illustration 1 is suggested by McAndrews v. Roy, 131 So.2d 256 (La.App.1961). Illustration 2 is based on *National Bank of Commerce, supra*.

Comment c. Monetary relief will not be awarded for an infringement of the right of publicity in the absence of evidence establishing pecuniary loss to the plaintiff or pecuniary gain to the defendant. See Zim v. Western Pub. Co., 573 F.2d 1318 (5th Cir.1978) (limiting plaintiff to nominal damages); U.S. Life Ins. Co. v. Hamilton, 238 S.W.2d 289 (Tex.Civ. App.1951) (same). However, the amount of damages need not be proved with exactness, and courts have broad discretion to determine appropriate compensation. See, e.g., Bi–Rite v. Button Master, 578 F.Supp. 59 (S.D.N.Y.1983); Hogan v. A.S. Barnes & Co, 114 U.S.P.Q. 314 (Pa.C.P.1957) (requiring only a "reasonably fair basis" for calculating damages).

Cases awarding compensatory damages for unintentional infringements include, e.g., Genesis Pub., Inc. v. Goss, 437 So.2d 169 (Fla.App.1983); Welch v. Mr. Christmas Inc., 57 N.Y.2d 143, 454 N.Y.S.2d 971, 440 N.E.2d 1317 (1982); Myers v. U.S. Camera Pub. Corp., 9 Misc.2d 765, 167 N.Y.S.2d 771 (N.Y.C.Ct.1957). Monetary relief was denied and the plaintiff limited to an injunction against an innocent retailer of infringing posters in Brinkley v. Casablancas, 80 A.D.2d 428, 438 N.Y.S.2d 1004 (1981). Cf. Flake v. Greensboro News Co., 212 N.C. 780, 195 S.E. 55 (1937) (nominal damages awarded against a newspaper for the mistaken use of the plaintiff's photograph in advertising).

The cases that award an accounting of the defendant's profits involve intentional infringements. For the justification, in a trademark context, for limiting an accounting of profits to cases of intentional infringement, see George Basch Co. v. Blue Coral, Inc., 968 F.2d 1532 (2d Cir.), cert. denied ___ U.S. ___, 113 S.Ct. 510, 121 L.Ed.2d 445 (1992) (citing Restatement Third, Unfair Competition § 37 (Tent.Draft No.3 (1991))).

Comment d. Cases awarding damages based on the pecuniary loss to the plaintiff include, e.g., Waits v. Frito–Lay, Inc., 978 F.2d 1093 (9th Cir.1992), cert. denied ___ U.S. ___, 113 S.Ct. 1047, 122 L.Ed.2d 355 (1993) (damages awarded for both injury to good will and the fair market value of the use); Big Seven Music Corp. v. Lennon, 554 F.2d 504 (2d

Cir.1977) (damages awarded for injury to market reputation resulting from a use with inferior merchandise); Clark v. Celeb Pub., Inc., 530 F.Supp. 979 (S.D.N.Y.1981) (model awarded damages for the diminished value of her services resulting from the defendant's use of her photograph in a pornographic magazine). See also Hirsch v. S.C. Johnson & Son, Inc., 90 Wis.2d 379, 280 N.W.2d 129 (1979) (recognizing the potential for damage to reputation and dilution of the market value of the plaintiff's identity); Lugosi v. Universal Pictures, 25 Cal.3d 813, 160 Cal.Rptr. 323, 603 P.2d 425 (1979) (Bird, J., dissenting) (recognizing that overexposure and harm to the plaintiff's image can cause a loss of future economic opportunities); Continental Optical Co. v. Reed, 119 Ind.App. 643, 86 N.E.2d 306 (1949) (loss in the value of the plaintiff's likeness for use in the plaintiff's business could be compensable) (dictum).

A majority of the right of publicity cases measure damages by the value of the unauthorized use. See, e.g., National Bank of Commerce v. Shaklee Corp., 503 F.Supp. 533 (W.D.Tex. 1980); Grant v. Esquire, Inc., 367 F.Supp. 876 (S.D.N.Y.1973); Apple Corps Ltd. v. Leber, 229 U.S.P.Q. 1015 (Cal.Super.1986); Alonso v. Parfet, 253 Ga. 749, 325 S.E.2d 152 (1985); Cabaniss v. Hipsley, 114 Ga. App. 367, 151 S.E.2d 496 (1966). See also Fla.Stat. § 540.08(2) (damages "including an amount which would have been a reasonable royalty"). The defendant is liable for the value of the use even if the use did not produce a profit. Hogan v. A.S. Barnes & Co, 114 U.S.P.Q. 314 (Pa. C.P.1957). In some circumstances even non-celebrities may recover the commercial value of the defendant's use. See Canessa v. J.I. Kislak, Inc., 97 N.J.Super. 327, 235 A.2d 62 (1967); McCarthy, The Rights of Publicity and Privacy § 4.3.

The value of an unauthorized use is sometimes determined by the plaintiff's customary fee for similar uses. See Clark, *supra* (value based on prior modeling fee); Welch v. Mr. Christmas Inc., 57 N.Y.2d 143, 454 N.Y.S.2d 971, 440 N.E.2d 1317 (1982) (damages apparently measured by the fee under an earlier license between the parties). Expert testimony on the value of the use is also admissible. See National Bank of Commerce, *supra*; Grant, *supra* (also suggesting that there may be an enhanced first-time value associated with the use if the celebrity has not previously endorsed a product).

Although there is little case law, it is widely assumed that the defendant's profits are an appropriate measure of relief in right of publicity cases under rules analogous to the recovery of profits in trademark, trade secret, and copyright cases. See McCarthy, The Rights of Privacy and Publicity § 11.8D. See also Restatement of Restitution § 136 (1937). Defendant's profits from the unauthorized use of the plaintiff's identity were awarded in Bi–Rite v. Button Master, 578 F.Supp. 59 (S.D.N.Y. 1983); Factors Etc., Inc. v. Pro Arts, Inc., 496 F.Supp. 1090 (S.D.N.Y. 1980), reversed on other grounds 652 F.2d 278 (2d Cir.1981), cert. denied 456 U.S. 927, 102 S.Ct. 1973, 72 L.Ed.2d 442 (1982). See also McFarland v. E & K Corp., 18 U.S.P.Q.2d 1246 (D.Minn.1991) (recognizing the possibility of an unjust enrichment claim); Lugosi, *supra* (Bird, J., dissenting) (supporting an accounting of the defendant's profits, with the burden of apportionment on the defendant). Cf. Nossen v. Hoy, 750 F.Supp. 740 (E.D.Va.1990) (recognizing a quasi-contract claim for unjust enrichment resulting from the defendant's use of the plaintiff's name and reputation). But see Price v. Hal Roach Studios, Inc., 400 F.Supp. 836 (S.D.N.Y.1975) (denying an accounting of the defendant's profits). For state statutory provisions authorizing the recovery of defendant's profits, see Cal.Civ.Code § 3344(a) (burden is on the defendant to establish any deductible expenses); Okla.Stat. tit. 21, § 1449(A) (same); Tenn.Code Ann. § 47–25–1106; Tex.Prop.Code Ann. § 26.013; Wis.Stat. § 895.50(1)(b) (authorizing damages based on defendant's unjust enrichment).

Comment e. Punitive damages may ordinarily be awarded in right of publicity cases if there is evidence of malice or a conscious disregard for the plaintiff's rights. See, e.g., Waits v. Frito–Lay, Inc., 978 F.2d 1093 (9th Cir.1992), cert. denied ___ U.S. ___, 113 S.Ct. 1047, 122 L.Ed.2d 355 (1993) (upholding an award of punitive damages based on a finding of malice); Frazier v. Norwegian Cruise Line, Inc., 945 F.2d 395 (3d Cir.1991) (applying Restatement, Second, Torts § 908 to deny punitive damages absent evidence of conscious or reckless disregard); Bi–Rite v. Button Master, 578 F.Supp. 59 (S.D.N.Y.1983) (denying punitive damages absent intentional infringement); Clark v. Celeb Pub., Inc., 530 F.Supp. 979 (S.D.N.Y.1981) (continued distribution of infringing magazine after the plaintiff's objection justified punitive damages); Staruski v. Continental Tel. Co., 154 Vt. 568, 581 A.2d 266 (1990) (punitive damages held appropriate for a publication by the defendant made despite the plaintiff's objection); Genesis Pub., Inc. v. Goss, 437 So.2d 169 (Fla.App.1983) (denying punitive damages absent conscious infringement).

A majority of the state statutes that recognize the right of publicity expressly authorize the award of enhanced or punitive damages, often upon proof that the defendant "knowingly" used the plaintiff's identity in a prohibited manner. The latter standard has been interpreted under New York Civil Rights Law § 51 as eliminating the need to establish malice or recklessness. See Welch v. Mr. Christmas Inc., 57 N.Y.2d 143, 454 N.Y.S.2d 971, 440 N.E.2d 1317 (1982).

Comment f. Recovery of attorney's fees in right of publicity actions is authorized in Cal.Civ.Code § 3344(a) (prevailing party); Okla. Stat. tit. 12, § 1449(A) (prevailing party); R.I.Gen.Laws § 9–1–28.1(b) (prevailing party); Tex.Prop.Code Ann. § 26.013(a)(4) (prevailing plaintiff); Wis.Stat. § 895.50(1)(c) (prevailing plaintiff).

TABLE OF CASES

A

TABLES

TABLE OF CASES

TABLE OF CASES

TABLE OF CASES

B

TABLE OF CASES

C

D

TABLE OF CASES

E

F

G

TABLE OF CASES

H

I

K

TABLE OF CASES

L

M

TABLE OF CASES

N

TABLE OF CASES

O

P

Q

R

S

U

V

W

Y

Z

*

TABLE OF STATUTES

(Including references to U.S. Constitution)

UNITED STATES

UNITED STATES CONSTITUTION

UNITED STATES CODE ANNOTATED

5 U.S.C.A.—Government Organization and Employees

15 U.S.C.A.—Commerce and Trade

TABLE OF STATUTES

UNITED STATES CODE ANNOTATED

15 U.S.C.A.—Commerce and Trade

UNITED STATES CODE ANNOTATED

15 U.S.C.A.—Commerce and Trade

TABLE OF STATUTES

TABLE OF STATUTES

UNITED STATES CODE ANNOTATED

17 U.S.C.A.—Copyrights

Sec.	This Work Sec.
301 (Cont'd)	38, Com. *d,* p. 415
	38, RN, p. 419
	38, RN, p. 422
	46, Com. *i,* p. 535
	46, RN, p. 546
302	38, Com. *d,* p. 413
	39, Com. *c,* p. 428
408	39, Com. *c,* p. 429
408(b)(1)	39, Com. *c,* p. 429
506(c)	3, RN, p. 46
507(b)	31, RN, p. 324
705	39, Com. *c,* p. 429

18 U.S.C.A.—Crimes and Criminal Procedure

Sec.	This Work Sec.
1341	39, Com. *b,* p. 427
	39, RN, p. 441
1343	39, Com. *b,* p. 427
	39, RN, p. 441
1905	39, RN, p. 441
	40, RN, p. 464
2314	39, Com. *b,* p. 427
2314—2315	39, RN, p. 441

19 U.S.C.A.—Customs and Duties

Sec.	This Work Sec.
1526	24, Com. *e,* p. 258
	24, RN, p. 263

UNITED STATES CODE ANNOTATED

35 U.S.C.A.—Patents

Sec.	This Work Sec.
101	39, Com. *c,* p. 427
103	39, Com. *c,* p. 427
111	39, Com. *c,* p. 428
112	39, Com. *c,* p. 428
122	39, Com. *c,* p. 428
135	39, Com. *c,* p. 427
171	17, RN, p. 180
271	39, Com. *c,* p. 427
292	3, RN, p. 46

47 U.S.C.A.—Telegraphs, Telephones, and Radiotelegraphs

Sec.	This Work Sec.
151 et seq.	38, RN, p. 419

49 U.S.C.A.—Transportation

Sec.	This Work Sec.
1305(a)(1)	2, RN, p. 32

STATUTES AT LARGE

Year	This Work Sec.
1905, Feb. 20, c. 592, § 16, 33 Stat. 728	21, RN, p. 237
1946, July 5, c. 540, 60 Stat. 437	20, RN, p. 221
1946, July 5, c. 540, § 32(1), 60 Stat. 437	21, RN, p. 237
1984, Oct. 11, P.L. 98–469, 98 Stat. 1837	36, RN, p. 394

ALABAMA CODE

Sec.	This Work Sec.
8–12–6 et seq.	9, SN, p. 83

TABLE OF STATUTES

ALABAMA CODE

Sec.	This Work Sec.
8–12–6 et seq. (Cont'd)	12, SN, p. 100
8–12–17	25, SN, p. 275
8–19–1 et seq.	1, SN, p. 13
8–27–1 et seq.	39, SN, p. 437

ALASKA STATUTES

Sec.	This Work Sec.
10.35	12, SN, p. 100
10.35.040	12, RN, p. 103
45.50.010 et seq.	9, SN, p. 83
45.50.471 et seq.	1, SN, p. 13
45.50.910 et seq.	39, SN, p. 437

ARIZONA REVISED STATUTES

Sec.	This Work Sec.
10–108(3)	12, SN, p. 100
44–401 et seq.	39, SN, p. 437
44–1441 et seq.	9, SN, p. 83
44–1460 et seq.	12, SN, p. 100
44–1521 et seq.	1, SN, p. 13

ARKANSAS CODE ANNOTATED

Sec.	This Work Sec.
4–70–201 et seq.	12, SN, p. 100
4–71–101 et seq.	9, SN, p. 83
4–71–113	25, SN, p. 275
4–75–601 et seq.	39, SN, p. 437
4–88–101 et seq.	1, SN, p. 13

WEST'S ANNOTATED CALIFORNIA BUSINESS AND PROFESSIONS CODE

Sec.	This Work Sec.
14200 et seq.	9, SN, p. 83
14330	25, SN, p. 275
14411	12, RN, p. 103
14415	12, RN, p. 102
14492—14495	12, RN, p. 102
17000 et seq.	1, SN, p. 13
17900 et seq.	12, SN, p. 100

WEST'S ANNOTATED CALIFORNIA CIVIL CODE

Sec.	This Work Sec.
980	38, RN, p. 423
990	46, SN, p. 536
	46, RN, p. 544
	46, RN, p. 545
	49, RN, p. 569
990(b)	46, RN, p. 543
990(h)	46, RN, p. 545
990(n)(*l*)	47, RN, p. 559
990(n)	47, RN, p. 558
990(n)(1)	47, RN, p. 556
990(n)(4)	47, RN, p. 553
3344	46, SN, p. 536
	46, RN, p. 539
	47, RN, p. 552
	47, RN, p. 558
	49, RN, p. 569
3344(a)	46, RN, p. 541

WEST'S ANNOTATED CALIFORNIA CIVIL CODE

WEST'S ANNOTATED CALIFORNIA LABOR CODE

WEST'S COLORADO REVISED STATUTES ANNOTATED

CONNECTICUT GENERAL STATUTES ANNOTATED

DELAWARE CODE

DISTRICT OF COLUMBIA CODE

WEST'S FLORIDA STATUTES ANNOTATED

TABLE OF STATUTES

WEST'S FLORIDA STATUTES ANNOTATED

Sec.	This Work Sec.
540.08(3)(a)	47, RN, p. 555
540.08(3)(b)	47, RN, p. 553
540.08(3)(c)	46, RN, p. 540
540.08(4)	46, RN, p. 545
540.08(6)	46, RN, p. 539
688.001 et seq.	39, SN, p. 437
865.09	12, SN, p. 100

OFFICIAL CODE OF GEORGIA ANNOTATED

Sec.	This Work Sec.
10–1–370 et seq.	2, SN, p. 32
10–1–390 et seq.	1, SN, p. 14
10–1–440 et seq.	9, SN, p. 83
10–1–451(b)	25, SN, p. 275
	25, RN, p. 278
10–1–490 et seq.	12, SN, p. 100
10–1–760 et seq.	39, SN, p. 437

HAWAII REVISED STATUTES

Sec.	This Work Sec.
480–1 et seq.	1, SN, p. 14
481A–1 et seq.	2, SN, p. 32
Ch. 482	12, SN, p. 100
482–1 et seq.	9, SN, p. 83
482B–1 et seq.	39, SN, p. 437

IDAHO CODE

Sec.	This Work Sec.
48–501 et seq.	9, SN, p. 83
48–512	25, SN, p. 275
48–601 et seq.	1, SN, p. 14
48–801 et seq.	39, SN, p. 437
53–501 et seq.	12, SN, p. 101

ILLINOIS COMPILED STATUTES

Sec.	This Work Sec.
765 ILCS 1035/0.01 et seq.	9, SN, p. 83
765 ILCS 1035/15	25, SN, p. 275
	25, RN, p. 278
765 ILCS 1060/1	42, RN, p. 490
765 ILCS 1065/1 et seq.	39, SN, p. 437
765 ILCS 1065/2(d)	42, RN, p. 491
765 ILCS 1065/8	41, RN, p. 477
805 ILCS 405/0.01 et seq.	12, SN, p. 101
815 ILCS 505/1 et seq.	1, SN, p. 14
815 ILCS 510/1 et seq.	2, SN, p. 32

WEST'S ANNOTATED INDIANA CODE

Sec.	This Work Sec.
23–15–1–1 et seq.	12, SN, p. 101
24–2–1–1 et seq.	9, SN, p. 83
24–2–3–1 et seq.	39, SN, p. 437
24–5–0.5–1 et seq.	1, SN, p. 14

IOWA CODE ANNOTATED

Sec.	This Work Sec.
547.1 et seq.	12, SN, p. 101
548.1 et seq.	9, SN, p. 83

TABLE OF STATUTES

IOWA CODE ANNOTATED

KANSAS STATUTES ANNOTATED

KENTUCKY REVISED STATUTES

LOUISIANA STATUTES ANNOTATED—REVISED STATUTES

MAINE REVISED STATUTES ANNOTATED

MARYLAND CODE, BUSINESS REGULATION

MARYLAND CODE, COMMERCIAL LAW

MARYLAND CODE, CORPORATIONS AND ASSOCIATIONS

MASSACHUSETTS GENERAL LAWS ANNOTATED

MASSACHUSETTS GENERAL LAWS ANNOTATED

Ch.	This Work Sec.
214, § 3A (Cont'd)	46, RN, p. 539
	46, RN, p. 542
	46, RN, p. 545
	47, RN, p. 552
	47, RN, p. 553
266, § 71A	12, RN, p. 102

MICHIGAN COMPILED LAWS ANNOTATED

Sec.	This Work Sec.
15.361—15.369	40, RN, p. 465
429.31 et seq.	9, SN, p. 84
445.1 et seq.	12, SN, p. 101
445.901 et seq.	1, SN, p. 14
450.1217	12, SN, p. 101

MINNESOTA STATUTES ANNOTATED

Sec.	This Work Sec.
181.78	42, RN, p. 490
325C.01 et seq.	39, SN, p. 438
325D.43 et seq.	2, SN, p. 32
325F.68 et seq.	1, SN, p. 14
333.001 et seq.	9, SN, p. 84
	12, SN, p. 101

MISSISSIPPI CODE

Sec.	This Work Sec.
75–24–1 et seq.	1, SN, p. 14
75–25–1 et seq.	9, SN, p. 84

MISSISSIPPI CODE

Sec.	This Work Sec.
75–26–1 et seq.	39, SN, p. 438

VERNON'S ANNOTATED MISSOURI STATUTES

Sec.	This Work Sec.
407.010 et seq.	1, SN, p. 14
417.005 et seq.	9, SN, p. 84
417.061(1)	25, SN, p. 275
417.200	12, SN, p. 101

MONTANA CODE ANNOTATED

Sec.	This Work Sec.
30–13–203	12, SN, p. 101
30–13–301 et seq.	9, SN, p. 84
30–13–334	25, SN, p. 275
30–14–101 et seq.	1, SN, p. 14
30–14–401	39, SN, p. 438

NEBRASKA REVISED STATUTES

Sec.	This Work Sec.
20–202	46, SN, p. 536
	46, RN, p. 539
	47, RN, p. 552
20–202(1)	47, RN, p. 555
20–202(2)	47, RN, p. 553
20–202(3)	46, RN, p. 540
20–207	46, RN, p. 544
20–208	46, RN, p. 545
59–1601 et seq.	1, SN, p. 14
87–101 et seq.	9, SN, p. 84

TABLE OF STATUTES

NEW YORK, MCKINNEY'S CIVIL RIGHTS LAW

NEW YORK, MCKINNEY'S GENERAL BUSINESS LAW

NEW YORK, MCKINNEY'S LABOR LAW

NORTH CAROLINA GENERAL STATUTES

NORTH DAKOTA CENTURY CODE

OHIO REVISED CODE

OKLAHOMA STATUTES ANNOTATED

TABLE OF STATUTES

RHODE ISLAND GENERAL LAWS

SOUTH CAROLINA CODE

SOUTH DAKOTA CODIFIED LAWS

TENNESSEE CODE ANNOTATED

V.TEXAS C.A., BUSINESS & COMMERCE CODE

V.TEXAS C.A., PROPERTY CODE

TABLE OF STATUTES

V.TEXAS C.A., PROPERTY CODE

Sec.	This Work Sec.
26.012(c)	47, RN, p. 559
26.012(d)	46, RN, p. 545
26.013	49, RN, p. 569
	49, RN, p. 572
26.013(a)(4)	49, RN, p. 572
26.014	46, RN, p. 539

UTAH CODE ANNOTATED

Sec.	This Work Sec.
13–11–1 et seq.	1, SN, p. 14
13–24–1 et seq.	39, SN, p. 438
42–2–5 et seq.	12, SN, p. 101
70–3–1 et seq.	9, SN, p. 84

VERMONT STATUTES ANNOTATED

Tit.	This Work Sec.
9, § 2451 et seq.	1, SN, p. 14
9, § 2521 et seq.	9, SN, p. 84
11, § 1621	12, SN, p. 101
11, § 1623	12, SN, p. 101

VIRGINIA CODE

Sec.	This Work Sec.
8.01–40	46, SN, p. 536
	46, RN, p. 539
	46, RN, p. 542
	46, RN, p. 545
	47, RN, p. 552
59.1–69 et seq.	12, SN, p. 101

VIRGINIA CODE

Sec.	This Work Sec.
59.1–77 et seq.	9, SN, p. 84
59.1–196 et seq.	1, SN, p. 14
59.1–336 et seq.	39, SN, p. 438

WEST'S REVISED CODE OF WASHINGTON ANNOTATED

Sec.	This Work Sec.
19.77.010 et seq.	9, SN, p. 84
19.77.160	25, SN, p. 276
19.80.001 et seq.	12, SN, p. 101
19.86.010 et seq.	1, SN, p. 14
19.108.010 et seq.	39, SN, p. 438
49.44.140	42, RN, p. 490

WEST VIRGINIA CODE

Sec.	This Work Sec.
46A–6–101 et seq.	1, SN, p. 14
47–2–1 et seq.	9, SN, p. 84
47–8–2 et seq.	12, SN, p. 101
47–22–1 et seq.	39, SN, p. 438

WISCONSIN STATUTES ANNOTATED

Sec.	This Work Sec.
100.20 et seq.	1, SN, p. 14
132.01 et seq.	9, SN, p. 84
134.17 et seq.	12, SN, p. 101
895.50	46, SN, p. 536
	46, RN, p. 539
	46, RN, p. 545
	47, RN, p. 552

TABLE OF STATUTES

WISCONSIN STATUTES ANNOTATED

WYOMING STATUTES

POPULAR NAME ACTS

COPYRIGHT ACT OF 1976

FEDERAL TRADE COMMISSION ACT

LANHAM ACT

TABLE OF STATUTES

LANHAM ACT

LANHAM ACT

TABLE OF STATUTES

LANHAM ACT

LANHAM ACT

TABLE OF STATUTES

TABLE OF STATUTES

TABLE OF CROSS REFERENCES TO DIGEST SYSTEM KEY NUMBERS AND ALR ANNOTATIONS *

Section 1

1. Digest System Key Numbers

Torts ⚷10(5); Trade Regulation ⚷331, 401, 461, 870(2).

2. A.L.R. Annotations

Supreme Court's views regarding consent judgments, decrees, or orders in proceedings under federal antitrust laws or Federal Trade Commission Act. 43 L Ed 2d 807.

Propriety of ordering consolidation under Rule 42(a) of Federal Rules of Civil Procedure in actions involving patents, copyrights, or trademarks. 82 ALR Fed 719.

What constitutes impairment of proposed intervenor's interest to support intervention as matter of right under Rule 24(a)(2) of Federal Rules of Civil Procedure in actions relating to patents, copyrights, and trademarks. 76 ALR Fed 837.

Availability of permanent injunction under sec. 13(b) of Federal Trade Commission Act (15 USCS sec. 53(b)). 70 ALR Fed 716.

Modern status of pendent federal jurisdiction, under 28 USCS sec. 1338(b), over state claim of unfair competition when joined with related claim under federal trademark laws. 62 ALR Fed 428.

Modern status of pendent federal jurisdiction, under 28 USCS sec. 1338(b), over state claim of unfair competition when joined with related claim under federal copyright laws. 58 ALR Fed 875.

Federal regulation of competitive practices in liquor industry under sec. 5 of Federal Alcohol Administration Act (27 USCS sec. 205). 58 ALR Fed 797.

Modern status of pendent federal jurisdiction, under 28 USCS sec. 1338(b), over state claim of unfair competition when joined with related claim under federal patent laws. 57 ALR Fed 418.

* Prepared by West Publishing Company and Lawyers Co-operative Publishing Company.

TABLE OF CROSS REFERENCES

Validity, construction, and application of 39 USCS sec. 3009, making it an unfair trade practice to mail unordered merchandise. 39 ALR Fed 674.

Temporary relief against unfair trade practices under 15 USCS sec. 53. 34 ALR Fed 507.

Jurisdiction of Federal District Court to entertain attacks on Federal Trade Commission's actions. 16 ALR Fed 361.

Right to jury trial in suit in federal court for damages from infringement of trademark. 9 ALR Fed 853.

Liability in tort for interference with attorney-client relationship. 90 ALR4th 621.

Liability for interference with physician-patient relationship. 87 ALR4th 845.

Punitive damages for interference with contract or business relationship. 44 ALR4th 1078.

Award of attorneys' fees in actions under state deceptive trade practice and consumer protection acts. 35 ALR4th 12.

Liability of third party for interference with prospective contractual relationship between two other parties. 6 ALR4th 195.

Liability for interference with at will business relationship. 5 ALR4th 9.

Rights of attorneys leaving firm with respect to firm clients. 1 ALR4th 1164.

Liability for interference with franchise. 97 ALR3d 890.

Liability for interference with lease. 96 ALR3d 862.

Reasonableness of offer of settlement under deceptive trade practice and consumer protection acts. 90 ALR3d 1350.

Practices forbidden by state deceptive trade practice and consumer protection acts. 89 ALR3d 449.

Scope and exemptions of state deceptive trade practice and consumer protection acts. 89 ALR3d 399.

Right to private action under state consumer protection act. 62 ALR3d 169.

What statute of limitations governs action for interference with contract or other economic relations. 58 ALR3d 1027.

Liability of real-estate broker for interference with contract between vendor and another real-estate broker. 34 ALR3d 720.

Liability for inducing employee not engaged for definite term to move to competitor. 24 ALR3d 821.

Right to enjoin business competitor from unlicensed or otherwise illegal acts or practices. 90 ALR2d 7.

Punitive or exemplary damages as recoverable for trademark infringement or unfair competition. 47 ALR2d 1117.

Liability for procuring breach of contract. 26 ALR2d 1227.

Conflict of laws, with respect to trademark infringement or unfair competition, including area of conflict between Federal and state law. 148 ALR 139.

Actual competition as necessary element of trademark infringement or unfair competition. 148 ALR 12.

Section 2

1. Digest System Key Numbers

Libel and Slander ⚷130, 133; Trade Regulation ⚷403, 870(2).

2. A.L.R. Annotations

Restrictions on attorneys' advertisements regarding legal services as violating Federal Constitution's First Amendment—Supreme Court cases. 110 L Ed 2d 688.

Applicability to advertisements of First Amendment's guaranty of free speech and press—federal cases. 37 L Ed 2d 1124.

Advertising of "free gifts" and representations as to price of goods as unfair method of competition or practice within sec. 5(a) of the Federal Trade Commission Act (15 USC sec. 45(a)). 15 L Ed 2d 865.

Statute or ordinance regulating or prohibiting advertising as unconstitutional burden on interstate commerce—federal cases. 10 L Ed 2d 1386.

What constitutes "false advertising" of food products or cosmetics within secs. 5 and 12 of the Federal Trade Commission Act (15 USCS secs. 45, 52). 50 ALR Fed 16.

What constitutes "false advertising" of drugs or devices within secs. 5 and 12 of the Federal Trade Commission Act (15 USCS secs. 45, 52). 49 ALR Fed 16.

Power of Federal Trade Commission to issue order requiring corrective advertising. 46 ALR Fed 905.

TABLE OF CROSS REFERENCES

Propriety of Federal Trade Commission order under 15 USCS sec. 45 applying to all products sold by party, or to all products in broad category, where Commission has found false advertising of only one product or group of products sold by party. 45 ALR Fed 612.

Commercial tax preparer's advertising as unfair or deceptive act or practice under sec. 5 of Federal Trade Commission Act (15 USCS sec. 45(a)). 37 ALR Fed 81.

Advertising "free trial" of merchandise as deceptive act or practice or unfair method of competition violative of sec. 5(a)(1) of Federal Trade Commission Act (15 USCS sec. 45(a)(1)). 26 ALR Fed 795.

Actionable nature of advertising impugning quality or worth of merchandise or products. 42 ALR4th 318.

Validity, construction, and effect of statutes, ordinances, or regulations prohibiting or regulating advertising of intoxicating liquors. 20 ALR4th 600.

Validity and application of statute prohibiting use of name descriptive of engineering by business organization not practicing profession of engineering. 13 ALR4th 676.

Validity, construction, and effect of laws or regulations requiring merchants to affix sale price to each item of consumer goods. 7 ALR4th 792.

Validity, construction, and application of statute or regulation restricting use of terms such as "accountant," "public accountant," or "certified public accountant". 4 ALR4th 1201.

Practices forbidden by state deceptive trade practice and consumer protection acts. 89 ALR3d 449.

Scope and exemptions of state deceptive trade practice and consumer protection acts. 89 ALR3d 399.

Validity and construction of statute or ordinance prohibiting promotional games in connection with sale of gasoline. 57 ALR3d 1288.

Validity and construction of regulations dealing with misrepresentation in the sale of Kosher food. 52 ALR3d 959.

Validity, construction, and effect of state legislation regulating or controlling "bait-and-switch" or "disparagement" advertising or sales practices. 50 ALR3d 1008.

Validity of statute or ordinance forbidding pharmacists to advertise prices of drugs or medicines. 44 ALR3d 1301.

Rights and remedies with respect to another's use of a deceptively similar advertising slogan. 2 ALR3d 748.

Validity and construction of statute or ordinance requiring or prohibiting posting or other publication of price of commodity or services. 89 ALR2d 901.

What constitutes false, misleading, or deceptive advertising or promotional practices subject to action by Federal Trade Commission. 65 ALR2d 225.

Constitutionality, construction, and application of statute respecting political advertising. 168 ALR 886.

Validity, construction and application of statutes or ordinances directed against false or fraudulent statements in advertisements. 89 ALR 1004.

Constitutionality of statute or ordinance prohibiting or regulating advertising by physician, surgeon, or other person professing healing arts. 54 ALR 400.

Section 3

1. Digest System Key Numbers

Trade Regulation 🔑401, 870(2).

2. A.L.R. Annotations

Advertising of "free gifts" and representations as to price of goods as unfair method of competition or practice within sec. 5(a) of the Federal Trade Commission Act (15 USC sec. 45(a)). 15 L Ed 2d 865.

Advertising "free trial" of merchandise as deceptive act or practice or unfair method of competition violative of sec. 5(a)(1) of Federal Trade Commission Act (15 USCS sec. 45(a)(1)). 26 ALR Fed 795.

Actionable nature of advertising impugning quality or worth of merchandise or products. 42 ALR4th 318.

Disparagement of the quality of intangible property. 74 ALR3d 298.

Validity and construction of statute or ordinance prohibiting promotional games in connection with sale of gasoline. 57 ALR3d 1288.

Validity, construction, and effect of state legislation regulating or controlling "bait-and-switch" or "disparagement" advertising or sales practices. 50 ALR3d 1008.

TABLE OF CROSS REFERENCES

Section 4

1. Digest System Key Numbers

Trade Regulation ⚷404.

2. A.L.R. Annotations

Admissibility and weight of consumer survey in litigation under trademark opposition, trademark infringement, and false designation of origin provisions of Lanham Act (15 USCS secs. 1063, 1114, and 1125). 98 ALR Fed 20.

Making, selling, or distributing counterfeit or "bootleg" tape recordings or phonograph records as violation of federal law. 25 ALR Fed 207.

Validity and construction of state statutes penalizing "criminal simulation" of goods or merchandise. 72 ALR4th 1071.

Unfair competition by imitation in sign or design of business place. 86 ALR3d 884.

Trade dress simulation of cosmetic products as unfair competition. 86 ALR3d 505.

Use of "family name" by corporation as unfair competition. 72 ALR3d 8.

Unfair competition by direct reproduction of literary, artistic, or musical property. 40 ALR3d 566.

Rights and remedies with respect to another's use of a deceptively similar advertising slogan. 2 ALR3d 748.

Right, in absence of self-imposed restraint, to use one's own name for business purposes to detriment of another using the same or a similar name. 47 ALR 1189, supp 44 ALR2d 1156.

Right to enjoin competitor from selling his produce to dealers with whom plaintiff has exclusive contract or in such form as to enable dealers to palm off competitor's produce as that of plaintiff. 84 ALR 472.

Right of producer or distributor to protection against use of his containers. 60 ALR 285.

Right to protection against simulation of physical appearance or arrangement of place of business, or vehicle. 17 ALR 784, supp 28 ALR 114.

Section 5

1. Digest System Key Numbers

Trade Regulation ⚷404, 870(2).

2. A.L.R. Annotations

Making, selling, or distributing counterfeit or "bootleg" tape recordings or phonograph records as violation of federal law. 25 ALR Fed 207.

Unfair competition by direct reproduction of literary, artistic, or musical property. 40 ALR3d 566.

Commercial competitor's truthful denomination of his goods as copies of designs of another, using designer's name, as trademark infringement, unfair competition, or the like. 1 ALR3d 760.

Section 6

1. Digest System Key Numbers

Trade Regulation ⚿407, 411, 422.

2. A.L.R. Annotations

What constitutes "false advertising" of food products or cosmetics within secs. 5 and 12 of the Federal Trade Commission Act (15 USCS secs. 45, 52). 50 ALR Fed 16.

What constitutes "false advertising" of drugs or devices within secs. 5 and 12 of the Federal Trade Commission Act (15 USCS secs. 45, 52). 49 ALR Fed 16.

Practices forbidden by state deceptive trade practice and consumer protection acts. 89 ALR3d 449.

Scope and exemptions of state deceptive trade practice and consumer protection acts. 89 ALR3d 399.

Validity, construction, and effect of state legislation regulating or controlling "bait-and-switch" or "disparagement" advertising or sales practices. 50 ALR3d 1008.

What constitutes false, misleading, or deceptive advertising or promotional practices subject to action by Federal Trade Commission. 65 ALR2d 225.

Validity, construction and application of statutes or ordinances directed against false or fraudulent statements in advertisements. 89 ALR 1004.

Section 7

1. Digest System Key Numbers

Trade Regulation ⚿374, 445.

2. A.L.R. Annotations

Right to free speech and press as including right to refuse to foster, repeat, advertise, or disseminate views, messages, statements, or slogans repugnant to one's moral, religious, or political beliefs. 51 L Ed 2d 924.

Who, under Rule 65(d) of Federal Rules of Civil Procedure, are persons "in active concert or participation" with parties to action so as to be bound by order granting injunction. 61 ALR Fed 482.

Advertising agency as subject to FTC order under 15 USCS sec. 45 for false or deceptive representations in its advertisements for client's product. 47 ALR Fed 393.

Liability of telephone company for mistakes in or omissions from its directory. 47 ALR4th 882.

Right of publisher of newspaper or magazine, in absence of contractual obligation, to refuse publication of advertisement. 18 ALR3d 1286.

Section 8

1. Digest System Key Numbers

Trade Regulation ⚿374, 445.

2. A.L.R. Annotations

Who, under Rule 65(d) of Federal Rules of Civil Procedure, are persons "in active concert or participation" with parties to action so as to be bound by order granting injunction. 61 ALR Fed 482.

Section 9

1. Digest System Key Numbers

Trade Regulation ⚿1.

2. A.L.R. Annotations

Trademark protection under Lanham Act (15 USCS secs. 1501 et seq.) of name of musical group. 115 ALR Fed 171.

Restaurant name or mark as infringement of trademark under sec. 32(1) or sec. 43(a) of Lanham Act (15 USCS secs. 1114(1), 1125(a)). 95 ALR Fed 31.

Design on recreational object as valid trademark. 82 ALR Fed 9.

Letters, initials, or numerals as common-law trademarks. 56 ALR Fed 232.

Rights and remedies with respect to another's use of a deceptively similar advertising slogan. 2 ALR3d 748.

"Drive it yourself" and similar phrases in connection with business of renting automobiles as subject of trademark or protection upon ground of unfair competition. 43 ALR 213.

Right to protection in use of initials as a trademark or tradename, or upon ground of unfair competition. 11 ALR 1286.

Section 10

1. Digest System Key Numbers

Trade Regulation ⚷1.

2. A.L.R. Annotations

Trademark protection under Lanham Act (15 USCS secs. 1501 et seq.) of name of musical group. 115 ALR Fed 171.

Right of benevolent or fraternal society or organization to protection against use of same or similar name, insignia, or ritual by another organization. 76 ALR2d 1396.

Rights in union label, shop card, or other insignia denoting union shop or workmanship. 42 ALR2d 709.

Right of automobile association to exclusive use of name or insignia. 83 ALR 712.

Section 11

1. Digest System Key Numbers

Trade Regulation ⚷1.

2. A.L.R. Annotations

Rights in union label, shop card, or other insignia denoting union shop or workmanship. 42 ALR2d 709.

Section 12

1. Digest System Key Numbers

Trade Regulation ⚷1, 7.

2. A.L.R. Annotations

Trademark protection under Lanham Act (15 USCS secs. 1501 et seq.) of name of musical group. 115 ALR Fed 171.

Restaurant name or mark as infringement of trademark under sec. 32(1) or sec. 43(a) of Lanham Act (15 USCS secs. 1114(1), 1125(a)). 95 ALR Fed 31.

Use of "family name" by corporation as unfair competition. 72 ALR3d 8.

Incorporation of company under particular name as creating exclusive right to such name. 68 ALR3d 1168.

Right of charitable or religious association or corporation to protection against use of same or similar name by another. 37 ALR3d 277.

Right to protection of corporate name, as between domestic corporation and foreign corporation not qualified to do business in state. 26 ALR3d 994.

Right of automobile association to exclusive use of name or insignia. 83 ALR 712.

Section 13

1. Digest System Key Numbers

Trade Regulation ⚷10, 348, 478.

2. A.L.R. Annotations

Admissibility and weight of consumer survey in litigation under trademark opposition, trademark infringement, and false designation of origin provisions of Lanham Act (15 USCS secs. 1063, 1114, and 1125). 98 ALR Fed 20.

Application of secondary meaning test in action for trade dress infringement under sec. 43(a) of Lanham Act (15 USCS sec. 1125(a)). 87 ALR Fed 15.

Application of secondary meaning test in action for trademark or tradename infringement under sec. 43(a) of the Lanham Act (15 USCS sec. 1125(a)). 86 ALR Fed 489.

Unfair competition: geographical extent of protection of word or symbol under doctrine of secondary meaning. 41 ALR3d 434.

Doctrine of secondary meaning in the law of trademarks and of unfair competition. 150 ALR 1067.

Time as an element in determining whether a descriptive term has acquired a secondary meaning entitling it to protection against unfair competition. 40 ALR 433.

TABLE OF CROSS REFERENCES

Section 14

1. Digest System Key Numbers

Trade Regulation ⚿12.1, 13, 32.1, 34.

2. A.L.R. Annotations

Trademark protection under Lanham Act (15 USCS secs. 1501 et seq.) of name of musical group. 115 ALR Fed 171.

Letters, initials, or numerals as common-law trademarks. 56 ALR Fed 232.

Use of "family name" by corporation as unfair competition. 72 ALR3d 8.

Right, in absence of self-imposed restraint, to use one's own name for business purposes to detriment of another using the same or a similar name. 47 ALR 1189, supp 44 ALR2d 1156.

Unfair competition in use of geographic tradename by persons carrying on business elsewhere. 174 ALR 496.

"Drive it yourself" and similar phrases in connection with business of renting automobiles as subject of trademark or protection upon ground of unfair competition. 43 ALR 213.

Time as an element in determining whether a descriptive term has acquired a secondary meaning entitling it to protection against unfair competition. 40 ALR 433.

Section 15

1. Digest System Key Numbers

Trade Regulation ⚿23.

2. A.L.R. Annotation

When does product mark become generic term or "common descriptive name" so as to warrant cancellation of registration of mark, pursuant to sec. 14 of Lanham Act (15 USCS sec. 1064). 55 ALR Fed 241.

Section 16

1. Digest System Key Numbers

Trade Regulation ⚿43.

2. A.L.R. Annotations

Trade dress simulation of cosmetic products as unfair competition. 86 ALR3d 505.

Right of producer or distributor to protection against use of his containers. 60 ALR 285.

Section 17

1. Digest System Key Numbers

Trade Regulation ⚷43.

2. A.L.R. Annotations

Application of functionality doctrine under sec. 43(a) of Lanham Act (15 USCS sec. 1125(a). 78 ALR Fed 712.

Unfair competition by imitation in sign or design of business place. 86 ALR3d 884.

Right to protection against simulation of physical appearance or arrangement of place of business, or vehicle. 17 ALR 784, supp 28 ALR 114.

Section 18

1. Digest System Key Numbers

Trade Regulation ⚷61, 65.

2. A.L.R. Annotations

Requirements for trademark or service mark to become incontestable under sec. 15 of Lanham Act (15 USCS sec. 1065). 116 ALR Fed 615.

What constitutes "in commerce" within meaning of sec. 32(1)(a) of Lanham Trade–Mark Act (15 USCS sec. 1114(1)) giving right of action for infringement of trademark "in commerce". 15 ALR Fed 368.

Incorporation of company under particular name as creating exclusive right to such name. 68 ALR3d 1168.

Right of one to protection of tradename which he does not use. 48 ALR 1257.

Section 19

1. Digest System Key Numbers

Trade Regulation ⚷66.1, 67.

2. A.L.R. Annotations

Unfair competition: geographical extent of protection of word or symbol under doctrine of secondary meaning. 41 ALR3d 434.

Right to protection of corporate name, as between domestic corporation and foreign corporation not qualified to do business in state. 26 ALR3d 994.

Right to protection against use of trademark or tradename beyond the territory in which plaintiff operates. 36 ALR 922.

Sale under foreign trademark of product of foreign manufacturer as infringement of same trademark for same product registered in United States. 26 ALR 570.

Section 20

1. Digest System Key Numbers

Trade Regulation ⚷332.

2. A.L.R. Annotations

Parody as trademark or tradename infringement. 92 ALR Fed 25.

Right of owner of trademark for apparel or toiletries to protection under Lanham Act (15 USCS sec. 1114(1)) against infringement by another's use of similar mark for different items of apparel or toiletries. 38 ALR Fed 374.

Rights and remedies with respect to another's use of a deceptively similar advertising slogan. 2 ALR3d 748.

Conflict of laws, with respect to trademark infringement or unfair competition, including area of conflict between Federal and state law. 148 ALR 139.

Actual competition as necessary element of trademark infringement or unfair competition. 148 ALR 12.

Liability for innocent infringement of trademark or tradename. 96 ALR 651.

Section 21

1. Digest System Key Numbers

Trade Regulation ⚷334.1, 335, 336, 363.1, 367.

2. A.L.R. Annotation

Admissibility and weight of consumer survey in litigation under trademark opposition, trademark infringement, and false designation of origin provisions of Lanham Act (15 USCS secs. 1063, 1114, and 1125). 98 ALR Fed 20.

Section 22

1. Digest System Key Numbers

Trade Regulation ⚷333, 334.1, 335.

2. A.L.R. Annotation

Liability for innocent infringement of trademark or tradename. 96 ALR 651.

Section 23

1. Digest System Key Numbers

Trade Regulation ⚷335.

2. A.L.R. Annotation

Admissibility and weight of consumer survey in litigation under trademark opposition, trademark infringement, and false designation of origin provisions of Lanham Act (15 USCS secs. 1063, 1114, and 1125). 98 ALR Fed 20.

Section 24

1. Digest System Key Numbers

Trade Regulation ⚷368.1, 369, 370.

2. A.L.R. Annotation

Commercial competitor's truthful denomination of his goods as copies of designs of another, using designer's name, as trademark infringement, unfair competition, or the like. 1 ALR3d 760.

Section 25

1. Digest System Key Numbers

Trade Regulation ⚷366.

2. A.L.R. Annotation

Parody as trademark or tradename infringement. 92 ALR Fed 25.

Section 26

1. Digest System Key Numbers

Trade Regulation ⚷374.

2. A.L.R. Annotations

Who, under Rule 65(d) of Federal Rules of Civil Procedure, are persons "in active concert or participation" with parties to action so as to be bound by order granting injunction. 61 ALR Fed 482.

Liability as "vicarious" or "contributory" infringer under Federal Copyright Act. 14 ALR Fed 825.

Section 27

1. Digest System Key Numbers

Trade Regulation ⚷374.

2. A.L.R. Annotations

Who, under Rule 65(d) of Federal Rules of Civil Procedure, are persons "in active concert or participation" with parties to action so as to be bound by order granting injunction. 61 ALR Fed 482.

Liability as "vicarious" or "contributory" infringer under Federal Copyright Act. 14 ALR Fed 825.

Section 28

1. Digest System Key Numbers

Trade Regulation ⚷375.1.

2. A.L.R. Annotations

Commercial competitor's truthful denomination of his goods as copies of designs of another, using designer's name, as trademark infringement, unfair competition, or the like. 1 ALR3d 760.

Right, in absence of self-imposed restraint, to use one's own name for business purposes to detriment of another using the same or a similar name. 47 ALR 1189, supp 44 ALR2d 1156.

"Drive it yourself" and similar phrases in connection with business of renting automobiles as subject of trademark or protection upon ground of unfair competition. 43 ALR 213.

Section 29

1. Digest System Key Numbers

Trade Regulation ⚿375.1.

2. A.L.R. Annotation

Granting of "naked" or unsupervised license to third party as defense to trademark infringement. 118 ALR Fed 211.

Section 30

1. Digest System Key Numbers

Trade Regulation ⚿69.1, 375.1.

2. A.L.R. Annotations

Granting of "naked" or unsupervised license to third party as defense to trademark infringement. 118 ALR Fed 211.

What constitutes abandonment of trademark by discontinuance of use with intent not to resume it, under sec. 45 of Lanham Act (15 USCS sec. 1127). 83 ALR Fed 295.

What constitutes abandonment of trademark by conduct causing mark to lose significance as indication of origin, under sec. 45 of Lanham Act (15 USCS sec. 1127(b)). 81 ALR Fed 677.

Abandonment of trademark or tradename. 3 ALR2d 1226.

Right of one to protection of tradename which he does not use. 48 ALR 1257.

Section 31

1. Digest System Key Numbers

Trade Regulation ⚿385.1, 386, 387, 388.

2. A.L.R. Annotation

Laches as affecting claim for accounting and damages in federal action for infringement of trademark or tradename. 14 ALR Fed 342.

TABLE OF CROSS REFERENCES

Section 32

1. Digest System Key Numbers

Equity ⚿65(3); Trade Regulation ⚿375.1.

2. A.L.R. Annotation

Damages recoverable for wrongful registration of trademark. 26 ALR2d 1184.

Section 33

1. Digest System Key Numbers

Trade Regulation ⚿108.1.

2. A.L.R. Annotations

Granting of "naked" or unsupervised license to third party as defense to trademark infringement. 118 ALR Fed 211.

Trademark licensor's liability for injury or death allegedly due to defect in licensed product. 90 ALR4th 981.

Section 34

1. Digest System Key Numbers

Trade Regulation ⚿98.1, 103.1.

2. A.L.R. Annotations

Liability of transferor of business operated under tradename for supplies furnished to successor by one without notice of transfer. 70 ALR3d 1250.

Trademark or tradename as asset in case of bankruptcy, insolvency, or assignment for the benefit of creditors. 44 ALR 706.

Section 35

1. Digest System Key Numbers

Trade Regulation ⚿611.1, 628, 641.

2. A.L.R. Annotations

Rights and remedies with respect to another's use of a deceptively similar advertising slogan. 2 ALR3d 748.

Right to enjoin business competitor from unlicensed or otherwise illegal acts or practices. 90 ALR2d 7.

Right to enjoin competitor from selling his produce to dealers with whom plaintiff has exclusive contract or in such form as to enable dealers to palm off competitor's produce as that of plaintiff. 84 ALR 472.

Section 36

1. Digest System Key Numbers

Trade Regulation ⚷672, 676, 680.1.

2. A.L.R. Annotations

Award of attorneys' fees under sec. 35(a) of Lanham Act (15 USCS sec. 1117(a)) authorizing award in "exceptional cases". 82 ALR Fed 143.

Right to jury trial in suit in federal court for damages from infringement of trademark. 9 ALR Fed 853.

Rights and remedies with respect to another's use of a deceptively similar advertising slogan. 2 ALR3d 748.

Punitive or exemplary damages as recoverable for trademark infringement or unfair competition. 47 ALR2d 1117.

Section 37

1. Digest System Key Numbers

Trade Regulation ⚷673, 684.1.

2. A.L.R. Annotation

Recovery based on tortfeasor's profits in action for procuring breach of contract. 5 ALR4th 1276.

Section 38

1. Digest System Key Numbers

Torts ⚷10(5).

2. A.L.R. Annotations

Making, selling, or distributing counterfeit or "bootleg" tape recordings or phonograph records as violation of federal law. 25 ALR Fed 207.

Title insurance company's rights in title information. 38 ALR4th 968.

When statute of limitations begins to run against action for wrongful appropriation of literary property or idea. 79 ALR3d 820.

Right to republish advertising material originally appearing in plaintiff's publication. 55 ALR3d 180.

Unfair competition by direct reproduction of literary, artistic, or musical property. 40 ALR3d 566.

Allowance of punitive damages for invasion of common-law rights in literary property. 40 ALR3d 248.

Literary property in lectures. 38 ALR3d 779.

Common-law copyright in the spoken word. 32 ALR3d 618.

Rights and remedies as between originator of uncopyrighted advertising plan or slogan, or his assignee, and another who uses or infringes the same. 104 ALR 1357, supp 157 ALR 1436.

Application of principles of unfair competition to artistic or literary property. 19 ALR 949.

Right to protection against appropriation of advertising matter or methods. 17 ALR 760, supp 30 ALR 615.

Section 39

1. Digest System Key Numbers

Torts ⚷10(5).

2. A.L.R. Annotations

What are "trade secrets" within sec. 6(f) of the Federal Trade Commission Act (15 USCS sec. 46(f)) not subject to publication by the Commission. 50 ALR Fed 590.

What constitutes "trade secrets and commercial or financial information obtained from a person and privileged or confidential," exempt from disclosure under Freedom of Information Act (5 USCS sec. 552(b)(4)). 21 ALR Fed 224.

What is "trade secret" so as to render actionable under state law its use or disclosure by former employee. 59 ALR4th 641.

What is computer "trade secret" under state law. 53 ALR4th 1046.

What constitutes "trade secrets" exempt from disclosure under state freedom of information act. 27 ALR4th 773.

Section 40

1. Digest System Key Numbers

Torts ⚷10(5).

2. A.L.R. Annotations

Criminal liability for theft of, interference with, or unauthorized use of, computer programs, files, or systems. 51 ALR4th 971.

Disclosure or use of computer application software as misappropriation of trade secret. 30 ALR4th 1250.

Disclosure of trade secret as abandonment of secrecy. 92 ALR3d 138.

Criminal liability for misappropriation of trade secret. 84 ALR3d 967.

Disclosure of trade secret in court proceedings as abandonment of secrecy. 58 ALR3d 1318.

Section 41

1. Digest System Key Numbers

Torts ⚷10(5).

2. A.L.R. Annotations

Employee's duty, in absence of express contract, not to disclose or use in new employment special skills or techniques acquired in earlier employment. 30 ALR3d 631.

Former employee's duty, in absence of express contract, not to solicit former employer's customers or otherwise use his knowledge of customer lists acquired in earlier employment. 28 ALR3d 7.

Implied obligation not to use trade secrets or similar confidential information disclosed during unsuccessful negotiations for sale, license, or the like. 9 ALR3d 665.

Section 42

1. Digest System Key Numbers

Torts ⚷10(5).

2. A.L.R. Annotations

Disclosure or use of computer application software as misappropriation of trade secret. 30 ALR4th 1250.

Employee's duty, in absence of express contract, not to disclose or use in new employment special skills or techniques acquired in earlier employment. 30 ALR3d 631.

Former employee's duty, in absence of express contract, not to solicit former employer's customers or otherwise use his knowledge of customer lists acquired in earlier employment. 28 ALR3d 7.

Implied obligation not to use trade secrets or similar confidential information disclosed during unsuccessful negotiations for sale, license, or the like. 9 ALR3d 665.

Section 43

1. Digest System Key Numbers

Torts 🔑10(5).

2. A.L.R. Annotations

Access to confidential or privileged material in international trade cases under 19 USCS sec. 1516a(b)(2)(B). 73 ALR Fed 247.

Propriety of federal court's exclusion of public from criminal or civil trial in order to protect trade secrets. 69 ALR Fed 892.

Discovery of trade secret in state court action. 75 ALR4th 1009.

Criminal liability for theft of, interference with, or unauthorized use of, computer programs, files, or systems. 51 ALR4th 971.

Disclosure of trade secret in court proceedings as abandonment of secrecy. 58 ALR3d 1318.

In camera trial or hearing and other procedures to safeguard trade secret or the like against undue disclosure in course of civil action involving such secret. 62 ALR2d 509.

Discovery or inspection of trade secret, formula, or the like. 17 ALR2d 383.

Section 44

1. Digest System Key Numbers

Injunction 🔑138.33.

2. A.L.R. Annotations

Proper measure and elements of damages for misappropriation of trade secret. 11 ALR4th 12.

Propriety of permanently enjoining one guilty of unauthorized use of trade secret from engaging in sale or manufacture of device in question. 38 ALR3d 572.

TABLE OF CROSS REFERENCES

Section 45

1. Digest System Key Numbers

Damages ⚷88(1), 91(1), 114, 120(7).

2. A.L.R. Annotation

Proper measure and elements of damages for misappropriation of trade secret. 11 ALR4th 12.

Section 46

1. Digest System Key Numbers

Torts ⚷8.5(1, 2, 3, 4, 6).

2. A.L.R. Annotations

Supreme Court's views as to the federal legal aspects of the right of privacy. 43 L Ed 2d 871.

False light invasion of privacy, cognizability and elements. 57 ALR4th 22.

Name appropriation by employer or employee. 52 ALR4th 156.

Limitation of actions: invasion of right of privacy. 33 ALR4th 479.

Right to publicize or commercially exploit deceased person's name or likeness as inheritable. 10 ALR4th 1193.

Waiver or loss of right of privacy. 57 ALR3d 16.

Invasion of privacy by use of plaintiff's name or likeness for nonadvertising purpose. 30 ALR3d 203.

Invasion of privacy by use of plaintiff's name or likeness in advertising. 23 ALR3d 865.

Right of privacy. 14 ALR2d 750.

Validity and effect of contract, unconnected with transfer of any business or professional interest, purporting to grant exclusive right to use one's name or likeness for advertising purposes. 101 ALR 492.

Section 47

1. Digest System Key Numbers

Torts ⚷8.5(5.1, 6).

2. A.L.R. Annotations

Right to publicize or commercially exploit deceased person's name or likeness as inheritable. 10 ALR4th 1193.

Invasion of privacy by use of plaintiff's name or likeness in advertising. 23 ALR3d 865.

Validity and effect of contract, unconnected with transfer of any business or professional interest, purporting to grant exclusive right to use one's name or likeness for advertising purposes. 101 ALR 492.

Section 48

1. Digest System Key Numbers

Injunction ⚷96.

2. A.L.R. Annotation

False light invasion of privacy—defenses and remedies. 57 ALR4th 244.

Section 49

1. Digest System Key Numbers

Damages ⚷8, 15, 20.

2. A.L.R. Annotation

False light invasion of privacy—defenses and remedies. 57 ALR4th 244.

*

PARALLEL TABLE

RESTATEMENT OF TORTS SECTIONS TO RESTATEMENT THIRD, UNFAIR COMPETITION SECTIONS

Restatement of Torts (1938) Sec.	Restatement Third Unfair Competition Sec.
708	1
709	1 Com. *c*
710	1 Com. *a*
711	4, 20
712	4
713	8
714	6
715	9
716	12–13
717	20
718	18 Com. *d*
719	18
720	14 Com. *d*
721	14–15
722	14 Com. *e*
723	14 Com. *a*, 15 Com. *a*
724	14 Com. *a*
725	14 Com. *a*, 15 Com. *a*
726	32 Com. *c*
727	20, 28
728	20
729	21–23
730	21 Com. *j*
731	21–23
732	19
733	19
734	20 Com. *b*
735	15
736	24
737	24
738	27
739	26
740	28, 35 Com. *d*
741	16
742	17
743	16, 20
744	35
745	36
746	36
747	37
748	37
749	32
750	32 RN Com. *d*
751	31
752	30
753	30 Com. *a*
754	29
755	34
756	33–34
757	39–45
758	40 Com. *d*
759	41 Com. *c*
760	6
761	2–3

Cross-references to corresponding sections of the Restatement of Torts (1938) are included, where applicable, in the Reporters' Notes that accompany the sections in this Restatement.

*

INDEX

References are to Sections, Comments, and Reporters' Notes

A

References to Comments include the accompanying Reporters' Note.

INDEX

References to Comments include the accompanying Reporters' Note.

B

C

References to Comments include the accompanying Reporters' Note.

D

References to Comments include the accompanying Reporters' Note.

References to Comments include the accompanying Reporters' Note.

References to Comments include the accompanying Reporters' Note.

References to Comments include the accompanying Reporters' Note.

References to Comments include the accompanying Reporters' Note.

INDEX

References to Comments include the accompanying Reporters' Note.

References to Comments include the accompanying Reporters' Note.

R

References to Comments include the accompanying Reporters' Note.

References to Comments include the accompanying Reporters' Note.

References to Comments include the accompanying Reporters' Note.

References to Comments include the accompanying Reporters' Note.

U

References to Comments include the accompanying Reporters' Note.

†